# EUROPE
## 1450 TO 1789
### ENCYCLOPEDIA OF THE EARLY MODERN WORLD

## Volume 6
Tasso to Zwingli; Index

*Jonathan Dewald, Editor in Chief*

CHARLES SCRIBNER'S SONS®

THOMSON

GALE

New York • Detroit • San Diego • San Francisco • Cleveland • New Haven, Conn. • Waterville, Maine • London • Munich

THOMSON
———★———™
GALE

**Europe 1450 to 1789:**
**Encyclopedia of the Early Modern World**

Jonathan Dewald, Editor in Chief

For permission to use material from this product,
submit your request via Web at http://www.gale-
edit.com/permissions, or you may download our
Permissions Request form and submit your request
by fax or mail to:

*Permissions Department*
The Gale Group, Inc.
27500 Drake Rd.
Farmington Hills, MI  48331-3535

Permissions Hotline:
248-699-8006 or 800-877-4253, ext. 8006
Fax: 248-699-8074 or 800-762-4058

**LIBRARY OF CONGRESS CATALOGING-IN-PUBLICATION DATA**

Europe 1450 to 1789 : encyclopedia of the early modern world / Jonathan Dewald, editor in
chief.
        p. cm.
Includes bibliographical references and index.
    ISBN 0-684-31200-X (set : hardcover) — ISBN 0-684-31201-8 (v. 1) —
ISBN 0-684-31202-6 (v. 2) — ISBN 0-684-31203-4 (v. 3) — ISBN 0-684-31204-2 (v. 4) —
ISBN 0-684-31205-0 (v. 5) — ISBN 0-684-31206-9 (v. 6)
    1. Europe—History—15th century—Encyclopedias.  2. Europe—History—1492–1648—
Encyclopedias.  3. Europe—History—1648–1789—Encyclopedias.  4. Europe—Intellectual
life—Encyclopedias.  5. Europe—Civilization—Encyclopedias.  I. Title: Encyclopedia of the early
modern world.  II. Dewald, Jonathan.
    D209.E97 2004
    940.2—dc22
                                                                              2003015680

This title is also available as an e-book.
ISBN 0-684-31423-1 (set)
Contact your Gale sales representative for ordering information.
Printed in United States of America
10 9 8 7 6 5 4 3 2 1

# EUROPE
## 1450 TO 1789
### ENCYCLOPEDIA OF THE EARLY MODERN WORLD

# EDITORIAL BOARD

# CONTENTS OF THIS VOLUME

## VOLUME 6

# CONTENTS OF OTHER VOLUMES

## VOLUME 1

# VOLUME 2

## VOLUME 3

## VOLUME 4

## VOLUME 5

# USING THE ENCYCLOPEDIA

**Tables of contents.** Each volume contains a table of contents for the entire *Encyclopedia*. Volume 1 has a single listing of all volumes' contents. Volumes 2 through 6 contain "Contents of This Volume" followed by "Contents of Other Volumes."

**Maps of Europe.** The front of each volume contains a set of maps showing Europe's political divisions at six important stages from 1453 to 1795.

**Alphabetical arrangement.** Entries are arranged in alphabetical order. Biographical articles are generally listed by the subject's last name (with some exceptions, e.g., Leonardo da Vinci).

**Royalty and foreign names.** In most cases, the names of rulers of French, German, and Spanish rulers have been anglicized. Thus, Francis, not François; Charles, not Carlos. Monarchs of the same name are listed first by their country, and then numerically. Thus, Henry VII and Henry VIII of England precede Henry II of France.

**Measurements** appear in the English system according to United States usage, though they are often followed by metric equivalents in parentheses. Following are approximate metric equivalents for the most common units:

1 foot = 30 centimeters
1 mile = 1.6 kilometers
1 acre = 0.4 hectares
1 square mile = 2.6 square kilometers
1 pound = 0.45 kilograms
1 gallon = 3.8 liters

**Cross-references.** At the end of each article is a list of related articles for further study. Readers may also consult the table of contents and the index for titles and keywords of interest.

**Bibliography.** Each article contains a list of sources for further reading, usually divided into Primary Sources and Secondary Sources.

**Systematic outline of contents.** After the last article in volume 6 is an outline that provides a general overview of the conceptual scheme of the *Encyclopedia*, listing the title of each entry.

**Directory of contributors.** Following the systematic outline of contents is a listing, in alphabetical order, of all contributors to the *Encyclopedia,* with affiliation and the titles of his or her article(s).

**Index.** Volume 6 concludes with a comprehensive, alphabetically arranged index covering all articles, as well as prominent figures, geographical names, events, institutions, publications, works of art, and all major concepts that are discussed in volumes 1 through 6.

# MAPS OF EUROPE,
# 1453 TO 1795

The maps on the pages that follow show political boundaries within Europe at six important stages in the roughly three hundred and fifty years covered by this *Encyclopedia:* 1453, 1520, 1648, 1715, 1763, and 1795.

**Europe, 1453**

International border
• City

0    100    200 mi.
0  100  200 km

*Norwegian Sea*

N O R W A Y

S W E D E N

*Gulf of Bothnia*

*Gulf of Finland*

• Stockholm

*Baltic Sea*

**RUSSIAN STATES**

• Moscow

**TEUTONIC KNIGHTS**

SCOTLAND

• Edinburgh

*North Sea*

**DENMARK**
Copenhagen •

• Danzig

**POLAND-LITHUANIA**

IRELAND

E N G L A N D

• Dublin

Brandenburg

• Warsaw

• London

• Cologne

Bohemia
• Prague
Moravia

Silesia

*ATLANTIC OCEAN*

Brittany

• Paris

**HOLY ROMAN EMPIRE**

Vienna •
Austria

Buda • Pest

M O L D A V I A

F R A N C E

**HUNGARY**

*Bay of Biscay*

• Milan

Venice •

V E N I C E

**WALLACHIA**

*Black Sea*

NAVARRE

• Genoa

**BOSNIA**

• Florence
**PAPAL STATES**

*Adriatic Sea*

**SERBIA**

VENICE

O T T O M A N   E M P I R E

Bulgaria

• Constantinople

ARAGÓN

Corsica
(Holy Roman Empire)

• Rome

**NAPLES**

VENICE

Madrid •

Barcelona •

Minorca
(Aragón)

Sardinia
(Aragón)

*Tyrrhenian Sea*

Athens •

PORTUGAL

Lisbon •

**CASTILE**

Iviza
(Aragón)

Majorca
(Aragón)

*Ionian Sea*

VENICE

VENICE

GRANADA

Sicily
(Aragón)

Crete
(Venice)

*Mediterranean Sea*

**1453.** In the years around 1450, Europe settled into relative political stability, following the crises of the late Middle Ages. France and England concluded the Hundred Years' War in 1453; the Ottoman Turks conquered Constantinople in the same year and established it as the capital of their empire; and in 1454 the Treaty of Lodi normalized relations among the principal Italian states, establishing a peaceful balance of power among Venice, Florence, the duchy of Milan, the Papal States, and the Kingdom of Naples.

**Europe, 1520**

International border

• City

0    100    200 mi.

0  100  200 km

**1520.** In 1520, the Habsburg prince Charles V was elected Holy Roman emperor, uniting in his person lordship over central Europe, Spain, the Low Countries, parts of Italy, and the newly conquered Spanish territories in the Americas. For the next century, this overwhelming accumulation of territories in the hands of a single dynasty would remain the most important fact in European international politics. But in 1520 Habsburg power already faced one of its most troublesome challenges: Martin Luther's Reformation, first attracting widespread notice in 1517, would repeatedly disrupt Habsburg efforts to unify their territories.

**Europe, 1648**

— International border
• City

0    100   200 mi.
0   100  200 km

Norwegian Sea

N

Finland

SWEDEN

Helsingfors

DENMARK AND NORWAY

Christiania

Stockholm

Gulf of Bothnia

Gulf of Finland

Estonia (Sweden)

Livonia (Sweden)

Baltic Sea

RUSSIA

Moscow

SCOTLAND

Edinburgh

North Sea

Copenhagen

Königsberg  PRUSSIA

Lithuania

IRELAND

Dublin

UNITED NETHERLANDS

Amsterdam

Brussels

Brandenburg

Berlin

Hanover

Saxony

Dresden

Silesia

POLAND

Warsaw

ENGLAND

London

HOLY ROMAN EMPIRE

Bohemia

Spanish Netherlands

Paris

Bavaria

Munich

Vienna

Austria

Buda  Pest

Hungary

Transylvania

Moldavia

Wallachia

Brittany

FRANCE

ATLANTIC OCEAN

Bay of Biscay

SWITZERLAND

SAVOY  Milan

Turin  Parma

Genoa

VENICE

Venice

Modena

Florence

Lucca

TUSCANY

PAPAL STATES

Avignon (Papal States)

Bosnia

VENICE

RAGUSA

MONTENEGRO

Cattaro (Venice)

OTTOMAN EMPIRE

Black Sea

Constantinople

Anatolia

Adriatic Sea

Corsica (Genoa)

Rome

Naples (Spain)

Albania

Corfu (Venice)

PORTUGAL

Madrid

SPAIN

Lisbon

Minorca (Spain)

Sardinia (Spain)

Majorca (Spain)

Iviza (Spain)

Tyrrhenian Sea

Sicily (Spain)

Cephalonia (Venice)

Zante (Venice)

Ionian Sea

Athens

Crete (Venice)

Tangier (Spain)

Melilla (Spain)

Oran (Spain)

Algiers

Bona (Genoa)

Tunis

FEZ AND MOROCCO

BARBARY STATES

Mediterranean Sea

**1648.** The 1648 Peace of Westphalia ended the Thirty Years' War, one of the most destructive wars in European history. The peace treaty formally acknowledged the independence of the Dutch Republic and the Swiss Confederation, and it established the practical autonomy of the German principalities—including the right to establish their own religious policies. Conversely, the Holy Roman Empire lost much of its direct power; although its institutions continued to play some role in German affairs through the eighteenth century, the emperors' power now rested overwhelmingly on the Habsburg domain lands in Austria, Bohemia, and eastern Europe.

**Europe, 1715**

— International border
• City

0    100    200 mi.
0  100  200 km

*Norwegian Sea*

N

Finland

DENMARK AND NORWAY

S W E D E N

Helsingfors
St. Petersburg
Christiania
Stockholm
Estonia (Sweden)
Livonia (Sweden)
Moscow

*North Sea*

RUSSIAN EMPIRE

GREAT BRITAIN AND IRELAND
Edinburgh
Copenhagen
Königsberg
PRUSSIA
Lithuania

Dublin
Ireland
UNITED NETHERLANDS
Hanover
Berlin
POLAND
Warsaw

England
Amsterdam
London
Prussia

Brussels
Austrian Netherlands
HOLY ROMAN EMPIRE
Saxony
Dresden
Silesia
Bohemia

*ATLANTIC OCEAN*

Paris
Bavaria
Vienna
HUNGARY
Munich
Buda Pest
Transylvania

FRANCE
Berne
Austria
SWITZERLAND
Venice
VENICE
SAVOY

*Bay of Biscay*

Turin Parma
Avignon (Papal States)
Genoa
Modena
Florence
Lucca
TUSCANY
PAPAL STATES
Bosnia
VENICE
OTTOMAN EMPIRE

*Black Sea*

RAGUSA
MONTENEGRO
VENICE
Rumelia
Constantinople

Corsica (Genoa)
Rome
Naples
Naples (Austria)
Albania
Anatolia

Madrid
Minorca (Great Britain)
Sardinia (Austria)
*Tyrrhenian Sea*
Corfu (Venice)
Athens

PORTUGAL
SPAIN
Iviza (Spain)
Majorca (Spain)
Cephalonia (Venice)
Morea (Venice)

Lisbon
Sicily (Savoy)
*Ionian Sea*

Ceuta (Spain)
Algiers
Tunis
Crete (Ottoman Empire)

FEZ AND MOROCCO
ALGERIA
TUNIS
*Mediterranean Sea*

Gulf of Bothnia
Gulf of Finland
*Baltic Sea*
*Adriatic Sea*

**1715.** The Peace of Utrecht (1713) ended the War of the Spanish Succession, the last and most destructive of the wars of the French king Louis XIV. The treaty ended Spain's control over present-day Belgium and over parts of Italy, and it marked the end of French hegemony within Europe. In the eighteenth century, France would be only one of five leading powers.

**Europe, 1763**

—— International border
------ Internal border
• City

0    100    200 mi.
0  100  200 km

**1763.** The 1763 Treaty of Paris ended the Seven Years' War, a war that involved all the major European powers and included significant campaigns in North America and southern Asia, as well as in Europe. The war made clear the arrival of Prussia as a great power, at least the equal of Austria in central and eastern Europe.

## Europe, 1795

International border
- - - Internal border
● City

0    100    200 mi.

0  100  200 km

*Norwegian Sea*

Finland

DENMARK AND NORWAY

SWEDEN

*Gulf of Bothnia*

Helsingfors ●

St. Petersburg ●

Christiania ●

Stockholm ●

*Gulf of Finland*

Moscow ●

Scotland

*North Sea*

Edinburgh ●

Copenhagen ●

Königsberg ●

RUSSIA

*Baltic Sea*

Ireland
GREAT BRITAIN
Dublin ●

England

Amsterdam ●

UNITED NETHERLANDS

Hanover

PRUSSIA

Berlin ●

Warsaw ●

GALICIA

London ●

Prussia

Brussels ●
Austrian Netherlands

HOLY ROMAN EMPIRE

Saxony

ATLANTIC OCEAN

Paris ●

Bohemia

Munich ●

Vienna ●

HUNGARY

Buda ●
Pest ●

TRANSYLVANIA

Bavaria

Austria

*Bay of Biscay*

FRANCE

SWISS CONFED.

Milan ●
Venice ●

*Black Sea*

Genoa ●

Florence ●

*Adriatic Sea*

Constantinople ●

Corsica (France)

Rome ●

TUSCANY

Albania

OTTOMAN EMPIRE

PORTUGAL

Madrid ●

SPAIN

Minorca (Great Britain)

SARDINIA

Naples ●

SICILY-NAPLES

*Tyrrhenian Sea*

Corfu (Venice)

Athens ●

Lisbon ●

Majorca (Spain)

Iviza (Spain)

Cephalonia (Venice)

Zante (Venice)

Sicily

*Ionian Sea*

Algiers ●

Tunis ●

Crete (Ottoman Empire)

FEZ

ALGIERS

TUNIS

*Mediterranean Sea*

N

**1795.** By 1795, French armies had repelled an attempted invasion by Prussia, Austria, and England, and France had begun annexing territories in Belgium and western Germany. These military successes ensured the continuation of the French Revolution, but they also meant that European warfare would continue until 1815, when the modern borders of France were largely established. Warfare with France did not prevent the other European powers from conducting business as usual elsewhere: with agreements in 1793 and 1795, Prussia, Austria, and Russia completed their absorption of Poland.

cities, where architects and other artists were highly trained in practical mathematics, and constantly experimented, at least in sketches, with various combinations of machine elements. Leonardo da Vinci's (1452–1519) well-known breadth of interests—stretching from his designs of ingenious devices to sculpture to painting—was not uncommon. Francesco di Giorgio (1439–1502) also developed great expertise in the fields of engineering and hydraulics, along with his more decorative work. Architects directed sometimes dramatic refiguration of major cities. Rome was largely rebuilt in the sixteenth century and Paris in the seventeenth. Architects also designed dams and waterways, fortifications, and stage machinery.

As works of architecture and engineering gained greater cultural capital as markers of status and power, scholars and patrons themselves often came to seek the knowledge of the architects and to share their literate culture. Leon Battista Alberti (1404–1472) was a humanist who carved a new role for himself as the technical counselor to powerful men. His treatises detailing mathematical and conventional rules for painting, sculpture, and architecture became classics even in manuscript. Cooperation between elites and architects centered on military engineering and the study of ancient technical texts, works that promised the secrets of recreating the splendid world of the ancients. The duke of Urbino, Federigo Montefeltro (1422–1482), himself tried to aid Francesco di Giorgio in a translation of *De architectura* by the Roman architect Vitruvius. Alberti had given up making sense of this text, but the first editions came from practicing architects: Fra Giovanni Giocondo da Verona's (c. 1433–1515) Latin text of 1511, and Cesare Cesariano's vernacular edition in 1521. Other texts considered clues to ancient marvels of engineering were also routed to prominent architects and painters by their patrons. Texts of Archimedes, the hydraulics of Hero, and the mechanical collections of Pappus were books examined by scholars of both elite and artisanal status.

By the end of the sixteenth century, mathematicians such as Federico Commandino (1509–1575) and Guidobaldo del Monte (1545–1607) had developed their own elaboration of a classical rational mechanics. This work remained rooted to the world of the mechanic, but began to address a new sort of engineering professional that was just then beginning to emerge.

## NATURAL MAGIC AND ALCHEMY

No easy category existed during the late Renaissance in which to place figures who performed technological feats. The Syracusan Archimedes (c. 287–212 B.C.E.), for example, was famous as the maker of a wooden bird that flew all by itself, and as the engineer whose special mirrors burned Roman ships in the harbor—both accomplishments that early modern engineers attempted to recreate well into the eighteenth century. In the language of Renaissance Neoplatonism, the term *magus* often served best to characterize such figures. The magus was figured as a wise man whose knowledge of occult (hidden) natural properties allowed him to unleash operative forces and create amazing effects. Scholars of magic—among the most learned of the age—developed a doxography that linked magical, philosophical, and religious figures in historical progressions: from the legendary Egyptian magus Hermes Trismegistus, to Moses, to Pythagoras, to Platonic and Aristotelian philosophers, to Ptolemy as a judicial astrologer, and thence to the Hellenistic mathematician and reputed engineer Archimedes.

Meanwhile engineers themselves, military engineering writers such as Conrad Keyser (1366–1405) and Giovanni da Fontana (1395?–1455?), had cultivated a mixture of technology and magic. "Natural magic" pointed to the operative power inherent in technology, and offered a framework outside that of Aristotelian causality. By the turn of the seventeenth century, discussions of technology often adopted the name "magic" as "the practical part of natural philosophy." Influential writers such as Tommaso Campanella (1568–1639) and Giambattista della Porta (1535?–1615) continued to configure technological work as natural magic. Della Porta in particular had himself demonstrated success experimenting with lenses and was a key member of the Accademia dei Lincei before Galileo, with his mathematical-philosophical approach to technology, gained center stage among the academicians. In England the connection remained intact through Robert Fludd (1574–1637), whose work explicitly drew together mechanical technologies and divinatory arts within a mystical Christian framework. The work of John Wilkins (1614–

1672) is a late echo of the connection between mathematics, technology, and magic. His compendium of the most current work in rational and practical mechanics was entitled *Mathematical Magic,* but the "magic" was completely removed from occult overtones, and merely captured the transformative power of technology.

Another tradition of natural magic ran from Hermes to alchemical thinkers such as the medieval Islamic alchemist Geber and the learned friar Roger Bacon (c. 1220–1292). Alchemy was a repository of knowledge for a variety of distillation and metallurgical techniques. Before a more rationalized nomenclature could be instituted, alchemical lore was often veiled in occult language and bizarre images. Alchemy enjoyed something of a vogue in the sixteenth and seventeenth centuries and occupied some of the finest minds of the age, including the twenty-year concentrated studies of Isaac Newton (1642–1727). Alchemy consisted of distillation and metallurgical techniques, and created seemingly new substances through the combination and heating of reagents. These practices were often conceived within a theory of metals and a religious-spiritual view of nature and human labor. Probably due to the shapes of mineral veins, metals were believed to grow inside the earth; over long periods of time all metal would mature into gold. Alchemy was the art and labor by which nature could be hastened and perfected. While alchemists did indeed believe it was possible to turn base metals into gold, the operations of alchemy also provided both consumable products and an observable, experimental analog to the processes of nature. Metallurgists utilized the literature and techniques of alchemy, and Paracelsus (Philippus Aureolus Theophrastus Bombastus von Hohenheim, 1493–1541) developed a chemical medicine and alchemical view of nature that found numerous followers throughout the sixteenth and seventeenth centuries.

## BACONIANS AND THE DIRECTION OF PROGRESS

Francis Bacon (1561–1626) spent much of his forced retirement from politics writing on a reform of knowledge that would account for and extend the success of technological traditions but avoid the drawbacks of its current practices. His *Novum Organum* (1620; New organon) detailed both criticisms of the current state of knowledge and remedies. Bacon advocated the redirection of philosophy away from erudition and logical terminology, toward experience and the advancement of material wealth. Mechanics, mathematicians, physicians, alchemists, and magicians, Bacon noted, had hands-on knowledge of nature, "but all [have met with] faint success." Bacon had patience neither to wait for the happenstance of a lucky discovery or invention, nor to suffer the "fanciful philosophy" advanced by alchemists and others who presumed too much based on a narrow base of technical knowledge. "Knowledge and human power are synonymous," he proclaimed. While he advocated a program of experimentation, he was decidedly more articulate about a more descriptive collection of facts from the natural and technological worlds. For example, from a "history of trades" that would chart information from all manner of tradesmen, the philosopher would draw out axioms of principal import. The axioms could then be used to organize and further the trades.

Bacon's program, with the approach of the 1640 Puritan Revolution, appeared to some to offer the prospect of a "new Albion," an Edenic England created through technology in a great reform of religion, mind, and social organization. Samuel Hartlib (c. 1600–1662), for example, worked toward such a vision. Hartlib was in fact central to the circle of men who later founded the Royal Society.

The Royal Society, founded on explicitly Baconian inspiration, at first tried to fulfill the role of collectors of histories of trades. While this project was not successful, the society often centered around the experiments made by its curator. Information on mines, machines, and other technological news was assiduously collected along with accounts from physicians, mathematicians, and naturalists, and was printed in the *Philosophical Transactions.* Exhaustive histories of trades were finally realized at the end of the eighteenth century in France. The overt Baconians Denis Diderot (1713–1784) and Jean Le Rond d'Alembert (1717–1783) and the more staid Académie des Sciences both produced encyclopedias of arts and trades in the decades before the French Revolution.

## TECHNOLOGIES FOR SCIENCE; SCIENCE FOR TECHNOLOGIES

While Bacon had fully recognized the mutual relationship between the reform of natural philosophy and the progress of the arts, he had paid relatively little attention to the technologies that were themselves transforming the practices of science. While mechanics, architects, and craftsmen had always used mathematical measuring instruments in their work, and these themselves underwent great refinement in the sixteenth century, the new scientific instruments of the seventeenth century—the telescope, microscope, air pump, and to a lesser degree thermometers and barometers—depended on technologies and offered possibilities on a whole new level. The telescope and the microscope extended human vision enormously and produced experiential evidence in debates such as that over the Copernican hypothesis. The air pump, as it was developed by Robert Boyle (1627–1691) and his mechanic-client, Robert Hooke (1635–1703), consisted of a ratchet and piston system that could evacuate a glass receiver one cylinder-volume at a time. This served as a stage of observation for an artificial environment of evacuated air and allowed Boyle to make claims concerning the nature of the tiniest units of matter. This was a sort of instrument that had never been used in natural philosophy before. Such instruments were difficult to get to work dependably, and often relied on the skills of a mechanic like Robert Hooke.

Meanwhile, both elite and practical mathematicians developed mathematical skills that were meant to aid the design of ever more complicated technical tasks. Vernacular editions of Euclid had been available since Niccolò Tartaglia's (1499–1557) 1543 Italian edition. Above all, these editions spread and popularized geometrical proportioning techniques. Simultaneously, in the early seventeenth century the Scottish nobleman John Napier (1550–1617) and the Swiss watchmaker Joost Bürgi (1552–1632) developed logarithms that would make trigonometrical computations much easier. Napier in particular drew explicit attention to the ways logarithms would ease tasks in military engineering and survey. Napier also employed the decimal notation developed by the Dutch engineer and counselor to Maurice of Nassau (1567–1625), Simon Stevin (1548–1620). Decimal notation eased work with fractions. Proportional compasses and calculating sectors also eased practical calculations. The foundations of algebraic analysis were meanwhile made by Pierre de Fermat (1601–1665), and a century later the use of analysis became essential to the cadets of France's technical institutes, and made possible a new style of engineering. Meanwhile, projective geometry, always to some extent a tool of architects and engineers, had been highly developed and integrated into perspective by Gérard Desargues (1591–1661). Descriptive geometry was institutionalized in technical drawing, again at the French *écoles,* by Gaspard Monge (1746–1818).

## PROJECTORS, ARTIFICERS, AND THEIR PATRONS

In his fable of the ideal technological and moral society, the *New Atlantis* (1627), Francis Bacon had presented a kind of intellectual mirror opposite of mercantilist programs. In his imaginary Benthalem, technological secrets were constantly imported by explorers and developed by technicians; no technologies, however, would be exported to other nations. This speaks both to concerns about industrial espionage and difficulties caused by undeveloped patent laws that infected all states in Europe. It also indicates some of the enthusiasm political and cultural leaders had in the wholesale collection of technical knowledge, and their reliance on mechanical workers to feed their interests.

European rulers had long tried to prohibit the export of technologies on which their economies depended. Venice, for example, forced glassmakers to swear they would not take their art outside of the city's dominion. The importance of technological transference through the migration of skilled persons is most forcefully demonstrated in the case of Lucca's silk-throwing machine, the *filotoio.* Anyone carrying knowledge of this machine outside the confines of the city was threatened with death. Meanwhile, a design of the machine had been publicly available for years in Vittorio Zonca's *Novo Teatro di Machine et Edificii* (1607). It was not until the eighteenth-century industrial spy John Lombe spent two years studying the machine in Italy that the machine could be reproduced and operated.

Semi-itinerant mechanics often haunted baroque courts. Mechanicians such as Dutch-born Cornelis Drebbel (1572–1633) attracted attention in England (and for a short time in Prague) with perpetual motion machines, inventive skills for such devices as diving bells, and technical know-how for such major works as the draining of fens. As a projector in various German courts, the alchemist and mechanic Johann Joachim Becher (1635–1682) rose to something of a patron himself. He solicited secrets from a range of artificers, and probably used his alchemical skills to advertise his ideas for a new political economy based on trade and technology rather than agriculture. Numerous enthusiasts and scientific gentlemen cultivated relationships with their own artificers to construct machines.

## CLOCKS AND WATCHES

The first town clocks were constructed in the Middle Ages, usually as way of letting workmen know when shifts should change in new textile factories. While watchmakers themselves continually refined methods of gear-cutting throughout the period, scientists dramatically innovated clocks in the mid-seventeenth century. Clocks became more accurate and more convenient and promised a solution to the problem of determining longitude at sea—one of the most long-standing obstacles to navigation—as well as offering advantages to positional astronomy. If one could accurately keep track of the time of the home port and local time, longitude could easily be calculated. In 1656, the Dutch scientist Christiaan Huygens (1629–1695) designed a clock using a pendulum oscillator with a tautochronic, one-second period. The pendulum clock, however, proved inappropriate for the pitching deck of a ship. In the mid 1660s, Huygens turned to oscillators formed of a spiral hair spring—just as Robert Hooke was also investigating the use of a hair spring. This gave rise to a bitter, ultimately unresolved controversy over patents. However, neither watch proved accurate enough to serve the purposes of a marine chronometer. The government prize for the solution of the longitude problem, £20,000, was finally awarded in 1765 after the Yorkshire watchmaker John Harrison (1693–1776) improved accuracy through advances in workmanship rather than design.

## AUTOMATONS AND POPULAR DEMONSTRATIONS

In the sixteenth and early seventeenth centuries, mechanical devices for delight had largely been cul-

tivated in personal collections and gardens. Self-moving statues, ingenious fountains, and hydraulic devices designed by architects like Salomon de Caus (1576–1626) delighted visitors. Mechanical marvels were often placed next to exotic naturalia and antiquities. In the eighteenth century, automatons, such as those designed by Jacques de Vaucanson (1709–1782), were exhibited in shows and fairs.

More serious forms of enlightened infotainment were provided by popularizers of Isaac Newton's work. Jean Theophilus Desaguliers (1683–1744), for example, offered ten-week courses at a cost of two guineas a head. Demonstrators of "Newtonian" devices showed their wares from town to town. The abbé Jean-Antoine Nollet (1700–1770) made presentations of the new physics, and was a favorite in French salons. These popular mechanical demonstrations and lectures were probably one of the best venues in which to learn about applied mechanics. The automatons and demonstration devices, however, belonged to a larger cultural context in which machinery powered more tasks, and automation of labor was becoming more prevalent.

## MILLS: AGE OF WATER AND WOOD

If the nineteenth century was predominantly an age of coal and iron, the preceding centuries were largely characterized by water and wood. The vertical water wheel and the windmill were both imported to the Latin West in the Middle Ages. By 1450, these sources of power were already applied to brewing, hemp production, fulling, ore stamping, tanning, sawmills, blast furnaces, paper production, and mine pumping. Their use and development continued throughout the early modern period. The principle of translating circular wheel motion into other forms of translational motion was also applied through human or animal labor. Concern for milling and water-lifting machines is testified by the printed machine books of Agostino Ramelli (1531–c. 1600), Jacques Besson (1540–1576), and Vittorio Zonca (born c. 1580). These books present the intricate connection of wheels, gears, cams, and winches. Concurrent with the pressing need for machines to power manufactories was the need for machines that could pump or raise water. The latter were everywhere employed for drinking-water, for evacuating deep mines, for draining swamps, and for building canals.

The Netherlands, not surprisingly, led Europe in these technologies, both because of the superabundance of water and the need to drain the land and dredge ports. Because prevailing westerlies dependably blow over its lands, the Dutch also perfected windmills. Top sails could be rotated (either because mounted on a rotating cap or because the bottom of the tower could be rotated on wheels) to face wind. The *Wimpolen* drove bucket chains that drained water from the soil, then dumped it into the canals, and was part of land reclamation projects. Dutch experts in water reclamation and water wheel machinery were in high demand throughout the seventeenth century.

The main drawback of these early modern machines was that they were made of wood. By the late sixteenth century, Europe had been largely deforested, and wood became increasingly expensive. Wood also was a material in which precision tooling was limited, and which broke easily and required much maintenance.

## TEXTILES

Textiles were among the first products to be produced on a large scale through division of labor and mechanization. Important textile manufactories were well established in Italy and the Netherlands by the thirteenth century. In the sixteenth and seventeenth centuries, modest mechanized advances in ribbon weaving were introduced. In the 1730s, John Kay's (1704–1764) "flying shuttle" made weaving much faster and allowed broader cloth. This invention was soon followed by methods that mechanized jacquard weaving and repetitive pattern weaving.

Increased speed in weaving put heavier demands on the spinning of the yarns. Richard Arkwright (1732–1792) became one of the richest men in late-eighteenth-century England by mechanizing the spinning process of newly exploitable cotton imports. Arkwright's "waterframe" managed to imitate the touch of spinning and drawing out yarns by hand. Cotton fibers were drawn along through three pairs of rollers, each pair spinning at an increasingly faster rate. Arkwright began a spinning mill powering his invention with one horse in 1769, but established a water-powered mill only two years later. He continued to mechanize the industry with carding machines and a drawing frame.

## MINING, METALLURGY, AND THE STEAM ENGINE

With a demand for more intensive mining, and often entrepreneurial investment, sixteenth-century mining employed a vast array of machines and techniques, including the first form of the railroad. These were detailed in the elaborately illustrated volume *De Re Metallica* by the humanist Georgius Agricola (1494–1555). Deep ore deposits required pumps to evacuate water; the ore had to be raised; it was then roasted to make crushing easier. By the sixteenth century, most crushing was done by power-driven stamping mills. Ores were then fired in a blast furnace to extract the metals, and finally refined through a variety of metallurgical techniques, depending on the metals present.

The blast furnace was introduced by the beginning of the sixteenth century, and adopted across Europe. It was larger than its predecessor and required mechanical power to work the large bellows that provided the "blast" of hot air across the smelting metals. The furnace also had to be kept going around the clock. These alterations meant that blast furnaces needed to be built where there were plentiful supplies of water to run the water wheel, timber to make charcoal and fuel the furnace, plentiful labor, and exploitable ores. The blast furnace also made possible a new product: cast iron. While cast iron, particularly English cast iron, had a use in the making of ordnance, most cast iron was formed into wrought iron in a secondary process.

The iron trade was freed from the expense of charcoal fuel and the necessity and drawbacks of water-driven wheels in the mid-eighteenth century by the innovations of Henry Cort (1740–1800) and James Watt (1736–1819). Henry Cort developed a new style of furnace that made possible the use of coal in smelting iron by designing a way in which the sulfurous coke was kept out of direct contact with the metal. Watt improved the Newcomen steam engine used in mine drainage so that it was far more powerful. Thomas Newcomen's (1663–1729) steam engine was itself a variation of a philosophical curiosity invented by the mechanic Denis Papin (1647–1712?). The principle of both was to raise a piston in a cylinder by forcing it up with steam, then allowing condensation to create a vacuum so that atmospheric pressure would push the piston down. Watt added a separate condenser and a steam jacket around the cylinder, thus creating a far more rapid and powerful engine. Watt's steam engine was later adapted for use in many other manufactories, notably in textile and brass production, and made possible many new technologies. By the end of the eighteenth century, an average furnace consumed at least 2,000 tons of coke, processed 3,000 to 4,000 tons of iron ore, and produced 1,000 tons of iron per year.

## ENGINEERS, ENTREPRENEURS, AND ENLIGHTENMENT

As a generalization, one might say that the Renaissance gave rise to the great Italian architect-engineers; the baroque hailed the itinerant skilled mechanic from German and Dutch lands; and the Enlightenment saw the development of the highly trained French engineer and fostered the activities of the English entrepreneurial engineer.

By the end of the seventeenth century, Edmond Halley (1656–1742), otherwise beholden to various patronage networks and government service, set up his own ship-salvaging firm based on his innovative diving bell and diving suit. James Watt was one of the most successful (in part due to his association with Matthew Boulton [1728–1809]) and prominent of a number of engineers and inventors whose businesses flourished in eighteenth-century England. His association with the Birmingham "Lunar Society" is also instructive: a group composed of Watt, Boulton, the ceramics manufacturer Josiah Wedgwood (1730–1795), the botanist Erasmus Darwin (1731–1802), chemists James Keir (1735–1820) and Joseph Priestley (1733–1804), among others. These men saw the power of the connection between science and industry, and its possibilities for the improvement of society. They themselves had become engineers, curators of craftsmen, and scientists in eighteenth-century England's free mix of popular science and artisanal mechanics; however, they advocated a more rigorous scientific education for following generations. Whatever the workers in the mills, mines, and manufactories might have thought, members of the Lunar Society saw the values and products of science and technology as those most likely to lead to the moral, intellectual, and material liberation of humanity. This ideology they shared with many French Revolutionaries. Indeed, their forces were scattered in 1791 when a mob sacked the house of Priestley and others for their support of the French Revolution.

*See also* **Academies, Learned; Alchemy; Architecture; Artisans; Cartography and Geography; Ceramics, Pottery, and Porcelain; Chronometer; Clocks and Watches; Communication, Scientific; Design; Education; Engineering; Enlightenment; Firearms; Guilds; Industrial Revolution; Industry; Libraries; Magic; Medicine; Monopoly; Nature; Optics; Physics; Printing and Publishing; Scientific Instruments; Scientific Method; Scientific Revolution; Shipbuilding and Navigation; Textile Industry.**

BIBLIOGRAPHY

Braudel, Fernand. *The Structures of Everyday Life: The Limits of the Possible.* Translated and revised by Siân Reynolds. New York, 1981.

Bredekamp, Horst. *The Lure of Antiquity and the Cult of the Machine: The Kunstkammer and the Evolution of Nature, Art, and Technology.* Translated by Allison Brown. Princeton, 1995.

Cipolla, Carlo M. *Before the Industrial Revolution: European Society and Economy, 1000–1700.* 3rd ed. Translated and revised by Christopher Woodall. London, 1993.

———. *Guns, Sails, and Empires: Technological Innovation and the Early Phases of European Expansion, 1400–1700.* New York, 1965.

Eamon, William. *Science and the Secrets of Nature: Books of Secrets in Medieval and Early Modern Culture.* Princeton, 1994.

Goodman, David C. *Power and Penury: Government, Technology, and Science in Phillip II's Spain.* Cambridge, U.K., 1988.

Heller, Henry. *Labour, Science, and Technology in France, 1500–1620.* Cambridge, U.K., 1996.

Jacob, Margaret C. *Scientific Culture and the Making of the Industrial West.* New York and Oxford, 1997.

Jardine, Lisa. *Ingenious Pursuits: Building the Scientific Revolution.* New York and London, 1999.

Long, Pamela O. *Openness, Secrecy, Authorship: Technical Arts and the Culture of Knowledge from Antiquity to the Renaissance.* Baltimore, 2001.

McCray, Patrick W. *Glassmaking in Renaissance Venice: The Fragile Craft.* Aldershot, U.K., and Brookfield, Vt., 1999.

McNeil, Ian, ed. *An Encyclopaedia of the History of Technology.* London and New York, 1996.

Rossi, Paolo. *Philosophy, Technology, and the Arts in the Early Modern Era.* Translated by Salvator Attanasio. Edited by Benjamin Nelson. New York, 1970.

Schaffer, Simon. "Machine Philosophy: Demonstration Devices in Georgian Mechanics." *Osiris* 2nd ser., 9 (1995): 157–182.

———. "Natural Philosophy and Public Spectacle in the Eighteenth Century." *History of Science* 21 (1983): 1–43.

Singer, Charles, E. J. Holmyard, and A. R. Hall, eds. *A History of Technology.* Vol. 2, *From the Renaissance to the Industrial Revolution, c. 1500–c. 1750.* Oxford, 1957.

Smith, Pamela. *The Business of Alchemy: Science and Culture in the Holy Roman Empire.* Princeton, 1994.

Stewart, Larry. "A Meaning for Machines: Modernity, Utility, and the Eighteenth-Century British Public." *Journal of Modern History* 70, no. 2 (1998): 259–294.

———. *The Rise of Public Science: Rhetoric, Technology, and Natural Philosophy in Newtonian Britain, 1660–1750.* Cambridge, U.K., 1992.

MARY HENNINGER-VOSS

**TELESCOPE.** *See* **Scientific Instruments.**

**Teresa of Ávila.** Sixteenth-century gouache portrait. THE ART ARCHIVE/CARMELITE COLLECTION CLAMART/DAGLI ORTI

**TERESA OF ÁVILA** (1515–1582), founder of the Discalced Carmelites and a patron saint of Spain. Teresa of Ávila was born Teresa de Cepeda y Ahumada in Ávila, Spain, to Beatriz de Ahumada and Alonso Sánchez de Cepeda. Her mother came from an Old Christian family with a small estate in Gotarrendura, a village near Ávila. Her paternal grandfather, once a prosperous textile merchant in Toledo, moved to Ávila after the Inquisition convicted him of Judaizing, or practicing the Jewish religion or customs after having converted to Christianity, and sentenced him to a humiliating public ritual of penitence that usually resulted in loss of social reputation and business failure. In Ávila, Teresa's grandfather and his sons employed legal and financial routes to establish their right to the privileges of gentlemen, including a tacit agreement to overlook their genealogy. Teresa's contemporaries would have known of her *converso* heritage, but it was not publicly acknowledged until 1946. Teresa was the third child and first daughter born to Alonso and Beatriz, whose ten children joined two surviving offspring from Alonso's first marriage.

Teresa came to her career as a religious reformer relatively late in life. She joined the Carmelite Convent of the Incarnation just outside Ávila in 1535 and took vows in 1536 as Teresa of Jesus. In the *Book of Her Life* (1562–1565) she wrote that she withheld her wholehearted consent to the vocation until 1556, when she had two spiritual experiences that definitively turned her away from secular life. For these twenty years of irresolution, during which she suffered serious illnesses and experienced frightening visions that some confessors attributed to the devil, Teresa blamed the mitigated or relaxed rule in Carmelite convents, which among other liberties permitted nuns to come and go freely and to receive unlimited visitors. In condemning such lapses in monastic enclosure, Teresa participated in sixteenth-century movements to reform the Roman Catholic Church from within, or the Counter-Reformation. In 1560 Philip II (ruled 1556–1598) called on Spanish monasteries to contribute to his war against the Protestant Reformation by intensifying religious discipline.

On 24 August 1562 a house in Ávila was consecrated as the Convent of Saint Joseph under a constitution Teresa based on the 1247 formulation of Carmelite rule requiring strict asceticism and complete poverty. For the austere dress Teresa designed—habits of coarse fabrics and straw sandals—initiates were labeled Discalced (Barefoot) Carmelites. The new convent faced immediate threats to its existence. Some church officials considered that Teresa, known to practice a spirituality based on contemplation, might lead her nuns to abandon vocal prayer for mental prayer, which threatened both ecclesiastical authority and ecclesiastical income. Municipal officials of Ávila brought a lawsuit that was probably motivated by concern that a convent without an endowment could become dependent on civic financial resources.

Teresa's project of religious reform brought her allies as well as enemies in the church, monastic orders, and aristocracy. Giovanni Battista Rossi (1507–1578), the Carmelite prior general from Rome, found Saint Joseph's so impressive on his 1567 supervisory visit that he gave Teresa permission to found monasteries throughout Spain, with the explicit exception of Andalusia. Having secured this credential, Teresa began her travels around Spain in horse-drawn wagons. She eventually founded fifteen convents and monasteries herself and authorized other Discalced Carmelites to found two more. Teresa garnered much of her financial support and numerous recruits from *converso* families, who found most monastic orders, including the Carmelites after 1566, closed to them.

Teresa also continued to provoke controversy. Rossi eventually had to reprimand her for making foundations in Andalusia at Beas and Seville. By late 1575 the Inquisition was investigating her on several charges, and Carmelite officials had divested her of all leadership roles and had ordered her to stay in a Castilian convent. She probably owed permission to make more foundations, which came with the 1580 recognition of the Discalced as a separate province, to aristocratic friends holding high church and state positions.

Around 1562, Teresa began writing prolifically, both at the command of confessors and for her own purposes: first, the autobiographical *Book of Her Life* (composed 1562–1565; published 1588), fol-lowed by the devotional instruction in *Way of Perfection* (composed 1566–1569; published 1588), descriptions of her mystical experiences in *The Interior Castle* (composed 1577; published 1588), a chronicle of the origins of the Discalced Carmelites in *The Foundations* (composed 1582; published 1610), and several short works and numerous letters.

Teresa probably would be remembered only as a charismatic reformer but for reports that her body, when exhumed nine months after her death, had not deteriorated. Stories of other miracles accumulated, and in 1591 the bishop of Salamanca initiated the process that in 1622 made her a saint. In 1970 she became the first female doctor of the church.

*See also* **Catholic Spirituality and Mysticism;** *Conversos;* **Reformation, Catholic; Religious Orders.**

BIBLIOGRAPHY

*Primary Sources*

Teresa, of Ávila, Saint. *The Collected Works of St. Teresa of Ávila.* Edited and translated by Kieran Kavanaugh and Otilio Rodriguez. 3 vols. Washington, D.C., 1976–1985.

———. *The Complete Works of Teresa of Jesus.* Edited and translated by E. Allison Peers. 3 vols. London, 1944–1946.

———. *Santa Teresa de Jesús: Obras completas.* Edited by Efrén de la Madre de Dios and Otger Steggink. Madrid, 1951–1959.

*Secondary Sources*

Bilinkoff, Jodi. *The Ávila of Saint Teresa: Religious Reform in a Sixteenth-Century City.* Ithaca, N.Y., 1989.

Efrén de la Madre de Dios and Otger Steggink. *Tiempo y vida de Santa Teresa.* 2nd ed. Madrid, 1977.

Slade, Carole. *St. Teresa of Ávila: Author of a Heroic Life.* Berkeley, 1995.

Weber, Alison. *Teresa of Ávila and the Rhetoric of Femininity.* Princeton, 1990.

CAROLE SLADE

**TEUTONIC KNIGHTS.** The Teutonic Order was founded as a hospital in Acre (now 'Akko) in 1190. It became a military order in 1198 and expanded rapidly, particularly under the leadership of Hermann von Salza (1210–1239). In 1226 Frederick II's Golden Bull of Rimini granted Prussia to the Teutonic Order and this, together with the bulls of Gregory IX in 1230, laid the basis for the order's territorial power. Wars of conquest continued throughout the thirteenth century, and by 1290 the order had subjugated both Prussia and Livonia. After the fall of Acre in 1291 and the loss of the Holy Land, the order's headquarters moved to Venice, and then in 1309 to Marienburg. During the fourteenth century the focus of warfare switched to Lithuania, ruled by Grand Duke Gediminas (ruled 1315–1341) and his successors, and the order consolidated its power, which reached its apogee under Grand Master Winrich von Kniprode (1351–1382).

Prussia became the main resort for members of the European nobility intent on continuing the crusading tradition, notably King John of Bohemia in 1329 and Henry Bolingbroke (later Henry IV of England) in 1390 and 1392. By the end of the fourteenth century, however, the order was faced with rising unrest in the towns in Prussia, while the wars against the Turks, which began in 1396, diverted the flow of crusaders away from northern Europe. The baptism of Gediminas's grandson, Jogailo, and his election as Władysław II Jagiełło of Poland (1386–1434), saw the beginning of an attack by Poland and Lithuania on the order's territorial expansionism and on the legitimacy of the concept of military orders as such. The conflict culminated in the order's decisive defeat at the battle of Grünwald (Tannenberg) in 1410. The treaty of Toruń in 1466 compelled the order to return to Poland all the land on either side of the Vistula that it had conquered since 1309 and parts of Prussia conquered since 1250, including its headquarters at Marienburg. The remnants of East Prussia were ruled from Königsberg, but the grand masters had to swear an oath of allegiance to the kings of Poland. Finally, in 1525 the Grand Master Albert of Brandenburg implemented Luther's recommendation that he should establish a secular duchy in Prussia and that the knights there should renounce their vows and marry. A Catholic remnant of the order regrouped in Franconia with a new grand master and a residence in Mergentheim.

The order survived in Livonia until 1562, but the impact of the Reformation meant the loss of much of its land and infrastructure in the empire. During the second half of the sixteenth century it began fighting the Turks from its commanderies in eastern Austria, notably under Grand Master Archduke Maximilian of Austria (1585/1590–1618). However, the order suffered further losses in Alsace and Lorraine during the French Revolution and was abolished at the Peace of Pressburg in 1805. It was revived in Austria in 1834 and took on a charitative role, providing field hospitals and convalescent homes for soldiers until 1918. Following the collapse of the Austrian monarchy after World War I, it was recognized as a spiritual order by the Austrian state and the papacy, and it survives in that form.

*See also* **Lithuania, Grand Duchy of, to 1569; Poland to 1569; Prussia; Religious Orders.**

BIBLIOGRAPHY

Arnold, Udo. "Eight Hundred Years of the Teutonic Order." In *The Military Orders: Fighting for the Faith and Caring for the Sick.* Edited by Malcolm Barber. Aldershot, U.K., and Brookfield, Vt., 1994.

Christiansen, Eric. *The Northern Crusades: The Baltic and the Catholic Frontier, 1100–1525.* London, 1980.

MARY FISCHER

**TEXTILE INDUSTRY.** Between 1450 and 1800, textile production was second only to agriculture in economic importance. It employed more people and produced more profit than any other manufactured product. Production and trade existed at two levels. Everywhere peasants and villagers turned locally grown wool and flax into fabric and clothing for themselves and their neighbors. The cloth they produced was of poor quality and not designed for export to distant markets. On top of this local market sat a large and lucrative luxury trade in silk, wool, linen, and (eventually) cotton fabric, the most important of which were heavy woolens. The customers for these fabrics were wealthy landowners, government and church officials, merchants, financiers, aristocrats, and master craftsmen in Europe, Asia and the Levant.

Ireland and the Baltic region supplied much of Europe's flax, although it was widely grown and available. In the sixteenth century, Venice and other Italian cities acquired silkworms and mulberry trees, and began silk manufacturing. From there, the silk industry made its way north to Holland, Zurich,

Lyon, Cologne, and Spitalfields (East London), England. At the same time, cotton thread and fabric began to arrive from India and became wildly popular.

Most important of all the textile industries was the trade in raw wool and wool fabric. Sheep raising abounded everywhere. In the fifteenth century, the best fleeces came from England. In the sixteenth century, Spanish merino sheep knocked English sheep into second place. French sheep were considered to produce the third best wool. Two types of wool fabric were produced in Europe—woolens and worsteds. Of the two, the market for woolens was by far the larger. Woolens were made from short-staple wool fibers that were swirled together before spinning. The cloth had a soft-textured appearance and feel. Worsteds were made from long-staple wool and had a harder, smoother finish. Soft woolens were considered far more desirable than the harsher worsteds and dominated the wool trade.

Turning raw wool into fabric was a long, complicated process. The sheep's fleece was sheared in one continuous piece, rolled, sacked, and sold to merchants (drapers) or clothiers or their agents. The fleeces were dirty and greasy, not uniform, and far from ready for spinning and weaving. Fleece breakers opened up the fleece and removed the large pieces of debris that were caught in it. The fleece was then pulled apart, and the wool was sorted into three or four grades. Next, the sorted wool was cleaned. Any remaining debris was removed from the fleece by beating it with sticks, and then it was washed in alternating hot and cold, soapy and clean water. Some fleeces were dyed at this point, but dyeing raw wool produced dull colors, and it was common to dye fabric after it was completed rather than when the wool was raw. Whether it was dyed or not, the fleece was now lubricated with butter or oil to make it easier to work.

After breaking, cleaning, and oiling, the wool passed into the hands of combers and carders. Their task was to convert a mass of tangled, curling wool into long, straight, smooth fibers for worsteds by combing, or into a smooth ball of short wool fibers for woolens by carding. Spinners converted the combed or carded wool into continuous lengths of yarn by pulling, twisting, and turning it into a thin, continuous thread. This was the most labor-inten-

sive part of the process. Estimates vary, but six spinners (or more) seem to have been required for every loom that was in operation. Yarn that was spun with a drop spindle was stronger than wheel-spun yarn and was used for the looms' warps. Wheel-spun yarn was wound onto bobbins and used for the weft.

Weavers usually wound their own warps and prepared their own bobbins for the loom. The best woolens were woven on broadlooms that produced fabric that was 1 ¼ meters wide and 22 to 23 meters long. It commonly took two men and one child (most often, probably, a boy in training) to operate a loom and weave the cloth. Once the woolen cloth was woven, it passed into the hands of fullers who cleaned and softened it by dunking it in water that contained various kinds of detergents and soaps that dissolved or absorbed the fat that had been added to the wool before it was carded or combed. Lye, stale human urine, ashes, and fuller's earth were commonly used. Fullers placed the folded cloth in a vat and trod on it with their feet, periodically removing and refolding the cloth so it would be evenly fulled.

After fulling, the cloth was dried, stretched, bleached, and perhaps dyed. Teaselers raised the nap by brushing the cloth with the burr of the teasel plant to impart a soft finish. It was clipped smooth by shearmen, pressed, and returned to the merchant for sale. The entire process involved twenty people (not including dyers) for each piece of cloth produced and took at least six weeks. Women worked as carders, combers, and spinners, while men performed most of the other tasks. The finer the cloth, the larger the labor force and the longer the time it took to produce it. (More finely spun yarn required more spinners, for instance). The finishing of worsteds was much simpler (they did not require fulling, teaseling or shearing, for instance), but the market for them was much smaller.

In the fifteenth century, textile manufacturing was an urban industry, controlled by wealthy merchants (drapers) who purchased raw wool, had it turned into cloth, and then sold it, often to other craftsmen who performed the final finishing steps, including dyeing and teaseling. These were capital-intensive crafts, and cloth merchants often preferred not to be involved in them. Before the seventeenth century, most English cloth was dyed and finished in Holland. In England, in addition to merchants who only bought and sold, clothiers, themselves often master weavers, controlled a great deal of the woolen trade.

In the fifteenth and sixteenth centuries, textile workers dominated the population of towns like Venice and Leiden. By the sixteenth century, however, merchants had discovered that they could avoid the high wages, labor shortages, and quality controls imposed by urban guilds and governments by hiring peasants to do manufacturing work in their homes. Urban merchants continued to control production, but much of the work force was spread out through the countryside. Alternately referred to as the putting-out system, cottage manufacturing, and the *Verlag* system, merchants *(Verlagers)* found they could save money (rural workers could work for less because they produced much of their own food) and increase production at the same time. Trained cottage workers could be as skilled as urban workers, but many alternated farming and manufacturing and produced goods of lesser quality. The high-end woolen trade remained important, but many merchants began to reorient their businesses away from the luxury market and toward lower-quality, lower-priced, and more rapidly produced goods.

The building of fulling mills (first mentioned in accounts c. 1000) that beat the woven cloth with hammers raised by water wheels to replace the labor-intensive hand (or foot) fulling provided another incentive for merchants to put work out into the countryside and was a major determinant of the location of woolen production. In the eighteenth century, when merchants expanded employment to increase production, many rural villages became as much, or even more, dependent on the textile industry as they were on farming. Following the lead of Franklin Mendels, historians now call this intensification of cottage industry proto-industrialization to distinguish it from its earlier, perhaps more benign, manifestation, when cottage workers toiled fewer hours and produced goods for local markets.

### NEW MARKETS AND NEW FABRICS

Success in the textile industry was never permanent in the early modern world, and even the seemingly most secure industrial cities could watch their predominance and control of trade decline precipitously. Survival and growth depended on a host of

factors: access to raw materials, including raw wool and chemicals for dyeing; labor supply; access to trade routes and transportation systems, including ships and overland carriages; changing political allegiances; warfare; access to water for washing and fulling; demographic growth or stagnation; consumer demand; government laws and guild regulations; entrepreneurship; and fluctuating international markets.

In the sixteenth and seventeenth centuries, combinations of these factors inaugurated a series of important changes in the textile industry. Flanders, northern Italy, and southern Germany lost their dominance of woolen production to England, the Netherlands, and the Walloon region between the Meuse and Rhine Rivers. The woolen industries of Lille and Hondschoote disappeared rapidly. Venice, the largest producer of luxury broadcloths in the sixteenth century, saw its woolen industry wither away. One region's loss was often another's gain. England's woolen and worsted industries grew markedly with the government's decision to stop exporting wool fleeces in 1660. Leiden, adapting to a growing demand for lighter-weight fabrics, grew from a town of 12,000 in 1600 to a city of 80,000 in 1640, and then was outstripped by the nearby cities of Liège and Verviers, where labor costs were lower.

Often, the key to success was adaptability, especially in the eighteenth century. The economic downturn of the seventeenth century and changing consumer tastes had dampened demand for luxury woolens. Regions that had access to a variety of wool thread and flax or cotton began to produce "the new draperies," hybrid cloths made of both long and short staple wool (serges and says), wool and flax, wool and cotton, and cotton and flax (fustians and siamoises—that is, cotton and linen fabric produced in Normandy). Worsted production also profited from the demand for lighter-weight cloth.

Cotton fabrics from India and the Levant arrived in Europe in the sixteenth century or earlier. By the eighteenth century, the Dutch and English East India Companies began to import substantial amounts of pure cotton cloth (calicoes) from India and the Levant to Europe. To protect the woolen industry, England forbade the importation of pure cotton cloth in 1700. Other countries followed suit.

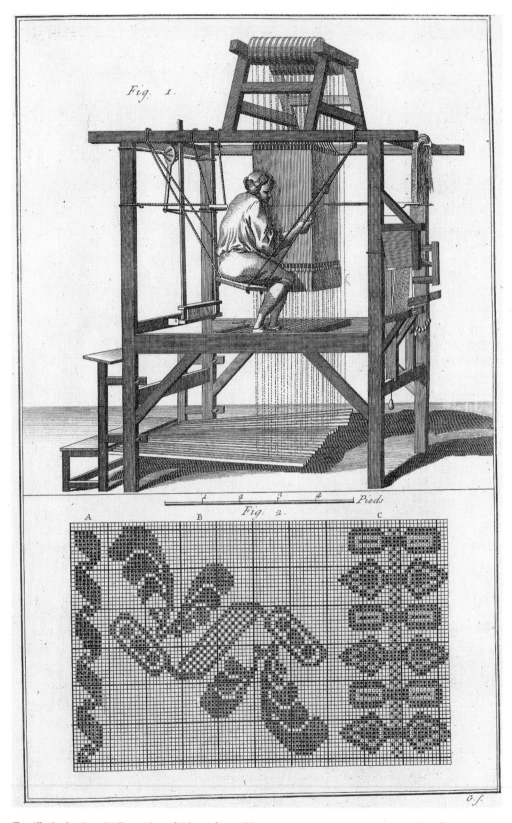

**Textile Industry.** An illustration of a loom for making passementerie lace and a template for a lace pattern, from the *Encyclopédie,* 1751–1772. Lace became popular in the mid-sixteenth century; by the mid-seventeenth century it was being produced commercially and was a particularly important textile product in several regions of France. THE ART ARCHIVE/DAGLI ORTI (A)

Raw cotton and cotton thread continued to arrive, however, imported not only from the Middle East and India, but also, beginning in the early eighteenth century, from the West Indies. The woolen industry remained the largest of the textile industries throughout the eighteenth century, but the market for cotton and linen fabric grew as fast as or faster than the supply of raw cotton. (Europeans were unable to spin cotton thread that was strong enough for warp threads until the introduction of the spinning frame in the 1770s.) The markets for these hybrid cloths of relatively modest quality were substantially different from those for woolen broadcloths. Many cloths were sent to Africa; others were purchased by European peasants, farmers, and urban workers. In both cases, the more brightly colored the cloth, the more it resembled the illegal calicoes and the more popular it was.

In English and Continental cities, woolen and worsted production continued to increase in the eighteenth century, despite the competition of the new draperies. In England this growth was fostered by the creation of urban cloth halls where the clothiers who oversaw the manufacturing of cloth sold their wares to merchants who, in turn, oversaw the finishing, transportation, and marketing of them. The most dynamic sector of the textile industry, however, was in cotton. The supply of raw cotton was far more elastic than the supply of wool and hence less expensive to purchase even though it had to be imported from Asia or the Western Hemisphere. The bulk of the heretofore untapped markets for European textiles lay in warm or temperate zones with hot summers—North America, Africa, south and east Asia, and the West Indies, where lightweight cloths were clearly more desired than heavy woolens.

## NEW TECHNOLOGIES

As the eighteenth century progressed, the invention of machines designed primarily to increase both the quantity and quality of cotton yarn made the manufacture of pure cotton fabric possible. Textile machines were not new in the eighteenth century. In 1598 William Lee invented a stocking frame for knitting. By the end of the seventeenth century, it had all but eliminated hand knitting. In 1604 William Dircxz van Sonnevelt invented a ribbon frame that allowed one person to weave twelve ribbons at

a time, and in the 1600s, Italians invented a machine for throwing silk that revolutionized silk manufacturing. At considerable risk, the plans for these machines were smuggled into England in 1717. Not all machines were immediately successful. John Kay's flying shuttle (1733) was slow to catch on because it speeded up weaving, which already consumed yarn faster than women could spin it. John Wyatt's and Lewis Paul's spinning frame (1738) was equally unsuccessful, but by mid-century the cultural climate was ready for innovation. The carding machines invented by Paul and others in the 1750s, James Hargreave's jenny (1765), Richard Arkwright's spinning frame (1769) (also known as the water frame), and Samuel Crompton's mule (1779) made it possible to produce stronger and finer cotton thread than ever before. With machinery came factories and the growth of cotton cities. Between 1760 and 1830, for instance, the population of Manchester, England, increased from 17,000 to 180,000. Edmund Cartwright devised a power loom in the 1780s, but its advantages over hand weaving were slight, and adoption of mechanical weaving came much more slowly than the adoption of mechanical carding and spinning. Finishing processes were also transformed. Chemicals replaced the sun as bleaching agents (sulfuric acid in 1756; chlorine in the 1790s) and cylinder printing replaced the old block press (1783).

Almost all of these machines were invented for the cotton trade, but they could be and were adapted for use in the production of wool fabric. Worsteds adapted more easily to the new technology than woolens did. The spinning frame was used to spin long-staple wool for worsteds. Short-staple wool used in woolens was more fragile and much more difficult to spin by machine, although it, too, was being spun by jennies by the 1780s. The same was true of mechanical weaving when it spread in the nineteenth century. Stronger threads made it easier to weave worsteds than woolens.

At the end of the eighteenth century, the textile industries of Europe were moving rapidly into the industrial era. The era of cotton had begun; worsteds were outpacing woolens; factory production was returning manufacturing to the cities; and markets had expanded well beyond the luxury trade of the fifteenth, sixteenth, and seventeenth centuries.

*See also* Capitalism; Clothing; Commerce and Markets; Enclosure; Industrial Revolution; Industry; Proto-Industry.

BIBLIOGRAPHY

Ashton, T. S. *The Industrial Revolution, 1760–1830.* Oxford, 1979.

Barnes, Edward. *Account of the Woollen Manufacture of England.* Introduction by K. G. Ponting. New York, 1970.

Berg, Maxine, Pat Hudson, and Michael Sonenscher, eds. *Manufacture in Town and Country Before the Factory.* Cambridge, U.K., 1983.

Clark, Alice. *The Working Life of Women in the Seventeenth Century.* London, 1982.

Coleman, D. C. "An Innovation and Its Diffusion: The 'New Draperies'." *Economic History Review,* 2nd series (1969): 417–429.

Davis, Ralph. *The Rise of the Atlantic Economies.* Ithaca, N.Y., 1973.

De Vries, Jan. *Economy of Europe in an Age of Crisis: 1600–1750.* Cambridge, U.K., 1976.

Gutmann, Myron P. *Toward the Modern Economy: Early Industry in Europe 1500–1800.* New York, 1988.

Hudson, Pat. *The Genesis of Industrial Capital: A Study of the West Riding Wool Textile Industry c. 1750–1850.* Cambridge, U.K., 1986.

Landes, David S. *The Unbound Prometheus: Technological Change and Industrial Development in Western Europe from 1750 to the Present.* Cambridge, U.K., 1969.

Mantoux, Paul. *The Industrial Revolution in the Eighteenth Century.* New York, 1961.

Smail, John. *Merchants, Markets and Manufacture: The English Wool Textile Industry in the Eighteenth Century.* London, 1999.

GAY L. GULLICKSON

---

**THEATER.** *See* Drama.

---

**THEOLOGY.** The common impression that the theological climate of late medieval and early modern Europe was monolithic is far from the reality. On the eve of the Renaissance and Reformation, theology was marked by a pluralism that created a state of ambiguity. The various theological schools of the day—nominalism, Scotism, Thomism, Augustinianism, Franciscanism, humanism, and others—vied for influence and dominance. On many levels, the differences among these schools were minimal, while on others they were profound, resulting in significant disagreements over church teaching.

As the changes of Renaissance society began to take hold, the theological approach of the Middle Ages no longer met the needs of the times and the spiritual longings of the people. The spirit of renewal that characterized the Renaissance called for an adaptation of traditional teaching, an appreciation of the historical context in the study of the Scriptures and the church fathers, and the application of the Gospel to the personal needs of the faithful. Scholasticism, which sought to bridge the gap between faith and reason by bringing reason to bear on theological matters, seemed to many in the Renaissance to be out of touch with contemporary realities. As Scholasticism immersed itself in dialectical speculations, it became more irrelevant, failing to move individuals to a more genuine living out of their Christian commitment. It was Scholasticism's orientation toward the abstract that drew the criticism of Renaissance thinkers such as Francesco Petrarch (1304–1374) and Desiderius Erasmus (1466?–1536), who proposed the "New Learning" associated with humanism as a means of revitalizing theology. For Erasmus, learning was to lead to virtue, scholarship to God, and thus, the restoration of theology was to be the means toward the revival of a living and lived Christianity.

**THOMISTIC REVIVAL**

Besides the humanist critique, Scholasticism also came under assault by the Protestant reformers. The *Summa Theologica* of Thomas Aquinas (1225–1274) was criticized for its treatment of Aristotle and the Holy Scriptures. Ironically, the polemical engagement with Scholasticism that came to characterize the Renaissance and the Reformation resulted in a rehabilitation of Thomism itself. Leading this rebirth of Thomism was the Dominican Jean Capréolus (c. 1380–1444), whose defense of the theology of Thomas sparked a new interest in his thought in the late fifteenth century. More important for this revival of Thomism was the work of another Dominican, Tommaso de Vio (1469–1534), known as Cajetan. Between 1507 and 1520 Cajetan wrote what was to become an extremely influential commentary on the *Summa Theologica* of Thomas, which exhibited a refreshing originality.

Thomism received a powerful stimulus and a wide dissemination from the Salamanca School, especially with the work of the Spanish Dominican Francisco de Vitoria (1486?–1546), who based his teaching largely on the *Summa Theologica*. Vitoria evolved his own method by considering questions rather than particular sayings of the *Summa Theologica*, initiating a new school of Thomistic thought. The popularity of his lectures and conferences allowed him to have far-reaching influence.

The new Scholasticism that resulted from the revival of Thomism sought, like its medieval counterpart, to reconcile faith and reason. But, unlike the abstractions and speculations of late medieval Scholasticism, it sought a theology that was simpler, clearer, and more relevant to the lives of people. In many ways it was more practical as it reexamined the method of theological proof, confronted the issues raised by the reformers, sought answers to the ethical issues raised by the colonization of the New World, and emphasized popular religious instruction and preaching. By the middle of the sixteenth century, Thomism seemed to have triumphed over other theological schools. Not only did Thomists dominate the Spanish universities, but at the Council of Trent (1545–1563), Thomism was clearly in ascendancy. Many of the Tridentine decrees reflected the teaching of Thomas, as did the Roman catechism and the theological manuals used by the seminaries. Many of the new religious orders of the period, especially the Society of Jesus, declared Thomas to be their official teacher. The constitutions of the society legislated Thomas, along with the Bible, as the basic text in theology. Given this Thomistic emphasis within the Society of Jesus, many of the leading Thomists of the late sixteenth-century were Jesuits—Robert Bellarmine (1542–1621), Francisco de Toledo (1515–1582), and Francisco Suárez (1548–1617). The climax of this Thomistic revival came with the declaration of Thomas as a "Doctor of the Church" by Pope Pius V in 1567.

## DOGMATIC THEOLOGY
Humanism's critique of Scholasticism along with its desire for a scripturally based theology led to the development of dogmatic theology as a distinct theological discipline. The major figure in this development was the Dominican theologian Melchior Cano (1509–1560). In his *De Locis Theologicis* (1563), he put forth the essential role of what he called *auctoritates* ('positive sources') in the work of theology—Scripture, the church fathers, and the councils. He demonstrated that theology took its principles from these sources. Thus, the quality of the conclusions in theology was determined by the quality and certitude of these sources. Cano's work looked to formulating these sources, establishing the criteria for assessing their value, and to positing the conditions under which they best served their purpose. The work created a theological methodology that was decisive in the development of a dogmatic theology that was positive in nature.

Dogmatic theology received an important impetus from the Council of Trent, which saw the need to provide an organized body of common doctrine. This need, together with the concern for the sources and the strong sense of dogma emerging from Trent, constituted the first stage of a recognizable dogmatic theology. The first aim of such a theology was to present the actual teaching of the church together with the theological note proper to it, followed by the exposition of that teaching. Hence its aim was pedagogical.

## PATRISTIC AND BIBLICAL THEOLOGY
Humanism's call for a return to the sources opened up new possibilities for theology. The importance placed on the study of the Bible, along with the revival of the writings of the church fathers, had a significant effect on theology in the Renaissance and the Reformation. In the Scholastic approach to theology, the Scriptures had lost their centrality and were relegated to an arsenal of evidence called upon to buttress the speculative arguments of the theologians. However, for the humanists, the concern was to restore Scripture to its place of centrality from which theology itself would emerge. For this to happen, theology needed to rely not on the Latin Vulgate, but rather on the original text of the Scriptures. Erasmus, in *Education of a Christian Prince* (1516), argues that the great weapon of the Christian is the knowledge of Holy Scripture, since it is the wellspring of Christian piety. Through a return to Scripture, theology would be reformed. In turn,

this scriptural revival would lead to a reform of Christian life and society.

The recovery of the patristic sources was an equally important contribution of humanism to theology. Here again, Erasmus played a significant role. He saw the fathers as engaged in genuine theology as opposed to the theologians of the day. Their authority derived from their closeness in time as well as in spirit to the divine source, and their chief value lay in their interpreting and helping to understand the Scriptures. Moreover, the writings of the fathers instructed and inspired individuals in living a Christian life. This reflects Erasmus's understanding of theology as practical in nature, as a guide to life rather than a subject for debate, and as a matter of transformation rather than speculation. Since Erasmus saw in the church fathers a more authentic and effective transmission of the teachings of Christ, he sought to make them better known through his patristic editions.

Besides the restoration of theology, the writings of the church fathers became the arsenal for controversial theology. This form of theology, which was seen as a first step toward the renewal of Catholic theology, developed as an answer to the doctrinal novelties of the reformers. The fathers provided the necessary witnesses for those aspects of Catholicism that were being challenged by the reformers. Controversial theology set a clear line of demarcation between the Catholic faith and the teachings of the reformers. Consequently, the teaching of theology entailed discriminating the true from the false—that is, that which is Catholic from that which is heretical—in order to prepare for the battle against the adversary. Controversialists rose up not only in Germany with Johann Eck (1486–1543) and Peter Canisius (1521–1597), but also in England with John Fisher (1469–1535) and Cardinal Reginald Pole (1500–1558). The most famous of the controversialists was Robert Bellarmine, who held the chair in controversial theology at the Roman College run by the Society of Jesus. Bellarmine's method was highly influential as he surveyed the whole field of Protestant-Catholic differences. A similar approach was employed by Francisco Suárez, who also taught at the Roman College. Suárez made clear distinctions between traditional church teachings and the novelties of the reformers. Suárez, along with Bellarmine, came to symbolize the long line of controversialists who championed the cause of the Counter-Reformation.

## MYSTICAL THEOLOGY

Another offshoot of the return to the sources was the deepening of mystical theology. The renewed interest in Pseudo-Dionysius (c. 500 C.E.), along with the scriptural revival, particularly of the Old Testament, fostered the mystical theology of the Renaissance. The mystical theologian focused on those Christians who, having conquered sin and its evil inclinations, and having grown in grace, drew near to Christ and were united to him. Mystical theology was not concerned with the good or the better so much as what was the best, which consisted in intimate union with God. Thus, mystical theology emphasized conforming the human will to the will of God through the successive stages of purgation, illumination, and contemplation. Mystical theology was especially vital in the life of St. Teresa of Ávila (1515–1582) and St. John of the Cross (1542–1591).

## MORAL THEOLOGY

Throughout the Middle Ages practical handbooks for confessors were always available to assist the faithful in the living out of a good life. The Thomistic revival of the fifteenth and sixteenth centuries was a step of considerable importance in the evolution of moral theology, which differed from its medieval counterpart. Moral theology came to be understood as the science of Christian life and action. It treated of the last end of the human person, of the morality of human acts, of natural and positive law, and of ecclesiastical sanctions within the context of theological reflection. Thus, it became a science distinct from dogmatic or speculative theology, embodied in a new literary genre, the *Institutiones morales* (Moral instructions).

Distinct from moral theology is ascetical theology, which is less concerned with the good and the evil, the licit and the illicit, the permitted and the forbidden, but is more interested in the greater and lesser good. The proper function of this branch of theology is to deal with the illuminative way.

## MARTIN LUTHER (1483–1546)

Overthrowing the Scholasticism that he knew, which was mostly nominalist in orientation, Martin Luther went back to the Scriptures to rediscover the message of salvation. Distrustful of human reason in fallen humanity, he sought to substitute for Scholastic theology a theology that was devout and scriptural. Proceeding from the authority of Augustine, Luther initiated a movement for reform of Christian doctrine and life that shattered the unity of Christendom.

The theological reformation initiated by Luther resulted from a rediscovery of God through Christ in the Scriptures. This rediscovery culminated in the twin banners of the Protestant Reformation—*sola fide* (by faith alone we receive Christ and his righteousness) and *sola scriptura* (authority resides in the Bible alone). The problem that plagued Luther was the concept of the *iustitia Dei,* which he understood as a punitive justice. In his view, God was a stern judge who weighed merit against sins. It was impossible, in Luther's mind, for sinners to stand before God in righteousness. This was the theological dilemma that culminated in the tower experience, so called because his new insight into the Gospel came to him in the tower of the Augustinian monastery in Wittenberg. The insight he gained in this experience led Luther to understand God's righteousness not as a demanding justice, rather as his mercy. The righteousness of God is no longer a demanding justice before which an individual may stand by virtue of his or her own good works and the forgiving grace of God. The righteousness of God is now primarily the grace which transforms and makes one righteous. Human activity no longer has any part in the ultimate determination of one's destiny. Grace alone enables one to stand before the righteousness of God. Humanity is righteous before God because of the atoning sacrifice of Christ. Belief in that act makes one just.

The essence of Luther's theology rested upon a different conception of the relationship between God and humanity. From his view of salvation based on faith grew most of the other doctrines of Protestantism. Good works played an important role in Luther's theology, but always as a result of faith, not the cause of it. Faith frees the individual by separating works from salvation. Once freed from the continual concern over salvation, the true believer could devote his or her life to doing good out of gratitude to God and not because it would contribute to salvation. Therefore, faith is not the end of Luther's theology, rather its beginning. From faith grows love, the active expression of the true Christian's faith. Thus, many elements of Catholicism were rejected as unnecessary.

## JOHN CALVIN (1509–1564)

The heart of John Calvin's theology, the core of which he acquired from Luther, was belief in the transcendent majesty and absolute sovereignty of God. The knowledge of God was the ultimate aim of life for Calvin. This knowledge was not an abstract knowledge, rather knowledge of God in relation to humanity; it could be acquired through creation and through Scripture. In the Scriptures we know God through Jesus and thus, Calvin understood the Bible as the only authority for our knowledge of God, which reveals all that should and can be known about Him.

However, Calvin insisted that the essence of God is inscrutable and that an infinite chasm separates the divine from the human. Due to the Fall, all humanity is corrupt and spiritually deformed. Therefore, humans are worthless in the sight of God. Yet, despite humanity's depravity, God did not abandon humans. The only mediator possible between God and humanity is Jesus. Through his atoning death on the cross, reconciliation was made possible. Through the redemptive grace of Christ and the gift of faith received from the Holy Spirit comes a spiritual union with Christ. This union brings about a regeneration or sanctification that renders the believer "born again," becoming a new creature in Christ and the inheritor of salvation. This results not from any human merit or effort but from faith in Christ.

Calvin took this idea one step further. The justifying grace of Christ is not for everyone, only for those whom God preelects. God's word germinates only in the elect, those whom he has already chosen for salvation even before their creation. Only on these individuals does Christ's redemption have any effect. The rest of humanity is predestined to perdition.

## CONCLUSION

Despite the critiques launched against the church by many Renaissance humanists, most remained within the institutional framework of Catholicism. Lutheranism and Calvinism diverged from the mainstream of the Renaissance when it exaggerated the Augustinian focus on the depravity of humanity and the servitude of the human will.

*See also* **Bellarmine, Robert; Bible; Calvin, John; Calvinism; Catholicism; Catholic Spirituality and Mysticism; Church of England; Erasmus, Desiderus; Humanists and Humanism; Luther, Martin; Lutheranism; Methodism; Pietism; Reformation, Catholic; Reformation, Protestant; Scholasticism.**

BIBLIOGRAPHY

Althaus, Paul. *The Theology of Martin Luther.* Translated by Robert C. Schulz. Philadelphia, 1966.

Bagchi, David V. N. *Luther's Earliest Opponents: Catholic Controversialists, 1518–1525.* Minneapolis, 1991.

Dowey, Edward A. *The Knowledge of God in Calvin's Theology.* New York, 1952.

George, Timothy. *Theology of the Reformers.* Nashville, 1988.

Gritsch, Eric, and Robert W. Jenson. *Lutheranism: The Theological Movement and Its Confessional Writings.* Philadelphia, 1976.

Kaiser, Edwin G. *Sacred Doctrine: An Introduction to Theology.* Westminster, Md., 1958.

MacKenzie, R. A. F. "The Concept of Biblical Theology." *Catholic Theological Society of America Proceedings* 10 (1955): 48–73.

Niesel, Wilhelm. *The Theology of Calvin.* Translated by Harold Knight. Philadelphia, 1956.

Olin, John C. *Six Essays on Erasmus and a Translation of Erasmus' Letter to Carondelet.* New York, 1979.

Pelikan, Jaroslav. *The Christian Tradition: A History of the Development of Doctrine.* 5 vols. Chicago, 1971–1989.

Wendel, François. *Calvin: Origins and Development of His Religious Thought.* Translated by Philip Mairet. Reprint. Durham, N.C., 1987.

FRANCESCO C. CESAREO

---

**THIRD ESTATE.** *See* **Bourgeoisie; Estates-General, French.**

---

# THIRTY YEARS' WAR (1618–1648).

The Thirty Years' War was one of the greatest and longest armed contests of the early modern period. Some historians have argued that it was a series of separate wars that happened to overlap in time and space rather than one coherent sequence of military campaigns in which a clearly defined set of issues was at stake throughout. If one looks at the Thirty Years' War in a European context, there is some truth in this argument. However, in central Europe, in particular in the Holy Roman Empire, the military and political events of the thirty years between the defenestration of Prague in May 1618 and the signing of the Westphalian peace treaties in October 1648 formed one continuous conflict and were in fact already perceived as such by most contemporaries.

## THE CAUSES OF THE WAR

For the outbreak of the war the deepening crisis of the Holy Roman Empire was of crucial importance. The crisis had a constitutional and political as well as a religious dimension. The emperor's prerogatives had never been clearly defined; a ruler who knew how to exploit his considerable informal powers of patronage could enjoy a great deal of authority, but a weak monarch could easily be reduced to a mere figurehead. This was very much Rudolf II's (ruled 1576–1612) fate during the last decade of his reign. The aging emperor, who was increasingly mentally unstable, was distrusted by both Catholics and Protestants. Moreover, he had managed to antagonize his own family. The power vacuum created by the collapse of his authority enabled ambitious princes such as Maximilian I, the duke of Bavaria, or Frederick V, the elector palatine, to pursue their own agenda. Their attempts to exploit the simmering religious conflict in Germany, which found its expression in the foundation of the Protestant Union, led by the Palatinate, in 1608 and the Catholic League *(Liga),* led by Bavaria, in 1609, were bound to undermine peace and stability. Germany had in the past been largely spared the horrors of religious warfare, thanks to the Religious Peace of Augsburg (1555). However, many problems had been left unresolved in 1555, such as the status of the ecclesiastical principalities that were ruled by Protestant prince-bishops, and of ecclesiastical property confiscated and secularized after 1555. The status of the Calvinists, who almost all Catholics and many Lutherans wanted to exclude from the benefits of the peace settlement as heretics, was also controversial. Initially the Imperial Chamber Court *(Reichskammergericht)*—one of the two highest law courts in Germany—had managed to settle disputes between the religious antagonists, but from the 1580s onward it became increasingly paralyzed, and the Imperial Diet *(Reichstag)* equally failed to provide a forum for compromise. The confessionalization of politics, culture, and society in the later sixteenth century had in fact created a climate of all-pervasive distrust that made such a compromise almost impossible. The enthusiastic adherents of both Counter-Reformation Catholicism and the eschatological worldview that most Calvinists and some Lutherans subscribed to saw the outbreak of armed conflict in the long run as both inevitable and even to some extent desirable.

However, whereas such mental attitudes were an important ingredient in the generally belligerent atmosphere that formed a crucial precondition for the outbreak of hostilities, their more immediate cause was the confrontation between the emperor and the Estates of Bohemia and its neighboring principalities, in particular Moravia and Upper Austria. Whereas Emperor Matthias (ruled 1612–1619) and his advisers wanted to recover the ground that had been lost by the Catholic Church and the ruling dynasty alike in the preceding years of domestic crisis, the Protestant opposition emphasized the elective character of the monarchy in Bohemia and its subjection to the control of the Estates. They vigorously defended the privileges of the Protestant Church that had been confirmed and extended during the last years of Rudolf II's reign. Reacting to the relentless Counter-Reformation offensive, which had, by a combination of missionary activity, generous imperial patronage for converts, and brute force already been successful in Styria, Carinthia, and elsewhere, they decided to kill the emperor's governors in Prague in the spring of 1618 by throwing them out of the windows of the imperial palace during a meeting of the Estates. The governors miraculously survived this defenestration, but armed conflict had now become unavoidable. Soon both sides tried to find allies both in Germany and in Europe. In Spain the fall of the duke of Lerma as royal favorite in 1618 marked the victory of those factions at court that favored a more assertive and warlike policy in central Europe, whereas at the same time in the Netherlands the adherents of rigid Calvinism and of an aggressively anti-Spanish policy gained the upper hand in 1618–1619 during and after the Synod of Dort (Dordrecht). Thus a renewal of the twelve-year truce between Spain and the Netherlands that had been signed in 1609 be-

came unlikely at the very moment when the Bohemian Estates rose against the Habsburgs. A war in Bohemia and Germany was therefore bound to become part of a wider European conflict sooner or later.

## THE FIRST DECADE OF THE WAR

In August 1619 the Estates of Bohemia deposed Ferdinand II, who had officially succeeded Emperor Matthias as king of Bohemia in March, and elected Frederick V, elector palatine, the leader of the Calvinists in Germany, in his stead. However, Frederick's rule was short lived. In November 1620 his army suffered a crushing defeat in the Battle of the White Mountain near Prague against the emperor's army, which had been reinforced by troops from the Bavarian-led Catholic League and by Spanish regiments. Whereas the Catholic League had decided to support Ferdinand, the Protestant Union preferred to stay neutral and was soon dissolved. In fact, some Protestant rulers, in particular John George of Saxony, openly supported the emperor. The fact that Ferdinand had managed to have himself elected emperor in the summer of 1619 gave him an authority that few German rulers dared to challenge openly for the time being. The next years were marked by an almost unbroken series of Catholic victories in central Europe. The Palatinate was occupied by Bavarian and Spanish troops in 1622, the palatine electoral dignity was transferred to Maximilian of Bavaria, and the army of the Catholic League led by Count Johann Tserclaes of Tilly threatened to dismantle the remaining Protestant strongholds in northern Germany. The troops of the Dutch Republic were too busy defending their own country to intervene in Germany. In fact, the important Dutch fortress of Breda had to surrender in 1625 to Spanish troops, a victory immortalized by Velázquez in his famous painting, *La rendición de Breda* (1634–1635; The surrender of Breda). However, King Christian IV of Denmark, who was also, as duke of Holstein, a prince of the empire and who hoped to acquire various prince-bishoprics in northern Germany for members of his family, decided to stop Tilly's advance in 1625. Hoping for financial and military support from the Netherlands and England—Charles I of England was the exiled elector palatine's brother-in-law—he mobilized the Imperial Circle *(Reichskreis)* of Lower Saxony for the Protestant cause. However, he had not antici-

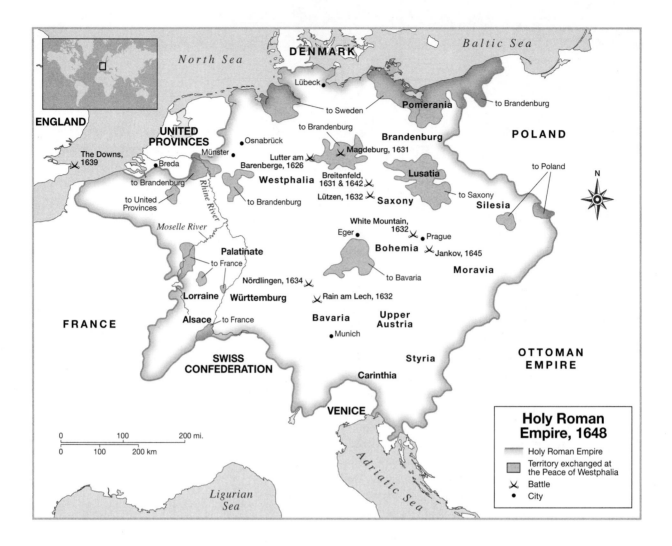

Holy Roman
Empire, 1648

Holy Roman Empire
Territory exchanged at
the Peace of Westphalia
Battle
City

pated that the emperor would raise an army of his own (counting initially 30,000 soldiers and growing fast), commanded by Albrecht von Wallenstein, a Bohemian nobleman and the greatest military entrepreneur of his age. Christian's troops were routed at Lutter am Barenberge (1626). Christian's ally Charles I of England was equally unsuccessful in his fight at sea against Spain, and France, which might have given support to the opponents of the Habsburgs, was paralyzed by a Protestant revolt during the years 1625–1628, in which England became involved in 1627. Thus Ferdinand II was able to crush his enemies. Christian had to withdraw from the conflict and signed the Peace of Lübeck in 1629, giving up his claims to several prince-bishoprics in northern Germany but retaining Holstein and Schleswig. However, Ferdinand failed to exploit his success adequately. His allies in Germany, in particular Maximilian of Bavaria, were, in fact,

increasingly apprehensive about the predominance of Habsburg power and the close cooperation between Ferdinand II and Spain. Moreover, they resented the arrogant and ruthless behavior of Ferdinand's commander-in-chief, Wallenstein, who had imposed enormous financial burdens on friend and foe alike, raising contributions for his 100,000-man army almost everywhere in Germany. Wallenstein had to resign in 1630 under pressure from Maximilian of Bavaria and other princes. Ferdinand tried to rebuild a united Catholic front in 1629 by passing the Edict of Restitution, which was designed to give all ecclesiastical property secularized since 1552/1555 back to the Roman Catholic Church. The potential consequences for Protestantism were disastrous. Protestantism was not outlawed but was likely to be reduced to the status of a barely tolerated and marginalized religious community in Germany.

## FROM CATHOLIC AND HABSBURG TRIUMPH TO ABORTIVE COMPROMISE, 1629–1635

At this stage, however, the Habsburg ascendancy in Europe, successfully reasserted in the early 1620s, was seriously challenged by France and Sweden. In 1628 La Rochelle, the stronghold of the French Huguenots, had been taken by a royal army led by Louis XIII and the prime minister, Cardinal Richelieu, in person. France was now free to intervene in central Europe. Initially, however, French troops confronted Spain only in Italy (the War of the Mantuan Succession, 1628–1631). Here they defied Spanish attempts to occupy the Duchy of Mantua after the main line of the native dynasty, the Gonzaga, had died out in 1628. The emperor had sent troops to northern Italy to help Spain, but withdrew these troops in late 1630. The troops were now badly needed in Germany itself, where Gustavus II Adolphus of Sweden landed his army on the coast of Pomerania in July 1630. Sweden felt threatened by plans to build an imperial fleet in the Baltic and by Habsburg support for its old enemy Poland. Moreover, the fight for Protestantism was an essential part of the claim to legitimacy of the Swedish dynasty, the Vasas, which had won the crown in the 1590s by ousting the older, Catholic branch of the family, which continued to rule in Poland.

The Edict of Restitution had antagonized even those Protestants who had preferred to stay neutral or had in fact supported the emperor for most of the 1620s. Their last doubts were dispelled when Magdeburg, a town of great symbolic importance to Protestants (it had resisted a long siege by Catholic armies in the late 1540s) was besieged by Tilly, taken by assault, sacked, and set on fire in May 1631. Brandenburg and Saxony now joined the king of Sweden in the fight against the Catholic forces. Having lost the battle of Breitenfeld in Saxony in September 1631, Tilly retreated to southern Germany and was decisively beaten at Rain am Lech in April 1632. Even Munich was now briefly occupied by Swedish troops, and an army from Saxony evicted the imperial garrisons from Silesia and Bohemia. In despair Ferdinand II decided to recall Wallenstein to reorganize his army. In the battle of Lützen in November 1632, Gustavus Adolphus won a last victory against Wallenstein but died in action. Sweden, however, maintained its superiority for a further two years. In 1634 Spain sent a fresh army to Germany across the Alps under the command of one of Philip IV's brothers, the Cardinal Infante Ferdinand. In February Wallenstein, who was reluctant to cooperate with Spain and was suspected of treasonous dealings with the enemy, was assassinated in Eger on the emperor's orders. Together with the future Emperor Ferdinand III, the Cardinal Infante inflicted a crushing defeat on the Swedes at Nördlingen in southern Germany in September. As far as Germany was concerned, Nördlingen might have been the end of the war. Ferdinand II did not repeat the mistakes he had made in 1629 by pursuing an Ultra-Catholic policy. Instead he reached a compromise with the moderate and essentially loyal Lutherans led by Saxony. The Peace of Prague (1635) did not revoke the Edict of Restitution, but suspended it for forty years. The position of Protestantism in northern and eastern Germany was now reasonably safe once more. However, no satisfactory settlement was reached in the Palatinate, in Hesse, or, for the time being, in Württemberg. In constitutional terms the emperor's authority had been considerably strengthened. He was now officially commander-in-chief of all armed forces in the empire. The Catholic League was dissolved, and only Saxony and Bavaria continued, with the emperor's permission, to maintain armies, which remained semi-independent. This change in the constitutional balance, however, was silently resented by many German princes and duly revised in 1648. In any case the Peace of Prague was deficient because it had failed to make provision for buying off the Swedes, who still maintained troops in many parts of Germany—in particular in the north—with territorial or financial concessions. In fact, the settlement of 1635 proved abortive, as it was rejected by both Sweden and France.

## THE LAST PHASE OF THE WAR AND THE ROAD TO SETTLEMENT

France was now faced by the prospect of a Spanish offensive supported by the emperor's army against the garrisons it had placed beyond its frontiers, in Lorraine, Alsace, and along the upper Rhine and Moselle rivers in the preceding years. In answer to an attack on the prince-bishop of Trier, who had become a French ally and client in 1632, Louis XIII declared war on Spain in May 1635. With the emperor's own declaration of war on France in March 1636, the war in Germany had, it seemed, finally fused with the all-European conflict between Spain and its enemies, which had already decisively influenced events in the empire in the past. Whereas French financial subsidies helped Sweden gradually recover from the defeat of Nördlingen, Spanish resources became increasingly inadequate to finance the worldwide war effort of the monarchy in the early 1640s. Spain suffered important naval defeats against the Dutch off the English coast in 1639 (Battle of the Downs) and near Recife in Brazil in 1640. Moreover, in 1640 both Catalonia and Portugal revolted against Castilian rule in an attempt to shake off the fiscal and political burden imposed on them by warfare. Spain did not recognize Portugal's independence until 1668 and managed to reconquer Catalonia in the 1650s. Nevertheless, it was no longer able to launch major offensive operations in central Europe. Emperor Ferdinand III (ruled 1637–1657), reluctantly supported by the majority of the German princes, was now virtually on his own in his fight against both France (which had committed a major army to operations in southern Germany) and Sweden. Nevertheless, the war dragged on for another eight years.

The logistics of warfare in a country that had been utterly devastated by continuous fighting and lacked the most essential provisions proved a major obstacle to large-scale offensive operations. For this reason, victories won in battles could rarely be fully exploited. Moreover, a war between Denmark and Sweden (1643–1645) gave the emperor's army time to recover after the devastating defeat it had suffered in the second battle of Breitenfeld in November 1642. However, in March 1645 the Swedes beat the imperial army decisively at Jankov in Bohemia. Although Ferdinand III was able to buy off Sweden's ally Transylvania, which had once more, as in the 1620s, intervened in the war (supported halfheartedly by the sultan), by territorial and religious concessions in Hungary, he was now forced to come to terms with his opponents. His allies in Germany became increasingly restless and either withdrew from active participation in warfare altogether or insisted on ending the war. Reluctantly the emperor entered into negotiations with Sweden in Osnabrück and with France in neighboring Münster in autumn 1645. Against his wishes, the German princes and Estates were allowed to participate in the peace conference, sending their own envoys to Westphalia. Partly because Ferdinand hesitated to abandon his old ally Spain, it was nevertheless three years before a settlement was reached. Peace between France and Spain proved elusive. So when the peace treaties were signed at Münster and Osnabrück on 24 October 1648, the Franco-Spanish conflict was deliberately excluded from the settlement. The treaties, known as the Peace of Westphalia, therefore failed to provide the basis for a truly European peace. The complicated legal arrangements that dealt with the various constitutional and religious problems of the Holy Roman Empire, on the other hand, proved remarkably long-lasting and stable, being invoked right up to the end of the empire in 1806.

## THE NATURE AND IMPACT OF WARFARE

Most countries—the Dutch Republic, which benefited from a flourishing economy in the midst of military conflict, was probably one of the few exceptions—waged war between 1618 and 1648 with financial resources that were grossly inadequate. Some countries such as Sweden nevertheless managed to finance their armies for long periods of time primarily out of contributions raised in areas under military occupation. Others tried, with limited success, to rely on taxation. France, for example, managed to double its income from domestic revenues in the 1630s and early 1640s. However, the enormous fiscal pressure provoked a series of popular revolts in France that prevented further increases in taxation and finally led to bankruptcy and civil war in 1648–1652. Most participants in the war entrusted the raising and maintaining of troops at least to some extent to military entrepreneurs who had their own sources of income and credit, thereby complementing the insufficient resources of the state. These entrepreneurs hoped to recoup their investments and to make a profit by extorting payments, not to mention downright plunder and confiscation, from occupied provinces. The hardship this involved for the civilian population was considerable. France, however, which was reluctant to rely on military entrepreneurs because of the dangerous domestic implications of such a system, was hardly more successful in asking noblemen to pay for the units under their command partly out of their own pockets without giving them, in compensation, full legal ownership of their regiments. Spain initially had a fairly sophisticated state-controlled system of organizing and financing warfare, but gradually more and more responsibilities such as the recruitment of soldiers were delegated to local magnates and urban corporations, and thereby decentralized. This phenomenon may be seen as a wider-ranging process of administrative refeudalization, as some historians have argued.

The often chaotic way in which armies were recruited and financed was at least in part responsible for the widespread lack of discipline among soldiers often remarked upon by contemporaries. Although some of the accounts of wartime atrocities, such as most or all tales of cannibalism, for example, have to be dismissed as unreliable, the excesses soldiers regularly committed when dealing with the local population in friendly as much as in enemy provinces were sufficient to severely disrupt civilian life. Combined with the rapid spread of infectious diseases among soldiers and civilians alike and the partial breakdown of trade, commerce, and agriculture, these effects of warfare had serious demographic consequences. This was true in particular for the Holy Roman Empire but to a lesser extent also for some areas of northern Italy and of France. In the empire population figures were reduced by at least 25 percent and possibly by up to 35 to 40 percent (about 6 million) during the course of the war. Some regions in northeastern Germany such as Pomerania and parts of Brandenburg, but also Württemberg in the southwest, had hardly more than a third of their prewar population in 1648. It took Germany almost a hundred years to recover demographically from the war. Nevertheless, older accounts that have seen the war, and also the Peace of Westphalia, as responsible for a general decline of the Holy Roman Empire and the German states no longer command widespread assent. Not only did the empire survive as a political and legal system providing reasonably effective protection and security to its members, but the rise of the Habsburg Monarchy after 1648, for example, and the flourishing baroque culture of many German courts in the later seventeenth century, show that in some areas at least the war had brought about changes that stimulated rather than stunted new growth once peace had been regained.

*See also* **Augsburg, Religious Peace of (1555); Bohemia; Dort, Synod of; Dutch Republic; Ferdinand II (Holy Roman Empire); Ferdinand III (Holy Roman** Empire); France; Gustavus II Adolphus (Sweden); Habsburg Dynasty; Habsburg Territories; Holy Roman Empire; La Rochelle; Louis XIII (France); Mantuan Succession, War of the (1627–1631); Military; Netherlands, Southern; Palatinate; Richelieu, Armand-Jean du Plessis, cardinal; Rudolf II (Holy Roman Empire); Saxony; Spain; Sweden; Tilly, Johann Tserclaes of; Wallenstein, A. W. E. von; Westphalia, Peace of (1648).**

BIBLIOGRAPHY

*Primary Sources*

*Briefe und Akten zur Geschichte des Dreißigjährigen Krieges, Neue Folge, Die Politik Maximilians von Baiern und seiner Verbündeten 1618–1651.* Part I, vol. I and II, edited by G. Franz and A. Duch; Part II, vol. I–X, edited by W. Goetz, D. Albrecht and K. Bierther. Leipzig, Munich, and Vienna, 1907–1997. Important edition of sources based mainly on the records of the Bavarian state archive in Munich; latest volumes so far deal with Peace of Prague (1635).

*Documenta Bohemica Bellum Tricennale Illustrantia.* Edited by J. Kocí et al. 7 vols. Prague, 1971–1981. Sources from archives in the Czech Republic.

*Germany in the Thirty Years' War.* Edited by Gerhard Benecke. London, 1978. Brief selection of sources in English.

*Secondary Sources*

Asch, Ronald G. *The Thirty Years' War: The Holy Roman Empire and Europe, 1618–1648.* Basingstoke, U.K., and New York, 1997. Concise survey, concentrates on central Europe without neglecting the role Spain and France played in the war.

Bireley, Robert, S. J. *Religion and Politics in the Age of the Counterreformation: Emperor Ferdinand II, William Lamormaini, S. J., and the Formation of Imperial Policy.* Chapel Hill, N.C., 1981. Excellent on the influence of court chaplains and on Counter-Reformation policy in general.

Burkhardt, Johannes. *Der Dreißigjährige Krieg.* Frankfurt am Main, 1992. Stimulating and well-argued account by a leading German scholar. Particularly good on propaganda and contemporary pamphlets. Occasionally somewhat idiosyncratic and fanciful in its assessment of the international situation.

Bußmann, Klaus, and Heinz Schilling, eds. *1648: War and Peace in Europe.* 3 vols. Münster/Osnabrück 1998. Important exhibition catalogue and two comprehensive volumes of essays covering almost all relevant topics, particularly rich on cultural history.

Elliott, John H. *The Count-Duke of Olivares: The Statesman in an Age of Decline.* New Haven and London, 1986. Majestic biography of the leading Spanish statesman of the age.

Israel, Jonathan I. *The Dutch Republic and the Hispanic World 1606–1661*. Oxford, 1982. Important work by one of the leading experts on Dutch early modern history.

Langer, Herbert. *The Thirty Years' War*. New York, 1980. Good on the social history of warfare.

Parker, Geoffrey, et al. *The Thirty Years' War*. 2nd ed. London and New York, 1997. Standard account in English, in which a number of scholars have cooperated; sees the war very much as an all-European conflict.

Parrott, David. *Richelieu's Army: War, Government and Society in France, 1624–1642*. Cambridge, U.K., and New York, 2001. Detailed study of French military organization which shows how ill prepared France was for the confrontation with Spain.

Redlich, Fritz. *The German Military Enterpriser and his Work Force: A Study in European Economic and Social History*. 2 vols. Wiesbaden, 1964–1965. Unrivaled account of the social and economic aspects of warfare and of recruitment in this period.

Stier, Bernhard, and Wolfgang von Hippel. "War, Economy and Society." In *Germany: A New Social and Economic History*. Vol. 2, *1630–1800*, edited by Sheilagh Ogilvie, pp. 233–262. London, 1996. Good survey of the impact of the war and the slow recovery after 1648, incorporating a great deal of recent research.

RONALD G. ASCH

# THIRTY-NINE ARTICLES. *See* Church of England.

# THOMASIUS, CHRISTIAN (1655–1728), German philosopher. Christian Thomasius was the leading legal theorist and university reformer in Protestant Germany during the early Enlightenment. A self-consciously controversial figure who built on the writings and influence of his mentor Samuel von Pufendorf (1632–1694), he developed a new philosophical outlook, eclecticism, which united all of his contributions to many intellectual fields. It also underpinned his high-profile assaults both on the outmoded Scholastic pedantry of German university life and on several contemporary instances of what he took to be intolerance and superstition in wider society, notably witchcraft prosecutions and the use of torture to extract confessions.

He was the son of Jakob Thomasius, himself an influential Aristotelian moral philosopher of the Altdorf School, which sought to introduce some of the ideas of Francisco Suárez (1548–1617) into German Protestant Scholasticism. Trained and educated at the Universities of Frankfurt an der Oder and Leipzig, he was a product of the intellectual synthesis between Lutheran Protestantism and Scholastic Aristotelianism, which had been brokered originally by Philipp Melanchthon (1497–1560). But Thomasius broke decisively with this intellectual orthodoxy when appointed as a young *Privatdozent* at Leipzig in the 1680s: he was the first academic to regularly give lectures in German as opposed to Latin, a practice he later carried through into his published writings. He was required to leave Leipzig in 1690 and sought employment in Prussia at the newly founded University of Halle, where he went on to hold senior chairs in philosophy and law. During this transitional period he developed his "practical philosophy" and initial proposals for reform of the traditional university curriculum. In a series of works, notably *Institutiones Jurisprudentiae Divinae* (1688; Institutes of divine jurisprudence) and *Introductio ad Philosophiam Aulicam* (1688; Introduction to court or civil philosophy) he transformed the innovative epistemological insights of Samuel Pufendorf's *De Jure Naturae et Gentium* (1672; On the law of nature and of nations) into a radical separation of moral philosophy from theology.

What drove this program was not a commitment to "Enlightenment rationality," as has been argued anachronistically by some historians, but a perception that the mingling of theology and moral and political sciences within the framework of metaphysics had produced a fundamental form of institutionalized corruption that was damaging both to true religion and to healthy philosophy. Only by separating theology and ethics could religion be saved from mere dogmatism, and a useful preparatory curriculum devised that would produce the jurists, administrators, and pastors appropriate for a coherently governed and properly ordered absolutist state. Educational reform, stemming from a revision of the traditional responsibilities of the faculties of philosophy, law, and theology, would thus usher in substantial changes for ecclesiology, political responsibility, and confessional coexistence. On this account Thomasius offered a powerful program for completing the desacralization of state forms, a process left incomplete in the political and philosophical debates that had followed the Peace of Westphalia in 1648. Yet this was undertaken not on behalf of the cause of secularization but rather so that Protestant Christianity could acquire once more a purified spiritual identity free from the accretions of "priestcraft." True religion was to be a matter of promoting the inward relationship of the individual with Christ in the manner of the early church. At first, these convictions naturally drew Thomasius close to the contemporary doctrines of the Pietists. However, he and his followers drew back from this assimilation once it became clear that Pietism would not accept his radical reduction of the state's right to intervene in religious affairs to the minimal level of threats to civil safety. In this respect too, Thomasius went well beyond the more conservative positions of Pufendorf.

Thomasius was considered as a thinker of weight and significance for much of the eighteenth century, and until the 1750s his views were propounded at German universities against the doctrines of Christian Wolff (1679–1754), Leibniz's most distinguished follower. However, the restriction of the publication of many of his works to German limited his intellectual influence beyond German borders, as was not the case with Pufendorf's Latin texts. Moreover, the antisystematic, practical, and problem-solving bias of his work left it more vulnerable to supercession once the debates of his own day had faded from the forefront of political and intellectual discussion. In sum, Thomasius can be considered as one of the first writers in Germany to place the individual at the heart of moral and legal theory, although he did not draw the same liberal consequences for political theory as were extracted elsewhere by John Locke (1632–1704) and other contemporary philosophers. In this respect, together with other thinkers in the German Enlightenment, he did not substantially shift his account of sovereignty far from that of Thomas Hobbes (1588–1679), a balance that emphasizes his transitional status between the thought-world of the baroque and the fully mature Enlightenment.

*See also* **Enlightenment; Melanchthon, Philipp; Pietism; Universities.**

BIBLIOGRAPHY

Hochstrasser, T. J. *Natural Law Theories in the Early Enlightenment.* Cambridge, U.K., and New York, 2000.

Hunter, Ian. *Rival Enlightenments: Civil and Metaphysical Philosophy in Early Modern Germany.* Cambridge, U.K., and New York, 2001.

Schröder, Peter. *Christian Thomasius zur Einführung.* Hamburg, 1999.

TIMOTHY HOCHSTRASSER

**3 MAY CONSTITUTION.** The first Polish constitution was adopted by the Four-Year Sejm (parliament) on 3 May 1791. It was the first such basic law in written form in Europe and the second in the world after the constitution of the United States (1787). The Constitution of 3 May was drafted at the Four-Year Sejm (1788–1792) by reformers led most actively by King Stanisław II August Poniatowski, Hugo Kołłątaj, and Ignacy Potocki. The constitution was preceded by two acts regarded as integral to it: the Reorganization of the *Sejmiki* [provincial diets] Act (adopted on 24 March 1791) and the Act on the Status of Towns and Townsmen's Rights (18 April).

In accordance with Enlightenment ideas, the Constitution and these two related documents introduced the principle of the nation's sovereignty and the separation of the legislative, executive, and judicial powers. Landless noblemen (usually dependent on magnates) were excluded from the Sejm and the *sejmiki,* and townsmen were given the opportunity to acquire nobility through the purchase of a landed estate or by virtue of services rendered to the country or professional work. The citizens of royal towns were guaranteed personal immunity and were granted the right to purchase landed estates and hold junior official posts. The towns received the right to send their representatives to the Sejm, where they would have an advisory voice on matters concerning towns. State protection of the Jews was confirmed. The constitution maintained serfdom, but peasants were to be put under the protection of the law and the government, *inter alia* with regard to contracts concluded with landowners.

The constitution abolished the election of kings; after the death of the current king, the throne was to be hereditary in the Saxon dynasty. Legislative power was vested in a bicameral Sejm (with a Chamber of Deputies and a Senate), which was to be responsible for legislation and taxation and would have broadly conceived control over the government as well as jurisdiction in offenses against the nation and the state. Laws were to be adopted by a majority vote; the deputies (204 plus 24 plenipotentiaries of towns) were to be elected for a term of two years. The competency of the Senate was restricted to a suspensory veto; if the Chamber of Deputies upheld its decision, the bill became law without the consent of the Senate. The role of the *sejmiki,* and indirectly also of the magnates, was restricted. The executive was strengthened: confederations (a form of legal rebellion) were banned and the *liberum veto* (the principle of unanimity that allowed a single deputy to dissolve the Sejm and invalidate its decisions or even to prevent it from assembling) was abolished.

The Council of Ministers, called the Guardians of the Laws, was to be the highest executive body. It was to be composed of the king, who had the decisive voice, the primate, and five ministers, and was to direct the central administration and supervise five commissions (ministries)—education, foreign affairs, justice, war, and treasury. The monarch was responsible to no one, while the ministers were responsible to the king and the Sejm for their policies and could be brought before the Sejm court if they broke the law—this was thus the world's first legally formulated principle of ministerial responsibility. The reform of the judiciary united the various noblemen's judicial courts into uniform collegiate country courts of first instance; courts of appeal were set up in towns. The constitution was a great step forward toward a centralized government. It laid the foundations for cooperation between landowners and rich burghers and opened possibilities for the further political and legal transformations that would be indispensable for the development of Poland's fledgling capitalism.

The Constitution of 3 May was supplemented on 20 October 1791 by the Mutual Pledge of the Two Nations, which emphasized the federal character of the state and the equal status of the Grand Duchy of Lithuania and the Polish Kingdom. The Duchy was to have the same ministerial posts as Poland, and it retained its separate system of laws.

This was a compromise between the Lithuanians' aspiration for sovereignty and reform of the political system, on the one hand, and the tradition of union between the two states and the preservation of the Commonwealth's federal character, on the other. The constitution gained the support of the majority of the nobility, townsmen, and many magnates. In 1792 its opponents set up the Targowica confederation in defense of the old system and asked Russia to intervene militarily. The achievements of the Constitution of 3 May were canceled by the fall of the Commonwealth with the Third Partition in 1795.

*See also* **Catherine II (Russia); Lublin, Union of (1569); Poland, Partitions of; Poland-Lithuania, Commonwealth of, 1569–1795; Poniatowski, Stanisław II Augustus.**

BIBLIOGRAPHY

Kowecki, Jerzy, ed. *Konstytucja 3 maja 1791: Statut Zgromadzenia Przyjaciół Konstytucji.* Warsaw, 1981.

Leœnodorski, Bogusław. *Dzieło Sejmu Czteroletniego 1788–1792: Studium historyczno-prawne.* Wrocław, 1951.

———. *Institutions polonaises au Siècle des Lumières.* Warsaw, 1962.

Rostworowski, Emanuel. *Ostatni król Rzeczypospolitej: Geneza i upadek Konstytucji 3 maja.* Warsaw, 1966.

MARCIN KAMLER

# TIEPOLO, GIOVANNI BATTISTA

(1696–1770), Italian painter, master of Venetian school. Tiepolo was famous in his own lifetime as a superb painter in fresco and a brilliant draftsman. A highly inventive artist, he could create spectacular effects in difficult sites, from the narrow gallery at the patriarchal palace at Udine in the mid-1720s to the vast staircase ceiling in the Residenz at Würzburg in the early 1750s. Contemporaries recognized his spirited, dynamic approach to subject matter and his frankly sensuous manner of painting. Tiepolo is comparable in his restless energy and imaginative power to Peter Paul Rubens, and essentially he worked with a similar baroque language of myth, allegory, and history, which he infused with a sense of freshness and modernity. His approach to religious art is characterized by candor and naturalism, while he was responsive to the different concerns of patrons and viewers at a time when the church was faced with new kinds of devotion and criticism. With the advent of neoclassicism, Tiepolo's art fell from favor: In an age that prized archaeological correctness, rationality, and ideals of improvement, his witty, Veronese-inspired conception of historical or classical subjects seemed frivolous, while his visually seductive qualities were seen as inimical to the serious intellectual aims of the new art. Nevertheless, his drawings and oil sketches continued to appeal to collectors, including Antonio Canova.

The son of a Venetian shipping merchant, Tiepolo was apprenticed in 1710 to Gregorio Lazzarini (1655–1730), an artist of international reputation patronized by prominent Venetian families. Before becoming an independent master, he worked in the household of Doge Giovanni Corner; members of the Corner family were to be his most steadfast and liberal patrons. Lazzarini encouraged his pupils to study Venetian sixteenth-century art, and Tiepolo made drawings of some famous works for publica-

tion in Domenico Lovisa's *Gran Teatro di Venezia* of 1717. His early involvement with the thriving Venetian engraving and publishing world was renewed in 1724 when he made drawings of antique sculpture as illustrations for Scipione Maffei's *Verona Illustrata,* an experience that gave Tiepolo an imaginative empathy with fragmentary antique remains, which recur in his drawings, etchings, and paintings. As well as studying the art of the past, Tiepolo looked to the tenebrism of Federico Bencovich (1677–1753) and the realism and monumentality of Giovanni Battista Piazzetta (1682–1754). In 1719 Tiepolo married Cecilia Guardi, with whom he was to have nine children. By then, the artist was working for a network of mercantile and noble patrons on religious and secular subjects.

Tiepolo's reputation was assured, however, with the success of his employment by Patriarch Dionisio Dolfin on a complicated iconographic program of fresco decoration at the patriarch's palace in

**Giovanni Battista Tiepolo.** Apollo and Europe, detail from the fresco cycle *Apollo and the Continents* in the main staircase at Würzburg Palace, created 1753. ©SANDRO VANNINI/CORBIS

Udine around 1725–1727; other members of the family commissioned a series of large oil paintings on martial Roman themes for the Ca'Dolfin in Venice, painted in 1726–1729. A variety of commissions followed in the north of Italy, with fresco decoration at the Archinto and Dugnani palaces in Milan (c. 1729–1731) and at the Villa Loschi near Vicenza (1734) of particular importance, generating further commissions from Milanese and Vicentine patrons. By 1736 Tiepolo was sufficiently renowned for the Swedish ambassador in Venice to invite him to decorate the new royal palace in Stockholm. Both local and foreign clients appreciated how his distinctive qualities of lucidity, gracefulness, and spirited handling contrasted with Piazzetta's more intense and rugged style. Thus, the newly elected archbishop elector of Cologne, who visited Venice in 1734, was to commission altarpieces from both artists. Among Tiepolo's celebrated works in Venice are the frescoes of 1737–1739 at the Dominican church of S. Maria del Rosario, and those of 1743–1745 at the Discalced Carmelite church of S. Maria di Nazareth (later destroyed), together with the decoration of the grand salon at the Palazzo Labia (c. 1746–1747) with sumptuous scenes from the story of Antony and Cleopatra. Francesco Algarotti became a close friend in the early 1740s, commissioning paintings and seeking his artistic advice; they shared a passion for the art of Paolo Veronese (born Paolo Caliari). Around this time, Tiepolo worked on two series of etchings, the *Vari Capricci* and the *Scherzi di Fantasia,* which contemporaries compared to the work of Rembrandt and Giovanni Benedetto Castiglione. He ran a busy studio, with his sons Giovanni Domenico (1727–1804) and Lorenzo (1736–1776) gradually taking on important roles.

In late 1750 Tiepolo traveled to Würzburg with Domenico and Lorenzo, working over the next three years on fresco decoration at the prince-bishop's residence and on a variety of altarpieces and cabinet paintings. After his return to Venice, Tiepolo's achievements included fresco decoration at the Villa Valmarana near Vicenza in 1757, where he painted themes from epic poetry, side by side with son Domenico's enchanting genre scenes, and the large, majestic Saint Thecla altarpiece (1759) for the cathedral at Este. Invited to Madrid in 1761 to decorate the throne room of the new royal palace at a time when he had numerous commissions in hand, Tiepolo was pressed by the Venetian government to accept. With Domenico and Lorenzo, he worked on various frescoes at the royal palace from 1762, and on religious commissions, until his death in Madrid in 1770.

*See also* **Baroque; Rubens, Peter Paul; Venice, Art in.**

BIBLIOGRAPHY

Aikema, Bernard. *Tiepolo and His Circle.* Translated by Andrew McCormick. Cambridge, Mass., 1996.

Barcham, William L. *The Religious Paintings of Giambattista Tiepolo: Piety and Tradition in Eighteenth-Century Venice.* Oxford and New York, 1989.

Brown, Beverly L., ed. *Giambattista Tiepolo: Master of the Oil Sketch.* Fort Worth, Tex., 1993.

Christiansen, Keith, ed. *Giambattista Tiepolo 1696–1770.* Venice and New York, 1996.

Gemin, Massimo, and Filippo Pedrocco. *Giambattista Tiepolo. I dipinti. Opera completa.* Venice, 1993.

Knox, George. *Giambattista and Domenico Tiepolo: A Study and Catalogue Raisonné of the Chalk Drawings.* Oxford and New York, 1980.

Krückmann, Peter O., ed. *Tiepolo in Würzburg: Der Himmel auf Erden.* Munich and New York, 1996.

Levey, Michael. *Giambattista Tiepolo: His Life and Art.* New Haven, 1986.

Puppi, Lionello, ed. *Giambattista Tiepolo: Nel terzo centenario della nascita.* Venice, 1998.

Whistler, Catherine. "Devozione e decoro nelle pale di Giambattista Tiepolo ad Aranjuez." *Arte Veneta* 52 (1998): 70–85.

CATHERINE WHISTLER

# TILLY, JOHANN TSERCLAES OF

(1559–1632), general of the army of the Catholic League (1620–1632). Johann Tserclaes of Tilly was probably born in February 1559 (we do not know the precise date) in Brabant (in the Spanish Netherlands), the son of Martin Tserclaes and Dorothea von Schierstädt. Because his father had been involved in the uprising of the Dutch noblemen (known as the "Gueux") against the Spanish crown, he spent his early years in exile. With his brother Jacob, young Tilly attended the Jesuit College at Cologne for a brief period. He did not join the order, but became a fervent supporter for the rest of his life.

After his family reconciled with the Habsburgs, Tilly entered military service. He began as a private but soon rose to higher ranks. Having fought under Alexander Farnese, duke of Parma, against the rebellious Dutch, he went to Hungary and led an imperial regiment against the Turks. He supported Rudolf II (ruled 1576–1612) in his struggle with his brother, Archduke Matthias (who succeeded Rudolf as emperor in 1612 and ruled until 1619), but in 1610 he left Prague and entered Bavarian service. Duke Maximilian I of Bavaria made him general lieutenant—commander in chief. In the Thirty Years' War, Tilly led the army of the Catholic League, while Maximilian was its political spirit.

Although we know little about his early years, the details of Tilly's life become more accessible with the beginning of the Bohemian campaign (1620). In the 1620s his victories helped to establish the military and political dominance of the imperial-Catholic rule throughout most of the Old Reich. He won the Battle of White Mountain (at Prague, 8 November 1620), had several encounters with Ernst of Mansfeld (he lost at Wiesloch/ Mingolsheim, 27 April 1622, but won at Wimpfen, 6 May 1622), crushed the army of Christian of Brunswick twice (Höchst near Frankfurt am Main, 20 June 1622, and Stadtlohn near the Dutch border, 6 August 1623), forced the Danish King Christian IV (ruled 1588–1648) to retreat (Lutter am Barenberge, 27 August 1626), and gained control of northern Germany. After A. W. E. von Wallenstein's dismissal in 1630, he took command of the imperial troops as interim general. In the Swedish campaign of 1631 he captured Magdeburg (20 May), but lost the battle of Breitenfeld against Gustavus II Adolphus (17 September). Trying to stop the Swedish invasion of Bavaria, he was defeated again at Rain am Lech (15 April 1632), where he was fatally wounded (he died at Ingolstadt on 30 April 1632).

Tilly's fame as a general derived from his successful campaigns throughout the 1620s, when he developed a unique battle-seeking strategy. The disastrous outcome of the Swedish war, however, tarnished his military reputation. Though he is normally characterized as belonging to the Spanish school (regarded as obsolete at the time) of military strategy, his failure against the Swedish cannot be adequately explained by invoking the more modern tactics of the Swedish army. Those defeats were at least partly due to the political tensions within the Catholic party, which prevented him from executing his planned offensives.

Tilly was also blamed for the sacking and burning of Magdeburg (20 May 1631), a catastrophe that did not reflect well on his military skills. Contemporary critics held him responsible for this disaster, but modern historians have refuted this verdict, pointing out that he would never have willingly destroyed a stronghold of such importance to his forthcoming campaigns.

Tilly can be regarded as a transitional figure, balanced between the classic type of military enterpriser and the emergent type of modern officer. Along with Wallenstein, he developed into one of the most successful enterprisers to make his fortune in a time of war. For his services, Tilly was remunerated with money and property (the most important was Breitenegg, a lordship in the Upper Palatinate), and in 1623 he was made a count. In contrast to Wallenstein, he confined himself strictly to military affairs and did not try to gain political influence. He remained absolutely loyal to his prince and was willing to obey even in controversial matters. Maximilian of Bavaria, as the undisputed political leader, and Tilly, as successful military commander, formed one of the most successful teams in the Thirty Years' War.

Because he never married and remained childless, Tilly's nephew Werner von Tilly continued his line in Bavaria.

*See also* **Gustavus II Adolphus (Sweden); Matthias (Holy Roman Empire); Parma, Alexander Farnese, duke of; Rudolf II (Holy Roman Empire); Thirty Years' War (1618–1648); Wallenstein, A. W. E. von.**

BIBLIOGRAPHY

Junkelmann, Marcus S. "Feldherr Maximilians: Johann Tserclaes Graf von Tilly." In *Um Glauben und Reich: Kurfürst Maximilian 1. Beiträge zur Bayerischen Geschichte und Kunst 1573–1651,* edited by Hubert Glaser, pp. 377–399. Munich, 1980.

Kaiser, Michael. *Politik und Kriegführung: Maximilian von Bayern, Tilly und die Katholische Liga im Dreißigjährigen Krieg.* Münster, 1999.

———. "Tilly in Köln: eine biographische Episode im Kontext der Traditionsbildung." *Geschichte in Köln, 41* (August 1997): 5–29. Especially useful for its discussion of Tilly's early years; also includes a bibliography on biographical works from the seventeenth century to the present.

Klopp, Onno. *Der dreißigjährige Krieg bis zum Tode Gustav Adolfs 1632.* 4 vols. Paderborn, 1891–1896. As there is no English biography yet, this German one remains the most comprehensive.

MICHAEL KAISER

---

**TIME, MEASUREMENT OF.** From being important in the mid-fifteenth century only to structured communities (monasteries, military camps, universities) and large-scale industrial undertakings (quarries, building sites, textile manufactories), measured time by the late eighteenth century had become the fundamental structural element of European social life. If the incidence of time control was felt more strongly in towns and industrial units than in the country, the sonorous hour indications of village church bells nonetheless brought it even to remote agrarian regions. This extension of time control in society was paralleled by major advances in the reliability and precision of time-measuring machines, but the causal relationship between the two is complex and only beginning to be investigated.

Time measurement was available in early modern Europe through the use of shadows (sundials and moon dials), gravity (water clocks, sandglasses, weight-driven clocks), or artificial force (spring-driven clocks and watches). Sundials and waterclocks derived from antiquity, mediated by humanist scholars; weight-driven clocks were an invention of medieval craftsmen, probably in the mid-thirteenth century. Spring-driven timekeepers can be claimed as an early modern invention, a response in the mid-fifteenth century to need for a portable timekeeper comparable with pocket sundials, which, known since antiquity, multiplied from the fourteenth century onward. Sandglasses were probably invented in Europe at about the same time as weight-driven clocks, in the mid-thirteenth century. For all, the ultimate time standard was that determined by the Earth's movements in relation to the Sun.

The various time-measuring instruments available had complementary functions. Sundials find time and display it; even if interrupted in their operation by lack of sunshine, they will immediately show time again once sunlight reappears. Weight- and spring-driven clocks and watches are timekeepers and time showers. Once set functioning, they count and display time without interruption. If deranged, however, they cannot of themselves find time again, but have to be set against a sundial. Throughout the early modern period, therefore, there was an essential complementary relationship between clocks, watches, and sundials, which are frequently found combined, or in close proximity to each other. Sandglasses are timekeepers but restricted to specific short periods, usually up to sixty minutes. They were used for measuring the often predetermined length of tasks such as university lessons, sermons, naval or military watches, and industrial activities.

Technical innovations in time-measuring machines during this period were many and fundamental. Although the usefulness of the force exerted by a coiled metal strip was recognized from at least the thirteenth century, it was not until the invention in the mid-fifteenth century of devices such as the fusee and the stackfreed, which equalized the force exerted as the spring uncoiled, that it could be useful in time measurement. Despite this, the behavior of sixteenth-century clocks and watches was affected by so many mechanical insufficiencies as to be highly erratic if not closely surveyed by the clock keeper, who was a regular appointment in towns and royal and noble establishments. Watches in the sixteenth century were as much valued as jewels as timekeepers, and public clocks were as important as symbols of social and economic status and for the astronomical/astrological indications they offered as they were for telling time. Indeed their behavior in the latter respect is frequently criticized in late-seventeenth and eighteenth-century literature.

The mathematical analysis of natural phenomena that characterized seventeenth-century research into the natural world, however, led to important innovations. Galileo (1564–1642), having recognized the isochronous nature of a pendulum, also recognized its potential as a controller for clock mechanisms and produced initial designs. Concurrently, but probably independently, Christiaan Huygens (1629–1695) produced different designs for this purpose and not only published its theory in his *Horologium Oscillatorium* (1672) but in 1676 revealed the isochronal properties of a flat spiral spring when applied to a watch balance.

These two fundamental innovations reduced the running error of clocks and watches from some twenty to thirty minutes a day to only a few minutes. Such precision allied with increased reliability in the performance of timekeepers, resulting from improvements in lubrication, bearings, and tooth profiles, meant that timekeepers now became viable machines for use in longitude determination, a task that had been proposed for them as early as 1532. Although immense technical difficulties remained to be overcome, by the 1780s viable longitude timekeepers existed and could be simplified for general use. Similarly, in the late eighteenth century, newly reliable timekeepers became an integral part of the development of timed industrial activity, and of the development of interlocking, time-tabled transport systems. None of this affected the watch as a status symbol, but it did transform its appearance as emphasis shifted from the watch as conspicuous jewel to the watch as elegant precision timepiece. Precision in the eighteenth century became the hallmark of quality, the equitable operation of the new timekeepers, of which Paris, London, and Switzerland were the chief producers, being both source and reflection of a new, absolute, Newtonian time.

*See also* **Calendar; Clocks and Watches; Galileo Galilei; Huygens Family; Newton, Isaac; Scientific Instruments.**

BIBLIOGRAPHY

Brusa, Giuseppe. *L'arte dell'orologeria in europa: Sette secoli de orologi meccanici.* Busto Arsizio, 1978.

Landes, David S. *Revolution in Time: Clocks and the Making of the Modern World.* Cambridge, Mass., and London, 1983.

Rossum, Gerhard Dohrn-van. *History of the Hour: Clocks and Modern Temporal Orders.* Translated by Thomas Dunlap. Chicago, 1996.

Thompson, E. P. "Time, Work-Discipline and Industrial Capitalism." *Past & Present* 38 (1967): 56–97.

A. J. TURNER

# TIME OF TROUBLES (RUSSIA).

The Time of Troubles (1598–1613), a complex political crisis manifested in repeated palace coups, civil war, and foreign occupation, nearly resulted in the shattering of the Muscovite state. The Time of Troubles (*smutnoe vremia*) had three interconnected causes.

The first and most crucial cause was the temporary delegitimation of royal authority following the extinction of the Riurikid dynasty in 1598, when Tsar Fedor Ivanovich died without an heir. Fedor's successor, Tsar Boris Godunov (ruled 1598–1605), was never able to fully legitimate himself because of court factionalism, his failure to marry into an eminent boyar family, and the suspicion that he had engineered the mysterious death of Tsarevich Dmitrii Ivanovich in 1591.

A second cause was economic dislocation and social unrest in Muscovy's northwestern and southern provinces. In the northwest, the Livonian War, border wars with the Swedes, and overtaxation had stripped the gentry of most of their peasant tenants. This greatly hampered Moscow's ability to mobilize troops from this region, traditionally the largest reservoir of military manpower. By contrast, the entire southern frontier from Seversk in the west to the Volga in the east was experiencing accelerated military colonization to protect against Crimean Tatar raids. Because the colonists were given smaller land and cash entitlements than prevailed in central Muscovy and because they settled among state peasants on crown frontier lands who paid *corvée*, considerable social discontent arose on the southern frontier. The upper stratum of the middle service class in Riazan' region was also increasingly alienated from Godunov's government because it felt denied the precedence honor and promotion opportunities due it.

The third cause was Muscovy's vulnerability to entanglement in the conflict between Sweden and the Polish-Lithuanian Commonwealth. War between King Sigismund III Vasa of Poland and Charles IX of Sweden (ruled 1604–1611) had broken out in 1600. This war eventually spilled over into northwestern Muscovy, because that region had been weakened during the last Livonian War and because of the growing weakness of Boris Godunov's regime.

The first phase of the Troubles (1598–1606) was primarily a dynastic crisis after the death of Tsar Fedor and took the form of boyar intrigues and then mass revolt against the "usurper" Boris Godunov. The spread of famine and banditry in 1601–1603 finally provided Godunov's old enemies—the Romanovs, Nagois, and other boyar clans—with the opportunity to turn the populace against him. They began circulating rumors that Tsarevich Dmitrii Ivanovich had not after all perished at Uglich in 1591 but had escaped Godunov's assassins and was returning to reclaim the throne. In 1603 a pretender Tsarevich Dmitrii surfaced in the grand duchy and received recognition and military support from several powerful Polish and Lithuanian magnates. This False Dmitrii invaded in 1604 and quickly won support across the southern frontier and into central Muscovy. When Tsar Boris died suddenly in April 1605, his generals came over to the False Dmitrii, abandoning Boris's heir Fedor Borisovich and allowing the False Dmitrii to take the throne in June 1605. The First False Dmitrii ruled less than a year. In May 1606 the boyar Vasilii Shuiskii, the Golitsyns, and Metropolitan Hermogen incited riots in Moscow against the presence of the large Polish retinue of Dmitrii's bride, Marina Mniszech, and in the course of these disorders Dmitrii was assassinated.

The second phase of the Troubles (1606–1610) was marked by a series of regional outbreaks against Tsar Vasilii Shuiskii, which ultimately provided both the Swedes and Poles grounds for military intervention. The first such insurrection began in Seversk in 1606 and spread across the south and into central Muscovy, much like the movement that had supported the late False Dmitri. Although led by Ivan Bolotnikov, a former military slave, and involving a significant number of peasant insurgents, it was not a "peasant war" but included many gentry. Bolotnikov was defeated at Tula in 1607, but his forces regrouped and joined with Cossacks and Polish and Lithuanian mercenaries to form a new army under the nominal leadership of a Second False Dmitrii. After an unsuccessful siege of Moscow, they established a rival government at nearby Tushino (1608). Several powerful boyars, most significantly the monk Fedor Romanov (who had been tonsured under Boris Godunuv), abandoned Tsar Vasilii and went over to the Tushinites. Vasilii responded by launching a counteroffensive using troops levied from Novgorod and the far north and a large number of Swedish mercenaries. The Second False Dmitrii was put to flight. But by inviting in Swedish mercenaries Tsar Vasilii had now given King Sigismund III pretext to invade Muscovy and place Smolensk under siege. Fedor Romanov and

those surviving Tushinite elites unwilling to seek Vasilii's forgiveness entered into negotiations with Sigismund and invited him to send Crown Prince Władysław to rule Muscovy. A Polish army under Hetman Stanisław Żółkiewski routed Tsar Vasilii's Russo-Swedish forces at Klushino (June 1610). The next month Vasilii was deposed by the Golitsyns, Riazan' gentry leaders, and agents of Fedor Romanov.

After the overthrow of Tsar Vasilii a council of seven boyars holding power in Moscow accepted the bargain offered by the Tushinites and Polish commanders and invited Władysław to rule on the condition that he take the Orthodox faith. But instead of Władysław they were sent a Polish occupation army. In this third phase of the Troubles (1610–1613) no tsar ruled in Moscow, but rather a Polish military dictatorship under siege by a succession of national liberation militias raised by Muscovite provincial elites (military town governors, wealthy merchants, Riazan' gentry) in uneasy alliance with cossack leaders. Smolensk fell to King Sigismund; a Swedish army occupied Novgorod. The Second False Dmitrii was assassinated by his own lieutenants; more new pretenders appeared (including an Infant Brigand, the son of the Second False Dmitrii and Marina Mniszech) but were unable to attract large followings. In 1611 a liberation militia led by Prince Dmitry Pozharsky established a provisional government at Iaroslavl; with Cossack support it finally drove the Poles from Moscow in October 1612. An Assembly of the Realm (*Zemskii Sobor*) in early 1613 elected Fedor Romanov's sixteen-year-old son, Michael, as tsar.

Incursions by Polish forces acting in the name of Władysław continued for another five years. An armistice signed at Deulino in 1618 required that Smolensk and parts of Seversk and Chernigov be restored to the commonwealth. Karelia was ceded to Sweden in return for the recovery of Novgorod. Much of northwestern and central Muscovy had been depopulated, and political reconstruction was hampered by the loss of several important chancellery archives in the great conflagration at Moscow in 1612.

The Troubles did not permanently alter the political and social order, however. The consultations of Tsar Michael with the *Zemskii Sobor* did not mean that patrimonial autocracy had given way to estate-representative monarchy; the power of the boyar elite had not declined, and there was no "ascendancy" of the provincial middle service class. Reconstruction (under the guidance of Tsar Michael's father, now patriarch) involved the expansion and refinement of mid-sixteenth-century institutions: the central chancelleries, the military town governors, and the *pomest'e* system of service-conditional land tenure.

*See also* **Boris Godunov (Russia); False Dmitrii, First; Livonian War (1558–1583); Michael Romanov (Russia); Romanov Dynasty (Russia); Russia; Russo-Polish Wars; Sigismund II Augustus (Poland, Lithuania); Vasa Dynasty (Sweden).**

BIBLIOGRAPHY

Dunning, Chester S. L. *Russia's First Civil War: The Time of Troubles and the Founding of the Romanov Dynasty.* University Park, Pa., 2001.

Platonov, S. F. *The Time of Troubles.* Translated by John T. Alexander. Lawrence, Kans., 1970.

BRIAN DAVIES

# TINTORETTO

**TINTORETTO** (Jacopo Robusti; c. 1518–1594), Italian painter. Jacopo Tintoretto was easily the most prolific painter in late-sixteenth-century Venice. The son of a Venetian cloth dyer, he advertised the fact in his professional nickname. Unlike certain other leading artists of the time, Tintoretto—"the little dyer"—did not seek to conceal his lower-class social origins. He was trained in an unidentified Venetian workshop during the 1530s. Early reports that he was summarily ejected from Titian's shop may represent nothing more than flattering legend. But the older master's professional hostility is nonetheless corroborated by a number of other early sources and was probably an important shaping factor in Tintoretto's career.

In very early works, such as the dramatic *Christ among the Doctors* (c. 1541–1542, Museo del Duomo, Milan), Tintoretto's style and technique pointedly depart from Titian's long-established naturalistic idiom. Forms twist and writhe in arbitrary fashion within a vertiginous spatial recession that relegates the protagonist to the far distance. In many of his earlier works, the painter's debt to the art of central Italy, and particularly to Michelangelo,

is evident. But Tintoretto's conceptual and formal individualism, like his penchant for leaving the broad (although thinly loaded) marks of his brush exposed on the picture surface, took his art beyond such sources and also beyond anything yet seen within Venetian Renaissance art. His production of paintings at high speed and in great volume, and his readiness to offer them at a low price, quickly became notorious. But the strategy proved very successful at a time in which demand for paintings was rapidly increasing.

Tintoretto did not select between patrons as Titian did: rather than prioritizing prestigious foreign clients, he concentrated on fulfilling local demands. By 1560 he was already the dominant painter across the city. From this point onward, he was almost constantly at work in the Ducal Palace. Following two disastrous fires in the palace (1574 and 1577), Tintoretto and his workshop undertook a series of large-scale commissions, culminating in the vast *Paradise* (c. 1588–1590) for the main State Room. He also produced many paintings for the city's non-noble lay confraternities (the so-called *Scuole*, or Schools). In 1548 he made his name with the startling *Miracle of the Slave* (Accademia, Venice) for the Scuola di San Marco, and between 1564 and 1588 produced more than sixty paintings for the meeting house of the Scuola di San Rocco.

These included wall paintings showing scenes from the Life of Christ and the Virgin, and typologically related scenes from the Old Testament on the ceiling of the upper room (Sala Superiore). The enormous *Crucifixion* (1565) is the most important work of Tintoretto's maturity, painted in an epic narrative style that brilliantly combines passages of earthy naturalism with more idealized formal sequences. In later paintings such as *The Baptism* and *The Agony in the Garden* (both 1578–1581), complex formal masses are cloaked in brownish shadow, illuminated only at certain points by angled shafts of golden light, which imply the immanent presence of the divine. But this spiritualized schema is brought alive by the inclusion of startling passages of naturalism, for example in the extraordinary *Annunciation* (1581–1582). The unprecedented formal manipulations exacted at San Rocco reflect Tintoretto's mature commitment to an ideal of sacred poverty, which brings together the selfless spiritual ideals of the commissioning confraternity with

**Tintoretto.** *The Crucifixion,* 1565. ©ARTE & IMMAGINI SRL/CORBIS

those of the wider Catholic Counter-Reformation, but also refers to his own lowly artistic identity as the "little dyer."

Tintoretto's dynamic manner dominated for only a short while in Venice: Veronese and even the old Titian were influenced by his art in certain ways, while El Greco and Palma Giovane were probably members of his workshop. After his death in 1594, the Tintoretto workshop continued to operate into the 1630s under the control of his painter sons, Domenico and Marco. But Tintoretto's artistic individualism, particularly in matters of technique, meant that his style was not easily emulated, and it was increasingly perceived as antithetical to the classicism of European artistic tradition. Despite John Ruskin's ecstatic appreciations in the post-Romantic era, Tintoretto has continued to be an elusive figure in the history of art. Recent attempts to see his work as mannerist typically founder on the passionate drama of his style and the radical abbreviations of his brushwork. And while his exposed paint surface owes something to the earlier Venetian Renaissance tradition of coloring *(colorito),* his ap-

proach is very different from that of artists such as Giorgione or Titian. It is, though, the very resistance of Tintoretto's manner to an easy integration within artistic tradition that makes it so interesting for the contemporary viewer.

*See also* **Painting; Titian; Venice, Art in.**

BIBLIOGRAPHY

Nichols, Tom. *Tintoretto: Tradition and Identity.* London, 1999.

Pallucchini, Rodolfo, and Rossi, Paola. *Tintoretto. Le opere sacre e profane.* 2 vols. Milan, 1982.

Rossi, Paola, and Puppi Lionello, eds. *Jacopo Tintoretto nel quarto centenario della morte.* Venice, 1996.

TOM NICHOLS

**TITIAN** (Tiziano Vecelli; 1488/1490–1576), Italian painter. Born in the Dolomite village of Cadore about 1490, Titian was trained in the Venetian workshops of Gentile and Giovanni Bellini in the early years of the sixteenth century. It was, however, the younger and more progressive Giorgione who had the greatest influence on his development. Titian's early paintings (for example, *Three Ages of Man*, c. 1512–1513, National Gallery, Edinburgh) are often set in lush pastoral landscapes and have a brownish Giorgionesque tonality. Titian also adopted Giorgione's improvising approach to painting, exploiting the special translucency of oil paint in building up forms and colors. Titian did, on occasion, make drawings, but typically preferred to work out his compositions in color on the picture surface.

Despite the similarities, Titian's early paintings are increasingly distinct from Giorgione's in their muscularity of form, clear placement of figures in space, and typically precise definition of surface texture. In the great altarpiece showing the Assumption of the Virgin (1516–1518, Sta. Maria dei Frari, Venice), the bulky forms of the protagonists recall the idealized figure types of Michelangelo and Raphael. But the intense vibrancy of Titian's color,

based on subtle modulations of red, gold, and silvery gray, nonetheless controls our apprehension of form. Titian went on to revolutionize the Venetian altarpiece in a sequence of outstanding paintings, culminating in the lost St. Peter Martyr altarpiece (1526–1530, destroyed 1867; formerly SS. Giovanni e Paolo, Venice). In the Pesaro altarpiece (1519–1526, SS. Giovanni e Paolo), he subverted the standard Venetian type of the *sacra conversazione* (sacred conversation) by making the donor family central to the iconography and spatial organization.

Between 1518 and 1524 he completed three so-called Bacchanals (*The Worship of Venus, The Andrians,* both Museo del Prado, Madrid; *Bacchus and Ariadne,* National Gallery, London) for Alfonso I d'Este, duke of Ferrara. The paintings were conceived as re-creations (*ekphrases*) of classical works of art described in literary texts by Philostratus, Catullus, and Ovid, and feature complex

**Titian.** *The Venus of Urbino*, 1538. ©Erich Lessing/Art Resource, N.Y.

nude or seminude figures that insistently recall classical friezes and relief sculptures. The antique world is here imagined as a place of sensual delight, the lighthearted tone owing little to the learned allegorical approach to mythological painting championed by earlier masters such as Sandro Botticelli or Andrea Mantegna.

It was Titian's brilliant transformation of the field of portraiture, however, that made his name with the aristocratic and royal houses of Europe. In portraits such as *Federico II Gonzaga, Duke of Mantua* (1529, Prado) Titian depicted his high-ranking sitter with an unprecedented degree of intimacy, showing him gently caressing a favored pet dog. Pendant portraits such as *Duke Francesco Maria della Rovere, Duke of Urbino* and his wife, *Eleonora Gonzaga* (both 1536, Galleria degli Uffizi, Florence) were more formal. But the duke's son Guidobaldo also acquired a mysterious erotic painting known as *The Venus of Urbino* (1538, Uffizi). Titian here referred directly to Giorgione's *Sleeping Venus,* a painting he himself had completed about 1510. But in the Urbino painting, the reclining woman is relocated to a contemporary bedroom, her knowing glance at the viewer and the bravura painting of her exposed flesh combining to generate an image of unprecedented erotic immediacy.

The painting is typical of the confident originality that characterizes Titian's mature work. In paintings such as *The Vendramin Family* (1545–1547, National Gallery, London) and *The Martyrdom of Saint Lawrence* (1547–1556, Gesuiti, Venice), Titian refers to existing visual and iconographic types in Venetian painting. But these are transformed by the master's brilliant awareness of the expressive possibilities of oil paint, and the sensual and emotive power of color. In the same period, Titian also worked for the Holy Roman emperor, Charles V (as in *Charles V at the Battle of Mühlberg,* 1548, Prado), and the patronage of the Habsburg family increasingly came to dominate his career. In 1551 Charles's son (the future king of Spain, Philip II) commissioned Titian to paint a series of mythologies (known as the *poesie)* based on Ovid's *Metamorphoses.* The resulting paintings are among the masterworks of sixteenth-century painting. But their relation to one another and their more precise meaning remain unclear. It appears that Titian enjoyed an unusual degree of autonomy in fulfilling Philip's commission, and this may have encouraged him to take an open-ended approach in which the free "poetic" association of ideas is preferred to more traditional iconography.

The paintings are loosely conceived in pairs, showing contrasting views of female nudes. But rather than being simply erotic, the *poesie* draw attention to the pain and suffering associated with sexual desire and love. This is the case, for example, in the extraordinary *Venus and Adonis* (1551–1554, Prado), in which the traditionally supine goddess of love turns puce-faced in restraining her mortal lover from his doom. As in many of the other *poesie,* her figure is modeled directly on a classical relief, yet the translation of the form into paint yields a new expressive intensity to her straining posture. Titian's abandonment of the Renaissance sense of the classical world as a place of innocent sensual delight is also evident in the *Diana and Acteon* and *Diana and Callisto* (both 1556–1559, National Gallery, Edinburgh). Here the dire consequences of crossing (even inadvertently) the goddess of chastity are made apparent. And yet these paintings possess an existential force that takes them beyond the redemptive schema offered by orthodox Christianity.

The two Diana paintings, along with subsequent *poesie* such as *The Rape of Europa* (1559–1562, Isabella Stewart Gardner Museum, Boston) and *The Death of Acteon* (c. 1560–1562, National Gallery, London) are painted in a remarkable summary manner that threatens to dissolve form into a myriad dabs of broken color. The mosaiclike effect provides a kind of technical analogue to the process of cataclysmic physical and emotional change described in the paintings. But Titian also used the technique in his religious imagery and portraiture from about 1560 onward (for example, *Portrait of Jacopo Strada,* 1567–1568, Kunsthistorisches Museum, Vienna; *Pietà,* 1575–1576, Accademia, Venice). Despite doubts about the status, or even the very existence, of Titian's "late style," it seems clear that it is best taken as a kind of intensification of the *colorito* (coloring) he had long practiced. The style developed organically as a result of his deepening response to the subject matter of his paintings.

Titian, who died in 1576, was easily the most successful painter in sixteenth-century Venice. The

**Titian.** *Assumption of the Virgin,* 1518, Santa Maria Gloriosa dei Frari, Venice.

international scope of his patronage meant that his influence was quickly transmitted across Europe, and his work had a major impact on painters as different as Peter Paul Rubens, Nicolas Poussin, Diego Velázquez, Rembrandt van Rijn, François Boucher, and Sir Joshua Reynolds. In the age of modernism, Titian's popularity has hardly diminished, the sensuous and emotional naturalism of his style, along with his experimentalism in matters of technique, assuring that his paintings continue to speak to a very wide audience.

*See also* **Giorgione; Painting; Poussin, Nicolas; Rembrandt van Rijn; Rubens, Peter Paul; Velázquez, Diego; Venice, Art in.**

BIBLIOGRAPHY

Crowe, J. A., and G. B. Cavalcaselle. *The Life and Times of Titian.* London, 1877.

Hope, Charles. *Titian.* London, 1980.

Joannides, Paul. *Titian to 1518: The Assumption of Genius.* New Haven and London, 2001.

Wethey, Harold E. *The Paintings of Titian: Complete Edition.* 3 vols. London, 1969–1975.

TOM NICHOLS

---

**TOBACCO.** Tobacco first attracted attention in Europe as an Amerindian curiosity. Christopher Columbus, Amerigo Vespucci, Jacques Cartier, and other European explorers reported the apparently omnipresent but varied use of a green herb by the people they encountered. For recreational, spiritual, and medicinal reasons, tobacco was externally applied to wounds, chewed (alone or with other substances), inhaled as a powder, or smoked (through canes, as rolled up leaves, or stuffed into a reed or a pipe). In the mid-sixteenth century, European scholars described the strange New World plant as part of the botanical renaissance. By the late 1560s, tobacco's medicinal properties were being widely investigated by people such as Conrad Gessner in Zurich, Pietro Mattioli in Bohemia and, most famously, by the French ambassador to Lisbon, Jean Nicot. In 1571, Nicolás Monardes, a physician of Seville, presented an influential assessment of the medical use of *Nicotiana.* His text, the English translation of which was entitled *Joyfull Newes out of the Newe Founde Worlde* (1577), became a standard medical textbook across Europe. Monardes told

physicians that tobacco had antiseptic and analgesic properties and could tackle a host of conditions from chilblains to intestinal worms and from halitosis to gout. Tobacco was used in a variety of ointments and poultices, formulas, and concoctions.

## SMOKERS AND SMOKING

While European science was discovering the medicinal potential of tobacco, Europeans in the New World were experimenting with more medicinally ambiguous patterns and modes of ingestion by smoking, snuffing, and chewing tobacco as part of their everyday lives. By 1550 smoking was prevalent in Spanish, Portuguese, and French colonial outposts. Sailors and adventurers returning from the New World brought their tobacco-consuming habits back with them to European ports. Particularly in London in the 1590s, putting dried leaves from a faraway land "in a pipe set on fire and suckt into the stomacke, and thrust foorth again at the nosthrils" became a popular pastime (Gerard, p. 287). Smokers such as Sir Walter Raleigh and Christopher Marlowe made smoking fashionable, particularly in male society. Numerous depictions of smoking soon appeared in poems and plays, such as Ben Jonson's *Every Man out of His Humour* (1600), in which smoking was often seen as a gentlemanly recreation. Perceptions of women smoking were generally negative but, as numerous seventeenth-century Dutch paintings, and plays such as Jonson's *Bartholomew Fair* (1611) illustrate, some women did smoke.

Smoking spread in England as a social activity (often in alehouses) and was commonly referred to as "drinking" tobacco. The practice quickly became controversial, prompting a medical and moral debate in the early seventeenth century. Smokers proclaimed tobacco's medicinal benefits: "nothing that harmes a man inwardly from his girdle upward, but may be taken away with a moderate use of Tabacco" (Chute, p. 19). Critics such as King James I & VI, who wrote *A Counterblaste to Tobacco* in 1604, condemned smokers for their wanton abuse of the new medicine and for their patently nonmedicinal, wasteful, and apparently compulsive consumption. Smoking had been identified as a vice. English physicians, while confirming the medicinal power of tobacco, warned against unnecessary and excessive smoking because it could disrupt humoral balance, provoking death "before either Nature urge, Maladie enforce, or Age require it" (Gardiner). Some commentators argued that smoking bred soot and cobwebs in the body, leading to enfeeblement, infertility, and a thirst for alcohol.

Despite such warnings, in the first half of the seventeenth century smoking and other recreational forms of tobacco use continued to spread in England and across Europe. The Dutch were particularly avid smokers and were soon growing tobacco and manufacturing distinctive pipes, such as the meerschaum. In France, state-regulated tobacco cultivation supplied French smokers and snuff-takers. By 1650, the use of tobacco as a medicine was widely accepted throughout Europe, but in many countries attempts were made to curb its recreational use. In Sicily, the pipe was declared illegal. In Denmark, Sweden, parts of Germany, Switzerland, Austria, and Hungary attempts were made to prohibit smoking, prevent tobacco cultivation, and inhibit its importation. The Russian patriarch considered smoking a deadly sin and in 1634 banned it on pain of execution for persistent offenders. In 1642, following a complaint by the dean of Seville that the entrance to his church was being defiled by tobacco juice, Pope Urban VIII threatened both clergy and congregation with excommunication if they smoked, chewed, or snuffed tobacco in church. Pope Innocent X issued another antismoking bull in 1650.

## TOBACCO AND ECONOMIES

Persistent and growing demand for tobacco in Europe promoted increasing crop cultivation in the New World. Spanish, Portuguese, and English colonies thrived by exporting vast quantities of the plant grown by slaves and indentured servants on large plantations. In 1626, 500,000 pounds of Virginia tobacco reached England. By the late 1630s, millions of pounds of tobacco were being shipped each year from Virginia, Maryland, and the English Caribbean, much of it re-exported to mainland Europe and beyond. As production increased, prices fell, making tobacco more readily available to all social classes. The growing international trade in tobacco attracted mercantile investment and presented governments with tax-raising opportunities. In England, where tobacco growing had been prohibited since 1619 (to aid colonial producers), substantial

revenues were generated from customs and other duties on tobacco. Ongoing complaints about the dangers of smoking to body and soul were subsumed by the vested interests of the governments, colonists, and merchants responsible for supplying tobacco to consumers.

Throughout the seventeenth and eighteenth centuries, Europeans continued to find medical uses for tobacco and to consume it for pleasure. Ornate tobacco pipes and snuffboxes were produced, offering opportunities for the display of status and refinement. In eighteenth-century England, snuff became particularly popular. Later, the cigars favored by Spanish consumers distinguished the gentlemen from the more plebeian smokers of clay pipes. Whatever the status of the consumer or the mode of ingestion, tobacco had become as integrated into European culture and society as it had been in pre-Columbian America. Like tea, coffee, and sugar, tobacco had become an integral part of European lifestyles.

*See also* **British Colonies: North America; Commerce and Markets; Consumption; Medicine; Public Health.**

BIBLIOGRAPHY

*Primary Sources*

Chute, Anthony. *Tabacco*. London, 1595.

Gardiner, Edmund. *The Triall of Tabacco*. London, 1611. Original title: *Phisicall and Approved Medicines*, 1610.

Gerard, John. *The Herball, or, Generall Historie of Plantes: Gathered by John Gerarde*. London, 1597.

James I & VI, King. *A Counterblaste to Tobacco*. London, 1604.

Monardes, Nicolás. *Joyfull Newes out of the Newe Founde Worlde*. London, 1577.

*Secondary Sources*

Dickson, Sarah A. *Panacea or Precious Bane: Tobacco in Sixteenth Century Literature*. New York, 1954.

Goodman, Jordan. *Tobacco in History: The Cultures of Dependence*. London and New York, 1993.

Price, Jacob M. *Tobacco in Atlantic Trade: The Chesapeake, London, and Glasgow, 1675–1775*. Aldershot, 1995.

Stewart, Grace. "A History of the Medicinal Use of Tobacco 1492–1860." *Medical History* 11 (1967): 228–268.

Walton, James, ed. *The Faber Book of Smoking*. London, 2000.

A. R. ROWLEY

**TOLEDO.** Toledo was an important city of Spain for much of the early modern period. Symbolic of this prominence are the large fortress (alcázar) built by the monarchs, the vast and richly decorated cathedral, and the impressive archdiocesan palace built by the prelates of Toledo, primates of the Spanish church.

Toledo's importance owes much to its geographic location. Security from outside attacks was enhanced by the deep, fast-flowing Tagus (Tajo) River, which offered a natural protective border on two-thirds of the city's perimeter and amplified the resistance offered by sturdy city walls and the heights of the interior space. Also, Toledo was at the center of the Iberian Peninsula, so it was a natural stopping-off point for travelers and merchandise, whether from Lisbon to the west or on the north-south routes in the crown of Castile. Within the region of New Castile, Toledo was the largest city and dominated the economy for much of the sixteenth century. This changed after Philip II (1527–1598) settled his court in the nearby city of Madrid in 1561. By the 1580s the two cities were competing for grain in local villages, and in the 1630s they competed over rights to plant vines and sell wine.

The population of Toledo expanded during the first three-quarters of the sixteenth century. According to the first census of 1528, some 30,000 people (5,898 households) lived in Toledo, and this figure doubled to approximately 62,000 people (12,412 households) by 1571. This appears to be the high point of the city's demographic expansion, as in 1597 only 54,665 people (10,953 households) were recorded. Baptismal records indicate a decreasing number of births in the first decade of the seventeenth century, when the city was struck by plague and then a subsistence crisis in 1605–1606. Population was also lost through emigration, especially to Madrid. Finally, among the city's wealthy families, fewer marriages were celebrated, in part because the crown's chaotic monetary policies ruined many and in part because numerous individuals of both sexes preferred celibacy and a church career. By 1632 the population had contracted to only 22,686 inhabitants, fewer that those recorded in the first census of 1528.

The oligarchy that governed Toledo consisted of a council of *regidores* and another council of *jurados,* both of which were supervised by a crown-appointed *corregidor.* The *jurados* did not vote on issues, but they could protest to the crown about injustices. They formed part of the small committees that did much of the actual work for the city, and they were entitled to supply one of the two deputies who attended the Castilian Cortes, the representative assembly. The *regidores* were divided into two benches, citizens and the more prestigious nobles, and into two factions according to the side on which they sat, the Silva on the right and the Ayala on the left. Frictions between the two benches and the two factions were constant, although after the *Comuneros* Revolt, which took a heavy toll on the Ayala faction, the battles were largely verbal and legal rather than physical. The crown added yet another division among the *regidores* in 1566, when a pure-blood statute was imposed on the citizens' bench. This ruling was directed against *conversos,* Jews who had converted to Christianity, whose bloodlines were seen as impure. Many citizen *regidores* were *conversos,* and a few openly protested to the crown about the new ruling, but to no avail. By 1639, however, the citizens bench was abolished, thus eliminating two of the three divisions that had previously divided the *regidores.*

Toledo had an active *converso* population that was especially visible in certain occupations. They accounted for two-thirds of the public notaries, probably a majority of the city's *jurados,* and certainly a majority of the local merchants and tax farmers. They built up the textile industries, most prominently silk and wool, of their native city. Many merchants kept a flock of sheep, and wool was sold to Toledo weavers, including cap makers, whose products were sold locally and were exported. Some merchants traveled to local fairs to buy wool cloth woven by villagers, which they took to Toledo to be finished. But Toledo is best known for the manufacture of silk products. Toledo families farmed the royal tax levied on Granada silk, and this post afforded Toledo merchants the opportunity to obtain the best silk of the Iberian Peninsula, although silk was also bought in Murcia and Valencia. In 1562 the master silk weavers of Toledo numbered 423. Unfortunately Toledo's textile industries followed the same downward path as the population.

*See also* **Conversos; Madrid; Spain.**

**Toledo.** *View of Toledo, 1604,* by El Greco.

BIBLIOGRAPHY

Brown, Jonathan. *El Greco of Toledo.* Boston, 1982.

Martz, Linda. *A Network of Converso Families in Early Modern Toledo: Assimilating a Minority.* Ann Arbor, Mich., 2003.

———. *Poverty and Welfare in Habsburg Spain: The Example of Toledo.* New York, 1983.

Montemayor, Julian. *Tolède entre fortune et déclin (1530–1640).* Limoges, France, 1996.

Ringrose, David R. *Madrid and the Spanish Economy, 1560–1850.* Berkeley and Los Angeles, 1983.

LINDA MARTZ

**TOLERATION.** Toleration (or its cognate, tolerance) denotes the readiness of an individual or a community to permit the presence and/or expression of ideas, beliefs, and practices differing from what is accepted by that individual or by the dominant part of the community. Toleration demands forbearance only; it does not require approval or endorsement of the tolerated ideas, beliefs, and practices. A tolerant person respects differences between him- or herself and other people; a tolerant community respects differences between groups and/or among individuals within the social totality. Toleration is thus antithetical to the persecution or repression (systematic or individualized) of ideas, beliefs, and practices that differ from one's own. Indeed, a tolerant person or society will protect the ability of such ideas, beliefs, and practices to persist even while acknowledging disagreement with them.

In early modern Europe, the main object of toleration in reality and as an ideal was difference of confession among religious communities, all of which claimed to be Christian. The Protestant Reformation had fragmented—permanently, as it turned out—the institutional and doctrinal unity of the Latin Christian Church that the faith had supposedly upheld since the time of St. Paul. During the sixteenth century, under the impact of Lutheran and Calvinist condemnations of the impurity of the visible Roman Church, not to mention the English Church's institutional break with Rome and the emergence of extreme sects such as the Anabaptists, Christianity was forced to reinvent itself as a creed united in faith but divided in rite. This situation has commonly led scholars to conclude that only in the post-Reformation context did the ideal vision and real conduct of tolerance enter into Europe, expressed by various proclamations of toleration as well as by the theoretical statement found in the *Epistola de Tolerantia* (1689; Letter on toleration) of John Locke (1632–1704).

Yet the assertion of the singular modernity of toleration, arising in the aftermath of the Protestant Reformation, masks the complexity of its history. Prior to the sixteenth century, certain voices at the core as well as on the periphery of European society were prepared to countenance the presence of dissenters and even heretics within Christianity as well as the existence of various non-Christian convictions. Moreover, other important issues, such as the discovery of the New World with its large population previously unexposed to the Christian faith, also drove the debate about the extension of forbearance to cultures and religious rites utterly alien to Europe. Finally, no particularly compelling evidence suggests that the desire to persecute forms of difference and dissent—in religion as in other fields of human endeavor—abated with the rise of modern Europe. Even those prepared to tolerate certain divergent Christian confessions were equally ready to exclude and brutally suppress other self-identified Christians—Roman Catholics, Anabaptists, Hutterites, millenarians—not to mention deists, atheists, and similar free thinkers.

This context needs to be considered when assessing the strengths and weaknesses of the modern European approach to toleration. Even before the monk Martin Luther (1483–1546) nailed his Ninety-Five Theses to the church door at Wittenberg in 1517, Europeans were grappling with the consequences of their encounter with the indigenous peoples of the Americas following the discoveries of the 1490s. Spain and Portugal in particular sought and received the authorization of the Roman Church to conquer and settle the lands of the Caribbean and Central and South America under the guise of evangelizing and converting the native populace. Some thinkers recoiled with considerable horror from the slaughter and enslavement that ensued. The towering figure of the School of Salamanca, Francesco de Vitoria (c. 1486?–1546), objected to the appropriation of the Aristotelian categories of barbarism and slavery by nature. Following de Vitoria, the Dominican bishop and former con-

quistador Bartolomé de Las Casas (1476–1566) composed a series of writings in Spanish as well as Latin defending the rights of the native population to maintain their cultural, political, and religious traditions and practices—even such controversial rites as human sacrifices, not to mention refusal of Christian missionaries and resistance to conquest. In a famous debate with the Scholastic advocate of Spanish dominion over the Indians, Juan Ginés de Sepúlveda, held at Valladolid in 1550, Las Casas used the materials of Aristotle's corpus, Thomism, and canon law to refute the assertion by the Spanish crown of its right to impose religion and civilization at swordpoint upon indigenous Americans. Rather, a Christian attitude toward the Indians—rooted in divine and natural law as well as the teachings of the pagan philosophers—demanded forbearance of their way of life, even if Europeans found their faith and rituals abhorrent.

At one time, scholars viewed the Reformation as a singularly positive stimulus to the promotion of toleration. It is true that Martin Luther, at least in some contexts, appears to defend tolerance on the grounds that the magistrate should be concerned only with the care of the body and does not have the tools at his disposal to control or alter the state of a person's soul. But other reformers, most notably John Calvin (1509–1564), were inclined to deny any measure of forbearance for religious positions that did not strictly conform to their new orthodoxy. Indeed, one of the important early defenders of toleration during the sixteenth century, Sebastian Castellio (or Sébastien Châteillon) (1515–1563), published pseudonymously a treatise entitled *De Haereticis, an Sint Persequendi* ('Of heretics, whether they should be persecuted') in reaction to Calvin's instruction to the city of Geneva in 1553 to burn a visiting Spanish heretic theologian, Michael Servetus, who opposed the doctrine of the Trinity. Castellio argued that coercion is an inappropriate tool for effecting a change of religious views, since Christian belief must be held with sincere conviction. Hence, clerics and magistrates must refrain from the persecution of convinced Christians who cling to doctrines that do not coincide with official teachings. While Castellio did not go so far as to license broad dissemination of heterodox theology, he maintained that a Christian's duties extended to tolerating the free and honest faith of fellow believers even in the face of disagreements of understanding and interpretation.

In the short term, voices such as Castellio's went unheeded. Rather, in places such as France and Germany, where the Reformation enjoyed greatest support, violent harassment of religious minorities—Catholic or Protestant—persisted and often threatened to erupt into full-scale religious warfare. It is true that some rulers and regions found ways to stamp out conflict, either by fiat or by negotiation. The most famous resolutions, such as the Religious Peace of Augsburg (1555) and the Edict of Nantes (1598), tended to be short-lived. But in Switzerland, where Reformed and Catholic communities often lived side-by-side, accommodation concerning the sharing of power and mutual respect for different rites succeeded in eliminating persecution in many areas. The Dutch Republic managed to achieve a similar arrangement, as did a number of eastern European states, including Poland, Transylvania, and Moravia.

These tolerant practices were certainly approved by many thinkers who subscribed to a range of confessions. Desiderius Erasmus (1466?–1535), one of the leading humanists of the age and a Catholic who nonetheless sympathized with the cause of reform, promoted a vision of toleration that he derived from the principles of classical rhetoric. According to Erasmus, violence was an inadequate, as well as un-Christian, means of dealing with unbelief. Only by speech might those who strayed from truth be convinced of the error of their ways. And both preaching and conversation—the two predominant ways in which the orthodox express truth to the errant—demanded that one tolerate the heterodox, if only in order to achieve conversion. Another humanist, Jean Bodin (1529/30–1596), pushed this discursive paradigm of tolerance even further. In his *Colloquium Heptaplomeres de Rerum Sublimium Arcanis Abditis* (1588; Colloquium of the seven about secrets of the sublime), Bodin adapted the standard literary genre of the interreligious dialogue, in this case between advocates of the major world religions and of various philosophical interpretations of divinity. Unlike previous texts of interreligious dialogue, however, Bodin's discussion produced a stalemate: no one changed his mind and no conversions occured. Bodin's point has been understood as the promo-

tion of tolerance, either because the relative merits of creeds cannot ultimately be demonstrated or because dialogue makes us realize that all religions have their merits and demerits. The text of the *Colloquium* was passed around secretly in manuscript for centuries, none daring to publish until the middle of the nineteenth century such a reputedly notorious challenge to the self-evident superiority of Christianity.

The cause of toleration became more visible as a political and intellectual force during the seventeenth century. As a practical aim, the Levellers in England during the 1640s made freedom to dissent from the established religion a central plank of their political program. Likewise, major figures in European philosophy weighed in on the side of freedom of religion. Thomas Hobbes (1588–1679) recognized the mischief that religion caused to the maintenance of public peace and order. His solution to the potential for religious conflict was not persecution of dissent but acknowledgment that, since faith was an inward matter, coercion of belief pertained to neither church nor state. So long as one's convictions about God and the afterlife did not produce external political dispute, Hobbesian logic required that the sovereign permit subjects to embrace whatever confession they liked. Baruch Spinoza (1632–1677) followed Hobbes in recognizing the inability of the government to control the inward faith of individuals. He therefore claimed a broad application for a right to liberty of thought and conviction without inference from a sovereign's (or a church's) determination of the truth or falsity of an individual's ideas. On the one hand, Spinoza proposed to employ the armed might of the state to rein in the activities of intolerant clergymen and mobs. On the other hand, he set clear limits on the power of the magistrate to persecute all forms of religious and intellectual dissent. The German jurist Samuel Pufendorf (1632–1694), too, advocated the protection of religious freedom in the name of the interests of the state. The sovereign must exercise control over the affairs of religion, not in order to impose "true" religion, but in order to ensure that "hotheads, pride, fame, and ambition" do not lead to civil conflict and sedition.

When viewed from the perspective of this intellectual backdrop, the concept of tolerance proposed by John Locke does not appear especially innovative or creative. Locke built his theory on a clear distinction between the aims of the church and the purposes of government. The church seeks to care for souls, whose condition cannot be changed by force but only by persuasion. Since the role of government is the protection of the life, liberty, and estate of subjects, its work cannot extend to the business of religion. For Locke, the magistrate should maintain public tranquility and defend individual rights. Thus, liberty of conscience was justified in the case of most Christian (and perhaps some non-Christian) rites. Of course, Locke insisted that government must take an appropriate interest in religious ideas and rites when they were capable of undermining social trust and political obedience. For this reason, he sought to exclude atheists and to ban any religious institutions that taught the superiority of the church to the temporal magistrate in civil affairs.

While Locke's account of toleration has received by far the most attention, the version proposed by the pre-Enlightenment thinker Pierre Bayle (1647–1706) is perhaps the most consistent and thoroughgoing of the late seventeenth century. Bayle is sometimes termed a *Calvinist* advocate of tolerance. Seeking to refute a range of arguments for persecution, Bayle baldly asserted that all forms of suppression of religious diversity encourage hypocrisy and erode social order. Indeed, to harass religious dissenters constitutes an affront to God. An erring conscience, if it be held in good faith, deserves as much protection as a correct one—a principle that Bayle extended even to atheists. Unlike many of his predecessors, he did not embrace a strict distinction between the inward and the outward, and he thus took seriously the ability of the threat of coercion to weaken the beliefs of individuals. But should a person be forced to surrender his or her inner convictions, an act of sacrilege has been committed because God forgives error on account of the purity of the intention. A false belief sincerely held was regarded by Bayle to be superior in the eyes of God to a true conviction held only as a result of external compulsion. Bayle did admit that rites which are likely to detract directly from civil order may be constrained or excluded, but his main concern seems to be fanatical sects that inspire their adherents to engage in conduct that endangers the health and well-being of other inhabitants of the community.

The themes highlighted by seventeenth-century proponents of toleration received further elaboration during the eighteenth century, in particular, the problem of balancing personal liberty of conscience against the need for public order and obedience. For instance, the journalist and novelist Daniel Defoe (1660–1731) railed in his writings against conformity, and he was only too happy to satirize the foibles of the persecutorial impulse. Although a dissenter himself, he once dared to publish a hoax pamphlet, "The Shortest Way with Dissenters" (1702), purportedly written by a High Church spokesman, that called for the hanging en masse of religious nonconformists.

The two most intellectually powerful eighteenth-century proponents of toleration were Christian Thomasius (1655–1728) and Immanuel Kant (1724–1804). Thomasius, a central figure of the so-called "civil Enlightenment," adopted a jurisprudential approach according to which all supposed heresies were framed in a historical light, and the charge of dissent was viewed simply as a means for different sects to vilify one another. Theological and metaphysical questions should be set aside in favor of a prudential law of religion *(Staatskirchenrecht)* that permitted and regulated expressions of religious diversity. Like Hobbes, Thomasius showed how an absolutist conception of government might yield a thoroughgoing principle of tolerance. Kant was certainly the more famous figure in the promotion of tolerant attitudes. His essay *Was ist Aufklärung?* (1784; What is enlightenment?) pronounced a human duty to become liberated from self-imposed mental chains and to develop an independent capacity for critical reflection. This requires a public sphere that is fully tolerant of differences in thought and action among individuals. Yet Kant also asserted the overriding duty that each person has to obey government, so that the subjects of a ruler have a supererogatory responsibility to refrain from public expression of ideas or doctrines that might promote disobedience to the sovereign will. For Kant, too, toleration did not necessitate the institutional primacy of rights associated with political liberalism.

Despite Kant's insistence upon obedience, a considerable number of Enlightenment thinkers in fact defended various forms of toleration in the eighteenth century. Thomas Paine (1737–1809) dismissed the terminology of "toleration" itself as inherently intolerant, since it depended upon the grant of the state, preferring to speak of basic rights associated with freedom of conscience and thought. The French philosophes, who were the main champions of enlightenment, likewise announced themselves to be defenders of tolerance. But perhaps it was with the "Declaration of the Rights of Man and the Citizen," approved by the National Assembly of France on 26 August 1789, that such a basic liberal conception of liberty of belief and worship received its characteristic statement.

*See also* Anabaptism; Bayle, Pierre; Bodin, Jean; Calvin, John; Defoe, Daniel; Dissenters, English; Enlightenment; Erasmus, Desiderius; Hobbes, Thomas; Jews, Attitudes toward; Kant, Immanuel; Las Casas, Bartolomé de; Locke, John; Luther, Martin; Nantes, Edict of; Philosophes; Reformation, Protestant; Revolutions, Age of; Salamanca, School of; Spinoza, Baruch; Thomasius, Christian.

BIBLIOGRAPHY

*Primary Sources*

Bodin, Jean. *Colloquium of the Seven about Secrets of the Sublime.* Edited by Marion Leathers Kuntz. Princeton, 1975.

Erasmus, Desiderius. *The Collected Works of Erasmus.* 22 vols. to date. Toronto, 1974–.

Las Casas, Bartolomé de. *In Defense of the Indians.* Edited by Stafford Poole. DeKalb, Ill., 1974.

Locke, John. *A Letter Concerning Toleration in Focus.* Edited by Susan Mendus and John Horton. London, 1991.

Pufendorf, Samuel. *Of the Nature and Qualification of Religion in Reference to Civil Society.* Translated by J. Crull. Edited by Simone Zurbuchen. Indianapolis, 2002.

*Secondary Sources*

Creppell, Ingrid. *Toleration and Identity: Foundations in Early Modern Thought.* New York, 2003.

Grell, Ole Peter, and Roy Porter, eds. *Toleration in Enlightenment Europe.* Cambridge, U.K., 2000.

Laursen, John Christian. *Religious Toleration: "A Variety of Rites" from Cyrus to Defoe.* New York, 1999.

Laursen, John Christian, ed. *Histories of Heresy in Early Modern Europe: For, Against, and Beyond Persecution and Toleration.* New York, 2002.

Laursen, John Christian, and Cary J. Nederman. *Beyond the Persecuting Society: Religious Toleration before the Enlightenment.* Philadelphia, 1998.

Murphy, Andrew R. *Conscience and Community: Revisiting Toleration and Religious Dissent in Early Modern England and America.* University Park, Pa., 2001.

Nederman, Cary J. *Worlds of Difference: European Discourses of Toleration, c. 1100–c. 1550.* University Park, Pa., 2000.

Nederman, Cary J., and John Christian Laursen, eds. *Difference and Dissent: Theories of Religious Toleration in Medieval and Early Modern Europe.* Lanham, Md., 1996.

Remer, Gary. *Humanism and the Rhetoric of Toleration.* University Park, Pa., 1996.

Waldron, Jeremy. *God, Locke, and Equality: Christian Foundations of John Locke's Political Thought.* Cambridge, U.K., 2002.

CARY J. NEDERMAN

---

**TOPKAPI PALACE.** The palatial complex built by the Ottoman Turkish sultan Mehmed II (ruled 1444–1446 and 1451–1481), completed in 1465, Topkapi occupied the site of the ancient acropolis of Byzantium at the northeastern tip of the Istanbul peninsula. Designed as the administrative center of a highly centralized imperial polity and as a royal residence, the Topkapi was inhabited by the Ottoman dynasty until the 1850s.

Located within a walled enclosure, Topkapi was built around three consecutive courtyards, each of which was entered through a monumental ceremonial gate. The layout and architecture of the structure were determined by several factors: notions of imperial seclusion, which underlined the divine and absolute authority of the sultan, and division of the structure into outer (public) and an inner (private) spaces, with strict rules governing the uses of all rooms and spaces. The administrative buildings in the second court, the council hall, the chancery, and the public treasury housed the government offices; architecturally these spaces bespoke the administration of justice by the sultan's extended household. Beyond the northern gate lay the inner palace, which featured the sultan's audience hall, the palace school and the dormitories for pages, a mosque, the privy chamber, and a treasury-bath complex where a lofty gallery offered spectacular views of the city. Lacking a strictly axial, geometric layout, Topkapi conveyed messages of imperial power through the use of symbolic elements such as the monumental

**Topkapi.** Aerial view of the palace. ©YANN ARTHUS-BERTRAND/CORBIS

gates and the belvedere tower, through the strictly codified and hierarchical use of space, and through rooms that commanded sweeping views, reflecting the monarch's dominion over the territories of the empire.

The main layout of Topkapi changed little throughout the following centuries. Nevertheless it became a repository of styles that reflected the changes in tastes and structure of the Ottoman house. The privy chamber was remodeled after 1517, to house the relics of the prophet Muhammad and his companions brought to Istanbul following the Ottoman conquest of Egypt. The expansions of the harem section during the reigns of Suleiman and Murad III corresponded to the royal family's move into the palace and to the growing role of women in the political realm. New kiosks and seaside residences were built beyond the central core, and former ones were replaced with more lavish structures, from the later sixteenth century onwards. In 1719 Ahmed III built a library in the third court, to house the palace's manuscript collection. The eclectic and westernized taste of the eighteenth

century was reflected in the extensive redecorations of this period. After being converted to a museum in 1924, Topkapi now also houses the palace archives and library.

*See also* **Constantinople; Mehmed II; Ottoman Empire; Suleiman I.**

BIBLIOGRAPHY

Çiğ, Kemal, Sabahattin Batur, and Cengiz Köseoğlu. *The Topkapi Saray Museum: Architecture, the Harem and other Buildings.* Translated and edited by J. Michael Rogers. Boston, 1988.

Necipoğlu, Gülru. *Architecture, Ceremonial, and Power: The Topkapi Palace in the Fifteenth and Sixteenth Centuries.* Cambridge, Mass., 1991.

Sözen, Metin. *Topkapi.* Istanbul, 1997.

ÇIĞDEM KAFESCIOĞLU

**TORTURE.** Torture (in Latin: *quaestio;* in German: *peinliche Frage, Folter,* or *Marter;* in French: *la question, gehene, gene*) was an integral part of medieval and early modern criminal procedure. Because a voluminous body of law covered every stage of torture, the system is called judicial torture. During the early modern period torture gradually lost its importance, and it was finally abolished at the end of the period.

## THE BACKGROUND OF JUDICIAL TORTURE

Judicial torture was no medieval or early modern invention. The Roman third-century lawyer Ulpian defined torture as "the torment and suffering of the body in order to elicit the truth." The actual jurisprudence of torture, however, only developed in connection with the twelfth-century "legal revolution," as the revival of Roman law at the newly founded universities of Northern Italy is often called. Before this, crimes were mostly prosecuted privately, with no public officials taking an active role in criminal investigations. The predominance of private prosecution came under threat as popes, kings, and princes increasingly centralized their political authority in the twelfth century. The process began in Northern Italy in the twelfth century and gradually spread to most other parts of Europe in the remaining centuries of the Middle Ages.

The inquisitorial procedure (inquisitio), as against the older accusatorial procedure (accusatio), was introduced to papal legislation as a means of controlling errant churchmen in the late twelfth century. In the inquisitorial procedure, the initiation of an action was entrusted to the court official, and the judge was actively involved in the investigation of the case. Inquisitorial procedure had been used in ancient Rome, and Charlemagne had also made use of it, but this type of procedure had fallen into disuse since the ninth century. In the thirteenth century, inquisitorial procedure was soon extended to the crime of heresy and other serious canon law crimes and soon spread to secular crimes as well. A parallel development (although not as yet thoroughly researched) was that serious crimes were categorized as exceptional (crimen exceptum), to which the normal rules of procedure did not apply.

The early medieval law of proof had left difficult cases to be decided by ordeal, oath, and judicial combat. Behind these archaic, "irrational" modes of proof lay the belief that God continuously intervened in the lives of the people and would let truth prevail in court as well. Leaving judicial problems for God to decide, however, ill suited the emerging conception of a rational, hierarchically organized judicial system. The result of the ordeal could not be challenged, nor could it be changed by the higher courts. The centralization of political power undermined the old European judicial systems, replacing lay judges with professional jurists. These professional judges were learned in Roman and canon law, distinct and alien from the system of proof based on ordeals, oaths, and combat. Many judges were probably familiar with formal logic and saw it as a basis for all legal decision making and law drafting. One of the most widespread forms of medieval legal scholarship became the so-called ordines iudiciarii, manuals of procedural law, in which both civil and criminal procedure, including the law of proof, were laid out in the minutest detail. The new procedure was based on learned law and written documents.

## TORTURE AS PART OF THE STATUTORY THEORY OF PROOF

A new law of proof emerged, then, as part and parcel of these developments. The Roman canon law of proof drew its elements, like medieval Roman law in general, from the materials of Emperor Justinian's Corpus Juris Civilis (Corpus of Civil Law; also spelled Corpus Iuris Civilis), which had originated in the sixth century. In canon law, ordeals were expressly prohibited at the Fourth Lateran Council in 1215. The building blocks of Roman law were combined with those produced by the emerging canon law to build what has been called Roman-canon law of proof, or the statutory or legal theory of proof. The theory then came to circulate as part of the European ius commune, 'common law', in the procedural law treatises of writers such as Albertus Gandinus (d. c. 1310) and William Durandus (c. 1237–1296). In contrast to the archaic system of oaths, ordeals, and combat, the new system assigned the decisions on evidence to human judges, not God, thus placing decisive emphasis on judicial torture. However, the change from one painful stage of criminal procedure to another—from ordeal to torture—may not have seemed as significant to ordinary people as it was to the theoretician.

Because the statutory theory of proof reached its maturity in the thirteenth century and remained virtually unchanged until the early modern period, it is convenient to describe the theory as it appears in sixteenth-century jurisprudence and legislation.

**Torture.** Engraving c. 1500 shows a prisoner being tortured on the wheel by clerics of the Spanish Inquisition. In this version of the widely used torture method, a fire below the wheel is used as the source of pain and injury. In other versions, the wheel was used simply to hold the victim while torturers beat him or her with metal bars. In some cases, the wheel was fitted with spikes. GETTY IMAGES

Among the many influential writers on criminal evidence embracing the statutory theory were the Italian Prosperus Farinaccius (1544–1618), the Dutchman Joost van Damhouder (1507–1581), and the German Benedict Carpzov (1595–1666). All these writers further elaborated and refined the theory of torture. The last important doctrinal defense of judicial torture was written by a Frenchman, Pierre François Muyart de Vouglans (1713–1791), in 1780.

Statutory theory of proof, as it was received from medieval literature in the works of Farinacius, Damhouder, Carpzov, and their colleagues, was based on the notions of full proof, half proof, and circumstantial evidence *(indicia)*. Full proof could consist only of the statements of two eyewitnesses or the defendant's confession. Circumstantial evidence, no matter how plentiful, could only amount to partial proof, and combination of one eyewitness and circumstantial evidence did not constitute full proof. Without full proof, however, the accused could not be convicted of a capital crime.

Sacramental confession had gained significance in the twelfth-century canon law and had been made an annual obligation on all Christians at the Fourth Lateran Council of 1215. Because of its increased cultural significance, it is no wonder that confession had become "the queen of proofs" *(re-*

*gina probationum)* in criminal procedure as well. The problem, however, was how to obtain full proof if no eyewitnesses were available. This is where judicial torture offered a solution. Judicial torture was never evidence in itself, but was a means of acquiring evidence in the form of confession.

## THE THEORY OF JUDICIAL TORTURE

At the beginning of the early modern period, the *ius commune* theory of torture was basically the same as it had been in the works of Gandinus and Durandus. The basic rules were similar across Europe. The use of torture was confined to capital crimes, for which the death penalty or mutilation could apply. Torture was intended as the last resort in situations in which no other means of gathering evidence was available. If there was already full proof in the form of two eyewitnesses or voluntary confession, torture was not necessary. The accused was to be threatened with torture before it was actually applied, for instance, by showing him the instruments of torture. The investigating judge was to follow the accused to the torture chambers and interrogate him as he was being tortured, while a notary recorded the findings. Sometimes a doctor's presence was also required; no advocate, however, was allowed for the accused.

Torture was meant to establish whether the accused had committed the crime, the commission of which *(corpus delicti)* had already been established by other means. This legal safeguard did not, however, apply to witchcraft cases. They were regarded as *crimina excepta,* 'exceptional crimes', in that their "traces disappeared with the act" *(facti transeuntis).* The law excluded certain classes of people from liability to judicial torture. Pregnant women, children below the age of twelve or fourteen, and old people (if torture might put their lives at risk) could not be tortured. Noble persons, public officials of a certain standing, clergy, physicians, and doctors of law were exempt from torture in some parts of Europe. Torture could not take place on Sunday or other legal holidays.

The most important legal safeguard in restricting the use of torture had to do with the amount of circumstantial evidence required to initiate it. According to the law, half proof in the form of the testimony of one eyewitness or a sufficient amount of circumstantial evidence was necessary to initiate

torture. Both in theory and in practice it was, however, largely left to the judge's discretion to determine when there was enough circumstantial evidence, although literature provided examples and guidelines. Compared to modern standards of proof necessary for conviction, the standard of evidence required for torture was often higher.

Other safeguards were provided to help material truth prevail as well. Contemporaries were well aware of the dangers that torture entailed from the point of view of finding out what had actually happened. Leading questioning was thus prohibited, and the confession extracted under torture was to be repeated in court within a certain time limit. Only the voluntary confession given thereafter, within twenty-four hours or so, served as proof, and not the confession given under torture. The practical significance of this safeguard was seriously undermined by the fact that the accused could be taken back to the torture chamber should he or she decide to recant the confession. Much of the literature recommended the practice of verifying the information obtained through torture, but many legal experts complained that courts paid too little attention to verification in practice. If the accused, nevertheless, managed to resist torture and did not confess, he or she had to be acquitted, at least until new incriminating evidence appeared.

The statutory theory of proof, together with judicial torture, was not only limited to legal literature but was incorporated into some of the major European legislative pieces of the early modern period, for example, the Constitutio Criminalis Carolina of imperial Germany (1532), the French Ordonnance Royale (1539) and Grande Ordonnance Criminelle (1670), and the Nueva Recopilación of Spain (1567). In some parts of Europe torture was used not only on the accused, but also on those against whom full eyewitness proof had already been produced. The idea was to secure confession, considered necessary for salvation, or to obtain evidence about possible accessories.

The legal literature was not greatly concerned with the form that judicial torture could take; this was largely a matter of local custom. In each case, the individual judge selected the method of torture, supposedly taking into consideration the seriousness of the charge. The most widespread torture device was the *strappado (corda, cola)*, "the queen of torments," in which the accused's hands were tied behind the back, and he or she was lifted up with a rope, sometimes with weights attached to the ankles. Or metallic devices, such as leg-braces, leg-screws, and thumbscrews, were used to press the accused's limbs or fingers and to crush them. Other widely used methods included keeping the accused awake; being stretched on the rack; and inducing the sensation of drowning by wetting a rag stuffed into the accused's throat.

## THE DECLINE OF TORTURE

In the seventeenth century, the system of judicial torture began to lose its practical significance, although it formally remained part of the law in most European countries until the late eighteenth and early nineteenth centuries. An important reason for its gradual disappearance was the erosion of its theoretical basis, the statutory theory of proof. In the sixteenth and seventeenth centuries, new forms of punishment were introduced as alternatives to death to cope with serious criminality, the most important being the galley, the workhouse, and the practice of exile and transportation. The new punishments called for more discretion in choice of punishment and sentencing. When the increased range of punishments and sentencing was combined with the different amounts of evidence available in practice, a revolution in the law of proof occurred. As John Langbein has shown, the "punishment upon suspicion" or "punishment for lying" (*Verdachtstrafe, Lügenstrafe*) developed as a result of this. For lesser evidence, a lesser punishment now followed. Although the death penalty still required full proof, both executions and incidents of judicial torture decreased from the sixteenth and seventeenth centuries in many European regions.

Thus, Sweden, where the statutory theory of proof was only adopted in the seventeenth century, and in its already changed form, could always boast of not having accepted judicial torture. In practice, however, torture was not completely unknown there. The same can be said of Aragón, another state that did not formally allow the use of torture. The English experience demonstrates particularly clearly the close connection between torture and the law of proof. The English jury system began to develop before the reception of Roman law in Europe. It was thus the jury, not the Roman canon law of proof, that replaced the archaic modes of evidence in the Middle Ages in England. The jury developed considerable freedom in evaluating evidence and condemning on circumstantial evidence, making torture to extort confessions unnecessary. A regularized system of judicial torture thus never developed, and its use was limited to political cases. Another reason for England's rejection of torture was that, unlike the Continent, England's judicial system developed on the basis of unpaid lay judges, to whom it would have been dangerous to entrust a system of torture.

## THE ABOLITION OF TORTURE

When Muyart de Vouglans wrote his treatise on criminal procedure in 1780, the medieval law of proof that had formed the basis of judicial torture had been eroded, and the philosophical and legislative attack on torture was already well under way. The best known critique of torture is Cesare Beccaria's (1738–1794) *On Crimes and Punishments* (1764), to which Muyart de Vouglans' work was in fact a response. Voltaire (1694–1778) joined Beccaria in fiercely condemning torture in some of his essays. According to the philosophes, torture could not secure correct judgments, since so much depended upon the ability of the accused to resist the physical pain involved. Torture was also wrong because it inflicted pain on people who had not been shown to deserve it. However, as Piero Fiorelli has demonstrated, these arguments were not the discoveries of the eighteenth-century philosophers, having been voiced by individual critics since the Middle Ages. Recent scholarship, especially the works of Fiorelli, Langbein, and Peters, has indeed shown that the historian of torture must look beyond the writings of the Enlightenment philosophers to understand why judicial torture was abolished.

European states abolished torture from their statutory law in the late eighteenth and early nineteenth centuries. Prussia was the first to abolish it in 1754; Denmark abolished it in 1770, Austria in 1776, France in 1780, and the Netherlands in 1798. Bavaria followed the trend in 1806 and Württemburg in 1809. In Spain the Napoleonic conquest put an end to the practice in 1808. Norway abolished it in 1819 and Portugal in 1826. The

Swiss cantons abolished torture in the first half of the nineteenth century. By the mid-nineteenth century, European legislators had thus harvested the fruits that the early modern revolution of proof, followed by Enlightenment philosophy, had produced. As Langbein and Peters observe, the final abolition of torture occurred gradually and in close connection with a general revision of criminal law. Legislative reforms took place partly simultaneously with, but in general slightly after, the Enlightenment philosophers' attack on judicial torture.

*See also* **Crime and Punishment; Inquisition; Law; Star Chamber.**

## BIBLIOGRAPHY

### *Primary Source*

Beccaria, Cesare. *On Crimes and Punishments and Other Writings.* Edited by Richard Bellamy. Translated by Richard Davies. Includes the translation of "Dei delitti e delle pene" (1764). Cambridge, U.K., 1995.

### *Secondary Sources*

Bartlett, Robert. *Trial by Fire and Water: The Medieval Judicial Ordeal.* Oxford, 1988.

Fiorelli, Piero. *La tortura giudiziaria nel diritto commune I–II.* Milan, 1953–1954.

Langbein, John H. *Prosecuting Crime in the Renaissance: England, Germany, France.* Cambridge, Mass., 1974.

———. *Torture and the Law of Proof: Europe and England in the Ancien Régime.* Chicago, 1977.

Peters, Edward. *Torture/Edward Peters.* New York, 1985.

HEIKKI PIHLAJAMÄKI

**TOURNAMENT.** Medieval tournaments had originally been serious exercises in martial training. As the introduction of firearms into warfare gradually made knightly armor obsolete, however, jousting lost much, although not all, of its practical rationale. The 1559 tilt at Paris in which French King Henry II received a fatal blow was already a

**Tournament.** Woodcut of knights practicing in the tilting ring, 1592. ©BETTMANN/CORBIS

somewhat archaic contest. Although tilts and other man-to-man encounters (often with blunted lances) continued to be held here and there into the eighteenth century, noncombative contests, such as runnings at the ring or at the head, became more common. With the decline of serious martial encounters, the medieval tournament tradition gave birth to several new theatrical genres that would flourish in early modern times.

The new genres, meant almost exclusively for courtly, aristocratic circles, may be said to have come into being by way of chivalric literature, whose popularity was undimmed by the progress of classical revival. Romances such as Sir Thomas Malory's *Le morte d'Arthur* (1485; The death of

Arthur) and Ludovico Ariosto's *Orlando furioso* (1515–1533; The madness of Roland) included episodes of jousting or tilting at the barrier. Planners of new, less earnest tournaments began to imitate situations or plots like those of the romances, so there were many variations on chivalric themes. For example, at Whitehall in 1581, courtier and poet Sir Philip Sidney (1554–1586) and three other knights apparently acted out a prearranged failure to capture the Fortresse of Perfect Beautie, which symbolized Queen Elizabeth's virginity and integrity. In 1605, after a poetic debate between allegorical ladies representing Truth and Opinion, sixteen knights who supported the proposition that marriage is superior to the single life tilted on foot across a barrier with sixteen others championing the opposite view. This

**Tournament.** Painting of a tournament in Turin by Antonio Tempesta, seventeenth century. ©ARCHIVO ICONOGRAFICO, S.A./CORBIS

English contest was planned by the poet Ben Jonson (1572–1637) and the architect Inigo Jones (1573–1652) as the second part of a whole entitled *Hymenaei: or the Solemnities of Masque and Barriers at a Marriage*. On the first day of the grand 1664 entertainments at Versailles, remembered as *Les Plaisirs de l'Île Enchantée* (Pleasures of the Bewitched Island), a troop of actors and dancers, including the young King Louis XIV, interpreted a chivalric episode of Ariosto's *Orlando*. The Versailles entertainments were apparently inspired in part by others held two years earlier at the court of Bavaria, the planners of which had been, in turn, inspired by Italian examples.

Despite such cross-influences, the evolution of tournament forms varied enormously across Europe. There were dramatic or literary tournaments, operatic tournaments, and many hybrids of tournament and ballet, including horse ballets, in which specially bred and highly trained horses executed graceful movements that sometimes simulated combat. Two of the most elaborate performances of the last kind, both of them put on at the Medici court in Florence during 1616, are handsomely represented in engravings by the artist Jacques Callot (1592–1635). By now, the grandest theatrical tournaments, having been extremely expensive to produce, were usually recorded in engravings and published accounts. There were also books on the art of planning such fêtes, the best-known of them being Claude-François Ménestrier's *Traité des tournois* (1669; Treatise on tournaments).

*See also* Festivals; Louis XIV (France); Prints and Popular Imagery; Versailles.

BIBLIOGRAPHY

*Primary Source*

Ménestrier, Claude-François. *Traité des tournois, ioustes, carrousels, et autres spectacles publics.* Lyons, 1669. (Photographic reprint with introductory notes by Stephen Orgel. New York and London, 1979.) Combined theoretical treatise and historical survey written by a scholar responsible for planning a number of courtly festivals in France.

*Secondary Sources*

Anglo, Sydney. *The Martial Arts of Renaissance Europe.* New Haven and London, 2000. A detailed study of the theory and practice of martial training covering most of the early modern period, by an author who has also written extensively on tournaments. See especially Chapters 8 and 9.

Watanabe-O'Kelly, Helen. "Tournaments in Europe." In *Spectaculum Europaeum: Theatre and Spectacle in Europe; Histoire du spectacle en Europe (1580–1750),* edited by Pierre Béhar and Helen Watanabe-O'Kelly, pp. 593–639. Wiesbaden, 1999. Easily the most comprehensive and systematic general study. Includes an extensive bibliography and a multilingual glossary of terms applying to tournaments (pp. 595–596).

Young, Alan. *Tudor and Jacobean Tournaments.* London and Dobbs Ferry, N.Y., 1987. An illustrated scholarly survey covering the whole period of the English Renaissance, with a bibliographical chronology extending to 1626.

BONNER MITCHELL

# TRADING COMPANIES.

The early seventeenth century saw the foundation of Dutch and English trading companies with exclusive rights over vast areas in various parts of the globe. These organizations were essentially merchant guilds that represented an "institutional innovation" that enabled them to conduct large-scale trade with distant shores. They came to exercise functions that were usually the prerogative of national states. The main companies were the East India Company, or EIC (1600–1858), the Hudson's Bay Company (founded in 1670 and still active) and the Royal African Company (1672–1750), all English, as well as the Dutch East India Company, or VOC (Vereenigde Oost-Indische Compagnie, 1602–1799) and the Dutch West India Company, or WIC (1621–1791). Imitation companies were established in numerous states, including Denmark, France, Genoa, Portugal, and Sweden.

The commercial success of Dutch fleets in Asia led to the foundation of the two foremost East India companies. The return of four Dutch ships from the Indian Ocean in 1599 laden with spices prompted the English Parliament to award a monopoly of trade with the East Indies to the EIC (31 December 1600). Whereas the English Russia and Turkey Companies had previously failed to get access to spices through the Asian land routes, the English would henceforth use only the route around the Cape of Good Hope. Across the English Channel, the so-called pre-companies, regionally based Dutch organizations that had actively traded with the East Indies since 1595, were liquidated to make way for the VOC. On 20 March 1602, the Dutch States-General granted the VOC a national monopoly that was similar in nature to that of the EIC.

## THE EAST INDIA COMPANIES

The Dutch and English East India Companies followed in the footsteps of the Portuguese merchants in Asia and learned from their experiences. Adopting the model that the Portuguese had successfully pioneered, the VOC created a string of "factories," fortified trading posts defended by garrisons, from Java to Japan and from Persia to Siam. These posts were linked by a regular exchange of information and commodities. The EIC established its own factories across a more limited area.

The EIC and VOC were not the first companies to enjoy national monopolies, but as chartered companies they did display some novel features. Investment in long-distance trade was no longer limited to overseas traders, as had been the case with regulated companies such as the Turkey Company, but the charters allowed domestic merchants to take part as well. What is more, the chartered companies evolved into joint-stock companies. This meant that shares were freely alienable and merchants no longer raised capital for one voyage, but created a permanent capital committed to the enterprise. Long-term considerations thus determined marketing policies. Nor was the working capital of the companies limited to their capital stock, since both resorted to the capital market to finance their operations.

A sound commercial policy underlay the VOC's remarkable performance. By minimizing its dependence on markets that it did not control, and becoming the largest buyer and seller, the company drastically reduced its risk. Success did not come overnight, but took decades to achieve. The company benefited from the general commercial crisis rocking Southeast Asia in the mid-seventeenth century, just as the Dutch partly owed their commercial hegemony in Europe to the prevailing regional political and economic crises. Yet the VOC was not universally successful. Its huge overhead costs proved detrimental when competing with Indian traders who operated at low cost and could accept a lower profit margin.

Military expenditures were one factor that raised overhead costs. From the outset, the VOC used force to further its objectives vis-à-vis Moluccan natives, Indian merchants, and Portuguese and English rivals to secure footholds, preempt foreign European settlement, and obtain spice monopolies. Superior military strength enabled the Dutch to conquer the spice islands, seize Portuguese forts, and oust the EIC from the Indonesian archipelago around 1623, the year in which the Dutch governor had ten English nationals tortured and executed. This "Amboina massacre" was a popular English propaganda tool against the Dutch in the years to come. Other noneconomic means helped the VOC to achieve near-total control of the production and marketing of nutmeg, mace, and cloves by the late 1660s. Clove production was, for instance, restricted to the island of Amboina, and trees and surplus stocks were destroyed. The spice monopsony, which enabled the VOC to fix prices, left the company with huge profits. By contrast, pepper remained elusive, since it was cultivated over a vast area. Besides, local princes did not always honor their agreements.

For lack of sufficient financial means, the EIC operated in the shadow of its Dutch counterpart for most of the seventeenth century. Its directors, however, made the best of the EIC's removal from the Spice Islands by concentrating operations on India, where the VOC's presence was small. While the VOC achieved some of its original aims, the EIC proved masterful in reinventing itself. In the eighteenth century, it discovered the marketability in Europe of Indian cloth and Chinese tea. In military matters, the EIC underwent a similar metamorphosis. Founded not as a war instrument like its Dutch rival, its fleets were relatively poorly equipped and offensive actions against Asians or Europeans virtually impossible. However, the company's new charter of 1661 stipulated that it could make war or peace with non-Christian princes or people, and very gradually, a more assertive line was adopted, in particular on the Indian subcontinent. By the 1760s, the EIC may be said to have assumed the role of a nation-state in India. It is debatable whether this expansion was based on a master plan, or whether the company was sucked into local power politics. The theory of reluctant imperialism has also been applied to the VOC, which was unable to achieve its objectives on Java without involving itself in a complex indigenous power struggle.

Wherever the chartered companies conducted a profitable trade, fellow nationals tried to benefit as interlopers. Exchanging goods from one part of Asia in another, EIC factors and private individuals carved out a niche for themselves. Although the EIC initially forbade such trade, considering those involved as rivals of its own intra-Asian trade, the costs that it entailed made the company withdraw from the trade, and its attitude toward the interlopers changed accordingly. "Free" merchants could begin to settle in port cities under English rule, after the EIC issued a series of indulgences, starting in 1667. Subsequent English commercial success in Asia cannot be understood without taking into account private "country trade." The VOC showed no such lenience, despite a statement by the secretary of its largest regional body, the Amsterdam Chamber, in the 1650s that intra-Asian trade were better left to private traders, whose overhead costs were modest compared with the company's, with its heavily armed ships. Not until 1742 did the VOC allow breaches in its monopoly. On the other hand, company employees enriched themselves by conducting private trade side by side with official company trade. Fraud and corruption were rampant in the Dutch factories.

In intra-Asian trade, the Portuguese had shown the way. Their country trade was more important than their trade to Europe. Like the Portuguese and the English private merchants, the VOC became active in this trade. Between 1640 and 1688 the Dutch company procured substantial amounts of Japanese silver and Taiwanese gold for the purchase of Indian textiles, which were then exchanged for Indonesian pepper and other spices, although some were sent to Europe. Most pepper and other spices were also sold in Europe, but a certain percentage was invested in Persia, India, Taiwan, and Japan. The profits made in the intra-Asian trade paid for Asian products, the sales of which in Europe yielded more than the dividend that the VOC paid to its shareholders in this period. The company's role in intra-Asian trade was eroded in the last quarter of the seventeenth century, when Indian merchants emerged as serious rivals in the trade to Java, Sumatra, and the Malay Peninsula. In addition, Japanese authorities curbed Dutch trade, effectively ending the VOC's role as chief supplier of precious metals in various Asian markets. Still, while the English became the main nation involved, the VOC easily remained the leading European company participating in intra-Asian trade.

What was the relationship between private trading companies and the home governments? Local magistrates were closely connected to VOC affairs in the United Provinces. They elected the directors of the regional chambers from among the principal investors. The States-General, for its part, had not only delegated sovereign powers to the VOC at the company's inception, but financially supported it afterward in time of need. This aid proved crucial in the VOC's early years, enabling the struggling company to make long-term investments in infrastructure and in military, maritime, and commercial affairs, which eventually paid off. The British government, on the other hand, arbitrarily exploited the financial resources of the EIC on several occasions. At the same time, it grew increasingly alarmed about the way the EIC conducted itself in India. Concluding alliances and treaties with native princes, and leading territorial expansion, the company resembled more a sovereign state than a trading company. Warfare was also thought to cut into profits from Asian trade, which was supposedly the company's chief business. The Dutch also debated the advantages of territorial expansion, but here it was the VOC's central board, not the States-General, that challenged the wisdom of company employees on the ground in Java.

Both companies contributed to national prosperity by employing thousands, stimulating the domestic shipbuilding and textile industries, and offering investment outlets. British financial leaders became involved in the EIC, while company men advised the British government on financial affairs. No such systematic crossovers occurred in the Dutch Republic, not even when the VOC faced serious financial problems in the second half of the eighteenth century. The fourth Anglo-Dutch War (1780–1784), in particular, had disastrous financial consequences. The curtain finally came down for the VOC following the French invasion of the Dutch Republic (1795). On 1 March 1796 a Committee of East Indian Trade and Possessions replaced the company directors. The EIC did not emerge as the great beneficiary of its rival's demise.

Not only had the French and Danish East India Companies emerged as competitors, the home front grew increasingly critical of the company's moral and economic record. In 1813 the British government stripped the EIC of all its monopolies, except for the tea trade with Canton, and in 1833 all company trade ceased. After the Great Rebellion in India (1857–1858), the British state assumed the company's affairs.

## THE ATLANTIC WORLD

Very different conditions obtained in the Atlantic world, where plantation companies such as the Virginia Company, licensed to establish colonies, were more prominent than pure trading companies, although in actual practice it is difficult to distinguish between the two. In 1621 the Dutch West India Company received privileges similar to those the VOC had in Asia. Founded expressly as a war machine that targeted Spanish and Portuguese ships and settlements, the WIC attracted little investment, as Dutch citizens feared the risks to which the company ships were exposed. They were proven wrong in the company's early days, in particular after the celebrated capture of the Spanish silver fleet of 1628, when the company paid a 50 percent dividend to its shareholders.

Soon, however, financial problems troubled the WIC and proved almost insurmountable. The company faced entirely different circumstances in the Atlantic from those experienced by the VOC. The creation of an intricate network of factories did not make sense in the Atlantic world. There was no Atlantic counterpart to the centuries-old intra-Asian trade in which to participate. Nor was the WIC able to obtain monopsony of the New World commodity it prized most: sugar. Not even the occupation (1630–1654) of northeastern Brazil, the world's largest producer, helped the company achieve that goal. The Dutch discovered that marketing Brazilian sugar was more difficult than was the case with East Indian spices, precisely because of the competition from other areas of sugar cultivation, including Java, Bengal, and the island of São Tomé off the African west coast.

Unlike its Asian counterpart, the WIC was unable to combine a vigorous commercial enterprise with warfare. The costly war with Habsburg Spain over Brazil, which began in 1630, forced the company to abandon some of its monopolies. By 1638, only the export of slaves from Africa and ammunition from the Netherlands, and the import of Brazilian dyewood, remained in company hands. Private merchants soon dominated the Brazil trade, although the dividing line between company interests and private concerns was, once again, not as clear as might be expected; WIC directors were among the principals of the free traders.

One argument used by advocates of the liberalization of trade was the need to people Dutch Brazil. The immigration of "free" settlers—artisans, merchants, and other colonists not in company service—so the argument ran, did more to guarantee the survival of a colony than the presence of soldiers. Besides, without trade the military was bound to become a liability, since soldiers' salaries and rations would eat away the company budget. A "free" population would create economic activity and pay import and export duties, as well as bear the burden of the soldiery. Free trade was also necessary to lure free settlers from the Dutch Republic.

At a slightly earlier stage, a similar discussion had erupted over New Netherland, the company's colony in North America. After the WIC assumed control of the colony in 1623, Manhattan and Fort Orange (now Albany) were established as trading posts to tap the vast hinterland for peltries. These posts resembled the VOC factories in Asia. A factory would seem to rule out large-scale migration, if only to curtail defense expenditures, as one company faction argued. Advocates of migration among the WIC directors emphasized the positive long-term effects of investments in agriculture and settlement. Their arguments carried the day, and by 1640 the company's fur monopoly was abolished.

The WIC remained in chronic financial trouble, as the war with the Iberian countries dragged on. In 1644 even a merger with the VOC was discussed, but the VOC refused, although it was forced by the States-General to pay its counterpart 5 million florins. In 1674, the WIC went bankrupt and was replaced by a new one with capable directors, recruited from the ranks of the shareholders. Outstanding shares and bonds were converted into new shares at a small percentage of their nominal value. In the eighteenth century, the WIC was transformed into an organization that managed the

Dutch colonies, after it lost its last monopolies, including the slave trade.

Whereas the WIC originally monopolized commerce in several products in the Atlantic world, monopolies in England were granted to various corporations. The English slave trade was exclusively conducted by the Royal African Company from 1672 until Parliament in 1698 yielded to the demands of other merchants and opened the slave trade to everyone. The Hudson's Bay Company started out as a fur-trading enterprise before undergoing a peculiar metamorphosis. It took up exploration on the west coast of North America and in the Arctic, branched out into land development and real estate, and remains to this day one of Canada's largest retailers.

**IMITATION COMPANIES**

If the Dutch and the English invented the typical chartered company, other Europeans were not far behind. Drawing inspiration from the pioneers, they imitated their examples down to the last detail. For example, the management of the Danish East India Company, founded in 1616, was entrusted to nine directors who received the Dutch title *bewindhebbers*. What may help to account for the adoption of Dutch terms was the role played by immigrants from Amsterdam and Rotterdam in establishing the Scandinavian companies. Nor was imitation confined to northern Europe; the Dutch West India Company served as the model for a Spanish privileged trading company, which was discussed at various times during the seventeenth century.

The imitation companies had one element in common. Their founders were obsessed with the particular structure of the English and Dutch models. They found to their cost that elaborate government initiatives only paid off when buttressed by mercantile activities. The latter, however, were often conspicuously absent. And even where there was sufficient support from merchants, undercapitalization prevented the companies from yielding the expected profits. In either case, private traders were allowed to break up the company monopolies within a few years.

What also stood in the way of success was the large degree of royal control over the imitation companies. The French East and West India Companies, in particular, were designed to increase state power abroad instead of running a business enterprise. The Portuguese East India Company (1628–1633) faced another problem. While the Dutch and English companies had set up the administrative apparatus in Asia from scratch, Portuguese company officials had to defer to existing authorities. They were forced to operate in a trading empire that had functioned for more than a century under its own political and military administration, which was not going to yield.

*See also* **British Colonies; Dutch Colonies; Dutch Republic; French Colonies; Fur Trade: North America; Portuguese Colonies; Shipping; Spanish Colonies.**

BIBLIOGRAPHY

Ames, Glenn J. *Colbert, Mercantilism, and the French Quest for Asian Trade.* DeKalb, Ill., 1996.

Blussé, Leonard, and Femme Gaastra, eds. *Companies and Trade: Essays on Overseas Trading Companies during the Ancien Régime.* Leiden and Hingham, Mass., 1981.

Brenner, Robert. *Merchants and Revolution: Commercial Change, Political Conflict, and London's Overseas Traders, 1550–1653.* Princeton, 1993.

Chaudhuri, K. N. *The Trading World of Asia and the English East India Company, 1660–1760.* Cambridge, U.K., and New York, 1978.

Disney, A. R. *Twilight of the Pepper Empire: Portuguese Trade in Southwest India in the Early Seventeenth Century.* Cambridge, Mass., and London, 1978.

Furber, Holden. *Rival Empires of Trade in the Orient, 1600–1800.* Minneapolis, 1976.

Gaastra, Femme S. *De geschiedenis van de VOC.* Zutphen, 1991.

Haudrère, Philippe. *La Compagnie française des Indes au XVIIIe siècle, 1719–1795.* Paris, 1989.

Heijer, Henk den. *De geschiedenis van de WIC.* Zutphen, 1994.

Lawson, Philip. *The East India Company: A History.* London and New York, 1993.

Prakash, Om. *The Dutch East India Company and the Economy of Bengal, 1630–1720.* Princeton, 1985.

Prakash, Om, ed. *European Commercial Expansion in Early Modern Asia.* Aldershot, U.K., 1997.

Steensgaard, Niels. *The Asian Trade Revolution of the Seventeenth Century: The East India Companies and the Decline of the Caravan Trade.* Chicago, 1974.

Thomson, Janice E. *Mercenaries, Pirates, and Sovereigns: State-Building and Extraterritorial Violence in Early Modern Europe.* Princeton, 1994.

Tracy, James D., ed. *The Political Economy of Merchant Empires: State Power and World Trade, 1350–1750.* Cambridge, U.K., and New York, 1991.

———. *The Rise of Merchant Empires: Long-Distance Trade in the Early Modern World, 1350–1750.* Cambridge, U.K., and New York, 1990.

WIM KLOOSTER

---

**TRANSPORTATION.** *See* **Communication and Transportation.**

---

# TRAVEL AND TRAVEL LITERATURE.

Travel writing was perhaps the most diverse genre of literature in early modern Europe. A single travel account contained nautical information including wind direction and speed, ocean depth, latitude and longitude, astronomical observations, and distance traveled each day. Coastlines were mapped, interiors explored, exotic plants and animals described for the first time by Europeans, or the observations of previous explorers confirmed. Accounts contained military intelligence regarding city fortifications, water supplies, populations, points of dissent that might be exploited, and notes on local commerce. Of great interest to European audiences were the customs and manners of indigenous populations encountered. All of this was rolled together and given a narrative form combining both adventure and philosophical reflection on Europe in the mirror of the other. European audiences were enthralled. Travel literature was the second-best-selling genre in the early modern era, behind only history.

Already in the sixteenth century enterprising editors began collecting the accounts of navigators and voyageurs. Richard Hakluyt's (1552–1616) *Principal Navigations, Traffiques and Discoveries* (1589) celebrated the English maritime tradition from the sixth to the sixteenth century; in a second edition he expanded his collection to include translations of French and Italian voyages as well. It is only through Hakluyt's edition that Sir Francis Drake's report of his privateering and circumnavigation of the globe survives, as the original report disappeared without being published shortly after he submitted it to Queen Elizabeth I. Hakluyt himself drew on the English precedents of Richard Eden's *Decades of the New World or West India* (London, 1555), which had been revised and expanded by Richard Willes in *The History of Travayle* (London, 1577). These in turn can be traced to the Italian collection by Giovanni Battista Ramusio, *Navigationi et viaggi* (Navigations and voyages, 3 vols; Venice 1550–1556). Hakluyt inspired several other collections and continuations of travel literature over the centuries, and in the nineteenth century a "Hakluyt Society" was founded, dedicated to the history of navigation and discovery, which exists to this day.

Useful for popular entertainment, moral edification, and scientific inquiry, travel literature also exerted direct influence on national policy. While neither Alvar Nuñez Cabeza de Vaca's (c. 1490–1557) urging of the Spanish crown to take a greater interest in proselytizing in Central America nor Sir Walter Raleigh's (1552–1618) advocacy of British exploration in greater Guiana were of direct consequence to national policy, other authors managed to get their message heard. William Dampier's *A New Voyage round the World* (1697), *Voyages and Descriptions* (1699), and *A Voyage to New Holland* (1704) were instrumental in directing England's attention to the Pacific, which previously had been ceded to the Spanish and the Dutch. John and Awnsham Churchill's *Collection of Voyages and Travels* (1704), modeled on Hakluyt and inspired by Dampier's commercial success, was a comprehensive plan for establishing naval bases in the Pacific for further exploration, commerce, and warfare. As the influence of Holland and Spain declined in the Pacific in the eighteenth century, England and France enjoined rivalry over Pacific hegemony.

England and France raced to be the first to discover the *Terra Australis incognita*, the southern continent believed to be a geographic necessity to balance the landmass of the northern hemisphere. In the late 1760s the British and French happened upon Tahiti nearly simultaneously. In 1767 Samual Wallis landed on the islands first, but Louis Antoine de Bougainville was in the area also from 1766 to 1769. He dispatched his scientific team to collect plant and animal specimens from the islands, and he even brought a native Tahitian named Ahutoru back to Paris. Immediately upon his return to France in 1769 Bougainville announced the discovery of the islands he named New Cythera, after the Aegean island where the goddess Venus first washed ashore. The discovery showed that the French navy could still compete with the British in the wake of the Seven Years' War (1756–1763), and thus it occasioned a great deal of national pride. The British responded with James Cook's first voyage (1768–1771), underwritten by the Royal Society, and in a separate expedition in 1774 Tobias Furneaux brought to London the Tahitian Omai, in answer to Ahutoru. Whether French, British, or Spanish, the voyages of discovery were always patriotic endeavors in addition to having geopolitical, military, and economic significance.

Travel literature created an odd association between men of action and men of letters. Shakespeare set his *Tempest* (c. 1611) on a spooky island, perhaps inspired by William Strachey's "True Repertory of the Wracke and Redemption of Sir Thomas Gates" in Bermuda (written 1610, published 1625). Strachey's shipmates initially found the island a desert, "onely fed with raine water, which neverthelesse soone sinketh into the earth and vanisheth away." Other places were populated by bats and indigenous people who did not respond well to the castaways' kindnesses. Shakespeare's "island seem to be a desert," (II. 1), Sebastian proposed to "go a bat-fowling" (II. 1), and the native Caliban returned Prospero's generosity by attempting to rape his daughter Miranda (I. 2). Even the sprite Ariel appeared in Strachey's account of "an apparition of a little round light, like a faint starre, trembling, and streaming along with a sparkling blaze, halfe the height upon the Maine Mast, and shooting sometimes from Shroud to Shroud, tempting to settle as it were upon any of the four Shrouds." It remained half the night and finally disappeared at dawn. Nevertheless Strachey wanted to disabuse the English of the image of Bermuda as islands that "can be of no habitation to man, but rather given over to devils and spirits"—but this is precisely the legend Shakespeare built upon.

In 1708–1711 one of the most influential travel writers, William Dampier, circumnavigated the globe with the privateer Woodes Rogers, who returned with both ships intact and his holds filled with exotic and expensive items, matching the success of Sir Francis Drake a century and a quarter earlier. Along the way they rescued Alexander Selkirk, who had been put ashore in the Island of Juan Fernandez in 1704 and marooned there for five years. They found Selkirk clothed in goat skins, looking "wilder than the original owners of them." He had survived by hunting and fishing and had passed the time "reading, singing Psalms and praying, so that he said he was a better Christian while in this solitude, than he ever was before." Selkirk was hailed in William Cowper's 1782 poem "The Solitude of Alexander Selkirk:" "I am monarch of all I survey." Selkirk's experience also formed the outline of one of the first English novels, Daniel Defoe's *Robinson Crusoe* (1719). Selkirk's island, some 500 miles west of Santiago, Chile, is still officially named Isla Robinson Crusoe. Even Samuel Taylor Coleridge's "Rime of the Ancient Mariner" (1798) has a core of truth, adopted from an episode described by George Shelvocke (*Voyage round the World*, 1726) of being stuck in the doldrums off Cape Horn, the only sign of life "a disconsolate black albatross, who accompanied us for several days, hovering about us as if he had lost himself, till Hatley, my second captain, imagining from his color that it might be some ill-omen, after some fruitless attempts, at length shot the albatross, not doubting, perhaps, that we should have a fair wind after it." Instead that minor atrocity brought Hatley no better luck than Coleridge's ancient mariner.

James Boswell caught the travel bug while speaking with Captain Cook between Cook's second and third voyages in 1776. He told Samuel Johnson that "while I was with the Captain, I catched the enthusiasm of curiosity and adventure, and felt a strong inclination to go with him on his next voyage. JOHNSON: 'Why, Sir, a man does feel so, till he considers how very little he can learn from such voyages.' BOSWELL: 'But one is carried away with the general and distinct notion of A Voyage Round the World.' JOHNSON: 'Yes, Sir, but a man is to guard himself against taking a thing in general.'" (Boswell, *Life of Samuel Johnson,* 3 April 1776)

"The enthusiasm of curiosity and adventure"— these were the allure of travel literature in the early modern period. Hardship and desperation brought out the best of human perseverance and intrepidity, whether it was the drama of Cook's crew desperately bailing water while trying to hoist the *Endeavor* off the Great Barrier Reef in 1771 or the exhilaration of William Bligh's arrival at Timor after sailing 1,200 leagues across the South Pacific with seventeen men in a twenty-three-foot open boat, after having been cast adrift by a mutinous crew of the *Bounty*. Just as exciting was George Anson's four-year *Voyage round the World* (1748), fraught with near disaster at every step. Storms off Cape Horn reduced a fleet of six raiders to one; raids on Spanish settlements on the west coast of South America as part of the War of the Austrian Succession (1740–1748) were beaten back; a treasure ship was captured; typhoon winds were so fierce that men lashed themselves to the fore-rigging to serve as sails, and one of the best was blown overboard and last seen treading water in the distance with no chance of rescue; advanced scurvy was healed with miraculous swiftness by fruit and fresh water on a South Pacific island. In scene after scene voyage accounts were a read as engaging as any modern thriller.

Only in rare cases like Dampier and Sir Walter Raleigh did men of action double as men of letters. Usually accounts of voyages around the world were ghostwritten (if not overtly so) by another author, and in the eighteenth century it was the policy of the British Admiralty board to confiscate the captains' logs and other officers' journals and turn them over to an author who collated the information and turned it into literature. In 1771, for example, John Hawkesworth was given a £6,000 advance to compile the scientific journals of Joseph Banks and Daniel Solander and Cook's logs in order to produce "the official" account of the voyage. J. Reinhold Forster thought he bore the right to fill Hawkesworth's role on Cook's second voyage for which he himself was the chief science officer, but after Hawkesworth's performance was panned in the British press, Cook asserted control over his logs and produced his own account. But even here the naval captain had considerable help from John Douglas, a canon of Windsor, in composing the narrative. Richard Owen Cambridge was assigned by the Admiralty to assist Forster, but Forster pulled out of the deal and turned his notes and journals over to his son George, who had also sailed with his father and Cook.

Not all travel in the early modern period involved overseas navigation, and many overland expeditions were specifically scientific in intent. Scientific travel marks a major change between the curiosity cabinets of the seventeenth-century collectors and the eighteenth-century project of botanical and zoological (and human) taxonomy. Following the lead of his teacher Olof Rudbeck, who in 1695 had made an overland journey to Lapland, in 1732 Carl Linnaeus crossed the Arctic Circle to the north coast of Norway, chiefly in search of plant specimens, the results of which were published as *Flora Lapponica* (1737). Several of Linnaeus's students traveled the globe in the taxonomic effort: Daniel Solander explored the South Pacific on Cook's first voyage; on his second voyage Cook picked up Anders Sparrmann at the Cape of Good Hope and took him around the world; Karl Peter Thunberg was the first European to visit Japan in over a century, where he offered medical information to the Japanese and took home numerous plant specimens; and Peter Forskål, traveling with a Danish Hebrew scholar and a German geographer funded by the Danish crown, sent home drawings and specimens from Egypt and Arabia before the expedition was wiped out by malaria in Yemen. J. G. Gmelin spent ten years (1733–1743) observing the flora and fauna of Siberia on the Russian payroll and published both a travel narrative and a scientific treatise, each in four volumes. The French also sent an expedition to Lapland in the 1730s, led by Pierre Louis Moreau de Maupertuis (1698–1759) not to collect plant specimens but to make astronomical observations to confirm the theory that, due to its rotation, the Earth is slightly flattened at its poles. These observations were coordinated with a simultaneous expedition to equatorial Peru led by Charles Marie de la Condamine (1701–1774). Most of the research journeys were government-funded and of national interest to the funding monarch, implicitly pitting the scientists against one another in competition. Yet there was a clear sense among the scientists themselves that they were members of an international republic of letters, and through their published travel narratives they shared their findings with each other.

As the volume of travel literature increased rapidly in the late eighteenth century, scholars began to put it to systematic use. Here the observations of travelers constituted the raw scientific data of geography and climate, of flora and fauna, and of human society and customs. In France Abbé Guillaume Thomas François Raynal (1713–1796) assembled a philosophical and political history of the settlements and trade of the Europeans in the East and West Indies on the basis of travel literature. Earlier in the century Anton Yves Goguet (1716–1758) brought a wealth of anecdotes from modern travelers to bear on ancient authors to construct a history of humanity in its earliest stages. Montesquieu's *Spirit of the Laws* (1748) was heavily dependent on travel reports. In Britain Henry Home, Lord Kames (1696–1782) and William Falconer (1744–1824) produced histories of global humanity from travel reports. In Germany the first glimmer of modern anthropology emerged in the reading of travel literature by Isaac Iselin (1728–1782), Johann Gottfried Herder (1744–1803), and Christoph Meiners (1747–1810), whose *Grundriß der Geschichte der Menschheit* (1785; Outline of the history of humanity) contained an eighty-page bibliography of cited travel literature.

*See also* **Botany; Cartography and Geography; Colonization; Ethnography; Europe and the World; Exploration; Herder, Johann Gottfried von; Linnaeus, Carl; Montesquieu, Charles-Louis de Secondat de.**

BIBLIOGRAPHY

*Primary Sources*

Bougainville, Louis Antoine de. *A Voyage round the World.* Translated from French by Johann Rheinhold Forster. London, 1772.

Cook, James. *A Voyage Towards the South Pole, and round the World Performed in His Majesty's Ships the Resolution and Adventure, in the Years 1772, 1773, 1774, and 1775.* London, 1777.

Dampier, William. *A New Voyage round the World.* 3 vols. London, 1697–1709.

Forster, Georg. *A Voyage round the World (1778).* Edited by Nicholas Thomas and Oliver Berghof. Honolulu, 2000.

Gmelin, Johann Georg. *Flora Sibirica.* 4 vols. St. Petersburg, 1747–1769.

———. *Reise durch Sibirien.* 4 vols. Göttingen, 1751–1752.

Hakluyt, Richard. *The Principal Navigations, Voiages, Traffiques and Discoveries of the English Nation.* 3 vols. London, 1598–1600.

Hawkesworth, John. *An Account of the Voyages Undertaken by the Order of His Present Majesty for Making Discoveries in the Southern Hemisphere.* London, 1773.

Raleigh, Walter. *The Discoverie of the Large, Rich, and Beautiful Empire of Guiana.* London, 1596.

Raynal, Abbé (Guillaume-Thomas-François). *Histoire philosophique et politique des établissements et du commerce des Européens dans les deux Indes.* 6 vols. Amsterdam, 1770.

Rogers, Woodes. *A Cruising Voyage round the World.* London, 1712.

Shelvocke, George. *A Voyage round the World.* London, 1726.

Strachey, William. "True Repertory of the Wracke and Redemption of Sir Thomas Gates." In Samuel Purchas, *Hakluytus Posthumous or Purchas His Pilgrims.* London, 1625. Reprinted in 20 vols. New York, 1965. Vol. 19, pp. 3–78.

*Secondary Sources*

Beaglehole, J. C. *The Life of Captain James Cook.* Stanford, 1974.

Elliott, J. H. *The Old World and the New, 1492–1650.* Cambridge, U.K., 1970.

Warner, Oliver. *English Maritime Writing: Hakluyt to Cook.* London, 1958.

MICHAEL CARHART

# TRENT, COUNCIL OF.

Considered the nineteenth general council of Western Christendom, the Council of Trent met after much delay in response to the call of both Lutherans and Catholics at the Nuremberg Reichstag of 1524 for "a general free Christian council in German lands" to reform the church. Paul III (reigned 1534–1549), having failed to assemble a council in the imperial city of Mantua in 1537 due primarily to inadequate security arrangements and in Venetian Vicenza in 1538 due to the attendance of only five bishops, ordered the council to meet in 1542 in Trent. This Holy Roman Empire city had a population of about six thousand, of whom a quarter were German-speaking, was ruled by a prince-bishop, and was situated on the Italian side of the Alps about eighty miles south of an imperial residence in Innsbruck. Hostilities between France and the empire delayed the opening of the council until 1545.

## GOALS AND SESSIONS OF THE COUNCIL

The goals formally assigned to the council by Paul III in 1542 were to define doctrine, correct morals, restore peace among Christians, and repel infidels. Pius IV in 1560 made explicit the goal that "schisms and heresies may be destroyed." The pope initially gave priority to a clarification of Catholic doctrine,

**Council of Trent.** Painting by Hermanos Zuccarelli, c. 1560–1566. ©Archivo Iconografico, S.A./Corbis

the emperor to a reform of abuses. The compromise was to treat simultaneously the removal of any abuses related to a teaching that was defined.

***Period I.*** The council can be divided into three periods. Period I, under Paul III, consisted of sessions 1 to 8 (13 December 1545 to 11 March 1547), which met in Trent. Claiming an outbreak of typhus, the pope had the council transferred to Bologna in the Papal States despite the opposition of the 27 bishops from Habsburg lands, who remained in Trent. Sessions 9 and 10 (21 April and 2 June 1547) issued no doctrinal or disciplinary decrees, and after the general congregation of 29 February 1548 the council was suspended. In subsequent periods the council would return to Trent. In

the first period, attendance varied from about 30 to 70 prelates per session; in all there were about 100 members with a deliberative vote: 5 cardinals, 12 archbishops, 76 bishops, 3 abbots, and 6 generals of religious orders, plus two procurators of absent German bishops who had only a consultative voice. Most prelates were Italians, the Spanish were well represented, and only a few came from other Catholic lands. During this period the prelates focused on the teachings of Martin Luther (1483–1546), Huldrych Zwingli (1484–1531), and their followers in Germany and Switzerland.

***Period II.*** Period II, under Julius III (reigned 1550–1555), included sessions 11 to 16 (1 May 1551 to 28 April 1552). Attendance varied between

44 and 51 prelates, with a total of about 59 prelates. As many as 13 German bishops were represented, including the personal presence of the powerful electoral archbishops of Mainz, Cologne, and Trier. Lutheran states agreed to send delegations: that from Brandenburg accepted the authority of the council and was incorporated at the 13th session; those from Württemberg and the imperial cities led by Strasbourg were allowed to read their mandates at the general congregation of 24 January 1552. Hopes that agreement could be found with so many Germans present were dashed by the reopening of military conflict.

***Period III.*** Period III, under Pius IV (reigned 1559–1565), consisted of sessions 17 to 26 (18 January 1562 to 3–4 December 1563) and was noteworthy for the arrival of a delegation of 13 bishops, 3 abbots, and 18 theologians from France and for the increased attention to the teachings of John Calvin (1509–1564) and the situation in France. There were 117 prelates at the 17th session, which rose to 228 at the 24th. About 270 bishops in all attended during this period, the vast majority being Italians (187), but Spanish (31) and French (26) were also well represented, and bishops from other Catholic lands attended too. The final decree was signed by 255 prelates and procurators. Altogether, the council sat for five years and one month.

## ORGANIZATIONAL STRUCTURE AND ATTENDEES

The organizational structures given to the council allowed it to achieve most of its goals. The popes were usually represented by cardinal legates, who served as council presidents and were in regular communication with the pope and congregation of cardinals in Rome, who set the agenda and at times made crucial decisions. "The Holy Spirit arrived in the saddle bags of papal couriers," quipped the historian Paolo Sarpi (1552–1623). The most important presidents were Cardinals Giovanni Maria Ciocchi del Monte (1487–1555, Tuscan canonist, administrator, and future Julius III), Reginald Pole (1500–1558, cousin of Henry VIII, friend of Sir Thomas More, conciliatory theologian, and archbishop of Canterbury under Mary Tudor), Girolamo Seripando (1493–1563, Neapolitan, conciliatory theologian, reformer, former general of the Augustinian friars, and archbishop of Salerno),

Stanislaus Hosius (1504–1579, Polish controversialist theologian and bishop of Warmia), and Giovanni Morone (1509–1580, Milanese diplomat, conciliatory theologian, former bishop of Modena, and target of the Roman Inquisition, whose diplomatic skills rescued the council after the deadlock over episcopal residence in 1563). The council presidents had the difficult task of resolving disputes—traditionalists versus conciliationists, papalists versus conciliarists and episcopalists, curialists and exempt religious versus diocesan bishops, Scholastics versus humanists, Scotists versus Thomists versus Augustinians, and rival national delegations eager for uniformity in teaching and practice (Spanish and Italians) or for reconciliation with the Protestants in their lands (Germans and French) or for preserving their ruler's patronage rights and prerogatives (Spanish, Portuguese, and French).

Among the other leading prelates at the council were the Italians: Pietro Bertano, O.P. (Fano), Tommaso Campeggio (Feltre), Giulio Contarini (Belluno), Cornelio Musso, O.F.M. (Bitonto, then Bertinoro), and Tommaso Stella, O.P. (Salpe, then Lavello, and finally Capodistria); the Spanish: Martín Pérez de Ayala (Guadix, then Segovia), Pedro Guerrero (Granada), Pedro Pacheco (Jaen), and Melchor Alváres de Vozmediano (Guadix); the Portuguese Bartolomé dos Martires, O.P. (Braga) and João Soarez, O.E.S.A. (Coimbra); the Frenchmen Antoine Filheul (Aix), Charles de Guise (Reims), and Nicolas Psaume (Verdun); the Germans Friedrich Grau [Nausea] (Vienna) and Julius von Pflug (Naumburg); the Scot Robert Wauchop (Armagh); the Croatian Georg Draskovich (Pécs); the Moravian Anton Brus von Müglitz (Prague); and the exiled Swede Olof Månsson Store (Uppsala).

Theologians, who had only a consultative vote in the proceedings, were sent by the pope and Christian rulers or brought along as advisers (*periti*) by the bishops and generals of religious orders. Known as "minor theologians" (*theologi minores*) to distinguish them from prelates who were also theologians, the vast majority were members of religious orders, and of these over half were Franciscans and about a quarter Dominicans. In the first period they numbered about 35; their numbers rose until in the last period there were about 100, of whom only 34 were allowed to speak on a topic, for a half-hour each; the others could submit their thoughts in writing prior to a debate. Among the leading theologians were the Jesuits and papal theologians Diego Lainez and Alfonso Salmeron; the Dominican Thomists Melchor Cano, Domingo de Soto, Bartolomé Carranza de Miranda, and Ambrogio Catarino (Lancellotto de' Politi); the Franciscan Scotists Alfonso de Castro and Andrés Vega; and the secular priests Johann Gropper, Francisco de Torres, and Ruard Tapper.

The council developed its own organizational structures. It began with classes or group meetings in which bishops and theologians together debated the theological issues, frequently in the form of suspect quotations extracted from the writings of the Protestants. When the bishops soon came to hate this procedure *(odiossima),* the legates had the theologians debate the topics on their own with the bishops listening. Once ideas were clarified and a consensus emerged, the bishops met on their own in particular congregations to draw up draft decrees. Reform decrees were drafted by commissions (nominated by the legates and approved by the prelates) from various proposals submitted by bishops and ambassadors. Drafts of decrees were debated in general congregations, where they were modified and approved. Formal approbation was done at a session, a liturgical ceremony with a mass, sermon, and formal vote on the decree. The decrees were issued in the name of the council with the papal legates presiding and not in the name of the council representing the universal church, as the more conciliarist types preferred. Beginning with the fifth session, the council condemned certain theological statements as anathema (contrary to Catholic teaching and practice) and then gave the reasons for the condemnation. From the sixth session onward the doctrinal decrees began with chapters that stated positively the Catholic position and ended with canons that condemned unacceptable teachings. The canons had the greater doctrinal weight.

## DECREES

The council issued a number of important doctrinal decrees. It affirmed that all the books of the Bible, including the Apocrypha or deuterocanonical books not found in the Hebrew bible and rejected by Luther, were inspired and that the Vulgate version was "authentic," that is, could be used in sermons and disputations. Critical editions and translations were subject to ecclesiastical censorship. The Bible was to be interpreted according to the sense given to it by the church over the centuries. Unwritten apostolic traditions, whether dictated orally by Christ or by the Holy Spirit, were also a source of saving truths and rules of conduct. It restated the teaching of the Council of Orange (529) on the existence, nature, and effects of original sin, rejecting both Pelagian optimism and Lutheran pessimism. It taught that justification, whereby one's sins were remitted and one became just and could grow in holiness through good works "done in God," was an unmerited gift of God, but that those with the power of discretion must freely cooperate with grace. The traditional seven sacraments (baptism, confirmation, Eucharist, penance or reconciliation, extreme unction or anointing of the sick, holy orders, and matrimony) were taught as having been instituted by Christ (whether immediately or mediately is not defined), to contain the graces they signify, and in the case of baptism, confirmation, and holy orders to leave an indelible mark on the soul so that they could not be repeated. Baptism by water even of children was necessary for salvation. In the Eucharist the bread and wine were changed into the true Body and Blood of Christ (transubstantiation), the pope was to decide when and where it was prudent to allow reception of the Eucharist under both forms, the Mass was a sacrifice, auricular confession of one's mortal sins to a priest was required, and marriage to be valid was henceforth to be contracted before a priest and witnesses. The existence of purgatory and the veneration of saints, relics, and sacred images were also decreed.

Among the principal reform decrees were those requiring a bishop to preach and reside in his diocese. A bishop was to conduct a visitation of his diocese and celebrate a synod annually. He was also to establish a lectureship on the Bible and to see that catechetical instruction was provided for the laity in parishes and that his clergy were properly trained in ecclesiastical disciplines in colleges—this led to the establishment of seminaries. Parish churches (and not confraternity churches and private chapels) were to be the settings for the laity's regular religious worship and instruction. Books were not to be published until their orthodoxy had been determined by the local ordinary or pope—this led to the issuance of lists or indices of forbidden books. Religious art was encouraged as a means for instruction and incitement of piety, but care was to be exercised that no false doctrine or unbecoming and confusing scene was depicted and no superstitious practices allowed. Avoiding more restrictive prescriptions, the council decreed that music was allowed in church provided it was not "base and suggestive," and it ordered seminarians to be taught to chant. The council entrusted to the pope the completion of a number of tasks it was unable to finish, and asked him to confirm its decrees.

By the bull *Benedictus Deus,* dated 26 January 1564 but issued on June 30th, Pope Pius IV confirmed all the decrees of the council unaltered and ordered their implementation. The first official edition of the decrees had been printed in Rome by Paolo Manuzio on 18 March 1564. The pope forbade the publication of any glosses or commentaries on them and established the Congregation of the Council on 2 August 1564 to interpret them. The principal doctrinal teachings of the council he summarized in the *Professio Fidei Tridentina,* to which all university professors (10 November 1564) and prelates (13 November 1564) were required to swear. Support for implementing the decrees was sought and secured from the rulers of Catholic states: Spain, Portugal, Venice, and Poland-Lithuania in 1564, the Catholic Swiss Cantons in 1565, and the Catholic Estates of the Empire in 1566. When the king and Estates-General of France repeatedly refused to confirm the decrees of Trent, French bishops met on their own and did so in 1615. Provincial councils applied Trent's decrees on the local levels. The decrees of the six Milanese provincial councils (1565–1582) held under Carlo Borromeo (1538–1584) and published together in 1582 as *Acta Ecclesiae Mediolanensis* became the model throughout Catholic Europe for much of the implementing legislation on the provincial and diocesan levels. The papacy brought to completion the tasks assigned to it by the council, issuing revised indices of forbidden books (1564 and 1596), the first Roman Catechism (1566), and corrected editions of the Breviary (1568) and Missal (1570). The decisions of the Congregation of the Council imposed on Catholicism a uniformity and passive deference to Rome that became known as Tridentinism. The implementation of Trent's decrees on the local level, pushed forward by papal nuncios, reforming bishops and religious, and dedicated Catholic rulers, took many generations to effect.

*See also* **Bible: Interpretation; Borromeo, Carlo; Catholicism; Clergy: Roman Catholic Clergy; Index of Prohibited Books; Jesuits; Lutheranism; Marriage; Paul III (pope); Pius IV (pope); Reformation, Catholic; Religious Orders; Ritual, Religious; Sarpi, Paolo (Pietro); Seminary.**

BIBLIOGRAPHY

*Primary Sources*

*Concilium Tridentinum: Diariorum, Actorum, Epistularum, Tractatuum Nova Collectio.* Edited by the Görres-Gesellschaft. 13 vols. Freiburg im Breisgau, 1901–2001. A critical edition of the primary sources for the council.

*Decrees of the Ecumenical Councils.* Original texts edited by Giuseppe Alberigo et al., translation editor Norman P. Tanner, S.J., 2 vols. London and Washington, D.C., 1990. Vol. II, pp. 657–799.

*Secondary Sources*

Alberigo, Giuseppe, and Iginio Rogger, eds. *Il concilio di Trento: nella prospettiva del terzo millennio.* Istituto di Scienze Religiose in Trento, Religione e Cultura, 10. Brescia, 1997.

Bäumer, Remigius, ed. *Concilium Tridentinum.* Wege der Forschung, 313. Darmstadt, 1979. Collection of the important articles on the council, plus useful bibliography.

De La Brosse, Olivier, Joseph Lecler, Henri Holstein, Charles Lefebvre, and Pierre Adnès. *Latran V et Trente.* Histoire des conciles oecuméniques, 10 and 11. Paris, 1975–1981.

Jedin, Hubert. *Geschichte des Konzils von Trient,* 4 vols. in 5. Freiburg, 1948–1975. Vols. 1 and 2 translated by Ernest Graf as *A History of the Council of Trent.* St. Louis and London, 1957–1961.

———. *Girolamo Seripando: Sein Leben und Denken im Geisteskampf des 16. Jahrhunderts.* 2 vols. Würzburg, 1937. Translated by Frederic C. Eckhoff as *Papal Legate at the Council of Trent: Cardinal Seripando.* St. Louis, 1947.

———. *Krisis und Abschluss des Trienter Konzils 1562/63: Ein Rückblick nach vier Jahrhunderten.* Herder Bücherei, 177. Freiburg im Breisgau, 1964. Translated by N. D. Smith as *Crisis and Closure of the Council of Trent: A Retrospective View from the Second Vatican Council.* London and Melbourne, 1967.

Tallon, Alain. *La France et le concile de Trente (1518–1563).* Rome, 1997.

NELSON H. MINNICH

# TRIANGULAR TRADE PATTERN.

The transatlantic slave trade involved more than the European purchase of slaves in Africa and their sale in the New World. Historians have identified as a triangular trade pattern a typical voyage of a slave ship consisting of three distinct legs: in the first, the ship would sail from a European port to coastal Africa and exchange its goods for slaves, who were then taken to the New World and sold for colonial produce. The ship then returned home to Europe laden with colonial cash crops, completing the triangle. The triangular trade found its classic, although not its original, expression in Eric Williams's seminal *Capitalism and Slavery* (1944). Williams argued that the triangular trade was Great Britain's primary trade in the seventeenth and eighteenth centuries, and gave a triple stimulus to British industry. British manufactures were used to buy slaves in Africa, and once the slaves were put to work on American plantations, they were dressed—along with their owners—by British industries and fed by New England agriculture and Newfoundland fisheries. Finally, the New World commodities that the slaves produced were processed in Britain, thus giving rise to new industries.

Williams went on to suggest that this multiple stimulus was so significant that the British triangular trade paved the way for the industrial revolution. There was a link, he argued, between the capital accumulated in the slave trade of Liverpool, Britain's largest slave-trading port, and the emergence of manufactures in Manchester. Up to 1770, one-third of Manchester's textiles exports went via Liverpool to the African coast, and one-half to the American and West Indian colonies. Other historians have pointed out that long-term credits from Manchester manufacturers were used to finance Liverpool's trade. However, it has not been possible to determine the extent to which industrial development was linked directly to the slave trade.

Africa was always the first stop in the triangular trade, and the Europeans quickly learned that they needed a variety of goods in order to do business there. The specific merchandise brought to barter differed according to the place of trade, and it was important for slaver merchants to keep up with local demand. European goods were highly valued in the local African economies, both for their usefulness and their exchange value. Cloth, for example, was popular in Senegambia (the area of modern day Senegal and Gambia), because it could serve as a kind of money or be made into clothes. The same was true of iron, which had a high exchange value but could also be made into tools, utensils, and weapons.

For lack of facilities to intern the slaves on the coast, the European purchase of slaves could take a long time. The average slaving vessel spent several months in Africa, the captain sailing up and down the coast or traveling inland until the ship's hold was filled. Once the so-called Middle Passage (the Africa-Americas run) had been completed, the slaves were sold. Payments were a perennial problem in the New World, since ships often arrived outside of the harvest season and, even when they arrived at the opportune time, most of their customers were heavily indebted planters. Due to the delay of payments, slave merchants were frequently compelled to advance credit to the planters, the interest for which was credited to the slave trader. Under this system, slave factors—traders in the employ of European merchant houses—served as intermediaries between the trader and the planter by arranging for the sale of slaves. In the British slave trade, the debt problem led to the adoption of a new system of remitting the proceeds of slave sales to England. This system, first introduced in the Caribbean in the 1730s, forced the slave factors to pay outstanding debts at specific times and to remit the proceeds of the slave sales in either cash, produce, or bills of exchange, effectively shifting the burden of supplying credit from the trader to the planter. If the factor cleared a debt with a bill of exchange, it had to be drawn against a British mercantile firm or guarantor.

Slave traders relied increasingly on these bills of exchange, as well as on the transport of produce on board ships other than slavers. The third leg of the triangular trade thus deviated from the model in that slave vessels did not usually carry large amounts of slave-produced goods from America to Europe. Many of the ships returning to the United Provinces from Suriname sailed in ballast, weighed down by sand and water. On the other hand, it was exceptional for slave vessels returning to British ports from Virginia and Jamaica to sail in ballast. Overall, it is hard to establish what percentage of the goods carried back represented payment for the slaves, although it is clear that the volume of goods that slavers transported from the New World to Europe was relatively small.

**SHUTTLE OR ROUND-TRIP VOYAGES**

In Atlantic trade generally, it was actually not the triangular trade that predominated, but the shuttle (also called round-trip) voyage, which did not include the New World–Europe leg of the triangle trip. Round-trip voyages produced experienced captains and increased the chance of a punctual delivery and of a landing around harvest time. By the last quarter of the seventeenth century, the transport of African slaves in the South Atlantic was partially a shuttle trade, in which the tobacco planters near Brazil's capital of Bahia exchanged their crop for bonded Africans on the Gold Coast. A similar bilateral trade developed between Rio de Janeiro and Angola. The largest of all slave trades, that of Brazil, was therefore not triangular at all.

Nevertheless, although the African slave trade was often conducted separately from the trade between Europe and the Americas, the services it supplied to the latter were indispensable. And while doubt has been cast on the overall effect of the triangular model on British industrialization, the triangular trade pattern forms part of the web of dependence that connected Europe, Africa, and the New World in the age of the slave trade.

*See also* **British Colonies: North America; Commerce and Markets; Slavery and the Slave Trade.**

BIBLIOGRAPHY

Klein, Herbert S. *The Atlantic Slave Trade.* Cambridge, U.K., 1999.

Minchinton, Walter E. "The Triangular Trade Revisited." In *The Uncommon Market: Essays in the Economic History of the Atlantic Slave Trade,* edited by Henry A. Gemery and Jan S. Hogendorn, pp. 331–352. New York, 1979.

Richardson, David. "The British Slave Trade to Colonial South Carolina." *Slavery & Abolition* 12, no. 3 (December 1991): 125–172.

Searing, James F. *West African Slavery and Atlantic Commerce: The Senegal River Valley, 1700–1860.* Cambridge, U.K., 1993.

Williams, Eric. *Capitalism and Slavery.* Chapel Hill, N.C., 1944.

WIM KLOOSTER

**TSERCLAES, JOHANN.** *See* Tilly, Johann Tserclaes of.

# TUDOR DYNASTY (ENGLAND).

Henry Tudor (ruled 1485–1509) traced his royal blood through his mother, Margaret Beaufort, who was a descendant of John of Gaunt, the younger son of Edward III (ruled 1327–1377). After the death of Henry, Prince of Wales, son of Henry VI (ruled 1470–1471), in 1471, Henry Tudor was the surviving male heir of the house of Lancaster. In 1485 he deposed the usurper, Richard III (ruled 1483–1485) at the Battle of Bosworth Field, and was crowned Henry VII. Henry survived numerous plots early in his reign but seemed secure on the throne by 1500. His heir, Prince Arthur (born 1486) died in 1502 and his brother, Henry, duke of York, succeeded to the throne in April 1509 as Henry VIII, shortly after marrying his brother's widow, Catherine of Aragón. Henry's desire for a male heir led him, in the late 1520s, to seek a divorce from his wife. This could only be achieved by breaking with the Roman Catholic Church and thus heralded the beginning of the English Reformation.

Henry died in 1547, leaving the throne to Edward VI, his nine-year-old son by his third wife, Jane Seymour. Edward actively supported Protestant reform but on his premature death in 1553, the throne passed to his elder sister, Mary, the daughter of Catherine of Aragón, despite efforts to place the Protestant Lady Jane Grey on the throne. Mary restored Catholicism and in 1554 married the Spanish prince, who became King Philip II in 1556. Mary died childless in 1558 and the throne passed to Elizabeth, Henry VIII's daughter by his second wife, Anne Boleyn. Elizabeth again broke from Rome and asserted her authority by refusing to marry or name her successor. The second half of Elizabeth's reign was dominated by war with Spain from 1585 over English support for Philip's rebellious Dutch subjects. Elizabeth survived the plots of her Stuart rival, Mary, Queen of Scots (whom she had executed in 1587) and the Spanish Armada of 1588. Despite a decade of war, factional intrigue at court, and economic crisis, it was Elizabeth's greatest achievement to pass the throne peacefully to her chosen successor, James VI of Scotland, who became James I of England in 1603.

*See also* Church of England; Edward VI (England); Elizabeth I (England); England; Henry VII (England); Henry VIII (England); James I and VI (England and Scotland); Mary I (England); Stuart Dynasty (England and Scotland).

BIBLIOGRAPHY

Brigden, Susan. *New Worlds, Lost Worlds: The Rule of the Tudors, 1485–1603.* London, 2000.

Guy, John. *Tudor England.* Oxford, 1988.

DAVID GRUMMITT

---

# TULIP ERA (OTTOMAN EMPIRE).

Lasting from 1718 to 1730, the Tulip Era was a transitory period in the Ottoman Empire that was marked by cultural innovation and new forms of elite consumption and sociability. The Tulip Era (in Turkish, *Lâle Devri*) coincides with the latter half of the reign of Sultan Ahmed III (ruled 1703–1730), specifically the twelve-year grand vizierate of Ahmed's son-in-law (*damad*), Nevşehirli Ibrahim (d. 1730). The period is known for several breakthrough achievements, including the first Muslim printing press in the empire, various innovations in the arts and urban design, and the first cultural embassies to Europe. It is also remembered for the extravagance of the imperial court and the emergence of a Western-inspired, elite pleasure culture. The period gets its name from court society's passion for tulips, which were especially prized as a cultivar and artistic motif. Grandees imported tulip bulbs at great expense, experimented with hybridization, and, planting them by the thousand, celebrated their blooms in candlelit "tulip illuminations" in gardens throughout Istanbul.

## COURTING EUROPE

In both domestic and foreign affairs, the sultan followed the lead of his grand vizier. Since the empire's disastrous defeats at the end of the seventeenth century, the Ottomans had been obliged to recognize the importance of diplomacy. Under Ibrahim's leadership, the regime pursued a policy of peace on the western front. Diplomatic relations with Europe were expanded, and European delegations in Istanbul were allowed to circulate more freely in Otto-

man society. The vivid account of Ottoman women by Lady Mary Wortley Montagu (1689–1762), wife of the British ambassador, is based on her unusual access to the harems of privileged Ottomans when she was in Istanbul with her husband, 1717–1718. It was France, however, that the regime regarded as a kindred state and looked to as a model during this period. The empire's most important embassy, to France in 1720, created a sensation in Paris—one of the earliest demonstrations of European "turcomania." In a reciprocal effect, the Ottoman court flirted with European exotica. Among the wealthy, and to some extent in society at large, there was experimentation with European entertainment styles and clothing fashions. The changes that Ottoman women introduced into their outdoor attire seemed minor to outsiders, but they provoked criticism in conservative circles, including the established guilds.

## FROM OPPOSITION TO REBELLION

The return of the Paris embassy fed the court's consumerist appetites with luxury goods, reports of French manners, and drawings of palaces and waterworks displays. Some features of the pleasure culture were extended to the larger public, which was treated to new amusement parks and new, nonreligious holidays on which to enjoy them. As with clothing fashions, the spread of public entertainments—in particular women's presence in mixed company—led to moralist objections. In 1727, prior to establishing the first Ottoman Muslim press under the direction of a Hungarian convert to Islam, Ibrahim Müteferrika (1674–1745), Ahmed III and Ibrahim took care to obtain an authorizing *fetva* ('edict') from the chief *mufti* ('judge') in order to hold down opposition to their innovation. In a further compromise, the press was restricted to publishing nonreligious works, such as historical chronicles, maps, and dictionaries. The regime's unpopularity increased during the late 1720s. The court's spending habits and social style became more and more contentious as economic problems worsened and the empire became enmired in war with Iran (Persia, as it was known to Westerners). When the empire suffered a military defeat on the eastern front and the government failed to act in 1730, there was a seditious uprising led by an Albanian seaman, later a bath attendant and janissary, Patrona Halil, and the regime was overthrown. The sultan was forced to abdicate, and along with his family was put under house arrest; Ibrahim and his closest associates, the main targets of the rebellion, were killed. The excesses of court society served as rallying cries for the mob, but the regime's other ventures—ill-conceived reforms and wartime misadventures—had already created important enemies, particularly within the military. Ahmed's successor, Mahmud I (ruled 1730–1754) all but closed the Tulip Era's cultural openings. Further experimentation with Europe as a cultural site would have to wait until the end of the century.

*See also* **Harem; Islam in the Ottoman Empire; Janissary; Ottoman Dynasty; Ottoman Empire; Paris; Printing and Publishing; Tulips; Vizier.**

BIBLIOGRAPHY

Göçek, Fatma Müge. *East Encounters West: France and the Ottoman Empire in the Eighteenth Century.* New York, 1987.

Refik, Ahmet. *Lâle Devri.* Istanbul, 1997.

Silay, Kemal. *Nedim and the Poetics of the Ottoman Court: Medieval Inheritance and the Need for Change.* Bloomington, Ind., 1994.

Zilfi, Madeline C. "Women and Society in the Tulip Era, 1718–1730." In *Women, the Family, and Divorce Laws in Islamic History,* edited by Amira El Azhary Sonbol, pp. 290–303. Syracuse, 1996.

MADELINE C. ZILFI

**Tulips.** Illustration of *Tulipa gesaeriana* by Jacopo Ligozzi (c. 1547–1632). ©SCALA/ART RESOURCE, N.Y.

**TULIPS.** The tulip made its first impact on European history in 1389 in Kosovo, when the son of the Ottoman sultan rode into battle against the Serbs wearing a shirt embroidered with tulips. The tulip is a plant native to Turkey and much revered in that country, where it is known as *lale.* The Western name probably derives from a mispronunciation of the Turkish word *tulband,* 'turban', which was reported back by early travelers as *tulipam.* It is possible that the similarity of the shape of the turban and the flower caused the linguistic confusion. In 1559 a Swiss physician and botanist, Conrad Gessner (1516–1565), published the first account and the first picture of tulips in western Europe.

In the sixteenth century tulips were cultivated in Europe by a mere handful of botanists. Most notable among them was Charles de L'Écluse, or Carolus Clusius (1526–1609), a native of Arras in the Habsburg Netherlands. Clusius helped establish the Imperial Botanical Garden at Vienna at the behest of Emperor Maximilian II and then created another botanical garden in Frankfurt before his appointment as Horti Praefectus at the recently established University of Leiden in the Netherlands in 1592. Clusius had the largest collection of tulip bulbs in Europe and ensured that the university's botanical garden included numerous varieties of tulips.

By then the tulip had already become a fashionable item in aristocratic gardens; in the Dutch Republic it was to become a truly popular flower. In 1612 Emanuel Sweerts (1552–1612) of Amsterdam published his *Florilegium,* the first sales catalogue that included tulips. Dutch agriculture was already highly commercialized and quick to pick up this new product. As it was, the soil directly behind the dunes in the vicinity of Haarlem proved exceptionally suitable for the growing of bulbs. The interest in tulips reached fever pitch during the 1630s, when a single bulb could change hands for the price

**Tulips.** *Flower Bouquet with Tulips,* painting by Ambrosius Bosschaert, 1609, Kunsthistorisches Museum, Vienna. ©ERICH LESSING/ART RESOURCE, N.Y.

of a sizable house on one of Amsterdam's fashionable canals. Especially in demand were the so-called broken varieties, which displayed flamed patterns of many colors, instead of the more common solid coloring. Twentieth-century laboratory tests would reveal that breaking occurred as the result of a viral infection of the bulb. In the seventeenth century it was only understood that the broken varieties were rare, and therefore valuable. Of the Semper Augustus, perhaps the rarest of them all, only twelve bulbs were known to exist, and at a certain point they were all owned by Adriaen Pauw (1581–1653), who was the pensionary, the most important civil servant, first of Amsterdam and later of Holland.

In 1637 the tulip bubble burst, and it took the Dutch authorities years to sort out the financial mess, which left numerous people bankrupt. Although observers at home and abroad insisted it had taught the speculators a lesson, the tulip mania turned out to be a publicity scoop. It would establish in the public mind, for centuries to come, the closest possible connection between Holland and bulbs. Thanks to its flowers, Dutch agriculture is still one of the largest exporters in the world.

*See also* **Botany; Commerce and Markets; Dutch Republic; Gessner, Konrad.**

BIBLIOGRAPHY

Dash, Mike. *Tulipomania: The Story of the World's Most Coveted Flower and the Extraordinary Passions It Aroused.* London, 1999.

Pavord, Anna. *The Tulip.* London, 1999. Both books contain extensive bibliographies.

MAARTEN PRAK

---

# TURKISH LITERATURE AND LANGUAGE.

The term *Turkish literature* refers to the literature produced in the Asian and Eastern European lands of the Ottoman Empire and composed in the Western Turkic, Oghuz-Turcoman dialects, of which the literary languages were Ottoman and Azeri Turkish. *Ottoman literature* here refers to the high-culture literature of the Ottoman period (c. 1326–1860). During early modern times, the Eastern Turkic, Kipchak-Chaghatai dialects produced their own distinctive literature, which flourished in Central Asia and the eastern parts of the Middle East. This literature is conventionally referred to by the general term *Turkic literature,* of which the predominant high-culture manifestation is called *Chaghatai literature.*

## OTTOMAN ORIGINS

Late in the eleventh century, Muslim Oghuz-Turcoman armies coming from the East had driven the Byzantines out of much of Asia Minor and established the Persianized sultanate of the Seljuks. In the aftermath of the Mongol invasions of the thirteenth century, Seljuk hegemony ended, and Asia Minor disintegrated into a hodge-podge of fiefdoms headed by local dynasts who favored the Turkish culture of their nomadic power base rather than the Persian high-culture focus of their Seljuk predecessors. The early Ottoman state originated in western Anatolia on the borders of Byzantium during the late thirteenth century as an assemblage of Turcoman seminomads under the command of a chieftain named Osman (Arabic *'Uthmān,* from which the name "Ottoman" derives). Successful incursions into Byzantine territory brought a flood of recruits into the Ottoman army and expanded Ottoman domination throughout western Asia Minor and into eastern Europe. With the capture of Constantinople (Turkish, Istanbul) in 1453, the Ottomans stood poised on the threshold of becoming the largest and arguably the most powerful empire of early modern times.

## LITERARY CURRENTS

Implicit in the origins of the Ottoman state are linguistic, literary, and cultural currents that resonate through almost six hundred years of Turkish literary history. The Turkic peoples who entered the Middle East in migratory military waves from Central Asia brought with them traditional literary forms, which had taken on an Islamic overlay. The territories they entered were dominated by a Perso-Arabic high culture that had developed in concert with the expansion of Islam. Legitimacy for any ambitious ruler depended upon his being perceived as the defender of the Islamic community and its traditions, which included Islamic high culture and its canonical languages—Persian and Arabic. Thus, the early Turkish rulers of Asia Minor drew their military support from the nomadic Turcoman tribes and therefore needed to speak their language and respect their traditions. However, as their domains extended, successful Turkish rulers came under increasing pressure to conform to the cultural norms associated with Islamic monarchical models.

As a result, Western Turkish literature diverged early onto two main trajectories. The leadership— the court, the court-dependent elites, the educated, educating, and administrative classes—adopted the genres, forms, themes, and rhetoric of the Islamic Perso-Arab tradition. Educated people were often trilingual and tended to think of the elite literary culture of what they called "the three languages" (Arabic, Persian, Turkish) as a single global culture with three voices. Ottoman poets wrote verses in Persian and Arabic as well as in Turkish, and the Ottoman court was lavish in its support of visiting Persian poets. Elite literature extensively employed Arabic and Persian vocabulary and elements of syntax within an overall Turkish grammatical scheme. As the Ottomans expanded into the Balkans and Greece, Turkish became a European language and imported some vocabulary from the many languages of the empire. Although a number of conquered Europeans adopted Ottoman language and culture, and former captives became noted Ottoman poets and authors, literary influences coming directly from Europe are impossible to trace with any certainty. The common people— villagers, nomads, urban non-elites, low-level military—continued a popular tradition of Central Asian Turkic literatures that was generally monolingual (Turkish), largely oral, most often sung, conservative, and local or tribal. However, despite the differences between these two trajectories, differences exaggerated by the tendency of academic institutions to distinguish between "literature" and "folklore," there was continual commerce between them, as exemplified by poet-musicians (*aşik,* 'lover'), who performed in both villages and urban areas, composing relatively accessible verses that moved easily between the forms, styles, themes, and base vocabulary of both traditions.

## THE POPULAR TRADITION

The literature of the village, the countryside, and the lower classes was based on a long tradition of Turkic poetry predating Islam. Popular poetry employed "syllable counting" rhythms (in Turkish, *parmak hesabi,* or 'finger counting'), which identified groups of syllables separated by minor caesuras (for example, the pattern 4 + 4 + 3 syllables). The folk poet *(aşik,* or *ozan)* most commonly composed in stanza forms, which were sung to the accompaniment of the "long lute" or *saz* and were often extemporized. The elite poetry of the Turks was urban and set in private gardens, parks, and taverns, while the popular poetry sang of mountains, forests, and fields, where a wandering minstrel sought his dream beloved and flirted with enticing village maids or sought mystical union with the Divine, who was imagined as a coy and inaccessible beauty. Popular literature included love songs, folk songs particular to various regions, poems about military heroism, religious verses reflecting the popular mysticism of villagers and nomads, songs of passages such as weddings and death, and a host of oral prose tales. The folk poet's verses had a counterpart in the prose of the *meddah* or 'storyteller', who enthralled audiences in villages, coffeehouses, bazaars, and taverns with a repertoire of tales in a variety of rhetorical styles. Although it is possible to discern when the elite early modern Ottoman literary tradition gave way to a distinctly modern literature, much of the popular tradition persisted substantially unchanged into the modern period, where it had a profound influence on the language, style, and themes of modern authors and poets who turned from the elite tradition.

## THE ELITE TRADITION:
## OTTOMAN LITERATURE

To the Ottoman elites, "literature" was, first and foremost, poetry. The elite literature adopted the genres of the Perso-Arab poetic tradition, including the rhythmical scheme, called *aruz*, which, via Persian, depended on metrical feet formed by the regular alternation of "long" and "short" syllables, which do not exist naturally in Turkish. A "long" syllable consists of either a consonant and a long vowel or a "closed" syllable (consonant-vowel-consonant); a "short" syllable is an "open syllable," a consonant, and a short vowel. The metrical feet are conventionally expressed as mnemonic word forms derived from the Arabic root meaning "to do." For example, one common metrical foot is symbolized by the word *fāilātun* (fā'i-lā-tun, long, short, long, long). The basic formal unit of elite poetry is the couplet *(beyt),* which is composed of two hemistiches *(misra),* based on set patterns of metrical feet. The most common rhyme scheme for lyric poetry and its relatives is a monorhyme with a rhyming first couplet (aa, ba, ca, da, etc.). There also exist stanzaic forms, which are thought of as expansions of couplets created by adding hemistiches to a base couplet. Longer narrative poems were written in rhyming couplets (aa, bb, cc, etc.). It was the custom for a poet's work, exclusive of narrative poems, to be collected into a single volume called a *divan,* which would contain hundreds and often thousands of poems. For this reason, elite Ottoman poetry is often referred to, especially in modern Turkey, as "Divan Poetry."

The dominant poetic genre of Ottoman literature was the short, approximately sonnet length (most often ten or fourteen hemistiches, five or seven couplets), erotic (and erotic-mystical) love poem called the *gazel* (Arabic, *ghazal* ). A respected

poet's collected works *(divan)* would commonly contain from a few hundred to thousands of *gazels.* Rooted in a generic Islamic mysticism expressed in the Neoplatonic imagery and understanding of love—differing only in minor details from what one would find, for example, in Ficino's *De Amore*—*gazel* poetry features a love-crazed, melancholic lover tormented by desire for a cruel and indifferent beloved who is at times a beautiful boy or (far less often) a beautiful girl, at times a beloved patron or ruler, at times God in the form of the mystical Divine, and many times a conflation of all three. The interactions of lover and beloved are carried out and reflected in conventional settings with a conventional cast of characters. Typically, there is a wine party, attended by a group of close friends who share an esoteric understanding of the universal, mystical meaning of the intoxications of passionate love and wine, which are misunderstood by ignorant and censorious outsiders. In the party, the carouser is served wine by an attractive boy in a tavern or in a secluded garden where each flower and tree, bird and animal also acts out the drama of lover and beloved. Beneath the esoteric and mystical pretenses of *gazel* poetry, however, lay direct connections to the actual erotic lives and entertainments of educated urban elites. Many *gazels* were composed to honor or attract famous beautiful boys. Poets caroused in taverns run by Jews or Europeans, who were not bound by Islamic prohibitions against wine.

The *kaside* (Arabic, *qasīdah*) is a long (often running to more than one hundred couplets), monorhyming, occasional poem, usually in praise of God, the Prophet Muhammad, the monarch, a highly placed official, or a patron. In addition, some *kasides* were composed to commemorate holidays, festivals, military victories, weddings, circumcisions, deaths, or buildings and monuments. A *kaside* usually begins with a prelude referencing a theme from erotic love poetry: love, a garden, a wine party, the heavens, a festival, and so forth. It then makes a transition linking the prelude to praise, which is followed by mention of the poet and, in many cases, by a specific request for favors. The *kaside* was expected to be a tour de force and *kasides* formed the second largest section in a poet's *divan.*

The narrative poem is known generically as *mesnevî* (Arabic, *mathnawī*), which means "rhyming couplets" and distinguishes this kind of poem from the monorhyming genres. Narrative poems in rhyming couplets told and retold the classical romantic tales of the Perso-Arab tradition, most of which, by Ottoman times, had taken on a distinct mystical, theosophical overlay. Poets also composed works such as verse histories, mystical and theological treatises, Islamic legends and tales of the Prophet, didactic works, and advice for princes in *mesnevî* form.

The minor genres of poetry included satire and invective, religious verse, riddles and enigmas, war poetry, and chronograms (verses in which the numerical values of Arabic script letters add up to a target date). Prose genres, like the poetry, contained a heavy burden of Persian and Arabic vocabulary and were generously larded with poetic interpolations. Some of the prominent prose genres were historical works, biobibliographical compendia, travel literature, legendary tales, interpretation of the Koran, essays, manuals on style, and treatises on religious, scientific, ethical, political, geographical, grammatical, and philological topics.

## HISTORICAL TRENDS

Mehmed II (the Conqueror, ruled 1451–1481) initiated a practice of lavish support for poets and litterateurs. He not only supported Ottoman poets but also is known to have patronized the master poets of the Timurid court in Herat: the Persian poet Djami and the famed Chaghatai poet Mir Ali Şir Nevayî. Through the early glory years of the reign of Suleiman (the Magnificent, 1520–1566), support for literary art remained high and literary talent was a key to upward mobility. For example, Necatî (d. 1509), considered the first great voice of Ottoman *gazel* poetry, began as a slave. One of Necatî's contemporaries was a woman named Mihrî (d. 1512), whose poems—delivered to the court by male intermediaries—won substantial cash rewards from the royal treasury. Bakî (d. 1600), the sixteenth century "sultan of poets" and model of rhetorical complexity for subsequent generations, was a low-level mosque functionary's son who became a chief magistrate. Hayalî (d. 1557), whose *gazel*s married mysticism, eroticism, and libertinism, started as a mendicant dervish youth and ended a provincial governor. The reach of Ottoman literature is attested to by the case of Fuzulî (d. 1556), an attendant of a shrine in Iraq,

who is considered today as one of the greatest Ottoman poets. Fuzulî compiled major poetry collections in Persian and Arabic and wrote in the Azeri dialect of Western Turkish.

The latter half of the sixteenth century and the early years of the seventeenth saw extensive regularization of appointments to the bureaucracy, economic crises, and social unrest, all of which served to lessen opportunities for literary talents from outside the educated and bureaucratic classes. This was the age of the greatest of the Ottoman court panegyrists, Nef'î (d. 1635), whose magnificent *kaside*s could not save him from being executed for indulging in the vicious lampooning of powerful courtiers. During the seventeenth century, the center of literary production moved from the court in the direction of the dervish lodges and the educated elites. High-culture poetry tended toward the complex mystical esotericism of the Persian "Indian Style," exemplified by the poetry of Na'ilî (d. 1666) and away from the cultural synthesis and public entertainments of the fifteenth and sixteenth centuries that had seen beloved shop boys and young soldiers as the recipients of rhetorically refined love poems. The synthesis was left to the burgeoning number of popular *aşiks* who performed in coffeehouses and taverns in both the elite and folk styles. During the so-called Tulip Era of the early eighteenth century—named after the tulip craze that swept the Empire—the court attempted to recapture the earlier synthesis and the support of a growing class of wealthy entrepreneurs by patronizing lavish entertainments, pleasure parks, and the work of such poets as the brilliant Nedim (d. 1730), who moved easily between the elite style and genres that reflected popular verses in simpler Turkish. The latter years of the eighteenth century saw the last great original mystical narrative poem *Beauty and Love* by Sheyh Galip, a Sufi master extensively patronized by the court. For the Turkish literature of the elites the early modern period does not end until the middle of the nineteenth century, when Ottoman intellectuals begin to adapt to European modernism.

*See also* **Ottoman Empire; Suleiman I; Tulip Era (Ottoman Empire).**

BIBLIOGRAPHY

Andrews, Walter G. *An Introduction to Ottoman Poetry.* Minneapolis, 1976.

———. *Poetry's Voice, Society's Song*. Seattle, 1985.

Andrews, Walter G., Najaat Black, Mehmet Kalpakli, eds. and trans. *Ottoman Lyric Poetry: An Anthology*. Austin, Tex., 1997.

Deny, Jean, et al. *Philologiae Turcicae Fundamenta*. Wiesbaden, 1965. Contains articles in several languages on Turkish and Turkic literatures. See especially the introductory chapter, "The Turkic Literatures. Introductory Notes on the History and Style" by Alessio Bombaci.

Gibb, E. J. W. *A History of Ottoman Poetry*. Vols 1–6. London, 1900–1909. The most comprehensive history but marred by nineteenth-century British imperial attitudes.

Holbrook, Victoria Rowe. *The Unreadable Shores of Love: Turkish Modernity and Mystic Romance*. Austin, Tex., 1994.

Silay, Kemal, ed. *An Anthology of Turkish Literature*. Bloomington, Ind., 1996.

WALTER G. ANDREWS

---

**TUSCANY.** *See* **Florence.**

---

**TYNDALE, WILLIAM.** *See* **Bible: Translations and Editions.**

---

**TYRANNY, THEORY OF.** The characteristics of tyranny were defined by Aristotle (384–322 B.C.E.) in his *Politics*. Tyranny was seen as a corrupt form of monarchy where the ruler acted despotically and preferred his own profit and pleasure to the common good. Tyrants were reputed to be greedy, lustful, and distrusting. They provoked flattery and conspiracy and employed foreign guards.

Among medieval thinkers whose writings on tyranny remained influential in early modern times were the jurists Bartolus of Sassoferrato (1314–1357) and Baldus de Ubaldis (1327–1400); the papal agent John of Salisbury (1115/1120–1180), whose *Policraticus* (1159) made the important distinction between a tyrant-usurper and a legitimate king who chose to rule by force rather than law; and the great Dominican theologian St. Thomas Aquinas (1225–1274), who allowed tyrannicide in extreme cases, but only if the consequences were likely to be better than the preceding oppression. A

less inhibited attitude to tyrannicide was held by another Dominican, Jean Petit, who justified the 1407 murder of Louis of Orléans, brother of Charles VI of France. Petit's assertions were criticized by the chancellor of the University of Paris, Jean Charlier de Gerson (1363–1429), who persuaded the ecclesiastical Council of Constance (1414–1418) to ban tyrannicide except in the circumstances outlined by Aquinas.

### THE SIXTEENTH CENTURY

Little was said about tyranny in the century following Petit, but the doctrine again became important during the Reformation, even though Martin Luther (1483–1546) taught that a tyrant was God's punishment for a sinful people, who should suffer and obey. Two Protestant exiles during the restoration of Roman Catholicism in England under Queen Mary I (ruled 1553–1558) had a different view. John Ponet, bishop of Winchester (1514–1556), was the author of *A Short Treatise of Politic Power* (1556), and Christopher Goodman, professor of divinity at Oxford (c. 1520–1603), wrote *How Superior Powers Ought to be Obeyed* (1558). Ponet answered his own question "whether or not it is lawful to depose an evil governor and kill him?" in the affirmative, and Goodman expressed similar views. A tyrant was defined not only as one who despoiled the people and refused them justice, but also as one who broke divine law.

Another advocate of tyrannicide was the Scottish Presbyterian humanist George Buchanan (1506–1582), who composed *De Jure Regni apud Scotos* (1579; Concerning the law of the kingdom among the Scots) when Mary, Queen of Scots, was deposed in 1567. Buchanan repeated the Aristotelian marks of tyranny and defined the concept as the treatment of a free people as if they were slaves. Among his classical authorities was Marcus Tullius Cicero (106–43 B.C.E.). His examples of tyrants were drawn from the Old Testament and Scottish history. In his posthumous *Rerum Scoticarum Historia* (1582; History of Scottish affairs), he made much of the deposition and killing of Scottish tyrants. He described tyrants in general as predatory wolves that any private individual could put to death.

During their armed resistance in the 1560s, the Huguenots made little use of the rhetoric of tyranny. However, their foremost polemicist, the Calvinist jurist François Hotman (1524–1690), employed such language against the Ultra-Catholic statesman Cardinal Charles de Lorraine in his *Epistre envoiée au tigre de la France* (1560; Letter sent to the tiger of France). In the late 1560s he drafted his celebrated *Francogallia,* demonstrating the long continuance of an ancient constitution in which the assembly of the realm could judge and depose tyrannical kings. Hotman cited several Frankish depositions, but his principal tyrant was a more modern king, Louis XI (ruled 1461–1483), who had allegedly subverted the constitution. When the *Francogallia* was published in 1573, the year after the massacre of St. Bartholomew, he added a preface listing the tyrants of classical antiquity and suggesting the relevance of tyranny to his own times.

The massacre of the Huguenots endorsed by Charles IX shifted their theory of resistance into a radical phase. However, the two other best-known works in this vein, *Du droit des magistrats* (1574; The right of magistrates) by Calvin's lieutenant Théodore de Bèze (1519–1605) and *Vindiciae contra Tyrannos* (1579; The defense of liberty against tyrants) by the Huguenot statesman Philippe Duplessis-Mornay (1549–1623), both displayed some caution about tyrannicide. Although Bèze said he would not discuss the Old Testament idea of God summoning an individual to kill a tyrant, he did provide some examples to this end. He distinguished between the tyrant-usurper and the legitimate king who became a tyrant, but he insisted that private individuals could not act without the leadership of lesser magistrates. In the case of the usurper, however, they might take arms if the magistrates failed to do so. Mornay's argument was similar in many respects. His greater juristic subtlety was probably due to the influence of Bartolus. While he stressed the need for collective action, he allowed greater freedom to private individuals under the natural right of self-defense.

Other Huguenot tracts responding to the massacre were less reticent about tyrannicide. The many-authored *Le reveille-matin* (1574; Alarm bell) directly attacked Charles IX as a tyrant and compared his mother, Catherine de Médicis, to Jezebel in the Old Testament, who had been killed by Jehu, the instrument of God in several tyrannicides.

The Italian queen mother was also denounced for introducing the supposedly perfidious doctrines of Niccolò Machiavelli (1469–1527), whose *Prince* was seen as a guidebook for tyrants. Perhaps the most remarkable tract on tyranny at this time was the *Discours de la servitude volontaire* (Discourse on voluntary servitude, also known as the *Contr'un*) by Michel de Montaigne's friend, Étienne de La Boétie (1530–1563). La Boétie's humanist essay was composed well before the religious wars. It was called into the service of Huguenot propaganda when it was published in part in the *Alarm Bell* and in full in a collection of resistance tracts titled *Mémoires de l'estat de France sous Charles neufiesme* (1576; Memoirs of the state of France under Charles IX). La Boétie rehearsed the vices and cruelties of the tyrants of antiquity, concentrating on the Roman tyrants portrayed by Cornelius Tacitus (c. 55–c. 120 C.E.).

In the second half of the religious wars the Holy Catholic League replaced the Huguenots as the main opponent of the French crown. After the murder of its leaders in 1588 by Henry III, the league's polemicists became enthusiastic proponents of tyrannicide. The league's best-known work on the theme was *De Justa Henrici Tertii Abdicatione* (1589; The just deposition of Henry III) by Jean Boucher (c. 1548–1644), rector of the Sorbonne. Apart from its religious and secular arguments about tyranny, the book was a violent personal diatribe against the last Valois king, who had in fact been assassinated by Jacques Clément shortly before it was published. In 1594 Boucher came out with his *Apologie pour Jean Chastel* (Apology for Jean Chastel), who had failed in his attempt to kill the next king, the Bourbon Henry IV. At this time the Jesuits were somewhat unjustly accused of preaching tyrannicide. The practice was, indeed, endorsed by the independently minded Spanish Jesuit Juan de Mariana (1536–1624) in his *De Rege et Regis Institutione* (1599; On the king and the education of the king). Henry IV was to be murdered by a fanatical believer in the doctrine, François Ravaillac, in 1610.

**THE SEVENTEENTH CENTURY**

The next notorious regicide was the execution of Charles I of England in 1649. The theory of tyranny, however, was seldom invoked against him before his trial, although it received mention in general works on political authority. Some so-called "Levellers," such as John Lilburne (1615–1657) and William Walwyn (1600–1680), made use of the concept, but they applied it to all and sundry—king, Parliament, church, and Cromwellian army council. In his *An Arrow against All Tyrants* (1646), for instance, Richard Overton (c. 1600–c. 1664) chose as his main targets the House of Lords and the Presbyterian clergy.

The strongest attack upon Charles I as a tyrant came from the pen of the republican poet John Milton (1608–1674). His *Tenure of Kings and Magistrates* (1649) was followed by his *Pro Populo Anglicano Defensio* (1650; Defense of the people of England), written in answer to the justification of Charles I by the French scholar, Claude de Saumaise (1588–1653). Milton discussed the tyranny and deposition of other kings, including those listed in the *Francogallia*, but his venom was reserved for Charles I and his champion.

In the next generation two renowned Whig republicans discussed tyranny in the context of the attempt to exclude Charles II's brother, the future James II, from the succession because of his Catholicism. *Plato Redivivus* (1680; expanded in 1681) by Henry Neville (1620–1694) and *Discourses concerning Government* (composed 1681–1683, first published 1698) by Algernon Sidney (1622–1683) showed familiarity with the Aristotelian tradition and the French resistance literature of the preceding century. They supported what had become known as "the Gothic constitution," based on Hotman's idea of the control of government by the sovereign assemblies of the Germanic peoples who had invaded France, Spain, and England in the fifth century. Like Milton, they both cited Hotman on the subversion of the ancient French constitution by Louis XI. They saw the tyranny of Charles II and his brother as likely to lead England to a regime comparable with Louis XIV's in France. Sidney had long been obsessed with tyranny. In 1660 he had inscribed the visitors' book at the court of Denmark with his Latin motto: "This hand, opposed to the sword of tyrants, seeks peace under liberty" (frontispiece to *The Works of Algernon Sidney*, 1772). Peace was not his forte. In 1683 he was tried and executed for plotting the assassination of Charles II, leaving to posterity the manuscript of his summa-

tion of the long tradition of the Aristotelian concept of tyranny in his *Discourses*.

## THE EIGHTEENTH CENTURY

In the eighteenth century it was the writings of John Locke (1632–1704), rather than those of Sidney, that influenced the political thought of the Enlightenment. Locke described the tyrant as one "whose commands and actions are not directed to the preservation of the properties of his people, but the satisfaction of his own ambition, revenge, covetousness, or any other irregular passion" (*Two Treatises of Government*, 1690). However much they admired Locke, the French philosophes tended to discuss the theme with a certain irony. In his *De l'esprit des lois* (1748; Spirit of the laws), Charles-Louis de Secondat, baron de Montesquieu (1689–1755) suggested that there was another kind of tyranny beside monarchical oppression: the force of cultural tradition. Voltaire (1694–1778) declared in an entry on tyranny in his *Dictionnaire philosophique* (1764; Philosophical dictionary) that there were no tyrants left in the Europe of his day, and in any case he preferred a royal tyrant to the tyranny of an assembly.

Thomas Paine (1737–1809) took tyranny more seriously in the context of the American and French Revolutions. His *Rights of Man* (1791) reduced all governments to two types, the hereditary ruler and the representative assembly. All hereditary government, he argued, was intrinsically a tyranny that had repressed natural rights in past centuries. Far more extreme were the ferocious accusations of tyranny leveled by the Jacobins Antoine Saint-Just (1767–1794) and François-Maximilien Robespierre (1758–1794) against Louis XVI in the proceedings that led to the king's execution in 1793. In the following year the accusers were themselves labeled tyrants and sent to the guillotine, an event that rendered Voltaire's preferences prophetic.

*See also* **Absolutism; Authority, Concept of; Autocracy; Bèze, Théodore de; Catholic League (France); Charles I (England); Democracy; Divine Right Kingship; English Civil War Radicalism; Henry IV (France); Law; Liberty; Locke, John; Machiavelli, Niccolò; Mariana, Juan de; Milton, John; Monarchy; Montesquieu, Charles-Louis de Secondat de; Natural Law; Political Philosophy; Reformation, Protestant; Republicanism; Revolutions, Age of; Rights, Natural; St. Bartholomew's Day Massacre;**

Sovereignty, Theory of; Voltaire; Wars of Religion, French.

BIBLIOGRAPHY

*Primary Sources*

Aylmer, G. E., ed. *The Levellers in the English Revolution.* London, 1975. Extracts from Leveller tracts.

Beza, Théodore (Théodore de Bèze). *Du droit des magistrats.* Edited by Robert M. Kingdon. Geneva, 1970.

Buchanan, George. *The Powers of the Crown in Scotland.* Austin, Tex., 1949. A translation of *De Jure Regni apud Scotos* by Charles Flinn Arrowood.

Franklin, Julian H., ed. *Constitutionalism and Resistance in the Sixteenth Century: Three Treatises by Hotman, Beza, and Mornay.* New York, 1969. Extracts from *Francogallia, The Right of Magistrates,* and *Vindiciae contra Tyrannos.*

Goodman, Christopher. *How Superior Powers Oght to be Obeyd of Their Subjects.* Edited by C. H. McIlwain. New York, 1931.

Hotman, François. *Francogallia.* Edited by Ralph E. Giesey and J. H. M. Salmon. Cambridge, U.K., 1972.

La Boétie, Étienne de. *Le discours de la servitude volontaire.* Edited by P. Léonard. Paris, 1976.

Locke, John. *Two Treatises of Government.* Edited by Peter Laslett. Cambridge, U.K., and New York, 1988.

Milton, John, *The Complete Prose Works of John Milton.* Vol. 4, *1650–1655.* Edited by Don M. Wolfe. New Haven, 1953–1982.

Mornay, Philippe Duplessis. *Vindiciae, contra Tyrannos: Or, Concerning the Legitimate Power of a Prince over the People, and of the People over a Prince.* Edited by George Garnett. Cambridge, U.K., and New York, 1994. Earlier English translations also known as *A Defense of Liberty against Tyrants.* See Franklin, above.

Neville, Henry. *Plato Redivivus.* In *Two Republican Tracts.* Compiled by Caroline Robbins. London, 1969.

Paine, Thomas. *The Rights of Man.* New York, 1961 [1791].

Ponet, John. *A Shorte Treatise of Politike Pouuer.* In *John Ponet (1516?–1556): Advocate of Limited Monarchy,* by Winthrop S. Hudson. Chicago, 1942.

Sidney, Algernon, *The Works of Algernon Sydney.* London, 1772.

*Secondary Sources*

Ford, Franklin L. *Political Murder from Tyrannicide to Terrorism.* Cambridge, Mass., 1985.

Kelley, Donald R. *François Hotman: A Revolutionary's Ordeal.* Princeton, 1973.

Kingdon, Robert M. *Myths about the St. Bartholomew's Day Massacres, 1572–1576.* Cambridge, Mass., 1988.

McFarlane, I. D. *Buchanan.* London, 1981.

Morrill, John. "Charles I, Tyranny and the Civil War." In *The Nature of the English Revolution.* London, 1993.

Ranum, Orest. "The French Ritual of Tyrannicide in the Late Sixteenth Century." *The Sixteenth Century Journal* 11, no. 1 (Spring 1980): 63–82.

Scott, Jonathan. *Algernon Sidney and the Restoration Crisis, 1677–1683.* Cambridge, U.K., and New York, 1991.

Walzer, Michael, ed. *Regicide and Revolution: Speeches at the Trial of Louis XVI.* Translated by Marian Rothstein. Cambridge, U.K., 1974.

J. H. M. SALMON

**UKRAINE.** Ukraine entered the fifteenth century with no independent state of its own, as the formerly powerful principalities of Galicia and Volhynia—heirs of the once mighty Kievan Rus'—succumbed to the rule of the Kingdom of Poland and the Grand Duchy of Lithuania. While the Rus' elites of the Galicia and Kholm regions, annexed by Poland in 1387, played little if any role in the political life of the Polish state, their counterparts in the rest of the Ruthenian (Ukrainian and Belarusian) territories, which were taken over by the Lithuanian princes in the course of the fourteenth century, became the most influential political force in the Grand Duchy of Lithuania. Their political clout was translated into cultural dominance, which was reflected in the status of the Ruthenian as the official language of the realm and in the conversion of numerous members of the Lithuanian ruling dynasty to Orthodoxy. The political, economic, and cultural dominance of the Ruthenian elites in the Grand Duchy of Lithuania was, nevertheless, short-lived, as Lithuania, threatened by its northern and eastern neighbors, strengthened its ties with the Kingdom of Poland.

A number of agreements proclaiming the union of the two states opened the door to growing Polish political, religious, and cultural influences in the Grand Duchy of Lithuania. The Union of Lublin (1569) concluded the process of the amalgamation of the two polities into one state, the Polish-Lithuanian Commonwealth. The union was opposed by the Ruthenian princes, as it significantly curtailed

their traditional powers in the region. It was supported nevertheless by the nobility, which as a result of the union received same political status as the Polish nobility *(szlachta)*. After the conclusion of union, the Kingdom of Poland effectively took control of most of Ukraine, adding to its earlier Ukrainian possessions the Podlasia, Volhynia, Kiev, and Bratslav regions. All of the Belarusian lands remained within the boundaries of the Grand Duchy of Lithuania. The border between the new Commonwealth partners, in the Pripet River basin, laid the foundations for the modern Ukrainian-Belarusian border. One of the consequences of the union in the cultural sphere was the gradual replacement of Ruthenian as the official language of the area by Latin and Polish. The Union of Lublin increased the Polish presence in Ukraine, as kings granted large latifundia there to Polish nobles. It also helped to initiate a mass migration of the Jewish population into central and eastern Ukraine.

From the late sixteenth century, the union of the Orthodox and Catholic Christians of the Commonwealth became the leitmotif of a controversial government policy. The union was proclaimed at the church council of Brest in 1596, and it provoked a strong negative reaction on the part of Ruthenian princes, Orthodox brotherhoods, and the majority of the monastic clergy. These groups had, in the decades leading to the Union of Brest, worked hard for the revival of Orthodox religious tradition and culture. The leading role in promotion of Orthodox learning was played by Prince Kostiantyn Ostrozky, who founded the Ostrih Academy (c. 1576) and

**Ukraine**

- ▨ Palatinates which joined Poland in 1569
- ▤ Hetmanate state, 1648–1782
- --- Border dividing Russian and Polish Ukraine, c. 1654
- ✕ Battle

sponsored the publication of the Church Slavonic Bible in 1580–1581. The Union of Brest provoked the rise of religious polemics in Ukraine. The writings of Catholic authors, among whom Piotr Skarga was most prominent, and Uniate writers, led by Metropolitan Ipatii Potii, were countered by Orthodox polemicists, who included the author of the first Church Slavonic grammar, Meletii Smotrytsky. In 1620 the Orthodox managed to restore their church hierarchy, and by 1633 they assured its recognition by the authorities. Peter Mohyla, the first "legitimate" Orthodox metropolitan of Kiev since the proclamation of the Union of Brest, played a leading role in the reform of Orthodox Christianity. He helped establish the Kiev College to raise the educational level of the clergy, standardized liturgical practices, and sponsored the composition of the Orthodox confession of faith, which was approved by the eastern patriarchs in 1643. The Kievan met-

ropolitanate under Mohyla led the entire Orthodox Church along the way to confessionalization.

## THE COSSACKS

An important role in the Uniate-Orthodox conflicts of the first half of the seventeenth century was played by the Ukrainian Cossacks, whose military clout assured the restoration of the Orthodox hierarchy in 1620. The Cossacks, whose existence is first recorded in historical sources at the end of the fifteenth century, grew by the mid-seventeenth century into an influential military and political force, which often raised the banner of Orthodoxy in its fight against the authorities. The growth of Cossackdom was closely associated with the colonization of the steppe areas of Ukraine, the construction of border castles and towns, and the advance of the magnates' latifundia, which resulted in the gradual enserfment of the peasantry. The transformation of Ukrainian Cossackdom from bands of fishermen, hunters, and freebooters to military formations in the service of Polish kings and a new social group striving for recognition on a par with the nobility was marked by a number of violent conflicts with the authorities. The latter tried to limit the number of Cossacks in the royal register and thus to curb the access of burghers and peasants to this socially and economically privileged group. Another reason for the authorities' desire to curb the growth of Cossackdom was constant Cossack interference in international affairs. The Cossacks' seagoing expeditions to the Ottoman possessions of the Black Sea littoral, their raids into the Crimea, and their interference into the internal affairs of Moldavia put the Commonwealth on a collision course with the High Porte and forced the Polish authorities to take a hard line against the Cossacks.

Between 1591 and 1638 there were five major Cossack uprisings against the Commonwealth and a number of smaller conflicts. By far the largest Cossack uprising started in the spring of 1648 under the leadership of the Cossack officer Bohdan Khmelnytsky. As with many earlier revolts, this one began at the Zaporozhian Sich—the Cossack headquarters in the lower Dnieper area. In a surprising move, the Cossacks united their forces with their traditional adversaries the Crimean Tatars and in the course of 1648 and 1649 scored a number of impressive victories over the armed forces of the Commonwealth. The Cossack military successes were accompanied by the massacre and expulsion of the Polish and Jewish population from the Cossack-controlled territories, as both groups were viewed by the rebels as close associates of the oppressive regime in Ukraine. In August 1649, after a successful battle against Commonwealth forces at Zboriv, the Cossacks made an agreement that recognized their control over three eastern palatinates of the Commonwealth and led to the foundations of a Cossack state known as the Hetmanate. Khmelnytsky's search for allies in his struggle with the Commonwealth led him first to the formal acceptance of Ottoman suzerainty in 1651. When the sultan failed to deliver the expected military assistance, Khmelnytsky turned to a Muscovite protectorate in 1654. He also sought other allies in his war against the Commonwealth, establishing especially close links with Sweden.

Khmelnytsky's policy of conducting an independent foreign policy irrespective of the wishes of Muscovy culminated during the tenure of his successor as hetman, former General Chancellor Ivan Vyhovsky. Disappointed with Muscovite policy, Vyhovsky turned to the Commonwealth, signing an agreement in September 1658 at Hadiach. This "union" would introduce the Ruthenian nation as a third partner in the Commonwealth, along with the Poles and Lithuanians. It expressed the strivings of the Ukrainian nobility but did not sit well with the Cossack rank and file. And the Polish side was not ready to accept the rebellious Ruthenians as equals. Both factors led to the collapse of the Hadiach agreement and the loss of power by Vyhovsky in 1659.

**"RUIN"**

The new hetman, Bohdan Khmelnytsky's son Iurii, initially sided with Muscovy, but in 1660 switched allegiance to the Commonwealth, thereby creating a split within the Cossack officer stratum. Some, led by Colonel Iakiv Somko, denounced the younger Khmelnytsky and remained loyal to the tsar. What followed was the period which in Ukrainian historiography is known as the "ruin." Muscovy fought Polish-Lithuanian and Ottoman armies, each side assisted by competing Cossack factions led by their own hetmans. The signing of Andrusovo agreement (1667) between Muscovy and the Commonwealth effectively divided Ukraine into two parts: territories on the left bank of the Dnieper together with Kiev (first temporarily and then permanently) went to Muscovy, while the rest of Ukraine remained under Polish control. An attempt to reestablish Cossack control over both parts of Ukraine was led by Hetman Peter Doroshenko, who relied on Ottoman help to achieve this goal. His attempt ended in failure in 1676 when Doroshenko was forced to abandon his office and surrender to the pro-Muscovite hetman of Left Bank Ukraine. The decades of continuous war brought devastation to Ukraine. The Right Bank, which was turned into a battleground between the competing Ottoman, Polish, and Cossack armies, suffered especially. Between 1672 and 1699 Podillia and parts of Right Bank Ukraine were ruled by the Ottomans, but they then returned to Polish control.

Cossack statehood and autonomy survived only in Muscovite-controlled Left Bank Ukraine. The relative security and stability of the region attracted numerous immigrants from Right Bank Ukraine. Among these was the Cossack officer Ivan Mazepa, who became hetman in 1687. Mazepa's name is linked to the Hetmanate's last attempt to play an independent role in international politics. Unhappy with the policies of Peter I of Russia, which aimed to further limit the Hetmanate's autonomy, in 1708 Mazepa joined the invading army of Charles XII of Sweden. Only part of the Cossack officers followed their hetman, and the defeat of Charles XII and Mazepa's forces at the hands of the Russian army in the battle of Poltava in 8 July (27 June o.s.) 1709 firmly reestablished Russian control over Left Bank Ukraine. Mazepa's "treason" was used by Peter to launch a decisive attack on the remnants of the Hetmanate's autonomy. The capital of the Hetmanate was moved closer to the border with Russia, the tsar took over the right to appoint Cossack colonels, his representative took up permanent residence at the hetman's court, and eventually the office of the hetman itself was abolished and replaced in 1722 by the rule of the Little Russian Collegium.

## ABSORPTION INTO RUSSIA AND THE RISE OF "LITTLE RUSSIAN" IDENTITY

In the course of the eighteenth century the Left Bank Cossack officer stratum developed a new identity, defined by loyalty to the "Little Russian" nation. That identity was deeply rooted in the loyalty to the Hetmanate's political traditions and institutions. It stressed cultural differences between Russia and Ukraine, but in most cases complemented the all-Russian identity of the Hetmanate's elite. The sons of Little Russia were among the architects of the all-Russian identity through most of the eighteenth century, and although they resented the abolition of their autonomy, after Mazepa they were reluctant to rebel against the tsar. Taking advantage of the change of rulers in St. Petersburg, the Cossack officers managed to restore the hetman's office twice, in 1727–1734 and 1750–1764. Nevertheless, these temporary successes in preserving the symbol of Cossack statehood could not reverse the slowly but evenly advancing process of the imperial absorption of the Hetmanate. This process culminated under Catherine II, who in the 1760s–1780s permanently abolished the hetman's office; liqui-

dated the Zaporozhian Sich, an autonomous Cossack Host in Lower Dnieper; and finally liquidated the Hetmanate altogether.

The successful wars with the Ottomans in the second half of the eighteenth century and the annexation of the Crimea by the Russian Empire in 1783 opened the steppes of southern Ukraine to further colonization and brought numerous settlers of Russian, Serbian, German, and Mennonite extraction into the region, apart from Ukrainian Cossacks and peasantry. The partitions of Poland (1772–1795) brought under Russian control most ethnic Ukrainian territories, with the exception of Galicia, Bukovina, and Transcarpathia, which were ruled by the Habsburgs. The Russian Empire took over territories settled mostly by Ukrainian and Belarusian peasants, the majority of whom adhered by that time to the Uniate church and were ruled by Polish, or heavily Polonized, Roman Catholic nobility.

*See also* **Andrusovo, Truce of; Belarus; Cossacks; Hetmanate (Ukraine); Khmelnytsky, Bohdan; Khmelnytsky Uprising; Lithuania, Grand Duchy of, to 1569; Lithuanian Literature and Language; Lublin, Union of (1569); Mazepa, Ivan; Orthodoxy, Russian; Poland to 1569; Poland-Lithuania, Commonwealth of, 1569–1795; Reformations in Eastern Europe: Protestant, Catholic, and Orthodox; Russia; Ukrainian Literature and Language; Uniates; Union of Brest (1596).**

BIBLIOGRAPHY

Frick, David A. *Meletij Smotryc'kyj.* Cambridge, Mass., 1995.

Gordon, Linda. *Cossack Rebellions: Social Turmoil in the Sixteenth-Century Ukraine.* Albany, N.Y, 1983.

Gudziak, Borys A. *Crisis and Reform: The Kyivan Metropolitanate, the Patriarchate of Constantinople, and the Genesis of the Union of Brest.* Cambridge, Mass., 1998.

Hrushevsky, Mykhailo. *History of Ukraine-Rus'.* Edited by Andrzej Poppe and Frank E. Sysyn. Translated by Marta Skorupsky. Edmonton, 1997–. See especially vols. 7 and 8.

Kaminski, Andrzej Sulima. *Republic vs. Autocracy: Poland-Lithuania and Russia, 1686–1697.* Cambridge, Mass., 1993.

Kohut, Zenon E. *Russian Centralism and Ukrainian Autonomy: Imperial Absorption of the Hetmanate, 1760s–1830s.* Cambridge, Mass., 1988.

Pelenski, Jaroslaw. *The Contest for the Legacy of Kievan Rus'.* Boulder, Colo., and New York, 1998.

Plokhy, Serhii. *The Cossacks and Religion in Early Modern Ukraine.* New York, 2001.

———. *Tsars and Cossacks: A Study in Iconography.* Cambridge, Mass., 2002.

Polonska-Vasylenko, Natalia. *The Settlement of the Southern Ukraine, 1750–1775.* New York, 1955.

Sevcenko, Ihor. *Ukraine Between East and West: Essays on Cultural History to the Early Eighteenth Century.* Edmonton, 1996.

Subtelny, Orest. *The Mazepists: Ukrainian Separatism in the Early Eighteenth Century.* Boulder, Colo., and New York, 1981.

Sysyn, Frank E. *Between Poland and the Ukraine: The Dilemma of Adam Kysil, 1600–1653.* Cambridge, Mass., 1985.

SERHII PLOKHY

# UKRAINIAN LITERATURE AND LANGUAGE.

The history of a literary language in Ukraine begins with the Christianization of Kievan Rus' about 988 and the adoption of the Church Slavonic language for use in liturgy and literature (chronicles, saints' lives, sermons). The Mongol Tatar destruction of Kiev in 1240 and the fourteenth-century partition of Ukrainian lands, chiefly among Lithuania and Poland, had profound effects on the development of languages and literatures in the area. In 1433 the Polish king Władysław II Jagiełło introduced Polish usage in Galician chanceries (at first Latin, then Latin and Polish) for court records and documents of state. In the Grand Duchy of Lithuania, on the other hand (which included what would become the Kiev Palatinate at this point), Ruthenian *(ruskii)* was employed in the chancery. Although the language came to have Belarusian features at its base, it tolerated Ukrainian dialect features as well and could serve as the "vulgar tongue" *(prostyi iazyk, prostaia mova)* for a "Ruthenian nation" that had not yet differentiated into Ukrainians and Belarusians.

After the "silence" of the late fifteenth and early sixteenth centuries, Ukrainian intellectuals helped to mount a Ruthenian revival. These activities came in reaction to the confessional and cultural challenges posed by the Reformation and Counter-Reformation in the Polish-Lithuanian Commonwealth. Among other things, the then Calvinist (and future Antitrinitarian) minister Szymon Budny

had published a Ruthenian catechism at Niasvizh (Nieśwież) in 1562. The architect of the Union of Brest, the Polish Jesuit Piotr Skarga, had asserted in 1577 that only Greek and Latin could function as languages of learning and religion, because only they possessed grammars and lexicons and thus "are always the same and never change." Responses came from centers in Ostrih (the Slavic-Greek-Latin Academy) as well as Lviv, Vilnius, and Kiev, where brotherhoods, schools, and printing presses were employed in the "national" cause.

Ruthenian scholars sought to answer Skarga's challenge by writing grammars and dictionaries of Church Slavonic, in which they wished to see a Ruthenian Latin. First attempts to produce a grammar (*Adelphotïs,* a Greek grammar with facing Slavonic translation, 1591; Lavrentii Zyzanii's *Slavonic Grammar,* 1596) culminated in Meletii Smotrytskyi's *Collection of Rules of Slavonic Grammar* (1618–1619), which served as the norm throughout the Orthodox Slavic world until the early nineteenth century. Pamvo Berynda (1627), Iepyfanii Slavynetskyi (1642), and Slavynetskyi together with Arsenii Koretskyi (1649) would offer lexicons and dictionaries.

Editions of Holy Scripture and liturgical books were a part of the revival. The Peresopnytsia Gospel (1556–1561), a sort of Slavonic-Ruthenian hybrid, remained in manuscript form. A Church Slavonic apostol (Acts and Epistles) was printed at Lviv in 1574, and a Bible, the first complete printing in the language, at Ostrih in 1580–1581. Metropolitan Peter Mohyla directed a project of correction and edition of Church Slavonic liturgical books in the 1630s and 1640s.

With the growth of Catholic and Protestant confessional propaganda and devotional literature (in both Polish and Ruthenian) came attempts to establish Ruthenian as a "national" vulgar tongue. Borrowing the argumentation of Protestant and Catholic discussions on the licitness and range of uses for popular languages, Meletii Smotrytskyi motivated his decision in 1616 to offer a Ruthenian translation of the old Slavonic Homiliary Gospel (a collection of sermons he hoped would stand in as an Orthodox postil) with the argument that, although he would rather use "the more noble, beautiful, concise, subtle and rich Slavonic language," he had listened to St. Paul and offered the work now in the "baser and more vulgar tongue," since "it is a more useful thing to speak five words in an intelligible tongue, than ten thousand in an unknown tongue (especially for the instruction of the people)" (1 Cor. 14:19). Although a certain number of works related to confession and devotion continued to appear in Ruthenian, Polish soon dominated in these areas of Ruthenian letters. The effects of the increasing Polonization that followed the Union of Lublin (1569) can be seen clearly in the history of the polemic leading up to and following the Union of Brest (1596). In the early stages, Orthodox, Uniates, and Catholics often employed Ruthenian in their tracts, sometimes issuing parallel Polish versions. By 1597 the Orthodox side had issued a first polemical treatise in Polish, and after 1628 all sides used Polish exclusively.

Thus by the early seventeenth century Ukrainians were using three literary languages: Church Slavonic in its new Meletian codification, Polish, and Ruthenian. Ruthenian usage began to accept more and more recognizably Ukrainian features; at the same time, Ruthenian texts came to look more and more like Polish written with Cyrillic letters. The program of Smotrytskyi and others had been to set Church Slavonic on a level with Latin as the language of Ruthenian culture, education, and high literature (including poetry), and to set Ruthenian next to Polish as a "vulgar tongue" with a wide range of usage in literature and private devotion. The program reached far beyond practice. Nonetheless, literature in Ruthenian experienced a modest flourishing in the seventeenth century. The archimandrite of the Kiev Caves Monastery Zahariia Kopystenskyi produced a monumental statement of the Orthodox position on the confessional debates in his *Palinodia* of 1620–1624, which, however, remained in manuscript until 1894. Monk Ivan Vyshenskyi used Ruthenian in the polemical tracts and epistles he sent to Rus' from Mt. Athos. The churchmen Leontii Karpovych, Meletii Smotrytskyi, Kyrylo Trankvilion-Stavrovetskyi, Ioannikii Haliatovskyi, Antonii Radyvylovskyi, Lazar Baranovych, Dmytro Tuptalo, and Stefan Javorskyi published Ruthenian sermons, individually and in large collections. Among exemplars of Ruthenian baroque poetry we may note Kasiian Sakovych's *Verses on the Sorrowful Funeral of the Noble Knight,*

*Petro Konashevych-Sahaidachnyi, Hetman of the Zaporozhian Army of His Royal Grace* (1622), as well as the many encomiastic poems with which Ruthenian churchmen and scholars prefaced their works. Among Cossack histories, the *Eyewitness Chronicle* (late seventeenth century) and the works of Hryhorij Hrabjanka (after 1709) and Samiilo Velychko (c. 1720) deserve mention. Ruthenian was also used in school dramas and intermedia. Still, it is important to note that Polish continued to function as a literary language for Ruthenians, even for the Orthodox: it was in this language that Mohyla printed Sylvester Kosiv's version of the lives of the Kievan Caves Fathers (1635) and Afanasii Kolnofoiskyi's collection of miracles connected with the Caves Monastery (1638).

Ukrainian Ruthenian was employed in the chancery of the Cossack Hetmanate, but its use declined in all areas with the now increasing Russianization of left-bank Ukraine and the continuing Polonization of the right bank. With Hetman Ivan Mazepa's defeat at Poltava in 1709, the Hetmanate became more and more a Russian province. In 1720 Tsar Peter I banned printing of church books in Ukraine. In 1723 the Cossack state lost the right to choose hetmans. In 1775 the Zaporozhian Sich was liquidated; in 1783 serfdom was introduced; and in 1785 the Cossack *starshyna* was incorporated into the Russian nobility. Church Slavonic was eventually replaced (except for liturgical uses) by the Slaveno-Russian that Ukrainian philologists helped to create. The Ruthenian vulgar tongue continued to find some use in Ukrainian administration until about 1780, during the reign of Catherine the Great; from that point the language would be relegated to mostly private use, allowed, with the advent of classicism's theory of the three styles, to function only in the "lowest" genres of belles lettres.

*See also* **Lithuanian Literature and Language; Mohyla, Peter; Polish Literature and Language; Reformations in Eastern Europe: Protestant, Catholic, and Orthodox; Smotrytskyi, Meletii.**

BIBLIOGRAPHY

*Primary Source*

Rothe, Hans, ed. *Die älteste ostslawische Kunstdichtung, 1575–1647.* Bausteine zur Geschichte der Literatur bei den Slawen, vol. 7. Giessen, Germany, 1976–1977.

*Secondary Sources*

Čyževs'kyj, Dmytro. *A History of Ukrainian Literature.* Translated by Dolly Ferguson, Doreen Gorsline, and Ulana Petyk. Littleton, Colo., 1975.

Martel, Antoine. *La langue polonaise dans les pays Ruthènes: Ukraine et Russie Blanche, 1569–1657.* Lille, France, 1938.

Voznjak, Mykhalo. *Geschichte der ukrainischen Literatur.* Translated by Katharina Horbatsch. Bausteine zur Geschichte der Literatur bei den Slawen, vol. 4. Giessen, Germany, 1975.

DAVID FRICK

---

**UNIATES.** Throughout the early modern period, the papacy received into communion with the Roman Catholic Church groups of Eastern Christians that retained their ecclesiastical structures and local practices. Unlike Protestants, whom the papacy viewed as break-away believers organized in sects devoid of sacraments and who should be reintegrated as individuals into the Latin Church, Orthodox and Oriental Orthodox Christians were considered bearers of the apostolic succession of bishops and valid sacraments; thus, these Christians could retain their traditions and ecclesiastical structures when reconciled with the Catholic Church. In contrast to the attempts for a universal union with the Orthodox Church attempted at the Second Council of Lyons (1274) and the Council of Florence (1439–1442), the unions of the early modern period were local unions of hierarchies, bishoprics, and even groups of believers. Post-Tridentine Catholicism viewed these groups not as local churches, but as Christians following specific rites that could be retained after proper submission.

The major stimuli for the unions were the policies of Catholic states that ruled over Orthodox and Oriental Christians, the desire of Eastern Christians to improve their situation under Catholic or even Islamic rulers by receiving the support of the papacy or Western Christian powers, and the attraction to the well-organized and dynamic Latin Christian world at a time of relative stagnation in Eastern Christendom. In most cases, programs for union initiated by either Rome or Eastern Christians were rejected by at least part of the clergy and laity, giving rise to competing ecclesial structures and fierce polemics. Orthodox responses to unionizing attempts often constituted a sharper definition of ecclesial traditions and dogmas, at times by adopting the tools and methods of their opponents.

The first and major union of the early modern period was that at Brest in the Polish-Lithuanian Commonwealth in 1596. Initiated by the metropolitan and bishops of the Kyiv metropolitanate, the Union of Brest held forth the promise of improving the situation of the Ruthenian (Ukrainian-Belarusian) Church in a Catholic-dominated state. Although supported by the monarch Sigismund III Vasa (ruled 1587–1632), the Uniates were unable to win over all the bishops to the union synod and were opposed by powerful nobles, the urban brotherhoods, numerous monasteries, and the Cossacks. They also suffered from the derisive attitude of many Latin clergy, who preferred outright conversion. Increasingly dependent on the civil authorities and Rome to combat the Orthodox opposition, the Uniates took on the spirit and institutions of the Latin Church, especially through the training of clergy in Roman and central-European seminaries. Led by dedicated hierarchs such as Metropolitans Ipatii Potii and Iosyf Rutsky and the Basilian Order, established in 1613 from the monastics who accepted the union, the Uniates survived the reestablishment of the Orthodox Metropolitanate in 1621 and the compromise of 1632, in which the state recognized the legality of the Orthodox and tried to divide the eparchies and churches between the two metropolitanates. The 1623 murder of Iosafat Kuntsevych, the archbishop of Polatsk, by the burghers of Vitsebsk who resisted his attempts to impose the union gave the Uniates a martyr and cult figure.

The Khmelnytsky Uprising, which began in 1648, put the very existence of the Uniate Church in question: in 1650, the king promised the rebels to return eparchies and churches to the Orthodox. Its situation worsened in 1654, when Muscovite and Ukrainian Cossack armies invaded the Grand Duchy of Lithuania and destroyed many Uniate centers on Belarusian territories. From 1655 to 1665 the Uniate Kyiv metropolitan see was left vacant; during the negotiations for the Union of Hadiach (1658) the Ukrainian side demanded the commonwealth abolish the union. Yet with the support of Rome and the restoration of Polish rule in the Belarus and right-bank Ukraine, the Uniates survived and increased in number in the late seventeenth century. By the turn of the century all the western Ukrainian eparchies accepted the union, and at the Synod of Zamość of 1720 the church's structure was strengthened, though Latinized at the same time. In the eighteenth century the Uniates comprised the overwhelming number of Eastern Christians in the commonwealth (approximately 4.6 million in the 1770s) and maintained a well-developed network of schools and printing presses. The partitions of the commonwealth in 1772, 1793, and 1795 radically worsened the Uniates' situation. Most came under Russian rule, and Catherine II (ruled 1762–1796) persecuted the church. Her successors in the nineteenth century abolished all the Uniate eparchies and converted all believers to Orthodoxy. In the western Ukrainian lands that went to the Habsburgs in 1772, the Uniates benefited from grants of equality with the Latin Church and were renamed the Greek Catholic Church and reorganized in the metropolitan province of Galicia in 1808. In the seventeenth century the Armenian archbishop of Lviv also entered into union with Rome.

The extension of Habsburg rule into central Europe and the Balkans created numerous Uniate communities. In 1610 a bishop was designated for Uniates in Croatia, and in 1646, at the Union of Uzhhorod, the Ukrainians of Hungary became Uniate. The most significant union was that of the Romanians of Transylvania at Alba Julia in 1700. Under the distinguished leadership of Bishop Ion Inochentie Micu-Klein (bishop 1729–1751), the church played a major role in defending Romanian cultural and political rights. Not all Transylvanians accepted the union, and Maria Theresa (ruled 1740–1780) was forced to permit them to have their own bishop in 1759.

In western Europe the major Uniate group was the Italo-Albanian, which was formed by the migration of Orthodox Albanians to southern Italy in the fifteenth century and later. In 1717 the Uniate Armenian Mechtarist fathers took up residence in Venice. Uniates also emerged in European colonies; one of the most important Uniate communities originated with the Christians of St. Thomas in the Malabar area of India, who were subordinated to the Latin Church by the Portuguese in the late sixteenth century. Missionary activities, some dating back to the Middle Ages and renewed in the early modern period, resulted in unions and the creation of ecclesiastical structures for Orthodox and Oriental Orthodox Christians, such as the union of parts of the Assyrian Church of the East in 1553, the election of a Catholic patriarch among the Syrian Orthodox 1662, the creation of an Armenian Patriarchate in Cilicia in 1742, and the creation of the Melkite Catholic Church in the early eighteenth century.

Current Catholic thinking has rejected the early modern form of conversion through union in deference to ecumenical contacts with the Orthdox. Nevertheless, Uniate groups have proved resilient in the Middle East and especially in eastern Europe, where they have reemerged after suppression by Communist governments. Most of these groups now view the term *Uniate* as derogatory.

*See also* **Khmelnytsky Uprising; Polish-Lithuania, Commonwealth of, 1569–1795; Reformations in Eastern Europe: Protestant, Catholic, and Orthodox; Ukraine; Union of Brest (1596).**

BIBLIOGRAPHY

Bieńkowski, Ludomir. "Organizacja Kosciola Wschodniego w Polsce." In *Kościół w Polsce*, Vol. 1. Edited by Jerzy Kłoczowski. Cracow, 1969, 733–1050.

Blažejowski, Dmytro. *Ukrainian and Armenian Pontifical Seminaries of Lviv (1665–1784)*. Rome, 1975.

Gudziak, Borys. *Crisis and Reform: The Kyivan Metropolitanate, the Patriarchate of Constantinople, and the Genesis of the Union of Brest*. Cambridge, Mass., 1998.

Macha, Josef. *Ecclesiastical Unification: A Theoretical Framework Together with Case Studies from the History of Latin-Byzantine Relations*. Rome, 1974.

Robertson, Ronald G. *The Eastern Christian Churches: A Brief Survey*. 5th ed. Rome, 1995.

FRANK E. SYSYN

---

**UNION OF BREST (1596).** The Union of Brest (Berestia) constituted the adherence of a major part of the hierarchy and part of the clergy and faithful of the Kyiv metropolitan see to the Church of Rome and its dogmas on condition of retaining its rites and elements of autonomy. In the late sixteenth century the Orthodox Church in the Polish-Lithuanian Commonwealth consisted of a Kyiv metropolitan subordinate to the patriarch of

Constantinople and seven bishops who had vast dioceses with millions of faithful. The subject of discrimination and of proselytization by Catholics and Protestants, the church was losing elements of its essential protectors, the Orthodox magnates and princes, to other creeds.

The arrival of Jesuits into the commonwealth in the 1560s revived discussion of church union, last attempted at Florence in 1439, prior to the fall of Constantinople. At the Florentine Union the Orthodox Church had accepted Roman dogmas on purgatory, the *filioque* (the procession of the Holy Spirit through the Son), the primacy of Peter's see, and the legitimacy of the form of Latin Communion but retained its ecclesiastical structure and rituals. The Florentine Union failed largely because it did not bring promised Western Christian support for beleaguered Byzantium. Temporarily accepted in the Ukrainian and Belarusian lands of the kingdom of Poland and the grand duchy of Lithuania but rejected in the Muscovite state, it resulted in the division of the Kyiv metropolitan see, with a separate metropolitan created in Moscow and the Russian church breaking away from the patriarchate of Constantinople. The calls of the Jesuits Piotr Skarga (1536–1612), Benedykt Herbest (c. 1531–1598), and Antonio Possevino (1533–1611) to make up Catholic losses to the Reformation by converting Eastern Christians found more favorable resonance at the court with the election of Sigismund III Vasa (ruled 1587–1632) as Polish king in 1587. At the same time the Orthodox bishops found themselves increasingly challenged by their laity (above all by newly forming urban brotherhoods) and by the interventions of the mother church, especially after the trip of Patriarch Jeremiah II (c. 1530–1595) through Ukraine and Belarus on his way to Moscow in 1588–1589, where he healed the breach with the Russian church and declared the Moscow see a patriarchate.

Religious ferment also followed the introduction of printing of Eastern Christian religious books (including the Ostrih Bible in 1580–1581) and the formation of an Orthodox academy under the patronage of the Volhynian magnate Prince Kostiantyn Ostrozky (1526–1608), who was open to the idea of ecumenical discussions among the churches. In the 1590s the Orthodox bishops met at a number of reform synods and, led by Bishops Ipatii Potii

of Volodymyr (1541–1613) and Kyrylo Terletsky of Lutsk (d. 1607), conceived a plan for strengthening the church and the role of the hierarchy within it through union with Rome. All hierarchs signed a letter to Pope Clement VIII (reigned 1592–1605) empowering the two bishops to negotiate for them in Rome.

After the bishops' profession of faith, the papal bull *Magnus Dominus* of 23 December 1595 declared the acceptance of the bishops and their flock, and the bull *Decet Romanum Pontificem* of 23 February 1596 guaranteed the terms. In return for accepting the Catholic interpretation of the *filioque* and purgatory and the primacy of the pope, the rites and traditions of the Ruthenian Kyivan Church, including the Slavonic liturgical language, married clergy, and local election of bishops and metropolitan, were permitted. Rome undertook to become an advocate for the Eastern Church to attain equality with the Western Church in the commonwealth, including admission of the Ukrainian-Belarusian bishops into the senate. While in practice the Union of Brest was a union of a local church with the see of Rome, post-Tridentine Rome's understanding of it was as a reception of a lost and sinful flock into the church, with a beneficent church permitting certain local customs.

The bishops from the first faced opposition to the union. Two of their ranks had earlier withdrawn their support when it became clear that Prince Ostrozky was opposed to any negotiations that did not include the patriarch of Constantinople and other Eastern churches. The Eastern patriarchs expressed their opposition, as did the urban brotherhoods and many monastic communities. Thus the council called to Brest in October 1596 soon split into two factions, one supporting and one opposing the union. The king's confirmation of the union and the presence of Roman Catholic bishops as papal emissaries did not intimidate the opposition, and the two opposing councils (synods) anathematized each other. Conflict between those who accepted the union, or Uniates, and those Orthodox who rejected it went on for generations, but through periods of advance (the late seventeenth century and early eighteenth century) and regress (the mid-seventeenth century and late eighteenth century) the union remained an enduring element in East

European church affairs and created the largest Eastern Christian community in union with Rome.

*See also* **Khmelnytsky Uprising; Orthodoxy, Russian; Reformations in Eastern Europe: Protestant, Catholic, and Orthodox; Ukraine; Uniates.**

BIBLIOGRAPHY

Gudziak, Borys A. *Crisis and Reform: The Kyivan Metropolitanate, the Patriarchate of Constantinople, and the Genesis of the Union of Brest.* Cambridge, Mass., 1998.

Halecki, Oscar. *From Florence to Brest (1439–1596).* Hamden, Conn., 1968.

Ševčenko, Ihor. *Ukraine between East and West: Essays on Cultural History to the Early Eighteenth Century.* Edmonton and Toronto, 1996.

Wlasowsky, Ivan. *Outline History of the Ukrainian Orthodox Church.* Vol. 1, *The Baptism of Ukraine to the Union of Berestye, 988–1596.* Bound Brook, N.J., 1956.

FRANK E. SYSYN

---

# UNITAS FRATRUM. *See* Moravian Brethren.

---

# UNITED PROVINCES OF THE NETHERLANDS. *See* Dutch Republic.

---

**UNIVERSITIES.** Universities played a vital role in the intellectual life of Europe from 1500 to 1789. They educated the intellectual elite and professional classes of Europe. An enormous number of political and religious leaders obtained university degrees or studied in universities without taking degrees even though the percentage of the population attending universities was extremely low. Universities provided the institutional home in which scholars carried on advanced research and created most of the humanistic, medical, legal, and scientific advances. The period from 1500 to 1650 was an era of unprecedented achievement for universities. They remained important, but to a lesser degree, from 1650 through the end of the eighteenth century.

## CHARACTERISTICS

A university had several linked components. Professors conducted research and taught theology, canon law, civil law, medicine, and the arts subjects of grammar, rhetoric, the classics of ancient Rome and Greece, logic, philosophy, mathematics, and astronomy, plus other subjects on occasion, such as medical botany and Hebrew. Written statutes told them which texts and disciplines to teach. A limited formal academic structure provided rules for instruction and student conduct. Students came, lived, studied, and obtained degrees. The university awarded degrees certifying that the recipient had a high level of expertise in a discipline with the approval of a supreme legal authority, such as emperor, pope, or the ruler of the state in which the university existed.

Europe had forty-seven universities in 1500, then added another twenty-eight new universities that survived by 1650. Thereafter the number of new university foundations slowed considerably, while some older ones were closed or merged. The net gain between 1651 and 1790 was ten, making a total of about eighty-five European universities in 1790. The lands that are now Germany, Italy, France, and Spain had, in that order, the largest number of universities, while another fifteen were to be found in the rest of Europe. Although any designation of the most important universities is open to disagreement, the list would include Bologna, Padua, Pavia, and Pisa in Italy; Paris in France; Cologne and Heidelberg in Germany; Vienna in Austria; Louvain in Belgium; Leiden in the Netherlands; Oxford and Cambridge in England; St. Andrews in Scotland; Alcalá de Henares and Salamanca in Spain; Coimbra in Portugal; and Cracow in Poland.

Universities were not the same across Europe. Universities in northern Europe and Italy differed greatly in the importance given to different disciplines, the level of instruction, and the age of students. Paris and Oxford, the prototypical northern universities, emphasized instruction in arts and theology. Most northern European universities had a majority of young students fourteen to eighteen or nineteen years of age studying for the bachelor's degree in arts, plus a smaller number of advanced students, often future clergymen seeking master's and doctoral degrees in theology. They had a handful of students studying for doctorates in law and medicine. Most northern European universities, especially those in German-speaking lands, had only one or two professors each for medicine and law.

Italian universities emphasized law and medicine at an advanced level and had many professors for these subjects. For example, the University of Bologna had an average of forty professors of law and twenty to twenty-five professors of medicine in the sixteenth century. They taught arts subjects such as logic and philosophy as well as preparation for medicine and law. But they taught little theology and did not award bachelor's degrees. The greatest number of students obtained doctorates in law, the next largest number doctorates of medicine, followed distantly by students winning doctorates of arts or theology. The master's degree with the right to teach was awarded with the doctoral degree without a separate examination. Students at Italian universities were typically eighteen to twenty-five years of age. Because of the emphasis on law and medicine at the doctoral level, many northern Europeans, especially Germans, obtained bachelor's degrees in the north, then came to Italy to obtain doctoral degrees in these disciplines.

The size of universities varied greatly, partly because the age of students differed. Paris, with an estimated 12,000 to 20,000 students, most of them young, was undoubtedly the largest university. Up to 500 teachers, the vast majority in arts instructing younger students while studying for advanced degrees, taught at Paris. Salamanca also had several thousand mostly younger students. The University of Bologna, the largest Italian university, had about ninety professors and 1,500 to 2,000 students, all studying for doctorates, in the sixteenth century. But the vast majority of universities were smaller: thirty to forty professors taught 300 to 800 students. Some universities had only ten to twenty professors teaching 100 to 300 students. Student enrollment fluctuated from decade to decade as war, disease, and the presence or absence of a famous professor caused students to move from one university to another. Students frequently began at one university and took a degree at a second or third. They could do this easily because the texts studied were the same from university to university, and all lectures, texts, disputations, and examinations were in Latin.

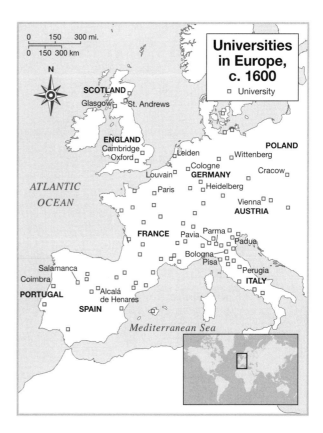

**Universities in Europe, c. 1600**
□ University

A course met five days a week, typically Monday, Tuesday, Wednesday, Friday, and Saturday, with the professor lecturing for an hour or longer. In a typical lecture, the professor began by reading a section from a standard authority, such as a scientific work of Aristotle, a medical text of Galen (c. 130–c. 200), a legal passage from the *Corpus iuris civilis,* the collection of ancient Roman law, or the New Testament for theology. The students sitting on benches normally had copies of the text or passages. The professor next delivered a detailed analysis of the text, explaining how it should be interpreted, rejecting some interpretations, reconciling others, bringing to bear other texts, and explaining its larger meaning. He might range far beyond the original text. This was the heart of university instruction. In due time the professor published these detailed analyses of authoritative texts. Other professors used them in their own research and teaching or published contrary interpretations. Students taking notes and annotating the passage in their own copies had useful professional information, such as a full explanation of a legal text and guidance about how it might be used in cases. The lecture concluded with questions and answers between students and professors. They sometimes moved into the piazza or atrium for this less formal part of teaching.

Another important academic exercise was the disputation. A student or professor posted a notice announcing that he would defend a series of positions in his discipline at a certain time and place. Anyone was free to come and argue. Disputations offered practice in learned argument, which was considered a valuable skill in all disciplines and professions. For medical students, the annual public anatomy was also essential. Students stood in tightly packed rows to watch as a dissector cut open a body as a professor explained the organs. Public anatomies were scheduled for the coldest time of the year and went on without stop until the body putrefied days and weeks later.

After three or four years of study, the student presented himself before a committee of examining professors as a candidate for the bachelor's degree. Examinations for the doctoral degree were more complex. After four to seven years of additional study, the candidate presented himself to an examining committee, appointed by a college of doctors of law, medicine, arts, or theology. Colleges of doctors consisted of professors and other local men holding doctoral degrees in a subject. A typical examination required the student to explain several passages (called *puncta* or points) chosen at random from the required texts in the discipline, followed by wide-ranging questions from the examiners. A candidate for a medical degree might also be required to give his opinion on a medical case proposed to him. Students who satisfied the examiners of their competence were awarded doctoral degrees recognizing them to be experts in a subject and authorized to teach it. The degree was conferred in public ceremonies marked by much rejoicing and considerable expense.

### HUMANISM

The introduction of humanism was the most important curricular change in the sixteenth century, and it involved much more than teaching the literary and historical classics of ancient Rome and Greece in their original languages. Humanists and professors with humanistic training transformed the study of several disciplines because they used their linguistic and historical skills and critical outlook of hu-

manism in their research and teaching. The use of the Greek text of Aristotle and ancient commentaries in place of medieval commentaries offered new insights in philosophy. The rediscovery of ancient mathematical texts aided mathematicians, including Galileo Galilei (1564–1642), a professor of mathematics at the University of Pisa (1589–1592) and the University of Padua (1592–1610). Applying the techniques of humanistic textual criticism to the *Corpus iuris civilis* led to a better understanding of the historical context of Roman law. Called humanistic jurisprudence, this new approach had great influence in French and German universities but little in Italian universities.

Humanism had the greatest impact in medicine through a series of developments sometimes called "medical humanism." Professors of medicine used humanistic skills to examine the medical texts of Galen and other ancients in the original Greek. They found the medieval Latin translations of Galen wanting, so they produced better Latin translations for classroom use. Their enhanced understanding of the texts soon led them to find fault with Galen himself. The medical humanists also placed greater emphasis on anatomical study achieved through more frequent and more knowledgeable dissections of human bodies. Italian universities added professorships of medical botany in order to improve the study of the medicinal properties of plants. The universities of Padua and Pisa simultaneously founded the first university botanical gardens in 1543. Henceforward, students came to the garden in springtime to examine plants and learn about their medicinal properties. Clinical medicine began in the 1540s when a Paduan professor took students to hospitals in order to lecture on a disease at the bedside of the ill patient. Even though universities remained dedicated to lecturing on authoritative texts, these innovations gave greater emphasis to hands-on study, a tendency that continued in the following centuries. Universities in Italy, especially Padua, pioneered the changes in teaching and research, while universities elsewhere quickly followed.

In many northern European universities, especially in Germany, the introduction of humanists and humanistic studies into universities at the beginning of the sixteenth century produced bitter conflict with theologians. The fundamental issue was, how should the sacred texts of Christianity be studied and interpreted? The theologians answered by traditional medieval Scholastic methods, using the tools of logic, the philosophical framework of Aristotle, and guidance from Thomas Aquinas, Duns Scotus, and other great medieval theologians. Only in this way could God's truth be uncovered and error avoided. The humanists answered, not through Scholasticism and medieval commentaries, but through careful linguistic, grammatical, and rhetorical analysis of the texts in their original language, Latin, Greek, or Hebrew. This enabled man to understand God's personal message and to be persuaded to follow him. The two sides fought bitterly. The humanists heaped scorn on university theologians for confusing the word of God with man's interpretations, while the Scholastic theologians dismissed the humanists as grammarians lacking the theological training to understand what they read. The differences were great, because the stakes were university positions in this life and salvation in the next. The advent of the Protestant Reformation exacerbated the conflict as many, but not all, younger German humanists joined Luther while older humanists and most Scholastic theologians remained Catholic. In Italian universities, by contrast, humanists and the few theologians who taught in universities there mostly ignored each other.

The sixteenth was a century of enormous achievement for universities. It is difficult to name another century in which university professors produced so much important scholarship. Numerous major religious leaders also held university professorships. Martin Luther (1483–1546), professor of theology at the modest, newly founded (1502), and geographically isolated University of Wittenberg, began a religious revolution. His chief lieutenant, Philipp Melanchthon (1497–1560), was a professor of Greek at Wittenberg. And many of their Catholic opponents were professors. Leaders with university training from other areas of life were equally important.

The eruption of the Protestant Reformation had both negative and positive impact on universities. Enrollment initially dropped sharply in German universities, especially those in lands that became Lutheran. But enrollment recovered by the end of the sixteenth century, and a few new universities, both Catholic and Protestant, were established. Despite their differences, students continued to move from university to university across religious boundaries. For example, German Protestant students continued to study and to get degrees in law from the Italian universities in Bologna, Padua, Pavia, and Perugia because the most famous professors of law taught there and because Italian civil governments protected them from prosecution for their religious beliefs.

## DECLINE: 1650 TO 1790

Universities continued to lead Europe in research and training leaders into the seventeenth century. But then new and different institutions of higher education rose to challenge them.

Protestants needed schools to train their clergymen in the new doctrines. Catholic universities obviously would not do this, and establishing new Protestant universities was difficult and expensive. Hence, small schools for theology and arts sprang up in the Protestant world. The Calvinist Genevan Academy (founded in 1559) was a famous example. It had seven or eight teachers for theology, Greek, Hebrew, arts, and law. The majority of the graduates became ministers. Some of these new schools sought to become universities teaching a broad range of subjects, but few succeeded.

In the Catholic world the new religious orders of the Catholic Reformation, led by the Jesuits, did the same on a much larger scale. The Society of Jesus, founded in 1540, originally established schools to train boys aged ten to sixteen in the humanities. A handful of Jesuit schools began to add upper-level classes in philosophy and theology in order to train members of the society. These schools, which were open to lay students, proved to be very popular because the Jesuits were excellent scholars and teachers and because the schools were free. Thus, a growing number of Jesuit schools with classes in logic, metaphysics, natural philosophy, mathematics, and theology appeared. Occasionally a Jesuit school also offered an introductory law course. Other religious orders of the Catholic Reformation followed the lead of the Jesuits.

Prodded by princes, the Jesuits also established boarding schools for noble boys and youths from about the ages of ten to twenty. These schools added classes in French, dancing, and horsemanship, all necessary skills for sons of the ruling classes, to the humanities, philosophy, and religion classes. Schools for nobles offering the opportunity to mix with peers attracted students who would otherwise have attended universities. They were expensive, but so were universities. Other Catholic Reformation religious orders again imitated the Jesuits.

Religious order schools offered a structured education in a morally upright and safe environment. By contrast, universities had loosely organized curricula, a licentious life style, and brawling students. Most university students carried swords, and many carried firearms. It is small wonder that many parents preferred religious schools, especially the boarding schools, for their sons. For example, the school for nobles at Parma, founded in 1601, rose from 550 students in 1605 to 905 in 1660, and a minority of the students were non-Italian. Approximately one-third of the students attended the higher classes, which duplicated the first year or two of university studies. Every young male from the ages of eighteen to twenty who attended a religious order school was a possible enrollment loss for universities. Protestant lands also established numerous highly regarded and socially selective schools that taught part of the arts curriculum of universities.

Learned societies offered intellectual and financial competition to universities needing scholars. A famous example was the Royal Society of London for the Advancement of Natural Knowledge, founded in 1662. Financially underwritten by member subscriptions, it supported scientific research, provided opportunities for contacts with other scholars, and published the results of research. Learned societies proliferated. Most Continental societies received funding from governments; some offered salaries to members who carried on studies in mathematics, astronomy, chemistry, and other subjects. And they did not have to teach. Overall, scientific societies offered attractive nonuniversity alternatives to scholars needing support. Scientific societies created an international network enabling scholars in a discipline to communicate their research.

The philosophes of the eighteenth-century Enlightenment attacked universities as not useful to society. They judged the traditional university curriculum to be incapable of training citizens to contribute knowledge to improve the state. So they persuaded rulers to create new, specialized institutions of higher learning to teach practical subjects, such as agricultural technology, engineering, military tactics, surgery, even the fine arts. These highly specialized and practically oriented schools competed with universities for students.

Some of the criticism of the philosophes was justified, but much was not. Universities had kept up with innovations in learning. Although Latin remained the common language of instruction and writing, and universities continued to teach traditional subjects, they had added professorships in new subjects such as history and geography. They had discarded Aristotelian science in favor of Galileo's mathematical physics and had then adopted experimental science, all in the course of a century. And university research in medicine continued to lead the way, as university professors produced all of the important medical advances of the seventeenth and eighteenth centuries. Professors in traditional subjects produced nontraditional works of scholarship. For example, Adam Smith (1723–1790), who taught logic and moral philosophy at the University of Glasgow from 1751 to 1764, produced *An Inquiry into the Nature and Causes of the Wealth of Nations* in 1776. Universities continued to award degrees certifying that the lawyer, judge, physician, clergyman, teacher, and civil servant were qualified to practice their professions. Learned societies, religious schools, and specialized schools could not do this. Overall, universities played essential intellectual and social leadership roles in European life that no other institution could replace.

*See also* **Academies, Learned; Classicism; Clergy; Education; Enlightenment; Humanists and Humanism; Latin; Law; Literacy and Reading; Medicine; Printing and Publishing; Reformation, Protestant.**

BIBLIOGRAPHY

Brockliss, L. W. B. *French Higher Education in the Seventeenth and Eighteenth Centuries: A Cultural History.* Oxford, 1987. Comprehensive study.

Curtis, Mark H. *Oxford and Cambridge in Transition 1558–1642: An Essay on Changing Relations between the English Universities and English Society.* Oxford, 1959.

De Ridder-Symoens, Hilde, ed. *A History of the University in Europe.* Vol. 2, *Universities in Early Modern Europe (1500–1800).* Cambridge, U.K., 1996. Information on all aspects of universities with emphasis on general patterns and the university in society. Good on northern universities.

Farge, James K. *Orthodoxy and Reform in Early Reformation France: The Faculty of Theology of Paris, 1500–1543.* Leiden, 1985. A detailed study of the personnel and activities of the major Catholic theological faculty.

Grendler, Paul F. *The Universities of the Italian Renaissance.* Baltimore and London, 2002. Comprehensive study of Italy's sixteen universities, 1400–1625, with extensive bibliography.

*History of Universities.* Avebury and Oxford, 1981–. Annual volume founded by the late Charles B. Schmitt. Includes articles, bibliographical surveys of recent research, and reviews.

Jurriaanse, M. W. *The Founding of Leyden University.* Leiden, 1965.

Maag, Karin. *Seminary or University? The Genevan Academy and Reformed Higher Education, 1560–1620.* Aldershot, U.K., and Brookfield, Vt., 1995. Important for Calvinist influence plus the universities of Heidelberg and Leiden.

McConica, James K., ed. *The History of the University of Oxford.* Vol. 3, *The Collegiate University.* Oxford, 1986. Excellent study of all aspects of Oxford between 1485 and 1603.

Rummel, Erika. *The Humanist-Scholastic Debate in the Renaissance and Reformation.* Cambridge, Mass., and London, 1995. Study of the battles between humanists and Scholastics, mostly in Germany.

Schmitt, Charles B. *Aristotle and the Renaissance.* Cambridge, Mass., and London, 1983. Short survey describing how Renaissance university scholars approached Aristotle in innovative ways.

Tyacke, Nicholas, ed. *The History of the University of Oxford.* Vol. 4, *Seventeenth-Century Oxford.* Oxford, 1997.

Wear, A., R. K. French, and I. M. Lonie, eds. *The Medical Renaissance of the Sixteenth Century.* Cambridge, U.K., 1985. Excellent collection of studies on medical humanism, anatomy, and other aspects of the medical Renaissance.

PAUL F. GRENDLER

---

# URBAN VIII (POPE)

**URBAN VIII (POPE)** (Maffeo Barberini; 1568–1644; reigned 1623–1644), Italian pope. After studies at Jesuit schools in Florence and Rome, he read law in Pisa (doctorate "in utroque jure" [both canon and civil law] in 1588), and entered the Roman prelature, backed by his uncle Francesco Barberini. He worked at the *Signatura* Tribunal, becoming prothonotary apostolic upon his uncle's resignation (1593) and then clerk of the Apostolic Chamber (1599). In 1592, his countryman Clement VIII appointed him governor of Fano, sending him later on important diplomatic missions. In 1604, he was consecrated titular archbishop of Nazareth and sent as nuncio to Paris. In this capacity, he was able to gain support for the Jesuits in France, but could not secure acceptance of the Tridentine decrees. Created cardinal by Paul V in 1606, he returned to Rome (1607), soon to be appointed bishop of Spoleto, a charge he held until 1617, adding for a time (1611–1614) the legation to Bologna. In both positions, he showed himself a strict administrator and a diligent reformer. In 1617, he resigned his diocese and returned to Rome as prefect of the Signatura Tribunal. A member of several important Roman congregations, he was also active in the intellectual and artistic circles of the city. His election to the papacy in the summer of 1623 was the result of a compromise between the different factions that supported stronger candidates, although he was perceived as favorable to France.

Soon after his elevation to the see of Peter, he manifested his intention to take charge as both a spiritual and a secular leader. This he achieved through nepotism, elevating to the cardinalate his brother Antonio and his nephews Francesco and Antonio, and giving administrative positions to his brother, Carlo, and his nephew Taddeo. As "Cardinal Nephew," administrator of the pontifical state, Francesco Barberini was to exert a great influence under the strict control of his uncle. Urban VIII was an absolute pope who wanted to ignore the college of cardinals, which he viewed as overly influenced by European powers (to compensate, the cardinals received the title of "Eminence" in 1630). In order to foster the independence of the Holy See, he strengthened the Papal States, building the stronghold of Castelfranco near Bologna, reinforcing Castel Sant'Angelo in Rome, and fortifying Civitavecchia's harbor. He was able to annex (1625–1631) the duchy of Urbino; however, his attempt to take over neighboring territories in Parma and Piacenza were thwarted by an Italian coalition (1644) that forced him to surrender the cities of Castro and Montalto, which had been occupied by papal forces in 1641.

Urban VIII's pontificate coincided with the Thirty Years' War (1618–1648). From the beginning of his pontificate, he had attempted to maintain a strict neutrality between the Habsburg and the Bourbons (Valtelline War, 1624–1626, War of

**Pope Urban VIII.** Portrait by Gian Lorenzo Bernini. THE ART ARCHIVE/PALAZZO BARBERINI ROME/DAGLI ORTI (A)

the Mantuan Succession, 1627–1631) as "Common Father" of all Catholics. During the war in Germany, he refused to support the imperial armies, seeking through his representatives to influence and control the process of re-Catholicization. Only in 1632 did he intervene by offering limited financial support and seeking diplomatic action. But the Holy See's efforts were hindered by the French alliance with Protestant powers and Urban's rejection of direct negotiation with heretics; on the eve of his death, the pope was able to foster a peace conference at Münster (1644).

On the religious level, Urban VIII took several important decisions. Probably the most famous one was to have his former friend Galileo Galilei prosecuted by the Roman Inquisition in 1633. He had to recant his heliocentric theories and was kept under house arrest until his death in 1642. By the bull *In Eminenti,* dated 1642, but published in 1643, Urban initiated a series of papal interventions in the Jansenist conflict, proscribing both Cornelius Jansenius' book *Augustinus* and the Jesuit theses that attacked it. The Barberini pope is associated with

the reform of the liturgical books (Breviary, Martyrologium, Missal, Pontifical); by revising the beatification and canonization processes he rendered sainthood more difficult to achieve. Urban VIII strengthened and expanded the competence of the *De Propaganda fide* congregation, giving his name to the college established to educate priests for mission territories.

More a prince than a pastor, Urban VIII was criticized during his lifetime for his visions of grandeur as manifested in the art work he commissioned (exemplified by Bernini's baldachin in St. Peter's). He was above all a political pope, whose goal was the independence of the Holy See through a strong papal state and active diplomacy. This goal was not achieved because of Urban VIII's resistance to confessional divisions in Europe and his deep misgivings about Habsburg Spain and Germany.

*See also* **Mantuan Succession, War of the (1627–1631); Papacy and Papal States; Rome; Thirty Years' War (1618–1648).**

BIBLIOGRAPHY

Blet, Pierre. "Un futur Pape, Nonce en France auprès d'Henri IV." *Études* 300 (1959): 203–220.

Fumaroli, Marc. "Cicéron pape: Urbain VIII et la seconde renaissance romaine." In *L'age de l'éloquence,* pp. 202–226. Geneva and Paris, 1980.

Hammond, Frederick. *Music and Spectacle in Baroque Rome: Barberini Patronage under Urban VIII.* New Haven and London, 1994.

Hook, Judith. "Urban VIII. The Paradox of a Spiritual Monarchy." In *The Courts of Europe: Politics, Patronage, and Royalty 1400–1800,* edited by A. G. Dickens, pp. 212–231. London, 1977.

Kraus, Andreas. *Das päpstliche Stadtssekretaria unter Urban VIII 1623–44.* Rome, Freiburg, and Vienna, 1964.

Lutz, G. "Rom und Europa während des Pontifikats Urbans VIII." In *Rom in der Neuzeit: Politische, kirchliche und kulturelle Aspekte,* edited by R. Elze, pp. 71–167. Vienna and Rome, 1976.

Nussdorfer, Lannie. *Civic Politics in the Rome of Urban VIII.* Princeton, 1992.

Scott, John Beldon. *Images of Nepotism: The Painted Ceilings of Palazzo Barberini.* Princeton, 1991.

Von Pastor, Ludwig. *History of the Popes from the End of the Middle-Ages.* Vol. XXVIII–XXIX. London, 1929–1938.

Westfall, Richard S. *Essays on the Trial of Galileo.* Vatican City State, 1989.

JACQUES M. GRES-GAYER

---

## URBAN LIFE. *See* Cities and Urban Life.

---

## URBAN PLANNING. *See* City Planning.

---

## USURY. *See* Interest.

---

**UTOPIA.** The impulse to wonder about a more perfect world is at least as old as Gilgamesh's search for the garden of Dilmun (c. 2500 B.C.E.). The dream of an earthly paradise seems to be widespread among the peoples of the earth, as a way of both imagining the ideal and expressing dissatisfaction with the here and now. Gilgamesh's perilous journey is prompted by his shock at the loss of his boon companion Enkidu and his own looming mortality. The propensity for utopian speculation is in part nostalgia for an idealized human existence, believed in the Islamic and Judeo-Christian tradition to have once existed in a paradise now lost. In times of social and political upheaval, such as existed in early modern Europe, authors also used the ideal for satiric purposes. As a result, utopian literature has flourished as a genre.

The first and most significant work of this kind is Sir Thomas More's *Utopia,* published in Latin at Louvain in 1516 (1551 in the first English translation). In letters to friends, More called his planned work "Nusquama," from the Latin adverb for 'nowhere'; however, when he chose the title, he transliterated the Greek negative *ou* into the Latin *u* and combined it with the Greek *topos* to create a new word, "utopia," or 'nowhere'. In the commendatory letters from his humanist circle printed with early editions of the work, several observed that this country also ought to be called "Eutopia" (from the Greek *eu* for 'good'). Thus "utopian" was seen at once as an intriguing but impossible ideal.

More (1478–1535), who served Henry VIII as an adviser and became chancellor in 1529, wrote his classic in the turbulent years just before the beginning of the Reformation. He cast his imaginative flight in the form of a dialogue, a rhetorical strategy that allowed him to express dissatisfaction with current social conditions while maintaining a comfortable distance rhetorically from such dangerous ideas as the abolition of private property. The first part is a discussion between Raphael Hythloday ('babbler of nonsense'), a mariner who had chanced upon a fabulous land where all goods were held in common, and More himself, about the problems of Christian Europe, which was plagued by greed and corruption. Part two (which was written first) is the actual discussion of the ideal society, where Christianity takes root among the Utopians with surprising ease because it is so consistent with the Utopians' communal way of life. At the end, the character More finally admits that he would like to see some aspects of Utopian society put into practice in England, but states that he believes it is unlikely ever to happen. Ultimately, *Utopia* attempts to negotiate a course between the ideal and the actual and implicitly recognizes that, given the fallibility of mankind, perfection is impossible.

In the aftermath of *Utopia,* which earned great renown for More, other descriptive works appeared that made use of some of the same literary devices: a shipwreck or other chance encounter with an ideal community, followed by a return to Europe. Ortensio Lando and Anton Francesco Doni's collaborative *Eutopia* in 1548 (its full title is *The Newly Discovered Republic of the Government of the Isle of Eutopia*) reverses this scenario by having a Eutopian citizen visit Italy to comment directly upon its excesses, which sparked interest in other utopian imitations.

### CHRISTIAN UTOPIAS OF THE SEVENTEENTH CENTURY
In the seventeenth century Francis Bacon's (1561–1626) advocacy of a "new" science based on inductive reasoning led others to dream of synthesizing human knowledge with religion to produce a universal knowledge, or "pansophia." This "utopian" myth became the driving force for a new vision of a Christian commonwealth. Bacon's utopian work, *The New Atlantis* (written c. 1614 and published posthumously in 1627) was a coda to *The Great*

*Instauration* (1620). It took the form of a voyage to the island of Bensalem, the centerpiece of which is Salomon's House, a research college where the new scientific method leads to discoveries and inventions that greatly enrich the commonwealth. A belief in pansophia had similarly inspired Tommaso Campanella (1568–1639) to put forth his vision of *The City of the Sun* (1623), a sea captain's account of an ideal Christian community, where a single ruler named Sun is assisted by three aides, Power, Knowledge, and Love (with an obvious indebtedness to the Christian Trinity of Father, Son, and Holy Spirit). The role of science is paramount, with the seven concentric walls that ring the city displaying pictorially the unity of all knowledge. By naming these walls for the seven planets orbiting the sun, Campanella clearly stands with Copernicus on the most important scientific debate of the age.

The vision of a Christian commonwealth founded on scientific principles is at the heart of one of the century's more influential utopianists, Johann Valentin Andreae (1586–1654), a Lutheran churchman who produced several works, notably *Christianopolis* (1619, published as *Reipublicae Christianopolitanae Descriptio* [Description of a Christian republic]), which garnered praise from learned readers such as Robert Burton. Framed as a traveler's tale, it describes a Christian city in which an elite brotherhood possesses a secret wisdom and oversees the further exploration of nature's secrets through scientific experimentation. Andreae had been part of a youthful circle at the University of Tübingen that had produced a series of utopian pamphlets around 1610 (*Fama Fraternitatis* and the *Confessio Fraternitatis* [The Fame of the Fraternity and the Confession of the Fraternity]), advocating a Protestant brotherhood to bring about reform within the Lutheran church. These pamphlets caused an extraordinary sensation when published in print, often called the Rosicrucian furor. Andreae's ideas greatly influenced the Moravian reformer Jan Comenius (c. 1592–1670) and passed into England through Samuel Hartlib (c. 1600–1662), who brought out an English translation of another treatise by Andreae (*A Modell of a Christian Society* [London, 1647]) to help reform England in the aftermath of the Civil War. With some justification, the Royal Society (founded in 1660) can be

considered the fruition of the dream of a Baconian research college to aid the commonwealth.

## UTOPIAN THOUGHT AMONG THE PHILOSOPHES

The rationalists of the Enlightenment who helped prepare the way for the revolutions of 1776 and 1789 did not produce any recognized utopian classics. There were, however, utopian elements in various works, such as Fénelon's *Adventures of Telemachus* (1699), Montesquieu's *Persian Letters* (1721), the sketch of El Dorado in Voltaire's *Candide* (1759), and Condorcet's *Esquisse* (1794), that were influential at the time.

*See also* **Bacon, Francis; Condorcet, Marie-Jean Caritat, marquis de; Fénelon, François; Montesquieu, Charles-Louis de Secondat de; More, Thomas; Philosophes; Progress; Rosicrucianism; Voltaire.**

BIBLIOGRAPHY

*Primary Sources*

Andreae, Johann Valentin. *Christianopolis.* Introduced and translated by Edward H. Thompson. International Archives of the History of Ideas, vol. 162. Dordrecht and London, 1999.

Bacon, Sir Francis. *The New Atlantis and the Great Instauration.* Edited by Jerry Weinberger. Arlington Heights, Ill., 1989.

Campanella, Tommaso. *The City of the Sun.* Translated by Daniel J. Donno. Berkeley, 1981.

More, Thomas. *Utopia.* Translated by Edward Surtz. New Haven, 1964.

*Secondary Sources*

Dickson, Donald R. *The Tessera of Antilia: Utopian Brotherhoods & Secret Societies in the Early Seventeenth Century.* Brill's Studies in Intellectual History, vol. 88. Leiden, New York, and Cologne, 1998.

Manuel, Frank E., and Fritzie P. Manuel. *Utopian Thought in the Western World.* Cambridge, Mass., 1979.

Negley, Glenn. *Utopian Literature: A Bibliography with a Supplementary Listing of Works Influential in Utopian Thought.* Lawrence, Kans., 1977.

DONALD R. DICKSON

# UTRECHT, PEACE OF (1713).

The Peace of Utrecht consisted of twenty-three treaties and conventions that ended the War of the Spanish Succession (1701–1714). Most, but not all, were signed in Utrecht in the Netherlands in 1713.

France and Austria ended hostilities with the Treaty of Rastatt in March 1714; the Treaty of Baden (September 1714) ended war between France and the Holy Roman Empire; Portugal and Spain concluded negotiations in Madrid in February 1715. Austria and the empire did not sign treaties with Spain until 1725, despite the cessation of fighting a decade before, largely because of Habsburg unwillingness to concede the Bourbon succession in Spain.

The contested Spanish succession fed fears of French hegemony after a Bourbon prince, Philip d'Anjou, grandson of Louis XIV, became Philip V of Spain in 1700. A Grand Alliance, comprising England, the Dutch Republic, Austria, and many smaller European powers, commenced war against France and Spain in 1702. Particularistic complaints underlying the allies' shared concerns made peace elusive. The French troops' occupation of towns in the southern Netherlands in 1701 threatened the security of the Dutch Republic. The English and Dutch feared French trade restrictions in Spanish

America after France received an *asiento* ('contract') to supply slaves to Spanish colonies, in 1701. An Austrian Habsburg prince, Archduke Charles, second son of Emperor Leopold I (ruled 1658–1705), was Philip V's chief rival for the Spanish throne.

Attempts at peace commenced in 1706 but faltered repeatedly. Negotiators failed to craft terms acceptable to multiple parties, and the fickle fortunes of war frequently reconfigured bargaining positions. In 1710, a change of government in Britain broke the impasse. War-weary Britons voted out the Whigs, and a Tory ministry headed by Robert Harley assumed power. Henry St. John, a new secretary of state, abandoned multilateral negotiations for bilateral negotiations with the French, and soon Britain and France had cut deals that promised peace but compromised the interests of Britain's allies.

On 29 January 1712, an international congress convened in Utrecht to negotiate a general peace between France and some members of the Grand Alliance. St. John wanted the semblance of a general

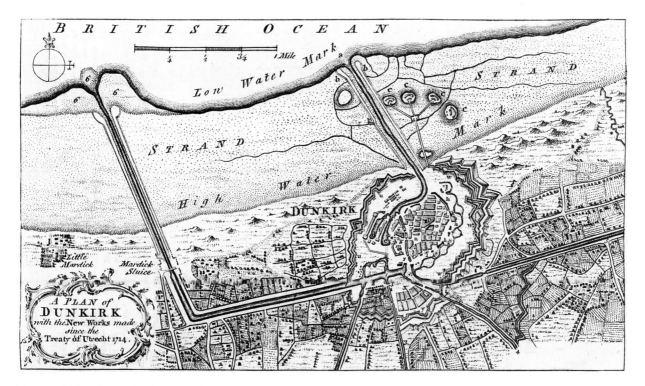

**Peace of Utrecht.** Under the treaty, France promised to demolish the fortifications at Dunkirk which were used as a base for attacks on English and Dutch shipping. This map from the October 1758 issue of *London Magazine* accompanied an article that accused the French of violating the treaty by refortifying the city: "It is too notorious, with how much chicanery they have been stealing work upon work, at this place, contrary to the most solemn engagements to the contrary." MAP COLLECTION, STERLING MEMORIAL LIBRARY, YALE UNIVERSITY settlement, even if most negotiating was bilateral rather than in congressional sessions. One of Britain's war aims was a balance of power in Europe, a goal that St. John suspected the French did not heartily support. A general peace between France and the allies, he believed, would forward that goal more than would a separate peace between France and Britain. By early 1713, the plenipotentiaries of Britain, the Dutch Republic, Savoy, Portugal, and Prussia had agreed to terms with France, and on 11 April signed treaties ending their participation in the war.

Spanish involvement in the congress was delayed until the April treaties acknowledged Philip V and his delegates' rights to negotiate for Spain, but treaties with some allies soon followed. Representatives from Austria and the empire left Utrecht without treaties because of unresolved differences with France or Spain. The Spanish succession remained their primary stumbling block, but its context had changed dramatically between 1702 and 1713. During those years, two Austrian emperors had died, Leopold I in 1705 and Joseph I in 1711. Archduke Charles, the contender for the Spanish throne as Charles III, was crowned Emperor Charles VI. In the Bourbon line, deaths claimed the French dauphin in 1711, putting Philip V of Spain fourth in line for the French throne. Two Bourbon deaths in 1712 left only a sickly boy between Philip and the French throne. These untimely deaths left both Charles and Philip with multiple dynastic claims, which, as the primary Spanish claimants, made them unattractive to many powers unless they renounced some of them. In 1712, Philip V renounced his French claims, which five allies, but not Austria and the empire, recognized in 1713.

The Peace of Utrecht redefined numerous dynastic conflicts. In addition to Philip V of Spain's renunciation of his French claims, the dukes of Berry and Orléans and their heirs were excluded from claims to the Spanish throne, thus precluding a future royal union of France and Spain. International acknowledgment of Philip V effectively ended a possible Habsburg union of Austria and Spain. France recognized the Protestant succession in Britain and agreed that the Stuart Pretender, James Francis Edward Stuart, and his heirs could not live on French soil. Frederick William I was acknowledged as king of Prussia. The house of Savoy re-

ceived Sicily from Spain (despite Austria's claim), and assurances that, if the Spanish Bourbon line failed, the Savoy line would succeed it. Emperor Charles VI received the other Spanish territories in Italy and the Netherlands. These arrangements curbed the hegemonic tendencies of dynastic unions, elevated state and national interests, and made a balance of power a shared European objective, if not a reality.

Colonial and commercial issues figured prominently in the Peace of Utrecht. France returned Rio de Janeiro in Brazil to Portugal and agreed to clarify the border between Portugal's and France's American claims. Rather than cede Iberian border towns, Spain gave Sacramento in South America to Portugal and acknowledged its Brazilian claims. France ceded Newfoundland, Acadia, St. Christopher, and the Hudson Bay territory to Britain, but insisted on exclusive seasonal shore rights in Newfoundland to exploit the cod fishery. The Anglo-Spanish treaty protected Spain's interest in the Newfoundland fishery. Spain transferred the *asiento* from France to Britain for thirty years, and allowed British trading stations on the Río de la Plata in South America. Gibraltar and Minorca, former Spanish possessions, guaranteed British commercial access in the Mediterranean.

Despite the achievements of the Peace of Utrecht, British machinations by Henry St. John, backed by Robert Harley, haunted European affairs for decades. In Britain, vitriolic criticism of St. John and Harley's treatment of allies forced both men into exile. British disregard of Dutch interests probably sped the Dutch Republic's decline as a European power. British abandonment of the Catalans left them vulnerable to Philip V's revenge for their support of the Grand Alliance. Newfoundland fishing concessions incensed opposition critics in Britain, and created international tensions that continue to the present. A fortified barrier in the southern Netherlands failed to hold back French forces in 1745, and festering boundary disputes in the colonies fueled the conflicts leading to the Seven Years' War. All contributed to the contested legacy of the Peace of Utrecht.

*See also* **Bourbon Dynasty (France); Bourbon Dynasty (Spain); Charles III (Spain); Frederick William I (Prussia); Habsburg Dynasty; Philip V (Spain);**

Seven Years' War (1756–1763); Spain; Spanish Succession, War of the (1701–1714).

BIBLIOGRAPHY

Frey, Linda, and Marsha Frey, eds. *The Treaties of the War of the Spanish Succession: An Historical and Critical Dictionary.* Westport, Conn., and London, 1995.

Hattendorf, John B. *England in the War of the Spanish Succession: A Study of the English View and Conduct of Grand Strategy, 1702–1712.* New York and London, 1987.

Kamen, Henry. *The War of Succession in Spain 1700–1715.* Bloomington, Ind., and London, 1969.

Pitt, H. G. "The Pacification of Utrecht." In *The New Cambridge Modern History,* Vol. 6: *The Rise of Great Britain and Russia, 1688–1715/25,* edited by J. S. Bromley, pp. 446–479. Cambridge, U.K., 1970.

ELIZABETH MANCKE

**VAGRANTS AND BEGGARS.** With the increase in the ranks of paupers in the late fifteenth and early sixteenth centuries, contemporary legislation began to discriminate between the deserving and the undeserving poor. The definition of the "true" poor (children, the aged, the sick, and the infirm) reflected the new policy of early modern governments all over Europe of refusing to recognize unemployment per se as an excuse for beggary. The magistrates held that, apart from those who were rendered incapable of earning a living by age or physical condition, all who begged should be considered willful idlers and treated severely. It was therefore declared that the beggary of the able-bodied poor was criminal. The intention was to help those unable to take care of themselves, whereas able-bodied persons unwilling to work were not entitled to poor relief, but, on the contrary, were subject to a variety of disciplinary measures. The dangerous poor were, according to a stereotype that developed in the sixteenth and seventeenth centuries, typically rootless, masterless, and homeless. The beggar who took to a life of crime, and abused the conventions of a Christian society of "orders" and "callings," became defined as a member of a deviant subculture, who had to be punished. In its justification of these punishments, which became even more severe during the seventeenth and eighteenth centuries, governments stressed the connection between beggary and criminality.

The equation between begging and crime became a commonplace in poor law legislation from the sixteenth century onward. It was used to justify harsh but futile measures against those who supposedly showed an ingrained laziness and a stubborn preference for living from charity, and, inevitably, went astray, becoming used in the end to a disorderly and criminal style of life (vagrancy, theft, smuggling, and prostitution).

### THE GROWING NUMBERS OF BEGGARS AND VAGRANTS

Vagrancy was a socially defined offense that reflects the dual problem of geographical and social mobility in early modern Europe. Offenders were arrested and punished not because of their actions, but because of their marginal position in society. The implication was that vagrants were not ordinary criminals but were regarded as a major threat to society, and therefore pursued by all authorities and stigmatized as deviants. The offense of which they were accused posed a serious challenge to the moral and physical well-being of the Christian commonwealth. Vagrants should not be confused with the outsiders known in medieval Germany as *fahrende Leute,* 'wayfarers'. Those included a variety of people, from wandering scholar to minstrels and knifegrinders. Many of them were engaged in itinerant trades or professions whose form of work involved wandering (entertainers, transient healers, hawkers, tinkers). They were also despised, ridiculed, stigmatized, and marginalized, but not prosecuted for their deviant way of life.

During the course of the fifteenth century a new social phenomenon grew up alongside these traditional "vagrants": the fraudulent beggar and the idle, sturdy vagabond. Their advent caused governments to react accordingly. In early modern Württemberg, for example, all officials were put on alert for idle vagrants from 1495, and by 1508 those arrested were increasingly charged with "suspicious wandering." The legal concept of vagabondage is based on the distinction between able-bodied and "impotent" poor, which had been propagated by the critiques of the traditional view of poverty since the later Middle Ages, but was only fully accepted by governments of all persuasions from the sixteenth century onward. The ideological underpinning was provided by the rhetorical flourishes of humanists and preachers and the attacks upon vagrants in popular literature.

The omnibus statutory definitions of vagrancy, and even those found in the learned or popular tradition, were not purely theoretical. Not every offender, of course, showed all the characteristics of the stereotype, nor were these traits absolutely necessary for prosecutions or arrests to take place. According to contemporary sources the number of vagrants had been increasing over the sixteenth century, but it is difficult to substantiate these estimates statistically. The clearest evidence of a real growth in vagrancy during the early modern period is the figures that refer to people who were arrested, convicted, or punished for vagrancy alone, and not for any other crime. In late-sixteenth-century England, vagrants numbering only in the hundreds were found in the special searches after the Rising in the North (1571–1572), while sixty years later reports to the Privy Council recorded the local arrest and punishment of many thousands of wandering rogues and sturdy beggars (nearly 25,000 in thirty-two English counties between 1631 and 1639). It is likely that the number of people that could be labeled as vagrants continued to increase well into the seventeenth century, not only in England but also in other European countries. But there was worse to come. In the eighteenth century vagrancy was exacerbated not only by deteriorating demographic and economic conditions but also by growing government efforts to eradicate the problem. Comparative statistics for the total number of vagabonds in various European countries are complicated by the variety of ways in which vagrants could be punished. Despite numerous uncertainties, it is possible, for

example, to compare the number of people detained as vagrants (broadly defined) and interned in "houses of correction" or *dépôts de mendicité* in England and France, respectively, in the later eighteenth century. While in England three to four thousand vagrants and idlers were interned annually, the French police arrested in the same period (1770s and 1780s) between ten and thirteen thousand vagrants each year. Comparing the rates of internment for every 10,000 inhabitants in the two countries, shows that, as far the repression of vagrancy was concerned, the French government was obviously more successful and its police more efficient in enforcing the vagrancy laws that had been in force in both countries since the sixteenth century. These numerical results are thus quite significant in terms of the capabilities of the two most powerful eighteenth-century European states and their respective policing organizations, but there can be no doubt that other countries made similar efforts to suppress vagrancy.

## THE STRUCTURE OF VAGRANCY

The sources also tell us something about the structure of vagrancy. Vagrants were more mobile and traveled longer distances than other migrants. According to an English study, the large majority of apprentices and journeymen moved less than forty miles, while among the vagrants whose place of origin can be determined, more than seventy percent had gone farther; a substantial number of them (22 percent) had even covered a distance of more than one hundred miles. It is often impossible to state the average age of those arrested as vagrants, because of the incompleteness of the data. The few statistics that we have for the sixteenth to eighteenth centuries, however, leave no doubt that vagrancy was mainly a young person's crime. In Tudor and Stuart England the proportion of vagrants below age twenty-one declined from 67 to 47 percent in the years 1623–1639 as compared to 1570–1622, but was still rather high. Most vagabonds were single and male. That is precisely the group that is underrepresented in listings of the resident respectable poor. The vagrants were distinguished from the latter also in being predominantly young.

Almost unanimously, contemporary observers and legislators assumed that vagabonds chose to be unemployed. The evidence of vagabonds' previous and present occupations suggests that unemployment was a growing problem and that opportunities were contracting, and that as a result the poor were taking up less secure positions such as casual labor, soldiery, and entertainment, which had at that time close links with vagabondage. According to a study on the profile of vagrancy in England in the sixteenth and seventeenth centuries, roughly one-third of all vagabonds who could report work histories were engaged in the production of food, leather goods, or cloth and metal wares, or in mining or building; at least one-quarter were servants, apprentices, journeymen, laborers, and harvest workers; almost one-fifth were petty tradesmen and tinkers; and one-tenth were soldiers and mariners. This profile of occupations is strikingly similar to that established for vagrants arrested in eighteenth-century Bavaria. The other major group that figures prominently in the German reports of arrest was a medley of tramping artisans and members of "dangerous trades," consisting largely of flayers and knackers' men and their families.

All these features and social traits provided ample grounds for abhorrence of the idle rogue and sturdy beggar and for his accidental confusion with the simple migrant or pauper.

### STIGMATIZATION

In early modern legislation the sturdy beggar was characterized as the incarnation of idleness. Flogging, branding, hard labor in the galleys, and all other penalties introduced against begging and vagrancy that involved public disgrace, were justified because they were meant to constrain the poor from following their unlawful and unchristian inclinations and impel them toward their moral and social duty, that is, to work. Branding and ear boring were ritual punishments that left everlasting marks of infamy on the body of the offender. According to the Edwardian statute of 1547 vagrants were to branded with a V on their breasts. Ear-boring is first mentioned in a statute passed in 1572. In France beggars and vagrants brought to court were subjected to the ritual of corporal punishment including branding (M for *mendiant*, V for *vagabond*) and public flogging. Both police and judges examined suspects' bodies for the marks of branding and whipping when they took their disposition. Sometimes the most obscure mark (e.g., the fact that a patch of skin on the

shoulder was lighter and of different texture from the rest) was used as proof of a criminal record.

Further forms of corporal punishment for deviant paupers included hair polling, the pillory, and ear cropping. Each of these rituals implied various degrees of public disgrace. The pillory, for example, had been employed against fraudulent beggars since the late Middle Ages. Other forms of degrading punishments for vagrants were of local origin, as for example the "ducking-stool," which was in use in some early modern English towns. This was a special instrument of punishment for prostitutes or dishonest tradesmen but also for other offenders, consisting of a chair in which an offender was tied and exposed to public derision or ducked in water.

Whipping, branding, and ear boring were for a long time and until the eighteenth century the easiest way of dealing with sturdy beggars and vagabonds. Whether these corporal punishments alleviated the problem of poverty and its concomitant, vagrancy, is doubtful. But it had at least one great advantage: it gave the local governments the feeling that they were at least doing something against the rising number of "masterless men" on the road.

### EXPULSION

Local authorities rather seldom used their legislative powers to lock up the wandering or deviant poor (confinement) or to restrict their freedom to move within the municipal area (segregation). More often than not, magistrates turned to the ancient remedy of expulsion. There was almost no town in early modern Europe that at one time or another did not prohibit begging and order the removal of all sturdy beggars and vagabonds. Gatekeepers and constables were admonished to redouble their efforts in order to keep the unwelcome poor outside the city. Some municipalities (e.g., Cologne and Bordeaux) were less successful in barring foreign beggars from entering the city because of the lack of police forces and gaps in their fortification systems. Other European cities managed better in keeping an eye on the floating populations.

In view of the various weaknesses connected with the expulsion or mass banishments of beggars, national governments tried more effective forms of removal for outcast rogues and sturdy beggars. In England the transportation of vagabonds to the colonies dates back to Elizabeth I's reign. The Vagrancy Act of 1597 stipulated that dangerous rogues should be banished overseas. A Privy Council order of 1603 mentioned various destinations: Newfoundland, the East and West Indies, France, Germany, Spain, and the Low Countries. Most of those exiled for vagrancy and other crimes were, however, sent to the American colonies.

## THE GREAT CONFINEMENT

Compared to stigmatizing corporal punishment and other traditional measures of social control such as expulsion and transportation, a new reformative policy of punishment in the form of so-called proto-penal institutions offered the authorities a kind of control over the offender without abusing his body. One should not forget, however, that despite this humanitarian impetus, in most "bridewells," houses of correction, or similar institutions founded in many European countries during the late sixteenth and early seventeenth centuries, chaining and beating of the inmates were common practice until the end of the *ancien régime.*

The most distinctive product of early modern thinking on social welfare was the creation of a new kind of hospital. The practice of confining beggars in jail-like institutions certainly gained favor in the eighteenth century, but as a means of providing work for the needy and punishing the disreputable and deviant, it had a long history, dating back to the second half of the sixteenth century. In 1553 Edward VI, influenced by Bishop Nicolas Ridley, conveyed an old, decayed palace, the Bridewell, to the city of London, for the purpose of safekeeping, punishing, and setting to work the idle poor and vagabonds. Other English towns (such as Norwich and Ipswich) followed in the 1560s. The poor-relief act of 1576 ordered the establishment of so-called houses of correction in all counties and corporate towns of the realm. In this prototype of an institution that was later to become known as the "workhouse," punishment by imprisonment was given a new importance. This means that labor was, for the first time, introduced as corrective discipline. The English statutes of 1576, 1597, and 1610 all listed punishment, work, and discipline as reasons for the establishment of such houses.

At about the same time when Bridewell became the English model for a new type of institution to combat vagabondage, the magistrates of the city of Amsterdam decided to establish a *tuchthuis* for men, to be followed by a similar institution for women known as a *spinhuis.* The name of the institution derived from the type of labor the inmates were compelled to perform. The men were forced to chop and rasp Brazilian dyewood, while the women and young children were required to spin, knit, or sew. The reformative program attached great importance to personal hygiene, industriousness, and piety.

The foundation of the Amsterdam *tuchthuis* was a landmark in the history of a vast program of social engineering, known since Michel Foucault's work in this field as "the Great Confinement." Whether or not one agrees with Foucault's theory of continuity of incarceration and the common disciplinary features of workhouses, asylums, prisons, and factories, there can be little doubt that all those institutions attempted to repress vagrancy and mendicity by segregating and putting to work those caught begging without permission. In the sixteenth century, labor still had strong religious-moral connotations as a remedy against sinful idleness. By the seventeenth century, when the workhouse movement had gained momentum all over Europe, the earlier quality of labor as the means to fight the supposed main cause of poverty (idleness) had been overlaid by a more pragmatic concept in which confinement and compulsory labor were seen as the appropriate instrument to punish and correct beggars and other deviants. Consequently, the workhouse became the distinctive feature of poor relief right to the nineteenth century, even if this English institution and its European adaptations and mutations failed to meet the high expectations of contemporaries.

*See also* **Charity and Poor Relief; Crime and Punishment; Poverty.**

BIBLIOGRAPHY

Ammerer, Gerhard. *Vaganten ohne Lyrik: Studien zur devianten, nichtsesshaften Lebensweise in Österreich 1750–1800—Ursachen und (Überlebens-) Strategien.* Habilitationsschrift. University of Salzburg, 2000.

Beier, A. L. *Masterless Men. The Vagrancy Problem in England 1560–1640.* London and New York, 1985.

Cubero, José. *Histoire du vagabondage: du Moyen Age à nos jours.* Paris, 1998.

Dartiguenave, Paul. *Vagabonds et mendiants en Normandie entre assistance et répression: histoire du vagabondage et de la mendicité du XVIIIe au XXe siècle.* Condé-sur-Noireau, France, 1997.

Finzsch, Norbert, and Robert Jütte, eds. *Institutions of Confinement: Hospitals, Asylums, and Prisons in Western Europe and North America, 1500–1950.* New York, 1996.

Fitzgerald, Patrick Desmond. *Poverty and Vagrancy in Early Modern Ireland.* Belfast, 1994.

Foucault, Michel. *Discipline and Punish: The Birth of the Prison.* Translated by Alan Sheridan. New York, 1979.

Geremek, Bronislaw. "Criminalité, vagabondage, paupérisme: la marginalité à l'aube des temps modernes." *Revue d'histoire moderne et contemporaine* 21 (1974): 337–375.

Hall, C. G. *A Legislative History of Vagrancy in England and Barbados.* Bridgetown, Barbados, 1997.

Hergemöller, Bernd-Ulrich, ed. *Randgruppen der spätmittelalterlichen Gesellschaft.* 2nd rev. ed. Warendorf, Germany, 2001.

Hippel, Wolfgang von. *Armut, Unterschichte, Randgruppen in der frühen Neuzeit.* Munich, 1995.

Hufton, Olwen H. "Begging, Vagrancy, Vagabondage and the Law: An Aspect of Poverty in Eighteenth-Century France." *European Studies Review* 2 (1972): 97–123.

Jütte, Robert. *Poverty and Deviance in Early Modern Europe.* Cambridge, U.K., and New York, 1994.

Küther, Carsten. *Menschen auf der Straße: Vagierende Unterschichten in Bayern, Franken und Schwaben in der zweiten Hälfte des 18. Jahrhunderts.* Göttingen, 1983.

Meneghetti Casarin, Francesca. *I Vagabondi, la società e lo stato nella republicca di Venezia alla fine del '700.* Rome, 1984.

Paultre, Christian. *De la répression de la mendicité et du vagabondage: en France sous l'ancien régime.* Reprint. Geneva, 1975. Originally published 1906.

Ribton-Turner, C. J. *A History of Vagrants and Vagrancy, and Beggars and Begging.* Reprint. Montclair, N.J., 1972. Originally published 1887.

Roeck, Bernd. *Außenseiter, Randgruppen, Minderheiten: Fremde im Deutschland der Frühen Neuzeit.* Göttingen, 1993.

Schwartz, Robert M. *Policing the Poor in Eighteenth-Century France.* Chapel Hill, N.C., 1988.

Sellin, Thorsten. *Pioneering in Penology: The Amsterdam Houses of Correction in the Sixteenth and Seventeenth Centuries.* Philadelphia, 1944.

Woodbrige, Linda. *Vagrancy, Homelessness, and English Renaissance Literature.* Urbana, Ill., 2001.

ROBERT JÜTTE

# VALOIS DYNASTY (FRANCE).

From its accession to the French throne in 1328 through its end in 1589, the Valois dynasty included thirteen kings: Philip VI (ruled 1328–1350); John the Good (1350–1364); Charles V (1364–1380); Charles VI (1380–1422); Charles VII (1422–1461); Louis XI (1461–1483); Charles VIII (1483–1498); Louis XII (1498–1515); Francis I (1515–1547); Henry II (1547–1559); Francis II (1559–1560); Charles IX (1560–1574); Henry III (1574–1589).

Over this period, the dynasty presided over some of the most violent years in French history. Its reign included the Hundred Years' War (1337–1453) and the Wars of Religion (1562–1598), two periods in which it seemed that France itself might break apart; and from 1495 through 1557 there were a series of wars with the kings of Spain, with each side seeking hegemony in Italy. The sixteenth-century Valois also confronted the advent of Protestantism, and their response to it continued to influence French society well into the nineteenth century. Despite the advantages that converting to Protestantism might have offered, Francis I and Henry II vigorously prosecuted all forms of heresy; and Charles IX endorsed the St. Bartholomew's Day Massacre of Protestants in 1572. As a result, to the end of the Old Regime the French monarchy would remain closely allied with Catholic ritual and belief.

The Valois included colorful characters to match the dramatic times in which they ruled. A patron of the arts and ambitious warrior, Francis I was a Renaissance monarch well suited to compete with his contemporaries Henry VIII of England (ruled 1509–1547) and the Emperor Charles V (ruled 1519–1556). But several other members of the dynasty showed signs of mental instability, and in both the fifteenth and the sixteenth centuries these had dire political consequences.

*See also* **Charles VIII (France); France; Francis I (France); Henry II (France); Henry III (France); Louis XII (France); St. Bartholomew's Day Massacre; Wars of Religion, French.**

BIBLIOGRAPHY

Baumgartner, Frederic J. *Henry II, King of France, 1547–1559.* Durham, N.C., 1988.

Knecht, R. J. *Francis I.* New York, 1982.

———. *The French Civil Wars, 1562–1598.* New York, 2000.

JONATHAN DEWALD

## VAN DYCK, ANTHONY (1599–1641),

Flemish painter. Born in Antwerp, Anthony van Dyck divided his career between his native Southern Netherlands, Italy, and England. Before he died at the age of forty-two, he had become the most influential portraitist in Europe. His portraits evoke the sitters' actual or desired rank as well as a sense of individuality, despite their idealization. Although he remains best known for his portraits, Van Dyck's ambition and talent extended to more prestigious history subjects, including religious and secular narratives in which he emphasized psychological states and relationships (for example, *The Mystic Marriage of the Blessed Herman Joseph,* 1630, Vienna, Kunsthistorisches Museum). Throughout his career Van Dyck departed from gender stereotypes more often than other artists, favoring subjects with passive men, and innovatively portrayed several women as glancing down at the viewer (for example, *Marchesa Elena Grimaldi,* 1623, National Gallery of Art, Washington, D.C.).

The son of a silk merchant, Van Dyck began his professional training at the age of ten with Hendrik van Balen, the most expensive figure painter in Antwerp. While still in his teens he produced accomplished works and apparently even ran his own studio at the age of sixteen before officially becoming a master in the Guild of St. Luke. Because the young Van Dyck shifted easily between different styles, the dating of his early works remains disputed. He could adapt to the style of the older Rubens, in whose studio he worked as an assistant helping in the execution of such works as the cartoons for tapestries illustrating the history of the Roman general Decius Mus. In such cases he applied paint smoothly and depicted massive, muscular figures in a more ambiguous space than was typical of Rubens. Spatial ambiguity remained a stylistic characteristic throughout Van Dyck's career as a means of intensifying his emphasis on psychological rather than corporeal presence. Early paintings done in his own style, with oil paint applied in broader, looser strokes, reveal his lifelong admiration for the work

**Anthony Van Dyck.** Self-portrait, c. 1630. HERMITAGE, ST. PETERSBURG, RUSSIA/BRIDGEMAN ART LIBRARY

of Titian (*Betrayal of Christ,* Prado, Madrid). Multiple versions exist of several early narrative subjects, the betrayal of Christ being a case in point. In planning such compositions, he made drawing after drawing to test alternative possibilities.

Portraits painted in Antwerp before 1620 (and again in 1628–1632) tend to be three-quarter length or smaller, a size suitable for the dwellings of Flemish burghers (*Frans Snyders,* The Frick Collection, New York). Props such as columns and flowing drapes, however, evoke the palatial settings of nobility, a status to which many of his fellow citizens aspired.

By the time Van Dyck left Antwerp in 1620, his works were as highly valued as Rubens's. He first went to England but by the end of 1621 had moved to Italy, remaining there for seven years and traveling extensively. His sketchbook (London, British Museum) records that he paid special attention to Titian. In Genoa, where he spent the most time, Van Dyck portrayed the city's nobility, such as Marchesa Elena Grimaldi (1623, National Gallery of Art, Washington, D.C.). Often shown full-length, they look down at the viewer, increasing the sense of elevated rank suggested by their reserved demeanor. Faces and hands stand out against the tonalities dominated by rich reds and blacks.

In 1628 Van Dyck resettled in his native Antwerp. Visitors to his house mention a "Cabinet de Titian" in which he displayed originals by and copies after Titian. Working with softer value contrasts, Van Dyck expanded his repertoire of portrait poses for compositional reasons and to characterize sitters more fully. This is especially evident in the *Iconography,* a print series portraying selected European notables, including heads of state, military leaders, scholars, and, unprecedentedly in such a prestigious context, fellow artists such as Jan Brueghel the Elder. At first Van Dyck etched the portraits himself, but had the prints made by engravers after his models.

In 1632 Van Dyck moved once again to England, where art patronage now flourished at a court ruled by Charles I, a discriminating and avid art collector. The king appointed Van Dyck his "principalle" painter and knighted him, raising the artist's status closer to that of the nobility he portrayed as well as entertained. The English portraits (*Portrait of King Charles I,* 1635, Louvre) differ from their Genoese counterparts in having a brighter palette, a tendency to more relaxed poses, and occasional pastoral associations. They were to have an enormous influence on later English painting. In 1634–1635 Van Dyck considered resettling permanently in Antwerp but returned to England, where he lived the rest of his short life. His works remain as integral to the history of painting in England and in Italy as in his native Southern Netherlands.

*See also* **Britain, Art in; Charles I (England); Netherlands, Art in the; Painting; Rubens, Peter Paul.**

BIBLIOGRAPHY

Brown, Christopher. *Van Dyck.* Oxford, 1982.

Martin, John Rupert, and Gail Feigenbaum. *Van Dyck as Religious Artist.* Exh. cat. Princeton, 1979.

Wheelock, Arthur K., Susan J. Barnes, and Julius S. Held, eds. *Anthony van Dyck.* Exh. cat. Washington, D.C., 1990.

ZIRKA ZAREMBA FILIPCZAK

**VASA DYNASTY (SWEDEN).** The Vasa Dynasty, which ruled Sweden from 1523 to 1654, included Gustav I Vasa (Gustav Eriksson), Erik XIV, John III, Sigismund I Vasa, Charles IX, Gustavus II Adolphus, and Christina. During their reigns, Sweden left the Kalmar Union and became an independent state, adopted Lutheranism, developed a more complex economy, built a Baltic empire and a place of importance in European affairs, and became increasingly European culturally. (The Vasa name derives from the *vase,* a sheaf of grain in the family's insignia or shield. The family's noble roots lie in the fourteenth century.)

Gustav I Vasa (ruled 1523–1560) established the dynasty. Aided by the Hanseatic League and important elements of the Swedish commons, he led the last of Sweden's rebellions against the Danish-controlled Kalmar Union. He became king in June 1523, and for thirty-seven years worked diligently and ruthlessly to ensure Sweden's independence and development. He made and maintained peace with Denmark, encouraged the Reformation, expropriated the properties of the Catholic Church to the crown's benefit, supported economic developments, built up a modest army and navy, curbed the Hanseatic League's influence, used the Parliament to ratify his actions, made Sweden a hereditary monarchy (1544), crushed domestic disturbances, and fostered the growth of a central administration. One of Europe's "new monarchs," he enhanced the power of the crown and curbed that of the nobility. Following his death in 1560, many of his achievements were eroded by the half-century of internal turmoil and foreign wars initiated by his sons Erik, John, and Charles.

Erik XIV (ruled 1560–1568) was temperamental, suspicious, and mentally unstable. He squandered the fiscal and political assets his father had bequeathed him. He launched Sweden's age of imperial adventures in the Baltic, helped to precipitate the Northern Seven Years' War (1563–1570) with Denmark, and even sought the hand of Elizabeth I of England. He also engaged in a running conflict with his half-brother, Duke John, who, from his duchy in Finland, acted like a king in his own right. This conflict peaked in 1568, when John, with the aid of their brother Charles, deposed Erik and imprisoned him in Gripsholm Castle, where he died in 1577.

John III (ruled 1568–1592), more stable, cultured, and politically astute than Erik, worked to restore peace and stability. His efforts were undermined by religious strife. His marriage to Catherine, daughter of Sigismund II Augustus of Poland, led to a drift towards Catholicism, and this was reinforced when their heir, Sigismund, who was raised a Catholic, became king of Poland as Sigismund III Vasa in 1587.

When Sigismund (ruled Sweden as Sigismund I Vasa 1592–1599) succeeded his father as king of Sweden, a political arrangement was forged to balance the interests of the crown, those of the last of the Vasa sons (Charles), and those of the high nobility. Fear of the king's Catholicism led to a reaffirmation of Lutheranism at Uppsala in 1593. Sigismund stacked the administration with his favorites, which alarmed Charles, and civil war erupted in 1597. Sigismund was defeated at Stångebro the following year and deposed in 1599. He remained king in Poland, however, until his death in 1632, and for over half a century the two lines of the Vasa dynasty were in conflict.

Charles IX (ruled 1599–1611) acted as regent until 1604, and he was not crowned until 1607. He ruthlessly eliminated his opponents (Linköping Bloodbath, 1600) and ruled personally or through favorites. He ignored complaints that he was violating the nobility's privileges. Following his death in 1611, the nobles took their revenge. Charles's heir, Gustavus II Adolphus, was only seventeen, and the price of his recognition was an accession charter that guaranteed noble power in the country.

Until relatively recently, Gustavus II Adolphus (ruled 1611–1632) has been viewed as one of Sweden's greatest kings—architect of Sweden's age of greatness; author of creative and positive developments in government, administration, economics, and education; one of history's best military leaders; and the man most responsible for the survival of Lutheranism in Germany. This interpretation usually paired him with his adviser and chancellor, Axel Oxenstierna. More recent assessments tend to assign greater influence to Oxenstierna in political, economic, and administrative matters. In military matters he was less a creative thinker than an efficient and effective applier of ideas originating elsewhere. Gustavus II Adolphus spent almost his entire reign at war (successively with Denmark, Russia, Poland, and the Catholic-Imperial forces in Germany). He died at the Battle of Lützen on 6 November 1632.

Christina (ruled 1632–1654), Gustavus II Adolphus's only legitimate heir, was six when her father was killed. Power therefore passed to a regency dominated by Axel Oxenstierna, and for the next twelve years the influence of the nobility was enhanced. Christina's personal rule covered a decade, and her importance has been variously interpreted. Oxenstierna's influence declined, and she effectively played competing factions against each other to achieve her desire for peace in Germany and the recognition of her cousin, Charles X Gustav, as her heir. Unwilling to marry, she abdicated and left Sweden in 1654. She converted to Catholicism and lived the rest of her life in Rome, where she pursued her cultural interests and dabbled in politics. She died in 1689.

The Vasa dynasty ended with Christina's abdication, as the crown passed to Charles X Gustav (ruled 1654–1660), son of Gustavus II Adolphus's half-sister, Katherine, and John Casimir of Pfalz-Zweibrücken.

*See also* **Charles X Gustav (Sweden); Christina (Sweden); Gustavus II Adolphus (Sweden); Kalmar, Union of; Oxenstierna, Axel; Sweden.**

BIBLIOGRAPHY

Kirby, David. *Northern Europe in the Early Modern Period: The Baltic World 1492–1772.* London and New York, 1990.

Nordstrom, Byron J., ed. *Dictionary of Scandinavian History.* Westport, Conn., 1986. This work contains articles on each of the rulers in the Vasa dynasty.

Robert, Michael. *The Early Vasas: A History of Sweden. 1523–1611.* Cambridge, U.K., and London, 1968.

Scott, Franklin D. *Sweden: The Nation's History.* Carbondale, Ill., 1988.

BYRON J. NORDSTROM

# VASARI, GIORGIO (1511–1574), Italian

biographer, painter, and architect. Born in the Tuscan town of Arezzo, Giorgio Vasari was brought in his early years to Florence, where he eventually became a prolific painter and highly accomplished architect. As an artist he is best known for his extensive historical and allegorical fresco decorations in the Palazzo Vecchio, made to celebrate the ruler of Florence, Duke Cosimo de' Medici. As an architect his most celebrated building is the Uffizi, the government "offices" built for his Medici patron.

Vasari's art and architecture are eclipsed, however, by his work as a writer. His monumental *Lives* (commonly known as *Lives of the Artists*), was first published in Florence in 1550 and was reprinted in a much revised and amplified version in 1568. Composed as a series of biographies, Vasari's book is a history of the progress of art, after its "rebirth," from Cimabue to the perfection of Michelangelo. Considered to be the first "history of art" as such, the *Lives* powerfully shaped the emergence of art history as a scholarly discipline in the modern era. Vasari's book is also a rich source of information about Renaissance artists and the world in which they worked. It is a valuable font concerning the theory, practice, criticism, and techniques of art.

Given the vast amount of attention Vasari's writing has received, what is still underestimated at this late date is the status of Vasari's book as an enduring masterpiece of imaginative literature and of historical art. Literary scholars have been insufficiently attentive to Vasari's relations to Homer, Ovid, and Virgil, to Dante, Petrarch, and Giovanni Boccaccio, to Politian, Marsilio Ficino, and Ludovico Ariosto, to Baldassare Castiglione, Pietro Bembo, and Pietro Aretino, and art historians are totally indifferent, if not hostile, to the literary virtues of the *Lives*.

Writing before the modern distinction between scientific history and historical fiction, Vasari produced a book that combined both—fables and *novelle* on the one hand and "factual documents," as we might call them, on the other. Although scholars have become increasingly attentive to the fictive character of the *Lives*, they have remained remarkably insensitive to the virtues of such fiction. Sometimes they still ignore or refuse to acknowledge the presence of fiction in Vasari's book, as when, for example, they treat his fable of Leonardo's fabulous buckler or his tale of Michelangelo's smiling faun made in the Medici garden as true stories, as documentation of what really happened. What is lost here is an adequate critical appreciation of Vasari's art, the poetic art and inventiveness of these and other stories.

The blind reading of Vasari, which talks around the fiction of his book or refers to it only as "poetic embellishment" when it is far more than that, is based on the misguided belief that history is an accumulation of facts when it is, in fact, shaped or formed, hence "fictive" in the root sense of the word. Fiction in Vasari is inevitably written in the service of the historical truth. Vasari reports, for example, that Piero di Cosimo was a "wild man," a fiction that is true to the character of the artist's primitive subjects, which are the inventions of a highly cultivated artist. The power of Vasari's fiction is so great that even modern scientific art historians have imagined him as a kind of caveman. Although Piero becomes a fictional character in the pages of Vasari, he is obviously not an invented character. Rather, he is a real person whose life is poetically imagined.

The poetry of Vasari endures in the modern fable of art, in Honoré de Balzac's *The Unknown Masterpiece*, the tale of a painter whose inability to complete a masterpiece echoes Vasari's portrayal of Leonardo's unfinished work. Vasari is alive in Robert Browning's poems on Fra Filippo Lippi and Andrea del Sarto, and in George Eliot's portrayal of Piero di Cosimo in *Romola*. The extent of Vasari's influence on the modern imagination is far greater than the provincial historiography of art history allows. Vasari's book is a classic of world literature in which the mythologized Piero di Cosimo, Leonardo, Raphael, and Michelangelo are characters of historical fiction who take their place as the subjects of history and the modern novel alike. Vasari often appropriated materials from other writers, far more than is generally realized; but, in the end, he was the superintending intelligence responsible for the making of a great literary and historical masterpiece, which will forever remain "Vasari's *Lives*."

*See also* **Art: Art Theory, Criticism, and Historiography; Biography and Autobiography; Florence, Art in.**

BIBLIOGRAPHY

*Primary Source*

Vasari, Giorgio. *Le vite de' più eccellenti pittori, scultori et architettori scritte da Giorgio Vasari*. Edited by Gaetano Milanesi. 9 vols. Florence, 1906.

**Giorgio Vasari.** Title page from *Lives of the Artists,* 1568. Yale Center for British Art, Paul Mellon Collection

*Secondary Sources*

Barolsky, Paul. *Why Mona Lisa Smiles and Other Tales by Vasari.* University Park, Pa., 1991.

Rubin, Patricia. *Giorgio Vasari: Art and History.* New Haven and London, 1995.

PAUL BAROLSKY

# VASILII III (MUSCOVY)

**VASILII III (MUSCOVY)** (1479–1533; ruled 1505–1533), grand prince of Muscovy. Vasilii III Ivanovich was the second son of Ivan III. His mother was the Greek princess Sofiia Paleologue. Coming to the throne in 1505, he pursued his father's policy of expansion and consolidation of territory. In 1510 he annexed the trading town of Pskov and in 1514 captured Smolensk from Poland-Lithuania. In 1520–1521 Vasilii imprisoned the last Ryazan prince for treasonous relations with the Tatars and absorbed his territory. Repeated raids by the Crimean Tatars on the southern border posed serious problems but did not prevent him from repeatedly trying to establish his candidates as khans of Kazan' on the Volga. A truce with Lithuania in 1522 allowed him to consolidate his gains, establishing Russia's western frontier for a century.

Internally Vasilii inherited the apparatus of his father's state and maintained it, at the same time asserting control over the small appanages of his junior kinsmen. His marriage to Solomoniia Saburova, the daughter of an important boyar clan, produced no heirs in twenty years, and in 1525, with the support of the church, Vasilii dissolved the marriage and forced her to become a nun. He quickly married Princess Elena Glinskaia, the daughter of a refugee prince from Lithuania whose uncle, Prince Mikhail Glinskii, had led a revolt against his sovereign, Sigismund I of Poland-Lithuania, in 1508. The Glinskii family were great magnates of Tatar origin who came to play an important role at the Russian court.

Religious issues intertwined with court rivalries marked the politics of Vasilii's reign. In 1507 Vasilii took Joseph of Volokolamsk and his monastery under his personal protection and supported Joseph in his conflicts with the church hierarchy. From 1509 Joseph's critic, the monk Vassian Patrikeev, son of the exiled prince Ivan Patrikeev, was also prominent at court, and he remained influential until about 1522. In those years Vasilii and Metropolitan Varlaam brought Maximus the Greek (Michael Trivolis, c. 1480–1556) to Russia to correct the Slavonic translations of Greek liturgical texts. Maximus combined philological skills acquired in Venice and Florence with traditional Orthodox belief, but he and Vassian both fell afoul of the new metropolitan, Daniil (1521–1539). Maximus was tried for heresy as well as for political comments in 1525 and again, with Vassian, in 1531, after which both were removed from their positions and sent into monastic exile. Maximus left a large body of devotional and theological writings. Though he was critical of excessive monastic wealth, his views remained within conventional teachings. During the same period Vasilii exiled several prominent boyars, the princes Shuiskii, Vorotynskii, and others, and Maximus's ally Ivan Nikoforovich Bersen'-Beklemishev was executed in 1525 for criticism of both the metropolitan and the grand prince.

The birth of an heir, Ivan Vasil'evich—the future Ivan IV, the Terrible—in 1530 ensured the succession, but Vasilii died in 1533. A regency, with its accompanying political instability, followed his death.

*See also* **Ivan III (Muscovy); Ivan IV, "the Terrible" (Russia); Russia.**

BIBLIOGRAPHY

Crummey, Robert O. *The Formation of Muscovy 1304–1613.* London and New York, 1987.

Solov'ev, Sergei M. *History of Russia.* Vol. 9, *The Age of Vasily III.* Translated by Hugh F. Graham. Gulf Breeze, Fla., 1976.

Zimin, A. A. *Rossiia Na Poroge Novogo Vremeni.* Moscow, 1972.

PAUL BUSHKOVITCH

# VAUGHAN, THOMAS

**VAUGHAN, THOMAS** (Eugenius Philalethes; 1622–1666), Welsh alchemist, Rosicrucian, Hermeticist, and Paracelsan. Twin brother of the poet Henry Vaughan, Thomas Vaughan was born in Newton, Wales. He studied at Jesus College, Oxford, graduating with a B.A. in 1642. Thereafter he became rector of Llansaintfraid and supported the Royalist cause in the Civil War. Ejected from his living by a parliamentary commission in 1649, he practiced as an alchemist, or chemical philosopher, in London. He published several books under the pseudonym Eugenius Philalethes: *Magia Adamica* (1650), *Anthroposophia Theomagica* (1650), *Anima Magica Abscondita* (1650), and *Lumen de Lumine* (1651). He was also responsible for publishing an English translation of the Rosicrucian manifestos *Fama* and *Confessio* in 1652. During the 1650s he became acquainted with Samuel Hartlib and two future fellows of the Royal Society: Thomas Henshaw, dedicatee of *Anima Magica Abscondita,* and Sir Robert Moray, with whom he conducted alchemical investigations. Vaughan is best remembered for his controversy with Henry More, who attacked him under the pseudonym *Alazonmastix Philalethes.* The vituperative character of the exchange can be gauged from the titles of Vaughan's replies: *Man-Mouse Taken in a Trap* (1650) and *The Second Wash, or the Moore Scour'd Once More* (1651).

*See also* **Alchemy; Hartlib, Samuel; More, Henry; Rosicrucianism.**

BIBLIOGRAPHY

*Primary Sources*

More, Henry (Alazonomastix Philalethes). *Anthroposophia theomagica, or a Discourse of the Nature of Man and His State after Death.* London, 1650.

———. *Observations upon Anthroposophia Theomagica.* London, 1650.

———. *The Second Lash of Alazonomastix.* London, 1651.

Vaughan, Thomas (Eugenius Philalethes). *The Fame and Confession of the Fraternity of R.C., commonly, of the Rosie Cross.* London, 1652.

———. *The Works of Thomas Vaughan.* Edited by A. Rudrum. Oxford, 1984.

*Secondary Sources*

Brann, N. L. "The Conflict between Reason and Magic in Seventeenth-Century England." *Huntington Library Quarterly* 43 (1980): 103–126.

Burnham, F. B. "The More-Vaughan Controversy: The Revolt against Philosophical Enthusiasm." *Journal of the History of Ideas* 35 (1975): 33–49.

Newman, William. "Thomas Vaughan, an Interpreter of Agrippa von Nettesheim." *Ambix* 29 (1982): 125–140.

SARAH HUTTON

# VEDUTA (VIEW PAINTING).

The golden age of *Vedutismo,* the art of painting views of Italian cities, towns, and villages, falls with some precision within the confines of the eighteenth century. The roots of the genre lie in printed and drawn topographical images produced in the previous century, particularly in Rome, of which the Flemish artist Lieven Cruyl produced an impressive series of drawings in the 1660s, and where landscape painters such as Paul Bril (1554–1626) and painters of ruins such as Viviano Codazzi (1603/4–1670) had important sidelines painting views of real locations. It was appropriately in Rome that the first specialist view painter, and the founding father of the Italian school of view painting, Gaspar van Wittel (1652/53–1736), known in Italy as Gaspare Vanvitelli, settled in the 1670s, and produced his first views, in gouache and oil, in the 1680s. Born at Amersfoort in Holland, Vanvitelli shows a Dutch sensitivity to light, meticulous technique, and delicacy in the treatment of detail, combined with a convincing perspective, which distinguish it from earlier, isolated examples. He also worked in Naples and Venice, where he similarly inspired the emergence of indigenous schools of view painting.

All the main practitioners of *Vedutismo* were also involved in the painting of *capricci,* imaginary assemblages of buildings, especially classical ruins, and it was from this tradition that Vanvitelli's greatest successor in Rome, the neoclassicist Giovanni Paolo Panini (1691–1765), emerged in the 1730s as the leading Roman view painter of his generation, his work being especially popular among the French. In addition, Naples had a significant school of view painters, unusual in that not only were few of its members Neapolitan by birth but many were not even Italian. Vanvitelli's views, second only to those he made of Rome, were followed by similar series of the city by the Modenese Antonio Joli (c. 1700–1777), the most widely traveled of all the Italian eighteenth-century view painters, and of towns on the Bay of Naples by the German Jakob Philipp Hackert (1737–1807).

It was in Venice that, following a visit by Vanvitelli in the 1690s, the one truly native school of view painting grew up. Luca Carlevarijs (also Carlevaris; 1663–1730), born in Udine but Venetian by adoption, published an influential set of 104

**Veduta.** *The Arch of Constantine* by Gaspar van Wittel. ©CHRISTIE'S IMAGES/CORBIS

engravings of Venetian views in 1703, and during the first decade of the century he painted a number of often large representations of particular events, the grandest form of view painting, for foreign visitors to the city. From this moment on, the development of view painting in Venice is inextricably linked to the demand for such work by foreign visitors, especially Englishmen on a grand tour. The career of Canaletto (born Giovanni Antonio Canal, 1697–1768) was established in the 1720s through his links with the Irish impresario Owen McSwinney, and above all with the English merchant banker, and later British consul, Joseph Smith, who was to be his greatest patron as well as his agent, ideally placed to organize commissions for souvenirs from eminent visitors to the city. By the late 1720s Canaletto had abandoned the vivid brushwork and dramatic light effects of his early work in favor of more precisely defined scenes invariably bathed in warm sunshine, presumably to cater better to his clients' tastes, and his tendency to work on an increasingly small scale was also motivated by commercial concerns. Much has been made of Canaletto's use of the camera obscura, but evidence of

this is limited, and Canaletto's views, despite appearances, often involve extensive distortions and lack topographical accuracy.

Although Canaletto showed a reluctance to leave his native city, he did visit Rome in his youth (1719–1720) and spent nine years in England (1746–1755). His nephew Bernardo Bellotto (1720–1780), no less an artist although one of a very different character, also left Italy in the 1740s, but in his case this was to be permanent. The cold light and dark brooding quality of his paintings, even his early views of Italy, were particularly well suited to his views of the northern cities, which he portrayed in series of large canvases during his residence at the courts of Dresden (1747–1758 and 1762–1766), Vienna (1759–1760), Munich (1761), and Warsaw (1767–1780). With the early death of Michele Giovanni Marieschi (1710–1743), the most talented of Canaletto's rivals in the 1730s, and the departure of Bellotto, Venice found itself without a significant view painter during Canaletto's years in England. It was left to Francesco Guardi (1712–1793), the last of the great Venetian view painters who only turned to view painting in the second half of the 1750s, to develop a highly individual new style, one of dramatic atmospheric effects over topographical representation, that carried the genre through to its conclusion on the eve of the fall of the Venetian Republic in 1797.

*See also* **Grand Tour; Netherlands, Art in; Painting; Rome, Art in.**

BIBLIOGRAPHY

Aikema, Bernard, and Boudewijn Bakker. *Painters of Venice: The Story of the Venetian "Veduta."* Amsterdam and The Hague, 1991.

Beddington, Charles. *Luca Carlevarijs: Views of Venice.* San Diego, Calif., 2001.

Briganti, Giuliano. *The View Painters of Europe.* Translated by Pamela Waley. London, 1970.

Kozakiewicz, Stefan. *Bernardo Bellotto.* Translated by Mary Whittall. London, 1972.

Links, J. G. *Canaletto.* 2nd ed. London, 1994.

CHARLES BEDDINGTON

---

**VEGA, LOPE DE** (1562–1635), Spanish dramatist. Lope Félix de Vega Carpio, the best-known and most influential dramatist of Spain's Golden Age of literature, was known as the "Freak of Nature" for the astonishing quantity and quality of his poetry, drama, and prose. His greatest legacy was to establish the genre of the *comedia,* a secular three-act play that reached enormous popularity on the public stages of Spanish cities in the late sixteenth and early seventeenth centuries.

Though Lope's family origins were humble, he soon drew attention for his unusual talents, being able to read Latin and compose poetry at an early age. He studied with the Jesuits in Madrid and at the University of Alcalá, served in a series of military expeditions, and performed occasional secretarial duties for a variety of marquises and dukes. Defining himself above all as a writer, he was one of the first Spanish playwrights to make a living from his art, although it generally brought him more fame than fortune.

Lope's life contained as much romance, adventure, and conflict as that of any of his fictional characters. He engaged in a series of tempestuous relationships, many of them adulterous, the earliest of which resulted in his exile from Castile for two years. He served on the ill-fated Armada expedition against England in 1588 and not only survived but composed poetry throughout the voyage. As a young man, Lope had considered the possibility of a religious calling, and he finally entered the priesthood in 1614 after the death of his second wife. He also served as an officer of the Inquisition and earned the favor of Pope Urban VIII. Passionately sensual and deeply religious, Lope often suffered the contradictions of his own personality. After his ordination, he continued to have a series of highly publicized affairs, and was said to have been in the habit of furiously scourging himself in penitence. He married twice and fathered more than a dozen children (legitimate and illegitimate). The turbulence of his life was echoed in his family: his last mistress suffered from blindness and fits of insanity, one of his daughters was seduced and abandoned, and a son who demonstrated great poetic talent suffered an untimely death at sea.

However unfortunate, the intensity of his personal experiences enriched Lope's art. Nearly all of the women with whom he was involved appeared in some incarnation in his poetic works: the "Filis" of his ballads was his first love, Elena Osorio; his first wife, Isabel de Urbina, appeared in verse as "Belisa"; Micaela de Luján, a longtime mistress, was immortalized in his sonnets as "Lucinda"; and "Amarilis" represented his last great love, Marta de Nevares. Lope's spiritual anguish was expressed most beautifully in his collection of sacred sonnets, *Rimas sacras* (1614; Sacred verses), and his best prose was encompassed in the largely autobiographical novel *La Dorotea* (1632).

As Lope's personal life was closely interwoven with his art, so was his literary career inseparable from the rise of the dramatic genre known as the *comedia.* Drama in sixteenth-century Spain had roots in a variety of traditions including classical Latin plays, medieval liturgical ceremony, folk traditions, and the Italian *commedia dell'arte.* Lope drew on all of these to create the *comedia,* mixing popular and erudite elements, favoring action and clever dialogue over character development, and disregarding the traditional distinction between comedy and tragedy. Though he was well trained in traditional literary techniques and the classic unities of time, place, and action, he argued that these were irrelevant to audiences who simply wished to be entertained. In 1609, he published *The New Art of Writing Plays in Our Time*, a tongue-in-cheek treatise written for the Academy of Madrid in which he criticized the uneducated tastes of the common people but argued that the style of popular drama must yield to the "tyranny of the audience." This approach was scorned by those who defended the Aristotelian precepts of drama, but it won Lope the adoration of the public. His dramatic career coincided with the opening of a number of public stages in cities across Spain, and under his guidance, the *comedia* gained enormous popularity and became the standard dramatic form of the Golden Age.

Lope claimed to have written nearly two thousand *comedias*, of which approximately five hundred survive. With a rich variety of subjects drawn from history, romance, religion, mythology, and adventure, their themes always reflected the principal concerns of early modern Spaniards: the tensions between love and honor, power and responsibility, and the individual and society. In a world very sensitive to status, Lope frequently demonstrated his sympathy for those who were excluded from the ranks of wealth and power. *Fuenteovejuna* (1614; The sheep well), *Peribáñez* (1621) and *El mejor alcalde, el rey* (1621; The best magistrate, the king), all portrayed the dignity and honor of rural villagers struggling against the tyranny and corruption of the nobility. Similarly, in plays such as *El perro del hortelano* (1613; The dog in the manger), Lope's spirited female characters resisted the expectations of the patriarchal world in which they found themselves (though his conclusions always reinforced the necessity of socially acceptable marriage). All of Lope's plays dealt with these themes in a vivid, energetic, and spontaneous style, demonstrating his preference for the passions and conflicts of real life over the academic abstractions and ideals favored by many of his contemporaries.

Lope's genius was best expressed in drama and lyric poetry, but he composed in nearly every literary genre, including sonnets, epic poems, prose, fables, treatises, short stories, and novels. In spite of his talent, his humble origins (and perhaps his scandalous behavior) prevented him from earning the patronage of the court that he had always hoped for, and he faced financial difficulties throughout his lifetime. This talent did, however, earn him the love of his audiences, both in his own time and in the

**Lope de Vega.** ARTE PUBLICO PRESS ARCHIVES, UNIVERSITY OF HOUSTON. REPRODUCED BY PERMISSION

centuries since his death, and it has guaranteed him a place among the greatest figures in literary history.

*See also* **Drama: Spanish and Portuguese; Inquisition, Spanish; Spanish Literature and Language; Urban VIII (pope).**

BIBLIOGRAPHY

*Primary Sources*

Vega, Lope de. *La Dorotea.* Translated and edited by Alan S. Trueblood and Edwin Honig. Cambridge, Mass., 1985.

———. *Five Plays.* Translated by Jill Booty. Edited with an introduction by R. D. F. Pring-Mill. New York, 1961. Translations of five of Lope's best-known plays: *Peribáñez, Fuenteovejuna, El perro del hortelano, El caballero de Olmedo,* and *El castigo sin venganza.*

———. *Obras completas de Lope de Vega,* edited by Jesús Gómez and Paloma Cuenca. Madrid, 1993.

*Secondary Sources*

Hayes, Francis C. *Lope de Vega.* New York, 1967.

Rennert, Hugo Albert. *The Life of Lope de Vega (1562–1635)*. New York, 1937.

JODI CAMPBELL

## VELÁZQUEZ, DIEGO (Diego Rodríguez de Silva y Velázquez; 1599–1660), the most important artist of the Spanish Golden Age. The son of parents of the lower nobility, Velázquez was born in Seville, where he lived until he was twenty-four. Between 1610 and 1616, he studied with Francisco Pacheco (1564–1654), the leading painter of the city. In 1618, he married Pacheco's daughter, Juana. Although profoundly influenced by Pacheco's commitment to the ideal of the learned painter, he did not imitate his master's dry, Italianate style.

His early genre scenes, including *An Old Woman Cooking Eggs* (1618, National Gallery of Scotland, Edinburgh) and *Waterseller* (1619, Wel-

**Diego Velázquez.** Self-portrait, 1623. ©ARCHIVO ICONOGRAFICO, S.A./CORBIS

lington Museum, London), constitute the first coherent group of secular figural paintings by a Spanish artist. These works probably were influenced by pictures of religious subjects with elaborate still life details by Flemish and north Italian artists such as Pieter Aertsen (c. 1508/09–1575) and Vincezo Campi (1536–1591). However, in contrast to these prototypes, Velázquez reduced the scenes to their essentials and focused upon a few naturalistically rendered figures and objects, strongly illuminated against a neutral background. The quiet dignity of the figures, and the monumental nature of the compositions, endow these images with a sense of transcendent importance.

In 1623, aided by courtiers from Seville, he obtained the opportunity to execute a portrait of Philip IV (ruled 1621–1665), which he revised a few years later (1623–1626, Museo del Prado, Madrid). Velázquez avoided the appearance of pomp so typical of baroque court portraiture of the time. The elegant pose, aloof gaze, and smooth, even illumination suffice to indicate the dignity of a king. Philip immediately appointed Velázquez royal painter; during subsequent decades, the two developed a close friendship, unprecedented between an artist and a Spanish monarch.

Interaction with Peter Paul Rubens (1577–1640) during Rubens's visit to Madrid in 1628–1629 decisively influenced the young artist, who sought to emulate the example of the painter-courtier. Rubens stimulated Velázquez's interest in the royal collection of Venetian paintings and encouraged him to expand his range of themes. Velázquez's first history painting, *The Feast of Bacchus* (1629, Museo del Prado, Madrid), introduced an unexpected melancholy note into the popular mythological subject. The beggar, seeking alms from the peasants gathered around Bacchus, evokes the transience of the pleasure of wine. Despite its originality, the uncertain definition of space and the overcrowded composition reveal artistic deficiencies.

To give him the opportunity to improve his skills, Philip sent Velázquez to Italy for over a year (1629–1630). In Rome, he met leading artists and studied ancient and Renaissance works. *The Forge of Vulcan* (1630, Museo del Prado, Madrid) demonstrated mastery of fundamental qualities of the Ital-

**Diego Velázquez.** *Las Meninas* (The Family of Philip IV). ©ERICH LESSING/ART RESOURCE, N.Y.

ian classical tradition, including accurate anatomy, dramatic expressions and gestures, and spatial perspective. Also in Rome, he produced two views of the gardens of the Villa Medici (both 1630, Museo del Prado, Madrid), among the first European paintings to have been created directly from nature. Superimposing "broken" brushstrokes over a reflective lead-white ground, he infused these seemingly casual images with a sense of atmosphere.

Returning to Madrid in 1631, Velázquez began the most productive decade of his career. By mid-decade, he had devised a highly original method of creating optical effects through the application of short, thick strokes of endlessly varied shapes and sizes. Thus, for example, when viewed from a distance, the jumbled brushwork covering the king's garments in *Philip IV of Spain in Brown and Silver* (1635, National Gallery, London) becomes resolved into a convincing record of the appearance of embroidered fabric. Although enlivened by free handling of paint and a brighter range of colors, the later royal portraits retain the directness and naturalness of his first works at court.

Throughout the 1630s, he supervised important decorative projects at royal palaces. For the Hall of Realms in the Buen Retiro, Madrid, he devised a coherent program of battle paintings, mythological images, and portraits. For this series, he produced the *Surrender of Breda* (1635, Museo del Prado, Madrid), the masterpiece of the period. By depicting the Spanish general with his arm upon the shoulder of the defeated Dutch leader, he visualized the ideal of mercy in victory, treated in several contemporary works by the court playwright Pedro Calderón de la Barca (1600–1681). Velázquez carefully studied portraits, battle plans, and other documentation in order to endow this imaginary conception of the event with an aura of authenticity. His paintings for the Torre de la Parada, a hunting lodge near Madrid, included two sympathetic and psychologically insightful portraits of dwarfs, Francisco Lezcano and Diego de Aceda (both 1636–1640, Museo del Prado, Madrid). Also created for the Torre, *Mars* (1640, Museo del Prado, Madrid) wittily depicted the ancient god of war contemplating his frustrations in love.

In the last two decades of his career, Velázquez reduced the scope (though not the quality) of his artistic production as he devoted himself to personal service to the king. His *Venus and Cupid* (c. 1648, National Gallery, London) is one of the few female nudes by a Spanish artist of the early modern era. The sensual pose, provocative use of the mirror image, and rich, luminous colors contribute to the erotic allure of this image. Between 1649 and 1651, Velázquez traveled in Italy to purchase art for the royal collection. His *Innocent X* (1649–1650, Galleria Doria-Pamphili, Rome) expressed the intense psychological energy of the aging pontiff. At the 1650 exhibition of Congregazione dei Virtuosi in Rome, he exhibited the recently completed *Juan de Pareja* (1650, Metropolitan Museum of Art, New York). Utilizing compositional formulae associated with aristocratic portraiture, he emphasized the dignity of his Moorish servant.

The exceptionally large *Las meninas* (1656; Maids of honor, Museo del Prado, Madrid) is regarded as the quintessential expression of his artistic aspirations. Velázquez depicted himself standing confidently at his easel, in the company of Princess Margarita and her attendants. Reflected in the mirror on the back wall are the king and queen, whose visit to his studio signifies royal approval of his art.

Intrigued by *Las meninas,* Pablo Picasso (1881–1973) created forty-four variations upon it in 1957 (all in Museo Picasso, Barcelona). Édouard Manet (1832–1883) is among the many other modernist artists who found inspiration in Velázquez's works.

*See also* **Calderón de la Barca, Pedro; Philip IV (Spain); Rubens, Peter Paul; Spain, Art in; Titian.**

BIBLIOGRAPHY

Brown, Jonathan. *Velázquez: Painter and Courtier.* New Haven and London, 1986. A vividly written and extensively illustrated study of all phases of the artist's career.

Brown, Jonathan, and John H. Elliott. *A Palace for a King: The Buen Retiro and the Court of Philip IV.* New Haven and London, 1980. This comprehensive study of a major decorative project examines Velázquez's position at court.

Domínguez Ortiz, Antonio, ed. *Velázquez.* Exh. cat. New York, 1989. This catalogue of the exhibition held 1989–1990 in New York and Madrid includes documentation on important works from all phases of the artist's career.

López-Rey, José. *Velázquez: A Catalogue Raisonné of His Oeuvre*. London, 1963. A useful catalogue of the artist's entire production.

RICHARD G. MANN

## VENALITY OF OFFICE. *See* Officeholding.

**VENICE.** One of the first cities in Italy to engage in international commerce after the devastations of the early Middle Ages, Venice established a maritime empire by 1300 and a territorial empire from the early 1400s. Its unique form of government, although not as perfect as its apologists claimed, was a model of a "mixed" constitution for the early modern world. Adapting to changing circumstances, its economy remained vibrant into the seventeenth century. It experienced little social turmoil, while its literary and artistic achievements were rivaled only by those of Florence and Rome. For most of its thousand years of existence, Venice was free and independent. One of the most successful states in Europe, it fell at last to Napoleon in 1797.

### MARITIME EMPIRE

Venice's unusual location and circumstances permitted its enterprising merchants to build a maritime empire by 1300. It was founded in the sixth and seventh centuries by refugees from the mainland, who had been forced by the invasions of the Germanic Lombards to flee northern Italian towns. They settled on a cluster of low, sandy islands in the Adriatic, where they were protected by the sea yet had access in their boats and barges to the river mouths that led to inland cities. Primarily fishermen, they also traded locally in fish and salt, which they manufactured from seawater. During the era of the Crusades (eleventh through fourteenth centuries), Venice (as well as Genoa, on the western coast of the Italian Peninsula) entered into Mediterranean commerce, establishing merchant depots on islands and seacoasts along the route to the Levant (Near East). In the late fourteenth century the rivalry between Venice and Genoa exploded into war. Venice

was victorious and retained mastery of its maritime empire.

The Ottoman conquest of Constantinople in 1453, however, signaled the beginning of the decline of Venice's maritime enterprise. Despite the victory by Venice and allies at the Battle of Lepanto (1571) against the Turkish fleet, the city's seaborne commerce was gravely injured. It was a commerce, moreover, based on the import of luxury goods from Asia, especially spices. By 1600 the tastes of European consumers were shifting. Sugar, tea, and tobacco became, more than pepper, the staples of world trade. In those markets Venice had no role.

### TERRITORIAL EMPIRE

In the meantime, however, Venice had won a territorial empire, beginning with the conquests of nearby Padua and Verona in 1405. By 1454 Venetian conquests reached far west on the Lombard Plain of northern Italy to Bergamo and Crema, almost to Milan, and northeast along the arc of the Adriatic Coast to Friuli and beyond to Dalmatia (modern Croatia). These territories included wealthy trading centers, drawing on the fertile lands

bordering the Po River, and gateways to the passes over the Alps and the commercial possibilities of the north. These conquests were made possible by the admirable military organization Venice developed. Heretofore, with only a maritime empire, Venice had provided both commanders and sailors, who also served as armed marines. On land Venice did not attempt to raise a citizen militia. Instead, it hired the best of the mercenary commanders (*condottieri*) then available but coordinated and systematized their efforts through a network of supervisors (*proveditori*) drawn from the governing elite. Venice was thus a pioneer of the rethinking of military organization that, in the sixteenth and seventeenth centuries, is sometimes considered a "military revolution."

The Peace of Lodi (9 April 1454) put an end, for the moment, to the rivalries among the great Italian powers, Venice, Milan, Florence, Naples, and the papacy, that had emerged from the crucible of warfare. The Italian League of the following year sought to maintain peace for a renewable twenty-five-year term by establishing a balance of

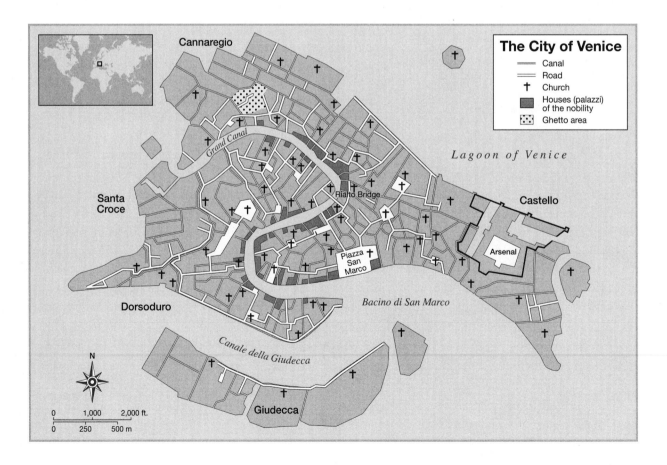

**Venice.** A sixteenth-century German bird's-eye view of Venice, with many buildings identified. The city, known as Queen of the Seas, reached the height of its commercial power in the fifteenth century, and at the time of this map was at the peak of its artistic glory. At the top of the map is the island of Murano, then, as now, the center of the Venetian glass industry. MAP COLLECTION, STERLING MEMORIAL LIBRARY, YALE UNIVERSITY

power. Some historians note that this agreement foreshadows the peace sought by the Congress of Vienna in 1815. Venice continued to seek commercial and political advantage where it could and fell into a damaging war with Ferrara (in the Papal States) from 1481 to 1484 that confirmed the impression of the larger city's aggressive behavior. When French, imperial, and Spanish armies began their long invasion of Italy in 1498 (with a pause in 1530 and no final resolution until the Treaty of Cateau-Cambrésis in 1559), Venice shifted its allegiance from side to side, attempting at times to maximize its advantage, at others simply to preserve the state.

In 1508, at the nadir of these conflicts, Venice faced the League of Cambrai. All of its sometime friends and enemies—France, Spain, the pope, and the empire—were united against the crafty republic. During a war that lasted from 1509 to 1517, Venice lost but then regained all of its mainland territories. It was saved by the commitment of its own people and the loyalty of mainland subjects. When the fog of war lifted at mid-century, Venice alone of the Italian states was capable of proceeding briskly to assume its accustomed preeminence. Venice withstood the Reformation and Counter-Reformation alike, weathering a papal interdict in 1606–1607. It remained an international power, although a waning one, until its 1797 demise.

Venice's success was due in part to its unique location and its energetic people. But it was the result as well of its system of government, which was sufficiently inclusive and sufficiently just to win the broad support of the citizenry.

**Venice.** *The Return of the Bucintoro to the Molo on Ascension Day,* by Canaletto. In an annual ritual, the citizens of Venice celebrate their close ties to the sea with a symbolic "marriage." The Bucintoro is the large boat at right which carries the doge. ©ALEXANDER BURKATOWSKI/CORBIS

## GOVERNMENT

By 1000 C.E. Venice's island communities had united into a single state ruled by an elected doge, whose election was a central part of Venetian political ritual. Soon thereafter the nominal obedience the Venetians paid to their presumed overlord, the Byzantine emperor, dropped away. By the thirteenth century the *Maggior Consiglio,* or 'Great Council', of prominent families made major decisions and limited the doge's effective power. In 1297 those families declared the *serrata,* or 'closing', of the Great Council. By that move, which took decades more to take full effect, they instituted a hereditary nobility of about 1,200 adult males (from some 150 families) with exclusive access to political power. With the exception of some eighty families admitted for exceptional service in 1388, there were no additions to the roster of noble fami-

lies until the seventeenth century (when nobility could be obtained by purchase).

The Great Council elected members from the same noble stratum to a senate, and the council or the senate elected members to a number of other councils, including the "Forty" of justice and the "Ten" for state security. They also elected the *avogadori di comun* (state attorneys), ambassadors, and military and other *proveditori.* Venetian government had many branches. A large part of the nobility spent a significant part of its time on the business of government, while a smaller elite of perhaps one hundred to two hundred exceptionally powerful men rotated in high office.

This government structure was by no means democratic. Yet it was admirable in many regards. It included elements of monarchy, of aristocracy, and of republican process. In the 1490s, when Florence was redesigning its government, it imitated the Venetian Republic, which also inspired English statesmen in the seventeenth century and even some of the American founders in the eighteenth century. Exaggerated statements of the justice and serenity of the Venetian state were made by proponents of the "myth of Venice" beginning in the fifteenth century. At the same time there prevailed a countermyth, voiced by the enemies of Venice, about that state's unique duplicity and cruelty.

## VENETIAN SOCIETY

A unique state was based on a unique society, of which no feature is more striking than the role of the nobility. From 1300 to 1500 the number of adult male nobles ranged from twelve hundred to twenty-five hundred and constituted 6 to 7 percent of the city's population. The population of Venice dipped to 50,000 after the plague of 1348 and reached a high of 190,000 around 1570, after which further rounds of epidemics took severe tolls. A secondary elite of *cittadini originari* ('original citizens', either native-born or so ranked by grant of privilege) provided the huge numbers of bureaucrats and secretaries (as well as merchants and pro-

fessionals) that a city of the complexity of Venice required. The artisan stratum was grouped in guilds that were less powerful than in some other cities but that were an important force for social cohesion. In addition the *scuole,* a uniquely Venetian version of the confraternity, provided charity and consolation for both members (of all social classes) and outsiders. A large pool of workers was employed by the Venetian state shipbuilding industry of the *Arsenale* (Arsenal). Below the strata of ordinary workers were the groups of prostitutes, beggars, and the poor found in most early modern cities. In addition Venice had a large population of resident foreigners, merchants in transit, visiting scholars, travelers, and refugees.

Women in Venice, as elsewhere in Italian society, were expected to obey their fathers and their husbands and dedicate themselves to childbearing, charity, and piety. Women of the middle and lower social ranks had more freedom than those of the nobility and high bourgeoisie. They were able to own property, participate in the public life of the marketplace, and defend themselves in court. Prostitutes and courtesans were numerous in a city with a large and mobile population, a large group of

**Venice.** A small engraved view of Venice as it was in 1765, from an early-nineteenth-century book published in New York. MAP COLLECTION, STERLING MEMORIAL LIBRARY, YALE UNIVERSITY

foreigners, and an elite of unmarried noble males (who remained bachelors so family wealth would flow to the next generation undivided). Venice also had a large number of women, committed nuns (including many forced as children into the convent as a cheaper alternative to marriage), abandoned children, widows, and former prostitutes, who lived in convents.

In this heterogeneous society there were also present those who dissented from the majority established religion, Catholicism. During the sixteenth century Venice was in many ways tolerant of heterodoxy. Its bookshops and taverns were homes to forbidden ideas. Venice cooperated with the Inquisition yet insisted on retaining its own investigators of religious dissent. In sum, in a diverse society the repressive hand of the Counter-Reformation was seen in Venice but could not act unrestrainedly.

**INTELLECTUAL AND ARTISTIC ACTIVITY**

During the same centuries of religious exploration, economic innovation, and empire building, Venice also was a center of intellectual and artistic activity. Historians, philosophers, mathematicians, and even humanists flourished from the fifteenth through the seventeenth century, although it was a humanism less critical of traditional structures of power than elsewhere. Venice became the major printing center of Italy, which means the most important printing center anywhere in the early years of that technological explosion. The work of Aldus Manutius (also Aldo Manuzio) (1449–1515), who opened his print shop in Venice in the 1490s, is especially notable. Among the many elegant Aldine editions are those of Greek and Roman authors thus printed for the first time anywhere in formats that made them accessible to scholars and amateurs. Venice participated in the artistic Renaissance in its own way, blending Gothic and classical styles in architecture and remaining loyal to traditional genres until fairly late. From the late fifteenth century to the sixteenth century, however, the Venetian masters Giovanni Bellini (c. 1430–1516), Giorgione (c. 1477–1511), Titian (1488 or 1490–1576), Tintoretto (c. 1518–1594), and Paolo Veneziano came to the fore with their characteristic sensitivity to color and light. In music, where Italy generally was laggard in the fifteenth century, needing to import composers and musicians from the Netherlands, Venice took a leading role from the sixteenth century. The city itself was a work of art. Its unique cityscape of breathtaking beauty, its ritual displays, and its interplay of costume and performance during the season of Carnival were magnets for all of Europe.

*See also* **Cateau-Cambrésis (1559); Genoa; Italy; Lepanto, Battle of; Printing and Publishing; Venice, Art in.**

BIBLIOGRAPHY

Brown, Patricia Fortini. *Venice and Antiquity: The Venetian Sense of the Past.* New Haven and London, 1996.

Davis, Robert C. *Shipbuilders of the Venetian Arsenal: Workers and Workplace in the Pre-Industrial City.* Baltimore, 1991.

Grendler, Paul F. *The Roman Inquisition and the Venetian Press, 1540–1605.* Princeton, 1977.

Lowry, Martin. *Nicholas Jenson and the Rise of Venetian Publishing in Renaissance Europe.* Oxford and Cambridge, Mass., 1991.

Mallett, M. E., and J. R. Hale. *The Military Organization of a Renaissance State: Venice c.1400–1617.* Cambridge, U.K., and New York, 1984.

Muir, Edward. *Civic Ritual in Renaissance Venice.* Princeton, 1981.

Pullan, Brian. *Rich and Poor in Renaissance Venice: The Social Institutions of a Catholic State, to 1620.* Oxford and Cambridge, Mass., 1971.

Romano, Dennis. *Patricians and Popolani: The Social Foundations of the Venetian Renaissance State.* Baltimore and London, 1987.

Ruggiero, Guido. *The Boundaries of Eros: Sex Crime and Sexuality in Renaissance Venice.* New York and London, 1985.

MARGARET L. KING

# VENICE, ARCHITECTURE IN.

According to Giorgio Vasari, the first historiographer of Italian Renaissance art, the modern era penetrated into Venice only with the arrival of the Florentine Jacopo Sansovino in the 1520s. Indeed, together with the Veronese Michele Sanmicheli and the Bolognese Sebastiano Serlio, who also arrived in the capital of the Venetian republic in the wake of the Sack of Rome of 1527, these architects were responsible for its Roman Renaissance. This is not to say that later fifteenth-century Venetian architects had not aspired to create a style *all'antica* or sought to bring glory to the city by emulating the architecture of the ancients. However, in its close trading ties with both Byzantium and the Levant, it is to Constantinople, as the second Rome, that Venice had traditionally looked. If the proud display of *spolia* such as the horses from the Hippodrome (looted from Constantinople and placed on the facade of San Marco) represented this veneration of antiquity, the lacy and ornate late Gothic style nevertheless persisted into the fifteenth century (Ca' d'Oro, begun 1421). This survival was due to a taste for rich materials and lavish decorations that was imported from the East and to the practices of stone masons imported from the West who had been trained in the tradition of a flamboyant Lombard Gothic style. Such was the case with architects like Mauro Codussi (St. Michele in Isola and the clock tower in the Piazza San Marco) and Pietro Lombardo (Santa Maria dei Miracoli), who were responsible for some of the most original buildings of the late fifteenth century in Venice.

## SIXTEENTH CENTURY

It is against this tradition favoring lavish surface decoration, colorful marble veneers, and effects of light and shade that the work of the great sixteenth-century architects must be understood. Although the fifteenth century saw the rise of Venetian economic power and the zenith of its maritime influence and the sixteenth the beginning of its gradual decline (after the wars with and defeat by the League of Cambrai between 1508 and 1529), it is paradoxically in the latter period that the most important monuments of the republic were built. The state sponsored major building campaigns—among which the complex surrounding the Piazza San Marco was the most conspicuous and important—precisely with the object of maintaining morale and projecting an image of security, power, and wealth at a difficult moment in its history. The architect of this *renovatio urbis* was Jacopo Sansovino (1486–1570), whose Zecca (the mint, begun 1536), Library of San Marco (begun 1537), Loggetta facing the Doge's palace (begun 1538), and Fabbriche Nuove di Rialto (market buildings, begun 1554), with their opulent and assertive classical style, displayed convincingly the importance and stability of the republic. The palaces he built for the patrician families (Dolfin, begun 1538, and Corner, begun 1545) as well as those by his contemporary Michele Sanmicheli (1484–1559) (Palazzo Grimani, begun

1556) which similarly relied on sequences of columns, tall facades, rich ornamentation, and equilibrium between horizontals and verticals, extended this image into the private domain.

In a city that had taken an early lead in the book publishing industry and where most of the principal Renaissance architectural treatises had first seen print (commentaries of *De architectura* by Vitruvius, the books on the orders and antiquities by Serlio, the treatises of Andrea Palladio, Giovanni Antonio Rusconi, and Vincenzo Scamozzi), patrons were both knowledgeable in matters of "modern" architecture and eager to see it built. This enthusiasm was reflected not only in the city but also in the countryside, toward which the patrician economic interests had turned after the mercantile fortunes of the republic had been threatened. Starting in the sixteenth century, the construction of villas, both as rural retreats and centers of estate management, rose dramatically. It is in villas such as Emo and Badoer, with their arcaded granaries flanking frescoed and meticulously proportioned central blocks set on a podium, that the Vicentine architect Andrea Palladio (1508–1580) consecrated the confluence of working farm and classical allusion that characterized the genre thereafter. Palladio's restrained interpretation of the temple front as church facade (San Giorgio Maggiore, begun 1566, and Il Redentore, begun 1577) also set the stamp on Venetian religious architecture of the late Renaissance and provided a model for churches into the eighteenth century. His intervention must be seen in contrast to the tradition of flamboyant facades particularly associated with the seats of lay confraternities attached to churches, such as the Scuola di San Rocco by Bartolomeo Bon and Antonio Scarpagnino (begun 1515).

## BAROQUE AND NEOCLASSICISM

If in the sixteenth century Venice was a center of architectural innovation and learning that could boast a great number of prominent architects, in the seventeenth century the uncertain fortunes of the elite and of the state led to something of a slowdown. Scamozzi, who succeeded Palladio, taking on the role of chief architect of the city, completed the remaining side of the square of San Marco with the Procuratie Nuove (the seat of the administrators of San Marco). Indeed, it was mainly the state and a

**Architecture in Venice.** *The Redentore Viewed from the Giudecca Canal,* by Canaletto. ©CHRISTIE'S IMAGES/CORBIS

few of the richest families who commissioned buildings of importance in this period. In this context the work of Baldassare Longhena, architect of Santa Maria della Salute (begun 1631) and of the Pesaro and Rezzonico palaces (begun 1652 and 1667, respectively), towers above the rest. His vocabulary drew on the Venetian traditional love of surface ornament and displayed rich sculptural decoration, heavy rustication, balustrades, masks, volutes, and keystone heads as well as dramatic effects of light and shade. Nevertheless, his architecture remained disciplined (drawing on Sansovino and Palladio) and resisted the scenographic effects associated with the Jesuit-inspired ecstatic religiosity current in Rome. His successor, Giuseppe Sardi, took the church facade type inherited from Palladio and refashioned by Longhena to an extreme of excessive ostentation from which no further development was possible (Santa Maria degli Scalzi, begun 1672, and Santa Maria del Giglio, begun 1678).

In the eighteenth century the economic fortunes of patrician families continued to decline and important architectural commissions came mainly from religious orders such as the Carmelites, Do-

minicans, and Jesuits. This reduction in wealth also led to a restraint in architectural vocabulary. Unlike other European countries where the baroque gave way to the rococo, in the Venetian republic this was only true of interiors. Their architecture, however, became increasingly sober and simple, and architects and theoreticians reacted more and more vociferously against the excesses of the baroque. Author-architects such as Antonio Visentini and Tommaso Temanza initiated a tradition of criticism as well as a renewed interest in the work of the great Renaissance architects. This Palladianism flowed easily into an incipient neoclassicism and marked the work of architects like Andrea Tirali, Giovanni Scalfarotto, and Giorgio Massari. Their buildings (San Nicolò da Tolentino, begun 1706, San Simeon Piccolo, begun 1718, and the Palazzo Grassi, begun 1748, respectively) display a move toward rationality, rigor, rules, and simplicity not only in the handling of ornament but also in floor plans and volumes.

Simultaneous with this trend was a rise in interest in the science of architecture. The tradition of military engineering (going back to the maritime power of the republic) and the work of Sanmicheli on the Arsenal, as well as the importance of hydraulic engineering in the city, contributed to this development. The work of Carlo Lodoli and Giovanni Poleni promoted an understanding of building science that ultimately saw a standardization of architectural training in Venice (as well as in Verona and Padua) and the development of a corps of military engineers educated on a model drawn from the French École des Ponts et Chaussées. Gianantonio Selva's theatre of La Fenice (finished 1792), severe and heavily dependent on the aesthetic of the plain wall, thus closes the century as a perfect illustration of the new classical sobriety and rationalism that pervaded both theory and practice.

*See also* **Architecture; Baroque; City Planning; Neoclassicism; Palladio, Andrea, and Palladianism; Venice.**

BIBLIOGRAPHY

Ackerman, James S. *The Villa: Form and Ideology of Country Houses.* Princeton and London, 1990.

Brusatin, Manlio. *Venezia nel Settecento: Stato, architettura, territorio.* Turin, 1980.

Concina, Ennio. *A History of Venetian Architecture.* New York, 1998.

Hopkins, Andrew. *Italian Architecture: From Michelangelo to Borromini.* London, 2002.

Howard, Deborah. *The Architectural History of Venice.* 2nd ed. New Haven, 2002.

Payne, Alina. *The Architectural Treatise in the Italian Renaissance: Architectural Invention, Ornament, and Literary Culture.* New York, 1999.

Tafuri, Manfredo. *Venice and the Renaissance.* Cambridge, Mass., 1989.

ALINA PAYNE

---

**VENICE, ART IN.** In about 1500 Venetian art bore an intimate relationship to its economic and political context. The traditional society of the Republic of Venice remained tied to the past, its conservative ideology reflected in well-established artistic conventions. Leading painters such as Giovanni Bellini (c. 1438–1516) worked mainly for local patrons, producing predominantly religious paintings of well-defined types (such as half-length devotional paintings and altarpieces). Their work was essentially public and patriotic in nature and reflected the nexus of religious and political values common to the wider populace of the city. The Venetian painter or sculptor was understood less as an individualistic genius than as a respectable civil servant. To a greater extent than elsewhere in Renaissance Italy, his professional life was controlled by the twin agencies of family workshop and guild. Certain of these traditional "core" conditions for the activity of artists in Venice did not change much over the following centuries (it is significant that a Venetian academy of painting was not founded until as late as 1754). And yet the history of Venetian art from 1500 onward must nonetheless map the gradual breakup of the integrated relationship between art and society in the city.

Giorgione (c. 1477–1511) was the first Venetian artist to radically challenge the traditional model for artistic activity in Venice. The small body of highly original paintings he produced in the first decade of the sixteenth century opened a new world for a generation of younger painters, including Palma Vecchio (c. 1480–1528), Vincenzo Catena (c. 1470/80–1531), Lorenzo Lotto (c. 1480–1556), Sebastiano del Piombo (1485–1547) and Titian. Perhaps most significant in this regard was Giorgione's partial withdrawal from the kind of painting that had previously tied Venetian artists to the cultural mainstream. Working primarily for a narrow elite of high-ranking patrons, Giorgione produced sophisticated "private" paintings, in which meaning was frequently rendered deliberately opaque or ambiguous. Giorgione's creation of a more intimate and secular kind of painting proved immediately inspirational. Artists made "portraits" of classical goddesses and courtesans in states of erotic dishabille (Palma, *Flora*, c. 1520–1525, National Gallery, London), or arcadian landscapes peopled by poeticized figures. A new type of Giorgionesque devotional imagery emerged, showing the Holy Family or *sacra conversazione* (sacred conversation) in wooded landscapes, often with a donor in attendance (Titian, *Madonna and Child, Saint John Baptist, and a Donor,* c. 1515, Alte Pinakothek, Munich). Titian, in particular, responded to Giorgione's exploitation of the special potentials of oil paint, adopting a similarly spontaneous approach, which ignored preparatory drawing on paper in favor of the manipulation of paint on the picture surface. It was through this special emphasis on coloring *(colorito)* that Venetian paint-

**Art in Venice.** *Bacchanal: The Andrians,* by Titian, painted c. 1516–1518. ©ARCHIVO ICONOGRAFICO S.A./CORBIS

ing of the early sixteenth century increasingly differentiated itself from that practiced elsewhere in Italy.

Titian, though, quickly developed a figure style that demonstrated his understanding of the monumental classicizing form of High Renaissance art in contemporary Florence and Rome. His frequent reference to antique and contemporary works in three dimensions may in part have been intended to show the ultimate superiority of painting to sculpture. But in works such as the *Bacchanals* (1518–1523, Museo del Prado, Madrid; National Gallery, London) he also responded to the developed classical taste of his high-ranking patron, Alfonso I

d'Este, duke of Ferrara. Titian's interest in classical form was fully shared by Tullio and Antonio Lombardo (c. 1455–1532; c. 1458–c. 1516), younger representatives of the family that had dominated the field of Venetian sculpture since about 1470. In a number of double bust-length portraits of young couples, for example, Tullio effectively bridged the gap between Giorgione's poetic mood and the revival of antique types: his so-called *Bacchus and Ariadne* (c. 1500, Kunsthistorisches Museum, Vienna) was clearly inspired by Roman reliefs. Antonio, meanwhile, carved more than thirty marble reliefs with classical subjects for Alfonso's private apartments in Ferrara (c. 1506–1516, State Hermitage Museum, St. Petersburg; Bargello, Florence). These works may not have been intended for the so-called Alabaster Room housing Titian's *Bacchanals,* but they are very similar in their attempt to revive an antique form of domestic decoration.

The d'Este commissions at Ferrara indicate that the developing interest in classicizing form was closely linked to the expansion of artistic patronage beyond the confines of Venice itself. The new type of courtly portraiture that Titian developed in the 1520s and 1530s was dependent on his contact with an increasingly international clientele of high-ranking aristocratic and royal families. But the new cosmopolitanism in Venetian art was certainly not confined to the work of Titian. Peripatetic painters such as Lotto and Pordenone (c. 1483–1539), who arrived in the city in 1527, brought styles that integrated formal ideas from other parts of Italy with more local conventions. The repeated references to antique sculpture and steep formal foreshortenings in Lotto's *Portrait of Andrea Odoni* (1527, Queen's Collection, London) reflect his experience of the art of central Italy, although the soft handling and warm palette recall the recent portraits of Titian. Pordenone's *Blessed Lorenzo Giustiniani* (c. 1532–1535, Gallerie dell'Accademia, Venice) refers pointedly to the quattrocento Venetian tradition of the *sacra conversazione* altarpiece. But Pordenone, who became an aggressive rival to Titian's hegemony in Venetian painting during the 1530s, shrinks the pictorial space and exaggerates the bodies of the main actors in a manner that pointedly recalls the Michelangelesque art of contemporary Florence and Rome.

The work of Jacopo Sansovino, the Florentine sculptor and architect who immigrated to Venice in 1527, owes relatively little to the kind of meticulous and prosaic classicism practiced by the Lombardi family in Venice in the early decades of the century. In works such as the bronze classical gods erected on the Loggetta in St. Mark's Square (1537–1542), Sansovino's manner is closer to the delicate and sophisticated mode of his Florentine contemporaries. Moreover, from about this time onward Venice was flooded with reproductive prints and statuettes after famous works by Raphael, Michelangelo, Parmigianino, and others. Perhaps inevitably, a "mannerist" phase followed, with even Titian's

painting briefly affected. But it was in the work of young painters such as Jacopo Bassano (c. 1510–1592), Andrea Schiavone (c. 1510–1563), and Jacopo Tintoretto that the mode really took root. These painters developed aggressively unorthodox styles, featuring complex, twisting figure groups, decentralized compositions, and heightened, sometimes non-naturalistic colors (Schiavone's *Adoration of the Magi,* c. 1547, Pinacoteca Ambrosiana, Milan).

It is no accident that this new intensity of response to foreign models coincided with the first concerted attempts to define a specifically "Venetian" tradition of art. Writing in response to the Tuscan Giorgio Vasari's disparagement of Venetian art in his *Lives of the Artists* (1st ed., Florence, 1550), local patriots such as Paolo Pino (fl. 1534–1565) and Ludovico Dolce (1508–1568) sought to define the local tradition. In his *Dialogue on Painting* (Venice, 1557), Dolce argued that Venetian art was quintessentially naturalistic and that this was achieved through the special skill of the city's painters in the use of color *(colore).* But while the idea of Venetian tradition as internally coherent and as essentially independent of the more idealizing design-based art of central Italy has often been restated, it does not really account for the wider diversity of manners practiced in the city after 1550. Tintoretto's work was deeply influenced by the formal idealism of Michelangelo, and careful preparatory drawings were central to the restrained manner of Veronese. Titian himself was soon to develop an unprecedented "late" style in which naturalistic features such as correct perspective and anatomical proportion were increasingly abandoned.

Many artists in mid- and later-sixteenth century Venice were visual opportunists, readily modifying their manner according to patron or picture type. Bonifazio de Pitati (1487–1553), for example, who ran a busy and influential workshop from the 1530s onward, took a pragmatic approach to painting in which consistency of style was sacrificed to flexibility. As the demand for visual imagery of all types increased (the vast majority of Venetian households possessed visual images by 1600), so artists diversified their products and devolved responsibility within their workshops to maximize production. Sansovino's own part in his later sculptural commissions was small: after sketching in clay, he typically

**Art in Venice.** *View of the Canal in Front of St. Mark's* by Canaletto. ©Archivo Iconografico S.A./Corbis

left the execution to his pupils, Alessandro Vittoria (1525–1608) and Danese Cataneo (c. 1509–1572). In like manner, Tintoretto employed specialist assistants to paint landscapes, still lifes, and even figures in his paintings as the scale of his pictorial commissions increased in the 1570s and 1580s. Artists, increasingly, marketed their work: Tintoretto may even have used his professional identity as "the little dyer" in this way, to suggest his readiness to paint for less prestigious patrons.

Two disastrous fires in 1574 and 1577 destroyed the main state rooms in the Ducal Palace and their pictorial decoration, resulting in an enormous commission for replacement ceiling and wall paintings for the workshops of Veronese and Tintoretto during the later 1570s and 1580s. But their work on this patriotic commission, devoted to the

"myth" of Venice as home of justice, peace, and liberty, ran alongside an increasing demand in the city's churches and lay confraternities for sacred imagery stressing the centrality of Christ and his sacraments to the faith. Under the impact of the Catholic Counter-Reformation, there was a marked upturn in commissions for paintings showing the heroic martyrdom of the saints or their acts of charity (Titian, *The Martyrdom of Saint Lawrence*, c. 1547–1556, Gesuiti, Venice; Bassano, *Saint Roch Healing the Plague-Stricken*, c. 1570–1573, Brera, Milan). In these works the Tridentine theologians' call for greater clarity of presentation was only partially answered. But the fiery spirituality of the imagery nonetheless reflects the deepening Catholicism of the age. Dramatic reduction in color, a lowering chiaroscuro, and a rough or unfinished painting surface combine to obscure all worldly form, as if to deny the viewer any enjoyment in mere external display.

The massive oeuvre of Palma Giovane (c. 1548–1628) is dominated by religious paintings. In works such as the cycle for the Oratory of the Crociferi hospital (1583–1592), Palma combined Titianesque naturalism in portraits and landscape with more idealized forms for the allegorical and sacred actors based on Tintoretto. Palma's stylistic pragmatism, like his constant reference back to the older generation of painters, was destined to become a kind of leitmotif of Venetian art in the seventeenth century. Pietro della Vecchia (1603–1678) made his name producing mock "Giorgionesque" paintings for collectors (*The Concert,* undated, Gemäldegalerie, Berlin), while the Fleming Nicolas Régnier (Niccolò Renieri, 1591–1667) combined painting with art dealing and collecting. But the internationalism of Venetian art also greatly intensified. The fame of the city's artistic tradition attracted important painters such as Bernardo Strozzi (1581–1644) from Genoa, along with Germans such as Johann Liss (c. 1595/1600–1631) and Johann Carl Loth (1632–1698). Strozzi and Liss, who arrived in the 1620s, used strong and varied color to produce an emotive stylistic hybrid of Venetian colorism and the international baroque. Later, in the 1660s, Loth, along with Giovanni Battista Langetti (1635–1676), introduced a darkened tenebrist manner, probably derived from paintings in Venice by Luca Giordano. But this in its turn quickly gave way, on the one hand, to the studious academism of Gregorio Lazzarini (1655–1730), and on the other to the decorative early rococo of Sebastiano Ricci (1659–1734).

The resulting stylistic potpourri has usually been seen as a reflection of the decline of Venetian artistic authority relative to other centers such as Bologna, Rome, and Naples. But art in Venice had long been responsive to other traditions, and the evident decline in quality in the seventeenth century had deeper causes. The aesthetic malaise reflected a more general social and economic one and is characterized by a kind of intense but ultimately debilitating retrospectivity. Early in the seventeenth century, Sansovino's pupil Vittoria was already busy collecting self-portraits of the famous Venetian masters, and later painters such as Carlo Ridolfi (1594–

1658) and Marco Boschini turned their efforts to writing ecstatic histories of the great Venetian tradition. The glorification of the Renaissance meant that the present constantly had to defer, and to this extent Venetian art of the seventeenth century became the victim of its own celebrated past.

If Venetian art had previously enjoyed a vital relation to the communal institutions and ideologies of the Republic, this was increasingly not the case. It is symptomatic that painting of the eighteenth century was dominated, on the one hand, by view painters working for a predominantly foreign clientele; and on the other, by those working in a decorative style in which form was more significant than content. The brilliant naturalism with which Giovanni Antonio Canaletto (1697–1768) and Francesco Guardi (1712–1793) represented Venice nonetheless served a growing pan-European idea of the city as a kind of miraculous survival or relic from a past age, whose special allure lay precisely in its "otherness." The intensely decorative paintings of Ricci, Giovanni Battista Piazzetta (1683–1754), and Giovanni Battista Tiepolo (1696–1770) similarly work their magic by detaching the viewer from the real and the present. Like their seventeenth-century predecessors, these artists were, in an obvious sense, deeply retrospective, their intense color harmonies referring back to the art of the Renaissance past, especially to that of Paolo Veronese. But in the case of Tiepolo, at least, the result was an art of revision rather than reversion, which transformed the conventions of Renaissance naturalism into an intensely self-contained decorative idiom that had no real precedents in Venetian art. In his vast decorative scheme for the Kaisersaal and grand staircase of the prince-archbishop's palace at Würzburg (1750–1753), Tiepolo's aesthetic dominance over the pretensions of his subject matter seems directly to anticipate the artistic autonomy of the artist of modern times.

*See also* **Painting; Tiepolo, Giovanni Battista; Tintoretto (Jacopo Robusti); Titian (Tiziano Vecelli); Vasari, Giorgio; Veronese (Paolo Caliari).**

BIBLIOGRAPHY

*Primary Sources*

Dolce, Ludovico. *Dolce's "Aretino" and Venetian Art Theory of the Cinquecento.* Translated and edited by Mark Roskill. New York, 1968. Includes text and translation of *Dialogo della Pittura* (1557).

Ridolfi, Carlo. *Le Maraviglie dell'Art*. Venice, 1648. Edited by Detlev von Hadeln. 2 vols. Berlin, 1914–1924.

*Secondary Sources*

Brown, Patricia Fortini. *Venice and Antiquity: The Venetian Sense of the Past*. New Haven and London, 1996.

Humfrey, Peter. *Painting in Renaissance Venice*. New Haven and London, 1995.

Huse, Norbert, and Wolfgang Wolters. *The Art of Renaissance Venice: Architecture, Sculpture and Painting, 1460–1590*. Chicago and London, 1990.

Levey, Michael. *Painting in XVIII Century Venice*. London, 1959.

Rosand, David. *Painting in Sixteenth-Century Venice: Titian, Veronese, Tintoretto*. Cambridge, U.K., 1997.

*Le siècle de Titien: L'âge d'or de la peinture à Venise*. Exh. cat. Paris, 1993.

*Venetian Seventeenth Century Painting*. Exh. cat. by Homer Potterton. London, 1979.

TOM NICHOLS

---

**VERMEER, JAN** (or Johannes, 1632–1675), Dutch painter. In 1653, Vermeer entered the Delft Guild of St. Luke as a painter, joining his father, who had registered with the guild as a picture dealer in 1631. It is not known with whom Vermeer learned his craft, but scholars have speculated that he studied either with Leonard Bramer (1596–1674) in Delft or with one of the Dutch followers of the Italian master Caravaggio who were active in Utrecht.

Only months before joining the guild, Vermeer married Catharina Bolnes (c. 1631–1688), a Roman Catholic from a distinguished family in Gouda. Vermeer, who was born to Protestant parents, probably converted to Catholicism at this time. *Allegory of Faith* of c. 1672–1674 is Vermeer's only painting with a specifically Catholic message. Here, the personification of faith takes communion before a painted crucifixion. An apple (signifying original sin) and a snake crushed by a stone (emblematic of the victory of Christ, the cornerstone of the church, over Satan) lie at her feet. As this work was likely tailored to adhere to the taste of the Catholic patron who commissioned the work, it is unwise to ascribe the meaning of the image to Vermeer's personal beliefs. It is not clear what, if any, impact Vermeer's religious orientation had upon his work.

The classical subject and large format of Vermeer's early *Diana and Her Companions* of c. 1655 suggest that Vermeer initially aspired to become a history painter, but by the late 1650s he shifted his focus to the genre interiors that would dominate his mature works. Vermeer first calmed the boisterous tavern scenes and curtailed the overtly sexual overtures of musical companies pictured by earlier Dutch genre painters. The girl in *Officer and Laughing Girl* (Frick Collection, New York), for example, sits calmly cupping her beverage in both hands; only her broad smile, and the soldier's bravura body language, indicate any attraction in this encounter. Similarly, Vermeer dispensed with melodramatic lighting in favor of more subtle plays of light. Many of Vermeer's early genre paintings are heavily dependent on the work of Pieter de Hooch (1629–after 1684), who was active in Delft until c. 1661. Vermeer followed de Hooch's innovative and illusionistic spatial recessions and surface effects sculpted from natural light before developing a personal aesthetic in the late 1660s based upon abstracted light and coolly crafted distances between viewer and subject. These later works, such as *Lady Writing a Letter with Her Maid* (National Gallery of Art, Dublin) that focus on women in domestic interiors seemingly provide entrée via the empty foreground but pen the figures behind middle ground obstructions. The light that pours in from the window fails to warm as it illuminates opaque, porcelain features and cool gray-green fabrics that hang straight in crystalline folds while it dissolves the table carpet into pools of unmodulated color. In this way, Vermeer gradually traversed the gulf between illusion and artifice.

Responses to Vermeer's paintings have focused most frequently on moralizing interpretations. Suspended from a larger narrative context, Vermeer's figures have been seen as behavioral models. Vermeer's women who entertain men away from Dutch society's watchful eye, like those in *The Concert* (Isabella Stewart Gardner Museum, Boston) may have been examples of unacceptable behavior, while his solitary, domestic women like *The Milkmaid* (Rijksmuseum, Amsterdam) may have been viewed as what Wayne Franits termed "paragons of virtue." Readings of this kind gain credence when positioned in relation to Vermeer's *Woman Holding a Balance* of c. 1662–1664, in

**Jan Vermeer.** *The Concert.* (See also the cover of Volume 5.) THE GRANGER COLLECTION

which the subject's ordinary activity takes on moral implications: her action is overshadowed by the representation of the biblical weighing of souls pictured immediately behind her.

Modern scholars have been as interested in how Vermeer painted as they have been in what he painted. Vermeer's spatial compressions and blurred perimeters suggest the influence of the camera obscura, a device that translated, but could not record, three-dimensional vignettes into two-dimensional reflections. Scholars concur that Vermeer was familiar with the device's optical effects, but a debate has arisen around the extent of Vermeer's use of the instrument. Some argue that Vermeer reproduced the camera's image in paint, while others have stressed a less dependent relationship. Delft was a center of optical experimentation due in part to the presence of the scientist Antoni van Leeuwenhoek (1632–1723), but as seventeenth-century Dutch art theory encouraged verisimilitude to be combined with artfulness, it seems unlikely

that an artist of Vermeer's stature merely replicated what was before him. In either case, Vermeer's canvases exhibit a meticulous buildup of forms and tones executed with a highly controlled brush.

Vermeer may have been able to practice such a labor-intensive method because he benefited from patronage, a rarity for Dutch painters of the period. John Michael Montias posited that as the Delft citizen Pieter Claesz van Ruijven (1624–1674) owned twenty of the approximately thirty-five known paintings by Vermeer, van Ruijven must have functioned as at least a de facto patron. He might, for example, have paid Vermeer for the right of first refusal on the artist's paintings. Such economic support would have freed Vermeer from the demands of the open market by enabling him to labor over each painting, confident that he would be adequately compensated for his efforts. Vermeer may have supplemented whatever income he generated from his painting by operating as an art dealer. These reasonably reliable sources of income would also explain Vermeer's extremely limited output, as he must not have felt pressure to produce his paintings in volume for the market.

The benefits of patronage apparently were not able to see Vermeer through the recession that followed the French invasion of the Netherlands in 1672. In 1676, a year after his death, his widow testified to her husband's creditors that Vermeer had amassed considerable debt in the 1670s because he had been unable to sell either his own paintings or those by other painters. She also stated that supporting their eleven children, all still minors, had exacerbated the family's financial situation. Like his fellow painters Rembrandt and Frans Hals, Vermeer apparently died in the throes of financial turmoil.

*See also* Camera Obscura; Leeuwenhoek, Antoni van; Netherlands, Art in the.

BIBLIOGRAPHY

Franits, Wayne E., ed. *The Cambridge Companion to Vermeer*. Cambridge, U.K., 2001.

Montias, John Michael. *Vermeer and His Milieu: A Web of Social History*. Princeton, 1989.

*Vermeer and the Delft School*. Edited by Walter Liedtke. Exh. cat. New York and London, 2001.

Wheelock, Arthur K. *Vermeer and the Art of Painting*. New Haven, 1995.

CHRISTOPHER D. M. ATKINS

# VERONESE (PAOLO CALIARI) (1528–1588),

Italian painter. Paolo Veronese (alongside Titian) was the most influential painter of the Venetian Renaissance. Trained in the 1540s in his native Verona by Antonio Badile and Giovanni Caroto, Veronese moved to Venice about 1551. He brought with him an intimate understanding of both Andrea Mantegna's spatial and structural precision in painting and Giulio Romano's more contemporary decorative mode (which drew heavily on the art of High Renaissance Rome, especially that of Raphael). These influences are already at play in early works such as *The Temptation of Saint Anthony* (1552–1553, Musée des Beaux Arts, Caen). But Veronese also proved immediately responsive to local artistic tradition in Venice. His first major commission in the city (the Giustiniani altarpiece of c. 1551, S. Francesco della Vigna, Venice) was modeled directly on Titian's Pesaro altarpiece, and many of his subsequent paintings of this type continue to refer to this seminal work. A few years later Titian recognized Veronese's deferential attitude by awarding him a golden chain for his contribution to a ceiling in the newly built Marciana Library (*Music*, 1556–1557).

Veronese quickly won favor with leading families among the Venetian nobility, and it was probably this connection with the upper classes that led him to change his name from Spezapreda (stonecutter) to Caliari (the name of a leading aristocratic family in Verona). His sensitivity to the values of Venetian patricians is evident in such portraits as *Giuseppe da Porto with His Son Adriano* (c. 1556, Contini-Bonacossi collection, Florence), which is characterized by a restrained magnificence. About 1560 the patrician brothers Daniele and Marcantonio Barbaro invited Veronese to fresco their new country villa at Maser, recently built by Andrea Palladio. Linking his images to one another—and also to the real space of the villa—by means of fictive architecture, Veronese provided a modern reconstruction of the kind of pictorial decoration found in ancient Roman country villas. To the somewhat obtuse allegorical program of his patrons, Veronese applied his usual light touch. His imagery manages to allude to all the main cultural, social, and economic functions of the house: as place of rural retreat, intellectual contemplation, family life, and agrarian productivity. But this content is constantly enlivened by playful trompe-l'oeil effects, intimate human and animal portraits, and humorous visual asides. The overt reference to classical models of domestic decoration is constantly underpinned (although never undermined) by the painter's special understanding of Venetian naturalism.

Between 1555 and 1565 Veronese worked on a series of paintings for the Hieronymite church of S. Sebastiano in Venice. Taken together, this ensemble (ceiling paintings, wall paintings on canvas and in fresco, painted organ-shutters, and an altarpiece) represents Veronese's masterwork in the field of sacred imagery. The nave paintings, showing scenes from the Book of Esther, offer a tour de force in illusionism and perspective foreshortening, but the tone remains festive and triumphal, and despite their religious content the compositions could serve well as models for subsequent works in a secular

**Veronese.** *Donna Giustiniani Barbaro with Old Nurse,* from the fresco cycle at Villa Barbaro, c. 1561. ©ARALDO DE LUCA/CORBIS

context. Veronese himself drew on these paintings in his later work for the Ducal Palace (for example, *Faith,* 1575–1578), while Peter Paul Rubens, Giovanni Battista Tiepolo, and many other painters over the next two centuries used the S. Sebastiano ceiling as a model.

Veronese's confident elision of secular and sacred modes in his paintings is most evident in privately commissioned works such as *The Supper at Emmaus* (c. 1559–1560, Musée du Louvre, Paris) in which patronal portraits crowd around the sacred figures under a Palladian loggia. In *The Marriage at Cana* (1562–1563, Louvre) for San Giorgio Maggiore, Veronese produced a scene of lavish contemporary feastmaking in an idealized Palladian setting. Among the group of finely dressed musicians are portraits of leading Venetian painters: Veronese shows himself (playing a viol) as prominent, along-

side the elderly Titian just to the right (playing a viola da gamba).

But such playful visual asides soon threatened to get the painter into trouble with the religious authorities. His inclusion of buffoons, dwarves, and German soldiers in the foreground of his *Last Supper* of 1573 (Gallerie dell'Accademia, Venice) landed him in front of the Catholic Inquisition who questioned the decorum of such additions. In response, the painter merely added an inscription identifying the subject as a less important one (the *Feast in the House of Levi*) and did not remove any of the offending figures.

Veronese's visual flamboyance did not markedly diminish in the 1570s, and it was only in the last decade of his life that he moved toward a more emotionally expressive approach (for example, *The Last Communion of Saint Lucy,* c. 1585–1586, National Gallery of Art, Washington, D.C.). But it was the integrated compositions of his earlier manner that were destined to be so influential on European artistic tradition over the following centuries. His sumptuous approach to picture making, underpinned by a clear grasp of perspective construction, offered a vital bridge between the scientific and naturalistic art of the early Renaissance and the decorative manner of the baroque and rococo periods. From the outset of his career, his pictorial lucidity reflected his special capacity for the absorption and integration of differing stylistic tendencies, and this gift for stylistic synthesis never deserted him.

*See also* **Venice, Art in.**

BIBLIOGRAPHY

*The Art of Paolo Veronese, 1528–1588.* Exh. cat. Edited by W. R. Rearick. Washington, D.C., 1988.

*Nuovi studi su Paolo Veronese.* Edited by M. Gemin. Venice, 1990.

Pedrocco, Filippo, and Terisio Pignatti. *Veronese catalogo completo.* Florence, 1991.

Pignatti, Teresio. *Veronese.* 2 vols. Venice, 1976.

TOM NICHOLS

---

**VERSAILLES.** The seat of the French monarchy from 1682 to 1789, Louis XIV's chateau at Versailles had its origins in a modest hunting lodge built in 1623 for his father, Louis XIII. When Louis XIV (ruled 1643–1715) assumed personal control of the government in 1661, he embarked upon a building program at the site that continued almost unabated until his death. Versailles was first an intimate retreat for the king and then a royal residence for a still itinerant court before it became the permanent seat of the French royal family, court, and government in 1682. Jean-Baptiste Colbert (1619–1683), Louis XIV's indefatigable finance minister, was responsible for procuring the staggering sums needed to build the chateau that became the model for royal palaces across Europe.

**ARCHITECTURAL HISTORY**

Louis XIV's magnificent chateau evolved in three major phases. The Sun King first intended Versailles to be a retreat from the responsibilities of government. Between 1661 and 1668, the architect Louis

Le Vau (1612–1670), the gardener André Le Nôtre (1613–1700), and the painter Charles Le Brun (1619–1690) collaborated to create a palace suitable for the Sun King to entertain favored courtiers. When Louis XIV decided in 1668 that Versailles was to become a royal residence, able to house his full court for months at a time, he ordered extensive additions. Le Vau drew up plans to frame the Old Chateau in a terraced "envelope" of white stone. The envelope included state apartments for the king and queen, the salons of which were each dedicated to one of the seven planets known to orbit the sun. The king's own bedchamber, echoing the theme articulated in the chateau's gardens, depicted scenes from the myth of Apollo.

Work on the chateau and its gardens was by no means complete when Louis XIV permanently installed his family, court, and government at Versailles in 1682. Jules Hardouin-Mansart (1646–1708) oversaw the final enlargement of the palace and adjacent buildings that would eventually house five thousand courtiers and as many government officials, guards, and servants. It was Mansart who designed the legendary Hall of Mirrors. Running almost the entire length of the chateau's western facade, the gallery was sheathed in mirrors, furnished with solid silver chandeliers, and crowned by ceiling panels by Le Brun that depicted pivotal episodes from the Sun King's life. Meanwhile, Le Nôtre continued to expand the gardens, adding grottoes, ornamental lakes, and a Grand Canal so vast the navy could perform maneuvers on it. Construction on Louis XIV's palace ceased only with the completion of the Chapel Royal in 1710.

The exterior of Versailles changed little over the course of the eighteenth century. Louis XV (ruled 1715–1774) came to loathe his great-grandfather's formal palace and added little to it. Although he commissioned the Royal Opera designed by Jacques-Ange Gabriel (1698–1782), he was far more interested in increasing the privacy of his own apartments. Louis XVI (ruled 1774–1792), the last of the Bourbons to rule at Versailles, also concentrated on interior renovations. His queen, Marie Antoinette (1755–1793), concerned herself with the Petit Trianon, a bucolic palace on the grounds of Versailles. After a revolutionary crowd triumphantly carried the ill-fated king and his family back to Paris in 1789, the chateau fell empty. The history

**Versailles.** Detail of a 1668 painting of the chateau and entrance court by Pierre de Patel. (See also the cover of Volume 6.)
THE ART ARCHIVE/MUSÉE DU CHÂTEAU DE VERSAILLES/DAGLI ORTI

of Versailles as the residence of the French kings officially ended in 1837, when Louis-Philippe declared that the royal chateau was to become a museum celebrating "all of France's glories."

**TOWN OF VERSAILLES**

The fortunes of the town of Versailles waxed and waned with the presence of the court. Louis XIV razed the original village to make room for his chateau's grand avenues and parks. He rebuilt the town on a new site, decreed that it was to become "the most frequented and flourishing in the world," and strictly regulated even the colors of building materials and decorations for its houses. With the court in permanent residence, Versailles became the administrative capital of France, the seat of all branches of government except the judicial. By the end of the seventeenth century, the town's population—swelled by those whose occupations or interests brought them to court—stood at over 30,000, and its inns could house hundreds more. With the death of Louis XIV in 1715, the court departed for Paris, and Versailles soon became a ghost town. It enjoyed a revival after 1722, when Louis XV returned to his great-grandfather's palace. Versailles lost its position as the administrative capital permanently in 1789 with the forced departure of Louis XVI for Paris.

**NOBLE LIFE AT COURT**

For many years, Versailles was seen as a gilded theater upon whose stage an all-powerful absolute

**Versailles.** The Galerie des Antiques at the Chateau of Versailles, c. 1688, painting by Martin des Batailles. THE ART ARCHIVE/ MUSÉE DU CHÂTEAU DE VERSAILLES/DAGLI ORTI

monarch entertained a captive audience of domesticated aristocrats. Recent research has shown, however, that Louis XIV could not arbitrarily dominate his subjects. His rule was limited by the fundamental laws of the realm, tradition, and the practical difficulties of enforcing his will on an extended country of twenty million people. Furthermore, without a police force or a standing army, the king relied upon his noble subjects to ensure order in the kingdom. Louis XIV's reign was consequently marked by cooperation with, rather than control over, the aristocracy. Similarly, the court of Versailles was a site of mutually satisfactory exchange between king and nobility. The king required the great nobles to attend court because he sought to ensure their loyalty. They came because they considered it their right and privilege and because they received social and material rewards for doing so.

The vast majority of the French nobility did not live at Versailles. Only the *grands,* the highest-ranking French nobles, were in residence. Even at the peak of noble attendance, the ten thousand court nobles represented only 5 percent of the hereditary nobility. Attendance was on a system of quarters that entailed residences of three months, twice a year. The privileged among this number were granted rooms within the chateau itself (which contained 220 apartments and 450 surprisingly small rooms); the less fortunate lived in the town of Versailles or were forced to travel back and forth to Paris each day. At the palace, the Sun King provided a continuous whirl of ballets, operas, fêtes, plays, and thrice-weekly gambling nights. While Louis XIV prevented members of the hereditary nobility from participating in affairs of state, courtiers did have more to do than attend entertainments, for many held offices in the royal households.

The primary duty of every courtier, however, was to attend the king. Accompanying the king conferred prestige but, even more important, allowed nobles to gain access to royal patronage. To secure the allegiance of his nobility and to prevent anyone else from gaining too much influence and power, Louis XIV distributed all royal patronage personally—no chief minister had control over the treasury, the distribution of estates, or the assignment of lucrative church posts or military commands. Those nobles who did not attend court seldom received any reward. Louis was known to say, when solicited for a favor on behalf of a noble who did not come to Versailles as often as the king liked, "I do not know him."

Louis XIV subjected his courtiers to a strict etiquette that governed their comportment, manners, and dress. This precisely graded code meted out privileges according to a noble's position in the court hierarchy. It determined, for example, who was allowed wear a hat and when, and who could sit in the presence of the royal family. The sociologist Norbert Elias has famously argued that the intricate rules and rituals that governed the members of Louis XIV's court facilitated the creation of the modern centralized state. The ordered society of Versailles became the European ideal of the well-run state.

Louis XIV performed the role of sacred kingship like an actor who never broke character. He calibrated his movements, gestures, and expressions at all times. The activities of his day—waking, dressing, socializing, eating—all followed a regimen so exacting that his every gesture took on a ritual status. This ceremonial elevated the status of the monarch at the same time that it limited access to him. The *lever,* the king's ceremonial awakening, serves as an example. During this daily "kingrise," six strictly designated sets of noblemen entered the royal bedchamber to dress the monarch. The highest-ranking noble present received the greatest privilege, that of handing the king his shirt. Courtiers vied to attend the *lever* (or its evening counterpart, the *coucher*) because it provided an opportunity to ask favors of the king. Those excluded could importune the monarch only as he traveled in his ritualized orbit from bedchamber to chapel to council chamber over the course of the day.

Without a monarch dedicated to the public performance of monarchy, the court of Versailles could not function so effectively as an instrument of rule. Through force of personality (and a renowned capacity for hard work), Louis XIV created a court that was simultaneously an irresistible social center for the high nobility and a seat of government for his ministry. This system, however, was largely dependent on the personality and abilities of the ruler. Louis XIV tirelessly performed the rituals of kingship, but neither Louis XV nor Louis XVI was willing to maintain such strict ceremonial. They also proved less able to divert members of the high nobility away from affairs of state or to maintain as effective a control over their ministers and state policies. Over the course of the eighteenth century, the court of Versailles, which had once been a celebration of divinely appointed monarchy, instead came to represent a center of despotism.

*See also* **Absolutism; Colbert, Jean-Baptiste; Court and Courtiers; France; Louis XIV (France); Louis XV (France); Louis XVI (France); Marie Antoinette; Monarchy; Saint-Simon, Louis de Rouvroy.**

BIBLIOGRAPHY

*Primary Source*

Saint-Simon, Louis de Rouvroy, duc de. *Historical Memoirs of the Duc de Saint-Simon: A Shortened Version.* Edited and translated by Lucy Norton. 3 vols. New York, 1967.

*Secondary Sources*

Adamson, John, ed. *The Princely Courts of Europe: Ritual, Politics, and Culture under the Ancien Régime, 1500–1750.* London, 1999.

Beik, William. *Absolutism and Society in Seventeenth-Century France: State Power and Provincial Aristocracy in Languedoc.* Cambridge, U.K., and New York, 1985.

Damien, André. "Versailles, Capitale?" *Revue des sciences morales & politiques* 151 (1996): 21–38.

Elias, Norbert. *The Court Society.* Translated by Edmund Jephcott. New York, 1983.

Le Roy Ladurie, Emmanuel. *Saint-Simon and the Court of Louis XIV.* Translated by Arthur Goldhammer. Chicago, 2001.

Mukerji, Chandra. *Territorial Ambitions and the Gardens of Versailles.* Cambridge, U.K., and New York, 1997.

Newton, William B. *L'espace du roi: La cour de France au château de Versailles, 1682–1789.* Paris, 2000.

Solnon, Jean-François. *La cour de France.* Paris, 1987.

Lynn Wood Mollenauer

---

**VESALIUS, ANDREAS** (1514–1564), Belgian anatomist. Born in Brussels, Vesalius came from a family of physicians with professional links to the courts of Austria and Burgundy. Between 1530 and 1536 he studied at the universities of Louvain and Paris. He acquired skill in the technique of dissection and a thorough comprehension of Galenic anatomy in Paris, where a deep philological and hermeneutical reassessment of the Galenic corpus was under way. Due to the outbreak of the war between Charles V and Francis I, Vesalius returned to Louvain in 1536, and there he published the *Paraphrasis in Nonum Librum Rhazae* (Paraphrase of the ninth book of Rhazes). After a brief stay in Venice as a surgeon, he settled in Padua, where he took a degree in medicine in 1537. In the same year he was appointed lecturer of surgery. As a teacher, he combined in a revolutionary way the functions of lecturer, demonstrator, and dissector. Between 1538 and 1539 he published the *Tabulae Anatomicae Sex* (Six anatomical plates), a set of six large sheets of anatomical woodcuts accompanied by brief explanatory notes, and the so-called Venesection letter, a defense of the humanist and Greek view on bloodletting against medieval and Arab interpretations. On the basis of both his outstanding knowledge of Galen's texts (Vesalius also collabo-

rated to the Giunta edition of Galen's *Opera Omnia*, published between 1541–1542) and his anatomical findings, he wrote *De Humani Corporis Fabrica Libri Septem* (Seven books on the structure of the human body), published in Basel by Joannes Oporinus in 1543. After the publication of the *Fabrica*, Vesalius sought employment in the imperial medical service. He became military surgeon and personal physician to Emperor Charles V (ruled 1519–1556). Between 1543 and 1544 he returned briefly to Italy, giving public anatomies in Padua, Bologna, and Pisa. In the *Epistola Rationem Modumque Propinandi Radicis Chynae Decocti* (1546; Letter on the manner of administering the china-root), he investigated the therapeutic value of the china-root. After Charles V's abdication in 1556, he was appointed physician to the Netherlanders at the Spanish court by Philip II. In the same year he published a revised edition of the *Fabrica* containing some relevant additions on cardiovascular physiology. He died in 1564 during a pilgrimage journey to Jerusalem.

*De Humani Corporis Fabrica* represents an extraordinary intellectual accomplishment that combines anatomical investigation, artistic ingenuity, woodcut craftmanship, and typographical expertise. Vesalius's intention was to give a most detailed and reliable account of the human body, an account purged of previous errors, based on direct reference to cadavers, and corroborated by the use of animal vivisection and comparative anatomy. The *Fabrica* can be viewed as both the foundation of modern anatomy and as a reference handbook for those practitioners who could not have direct access to dissection material. The anatomical illustrations were in all likelihood the product of artists and draftsmen from Titian's studio. Vesalius planned the enterprise and directed the execution, and it can be assumed that he had some share in the actual draftsmanship.

The *Fabrica* is more a correction of errors in Galen than it is an announcement of revolutionary discoveries. Vesalius was a formidable teacher and an outstanding performer of anatomical demonstrations, capable of entrancing observers with his manual dexterity. The importance of his work lies in his advanced pedagogical techniques and in his methodological views about anatomy. He introduced the use of anatomical drawings as a teaching device, mnemonic aid, and alternative source of information in the absence of a sufficient supply of cadavers. He revolutionized anatomical practice by establishing a reliable correspondence between the dissected body, the text of reference, and the illustrations. He contributed significantly to the standardization of anatomical nomenclature. From the religious point of view, Vesalius's work touched on some highly critical points in contemporary theological debates, such as the location of the faculties of the soul, the physical similarities between human and animal brains, the existence of the reticular plexus at the base of the brain, and the manufacture of animal spirits.

*See also* **Anatomy and Physiology; Medicine; Scientific Illustration; Scientific Method; Surgeons.**

BIBLIOGRAPHY

*Primary Source*

Vesalius, Andreas. *On the Fabric of the Human Body, Books I–II.* Translated by William Frank Richardson. San Francisco, 1998–1999.

*Secondary Sources*

Cushing, Harvey. *Bio-bibliography of Andreas Vesalius.* New York, 1943.

O'Malley, Charles D. *Andreas Vesalius of Brussels, 1514–1564.* Los Angeles, 1964.

Siraisi, Nancy G. "Vesalius and the Reading of Galen's Teleology." In *Medicine and the Italian Universities, 1250–1600.* Leiden, Netherlands, 2001.

GUIDO GIGLIONI

# VICO, GIOVANNI BATTISTA

(Giambattista Vico; 1668–1744), Italian philosopher of history, law, and culture. Vico was born in Naples on the eve of the Feast of St. John the Baptist (23 June). He lived all his life in and near Naples, where his father was the proprietor of a small bookshop, above which the family lived in a single room. Vico's mother was illiterate. In a society dominated by wealth, political power, aristocracy, and clergy, Vico was self-made and self-taught. From grammar school on he spent only short periods in formal instruction. The center of his mature education was a self-devised program of reading the ancients against the moderns, carried out while tutoring the children of the Rocca family for nine years at Vatolla (1686–1695). In 1699 he

won the concourse for the professorship of Latin eloquence (rhetoric) at the University of Naples, a position he held until succeeded in 1741 by his son Gennaro. As part of his duties Vico presented a series of orations to inaugurate the academic year, the two most prominent being "De nostri temporis studiorum ratione" (1709; On the study methods of our time) and "De mente heroica" (1732; On the heroic mind). This series of orations taken collectively constitutes a full doctrine of pedagogy.

In 1710 Vico published *De Antiquissima Italorum Sapientia* (On the most ancient wisdom of the Italians), the first part of a system of philosophy directed against Cartesianism. (The planned second and third parts were never completed.) The work contains one of Vico's best-known principles, "that the true is the made." He first applied this as a principle of mathematical reasoning; later he applied it in his science of history—because human beings make history, they can make a complete knowledge of it. In 1720–1722 Vico published a large, three-part work, *De Universi Juris Uno Principio* (Universal law), in anticipation of qualifying for a university chair in civil law. In 1723 he suffered the greatest disappointment of his career, his failure to succeed in the concourse for this position, described in his *Autobiografia* (1728–1731).

*Universal Law* was a prelude to his magnum opus, *Principi di una scienza nuova d'intorno alla comune natura delle nazioni* (1725, 1730, 1744; Principles of new science concerning the common nature of the nations). Failure of the concourse left him free to develop the versions of this work. Through an analysis of Roman law begun in *Universal Law* and in particular the concept of *ius gentium* (the law of the peoples)—that part of Roman law which it has in common with the laws of all other nations—Vico developed his conception of "ideal eternal history," according to which all nations develop through a natural law of three ages. The age of gods, in which all of nature and basic social institutions are ordered in terms of gods, is followed by the age of heroes, in which all virtues necessary to society are embodied in the character of the hero, followed by the age of humans, in which custom is replaced by written law and thought becomes abstract and rational.

This ideal eternal history stands against the seventeenth-century natural-law theories of Hugo Grotius (Huigh de Groot [1583–1645]), Samuel von Pufendorf (1632–1694), John Selden (1584–1654), and Thomas Hobbes (1588–1679). In place of a state of nature, from which human beings form a covenant, passing from a state of war of all against all to a state of rationally governed civility, Vico formulates his conception of "poetic wisdom" or, in modern terms, "mythical thought." Societal life first depends upon the human power of *fantasia* (imagination) to narrate the meanings of events through myths. From mythical commonalities, rational forms of understanding gradually develop. Against the Enlightenment principle of progress, Vico sees history as cyclic, that is, each nation passes through a *corso* (course) of the ages of ideal eternal history and falls, only to rise again in a *ricorso*.

Vico's influence on later thinkers is sporadic. Johann Gottfried von Herder (1744–1803), Karl Marx (1818–1883), Samuel Taylor Coleridge (1772–1834), and William Butler Yeats (1865–1939) discovered Vico and realized their connection to him after their own views were largely formulated. The major figure of the nineteenth century fully influenced by Vico was Jules Michelet (1798–1874), who translated Vico's works into French, making them the basis of his own philosophy of history. The two figures most influenced by Vico in the twentieth century and who in turn introduced Vico to many readers were Benedetto Croce (1866–1952) and James Joyce (1882–1941). Croce merged Vico's conception of history and society with his own philosophical idealism, making Vico into the Italian Georg Wilhelm Friedrich Hegel (1770–1831). Joyce was influenced by Vico throughout his career. Most prominently Joyce based the cycles of *Finnegan's Wake* (1939) on Vico's *New Science*, as he had based *Ulysses* (1922) on the ports of call of Homer's *Odyssey*.

*See also* **Cartesianism; Grotius, Hugo; Herder, Johann Gottfried von; Philosophy; Political Philosophy.**

BIBLIOGRAPHY

*Primary Sources*

Vico, Giambattista. *The Autobiography of Giambattista Vico.* Translated by Max Harold Fisch and Thomas Goddard Bergin. Ithaca, N.Y., 1975. Translation of *Vita di Giambattista Vico Scritta da se medesimo.*

———. *The New Science of Giambattista Vico.* Translated by Thomas Goddard Bergin and Max Harold Fisch. Ithaca, N.Y., 1984. Translation of *Principi di una scienza nuova d'intorno alla comune natura delle nazioni.*

———. *Opere.* 2 vols. Edited by Andrea Battistini. Milan, 1990. Edition of many of Vico's major works, including most helpful commentary and notes on each.

*Secondary Sources*

Berlin, Isaiah. *Three Critics of the Enlightenment: Vico, Hamann, Herder.* Edited by Henry Hardy. London, 2000. Treats Vico's philosophical ideas as the beginning of the Counter-Enlightenment.

Mazzotta, Giuseppe. *The New Map of the World: The Poetic Philosophy of Giambattista Vico.* Princeton, 1999. Connects Vico's thought to the basic figures and themes of the Renaissance.

Verene, Donald Phillip. *The New Art of Autobiography: An Essay on the "Life of Giambattista Vico Written by Himself."* Oxford, 1991. An analysis of Vico's autobiography and its connection to New Science.

———. *Vico's Science of Imagination.* Ithaca, N.Y., 1981. An assessment of Vico's philosophical ideas and their originality.

DONALD PHILLIP VERENE

# VICTORIA, TOMÁS LUIS DE (1548–1611), preeminent composer of the Spanish Renaissance. Rivaled only by Giovanni da Palestrina and Orlando di Lasso among his European contemporaries, Victoria produced an important body of work that was widely distributed, often reprinted, and highly praised from his time to ours. He is not only the most famous of the sixteenth-century Spaniards such as Cristóbal de Morales and Francisco Guerrero, but is arguably the most famous Spanish composer of all time.

An apparently proud Ávilan, who appended his name with "Abulense" in his publications, Victoria received his early musical training as a choirboy at Ávila Cathedral under Gerónimo de Espinar and Bernardino de Ribera. He may have known the illustrious organist Antonio de Cabezón during his Ávilan residence. With the help of his patron Cardinal Otto von Truchess of Augsburg, he went to Rome to study music and theology at the Collegium Germanicum in 1565. Four years later, he took charge of music at the Aragonese Church of Santa Maria di Monserrato, and soon afterward he took up positions at the two Jesuit colleges: the

Collegium Germanicum (1571) and the Collegium Romanum (1573, where he succeeded Palestrina, whom he knew and with whom he possibly studied), thus situating him at the intellectual and artistic heart of Jesuit activity during the height of the spiritual renewal sparked by the Council of Trent (1545–1563). His compositional and directorial activities in Rome and his association with Palestrina have led many historians to classify him as a "Roman School" composer, while others have emphasized his Spanish identity.

In 1572, Victoria published a collection of motets that would establish his fame, including "O magnum mysterium," "O vos omnes," and "Vere languores." His early motets were reprinted several times in his own lifetime. Ordained to the priesthood in 1575, he joined the Congregazione dei Preti dell'Oratorio (Congregation of the Oratory), and from 1578 to 1585 served as chaplain of S. Girolamo della Carità, where, free from the demands of a musical position and supported by lucrative Spanish benefices provided by Pope Gregory XII, he published several important collections of music while living in daily contact with Rome's great pastor, St. Philip Neri, for five years.

Victoria returned to Spain in 1587 to take up the position of chaplain to the Dowager Empress Maria at the Monasterio de las Descalzas de Santa Clara de la Cruz in Madrid, to which he was appointed by Philip II. He spent the rest of his life at the monastery, first as *maestro di capilla* and, after Maria's death in 1603, as organist. His return to his Castilian homeland saw him turn down prestigious positions at Spanish cathedrals in favor of his position at the royal monastery, where his music was performed by an expert choir and where he was allowed to oversee his publications abroad. He died in Madrid in 1611.

Victoria's reputation is based mostly on a somber collection of motets, a collection of music for Holy Week, and his Office for the Dead. These paint an unfairly morose picture of the composer whom some would regard as typically Spanish. His Masses paint a very different picture, being mostly based on motets with exultant texts. His cycle of sixteen Magnificats puts him in league with other Spaniards, such as Morales, Guerrero, and Alonso Lobo, who were unmatched in their attention to

the Canticle of Mary. His *Officium Hebdomadae Sanctae* (Office of Holy Week) was the first of its kind, and the Passions of Saints Matthew and John it contained were in constant use by the papal chapel into modern times. It also included his well-known *Lamentations of Jeremiah* and eighteen responsories for Tenebrae.

Like Claudio Monteverdi, Victoria stands at the end of the Renaissance and the beginning of the baroque period. His writing contains (indeed, exemplifies) much of the traditional church polyphony, consisting of several melodies that intertwine in a complex, harmonious web, but he also wrote simple psalm settings in the *falsobordone* style (such as Psalm 50 in the *Officium Hebdomadae Sanctae*) and polychoral works such as the *Missa Pro Victoria* (for double choir), which show the emergence of the baroque style with its emphasis on pitting parts of the ensemble against other parts. Beginning in 1600, he became the first significant composer to write independent keyboard accompaniments, anticipating the publications of the Venetian Giovanni Gabrieli by fifteen years. His later progressive compositions never achieved the fame of his early works, with the exception of the beloved *Officium Defunctorum* (Office of the dead, 1605), written upon the death of Empress Maria.

A genuinely religious man, Victoria wrote only sacred works. His output, while often understood as reflecting the mystical spirituality of El Greco and his fellow Ávilan St. Teresa de la Cruz, might be better understood in relation to the popular devotional spirituality of Neri and the Council of Trent's program of spiritual renewal, which was promoted with special zeal by the Jesuits who were responsible for his intellectual and musical formation.

*See also* **Catholic Spirituality and Mysticism; Jesuits; Monteverdi, Claudio; Music; Palestrina, Giovanni Pierluigi da; Trent, Council of.**

BIBLIOGRAPHY

Cramer, Eugene Casjen. "Some Elements of the Early Baroque in the Music of Victoria." In *De Musica Hispana et Aliis.* Vol 1, pp. 501–538. Santiago de Compostela, 1990.

———. *Studies in the Music of Tomás Luis de Victoria.* Aldershot, U.K., 2001.

Stevenson, Robert. *Spanish Cathedral Music in the Golden Age*. Berkeley and Los Angeles, 1961.

LEE MATTHEW ESCANDON

**VIENNA.** From the later thirteenth century, when Vienna and its surrounding territories were claimed by the Habsburg Dynasty, until the mid-fifteenth century, the Habsburgs slowly built up the old residence of their predecessors, the Babenbergs, and the one-time Roman legionnaires' camp into a sizable city complete with a church dedicated to Saint Stephen as well as a university and a castle residence built next to one of the old Roman roads leading to this important Danube River crossing. By 1500 the city may have had a population of approximately twenty to thirty thousand.

For some time during the fifteenth century, the Styrian branch of the Habsburg Dynasty held the upper hand among the Habsburg relations in central Europe, and their city, Wiener Neustadt, was the preferred residence of many of the Austrian dukes, including the important Habsburg Duke Frederick who was crowned Holy Roman emperor in Rome by Pope Nicholas V in 1452 and ruled until 1493. The emperor was able to achieve the long-standing Habsburg goal of elevating their church in Vienna, St. Stephen's, to episcopal status through papal permission in 1469. (The rival residence city of Wiener Neustadt was similarly honored in the same year.) Now Vienna would be not only a trading city, university town, and sometime archducal residence. It was the center of a modest ecclesiastical jurisdiction as well, one which often unhappily shared religious responsibilities with its

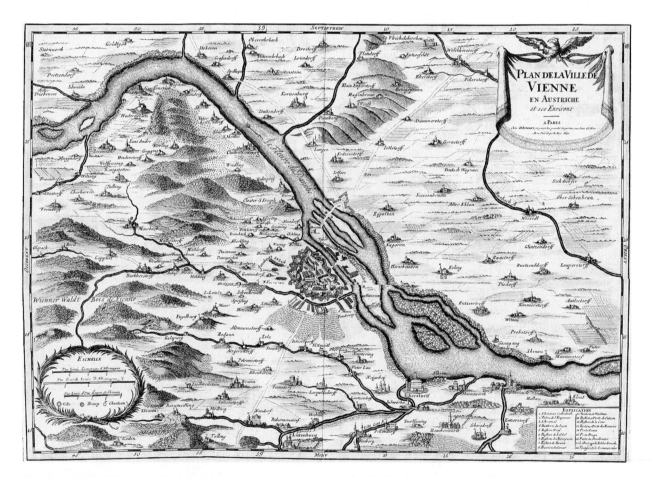

**Vienna.** A view of the city and the surrounding area based on a map by Nicolas Sanson, from a French atlas issued in 1692. The map shows the city's strategic location on the Danube, and identifies the neighboring cities and towns. Long the seat of the Habsburg Empire, Vienna had recently survived a bitter siege by the Ottoman Turks in 1683, and it was later transformed into a city of palaces and stately homes. A second line of fortifications was built in 1704–1706. MAP COLLECTION, STERLING MEMORIAL LIBRARY, YALE UNIVERSITY much more powerful neighbor, the Diocese of Passau, which also had administrative offices in Vienna.

For Vienna, the later fifteenth century meant a change in regimes: renewed claims over this area by the kings of Hungary led to an occupation of the city by the Hungarian King Mathias I ("Corvinus") Hunyadi beginning in 1485. King Mathias died in the city in 1490. The turbulent and multifaceted relationship with Hungary is an important aspect of Viennese history in this period.

The city on the Danube was again brought under Habsburg control through the efforts of Emperor Frederick's son, Archduke and later Emperor Maximilian I (ruled 1493–1519), who spent much of his time arranging Western marriages and residing in the Habsburg city of Innsbruck in Tyrol, among many other locations. For some time, the exact position of Vienna in the Habsburgs' plans was unclear. The Iberian and Burgundian inheri-

tances engineered by Maximilian necessarily meant that the dynasty's representatives were more tied to cities such as Ghent or kingdoms such as Castile than to the rather forgotten city on the Danube River.

When Maximilian's grandson and younger brother of Emperor Charles V, the Spanish-born Archduke Ferdinand (who ruled 1558–1564 as Holy Roman Emperor Ferdinand I) chose Vienna as his residence, the city fathers had already established a local regime with its own sense of autonomy. In the 1520s this urban regime was harshly suppressed by the archduke and his officials, and the city administration was reorganized under stricter dynastic control. Ferdinand had arrived in the city with a sizable retinue of Iberian nobles, military personnel, and other assorted hangers-on, and the Spanish-speaking community in the city and at the court endured at various levels for two centuries,

**Vienna.** *The Ceremonial Entry into Vienna of Isabella of Parma, Bride of Emperor Joseph II,* eighteenth-century painting by Martin Meytens. ©ERICH LESSING/ART RESOURCE, N.Y.

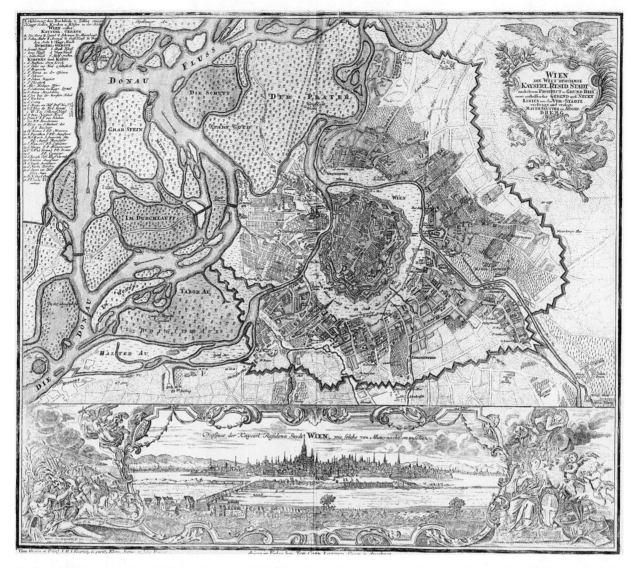

**Vienna.** A striking map from Mathaeus Seutter's 1745 *Atlas Novus* showing the imperial city of Vienna, the official residence of the Habsburgs. At bottom is a view of the skyline from across the Danube River. The new circle of fortifications around the outskirts of the city was built in the early eighteenth century; to the left of the old walled city is the Leopoldstadt, or second district, the center of Vienna's large Jewish community. MAP COLLECTION, STERLING MEMORIAL LIBRARY, YALE UNIVERSITY

reflecting the resident rulers' close ties to their dynastic kin in the West.

One of the pivotal years for the history of early modern Vienna was 1529, when Ottoman troops besieged the city, following on their successful campaigns of the previous years, which had succeeded in defeating the Hungarians and in advancing the Ottomans' control well into that nearby kingdom. The siege was successfully resisted, but the results of the destruction in the suburbs and the economic dislocation the siege had brought lasted for much of the century. The economic foundations of many of the

city's religious houses, which controlled properties outside of the old city walls, for example, were wrecked, and this, together with the increasing popularity of the teachings of Martin Luther and his followers, made the culture of the city increasingly Protestant, much to the dismay of Archduke Ferdinand, who resided in the Hofburg, the fortified Habsburg residence in the city.

Following the extinction of the Hungarian ruling dynasty in 1526, Habsburg claims to the Hungarian crown meant that Vienna maintained a certain dynastic importance because it was located so near to Bratislava, the newly relocated capital of Hungary, just down the Danube River. Military operations in the Hungarian kingdom were planned and administered from Vienna, even while the Habsburg rulers themselves increasingly gave in to the allures of Vienna's long-time rival, Prague, as their preferred place of residence. (Ferdinand and his two successors as Holy Roman emperor, Maximilian II and Rudolf II, were all buried in St. Vitus's cathedral in that Bohemian capital.) Ferdinand's grandson, the emperor Rudolf II (ruled 1576–1612), officially moved his residence up to the castle in Prague in the 1580s, leaving his brother Archduke Ernst and his sister Archduchess Elisabeth, the widowed queen of France, to reside in Vienna and attempt to regulate the increasingly unruly and Lutheran city population.

Conflicts over the Habsburg succession in Bohemia and Hungary eventually degenerated into the Thirty Years' War (1618–1648), but they had little direct effect on Vienna. For the most part, the fighting took place well away from the city, although in its earliest stages in late 1618 and early 1619, enemy troops reached the city's vicinity, as did Swedish troops in 1645. The continued rather uncertain status of Vienna in its rulers' imaginations was reflected in the decision of Emperor Ferdinand II (ruled 1620–1637) to return to his ancestral homeland, Styria, to be buried in 1637.

The true blossoming of Vienna as the baroque capital of central Europe and the undisputed capital of the Habsburg Dynasty came only later, in the eighteenth century. The city was once again besieged by Ottoman troops in 1683 and once again successfully withstood their attacks, with the help of King John III Sobieski of Poland. Unlike the aftermath of 1529, however, subsequent Habsburg military campaigns pushed the Ottoman frontier well into Hungary and farther to the southeast. Vienna changed in character from a border fortress to a centrally located administrative and trading center, well located on the Danube for trading downstream with the newly conquered Hungarian territories. The Habsburgs' loss of their Iberian inheritance through the War of the Spanish Succession (1701–1714), as well as their earlier setbacks in the Holy Roman Empire during the Thirty Years' War, combined to redirect the dynasts' attention toward the south and east. Vienna was well situated to benefit from this reorientation.

The alliance of the Habsburgs and their supporters with a reinvigorated Roman Catholicism during the Counter-Reformation also provided an ideology and a cultural program that were physically reflected in the triumphant, new post-1683 city. New convents and monasteries abounded, and a much more extensive (although less militarily effective) wall (the 1704 *Linienwall*) was constructed. Noble palaces and Habsburg summer residences were constructed outside the confines of the walls as well, reflecting a new optimism and sense of security that would only be challenged when Napoleon's troops neared the city in the early nineteenth century. Vienna was now the capital of one of Europe's most important powers. It remained so until the demise of that power in the early twentieth century.

*See also* **Austria; Ferdinand I (Holy Roman Empire); Ferdinand II (Holy Roman Empire); Frederick III (Holy Roman Empire); Habsburg Dynasty: Austria; Holy Roman Empire; Hungary; Maximilian I (Holy Roman Empire); Prague; Rudolf II (Holy Roman Empire); Vienna, Sieges of.**

BIBLIOGRAPHY

Barker, Thomas Mack. *Double Eagle and Crescent: Vienna's Second Turkish Siege and its Historical Setting.* Albany, N.Y., 1967.

Csendes, Peter. *Historical Dictionary of Vienna.* Lanham, Md., 1999.

Lorenz, Hellmut. "The Imperial Hofburg: The Theory and Practice of Architectural Representation in Baroque Vienna." In *State and Society in Early Modern Austria,* edited by Charles W. Ingrao. West Lafayette, Ind., 1994.

Spielman, John P. *The City and the Crown: Vienna and the Imperial Court, 1600–1740.* West Lafayette, Ind., 1993.

Weigl, Andreas, ed. *Wien im Dreißigjährigen Krieg: Bevölkerung, Gesellschaft, Kultur, Konfession.* Vienna, 2001.

JOSEPH F. PATROUCH

---

# VIENNA, SIEGES OF.

The city of Vienna was the object of two unsuccessful sieges by Ottoman forces during the early modern period.

## THE FIRST SIEGE, 1529

When, at the battle of Mohács in 1526, the troops of Sultan Suleiman I (ruled 1520–1566) wiped out the Hungarian army and killed King Louis II, they cleared the way to the Hungarian throne for their main rival, the Habsburgs. After Suleiman's protégé, János Szapolyai (ruled 1526–1540), was ousted from Hungary by his rival, Ferdinand I of Habsburg, also elected king of Hungary (1526–1564), Suleiman was eager to redress the unintended consequences of his victory at Mohács. The Ottoman army of 80,000 to 100,000 men retook Buda, Hungary's capital, from the Habsburgs in September 1529 and gave it back to their ally János. Suleiman, however, wanted the resolve the Habsburg-Ottoman rivalry in Central Europe by conquering Vienna, the capital of the Habsburgs' Danubian Monarchy. Vienna was defended by some 18,000 to 25,000 soldiers under the able leadership of Niklas Graf zu Salm and Wilhelm Freiherr von Roggendorf, who had ordered the city's medieval and obsolete defenses substantially strengthened. The siege lasted for some two weeks (27 September–15 October 1529). The Ottoman bombardment was not effective, for the attackers had had to leave their siege artillery in Bulgaria and Hungary owing to unusually rainy weather and muddy roads. The defenders discovered or disarmed most of the Ottoman mines, and when some mines did succeed in opening significantly large holes, the attackers were repulsed by pikemen and harquebusiers. With winter approaching, the Ottomans raised the siege. After another failed attempt in 1532, when the small Hungarian castle of Küszeg (Güns) stopped Suleiman's army, the sultan and Ferdinand accepted the status quo in Hungary.

## THE SECOND SIEGE, 1683

In 1683 Vienna was besieged for the second time by the Ottomans, who by 1541 had conquered central Hungary, bringing the frontier dangerously close to the Austrian capital. The 1660s saw new Ottoman conquests in Hungary (1660 and 1663), Crete (1669), and Poland-Lithuania (1672 and 1678) under the able leadership of the Köprülü grand viziers. The recent revival of Ottoman military fortunes, the renewed Franco-Habsburg rivalry, and, more importantly, the weakness the Habsburgs had shown in Hungary against Imre Thököly's *Kuruc* insurrection (1681–1683), persuaded Kara Mustafa Paşa, the ambitious grand vizier (1676–1683), that the time had come to conquer Vienna. With the auxiliary troops of Crimean, Walachian, Moldavian, and Transylvanian vassals, the army that reached the outskirts of Vienna by early July numbered some 150,000 men, although only 40,000 were central troops of the standing army and although, as in 1529, the Ottomans lacked heavy siege artillery. Count Ernst Rüdiger von Starhemberg ably directed the 15,000-strong defense forces, but by early September heavy Ottoman bombardment and mining opened numerous breaches in the walls, and the defenders were running short of supplies. The fifty-nine-day siege ended with the arrival of the imperial and Polish relief army under the command of Charles V, duke of Lorraine, and King John III Sobieski (ruled 1674–1696) on 11 September 1683. The decisive battle of Kahlenberg, at the edge of the Vienna Woods, took place the next day when the relief army of 75,000 destroyed the unprotected attackers' camp. Kara Mustafa and his army fled, leaving rich booty for the Christians. Vienna was saved by a coalition of Central European countries, whose army proved to be tactically superior and was, for the first time in the history of Ottoman-European confrontations, able to match the Ottomans in terms of deployed manpower and weaponry, as well as in logistical support.

*See also* **Ottoman Empire; Suleiman I.**

BIBLIOGRAPHY

Barker, Thomas M. *Double Eagle and Crescent: Vienna's Second Turkish Siege and Its Historical Setting.* Albany, N.Y., 1967.

Broucek, P., E. Hillbrand, and F. Vesely. *Historischer Atlas zur Zweiten Türkenbelagerung: Wien 1683.* Vienna, 1983.

Kreutel, Richard F., ed. *Kara Mustafa vor Wien.* Graz, 1982.

Leitsch, Walter. "Warum wollte Kara Mustafa Wien erobern?" *Jahrbücher für Geschichte Osteuropas* 29, no. 4 (1981): 495–514.

GÁBOR ÁGOSTON

# VIÈTE, FRANÇOIS (1540–1603), French mathematician. Viète is widely viewed as the founder of modern algebra. Born in Fontenay-le-Comte in the province of Poitou, he studied law at the

University of Poitiers and received his degree in 1560. Shortly thereafter he entered the service of the noblewoman Antoinette d'Aubeterre and served as legal adviser as well as educator of her daughter, Catherine of Parthenay (later Rohan). His position in the household of this leading Huguenot family involved him with increasing prominence in the tense religious rivalries of the time. In 1573, following several years in Paris, he was appointed counselor to the Parlement of Brittany in Rennes by King Charles IX, and in 1580 he became a member of Henry III's privy council. Following a period of political eclipse in the late 1580s, he was recalled to court in 1589 and served as counselor to Henry III and Henry IV until his death on 23 February 1603. During his years as royal counselor Viète specialized in cryptanalysis, becoming one of the leading code breakers in Europe. His success in decoding secret Spanish communications famously brought upon him the accusation of being in league with the devil.

Despite his active career at court, Viète found time to research and publish an impressive number of mathematical works in a range of different fields. His most influential work, however, was undoubtedly in algebra. The field known as "algebra," he contended, was not, in fact, an achievement of Arab mathematicians, but was a corruption of the ancient "Art of Analysis" which was known in classical times. Unlike synthesis, which begins with self-evident assumptions and proceeds deductively to necessary conclusions, analysis proceeds in the reverse direction. In analysis, one assumes that the desired conclusion is true and then proceeds to deduce the implications of this assumption. If this leads to a known true relationship, it is a good indication (although no proof) that the original assumption was true. The mathematician can then reverse course and use the analysis as a guide for a synthetic proof of the theorem. If, on the other hand, the assumption leads to a falsehood, it is also necessarily false.

Classical mathematicians, Viète believed, used analysis extensively in their research. Unfortunately, as they only considered synthetic proof to be proper and incontrovertible, they proceeded to suppress the analytic part of their research in their published works. This left their modern-day successors with beautiful and elaborate synthetic constructions, such as can be found in the writings of Euclid and Archimedes. The method used by the ancients to discover their theorems—namely analysis— appeared to be lost. Viète set out to correct this unfortunate state of affairs by recovering the ancient "Art of Analysis." Beginning with his *Introduction to the Analytic Art* of 1591, and continuing in a series of subsequent works, he laid down the basic outlines of the ancient method as he perceived it.

Viète's fundamental insight was that the "Art of Analysis" was none other than the algebra. In algebra, he pointed out, one proceeds analytically: when presented with a mathematical problem, one assumes that the solution has already been found, and sets up a mathematical relationship accordingly. One then proceeds to analyze this relationship, arriving ultimately at a true solution if such exists. This, he claimed, was precisely the approach used in ancient analysis.

Viète realized, however, that the algebra of his time was inadequate to the task. It consisted of a long and increasing list of solutions to specific problems and practical rule-of-thumb methods to help with the solution of others. This, for Viète, was evidence of the corrupt state of algebra and the need for restoration. He therefore sought to replace the haphazard algebraic practices with general rules of analysis that would guide the solution of all problems.

To accomplish this, Viète proposed a novel system of notation. For the first time, he distinguished between the given magnitudes of a problem and the unknown ones, which must be sought out. The given magnitudes, he proposed, should be signified by consonants (B, C, D, F . . . ) and the unknown ones by vowels (A, E, I, O, U, Y). This simple innovation enabled Viète to write down not just specific linear, quadratic, and cubic problems, but general types of linear, quadratic, and cubic equations. Consequently, once a general type of equation was analyzed and solved, any particular instance of this type could be solved as well. With considerable justification, Viète referred to his "recovered" Art of Analysis as "the doctrine of discovering well in mathematics" (*doctrina bene inveniendi in mathematicis*).

In addition to algebra, Viète contributed to numerous other mathematical fields including trigonometry, conic sections, and astronomy. His enduring reputation, however, rests firmly on his algebraic work. Despite his claim that he was merely recovering an ancient method, his approach was in fact very different from the geometrical analysis practiced in antiquity. It is ironic, but telling, that Viète, who sought to replace the corrupt "algebra" with pure "analysis," has become known to subsequent generations as the father of modern algebra.

See also Henry III (France); Henry IV (France); Mathematics.

BIBLIOGRAPHY

*Primary Sources*

Viète, François. *The Analytic Art.* Translated by T. Richard Witmer. Kent, Ohio, 1983.

————. *Oeuvres Mathematiques.* Edited by Jean Peyroux. Paris, 1991–1992.

*Secondary Sources*

Klein, Jacob. *Greek Mathematical Thought and the Origin of Algebra.* Translated by Eva Brann. New York, 1968.

Mahoney, Michael S. "Nullum Non Problema Solvere: Viète's Analytic Program and its Influence on Fermat." In *The Mathematical Career of Pierre de Fermat,* pp. 26–71. 2nd ed. Princeton, 1994.

AMIR ALEXANDER

# VIGÉE-LEBRUN, ELISABETH (1755–1842), French painter.

Known primarily for her portraits, Vigée-Lebrun was a favorite artist of aristocratic patrons throughout Europe at the end of the eighteenth century, the most famous of whom was Queen Marie Antoinette of France (1755–1793). Vigée-Lebrun was born in Paris, the daughter of a hairdresser from the province of Luxembourg, Jeanne Maissin, and a minor portraitist, Louis Vigée, who was a member of the Académie de Saint-Luc. Her father gave her drawing lessons in his studio when she was twelve, although he died shortly after they began. She then studied drawing with two minor artists, Blaise Bocquet and Gabriel Briard. By her own account, she was largely self-taught, copying Old Master paintings in private collections she visited in the company of her mother. By the age of fifteen, she had established herself as a professional portraitist but practiced without a license. In 1774, after her studio had been seized by officers of the Châtelet (royal tribunal in Paris), she applied for membership in the Académie de Saint-Luc, exhibiting several works in the Salon de Saint-Luc that same year. Her ambition, however, was to be received as a history painter by the Académie Royale de Peinture et de Sculpture.

During the late 1770s, Vigée-Lebrun completed several history paintings but remained barred from acceptance into the Académie Royale because of the commercial dealings of husband, Jean-Baptiste-Pierre Lebrun, an art dealer. Upon Marie Antoinette's intervention, however, the honor of full membership was granted on 31 May 1783. (Her reception piece, *Peace Bringing Back Abundance* (1780), is now in the collection of the Louvre Museum). The minutes of the meeting at which Vigée-Lebrun was accepted for membership state that the academicians acted to execute "with profound respect the orders of its Sovereign." However, her painting was assigned no category.

Although Vigée-Lebrun was never apprenticed to a master painter and was prohibited by her sex from becoming a student at the Académie Royale, she nevertheless profited from her study of leading artists from the French school. She was greatly influenced by Jean-Baptiste Greuze (1725–1805), particularly in terms of her technique, which uses a buildup of transparent glazes to generate highly polished surface textures in areas of flesh and drapery. As with Greuze, her lack of academic training contributed to this reliance on the use of color, rather than line, to define form. Her approach to composition in many of her large state commissions, such as the *Portrait of Marie Antoinette* (1778; Musée national du Château de Versailles) follows the illustrious examples of portraits by Hyacinthe Rigaud and Jean Marc Nattier, favorite court artists during the reigns of Louis XIV and Louis XV, respectively.

Vigée-Lebrun's debt to the Old Masters is evident in her highly sought-after *maternités* (mother and daughter images), which register a direct lineage back to the Madonnas of Raphael, and in her *Self-Portrait in a Straw Hat* (1783; National Gallery of Art, London), which deliberately quotes a portrait by Peter Paul Rubens. While some scholars consider this work to be a straightforward tribute to the celebrated courtier-artist, others regard it as a clever assertion on the part of Vigée-Lebrun of her ability to assume a similar place in history. Indeed,

**Elisabeth Vigée-Lebrun.** Marie Antoinette with her children, 1787. THE ART ARCHIVE/MUSÉE DU CHÂTEAU DE VERSAILLES/DAGLI ORTI (A)

her aspirations to enjoy the elevated status of a history painter would be satisfied not by following the usual paths of academic progress, but through her novel conceptions in the realm of portraiture that challenged notions of conventional subject hierarchies and divisions between genres.

## PATRONAGE AND PRESTIGE

Vigée-Lebrun received her first royal commission in 1776, executing several portraits of the king's brother, the comte de Provence (whereabouts unknown). Two years later, she was called upon to paint the queen. Marie Antoinette had been searching for an artist who would best capture her likeness, and she responded to Vigée-Lebrun's singular ability to lend an informal air to the requirements of royal portraiture. Her *Portrait of Marie-Antoinette with Her Children* (1787; Musée national du Château de Versailles) is a brilliant combination of tradition and innovation. In this painting, Vigée-Lebrun follows the conventions of state portraiture by looking back to Nattier's portraits of Queen Marie-Leczinska and Madame Adélaïde (the wife and daughter of Louis XV) in the construction of her composition; however, she adds a contemporary reference to the popular idea of the "good mother" by merging the ceremony of state with the intimacy of family. This painting also transcends the limitations of a single genre by treating the portrait as both a history painting and a scene of everyday life.

Equally novel was the *Portrait of Marie-Antoinette* (1783; private collection, Germany) *en chemise* in which the sitter wears a simple, sheer white muslin dress and straw hat. This remarkably casual portrait caused a sensation at the salon, where it was said that the queen appeared in her underwear. While many critics commented on the impropriety of such a representation, which was not formal enough to suit contemporary standards, this painting and others like it influenced the course of costume development in France. Such portraits popularized a new look of loosely constructed garments, unpowdered hair, and natural curls—as opposed to the conventional French dress that required corsets and ornate wigs.

In addition to her activities as a painter, Vigée-Lebrun hosted one of the most fashionable salons in Paris, where music, literature, and the arts were topics of conversation. Her famous *souper grec*

(Greek supper) took place in 1788, an impromptu event inspired by literary recitations at which guests donned Greek attire and dined on a menu prepared from ancient recipes, served on a collection of archaic pottery. The entire affair was orchestrated by Vigée-Lebrun and took on the character of a *tableau vivant* (living painting). The expense of the event was greatly exaggerated by rumors, resulting in her vilification in scandal sheets. In the late 1780s, she increasingly became a figure of controversy.

A staunch royalist throughout her life, Vigée-Lebrun profited from her service to the French court, but this allegiance also forced her into exile during the Revolution of 1789, accompanied by her only child, Jeanne Julie Louise (born 12 February 1780). Her prestigious reputation did not fail her, and she continued to work in aristocratic circles, traveling first to Italy, then Austria, Germany, and Russia. She enjoyed great success at these foreign courts, securing her fortune before she was repatriated in 1801. While she continued to paint late in life, the energies of her last years were devoted to composing her memoirs, the first installment of which was published by Hippolyte Fournier in 1835. Vigée-Lebrun died in Paris at the age of eighty-seven.

*See also* **Art: Artistic Patronage; France, Art in; Marie Antoinette; Women and Art.**

BIBLIOGRAPHY

*Primary Source*
*The Memoirs of Elisabeth Vigée-Le Brun.* Translated by Siân Evans. Bloomington, Ind., 1989.

*Secondary Sources*
Baillio, Joseph. *Elisabeth Louise Vigée Le Brun 1755–1842.* Exh. cat. Fort Worth, 1982.

——. "Le dossier d'une oeuvre d'actualité politique: Marie-Antoinette et ses enfants par Mme Vigée Lebrun." *L'oeil* 308 (March 1981): 34–41 and 74–75; and *L'oeil* 310 (May 1981): 53–60; 90–91.

Goodden, Angelica. *The Sweetness of Life: A Biography of Elisabeth Louise Vigée Le Brun.* London, 1997.

Radisich, Paula. "Qui peut definer les femmes? Vigée-Lebrun's Portraits of an Artist." *Eighteenth-Century Studies* 25 (Summer 1992): 441–468.

Sheriff, Mary D. "The Cradle Is Empty: Elisabeth Vigée-Lebrun, Marie-Antoinette, and the Problem of Intention." In *Women, Art and the Politics of Identity in Eighteenth-Century Europe.* London, 2003.

————. *The Exceptional Woman: Elisabeth Vigée-Lebrun and the Cultural Politics of Art.* Chicago and London, 1996.

JENNIFER D. MILAM

# VILLAGES.

**VILLAGES.** The village, alongside the parish and the family, was the most widespread unit of social organization throughout the early modern period. There were well over 130,000 villages in western Europe, each a largely self-sufficient rural community with a population that averaged between 100 and 500 inhabitants. Flexibly adapted to a wide range of state structures and environments, villages often enjoyed high degrees of self-government. Many also performed essential state services, including tax collection, poor relief, and the maintenance of order. Although far from democratic in modern terms, village assemblies at times displayed the most broad-based political participation of any governing institution in western Europe. Villages were anything but static communities; rates of mobility and exogamy were significantly higher than once thought. This mobility in turn reflected major changes in land exploitation patterns and in world markets, which permanently altered the economic balance of communities between 1450 and 1789. By 1550, the polarization of villages into a minority of prosperous peasants exploiting large holdings and a majority of nearly landless rural laborers had dramatically changed the social landscape. By the end of the seventeenth century, the economic division of Europe into regions closely connected to the Atlantic and world economies and regions left behind affected patterns of wealth and power within villages.

## VILLAGE ORGANIZATION AND SOCIAL STRUCTURE

Social hierarchy in the village was well defined in most regions. As serfdom or villeinage declined by 1450, a new pyramidal social structure had emerged over a broad swath of western Europe. At the base of the peasantry were landless day laborers, joined by cottagers who rented or sharecropped less than enough land to live on in bad years. In many regions they constituted 50 to 60 percent of the village population, and increasingly depended upon weaving and cottage industry to eke out a subsistence living. One grade above were those who leased, rented, or sharecropped a self-sufficient holding. In upper Normandy, a relatively prosperous region, these modestly independent farmers represented only about 20 percent of the village households in the late seventeenth century, and they leased fewer than twenty-five acres apiece. But this middling sort (in England, husbandmen) were universally shrinking in numbers. Provinces as diverse as Languedoc and Normandy in France, as well as much of England and Scotland, the maritime provinces of the Dutch Republic, and northwestern Germany, all experienced significant losses of middling peasantry beginning in the mid-fifteenth century.

At the pinnacle of village society a new peasant elite had fully developed by 1550, composed of large leaseholders (copyholders) or freeholders (owners). Known as *laboureurs* in France, yeomen in England, or *Vollbauern* in Germany, they typically owned their own plow and team, employed other villagers as day laborers, and exploited a minimum of about 50–100 acres. Strongest in wealthier regions along the cereal plains of Europe and in England, these substantial peasant exploiters typically represented between 5 and 15 percent of village households. But they were surprisingly evident in poorer regions as well; they made up nearly 10 percent of the population in parts of Naples, for example. This peasant elite was essential to the stability of the community as a whole. They often lent seed, livestock, and cash to their poorer neighbors, though often at ruinous interest rates. Landless villagers in turn depended upon casual wage labor from wealthy peasants and landlords for their survival. In larger villages, the nucleus of cultivators and laborers was complemented by a small group of rural artisans (especially coopers and blacksmiths) and service providers (millers and innkeepers).

This core of peasants, artisans, and wage laborers was topped by a thin layer of privileged rural elites. These were men (and occasionally women) who were of the village, but not entirely in it. Noble lords or seigneurs resided in some villages, although they were increasingly absentee landlords by the seventeenth century. Their estate stewards and seigneurial court judges, along with well-to-do landlords who were not yet noble (gentry or *sieurs*), priests and pastors, royal judges, and rural merchants all exercised substantial control over land use

**Villages.** *A Village Street with Peasants and Travelers, a Canal Beyond,* by Jan Brueghel the Younger. ©CHRISTIE'S IMAGES/CORBIS

and wages in the village. This group also collectively controlled civil, canon, and customary laws; criminal punishment; public works; and some poor relief—powers that affected villagers on a daily basis.

The physical maps of western European villages varied greatly, but tended to fall into two main patterns. Across the broad band of open cereal plains like the Beauce, the nucleated village with its outlying fields cut up into plow strips or furlongs was typical. In wooded areas like Shropshire, England, or mountainous regions like the Pyrenees, Alps, and Apennines, isolated farms and scattered hamlets were common. They enjoyed some of the highest levels of autonomy and self-government, remote as they were from the central state. But these scattered settlements were intimately tied together by common social institutions, particularly the parish church, the local market, and the law courts.

From the sixteenth through the eighteenth centuries, however, the twin processes of enclosure and engrossment (consolidation) of fields wrought sig-

nificant changes in village land-use patterns. The English enclosure movements of the sixteenth and eighteenth centuries, like the notorious highland clearances in Scotland, fenced off common lands for sheep runs or agricultural improvements. Engrossment allowed larger blocks of fields to be brought under the management of one owner or lessor, which made enclosures easier. The social consequences were often dire: increasing pauperization or flight of villagers who no longer had crucial access to the common lands. Even without these new stresses, village communities were the sites of a delicate balancing act between resources and population throughout the early modern period. Late marriages, low rates of illegitimacy, and limitation of family size were the key factors that allowed villages to survive under near-subsistence conditions.

Despite their small size, there was a high degree of social and economic mobility bubbling below the surface of western European villages. Some was downward mobility, driven by growing rural stresses from the mid-sixteenth to the eighteenth century. Economic polarization that pushed more peasants into the landless category, population growth that overburdened villages, and the enclosure and engrossment of land caught many in the economic downdraft. Villages across Europe expressed increasing concerns about (and often a hardening of attitudes toward) vagabonds, "sturdy beggars," and the settled poor. Expanding cities like London and Paris were one of the safety valves for the rural needy. The resultant rates of mobility are sometimes striking: One English village in Northamptonshire experienced a 52 percent turnover in households in just the twenty years before 1638.

Upward mobility was still in the grasp of other village groups, however. Prosperous peasants became the feeder school for the gentry. Those who had acquired roughly a hundred acres or more could begin the delicate process of insinuating themselves into the landlord class of the village by ceasing to work with their hands, educating sons in the law, marrying into gentry families, and having themselves duly noted down in the parish records as *sieurs* or "gentlemen." Indeed, the wealthy peasantry and the gentry often formed a kind of social convection zone in the village, where gentry who failed to maintain their position sank back into the peasantry, and careful peasants moved up to replace them. In the parish of Myddle in seventeenth-century England, only half the gentry were able to maintain their status over two or three generations; the rest were replaced by yeomen and merchants. The most difficult step upward was from the day laborer or cottager class into the ranks of the wealthy peasantry. One expert has estimated that it required an English day laborer's wages for a hundred years to acquire a self-sufficient farm holding. Moreover, the numerous advantages held by village elites made it difficult to become a self-sufficient landowner. Through strategic marriages, command of property law, control of the village assembly and common lands, and usurious loans secured by farms, land was magnetically attracted toward those who already had land.

## COMMUNAL BONDS

The organization of western Europe into villages, as opposed to tribal or kinship organization, was based on neighborhood solidarities among distinct fami-

lies. This sense of neighborhood emerged in the language as *voisinage* in France and *Nachbarschaft* in Germany, and it was cemented by a number of institutions and traditions. At the center was the parish church, which united even scattered farms and hamlets into the village community. (In many regions parish and village boundaries were largely coterminous, but they were not always so.) Sunday services were only one of the occasions for creating parish bonds. Religious confraternities, celebrations of holy days, marriages, and baptisms all helped to cement communal bonds across family lines. The parish church, in tandem with the village assembly, organized poor relief for the community. Even the arrangement of the church served to remind villagers of their assigned place in the social hierarchy: church benches, for those important enough to sit during services, were strictly arranged according to rank.

Beyond the doors of the parish church, taverns, alehouses, and weekly markets served as vital centers of sociability. On winter evenings, villagers often congregated together to save light, repair tools, and tell stories. Seigneurial and royal assizes regularly brought villagers together to resolve (or occasionally inflame) their disputes in court. Many of these institutions and traditions cut through social hierarchies and regularly brought poorer and wealthier members of the village into contact with each other. But villages were also arenas of conflict, which was expressed in endemic lawsuits, physical violence, *charivaris,* and witchcraft accusations. The inherent tensions created by wide gulfs in economic, honorific, and power status were always latent. Even a relatively small community of forty or fifty families might encompass a family of supernova aristocrats and landless paupers.

The village in turn was more deeply embedded in larger economic and social circuits than was once believed. Annual fairs brought into the village country dwellers from a wide circumference, as well as merchants from urban areas; in France these often included theater troupes and peddlers of cheap popular books (the famous Bibliothèque Bleue). Royal courts on the Continent, and circuit assizes in England, drew university-trained lawyers and judges into the countryside. English justices of the peace, drawn almost exclusively from the rural gentry class, had become fixtures in the House of Commons by

**Villages.** A seventeenth-century engraving depicts commercial activities at the edge of a village. THE GRANGER COLLECTION, NEW YORK

the seventeenth century and were expected to help control elections to Parliament in the county. Aristocrats and nobles took rural servants, particularly women and girls, into the cities with them; many of them returned to the village as young women with dowries. In transhumance areas and coastal regions, it was the young men who typically left home for months at a time, to follow herds of sheep or to fish as far away as Newfoundland. Above all, the production of both bulk goods and luxury goods for the Atlantic trade tied villages into global cycles of boom and bust. Production of cotton, linen, and flax, the weaving and dying of fabric and lace, cheese making, wine making, and glassmaking became central to village economies from the Veneto in Italy to western France to Flanders and the Dutch Republic. As both the state and impersonal economic forces made a wider impact on village life, they became the source of new discontents.

Their solidarity helped to make villages the natural locus of rural riots and protests against these wider powers. Enclosure riots in England and Scotland, periodic tax and bread riots, and poaching and smuggling everywhere expressed the villagers' firm sense of their customary rights against landlords, tax

officials, and grain suppliers. One need only think of the German Peasants' War of 1524–1525, the revolt of the Nu-Pieds in Normandy in 1639–1640, or the rebellion of the *Bonnets Rouges* in Brittany in 1675 to see that grievances over seigneurial exactions and innovative tax schemes were always simmering in rural communities. Moreover, these disturbances were almost never led by the landless poor, but rather by those who had something to lose in the village: the natural peasant leadership.

## VILLAGE GOVERNMENT AND FUNCTIONS

Villages were composite entities made up of overlapping institutions, above all the family, the parish, the seigniory (or lordship), and the village assembly. This last institution is what gave the village community its formal coherence; it developed special characteristics in the West. In France, village communes or assemblies *(communautés, assemblées)* had received formal charters by the thirteenth century in some areas; in others, they remained informal but recognized institutions. They were composed of heads of households, since the household, not the individual, was the fundamental social unit. But within the assembly, the hierarchical village social structure was instantly apparent. The households of *laboureurs* or yeomen normally dominated land-use issues, tax matters, and village offices. Assemblies were predominantly male, although evidence indicates that widows with substantial holdings were sometimes admitted.

Although the constellation of powers in any given village was unique, their local functions were quite similar. The *Gemeinde* in northwestern Germany, like the assembly in England and the commune in France, met periodically after Mass to elect syndics or council members and other minor officials. They managed most communal aspects of life, from grammar schools to ale quality, by appointing schoolmasters, aleconners, shepherds, and harvest guards. Through the *fabrique* (vestry), they jointly shouldered responsibility for the upkeep of the parish church. Above all, the assembly controlled crucial aspects of land use and labor. They set the dates of the grain or wine harvest, fixed wages for day laborers, and controlled the sale, lease, or rental of the common lands. Waters, woods, wastelands, and meadows were collectively managed, which provided a crucial margin of survival for many villagers.

The village assemblies also performed critical functions for the early modern state, which had only a thin presence at the local level. By far their most contentious task in regions like France and the Italian city-states was apportioning and collecting royal taxes in the village. In France, the community was then burdened with collective responsibility for making up any shortfall in uncollected taxes. Villages often exercised important legal and policing powers at the local level. Some German assemblies were allowed to set their own weights, measures, and prices. French assemblies increasingly used lawsuits in the seventeenth and eighteenth centuries to contest their rights with other villages, their lords, or even with royal officials. Drunken or disorderly behavior, domestic fights, scolding, and marketplace fraud were typically handled through local seigneurial courts, in petty sessions, or by village arbiters.

While communes or assemblies provided a significant measure of self-government under normal conditions, they were nevertheless sharply circumscribed in their ability to protect the village from environmental or political disasters. Cycles of famine and disease, escalating tax demands from the central state, and marauding armies spawned by the civil, religious, and international warfare of the age regularly decimated individual villages. Nevertheless, villages collectively remained a resilient and adaptable social unit throughout the early modern period, and one on which the wealth of most of Europe depended.

*See also* **Agriculture; Landholding; Mobility, Geographic; Mobility, Social; Peasantry; Peasants' War, German; Popular Protest and Rebellions; Wages.**

BIBLIOGRAPHY

*Primary Source*

Gough, Richard. *The History of Myddle*, edited by David Hey. Harmondsworth, U.K., and New York, 1981. Printed version of manuscript (1703).

*Secondary Sources*

Davis, Natalie Zemon. *The Return of Martin Guerre*. Cambridge, Mass., 1983.

Forster, Robert, and Orest Ranum, eds. *Rural Society in France: Selections from the Annales; économies, sociétiés, civilisations*. Translated by Elborg Forster and Patricia M. Ranum. Baltimore, 1977.

Ginzburg, Carlo. *The Cheese and the Worms: The Cosmos of a Sixteenth-Century Miller*. Translated by John and Anne Tedeschi. Baltimore, 1980.

Goubert, Pierre, and Daniel Roche. *Les Français et l'Ancien Regime*. Paris, 1984.

Huppert, George. *After the Black Death: A Social History of Early Modern Europe*. Bloomington, Ind., 1986.

Le Roy Ladurie, Emmanuel. *The French Peasantry, 1450–1660*. Translated by Alan Sheridan. Berkeley, 1987.

Porter, Roy. *English Society in the Eighteenth Century*. London, 1982.

Sabean, David Warren. *Power in the Blood: Popular Culture and Village Discourse in Early Modern Germany*. Cambridge, U.K., and New York, 1984.

Underdown, David. *Revel, Riot, and Rebellion: Popular Politics and Culture in England 1603–1660*. Oxford and New York, 1985.

Vardi, Liana. *The Land and the Loom: Peasants and Profit in Northern France, 1680–1800*. Durham, N.C., 1993.

Wegert, Karl H. *Popular Culture, Crime, and Social Control in Eighteenth-Century Würtemberg*. Stuttgart, 1994.

ZOË A. SCHNEIDER

**VILNIUS** (Polish, Wilno; Yiddish, Vilna). Vilnius was the capital of the Grand Duchy of Lithuania, thus the second capital of the Commonwealth of Poland-Lithuania. Established at a crossroads between East and West, it imported Muscovite furs and reexported them, along with local forest products, by river to the Baltic (Königsberg, Riga, and Gdańsk were among its trading partners), whence it imported fabrics, salt, spices, fruit, and metals. Vilnius received the Magdeburg Law for municipal self-government in 1387 following the Grand Duchy's acceptance of Christianity and entry into federation with Poland. The city had long had a mixed population (pagan Lithuanians, Orthodox Ruthenians [Ancestors of Ukrainians and Belarusians], Catholic Germans). In 1536 a royal decree established "Greek" and "Roman" parity for elections to the magistracy. Lutherans (largely burgher and German in origin) date their continuing presence from 1555, Calvinists (led by increasingly Polonized nobles) from the 1560s, and Greek Catholics from the Union of Brest (1596). Islamic Tatars had settled in the Lukiškės (Łukiszki) suburb around 1400. Jews came relatively late, receiving their first privilege for settlement within the walls in 1593.

All five recognized Christian confessions competed for office in the magistracy under Greek (Orthodox and Uniate) and Roman (Catholic, Lutheran, Calvinist) rubrics until 1666, when a royal decree limited membership in the ruling elite to Catholics and Uniates. "Dissidents" (Orthodox, Lutherans, Calvinists) remained a significant presence in the merchants' and artisans' guilds, where parity arrangements mirroring those of the magistracy continued to function without the new restrictions. The competing Uniate and Orthodox confraternities made the city an early center of a Ruthenian spiritual and cultural revival. Jews governed themselves autonomously through their *kahal* and the *vaad* or Council of the Chief Lithuanian Communities. Tatars went to their mullah for decisions on internal affairs. Both Jews and Tatars turned to the nobles' Castle Court (rather than the burghers' magistracy) for law in cases involving the Christian world.

Although Vilnians spoke Polish, Ruthenian, Lithuanian, German, and Yiddish, Polish was the city's lingua franca by the early seventeenth century, and all Christians (and some of the Tatars who tended toward assimilation) felt the draw of Polish cultural norms.

Lutherans and Calvinists established schools in the middle of the sixteenth century, but the Jesuits (introduced here in 1569) soon offered effective competition. Stephen Báthory made their *collegium* (established in 1570) into an academy in 1578. It would become Poland-Lithuania's second university (after Cracow), eventually bearing the name of its royal founder. The academy welcomed the sons of the grand duchy's "dissidents" and played an important role in the Catholicization of society in the seventeenth century.

Vilnius was home to early Cyrillic printing houses (the earliest that of Francysk Skaryna, in 1524), and a Calvinist shop (Daniel of Łęczyca) functioned in the years 1581–1607. Here, too, the Jesuits' Academy Press (1592–1804) soon took over the local market, also printing for Vilnius Uniates. Vilnius became a center of Jewish culture in the eighteenth century, during the life of the Gaon Rabbi Elijah (1720–1797).

The general decline of Vilnius began with the Muscovite occupation of the city (1655–1661) and was deepened with the depredations of the Northern War (1700–1721). Vilnius's status as capital of the Grand Duchy of Lithuania ceased with the third partition of Poland (1795), when it became a provincial city of the Russian Empire.

*See also* **Belarus; Jews and Judaism; Lithuania, Grand Duchy of, to 1569; Poland-Lithuania, Commonwealth of, 1569–1795; Poland to 1569; Reformations in Eastern Europe: Protestant, Catholic, and Orthodox.**

BIBLIOGRAPHY

Cohen, Israel. *Vilna*. Philadelphia, 1943.

Frick, David. "The Bells of Vilnius: Keeping Time in a City of Many Calendars." In *Making Contact: Maps, Identity, and Travel,* edited by Glenn Burger, Lesley B. Cormack, Jonathan Hart, and Natalia Pylypiuk, pp. 23–59. Edmonton, 2003.

Ragauskas, Aivas. *Vilniaus miesto valdantysis elitas XVII a. antrojoje pusėje (1662–1702 m.).* Vilnius, 2002.

Schramm, Gerhard. "Protestantismus und städtische Gesellschaft in Wilna (16.–17. Jahrhundert)." *Jahrbücher für Geschichte Osteuropas* 17 (1969): 187–214.

DAVID FRICK

**VINCENT DE PAUL** (1581–1660), founder of the Congregation of the Mission and of the Daughters of Charity. Vincent de Paul was not only one of the main figures of the Catholic Reformation but also one of the most popular French saints of the seventeenth century. His reputation as philanthropist and pragmatic protector of the underprivileged, already secured during his life, somewhat overshadows the political, spiritual, and mystical aspects of his life, revealed in his extensive correspondence.

Born in 1581 in a modest peasant family of Pouy (Aquitaine), Vincent found in the church the most likely means of social promotion. Subsidized by the judge of his hamlet, Monsieur de Comet, he was sent to the Cordeliers' college of Dax (1595–1597). In 1600, he was ordained priest and in 1604, he vanished for two years. Many historians speculate on this disappearance. According to what Vincent de Paul himself wrote to his protector Comet, during a sea trip from Marseille to Toulouse, he was captured and sold as a slave in Tunis, where he stayed for two years. He managed to convert his slave master, a renegade, and to flee with him back to France. After traveling to Rome and Avignon, he finally settled in Paris in 1608, was made chaplain to the queen Marguerite de Valois (1610), and began to move in the *dévot* circles, becoming very close to Pierre de Bérulle and the Oratorians. In 1612, he became the parish priest of Clichy, following the post-Tridentine line: renovating the church, catechizing its people, erecting the Confrérie du Rosaire (brotherhood of the Rosary). A year later, he became chaplain to the family of Philippe-Emmanuel de Gondi, and his life changed.

In 1617, Vincent de Paul was shocked by the deep ignorance of the faith he found among the inhabitants of the hamlet of Folleville, on the domain of De Gondis's family. This awareness, described by many as a true conversion, seemed to dictate his calling. He decided to instruct the poor and become a missionary. Contrary to Pierre de

**St. Vincent de Paul.** Nineteenth-century portrait engraving. GETTY IMAGES

Bérulle and François de Sales, whom he considered his most influential masters, Vincent de Paul was less speculative and more inclined toward action. He considered that true Christian perfection did not consist of mystical ecstasies but of charitable field enterprises. With De Gondi's financial help, Vincent de Paul founded the Congregation of the Mission. The so-called Lazarists (named after the priory of Saint-Lazare where the community settled in 1632; approved by pope Urban VIII in 1633) devoted themselves to the parish missions (described by Vincent de Paul in his letters as "the salvation of the poor people of the countryside") and to the training of the local priests, for it was seen "necessary to maintain the people and to keep the fruit of the missions made by good ecclesiastics, imitating in this the great conquerors, who leave garrisons in the places they take, by fear to lose what they have acquire with so much effort." To this end, the Tuesday Conferences were launched in 1631—a kind of continuing education for priests that allowed them to reflect, pray, and work in common and that gathered the elite of the Parisian clerics. The same ideal guided the opening of the Lazarist seminary for ordinands in 1642 in the College des Bons Enfants. The idea was less to give a high theological culture than to give a solid moral, spiritual, and pastoral education to the future priests who would be called, as Vincent de Paul wrote in his *Colloquium to the Missionaries,* "to preach simply and familiarly as did the apostles." The expansion of the Lazarists was remarkable, first in France (in 1660, 131 priests and 52 coadjutors lived in 25 residences and had organized some 840 missions in the countryside) then in the field of the foreign missions (Madagascar in 1648), for the Lazarists added to their former objectives the conversion of the "pagans."

From the beginning, each Lazarist mission concluded with the creation of Confréries de Charité (Brotherhoods of Charity), which gathered and organized local noblewomen to care for the poor. In 1633, Vincent de Paul and his closest collaborator, the widow Louise de Marillac (1591–1660), founded the Daughters of Charity in order to support the Brotherhoods of Charity and to achieve charitable work on a larger scale, combining spiritual salvation with material help in keeping with the recommendations of the Council of Trent. Noncloistered and dressed as peasant women, the "grey nuns" contributed to implement in France the basis of health and social service (there were sixty houses in 1659). Similarly, Vincent de Paul founded L'Oeuvre des Enfants Trouvés (Care of Foundlings), which aimed to rescue abandoned children, and he supported various charitable undertakings for the sick, the disabled, and beggars, activities that were centralized in the network of the general hospitals that developed in the 1650s.

Until his death in 1660, the influence of "the father of the poor" was considerable. He was associated with the main *dévot* circles, in the secret Compagnie du Saint Sacrement (Company of the Holy Sacrament), and in the Visitation Sainte Marie (where he replaced François de Sales as superior). Queen Anne of Austria chose him as her confessor and placed him in 1643 at the Council of Conscience initiated by Cardinal Richelieu, who, like King Louis XIII, had held him in great esteem. Since he avoided the various spiritual conflicts of his time, he managed to stay close to parties who were adversaries: the old families of the Catholic League such as the Marillacs, the abbot Saint-Cyran (1581–

1643)—though he vigorously condemned his Jansenist ideas—and the Jesuits, with whom he never hesitated to collaborate and among whom he found inspiration.

*See also* **Bérulle, Pierre de; Catholic League (France); François de Sales; Jansenism; Reformation, Catholic; Religious Orders; Trent, Council of.**

BIBLIOGRAPHY

Dodin, André. *La légende et l'histoire: De monsieur Depaul à saint Vincent de Paul.* Paris, 1985.

———. *Vincent de Paul and Charity: A Contemporary Portrait of His Life and Apostolic Spirit.* Translated by Jean Marie Smith and Dennis Saunders. New Rochelle, N.Y., 1993.

Dubois, Raymonde, and Luigi Mezzadri. "Evangelization and charité; Reformation and Counter-Reformation." *History of European Ideas,* 9, no. 4 (1988): 479–488.

Foucault, Michel. *Folie et déraison: Histoire de la folie à l'âge classique.* Paris, 1961.

Gutton, Jean-Pierre. *La société et les pauvres: L'exemple de la généralité de Lyon, 1534–1789.* Paris, 1971.

Jones, Colin. *The Charitable Imperative: Hospitals and Nursing in Ancien Régime and Revolutionary France.* London and New York, 1989.

Mezzadri, Luigi. *Histoire de la Congrégation de la mission.* Paris, 1994.

———. *Vincent de Paul (1581–1660).* Paris, 1985.

Miquel, Pierre. *Vincent de Paul.* Paris, 1996.

Salem-Carrière, Yves-Marie. *Saint Vincent de Paul et la politique.* Bouère, France, 1992.

DOMINIQUE DESLANDRES

# VIOLENCE.

**VIOLENCE.** Violence was endemic in early modern Europe, from Scandinavia to the Mediterranean, and from the Urals to the British Isles. Serfs and peasants wielded knives and staffs, most gentlemen and merchants wore swords and/or pistols, and nobles and their numerous retainers were similarly armed. Even teenaged students carried knives in their schools, brawled in the streets, and operated as gangs. The weapons used were often determined by class, as were the instruments of public death. Thus while serfs and peasants were hanged, the aristocracy had the privilege of death by the sword; women were burned alive or drowned. Tempers were short in this society, and weapons were easy to hand. The propertied classes, especially, lacked self-control until the waning of the seventeenth century. They encouraged gangs of retainers or hired thugs, or they formed groups of brigands, to assault enemies in paying off grudges or pursuing local or political power.

Rates of violent activity that can be quantified from official records in western Europe suggest a large rise from the fifteenth to the seventeenth centuries, followed by a long decline to the late eighteenth century. Rates of violent crime based on indictments and inquests rose sharply from the 1560s to the 1620s, peaking at the turn of century at ten per hundred thousand. They then declined greatly in the mid-seventeenth century, when they reached six per hundred thousand, drifted lower in 1700, when they reached three per hundred thousand, and then declined significantly in the mid-eighteenth century, when they reached two per hundred thousand. In all countries, however, rates were highest in the borderlands and lowest in central urban areas.

## PERSONAL VIOLENCE

The sixteenth century represented the apex of a long-term acceleration in personal violence that began in the decades following the Black Death of the mid-fourteenth century. Social, economic, and religious conflict nurtured violent solutions in an age where there were few institutions to control human activity. Thus personal violence rose in the midst of the decline of medieval institutions and the cobbling together of new ones that would form the early modern state. Personal violence, whether reactive, instinctive, or ritualized, became an acceptable form of human behavior.

However, a growing intolerance of brutality marked a shift in social psychology that developed in England, the Low Countries, Scandinavia, France, and Switzerland, and which later spread first throughout western Europe, and more slowly across the Mediterranean, in the course of the seventeenth and early eighteenth centuries. An increasingly civilized and sophisticated view of the behavior of middle class citizens, together with a stronger sense of "the peace of God" in Catholic and Protestant churches of the Reformation and Counter-Reformation, caused a movement away from violence as a means for the resolution of personal quarrels and disputes. Distressed by sensa-

tionalist literature boasting graphic representations of murder and mayhem, the aristocratic and middle classes of Europe began to reform their behavior in what Norbert Elias termed "a civilizing process." Without social support, many traditional forms of personal violence inevitably declined. At the same time, growth in the state's control of violence through policing (particularly in France and Spain) and weapons licensing had a profound effect on communities, limiting opportunities for violence. Finally, with the decay of a popular culture grounded in violence and new expectations of social comportment enforced by the state's judicial system, both group and interpersonal violence receded into the background.

However, perceptions of violence were not easily changed. The late seventeenth and early eighteenth centuries witnessed a surge of popular literature in the form of pamphlets and ballads that told gruesome tales of horrid violent acts; these materials were republished throughout the eighteenth century. This perception was also promoted by women who wrote best-sellers on sensational and scandalous violent acts by women, which became stereotypes in the literature of the era. Moreover, while group violence at the hands of the aristocracy was in decline, the rise of the duel among aristocrats came into vogue in the course of the seventeenth century, most significantly in France, Italy, and England, in spite of the admonitions of churchmen, lawyers, judges, and moralists. And while plebeian and gentlemanly delinquency was on the decline, individual aristocratic delinquency in the form of sexual and roisterous debauchery was on the rise. Thus while interpersonal violence had declined sharply in the overall population by the mid-eighteenth century, in its growing absence the public appetite for stories of violence had increased dramatically.

Much violence, however, was spontaneous. The Paduan artist Niccolò Pizzolo was murdered in a quick-tempered argument; the Mantuan painter Andrea Mantegna hired thugs to beat up rivals who pinched his designs; the Swiss artist Urs Graf displayed bouts of brutal beatings; the sculptor-painter Michelangelo of Florence had his nose broken in a fight with a fellow sculptor; and Christopher Marlowe was stabbed to death in a tavern brawl, as was the actor Gabriel Spencer by the London playwright Ben Jonson. Fencing grew in popularity in the sixteenth century as the rapier became a favourite weapon of fashionable society because of its more flexible and lightweight qualities in violent confrontations. Many towns enacted legislation to ban the carrying of arms in public places, all to little avail. But most standards of behavior were flaunted, especially by youths at a time (late sixteenth and early seventeenth centuries) when male adolescents and young bachelors comprised a significant proportion of the population increase.

Violence was also embedded in the extreme passions of the fifteenth century, which continued into the sixteenth. Rapes, murders, fisticuffs, and knifings followed adulteries or rejections, as recounted in the stories of Margaret of Angoulême, Queen of Navarre, in the 1530s and 1540s. These passions also influenced perceptions that violent crime was "situationally determined": they can be seen in the activities of cunning women in England, *muchachos* and *caballeristas* in Spain, *strollica* in Italy, *znakhar* in Russia, and *charivari* in France. They also can be found in the activities of people on the margins, such as suicides and witches, and the unrecorded inhabitants of marshes, forests, and moors.

Other examples of personal violence were clearly ritualized. These included, for continental Europe, punching a debtor until he agreed to pay, hiring assassins in family vendettas, and gathering armed bands to redress wrongs real or imagined. In German towns, initiation riots for journeyman aspirants to the Hanseatic merchant guilds included being hanged from a chimney until out of breath, thrown three times from a boat in the harbor and pushed back into the sea upon climbing in each time until the last, and being whipped bloody in the guildhall. Erasmus noted from his enlightened Rotterdam and Paris that the initiation ceremonies for schools were "fit for executioners, torturers, pimps or galley-slaves."

Youth were often regarded by authorities as primary agents of personal violence. In Swiss and Italian towns, youthful vigilantes used violence upon older citizens who committed immoral sins such as gambling and the ostentatious display of wealth. In French towns, intervillage combat games led to beatings and killings, which were regarded as part of the culture of sport. In England, there are recorded examples of youthful cricketers beating one another with their bats, and a statute from 1563 stated that a man under age twenty-four "is wild, without judgment and not of sufficient experience to govern himself." Much of this violence was conditioned by their exposure to extreme cruelty early in life. Throughout Europe, cats were stoned to death, and bulls and bears were baited and maimed, as were individuals accused of criminal offences. It was not unusual for crowds to see impaled men on stakes thrown to the ground to be eaten by dogs and crows. As Juan de Mariana of Toledo wrote in 1599, killing beasts brutally was a short step from killing men.

Finally, women throughout Europe were responsible for their own violent acts. These acts were accepted because of the perception of sex: women, ruled by their physical body rather than by rational capacity, and aggressive in their actions, possessed magical powers over men. This was seen in the role of women in murder, rape, and suicide in contemporary writing, prose fiction, and drama. Sexual violence became a defining element in male-female relations through rape, ravishment, and seduction. Older women were also active in violence, especially in Ireland, Holland, and France in riots and rebellions against communities and the state. In Germany they were as apt as men to be tortured by church or state for acts asof ill conduct. Their violence, however, was more pronounced in towns than in the countryside.

### STATE-SPONSORED VIOLENCE

Meanwhile, institutions of the state, through war, interrogation, and the courts, became major players in dispensing acts of violence against their own and neighboring peoples. While unquantifiable, it would be safe to assume that interpersonal relations became more peaceful in the course of the early modern era, especially in the second half of the seventeenth century, but that society as a whole became more violent with the actions of city- and nation-states from the late sixteenth to the early eighteenth centuries.

The sixteenth and seventeenth centuries were a time of ubiquitous violence unleashed by new nation-states. This was violence inflicted upon civilians by employed or discharged soldiers living in their midst; institutionalized violence such as torture and execution; violence associated with extra-legal dispute resolution in the form of duels, feuds, and arbitration; interpersonal violence as assault, homicide, domestic violence, rape, and infanticide; group violence in the rituals of youth gangs, carnival, and sports; popular protest displayed in enclosure, food, and tax riots; and the organized crime of bandits and highwaymen. In the end, violence was never far from the consciousness of early modern Europeans.

War could be especially violent for civilian noncombatants. As Francesco Guicciardini wrote in 1525, "all political power is rooted in violence." In the Schmalkaldic War of 1546–1547, Spanish troops suspended male civilians by their genitals, then tortured them to reveal where they had hidden their money and valuables; women and girls were raped. The link between personal and public violence was well expressed by Pierre de la Primaudaye in 1577: out of quarrels and dissension come sedition, civil, and open wars, and men, under the influence of war, "become savage."

Violence was also a result of the growth of wealth in the era as it came to a few, while poverty worked its way into the many. Enclosure and the commercial cultivation of land caused rural depopulation and dearth, while swelling populations in towns and cities caused job competition and low salaries in an age of rising prices for food. Thus Leonardo da Vinci's plan for an ideal town had upper walks for the gentility to protect them from the plebs. This idea came to symbolize one of the primary aims of the new seventeenth-century state: the suppression of disorder and the monopolization of violence in the form of ritualized public punishment. It proved workable in the new monarchies of France, Netherlands, and the British Isles, moderately feasible in Italian and German areas, and only partly possible in the Iberic world, Helvetic cities, and Nordic countries.

In the end, the dawn of the modern era of violence occurred in the late eighteenth century with the disintegration of monarchial governments and the rise of secular nation-states, organized bandits and brigades, and modern warfare. These institutions precipitated a professional police, central courts, and the prison as the royal power of the early modern era gave way to the state power of modern times. Thus the growth of the modern state from the sixteenth to the early eighteenth century con-

tributed to a shift in violence from personal to state controlled.

## REGIONAL VARIATIONS

Europe comprises an area of diverse regions, and its geography has led to the work of the Annales School of quantitative research that has included violence as one of its subjects. In France and Italy, each region has a research leader and team. In other regions the focus has been on towns, as with the Burgundian, Flemish, Helvetic, Dutch, German, and Swiss. In the British Isles and Scandinavia, it has been a combination of both regions and towns. Most of the published research, however, has been on Italy, France, the Netherlands, Swiss and German towns, the British Isles, and Nordic countries. Results reveal that England, France, and the Netherlands were the most violent societies from the sixteenth to the mid-eighteenth century.

In England, there were various high points from the alleged execution of 70,000 rogues during the reign of Henry VII to the "crime wave" of the early 1600s. While criminal gangs were being eliminated and the violence of private warfare waged by the nobility was replaced with war in the courts (litigation), petty violence seems to have continued unabated, stimulated by the social and economic dislocations of the first agricultural and industrial revolution beginning in the late sixteenth century. In criminal acts, there was also a significant change from violent acts against persons (personal crime) to acts against property (property crime). But while noble violence was diluted by resort to the courts, violence was waged incessantly among the peasantry.

In Scandinavia, violence stemmed from personal conflicts, as is visible in the famous witch trials of the 1660s and 1670s that involved mostly old women. Here, in the Nordic countries, crimes of violence, especially lethal violence, underwent a major decline during the late seventeenth and early eighteenth centuries. As in England, violence became more tied to economic disputes, both rural and urban. Much of the violence caused by "honor" disappeared as disputes came to be resolved in nonviolent ways. However, by the late seventeenth century women came to be charged with one-third of all offenses because of sexual crimes that were first prosecuted during Reformation efforts to curb extramarital sex, infanticide, and witchcraft. Violent offenders were often goldsmiths, shoemakers, peasants, and farmhands; only soldiers were overrepresented after wars.

In poor and isolated regions of France, violence was directed downward, rarely upward, in the social order. Much of the violence was that of a riposte—informal justice administered by someone provoked into violent action. Here magistrates showed little interest in investigating popular traditions of "self-help." A similar situation existed in Italy with the popular vendetta. This was demonstrated by the Zambarlini family, who turned their victims into "dogmeat." They dismembered corpses, leaving them unburied to be consumed by dogs or pigs, thereby denying their victims the rites of Christian burial and the hope of eternal salvation.

Regional variations also involved distinctions between violence in rural and urban settings. In the county of Essex, England, for example, the rate of interpersonal violence has been estimated as three times the national average. However, that may be due to the fact that Essex was the center of the Puritan movement, where local clergy were vigilant in having acts of violence reported, and where human acts previously regarded as nonviolent (such as child- and wife-beating) were now regarded as violent in nature and to be strongly condemned and eliminated. In major urban areas such as London, however, local authorities took a strong hand in highlighting major violent acts and creating institutions to reduce violence. Therefore, Londoners came to recognize the limits of terror with a new concern over violence associated with public hangings and their processions and public whippings in the streets; Londoners thus became advocates of the end of state-sponsored violence.

## CONCLUSION

The historiography of violence has seen parallel developments with social history since the mid 1970s, where there are distinct typologies linked to politics and society and integrated into the wider historical context. Currently, there is an outpouring of theses, mostly on violence associated with homicide, infanticide, sexual offences, gender, dearth, and forms of punishment. Recent publications emphasize the role of the state, the deployment of central authority, and ideology. But there are few studies of vio-

lence from the view of the perpetrator, apart from London historians who have interpreted violent acts as strategies of the poor to aid their quest for survival in the eighteenth-century city.

*See also* **Assassination; Cities and Urban Life; Class, Status, and Order; Crime and Punishment; Duel; Passions; Police; Torture.**

BIBLIOGRAPHY

Beattie, John. *Policing and Punishment in London, 1660–1750: Urban Crime and the Limits of Terror.* Oxford, 2001.

Burke, Peter. *Popular Culture in Early Modern Europe.* New York, 1978.

Egmond, Florike. *Underworlds: Organized Crime in the Netherlands, 1650–1800.* Cambridge, U.K., 1993.

Elias, Norbert. *The Civilizing Process.* 2 vols. Translated by Edmund Jephcott. 1st ed. 1978. New York, 2001.

Emsley, Clive, and Louis A. Knafla, eds. *Crime History and Histories of Crime: Studies in the Historiography of Crime and Criminal Justice in Modern History.* Westport, Conn., 1996.

Evans, Richard J., ed. *The German Underworld: Deviants and Outcasts in German History.* London, 1988.

Greenshields, Malcolm. *An Economy of Violence in Early Modern France: Crime and Justice in the Hauite Avergne, 1587–1664.* University Park, Pa., 1994.

Kiernan, V. G. *The Duel in European History: Honour and the Reign of Aristocracy.* Oxford, 1988.

Österberg, Eva, and D. Lindström. *Crime and Social Control in Medieval and Early Modern Swedish Towns.* Uppsala, 1988.

Ruff, Julius R. *Violence in Early Modern Europe, 1500–1800.* Cambridge, Mass., 2001.

Sharpe, James. *Crime in Early Modern England, 1550–1750.* London, 1984; rev. ed., 1998.

Stone, Lawrence. "Interpersonal Violence in English Society, 1300–1980." *Past & Present* 101 (1983): 22–33.

LOUIS A. KNAFLA

---

**VIRTUE.** Virtue refers to a valued human characteristic or to excellence, or to the sum of such qualities. Hence, the term has an inherently normative or evaluative connotation, since it selects out forms of knowledge and action that are approved and commended. The notion of virtue in Western thought stems from the Greek word *arete* as translated into the Latin *virtus*. The concept has a long history in Europe and was widely employed in a number of contexts—social and political as well as moral—during the early modern period.

In its earliest Greek expressions, "virtue" denoted the superlative prowess of the heroic warrior and thus possessed both highly individualistic and gendered implications. Although the latter never fully disappeared (hence the etymological connection between virtue and virility, both derived from the root *vir*, 'man'), the former was subsumed into the communal sphere with the rise of the classical polis. Virtue and the virtues came to be regarded in the city-states of the ancient world as coordinate with the laws and customs of a given community. Thinkers as diverse as Pythagoras, Plato, and Aristotle agreed that the moral character of the individual constituted a microcosm of the political character of the city. The Greeks commonly identified four so-called cardinal virtues—courage, wisdom, justice, and temperance—although they also upheld the worthiness of many other qualities.

The ancient Romans and the European Christians generally embraced both the private and the public aspects of virtue. The popularity of philosophical schools such as Stoicism and Epicureanism among cultivated Romans and the other-worldliness and asceticism of Christianity tended to locate forms of virtue in the individual and to promote the priority of personal happiness over public good. Yet the Romans (particularly in the period of the Republic) also hailed the sacrifices of leaders and fellow citizens who were motivated by purely civic goals. Likewise, medieval Christians expected that government would be conducted by rulers whose actions fully accorded with standards of earthly rectitude, justice primary among them. To the list of cardinal virtues came to be added the so-called Christian or theological virtues of faith, hope, and charity.

The conventional wisdom about the fate of virtue in modern Europe charts an arc of its repoliticization during the Renaissance (in the guise of so-called civic humanism), followed by a period of redefinition and disappearance from the public sphere occasioned by the Protestant Reformation, the emergence of liberalism, the rise of commercial society, and the spread of Enlightenment values. This interpretation requires some qualification, however, inasmuch as the process was less one of straightforward decline than of complex transformation.

The association of the Renaissance itself (especially in Italy) with the glorification of civic-minded virtue—the ethos of sacrifice for the sake of one's fellow citizens and city—shared by members of a community (the so-called "civic humanism" thesis pioneered by Hans Baron) has come under serious and deserved challenge. While it is true that many of the greatest humanists of the fifteenth and sixteenth centuries embraced citizenship as the fullest expression of a virtuous human life, taking the Roman statesman-orator Cicero as their exemplar, others adopted alternative views. Praise of Caesar and the Roman Empire, and hence devaluation of civic virtue, was quite common among leading humanists. A further group of Renaissance thinkers maintained a more orthodox Christian account of virtue as essentially a mark of God's grace or a trait that demonstrated one's worthiness for salvation. Moreover, there was nothing essentially urban about the idea of public virtue as the foundation for a good state; such a view was as widespread at the courts of territorial monarchs as in the cities of the Italian peninsula. Conceptions of virtue in Renaissance thought simply lacked the uniformity implied by the civic humanism thesis as commonly stated.

Early modern Europe witnessed numerous attempts to redefine, challenge, or criticize both conventional public and private ideals of virtue. Perhaps the most famous example of this is Niccolò Machiavelli (1469–1527), who enjoys an infamous reputation for his attack on virtue, especially in its standard classical and Christian versions. In his *Il principe* (1513–1514; The prince), Machiavelli argues that virtue as taught by ancient philosophers and preached from pulpits is very often incompatible with effective use of political power. A ruler who seeks to govern according to the cardinal and theological virtues will lose his office, since others who are prepared to employ tactics that lack moral sanction will oust him in their own quest for position and glory. Machiavelli peppers his little book with tales of virtuous magistrates who have been ruined and vicious ones who have succeeded. According to Machiavelli, the only assurance that the prince can overcome the vicissitudes of politics is a readiness to act in a manner inconsistent with virtue when circumstances require it. The Machiavellian ruler is not above counseling murder, deception, manipulation, and nearly every other mode of conventionally immoral conduct, if these acts prove efficient in maintaining hold on the levers of power. Machiavelli calls this moral flexibility *virtù* (the standard Italian word for 'virtue'), thus apparently turning the conventional discourse of ethics on its head.

Yet Machiavelli is not guilty of "teaching evil," despite the accusation made against him. In fact, his conception of *virtù* suggests that the ruler should always act according to commonplace virtue whenever he can do so without undermining his own power. Conventionally evil means should only be used when absolutely necessary, and even then the prince must do his best to ensure that people do not perceive him to be acting immorally, lest his reputation be harmed. Moreover, Machiavelli seems to think that this advice pertains only in the case of holders of public office; Machiavellian *virtù* is, one might say, a distinctively political way of acting, not to be commended to private persons in their interactions with one another. Nor ought it be forgotten that in his own political loyalties and other political writings, Machiavelli stood for a republican conception of civic virtue that lauded the sacrifice of personal goals and desires for the sake of attaining the communal glory of one's city.

Machiavelli was not alone among early modern European authors in reformulating ideas about virtue inherited from the classical and Christian past. For example, many humanists posed questions about the connection between virtue and nobility as it had customarily been conceived. In this period, as in early times, blood and birth were regarded as bestowing nobility upon an individual, and nobility in turn qualified a person to wield power and rule over natural inferiors. But humanist writers proposed that virtue alone prepared men for political office, since those who were most virtuous were most likely to act for the common good. Hence, it was the virtuous who possessed true nobility *(vera nobilitas)*, and virtue was by no means coextensive with paternity and landed wealth. In Italy and even more noticeably in northern Europe, invocations of virtue could easily be translated into challenges to the cherished principle that some people were "naturally born" to rule.

Another modification of traditional conceptions of virtue came with the continuing commercialization of European economic relations and social values. Whereas for the ancient philosophers and medieval Christian theologians the private accumulation of liquid wealth had been widely viewed as incompatible with virtue, early modern authors began to reevaluate this doctrine. Some thinkers, such as the Italian civic humanists Leonardo Bruni (c. 1370–1444) and Gian Francesco Poggio Bracciolini (1380–1459), contended that citizens should proudly acknowledge industriousness and self-acquired possessions as the foundation of morality and the greatness of their cities. Other authors went further. The Dutch-born Bernard de Mandeville (1670–1733) proposed in his *Fable of the Bees* (1714/1729) the famous principle that private vices yield public goods, which is to say that the pursuit of personal gain, and indeed the desire for comfort and luxury, lead directly to the enrichment of society as a whole and the consequent benefit of all its members.

In spite of recent claims that the Enlightenment project of grounding morality on human reason alone led to the erosion of virtue-based ethics, thinkers of the eighteenth century continued to uphold virtue as central to the worthwhile human life. The central document of the Enlightenment, the *Encyclopédie* (1751–1758) compiled by Denis Diderot and Jean Le Rond d'Alembert, treated virtue as an indwelling sense given to all members of mankind universally and without exception and thus invariable in its content across time and place. While the *Discours sur l'origine et les fondements de l'inégalité parmi les hommes* (1755; Discourse on the origins of inequality) and the *Émile* (1762) of Jean-Jacques Rousseau (1712–1778) seem to treat the conventional virtues as affectations imposed artificially and detrimentally upon naturally good humanity, their author still insisted upon virtue as indispensable for a free society. Using language that any civic republican might endorse, Rousseau stipulated in *Discours sur l'économie politique* (1755; A discourse on political economy) that virtue is realized when citizens conform their particular wills to the determinations of the general will. While the discourse of virtue may have been further transformed during the early Enlightenment, it by no means disappeared.

See also *Encyclopédie*; Enlightenment; Machiavelli, Niccolò; Political Philosophy; Rousseau, Jean-Jacques.

BIBLIOGRAPHY

*Primary Sources*

Kohl, Benjamin G., and Ronald G. Witt, eds. *The Earthly Republic: Italian Humanists on Government and Society.* Philadelphia, 1978.

Kraye, Jill, ed. *Cambridge Translations of Renaissance Philosophical Texts.* Vol. 2, *Political Philosophy.* Cambridge, U.K., and New York, 1997.

Rousseau, Jean-Jacques. *The Social Contract and Discourses.* Edited by G. D. H. Cole. Revised by J. H. Brumfitt, and John C. Hall. New York, 1993.

*Secondary Sources*

Baron, Hans. *The Crisis of the Early Italian Renaissance: Civic Humanism and Republican Liberty in an Age of Classicism and Tyranny.* Rev. ed. Princeton, 1966.

Burtt, Shelley. *Virtue Transformed: Political Argument in England, 1688–1740.* Cambridge, U.K., and New York, 1992.

Hankins, James, ed. *Renaissance Civic Humanism: Reappraisals and Reflections.* Cambridge, U.K., and New York, 2000.

MacIntyre, Alasdair. *After Virtue: A Study in Moral Theory.* 2nd ed. Notre Dame, Ind., 1984.

Pagden, Anthony, ed. *The Languages of Political Theory in Early-Modern Europe.* Cambridge, U.K., and New York, 1987.

Skinner, Quentin. *Visions of Politics.* Vol. 2, *Renaissance Virtues.* Cambridge, U.K., and New York, 2002.

CARY J. NEDERMAN

**VITALISM.** *See* Matter, Theories of.

# VIVALDI, ANTONIO (1678–1741), Venetian composer and violinist.

Vivaldi produced numerous instrumental and vocal works during his lifetime, but he is best known for his concertos for a diverse group of instruments. An important and influential musician during his career, his music figured prominently in the baroque revival of the 1950s and 1960s.

Born in Venice on 4 March 1678, Vivaldi suffered from what was described as *strettezza di petto* (tightness of the chest), which was probably bron-

**Antonio Vivaldi.** Portrait by an unknown artist. DAMIANO/GETTY IMAGES

chial asthma. This illness plagued him throughout his life and exerted a strong influence on his personal and professional behavior. Vivaldi studied the violin with his father, and he was also trained as a priest, but his asthma prevented him from effectively saying mass. Because of the red hair he inherited from his father, Vivaldi was known throughout his career as *il prete rosse* ('The Red Priest').

In September 1703, Vivaldi accepted his first position, as *maestro di violino* for the Pio Ospedale della Pietà, one of four "hospitals" established in Venice to care for poor orphaned children, and he would remain intermittently associated with this institution for much of his career. Musical training was an integral part of the curriculum for the young girls at all of the *ospedali,* and Vivaldi's responsibilities included teaching violin, buying new instruments, and maintaining the collection. He was dismissed from this position on 24 February 1709—the first of several dismissals and rehirings, largely the result of the precarious financial conditions at the hospital—but used the freedom to meet both

George Frideric Handel (1685–1759) and Domenico Scarlatti (1685–1757), who were in Venice at the time, and to begin writing operas. He returned to the Pietà in 1711, becoming *maestro de' concerti* in 1716, and successfully produced sacred and instrumental music, including trio sonatas, violin sonatas, the set of twelve concertos for one, two, and four violins called *L'estro armonico* (1711), and the oratorio *Juditha Triumphans* (1716).

Vivaldi spent 1718–1720 in Mantua, devoting himself to opera composition, and later traveled to Rome to produce three operas for the 1723 and 1724 carnivals, but he also wrote 140 concertos for the Pietà. Among these are *Il cimento dell'armonia e dell'inventione* (in which we find his most famous work, the violin concerto *The Four Seasons* [*Le quatro stagione*]), *La Cetra,* flute and string concertos, and *Il pastor fido.*

Vivaldi's questionable relationship with the singer Anna Girò and her half-sister Paolina dates from this period. Vivaldi vigorously denied all accusations of sexual impropriety, but the widespread rumors had a detrimental effect on his career and reputation.

Between 1729 and 1735 Vivaldi traveled widely to Vienna, Prague, and several Italian cities to supervise productions of his operas, and he ultimately returned to Vienna at the age of sixty-two, in the hope of securing patronage from Charles VI. His efforts met with limited success, and he died on 28 July 1741, receiving a pauper's funeral at Vienna's Cathedral of St. Stephen.

Vivaldi was extraordinarily prolific, producing over five hundred concertos for almost every combination of instruments, solo and trio sonatas, instrumental sinfonias, and an impressive body of sacred music, including oratorios, masses and motets. Twenty-one of his operas have survived, at least in part, although their full artistic and dramatic power has yet to be evaluated.

Vivaldi's highly distinctive and recognizable musical style had a profound impact on his contemporaries and future composers such as Giuseppe Tartini (1692–1770). His greatest influence was in the development of the concerto. Vivaldi has been credited with inventing or at least regularizing "ritornello form," usually employed in fast movements, in which a "refrain" played by the full ensemble alternates with freer, modulatory episodes played by the solo instruments. His deft coordination of melody and harmony was much admired by Johann Sebastian Bach (1685–1750), who absorbed Italian style through his study and transcription of Vivaldi's concertos and trio-sonatas; this influence is particularly apparent in Bach's *Brandenburg Concertos.* Other distinctive elements of Vivaldi's style include a fluid alternation of major and minor tonalities, a highly progressive use of dissonance and rich harmonies, and an innate melodic gift, particularly in slow movements. His vocal music has been criticized for perfunctory text-setting and violinistic vocal writing, but there are examples of great skill and inspiration in this genre, such as his *Gloria* (RV 588) or *Magnificat* (RV 610), and his virtuosic and highly expressive motets for solo voice. Vivaldi was unquestionably a master orchestrator who explored the idiomatic potential of the many instruments for which he wrote. *The Four Seasons,* for example, not only illustrates his skill in writing for the virtuoso violinist, but also his ability to depict extramusical or programmatic ideas in a manner that anticipates the Romantic era.

*See also* **Bach Family; Music; Venice.**

BIBLIOGRAPHY

Heller, Karl. *Antonio Vivaldi: The Red Priest of Venice.* Translated by David Marinelli. Portland, Ore., 1997. Translation of *Antonio Vivaldi* (1991).

Landon, H. C. Robbins. *Vivaldi: Voice of the Baroque.* London, 1993.

Talbot, Michael. *Antonio Vivaldi: A Guide to Research.* New York, 1988.

———. *The Sacred Vocal Music of Antonio Vivaldi.* Florence, 1995.

———. *Venetian Music in the Age of Antonio Vivaldi.* Aldershot, U.K., 1999.

WENDY HELLER, MARK KROLL

# VIVES, JUAN LUIS

**VIVES, JUAN LUIS** (1492–1540), sixteenth-century Spanish humanist. Juan Luis Vives spent most of his life outside Spain. Born in Valencia to a family of Jewish converts to Christianity, Vives began his studies in his native city but eventually chose to move to Paris in 1509, possibly fearing the Inquisition, whose severity would eventually take a toll on his family. In Paris he studied in the colleges of Beauvais and Montaigu along with other Spanish scholars like himself. In 1512 Vives left Paris and settled in Bruges, which he would call his home for the rest of his life. In 1516 the scholar from Valencia met Erasmus of Rotterdam, an encounter that initiated a decades-long association between the two and helped bring Vives into the circle of humanist thought.

In 1519 Vives was teaching at the University of Louvain, where, under Erasmus's influence, he undertook one of his most important works, a commentary on St. Augustine's *City of God,* published in Basel in 1522 and dedicated to Henry VII of England. It seems Vives's fame was extensive, for that same year he was offered a chair at Spain's prestigious University of Alcalá, recently vacant due to the death of the godfather of Spanish humanists, Antonio de Nebrija. He refused the honor and instead found himself one year later in England, teaching at Corpus Christi College, Oxford. He was named tutor to the princess Mary and reader to the queen, Catherine of Aragon, by Henry VIII. In 1523 he dedicated his *De Institutione Feminae Christianae* (On the education of a Christian woman) to the queen. His relationship with the royal family would become complicated, however, when he sided with Catherine in the dispute over Henry VIII's wish to divorce her for Anne Boleyn. Although he did not lose his life, as did his friend Sir Thomas More, Vives was eventually banished from England by the king. By then a married man, Vives returned to Bruges in 1528, where he would remain until the end of his life, resuming his post as professor at Louvain.

A prolific writer, Vives focused his formidable intelligence on a wide range of subjects. He had specific ideas about education, to which he devoted a number of works, railing against the utilitarian concept of knowledge as information as well as the idea of studying in order to obtain fame. In *De Institutione Feminae Christianae,* he defended the education of women, but it would be an exaggeration to label him a proto-feminist. Perhaps one of the best-known traits of Vives's thought is his criticism of a type of Scholasticism that had degenerated into a fixation on dialectics and syllogisms. In his monumental encyclopedia *De Disciplines Libri XX* (1531; Twenty books on the disciplines) Vives insisted that dialectics be subordinated to the other

**Juan Luis Vives.** Anonymous sixteenth-century portrait. ©Archivo Iconografico, S.A./Corbis

branches of philosophy such as morals and metaphysics. He also leveled frequent criticisms at his contemporaries' slavish reliance on ancient philosophical authorities to the detriment of the exercise of human reason, though he always did so with a genuine respect for Aristotle and his commentator Thomas Aquinas.

Vives's treatise *De Anima et Vita* (1538; On the soul and life) is recognized as a foundational text in the study of the inner life of the human being. In Vives's view, in order to know the soul, one must study its operations and functions, a study that is founded on a thorough knowledge of earthly life in its different forms. The third book of *De Anima et Vita,* an examination of the passions, takes much of its inspiration from the Scholasticism of Thomas Aquinas, but it has also gained Vives a place among the precursors of modern psychology, thanks to its employment of introspection and self-observation.

Thoroughly interested in the affairs of his times, Vives was an avid letter writer and corresponded with kings, cardinals, and emperors. Later dubbed a pacifist because of his desire for peace among peoples and his special concern for ending the fratricidal wars afflicting Europe, Vives also pointed out the threat to Christendom posed by Turkish expansion in the Mediterranean in works such as *De Conditione Vitae Christianorum sub Turca* (On the conditions of Christians under the Turks).

Though an educator by vocation, Vives was also a commercially successful author, and some of his most popular works were dedicated to the subject of Christian apologetics and devotion. His last book, which he was working on at the time of his death in 1540, was entitled *De Veritate Fidei Christianae* (On the truth of the Christian faith).

*See also* **Erasmus, Desiderius; Henry VIII (England); Humanists and Humanism; More, Thomas; Scholasticism**

BIBLIOGRAPHY

*Primary Sources*

Vives, Juan Luis. *Declamationes Sullanae.* Edited and translated by Edward V. George. Leiden, Netherlands, 1989.

———. *The Education of a Christian Woman: A Sixteenth-Century Manual.* Translated by Charles Fantazzi. Chicago, 2000.

———. *On Assistance to the Poor.* Translated by Alice Tobriner. Toronto, 1999.

———. *The Passions of the Soul: The Third Book of* De Anima et Vita. Translated by Carlos G. Noreña. Lewiston, N.Y., 1990.

———. *Somnium et Vigilia in Somnium Scipionis. The Library of Renaissance Humanism, Vol. 2.* Edited by Edward V. George. Greenwood, S.C., 1989.

*Secondary Sources*

Abellán, José Luis. *Historia crítica del pensamiento español.* Vol. 2, *La edad de oro.* Madrid, 1979. An in-depth reference work on the major figures in Spanish philosophy.

Bataillon, Marcel. *Erasmo y España.* Mexico City, 1997. A classic text on Spanish humanism.

Copenhaver, Brian P., and Charles B. Schmitt. *Renaissance Philosophy.* Oxford, 1992.

Fraile, Guillermo. *Historia de la filosofía española.* Madrid, 1971. A concise historical introduction to Spanish philosophy.

Noreña, Carlos G. *Juan Luis Vives and the Emotions.* Carbondale, Ill. 1989.

———. *A Vives Bibliography.* Studies in Renaissance Literature, vol. 5. Lewiston, N.Y., 1990.

Schmitt, C. B., ed. *The Cambridge History of Renaissance Philosophy.* Cambridge, U.K. 1991.

DAMIAN BACICH

**VIZIER.** Vizier, 'helper' or 'deputy', a term first employed in the Koran, evolved to mean 'chief minister' in early Islamic history, possibly becoming an office of Arab administration with the Abbasid Caliph al-Mahdi (775–785). The title vizier was applied widely as an honorific for representatives of the caliph or sultan. The term "grand vizier" denoted those chief, or prime, ministers who served the Ottoman sultans from 1300 to 1923.

### ORIGINS OF THE INSTITUTION

The Perso-Turkish word vizier (also "vezir," or "vizier") originates in the Arabic *wazīr,* and appears in the Koranic verse "We gave Moses the book and made his brother Aaron his wazīr," (Koran, chapter XXV: 35), denoting a helper. Viziers quickly assumed the role of second-in-command in early Islamic history, the most famous among the Abbasids being the Barmakid family of advisers and secretaries under Caliph Harun al-Rashid (786–809). By the eleventh century, the power and obligations of the vizier were delineated in Muslim administrative manuals, which frequently described the office as subordinate only to the caliph or sultan. Vizierial households, in imitation of those of caliph or sultan, became centers of tremendous wealth, ostentation, and intellectual and artistic patronage. The tension between the two most powerful figures of Muslim courts, the ruler and his vizier, is one of the most common struggles represented in early histories and transmitted into western literature, as Shakespeare's *Othello* attests.

The title of vizier could be differentiated, as it was under the Fatimid dynasty in Egypt (969–1171), and was sometimes carried by military officials, who developed an independence of action in the latter years of that dynasty. In Muslim Spain (Andalusia), where the term *hājib* was the equivalent of vizier, multiple viziers abounded, with as few as ten or as many as twenty-nine in place at one time

In Persia, viziers were perceived as servants of the ruler rather than the state, and often they were charged with overseeing financial affairs. Mahmud, founder of the Ghaznavids (998–1030), had six viziers, of whom three were dismissed and died violently, two were dismissed and stripped of their wealth, and the sixth executed; such treatment was testimony to the hazards of the position. Inheritors of Ghaznavid court practices, both the Seljuk and the Ottoman dynasties maintained the office as a well-defined and extremely powerful position. Of special note is Nizam al-Mulk (vizier 1063–1092), who served two Seljuk sultans and exercised the greatest of powers of any vizier up to that time. Beyond tending to the general affairs of the sultan, Nizam al-Mulk was also responsible for religious affairs and for diplomatic relations with foreign rulers. He also on occasion led the army on campaign. Nizam al-Mulk amassed legendary wealth and armies of slaves, founded an educational system known as the Nizamiya, and compiled one of the best-known pre-Ottoman manuals on administrative practice, *Siyasetname* (The Book of government).

## GRAND VIZIERS UNDER THE OTTOMAN EMPIRE

Historians have made much of the Seljuk and Ottoman practice of staffing the administration from non-Turkish stock, as was the case with Nizam al-Mulk. The Ottomans, especially after the conquest of Istanbul in 1453, were also inclined to choose the grand vizier from its officials who had been conscripted and converted from the Christian populations of the Balkans (called *kul kapikulu*, 'slaves of the court'); these were mainly Albanian or Serbian peoples. After the 1550s, when the Ottomans colonized Hungary, Croatians and Hungarians populated the *kul* ranks. Similarly, in the eighteenth and nineteenth centuries, sultans Selim III (ruled 1789–1807) and Mahmud II (ruled 1808–1839) preferred Georgians or Circassians for their grand viziers, since the trans-Caucasus region was then a ready source of slaves. Ethnic preferences may have influenced the sultans' choice of servants, but at least in the early days of the empire, the administrative experience of the non-Turkic populations was especially valued. In any case, unquestioning loyalty was seen as more forthcoming from slave converts than from freeborn Muslims.

Under the Ottomans, as elsewhere, the title of vizier distinguished lesser officers of the empire, often in hierarchical order (as part of the *erkân-i devlet*, 'pillars of the state', of the *divan-i hümayun*, 'imperial council'), but grand vizier or *sadrazam* (also *vizier-i azam*) was the most powerful officer after the sultan. Before 1453, the grand vizier was appointed from among the religious class and was often a judge *(kadi* or *kazi)*. Between 1385 and 1453, the Candarli family held the office, and all were judges. After 1453, the *kul*, military rather than religious men with expertise in financial and chancery affairs, dominated the office (Inalcik, p. 195). Palace factions of new sultans tended to influence the appointments of the grand vizier, and there was frequently a complete restaffing of the bureaucracy after a new accession. In the second half of the seventeenth century, a severe crisis led the sultan to grant Grand Vizier Mehmed Köprülü extraordinary powers, and a separate administrative office, the Babiali (the Sublime Porte), was created to restore the stability of the empire. For half a century, the Köprülü family dominated the office, reorganized the economy, restored order throughout Ottoman territories, and dealt increasingly with foreign affairs. Grand viziers in the eighteenth century were often appointed after serving as *reisülküttab* (head of the chancery, later foreign affairs minister). Especially notable was Koca Ragib Pasha (ruled 1757–1763), who served two sultans after negotiating earlier treaties with Nadir Shah of Persia and the Habsburgs at Belgrade in 1739. Koca Ragib associated with a large circle of intellectuals and built his personal library, which was opened to the public and still operates in Istanbul.

The grand vizier led all military campaigns after 1700 and served as head of the imperial council, where he and the other viziers, as the primary representatives of the sultan's authority, discussed state affairs. Many viziers married daughters and sisters of the sultan and were subsequently called *damad*, 'bridegroom', acquired rights to revenues of vast estates, and were granted stature matched only by that of the royal house. Some, such as the famous Damad Ibrahim Pasha, who was grand vizier to Suleiman the Magnificent (ruled 1520–1566) from 1523 to 1536, lost their lives when they overstepped their bounds in emulating the sultan. The office was always precariously secured and held and very often ended with confiscation of wealth, exile, and/or death. By the mid-nineteenth century, the power and prestige of the vizier had declined; the office had assumed the proportions of a modern-day minister.

*See also* **Ottoman Empire; Sultan.**

BIBLIOGRAPHY

Dankoff, Robert. *The Intimate Life of an Ottoman States-man: Melek Ahmed Pasha (1588–1662), as Portrayed in Evliya Çelebi's* Book of Travels (Seyahat-name). Albany, N.Y., 1991. A wonderfully evocative view of the trials and tribulations of Grand Vizier Melek Ahmed.

Imber, Colin. "Khalil Pasha, Djandarli," in *Encyclopedia of Islam.* 2nd ed. Vol. 3. CD-ROM edition. One of numerous individual entries for well-known Ottoman grand viziers.

Inalcik, Halil. *The Ottoman Empire: The Classical Age 1300–1600.* London, 1973.

Sourdel, Dominique. *Le vizierat abbaside de 749 à 936.* 2 vols. Damascus, 1960.

Stavrides, Theoharis. *The Sultan of Vezirs: The Life and Times of the Ottoman Grand Vezir Mahmud Pasha Angelović (1453–1474).* Leiden, 2001. Includes a comprehensive introduction to the history of the office.

"Wazīr," in *Encyclopedia of Islam.* 2nd ed. Vol. 11. Leiden, 2001. Articles for several dynasties with individual authors, including Halil Inalcik on the Ottomans.

Virginia H. Aksan

---

**VOLTAIRE** (François-Marie Arouet; 1694–1778), French philosopher, historian, dramatist, and poet. Voltaire was born in Paris 21 November 1694, the son of a successful notary. A prolific philosopher, historian, and writer in numerous genres and a tireless champion of freedom of thought and expression, no figure better represents the spirit of the French Enlightenment than Voltaire.

Three years after the death of his mother (née Marguerite Daumard), Voltaire entered the Jesuit Collège Louis-le-Grand in Paris, in 1704, where he spent the next seven years. Following his studies, Voltaire frequented the libertine society of the Temple and began to exercise his literary talents by composing satirical light verse as well as his first play, *Oedipe,* completed in manuscript in 1715. In 1716 Voltaire was exiled from Paris because of an epigram against the regent, and in May 1717 was sent to the Bastille, accused of further inflammatory writings. Shortly after his release, *Oedipe* was staged

in November 1718, its brilliant success making him an overnight celebrity, considered France's preeminent poet. It was at this point that he adopted the name Monsieur de Voltaire, not only a *nom de plume* but also an index of his lifelong aristocratic aspirations.

The self-styled nobleman received a harsh but transformative lesson in 1726, when following a quarrel with the chevalier de Rohan, Voltaire once again found himself imprisoned in the Bastille and then was exiled to England for two years. Rightly or wrongly, Voltaire saw in England a model of political freedom and, above all, religious tolerance, which was to result in his hugely popular and influential *English Letters* (published first in England in 1733, in English and French versions, then in France in 1734). During his British sojourn, Voltaire, having acquired reasonable competence in English, read numerous English writers and thinkers, but it was above all the works of John Locke and Isaac Newton that earned his enduring admiration.

While a number of biographers and critics have overstated the intellectual impact England was to have on Voltaire—his deism and skepticism certainly predated his exile—it is clear that England had the effect of consolidating his militant opposition to intolerance and dogma in politics and religion, and just as importantly, made him a partisan of British sensualism (in Locke), and the "new philosophy" of scientific method (in Newton and his precursor, Francis Bacon). In France Voltaire became the greatest popularizer of Newtonian physics (publishing *Elements of Newton's Philosophy* in 1738) and a driving force behind the Enlightenment's antimetaphysical, positivistic, and scientific bent in which the Cartesian rationalism of the French classical age gave way to the influence of English empiricism.

The English exile set the stage not only for Voltaire's abiding philosophical concerns but also for a life spent mostly outside Paris. From 1734 he lived at Cirey with his mistress, Émilie du Châtelet, until her death in 1749. For a number of years prior to her death, Frederick the Great of Prussia (ruled 1740–1786) had sought to bring Voltaire to Potsdam and Berlin, and in 1750 Voltaire took up the offer; but the nearly three years he spent with Frederick ended in bitter disillusionment for both par-

**Voltaire.** Portrait after Maurice Quentin La Tour. THE ART ARCHIVE/MUSÉE DU CHÂTEAU DE VERSAILLES

ties. After five years moving from one side of the Franco-Swiss border to the other, in 1759 he purchased the chateau of Ferney, just outside Geneva, which over the years he built into a sprawling estate, home to various cottage industries that added to his already considerable fortune, and a cultural crossroads where Voltaire hosted innumerable guests. He lived and worked there until the last year of his life. In February 1778, he returned to Paris to produce his last play, *Irène,* and his triumphant return to the capital was a legendary moment in French cultural history, so overwhelming that the eighty-four-year-old Voltaire remarked that he was being "killed with glory." After a long life of notorious ill health and hypochondria, he died during the night of 30 May.

Today Voltaire is read above all as a philosopher—in the restricted sense that word had in the French eighteenth century—and as an acerbic social critic who railed against injustice, metaphysical absurdity of every ilk, clerical abuse, prejudice, and superstition. Those threads came together bril-

liantly in his 1759 philosophical tale, *Candide,* in which he lambasted the idealist doctrine of pre-established harmony and the "best of all possible worlds" promulgated by Gottfried Wilhelm Leibniz and his followers Alexander Pope and Christian Wolff. *Candide* was written largely in response to the death of thirty thousand victims of the 1755 Lisbon earthquake and as an exposition of the problems raised in his hastily drafted 1755 *Poem on the Lisbon Disaster.* In response to the question of evil, Voltaire abandoned any claim on a metaphysical explanation of human affairs, proposing instead that we "cultivate our garden," that is, that we focus on local and practical concerns, faced with an order of experience that may in some sense be providential but whose mechanism escapes our reason. Voltaire had explored the problem of theodicy and providence in his earlier tale, *Zadig* (1747), which along with *Micromégas* (1752) and more than twenty other philosophical tales, made Voltaire the master of one of the French Enlightenment's most fecund and innovative literary forms.

Yet Voltaire thought of himself perhaps more as a poet, playwright, and historian than as the mordant satirist acknowledged today. His career began and ended with the theater; in between, he produced a dozen or so plays, with varying degrees of success. Today they are rarely read or staged. From the light verse of his youth to the epic *Henriad* and the bawdy *Maid of Orleans,* the epicurean *Mondain,* and his *Poem on Natural Law,* among many others, poetry also held a central place in his oeuvre. In the domain of history, Voltaire (who was appointed royal historiographer in 1745 and elected to the French Academy in 1746) composed works on Charles XII, Louis XIV, and Louis XV. As with his plays and poetry, these books are today little read. Other works of nonfiction have fared better: the *Essay on Manners* (1754), the *Treatise on Tolerance* (1763, written after Voltaire had intervened in the Calas affair, in which a Protestant man was wrongfully executed on the charge of killing his son who wished to convert to Catholicism), and the *Philosophical Dictionary* (first volume published 1764) remain enduring classics.

Voltaire's overwhelming importance and influence in the eighteenth century lie in his promotion of the force of reason and justice, his ironic wit, and his unparalleled skills as a propagandist of the ideals of the Enlightenment. In a career ranging from the end of the reign of Louis XIV to the reign of the last king of the *ancien régime,* Voltaire was France's clearest, most prolific, and most enduring voice of dissent.

*See also* *Encyclopédie;* **Enlightenment; French Literature and Language; Philosophes.**

BIBLIOGRAPHY

*Primary Sources*

Voltaire. *The Complete Tales of Voltaire.* Translated by William Walton. New York, 1990.

——. *Correspondance.* Edited by Theodore Besterman. 13 vols. Paris, 1977–.

——. *Les oeuvres complètes de Voltaire.* Edited by Theodore Besterman and W. H. Barber. 64 vols. Geneva and Toronto, 1968–1984.

——. *Political Writings.* Edited and translated by David Williams. Cambridge, U.K., 1994.

——. *The Portable Voltaire.* Edited by Ben Ray Redman. New York, 1977.

——. *The Selected Letters of Voltaire.* Edited by Richard A. Brooks. New York, 1973.

——. *The Works of Voltaire.* Translated by William F. Fleming, et al. 22 vols. Reprint. New York, 1988.

*Secondary Sources*

Knapp, Bettina L. *Voltaire Revisited.* New York, 2000.

Mason, Haydn Trevor. *Voltaire: A Biography.* Baltimore, 1981.

Pearson, Roger. *The Fables of Reason: A Study of Voltaire's "Contes philosophiques."* Oxford, 1993.

Pomeau, René. *D'Arouet à Voltaire, 1694–1734.* Oxford, 1985.

PATRICK RILEY, JR.

**VOUET, SIMON** (1590–1649), French painter. Since the late seventeenth century, most historians of French art have justifiably considered Vouet to be the founder of the early modern school of French painting. Born in Paris, the son of a minor court painter and grandson of the Master of the King's Falcons, Vouet was a child prodigy who was perfectly situated to receive the best possible exposure to great works of art, and the best training, which probably began with his father. At the age of fourteen he was already recognized as a successful portraitist, and at the age of twenty-two he was selected by the crown to travel to Constantinople with the French ambassador to paint portraits of important foreign dignitaries.

On his return from the Near East, Vouet traveled through Italy and settled in Rome, which was at that time the center of the art world. There, like so many artists of his generation, he painted in a Carravaggesque mode, but one that sought to infuse this tenebrist approach with delicacy and refinement (*St. Jerome and the Angel,* c. 1622, National Gallery of Art, Washington, D.C.). His commissions at this time included altarpieces or complete decorations for the Raggi Chapel of the Gesù in Genoa, the Alaleoni Chapel in St. Lorenzo in Lucina in Rome, and the Charter House of St. Martin in Naples. He achieved so much success in Rome that in 1624 he became the first non-Italian to be elected director, or prince, of the Accademia di San Luca, where his insistence on a solid grounding in principles of good draftsmanship—that is, figure drawing—was greatly admired. Cardinal Richelieu and Louis XIII kept a close watch on this precocious talent by supporting him in Rome, and by 1626, he was offered a *brevet du roi,* accompanied by a lucrative pension and suitably noble housing in the Louvre for himself, his family, and his atelier.

Upon his return to Paris in late 1627, knowing that Carravaggio (1571–1610) and his followers were never really appreciated in the French capital, Vouet gradually altered his manner. During his four-month stop in Venice on his return journey from Rome, he modified his heavy chiaroscuro with the grace, fluidity, and color of northern Italian painting. As a result, Vouet became unequaled in Paris for grand decorative painting, where slightly elongated monumental figures with swirling draperies slowly float across the surfaces of his large canvases (*Allegory of Wealth,* Louvre, Paris). His manner was an astute blend of sixteenth-century mannerist French court art at Fontainebleau, the Romano-Bolognese classicism of the Carracci, the naturalism of Carravaggio, and the extravagant color, lively facture, and dazzling light of sixteenth-century Venetian artists. The genius of Vouet's elegant inventions was conveyed by the power of his draftsmanship, as is evident in the numerous drawings that survive. Most of them are elegant figure studies that reveal his use of firm, sweeping contours

**Simon Vouet.** *St. Jerome and the Angel,* c. 1622. NATIONAL GALLERY OF ART, WASHINGTON, D.C.

that effortlessly render the human form in motion. Only a small number of composition studies enable us to comprehend the genesis of his designs.

Vouet's ever-increasing success led to numerous ecclesiastic commissions for altarpieces (St. Nicolas-des-Champs, St. Eustache, and the Novitiate of the Jesuits), and an even greater number of royal and private commissions for both religious and secular decorations at the Louvre, the Palais Royal, the Palais du Luxembourg, the Hôtel Séguier and the chateaux at Chilly, Chessy, Fontainebleau, Poitou, Rueil, Saint-Germain-en-Laye, and Wideville. Being in such demand required an increasing number of skilled hands in a remarkably organized studio. His extraordinarily busy atelier utilized, trained, and influenced more than a generation of painters and printmakers. These artists included François Perrier, Nicolas Chaperon, Charles Poërson, Pierre Daret, Michel I Corneille, Nöel

Quillerier, François Bellin, Pierre Patel l'aîné, Eustache Le Sueur, Michel Dorigny (1616–1665), and François Tortebat (1616–1690). These last two became his sons-in-law and made etching or prints of many of his works. As each of these artists matured, they actively participated in the master's vast decorative campaigns. A generation later, the possibilities of this well-run enterprise would be taken to even greater heights by his most famous student, Charles Le Brun, in the service of Louis XIV.

Unfortunately, most of Vouet's decorative ensembles have been destroyed or dismantled. However, well aware of his posterity, Vouet owned his own printing press and was granted a royal privilege to replicate his designs. This encouraged an atmosphere of experimentation with printmaking that led Perrier, Dorigny, Tortebat, and others to interpret in etchings and engravings a large portion of his most celebrated commissions.

*See also* **Caravaggio and Caravaggism; Carracci Family; Le Brun, Charles; Louis XIII (France); Mannerism; Painting; Richelieu, Armand-Jean Du Plessis, cardinal.**

BIBLIOGRAPHY

Brejon de Lavergnée, Barbara. *Dessins de Simon Vouet, 1590–1649. Musée du Louvre, Cabinet des dessins.* Paris, 1987.

Clark, Alvin L. "Simon Vouet and His Printmakers: Posterity, Prosperity, and Process." In Museum of Fine Arts, *French Prints from the Age of the Musketeers,* exh. cat., edited by Sue Welsh Reed. Boston, 1998.

Crelly, William. *The Painting of Simon Vouet.* New Haven, 1962. Contains catalogue raisonné.

Galeries nationales du Grand Palais. *Vouet.* Exh. cat. Texts by Jacques Thuillier, Barbara Brejon de Lavergnée, and Denis Lavalle. Paris, 1990.

Loire, Stephane. *Simon Vouet: Actes du colloque international.* Galeries nationales du Grand Palais, 5–7 February 1992. Paris, 1992.

Staatliche Graphische Sammlung der Neue Pinakothek. *Simon Vouet: 100 Neuentdeckte Zeichnungen aus den Bestanden der Bayerischen Staatsbibliothek.* Exh. cat. Richard Harprath and Barbara Brejon de Lavergnée, eds. Munich, 1991.

ALVIN L. CLARK, JR.

**WAGES.** The history of wages in early modern Europe is a study of contrasts. To begin with, most people toiled on family farms or in family enterprises. Hence wages were a dominant part of income for only a small fraction of the population. Nevertheless, hiring workers for wages and working for someone else part of the time were extremely common. The tension between these two facts has informed the two key debates about wages in the early modern period. The first debate, accepting the ubiquity of paid labor, uses wages to infer standards of living and thus examine Malthusian cycles. The second debate involves both the extent of wage labor and the institutions that made it respond or not respond to the laws of supply and demand.

In 1798, the British social theorist Thomas Malthus (1766–1834) argued that in agrarian economies (agriculture absorbed two-thirds of all workers in nearly all European regions prior to 1800) incomes depended on the ratio of land to population. More land allowed higher output per person; more people drove down the output per person. Because land rents increase when land is scarce, wages are even more sensitive to scarcity than output per person. This narrative has been adopted, with slight variation, by many different scholars who believe that these iron laws held firm for millennia. For some, these shackles were eventually broken by the increased use of coal, for others by access to the agricultural output of the New World, or even by technical change broadly defined and dated to sometime in the mid-eighteenth cen-

tury. From the time of the Black Death (mid-fourteenth century) to the 1750s, wage series did follow a broad Malthusian pattern. In England, for instance, wages started from a low in the mid-1300s, rose for nearly a century and a half in response to the epidemic's massive mortality rate, then fell for an equally long time, bottoming out in the seventeenth century. The rise of wages in the eighteenth century was not pronounced, but wage stability in the face of massive population growth was nonetheless an important achievement. Bits and pieces of this story can be seen in all European countries, though each in its fashion raises questions about the standard Malthusian model.

In recent years, Malthus has been under strong challenge. First, as Van Zanden states, wages are not income. At the individual level, nonwage compensation—from common rights, or home manufacture, for instance—was an important element of most families' income in the early modern period. At the national level, earnings from land, capital, skills, and entrepreneurship were of considerable value, even though their distribution was quite different from that of wages. As the recent historical record suggests, economies can experience massive growth without witnessing much real wage increase for the unskilled. In the past as in the present, one should investigate wages with some concern for inequality.

Second, and more problematic, is the evidence that comes from examining regional patterns in wages. Regional variation in wages at any point in time is of the same order of magnitude as the two-century variation in wages of a local Malthusian cycle. If we compare high wage regions to low wage regions Malthus's theory fails again. In fact, high population areas did not have low wages. On the contrary, economically leading areas were most often very densely populated relative to the European hinterland. Northern Italy, the Low Countries, and England all were or became densely populated in their period of economic leadership; and they were all also high wage economies. Economic historians now argue that Malthus's emphasis on endowments and demography explained in part the evolution of economies and wages. Political institutions and economic institutions have at least as much importance.

The second debate arrays two sides. On one side scholars argue that families in the early modern era preferred self-sufficiency to the uncertainty or unfairness of market interaction. Therefore they avoided labor markets. These scholars also argue that, unlike in modern society, workers and their employers were enmeshed in a web of social relations that only capitalism would break. In this view, labor exchange was relational rather than market-driven. In such a situation, one would prefer to employ an acquaintance at a higher wage rather than hire an outsider for less. In contrast, the argument continues, modern factory workers have no social relations either with management or with the distant shareholders of the corporation they work for; hence wages are free to reflect the iron law of supply and demand.

That view has come under repeated challenge. In part, this is because the arguments that seek to differentiate early modern from modern labor markets have been made on unsound quantitative evidence and are based on a very naive view of how labor markets operate. When scholars take into account that labor markets are always imperfect, differences between those of the preindustrial and contemporary eras cease to be differences in kind.

The market-avoidance argument fails for empirical reasons: only a small fraction of farms and enterprises were the right size to have an exact balance between their labor demand and their family labor supply. Imbalances arose for different reasons, including seasonal peaks in labor demand at harvest, the demographic cycle in crafts, and the difficulty of adjusting farm size to family size. Therefore many,

probably most, families either bought or sold days of labor, earning or paying wages. These wages did reflect supply and demand, rising in summer as demand for labor increased, and falling when population growth was rapid and during bad harvests, when the amount of work was reduced, and so on.

There were some important exceptions. For instance, in eastern Europe the strengthening of serfdom stymied labor markets. But there were other areas, like the Low Countries, where wage labor was quite prevalent by the end of the Middle Ages. Overall, the extent of wage labor seems to have paralleled the extent of markets in general: where trade and commerce were more active, one could observe more active labor markets.

*See also* **Capitalism; Commerce and Markets; Laborers; Servants.**

BIBLIOGRAPHY

Allen R. C. "The Great Divergence in European Wages and Prices from the Middle Ages to the First World War." *Explorations in Economic History* 38, no. 4 (October 2001): 411–448.

Brown, Henry Phelps, and Sheila V. Hopkins. *A Perspective of Wage and Prices.* London, 1981.

Campbell, B. "Agricultural Progress in Medieval England: Some Evidence from Eastern Norfolk." *Economic History Review* 36, no. 1 (February 1983): 26–46.

de Vries, J., and A. van der Woode. *The First Modern Economy: Success, Failure and Perseverance of the Dutch Economy 1500–1815.* Cambridge, U.K., 1997.

Epstein, S. "Craft Guilds, Apprenticeship, and Technological Change in Preindustrial Europe." *Journal of Economic History* 58, no. 3 (September 1998): 684–713.

Grantham, G. "Contra Ricardo: On the Macroeconomics of Pre-Industrial Economies." *European Review of Economic History* 3, no. 2 (August 1999): 199–232.

Hoffman, P. T. *Growth in a Traditional Society.* Princeton, 1998.

Hoffman, P. T., D. Jacks, and P. Lindert. "Real Inequality in Europe Since 1500." *Journal of Economic History* 62, no. 2 (June 2002): 322–355.

Jones, E. L. *The European Miracle: Environments, Economies, and Geopolitics in the History of Europe and Asia.* 2nd ed. Cambridge, U.K., 1987.

Malthus, T. R. *An Essay on the Principle of Population.* 1798.

Mokyr, J. *The Lever of Riches: Technological Creativity and Economic Progress.* New York, 1990.

North, D. C. *Structure and Change in Economic History.* New York, 1981.

Ozmucur, S., and S. Pamuck. "Real Wages and Standards of Living in the Ottoman Empire 1489–1914." *Journal of Economic History* 62, no. 2 (June 2002): 293–321.

Reddy, W. M. *The Rise of Market Culture: The Textile Trade and French Society, 1750–1900.* Cambridge, U.K., 1984.

Van Zanden, J. L. "Rich and Poor before the Industrial Revolution: A Comparison between Java and the Netherlands at the Beginning of the Nineteenth Century." *Explorations in Economic History* 40, no. 1 (January 2001): 1–23.

Wrigley, E. A. *Continuity, Chance and Change: The Character of the Industrial Revolution in England.* Cambridge, U.K., 1988.

Wrigley, E. A., and R. S. Schofield. *The Population History of England 1541–1871: A Reconstruction.* Cambridge, Mass., 1981.

JEAN-LAURENT ROSENTHAL

# WALLENSTEIN, A. W. E. VON

(originally Waldstein; 1583–1634), Bohemian noble, soldier, and statesman who played an important role in the Thirty Years' War (1618–1648). Albrecht Wenzel Eusebius von Wallenstein was born in Bohemia (today the Czech Republic). Given a Protestant upbringing, he converted to Catholicism in 1606. In 1609, his Jesuit confessor arranged his marriage to a wealthy widow who may have been some ten years his senior. When she died in 1614, he inherited all her estates. During the Bohemian rebellion that began in 1618, he remained loyal to the ruler, the Holy Roman emperor Ferdinand II (ruled 1619–1637), and profited enormously from the latter's victory over the rebels. He was appointed governor of the kingdom of Bohemia and bought up a large number of confiscated estates so that he came to possess most of northeastern Bohemia. These estates were consolidated into Friedland, of which he became duke in 1623.

In 1625, when the emperor decided to raise an army of his own to counter the threat from Christian IV of Denmark (ruled 1596–1648), Wallenstein was the obvious choice to be commander in chief; he was appointed on 7 April. It is often said that he raised and paid for this army at his own expense, and there is certainly some truth to it: he was able to put together a force of over 24,000 without recourse to the imperial treasury. His great

personal wealth and his ability to obtain loans were important factors, but Wallenstein's primary aim was to sustain his forces with requisitions from any territory they occupied. He also used his duchy of Friedland as a source of supplies.

During the Danish phase of the war (1625–1629), Wallenstein enjoyed considerable military success. He defeated the Protestant commander, Count Ernst of Mansfeld, at Dessau in 1626, and early in 1627 he marched into Holstein and Jutland (the Danish mainland) before turning east into Mecklenburg and Pomerania. The dukes of Mecklenburg had supported Christian IV, so the emperor deprived them of their titles, transferred their confiscated estates to Wallenstein (February 1627), and the following year made him the sole duke of Mecklenburg (January 1628). This arbitrary move caused some disquiet among all hereditary rulers.

The campaign of 1628 was anticlimactic. The complete defeat of Denmark turned out to be an impossibility: although the emperor appointed Wallenstein "General of the Oceanic and Baltic Seas" in February 1628, without a fleet the Danish islands were beyond his reach. He attempted to capture the port of Stralsund in the summer of 1628 (May–July), but without success. Although he defeated Christian again at Wolgast in September, Wallenstein warned the emperor that if peace were not made, Sweden might undertake a full intervention. He also warned that the cost of maintaining his 100,000-strong army was placing an intolerable burden on the north German states. Peace was made at Lübeck (July 1629).

Wallenstein's success and his financial exactions from friend and foe alike created enormous resentment and, with the coming of what was thought to be peace, the princes turned on him at the Electoral Diet in Regensburg and made a formal request for his dismissal on 16 July 1630. Surprisingly, Ferdinand agreed to comply; the general was dismissed on 13 August. Equally surprising was the fact that Wallenstein also complied. Indeed, it would appear that he had come to feel that the maintenance of such a large army was unsustainable and greeted the end of his responsibility with relief. Although there are some indications that Ferdinand had come to distrust his general, his dismissal deprived the emperor of military power just as he faced invasion from the Swedish king, Gustavus II Adolphus.

The success of Gustavus II Adolphus in 1631 forced the emperor to recall Wallenstein, and he was appointed commander in chief (with considerable powers) once again in April 1632. Although he was not victorious at the Battle of Lützen in November, the death of the Swedish king in that battle created a new political situation. Surprisingly, Wallenstein did not go on the offensive, but sought to conduct negotiations with all concerned parties in an effort to bring peace (and probably to obtain territory and titles for himself). However, his independence, his alleged double-dealing, his reliance on astrological predictions, and his bizarre behavior (it was asserted that on arrival in any town he ordered all dogs and cats to be killed because he did not like the noise they made) undermined his credibility with everyone. By now he had become a liability to the emperor, who saw him as a traitorous conspirator (and dispensable now that Spanish aid was imminent). Accordingly, in January 1634 he ordered Wallenstein's capture (or liquidation), and the following month he was assassinated—by an Englishman, an Irishman, and a Scotsman.

Wallenstein was the most important military entrepreneur in the Thirty Years' War, and his alleged treason and murder have overshadowed the considerable success he had in his first imperial generalship (1625–1630), when he raised the emperor to the zenith of his power. An enigmatic figure, his life became the subject of a dramatic trilogy by the German poet, Johann Christoph Friedrich von Schiller.

*See also* **Ferdinand II (Holy Roman Empire); Gustavus II Adolphus (Sweden); Lübeck; Schiller, Johann Christoph Friedrich von; Thirty Years' War (1618–1648).**

BIBLIOGRAPHY

Asch, Ronald G. *The Thirty Years' War: The Holy Roman Empire and Europe, 1618–1648.* New York and London, 1997. An up-to-date survey of the war of manageable length that keeps the focus on Germany. Wallenstein is not neglected.

Benecke, Gerhard, ed. *Germany in the Thirty Years' War.* London, 1978. A collection of documents; for Wallenstein's reappointment in 1632 and his assassination in 1634, see pp. 89–92.

Darby, Graham. *The Thirty Years' War.* London, 2001. A concise introduction to the conflict; a good place to start.

Mann, Golo. *Wallenstein: His Life Narrated.* New York, 1976. Translated from the German edition of 1971 by Charles Kessler, this runs to over 900 pages, without the notes and bibliography of the original.

Parker, Geoffrey, ed. *The Thirty Years' War.* 2nd ed. London and New York, 1997. Currently the definitive work on the war, with a full set of notes and a comprehensive bibliography that lists all the essential works in German. For Wallenstein, see especially pp. 262–263 of the bibliographical essay.

GRAHAM DARBY

# WALPOLE, HORACE (1717–1797), English statesman and man of letters.

Although Horace Walpole sat in the House of Commons from 1741 to 1768, he did not pursue an orthodox career as a statesman. An intense and acutely sensitive man, Walpole was temperamentally unsuited to the cut and thrust of political battle, and preferred to work behind the scenes as a pamphleteer, a gossip, a networker and, ultimately, a historian.

Walpole was fiercely loyal to his family and friends, and herein lies the key to all his politics. He never failed to support his friend and cousin, Henry Seymour-Conway, while disliking all critics and enemies of his father (Sir Robert Walpole). All but one account of Horace Walpole's political career have been marred by a failure to recognize his homosexuality, without which it is impossible to understand the depth of his hatred for Henry Pelham and the duke of Newcastle, the brothers of Catherine Pelham, whose arranged marriage to Walpole's onetime lover Henry Fiennes-Clinton, earl of Lincoln, took place in 1744.

Horace Walpole's hostility to the Pelhams has usually been explained in terms of his belief in their disloyalty to Robert Walpole, whom they "deserted" when his ministry began to crumble. Although the Pelhams succeeded Robert as leaders of the Court Whigs, Horace did not join them after his father's death, aligning himself instead with Richard Rigby and Henry Fox. When Fox joined a ministry in partnership with Newcastle in 1756, Walpole operated behind the scenes to annoy and frustrate both while remaining on ostensibly friendly terms with Fox. Walpole's unsuccessful attempt to prevent the execution of Admiral John Byng for failing to prevent the loss of Minorca may have been partly motivated by the desire to embarrass Fox and Newcastle, suspected by many of having found a scapegoat for a more serious error of military judgment. At any rate, Walpole's *Letter from Xo Ho, a Chinese Philosopher at London, to his Friend Lien Chi at Peking* (1757), which pithily summarized the hypocrisies of Byng's impeachment, established Walpole as a witty and dangerous pamphleteer.

Walpole was most active from 1763 to 1767, when he acted as a political mentor to Conway. Both men had voted against George Grenville's ministry to defend the freedom of the press, then threatened by government action against the opposition M.P. John Wilkes, an outspoken critic of the crown, and the *North Briton,* a newspaper that printed his articles. George III, angered by what he perceived as insubordination, ordered Conway's dismissal from his regiment and court position, whereupon Walpole joined the opposition and began intriguing to bring down the Grenville ministry. When the Rockingham Whigs took office in 1765, Conway became secretary of state for the Southern Department and leader of the House of Commons. Walpole, however, was offered nothing, and a brief estrangement took place between the two. In April 1766, he resumed his place as Conway's adviser, notwithstanding the latter's cooling enthusiasm for politics, and became an inside observer of the Rockingham and Chatham ministries. When Conway decided to resign the lead in the Commons at the end of 1767, Walpole also decided to leave political life, and returned to his other occupations as author, publisher, art critic, and antiquarian.

Although Walpole is one of England's greatest letter writers, whose correspondence is an invaluable source for the political, social, and cultural history of mid-Hanoverian England, his *Memoirs of the Reign of George II* and *Memoirs of the Reign of George III,* written for posterity and published after his demise, provide a lively narrative of political events and personalities from 1751 to 1772. Both were much maligned—unjustifiably so—by nineteenth-century critics. Of the two works, the *Memoirs of the Reign of George III,* written between 1766 and 1772, are the more valuable, for they describe

**Horace Walpole.** Portrait engraving by J. McArdel after a painting by Sir Joshua Reynolds. ©BETTMANN/CORBIS

events in which Walpole was a central participant. Although the *Memoirs of the Reign of George II* are less reliable, they still constitute the most important source in existence for the parliamentary debates of 1754–1761.

The memoirs are not without bias. Walpole's loathing of the Pelhams manifests itself in the representation of the Duke of Newcastle as a time-serving incompetent. Henry Fox was traduced as a greedy and unscrupulous careerist. Walpole was also responsible for creating the myth of a sinister plot hatched by the princess dowager and Lord Bute, George III's first prime minister, to revive the royal prerogative and employ it against opponents of the crown. The memoirs, in effect, encapsulated the Whig perspective on crown and Parliament usually attributed to English historians of the nineteenth century.

*See also* **English Literature and Language; George II (Great Britain); George III (Great Britain); Parliament; Pitt, William the Elder and William the Younger; Political Parties.**

BIBLIOGRAPHY

Hunting, Warren Smith, ed. *Horace Walpole: Writer, Politician and Connoisseur: Essays on the 250th Anniversary of Walpole's Birth*. New Haven and London, 1967.

Ketton-Cremer, Robert Wyndham. *Horace Walpole: A Biography*. London, 1946.

Mowl, Timothy. *Horace Walpole: The Great Outsider*. London, 1996.

JENNIFER MORI

**WARFARE.** *See* **Military.**

**WARS OF RELIGION, FRENCH.** The rapid growth of Protestantism in France that began in the 1530s reached a climax around 1560, when roughly one in every twenty French men and women had converted to the new faith. This extraordinary growth resulted in a predictable backlash by French Catholics, whose church and monarchy declared all Protestants—and in France they were overwhelmingly Calvinists, who came to be called Huguenots—to be heretics. For Catholics, Protestants living in their midst not only threatened their eternal souls, but were believed to threaten their earthly existence as well. In an age when every major outbreak of plague, famine, and disease tended to be interpreted as a sign of God's punishment for their sins, most French Catholics believed that heresy within their midst was an open invitation for God's wrath to be visited upon them. Thus, the majority of French Catholics were openly hostile to the Reformation. These popular feelings were reinforced by the French monarchy, as kings Henry II (ruled 1547–1559) and Francis II (ruled 1559–1560) sought to eliminate heresy in their kingdom via both persecution and prosecution. The surge in Protestant growth in the late 1550s, however, meant that the official royal policy of suppression was never likely to succeed. And when the Huguenots seized several major towns by force in 1561–1562, it was clear that suppression had not worked.

Moreover, by 1562 several key members of some prominent noble families such as the Bourbons and the Albrets had converted to the new religion, further exacerbating political tensions and rivalries at court. Their chief rivals, the Guise family, had long championed the Catholic cause; and since the young King Francis II's wife was Mary Stuart of Scotland, whose mother was Mary of Guise, the Guises found themselves in a position of authority during Francis's reign. When the king died of an ear abscess in December 1560, however, his successor was his nine-year-old brother, Charles IX (ruled 1560–1574). The unwritten French constitution required a regent to be appointed until the young king reached his fourteenth year, when he could then govern in his own right. Catherine de Médicis, Henry II's widow, as queen mother of both Francis II and Charles IX, accepted this position, and it was she who had to face the prospect of dealing with the Protestant problem, given that suppression as a policy had simply not worked. Although she was not in favor of religious toleration in principle—indeed, it was very difficult in the sixteenth century even to imagine such a concept—Catherine attempted to work out some kind of limited coexistence. First, she called together leaders of both the Huguenot and Catholic churches at the Colloquy of Poissy in 1561 to see if a compromise were possible. But both the cardinal of Lorraine on the Catholic side and Théodore de Bèze, Calvin's lieutenant from Geneva on the Protestant side, recognized that significant compromise on either the doctrinal or liturgical issues that divided them was impossible. Despite the lack of success at Poissy, however, Catherine went ahead and issued an edict in January 1562, recognizing the legal right of French Protestants to exist and even worship in a few limited areas of the kingdom for the first time. This milestone was far from religious toleration, but it marked a sharp break with the previous royal policies of persecuting Protestants as heretics. French Catholics, however, refused either to accept or enforce the edict. When the prince of Condé, a Protestant member of the Bourbon family, raised troops to enforce the edict on his own, civil war was the result. Over the next thirty-six years, not only did French Huguenots and Catholics raise armies to fight each other on the battlefield, they also fought each other as civilians in towns and cities across the kingdom. Thus, violence in the streets among civilians became a hallmark of the French Wars of Religion for an extended period, imposing on France an experience unmatched by other territories affected by the Reformation: two generations of civil war.

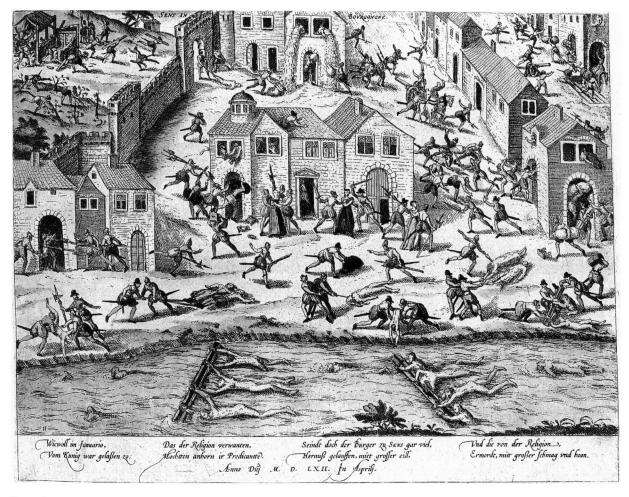

**French Wars of Religion.** The massacre of Huguenots by Catholics in Sens, Burgundy, April 1562; engraving by Hogenberg, late sixteenth–early seventeenth century. THE ART ARCHIVE/UNIVERSITY LIBRARY GENEVA/DAGLI ORTI

The outbreak of civil war in the spring of 1562 began a long series of armed conflicts, followed by brief periods of siege or battlefield confrontation between the two armies, and concluded by extended peace negotiations and a peace treaty. Each of these successive civil wars followed a similar pattern. While one side might manage to defeat the other's army on the battlefield, there was no way that either could effectively administer a heavy enough defeat to disarm all the civilians and nobles on the other side, much less occupy its opponent's cities and towns. Thus, each successive peace treaty had to be a forced compromise, offering very limited rights and legal guarantees that were never enough to provide complete security and freedom of worship for French Protestants. But even limited rights were far too numerous for French Catholics, and each period of peace was soon followed by

another outbreak of war. In all, France was to suffer through eight separate civil wars between 1562 and 1598.

### THE ST. BARTHOLOMEW'S DAY MASSACRES

The first major turning point in the religious wars came in August 1572 with the massacres in Paris that began in the early morning hours of 24 August, St. Bartholomew's Day. Two days earlier, members of the Guise family, probably with the tacit support of Catherine de Médicis, had come to the decision to assassinate Gaspard de Coligny, admiral of France and the military leader of the Huguenots, because of fears of a Huguenot military reprisal in Paris, where many Protestant nobles had gathered for the royal wedding between the king's sister Margaret and Henry of Navarre, son of the Protestants Anthony de Bourbon and Jeanne d'Albret, king and queen of Navarre. Though there was no Protestant coup being planned by Coligny, the assassination attempt nevertheless took place. Because it failed, however, only seriously wounding Coligny, the many Huguenot nobles in Paris began to fear for their lives. This only exacerbated the fears of the Guise family and the queen mother, who managed to persuade the king, Charles IX, and the rest of his council on 23 August to undertake another murder attempt on Coligny, this time accompanied by the killing of roughly two dozen of the leading Huguenot nobles in Paris. When these murders were duly carried out in the early morning hours of 24 August, the feast day of St. Bartholomew, many Catholics in Paris misunderstood the killings as a sign that the king wished all Huguenots in Paris to be killed. Since there had already been violence between Protestants and Catholics in Paris the previous year, it did not take much to set off widespread attacks against all Huguenots in the capital. Over the next two days Parisian Catholics killed upwards of 2,000 French Protestants. The events in the capital sparked similar massacres in a dozen provincial towns across the kingdom over the next few weeks. By October 1572 as many as six to eight thousand Huguenots had been killed. These massacres marked an end to Protestant growth in France, not so much because of the loss of life, as considerable as it was, but because of the chilling symbolic impact of the massacres. It appeared to many that the crown had returned to a policy of cruel suppression, while many Huguenots saw the massacres as a sign that God had abandoned them. A significant number of them began to abjure their religion and convert to Catholicism as a result. Most Huguenots did not convert, however, and the intermittent cycle of war and peace soon commenced once again.

## THE CATHOLIC LEAGUE

The second major watershed in the civil wars occurred in June 1584 when the last surviving Valois heir to the throne, Francis, duke of Anjou, died from tuberculosis at the age of 29. King Henry III (ruled 1574–1589), who had succeeded his brother Charles IX two years after the St. Bartholomew's Day Massacres, was childless. The death of his younger brother Anjou, who was the last and youngest of Catherine de Médicis's and Henry II's four sons, meant that the next in line to the throne was Henry of Navarre, a Protestant. This unfortunate conse-

quence resulted in the Guise family's organizing a Holy Catholic League, backed by money and troops from King Philip II of Spain, to pressure the king to disavow Navarre, who, despite his legitimacy as heir by birth, was rendered illegitimate because of his religion. The political pressure mounted by the league was so great, in fact, that in 1585 these militant Catholics even managed to get Henry III to issue an ordinance making it illegal to be Protestant in France, revoking all the limited rights of existence that Huguenots had won since Catherine de Médicis's original edict in January 1562. It certainly appeared that the policies of suppression of the 1550s had returned once again. Moreover, when Henry, duke of Guise, entered Paris against Henry III's will in May 1588, Guise's reception was so warm and his popularity among the Parisian people so great that the king was forced to flee his own capital. He gained his revenge by having Guise and his brother murdered in December 1588. Victory was only temporary, however, as Henry III himself was murdered the following August by a disgruntled Catholic monk. Thus, from August 1589 Henry of Navarre was recognized as the legitimate king of France—as King Henry IV (ruled 1589–1610)—only by French Protestants and a small minority of Catholics who were willing to place his legitimacy by birth above his Calvinist religion. The overwhelming majority of French Catholics, however, urged on by the league, refused to accept Navarre's claim to the throne and held out against him. The cycle of civil war was destined to continue.

## THE EDICT OF NANTES

The final watershed in the French Wars of Religion occurred in July 1593, after four long years of indecisive fighting between the armies of King Henry IV and the Catholic League. The city of Paris had been besieged by the royalist forces of the king in 1590, and some Parisians even starved to death in a long, ruinous summer. The turning point came when Henry made the decision to abjure his Protestant religion and take instruction in the Catholic faith. It was certainly not a cynical decision, as his enemies claimed, nor one made lightly. Henry had been a devout Calvinist ever since he was first instructed in the faith by his mother. He was forced to recognize, however, that the French constitution required the king to be Catholic. To resolve the long religious conflict and bring the disorders in the kingdom to

Casles Ducis Guisij, fratricq; ipsius Cardinalis, duorii Episcoporii,
Lugduneisium et alior; aliquot procerum Blesij in Gallia fac
ta 23. et 24. Decemb, Anno 1588.

Ecce Ducis Guisij fratrisq; miserrima cædes
Totq; vereubrum vincla necėsq; patrum . .
Que sit .auśa rei, non est tibi dicere nestrů:
Justa sed est summi vindicis ira Dei .

Scher an des Herrn von Guisø Mordt
Vnd ander Herrn an diesem ordt:
Deß handels vrsach, mellờ ich nicht:
Ellein recht ist Gottes gericht

**French Wars of Religion.** Assassination of Duke Henry of Guise by the guard of King Henry III, 23 December 1588, engraving by Hogenberg, late sixteenth–early seventeenth century. THE ART ARCHIVE/UNIVERSITY LIBRARY GENEVA/DAGLI ORTI

an end, Henry publicly converted to Catholicism in the summer of 1593. When the pope formally absolved the king shortly thereafter, the many nobles and towns loyal to the league began to submit to his authority and accept him as their new monarch. But Henry IV still faced the same problem as all his predecessors: how to produce a peace treaty that was acceptable to both sides with a chance of survival. The Edict of Nantes, published in the spring of 1598, looked on paper to be very similar to many of the numerous earlier edicts of pacification, none of which had proved very durable. France had suffered horribly during the wars of the league, however, as increased warfare combined with economic and agrarian crises in the 1590s to create loud demands from within various elements of the population to stop the fighting. Bands of armed peasants in

Burgundy, Perigord, and Limousin, some of whom may have been organized by elites, organized to keep soldiers out of their villages whether they were Huguenots or Catholics. Thus, the situation was very different from the earlier peace edicts, as the entire kingdom's resolve to continue to wage war in such dire economic circumstances began to waver.

Another principal difference between the Edict of Nantes and the seven earlier edicts of pacification is that Henry IV explicitly appealed to both sides. To the Catholic majority, he promised in the preamble of the edict that France would forever remain a Catholic country, and that one day God would bless his kingdom by reuniting all French men and women in the one true Catholic faith. The various articles of the edict spelled out that the monarchy, the state, and all French institutions would also remain Catholic, thus ensuring that Catholicism would never be jeopardized as the official religion of the kingdom. The edict also restored the Catholic Mass in all Protestant areas where it had been banned, introducing it into some areas for the first time in forty years. In addition, the edict required all Huguenots to begin paying the ecclesiastical tithe to the Catholic Church, just as their Catholic counterparts had always done, in order to provide for the salaries of parish priests throughout the kingdom. On the surface, then, the Edict of Nantes was meant to appease French Catholics, especially those former members of the league who had opposed the king prior to his conversion.

On the other side, the edict made clear that Huguenots had freedom of conscience in France,

meaning they would not be persecuted for simply being Protestant. Their right to freedom of worship, however, was severely restricted, limited to those towns mainly in the south of France already under Huguenot control in August 1597. Moreover, all former Catholic churches in these areas were to be turned back over to the French Catholic Church. The Huguenots would have to build their own churches, or worship in private (meaning largely aristocratic) homes in the towns they controlled. But the king also granted the Huguenots concessions not made public in the edict. First, they were given a special subsidy to pay the salaries of their ministers, offsetting the ecclesiastical tithe required in the edict itself. More importantly, Henry granted the Huguenots the right to garrison troops in the towns they controlled, thereby guaranteeing

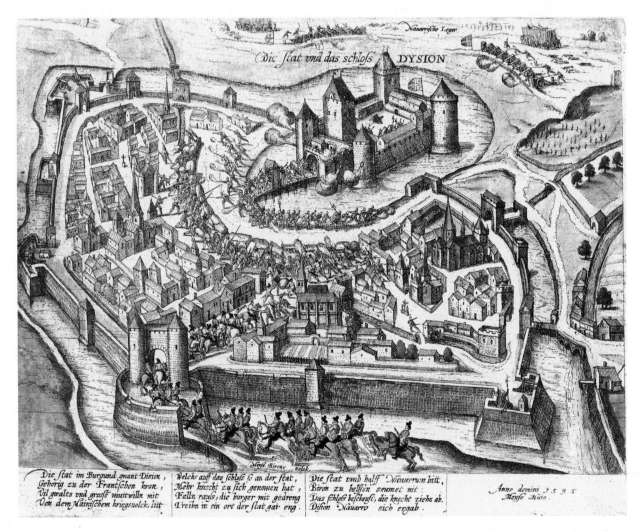

**French Wars of Religion.** Dijon, Burgundy, surrenders to King Henry IV, May 1595, engraving by Hogenberg, late sixteenth–early seventeenth century. THE ART ARCHIVE/UNIVERSITY LIBRARY GENEVA/DAGLI ORTI

their own safety and defense. Thus in a variety of ways, while the Edict of Nantes initiated a period of religious coexistence, it was far from a policy of religious toleration. And for most among the French Catholic majority, even this religious coexistence was thought to be only temporary, until those remaining Protestants might be won back to the true faith, following the example set by King Henry IV. For them, the future of France was as a kingdom of Catholic uniformity of religion. The Huguenots, however, recognized that their gains in the edict would last only as long as they were loyal to the crown and only as long as their newly converted king chose to enforce them. Henry's son Louis XIII (ruled 1610–1643) sought to dismantle the subsidies and military protection of the Huguenots, while Henry's grandson Louis XIV (ruled 1643–1715) revoked the Edict of Nantes altogether in 1685.

*See also* **Catherine de Médicis; Catholic League (France); Coligny Family; Condé Family; France; Guise Family; Henry IV (France); Huguenots; Nantes, Edict of; St. Bartholomew's Day Massacre.**

BIBLIOGRAPHY

*Primary Source*

Potter, David, ed. and trans. *The French Wars of Religion: Selected Documents.* New York, 1997.

*Secondary Sources*

Benedict, Philip. *Rouen during the Wars of Religion.* Cambridge, U.K., and New York, 1981.

Davis, Natalie Zemon. *Society and Culture in Early Modern France: Eight Essays.* Stanford, 1975.

Diefendorf, Barbara B. *Beneath the Cross: Catholics and Huguenots in Sixteenth-Century Paris.* New York, 1991.

Greengrass, Mark. *France in the Age of Henri IV: The Struggle for Stability.* 2nd ed. London and New York, 1995.

Holt, Mack P. *The French Wars of Religion, 1562–1629.* Cambridge, U.K., and New York, 1995.

Holt, Mack P., ed. *Renaissance and Reformation France, 1500–1648.* Oxford, 2002.

Knecht, Robert J. *The French Civil Wars, 1559–1598.* London, 2000.

Roberts, Penny. *A City in Conflict: Troyes during the French Wars of Religion.* Manchester, U.K., and New York, 1996.

Salmon, J. H. M. *Society in Crisis: France in the Sixteenth Century.* London and New York, 1975.

MACK P. HOLT

**WARSAW** (Polish, Warszawa). A small late medieval settlement on the left bank of the middle Vistula, Warsaw became the capital of the Principality of Mazovia during the reign of Janusz I the Elder (ruled 1374–1429). "Old Warsaw" was founded c. 1300 on the escarpment overlooking the Vistula, just north of an existing castle. By 1408 a "New Warsaw," lying due north of Old Warsaw, had established its own autonomous municipality, with a separate magistracy and market square. Old Warsaw was the more populous and affluent, with the bricked houses of the patriciate and wealthier tradesmen. Artisans, shopkeepers, and small farmers occupied the mostly wooden structures of New Warsaw.

The last Mazovian prince, Janusz III, died in 1526, and from that time Mazovia and Warsaw came under the Polish crown. No longer the small capital of an independent principality, Warsaw nonetheless continued to grow modestly, thanks partly to its expanding ties with Cracow and the kingdom. In 1527 and 1529, Sigismund I (ruled 1506–1548) granted charters to eleven Warsaw guilds, removing them from the jurisdiction of the Cracow brethren. By 1564, Old Warsaw encompassed 486 stone houses, New Warsaw 204 still mostly wooden houses. Jews were expelled from Warsaw in 1483, and a privilege *de non tolerandis Judaeis,* granted its burghers in 1527, forbade Jewish settlement in the town itself, relegating them to the suburbs for most of the early modern period.

Warsaw grew quickly in significance toward the end of the sixteenth century. From 1569 it was the site for meetings of the General Parliament, and from 1573 for the Election Parliaments that chose the kings of Poland and the grand dukes of Lithuania. A fire in the Wawel Castle in Cracow in 1596 moved Sigismund III Vasa (ruled 1587–1632) to begin expanding the Warsaw castle and to make it into the residence of Polish kings and their courts beginning in 1611. (Cracow would remain the capital and coronation city.) With the transfer of the royal court to Warsaw, the city began to draw magnates and gentry, who established residences in privately owned suburban "jurisdictions," which formed a chain of autonomous towns around Old and New Warsaw and offered competition to Warsaw's patriciate and guild artisans. The right-bank

Praga suburb, the site of breweries, warehouses, and granaries, received its municipal privilege in 1648.

The wars of the mid-seventeenth century interrupted Warsaw's rapid growth from modest sixteenth-century numbers (its population had reached 20,000 by 1655). Swedish and Transylvanian armies finally left the city on 23 June 1657, and the rebuilding of Old and New Warsaw was largely completed by 1670. Under John III Sobieski (ruled 1674–1696) the center of gravity moved to the west, beyond the old walls, and settlement expanded into the magnates' suburban jurisdictions to the north and south along the river. The city again rebuilt after the Northern War (1700–1721). Warsaw became the center of Polish commerce and enlightenment under the last Polish king, Stanisław II Augustus Poniatowski (ruled 1764–1795). A "Black Procession" of burgher leaders to the Royal Castle on 2 December 1789 paved the way for belated urban reform in the Commonwealth of Poland-Lithuania. The autonomy of the "jurisdictions" was finally abolished, and Old and New Warsaw, plus the suburbs, now formed one urban legal unit. Warsaw's growth (to 110,000 in 1792) was delayed with the sacking of Praga by Russian armies on 5 November 1794 and the third partition of Poland (1795), which initially gave part of Mazovia, including Warsaw, to Prussia. In 1799, the city's inhabitants numbered 64,000.

*See also* **Jews and Judaism; Northern Wars; Poland, Partitions of; Poland-Lithuania, Commonwealth of, 1569–1795; Poland to 1569.**

BIBLIOGRAPHY

Berdecka, Anna, and Irena Turnau. *Życie codzienne w Warszawie okresu Oświecenia.* Warsaw, 1969.

Drozdowski, Marian M., and Andrzej Zahorski. *Historia Warszawy.* Warsaw, 1997.

DAVID FRICK

---

**WATCHES.** *See* **Clocks and Watches.**

---

**WATTEAU, ANTOINE** (born Jean-Antoine; 1689–1721), French painter. Antoine Watteau was born in Valenciennes in northern France in humble circumstances. By the end of his short life (he died at 32 of tuberculosis), he was a celebrated painter in Paris. Today, he is generally considered to be the father of the rococo style because he developed the *fête galante*, 'gallant party', as a subject; it became a hallmark of the era's painting. Watteau's work in particular, and the rococo style in general, reflect a major transformation of the French art world. At the beginning of Watteau's lifetime, King Louis XIV (ruled 1643–1715) controlled the production of culture through the establishment of academies and state-supported patronage of the arts. By the time of his death, patronage of the arts had shifted to private individuals who were no longer interested in the highly didactic and often propagandistic art demanded by royal patronage. Although Watteau was a member of the Royal Academy of Painting and Sculpture, it was a group of private collectors who collected his work and cultivated his reputation.

The *fêtes galantes* were contemporary scenes of elegant men and women, usually in an outdoor setting and sometimes dressed in masquerade, engaged in conversation, flirtation, music making, and dancing. Watteau's *fêtes galantes* were intimate in scale; the pictures were the appropriate size to be enjoyed in a private space, rather than the monumental paintings of subjects taken from classical mythology and history that decorated the public spaces of Louis XIV's palaces. The *fêtes galantes* mirrored the kinds of social activities enjoyed by Watteau's elite collectors and also reinforced their image of themselves.

The appearance of some figures dressed in theatrical costumes and others in contemporary everyday garb is another trait of Watteau's *fêtes galantes*. Watteau absorbed the theatrical milieu under the tutelage of his first teacher in Paris, Claude Gillot (1673–1722), who illustrated theatrical troupes. Claude Audran (1658–1734), who did decorative painting in the homes of Parisian high society, taught Watteau his highly ornamental style and introduced him to his future patrons. Watteau himself later had two students, Nicolas Lancret and Jean-Baptiste-Joseph Pater, who also specialized in *fêtes galantes*.

Perhaps Watteau's most famous *fête galante* is *Pilgrimage to Cythera* (1717, Louvre). The painting

**Antoine Watteau.** *The Pilgrimage to Cythera.* ©ARCHIVO ICONOGRAFICO S.A./CORBIS

represents a lighthearted topic that was popular in theatrical and musical performance—a pilgrimage to Venus's Island of Cythera, where everyone would fall in love. In Watteau's painting, a statue of Venus indicates the pilgrims are on the island of Cythera. Three couples are arranged on a hillock and this can be read as a narrative of departure. The couple closest to the statue is most fully under Venus's spell of love; the next couple to the left is getting up, emerging from the spell of love; and the third couple is already standing. The woman glances back, as if wistfully remembering the spell of love already gone. On the other side of the hillock, a group of people heads toward a boat. Their pilgrimage is over and they will return to the real world. Watteau's *fêtes galantes* have often been characterized as melancholy, containing a subtext that alludes to the passing of love and of life.

The passing of the era of King Louis XIV is represented in another of his celebrated works, *The Signboard of Gersaint* (1721, Staatliche Museum,

Berlin). This work shows the interior of the shop of Watteau's friend, the art dealer Edmé Gersaint. On the left side, workmen pack away a portrait of Louis XIV, and the walls are covered with paintings representative of an older style associated with his reign. On the right side, elegantly dressed customers admire paintings representative of the new, or rococo, style preferred by elite private patrons. This painting also celebrates the collection and enjoyment of art, which had become part of the social rituals enacted among the elite.

Watteau's paintings are often very witty. In *The Signboard of Gersaint*, the painting of Louis XIV being stored not only represents the passing of an era, but is also a visual pun, referring to the name of Gersaint's shop, "The Grand Monarch." In *Pilgrimage to Cythera*, the cherubs who flutter above the ship cavort erotically, perhaps acting out what the more decorous pilgrims below are thinking about. Wittiness, whether in art or in conversation, was a trait much esteemed in eighteenth-century high society.

Today, as in the eighteenth century, Watteau's works are highly prized. He managed to combine superb draftsmanship with deft painting to subtly represent facets of both the complex social life and the attitudes of those who came to dominate early modern European society.

*See also* **France, Art in; Louis XIV (France); Rococo.**

BIBLIOGRAPHY

Grasselli, Margaret, and Pierre Rosenberg, with the assistance of Nicole Parmantier. *Watteau: 1684–1721.* Washington, D.C., 1984.

Plax, Julie Anne. *Watteau and the Cultural Politics of Eighteenth-Century France.* New York, 2000.

Posner, Donald. *Antoine Watteau.* Ithaca, N.Y., 1984.

Vidal, Mary. *Watteau's Painted Conversations: Art, Literature, and Talk in 17th and 18th Century France.* New Haven, 1992.

JULIE ANNE PLAX

---

**WEALTH.** *See* **Aristocracy and Gentry; Class, Status, and Order; Consumption.**

---

**WEATHER AND CLIMATE.** The history of the climate during the early modern age is largely centered on the climatic deterioration known as the "Little Ice Age." Much evidence testifies to a significant degradation of atmospheric conditions from the perhaps uniquely favorable circumstances of the High Middle Ages to the cooler, wetter, and less stable weather of the early modern period. No consensus exists with regard to the nature or the chronology of this phenomenon, the value of the sources available to investigate it, or its impact upon European societies. Nevertheless, the recognition of the importance of climate as a historical factor has led researchers to revisit many well-traveled paths of European history. Their efforts have become particularly relevant considering twenty-first-century fears of global warming.

The sources that historians draft to document the climate of the fifteenth to eighteenth centuries may be arranged in two main categories: literary and iconographic documents and serial and/or quantifiable data. In turn, this second group of sources may itself be divided into direct and indirect records. The value and the limitations of all relevant sources are still debated. References to weather conditions are found in many diaries, almanacs, chronicles, letters, professional accounts, and scientific and military logs. Yet this information is very heterogeneous and thinly and unevenly distributed across the continent and the centuries. It is inevitably subjective and likely to recall extreme or rare occurrences (similar comments may be directed at the pictorial records that testify to various effects of the weather). More systematic and more intentional direct records of weather conditions are rare, particularly early in the period. Their great merit is to enable the construction of data series, yet the lack of standardized measures of temperatures and other climatic variables greatly complicates the task of researchers.

To complete this rich yet insufficient medley of references, historians turn to indirect evidence. Some of it requires refined scientific analyses, ranging from the mapping of tree rings to carbon dating and the assaying of soil or ice cores. A second category of proxy sources includes evidence of weather-dependent economic output, principally crops. Municipal rolls of market prices, institutional accounts of harvests, church tithes registers, or seigneurial records may all reflect variations in local weather conditions. However, both agricultural production itself and the transactions that produced these records were also shaped by economic, political, and cultural tensions. (Agronomists also warn of the intrinsic complexity of the relation between weather and output.) For instance, the dates of grape harvests have always been linked to competitive pressures and evolving tastes as well as spring and summer conditions, just as flood reports are shaped by water levels but also by demographic pressures, hydraulic works, or fiscal imperatives. Increasingly rigorous standards have been applied to the reconstitution of early modern climates, demanding advanced dissections of the effect of weather upon the documented variables and sophisticated statistical testing of the resulting figures.

Several significant cross-disciplinary collaborations substantiate the existence of a negative turn in the weather during the early modern era and also expose its complexity. Its outside limits range from the fourteenth to the nineteenth centuries, although its beginnings are obviously less documented than its end. Naturally, no uniform weather pattern stretched across this long period or across all regions of Europe; this calls for the study of fine regional and chronological distinctions. Temperatures are perhaps better known than precipitation amounts, and great variability as well as episodes of extreme weather are emerging as key findings. Charts of growing seasons and growing ranges have been drawn and compared with the more favorable conditions of the High Middle Ages and the well-documented contemporary era. To date, the geography and chronology of the early modern climate "pessimum" (severe deterioration) remain the object of much valuable work.

Historians speculate on the origins of this climatic deterioration, notably turning to factors such as solar, volcanic, or even human activity, but they are chiefly interested in its consequences. Its impact upon food production is at the center of many debates, because of its crucial importance to many aspects of early modern social, economic, and even political life. Inquiries into the demographic impact of the Little Ice Age continue to enrich our understanding of related subjects such as famines, epidemics, and epizootics. Increasingly, historians separate the consequences of sharp and brutal but short events from those of medium-term, interannual, and decadal or secular trends and underscore the distinctions to be made between the great climatic zones of Europe. They also contrast the impact of weather in secure agricultural areas with that in marginal lands of all sorts and have started to acknowledge the importance of microclimates. New knowledge of climatic patterns is also being applied to many long-standing historical concerns: the "general crises" of the fourteenth and seventeenth centuries; large-scale migration patterns, and, occasionally, the disappearance of whole communities; popular rebellions; economic trends ranging from the southward retreat of vineyards to the shifting of fishing grounds and the great inflation of the sixteenth century; and some of the key advances of the early modern age, such as the agricultural revolution. Finally, climate history has also entered the field of cultural studies, with explorations of the role of climate in shaping popular beliefs and traditions reflected in language, ceremonies, superstitions, and even witch-hunts.

The implications of research on the history of climate are many. Even those who remain skeptical of the solidity of such probes will agree that they serve to highlight and explain the importance and the diversity of human responses to environmental challenges. Research devoted to the early modern climate can also speak to early modern communities' ability to diversify their crops, their landholding patterns, the attempts of authorities to mitigate the impact of brutal episodes, the role played by growing commercial networks and related levels of specialization, the flexibility or rigidity of certain social structures, and the reasons behind important evolutions of landscapes. In the course of these investigations, several fundamental assumptions have been questioned, such as the vulnerability of preindustrial communities to climatic fluctuations, and even the stability of the natural environment in which they functioned.

The strongest objections to the work of climate historians revolve around the value of the data and methods used. But there are also regular denouncements of the risks of determinism associated with these (and other) probes into environmental history. This is particularly so because of a long-standing tradition linking the supposedly favorable climate of Europe with the successful projection of European power across the oceans. Many aspects of the European environment have been and are still advanced to justify what has been called the "European Miracle," ranging from its (mostly) temperate nature and the (relative) absence of large-scale destructive episodes, to its very diversity. All such theses stand accused of ignoring or underestimating the historically crucial element of human agency and, most significantly, of simplifying the great complexity of climate patterns and their impact upon land and people.

Such Eurocentric interpretations of the influence of climate upon societies are not new. Emboldened by the growing reach of their information networks, early modern thinkers linked geography and climate with social and cultural development in several ways, just as they started to reflect on the possibility of climatic variations over time. These reflections could join speculations on the relative merits of ancient and modern societies, or the clustering of geniuses. They could also enter the realm of religious thought, through hypotheses on "geological times" or the universal decline of the earth's ability to support life, as well as daring interpretations of some key episodes of the Scriptures; those, on the contrary, who argued the immutability of climate opened the door for more enlightened plans for improving lives. The same period also marked the beginnings of a more systematic and more scientific interest in recording weather patterns. This trend made clear the need for more reliable thermometers and other instruments and heralded the eventual science of meteorology, although, as is common during the early modern era, cultural groups other than the elite of princely scientific societies remained active in their own ways. The interest in climate, like that in many other aspects of nature, helped mark social and regional identities. Late in the period, attention turned to the potential impact of human activities upon the natural environment and climate. Large-scale or particularly acute instances of deforestation fueled the theory of desiccation, predicated upon the idea that forests attracted, retained, and redistributed atmospheric moisture. Some applied it on a grand scale, speculating, for instance, on the decline of Classic societies or the future of the North American climate after settlement. Others turned to the small but revealing scale of tropical islands. In these settings, free of some of the traditional bounds that had developed in Europe, novel measures emerged that may be seen as forerunners of the science of ecology and the protectionist measures that would grow in the nineteenth and twentieth centuries.

Research in climate history is an established component of environmental history. Like other aspects of this new field, it calls for decidedly multidisciplinary approaches, and it struggles to overcome the fundamental objections associated with the ever-recurrent temptation of deterministic interpretations of history. In the context of an early modern era rich in sources, it greatly enriches our understanding of material and social life and contributes to the development of ever more refined models of the links between nature and culture.

*See also* **Agriculture; Environment; Forests and Woodlands; Scientific Instruments.**

BIBLIOGRAPHY

Blaut, James M. "Environmentalism and Eurocentrism." *Geographical Review* 89 (July 1999): 391–408.

Flohn, Hermann, and Roberto Fantechi, eds. *The Climate of Europe, Past, Present, and Future: Natural and Man-Induced Climatic Changes, A European Perspective.* Dordrecht and Boston, 1984.

Jankovi'c, Vladimir. *Reading the Skies: A Cultural History of English Weather, 1650–1820.* Chicago, 2000.

Jones, P. D., et al., eds. *History and Climate: Memories of the Future?* New York, 2001.

*Journal of Interdisciplinary History* 10, nos. 2 and 4 (1979–1980).

Le Roy Ladurie, Emmanuel. *Times of Feast, Times of Famine: A History of Climate since the Year 1000.* Translated by Barbara Bray. Garden City, N.Y., 1971.

Pfister, Christian, Rudolf Brázdil, and Rüdiger Glaser, eds. *Climatic Variability in Sixteenth-Century Europe and Its Social Dimension.* Dordrecht and Boston, 1999.

PIERRE CLAUDE REYNARD

**WEIGHTS AND MEASURES.** Weights and measures throughout Europe during the early modern period were characterized by complexity and confusion and dominated by customary practices. Numbering in the hundreds of thousands, they arose originally from Greek, Roman, Celtic, Germanic, Slavic, and other roots and multiplied on local, regional, and state levels at a rapid pace after 1450. Among the principal causes for this proliferation were economic development, commercial competition, population growth, urbanization, taxation manipulations, territorial expansion, and technological progress. Contributing also were ineffective governmental decrees and legislative acts, the paucity and inferior workmanship of the physical standards manufactured to serve as prototypes, and the overwhelming number of poorly trained officials entrusted with inspection, verification, and enforcement duties.

Central governments contributed to weights and measures proliferation by promulgating multiple state standards for individual units, depending on where they were used and by whom. Sizes of units in capital cities were often different from those in the provinces or in rural areas. They even differed among social classes. On the other hand, common local units occasionally became so popular that they gained unit standardization. They then competed with state units, producing further confusion.

With the rapid growth of cities, weights and measures frequently separated into different standards depending on whether they were employed within the cities or outside their walls. A sharp division arose between urban and suburban measures. Similarly, some measuring units differed according to their use on land or on sea. A general rule throughout Europe was that measures always increased in size or distance once land was no longer in sight.

Product variations were the most important source for metrological proliferation. Those based on quantity measures varied by number or by an odd assortment of human, animal, and other capabilities. Even when these measures had standardized counts, capacities, or weights, the actual sizes depended on the characteristics of the products involved. Compounding this situation was the centuries-old practice of dividing existing units into halves, thirds, and fourths or into an irregular assortment of diminutives. Similar problems were assigning the same name to different units, basing one unit on a multiple or submultiple of another, bestowing more than one name on the same unit, and authorizing various methods of submultiple compilations for a given unit.

Further examples were units of account that were simply computational units for record keeping and other business purposes. Similarly, there were measures reserved for wholesale trade that referred to any number of other better-known units without any correlation to existing standards. Measures were also based on the monetary values of coins, on units of income derived through production, on crop yields and tax assessments, and on work functions, dimensions, and time allotments of humans and animals. The sizes of such units rested on a myriad of imprecise factors.

Regardless of such conditions, Europe in the seventeenth and eighteenth centuries produced a climate of change ushered in by the age of science and the Enlightenment. During this critical period, a number of developments occurred that altered metrological history profoundly, and eventually led to the creation and implementation of the metric system in France in 1793 and the imperial system in England in 1824.

First, there was the dynamic of scientific and technological invention and innovation that overthrew the rigid reliance on past traditions. The introduction of numerous new concepts, instruments, and procedures linked theoreticians with craftsmen for the first time and led to profound advancements in lenses, magnification glasses, microscopes, navigational, astronomical, and triangulation instruments, and clocks. These and hundreds of other breakthroughs, spearheaded chiefly by English, French, and Italian scientists, played a critical role in the reformation of weights and measures.

Second, many of these successes received stimulus and support from the European scientific societies that developed rapidly during the 1600s. By the end of the century, most serious scientists in Europe had become members of these societies, and their journals disseminated knowledge of new discoveries and inventions. In Italy the Roman Accademia dei Lincei and the Florentine Accademia del Cimento made significant scientific strides, the latter especially in its technological apparatus.

The most important societies for the future development of metrology, however, were the Royal Society of London and the Academy of Sciences of Paris and their offshoots, the Greenwich and Paris observatories. The English organizations cast their scientific net far and wide and made giant advancements in physics, astronomy, chemistry, and natural science which, coupled with their pioneering work in technological instruments, helped create a new era in weights and measures. Even more important were the Parisian groups whose scientists introduced the practice of using telescopes in conjunction with graduated circles for the precise measurement of angles. This led to measurements of the meridian arc and the computation of the radius of the Earth. This seminal work provided metrologists with possibilities for a natural physical standard that eventually became the basis for the metric system.

These and other advances led to the creation of hundreds of metrological reform proposals. In England the pendulum was given special emphasis. Since the second unit (of time) is determined by the motion of the earth, it was believed that the length of the second's pendulum in a given latitude would be an invariable quantity that could always be recovered or duplicated. Others proposed altering the existing system to conform to a decimal scale, eliminating all units except for a select few, and coordinating all units to a strict series of ratios. Unfortunately, the revamped English system of 1824 excluded any natural standard and opted only for streamlining the old system and establishing more accurate physical standards. The French proposals concluded far more successfully. After numerous experiments, France settled on a standard determined by the triangulation measurements of that portion of the meridian arc that ran from Dunkirk through Paris to Barcelona. In the process they established a new measure—the meter—as one ten-millionth of the distance from the North Pole to the equator. Even though there eventually were some problems with the final measurements, a new era in world metrology had begun.

See also Enlightenment; Mathematics; Scientific Instruments.

BIBLIOGRAPHY

Berriman, Algernon E. Historical Metrology. London, 1953. An excellent study of the major issues in European metrological history.

Daumas, Maurice. Scientific Instruments of the Seventeenth and Eighteenth Century. New York, 1972. Shows the impact of technology on numerous metrological developments.

Kula, Witold. Measures and Men. Translated by Richard Szreter. Princeton, 1986. Important for the historical correlation between metrology and society.

Zupko, Ronald E. Revolution in Measurement: Western European Weights and Measures since the Age of Science. Philadelphia, 1990. Extensive coverage of medieval and early modern European weights and measures with a comprehensive bibliography on all issues.

———. "Weights and Measures." In Encyclopedia of the Renaissance. Vol. 6. New York, 1999. Tables of principal European units of measurement.

———. "Weights and Measures: Western European." In Dictionary of the Middle Ages. Vol. 12. New York, 1989. Europe-wide in scope with tables of equivalents; see also author's metrological articles in the other eleven volumes.

RONALD EDWARD ZUPKO

**WESLEY FAMILY.** The Wesley family included John Wesley (1703–1791) and his brother Charles Wesley (1707–1788), leaders in the eighteenth-century evangelical movement in England called Methodism. The Wesleys' ancestry included Puritans and Nonconformists on both sides, although their parents were staunchly committed to the Church of England. Their paternal great-grandfather Bartholomew Westley (c. 1596–1671), grandfather John Westley (c. 1636–1770), and maternal grandfather Samuel Annesley (c. 1620–1696) were clergy removed from their positions after the Restoration because they were Anglican dissenters.

The parents of the brothers were Samuel Wesley (1662–1735) and Susanna Annesley Wesley (1669–1742). An ordained Anglican priest, Samuel Wesley became rector of Epworth parish in Lincolnshire in 1695. Although he was a talented scholar and poet, he was unpopular with his parishioners because of his strict demands that they live holy lives. It is believed that disgruntled parishioners, among other spiteful acts, set fire to the rectory in 1709. The building was destroyed with no loss of life.

The Wesley family included nineteen children, ten of whom lived into adulthood. With a large family, life in the Epworth rectory was busy. Susanna Wesley possessed considerable intellectual ability and skillfully managed the household. She supervised the children's earliest education, teaching each how to read and write. Circumstances for Susanna became quite difficult in 1705, when Samuel was imprisoned for several weeks in Lincoln Castle for debt he could not pay. Both parents instructed their offspring in the essentials of the Christian faith, including respect for the Bible and the traditions and practices of the Anglican Church. It would be difficult to underestimate the lasting influence of Samuel and Susanna on their children.

The three sons Samuel Jr., John, and Charles were ordained into the ministry of the Church of England. They were graduates of Christ Church College, Oxford University. After service on the staff of Westminster School in London, Samuel Jr. was named headmaster of Blundell's School in Tiverton. John, who was elected a fellow of Lincoln College, Oxford, in 1726, also served as his father's parish assistant and was a missionary to the American colony of Georgia in 1736–1737. His ministry among the settlers and Native Americans was disappointing. He returned to England in 1737 in spiritual despair. His despondency ended with his evangelical conversion on 24 May 1738. Charles accompanied John to America and for a short time was secretary to General James Oglethorpe (1696–1785), Georgia's colonial governor. Ill health and misunderstandings with the governor and colonists forced Charles to return to England in 1736 and laid the groundwork for his conversion on 21 May 1738. In the months that followed their religious renewals, John and Charles became principal leaders in that part of the evangelical revival known as Methodism.

The lives of the seven daughters, Emilia, Susanna, Mary, Mehetabel, Anne, Martha, and Kezia, were mostly marked by difficulty and unhappiness. Mehetabel, or Hetty, the most talented of the daughters, published poetry in various magazines. The Wesley family was noteworthy in eighteenth-century England largely through the evangelical ministry of John Wesley and Charles Wesley.

See also **Church of England; Methodism.**

BIBLIOGRAPHY

*Primary Source*

Wesley, Susanna. *Susanna Wesley: The Complete Writings.* Edited by Charles Wallace Jr. New York, 1997.

*Secondary Sources*

Edwards, Maldwyn Lloyd. *Family Circle: A Study of the Epworth Household in Relation to John and Charles Wesley.* London, 1949.

Maser, Frederick E. *The Story of John Wesley's Sisters; or, Seven Sisters in Search of Love.* Rutland, Vt., 1988.

Newton, John A. *Susanna Wesley and the Puritan Tradition in Methodism.* London, 2002.

CHARLES YRIGOYEN, JR

---

# WESTPHALIA, PEACE OF (1648).

The Treaties of Münster and Osnabrück, which ended the Thirty Years' War, are known collectively as the Peace of Westphalia. The main obstacles to a general peace in Germany after 1635 were the ambitions of France and Sweden and changing military fortunes. Sweden wanted territorial and financial compensation while France, under the cardinals (Richelieu to 1642, Mazarin thereafter), envisaged something altogether more ambitious that involved a considerable reduction in both Spanish and Austrian Habsburg power. In addition, matters were complicated by the individual ambitions of various German princes and separate negotiations between the Spanish and the Dutch. Ultimately, 176 plenipotentiaries representing 196 rulers attended the peace negotiations.

Despite these problems, talks began in 1643 at Münster and Osnabrück, the two cities specified for negotiations by the Franco-Swedish Treaty of 1641. France, Spain, and the other Catholic participants were based at Münster, Sweden and her allies at Osnabrück. Although Emperor Ferdinand III (ruled 1637–1657) initially delayed negotiations, the collapse of his military position in 1645 forced him to undertake serious discussions in 1646. However, that a settlement was not reached until the autumn of 1648 was largely due to Mazarin rather than the emperor. In fact, the war only really came to an end at that time because of France's inability to carry it on.

## NEGOTIATIONS

With so many participants and so many conflicting interests, it is hard to discern any pattern of negotiation, but the aims of the major participants can be identified. The emperor clearly wanted a full and final peace settlement. Because his situation was desperate, he was prepared to make far-reaching religious and territorial concessions if necessary. Mazarin's wish for a universal peace was scuttled by the collapse of negotiations with Spain in 1646. The Spanish preferred to work out a deal with the Dutch (achieved in January 1647, ratified at Münster in January 1648) and keep fighting. As far as Germany was concerned, France wanted to destroy the emperor's influence by strengthening the autonomy of the individual princes and by replacing the existing imperial institutions with a French-led federation. However, these plans were unpopular with the German princes, who valued the Holy Roman Empire and preferred an emperor limited in authority to dominance by France and Sweden. Count Maximilian von Trauttsmannsdorf, the imperial envoy, had little difficulty in resisting these French demands. French demands for most of Alsace and parts of

Lorraine, on the other hand, were quite modest because France mainly wanted Spanish territory. Mazarin was able to obtain Habsburg domains in Alsace in return for 1.2 million thalers in a deal with the emperor in September 1646.

The Swedes were prepared to compromise because Queen Christina was eager for a quick settlement. In any event her erstwhile allies, the French, did not want to see Sweden become too powerful. Accordingly, Mazarin decided to build up Brandenburg as a counterweight to Swedish power, and in February 1647 the Swedish envoys were persuaded to agree to a partition of Pomerania with the elector. Trauttmannsdorf was able to exploit this tension between the allies in other ways, too. For instance, Sweden demanded religious toleration within the Habsburg lands, for the Bohemians in particular. Knowing that the French had little sympathy for Bohemian Protestants, and would not support Sweden on this issue, the emperor resisted this demand quite firmly.

As far as religion was concerned, matters of territory and allegiance had been addressed in the Peace of Prague and at the Diet of Regensburg, but the status of Calvinism and secularized lands still had to be resolved. Although the delegates were divided according to confessional lines, even within the same denomination there was no agreement. However, because the Protestants proved to be more united overall, the final agreement on religious issues reached in March 1648 was more favorable to them.

Final agreement was postponed because Mazarin, unnerved by Spain's deal with the Dutch (which he had tried to sabotage), decided to increase French demands. This rekindled the war, though with the onset of civil unrest in France in the summer of 1648 (the Fronde), Mazarin reluctantly changed his tune and by August was convinced of "our need to make peace at the earliest opportunity." Consequently, he dropped his extra demands and agreed to a settlement (though the emperor did agree not to aid his Spanish cousin).

## TERMS

The Peace of Westphalia was signed simultaneously at Münster and Osnabrück on 24 October 1648 and consisted of 128 clauses. The main parts can be summarized as follows:

1. The principle of *cuius regio, eius religio* ('whoever rules the territory determines the religion') was reaffirmed, but construed to relate only to public life.

2. Calvinism was finally recognized within the Confession of Augsburg and, except within the Bavarian and Austrian lands (including Bohemia), Protestant retention of all land secularized before 1624 was guaranteed.

3. In matters of religion there were to be no majority decisions made by the diet. Instead, disputes were to be settled only by compromise.

4. To all intents and purposes, the separate states of the Holy Roman Empire were recognized as sovereign members of the diet, free to control their own affairs independently of each other and of the emperor.

5. Maximilian of Bavaria (1573–1651) retained his electoral title and the Upper Palatinate.

6. A new electoral title was created for Karl Ludwig (1617–1680), the son of the former elector palatine, on his restoration to the Lower Palatinate.

7. John George of Saxony, a leading German Protestant prince who had supported Ferdinand, was confirmed in his acquisition of Lusatia (a region of eastern Germany and southwest Poland).

8. Frederick William of Brandenburg (1620–1688) acquired Cammin, Minden, and Halberstadt, along with the succession to Magdeburg.

9. The emperor's claim to hereditary rights in Bohemia, Moravia, and Silesia was established. The Habsburg Sundgau was surrendered to France.

10. The Peace of Westphalia confirmed Swedish control of the river mouths of the Oder, the Elbe, and Weser—virtually the entire German coastline—by the occupation of western Pomerania, Stettin, Stralsund, Wismar, the dioceses of Bremen and Verden, and the islands of Rügen, Usedom, and Wollin. Sweden was also paid an indemnity of 5 million thalers.

11. France acquired Habsburg territory and other jurisdictions in Alsace. Other acquisitions included Pinerolo in Savoy and Breisach and Philippsburg on the right bank of the Rhine.

12. The United Provinces of the Netherlands (Dutch Republic) were declared independent of both Spain and the Holy Roman Empire (Switzer-

land was also acknowledged as independent of the empire).

13. No prince of the empire, not even the emperor, could ally with the Spanish monarchy.

## ASSESSMENT

An overall assessment is not easy to make. By and large the treaties defused those problems largely responsible for the war. Although confessional loyalties remained important, the age of religious wars was over in Germany. The religious settlement proved to be realistic and lasting, though the pope, Innocent X (reigned 1644–1655), was unambiguous in his condemnation. Whether or not this was the "last religious war," as some claim, and whether or not religion ceased to be so important in political and international affairs after this war, are moot points.

As far as the political settlement is concerned, the peace was remarkably conservative and legalistic. It was intended more as a restatement of old rights than as anything new. Much that had been a matter of fact or common practice, such as the autonomy of the princes, was now de jure (legal). Of course, that is not to say there were no innovations—the creation of an eighth electorate was new, the first extension of the number of imperial electors since 1356—but established custom and legal rights were usually preferred.

Within the empire, Saxony, Bavaria, and Brandenburg had all grown in size and importance. The tendency was toward fully sovereign independent states. However, these larger states were still not a match for the emperor, who among other things retained the prestige of precedence. Ferdinand III undoubtedly lost power—for instance, he lost the right to levy taxes outside his homelands and to declare war without the consent of the diet—but he remained the foremost prince in Germany. Moreover, many of the smaller states were too small to exploit the rights and liberties they had been granted; they preferred the security of the Holy Roman Empire. They relied on the emperor and were happy to seek his protection, particularly now that he could not be a predator. For these reasons Franco-Swedish attempts to destroy imperial institutions had been resisted. After 1648 the imperial bureaucracy became more cumbersome and made Habsburg control less practical; however, recent research is beginning to question the idea that Westphalia fixed the empire's constitution in its final form. It is now thought to have been more adaptable to change, and, in fact, imperial policy continued to be decided by the emperor.

The emperor himself was now very much strengthened within his hereditary territories: both religious and political opposition in Bohemia and Austria had been crushed and the hereditary lands were now ruled as a single unit. Accordingly, the emperor was in a far better position than he had held in 1618. Of course, compared with the dizzy heights of 1629 there had been reverses—Ferdinand III had undoubtedly lost the last part of the war—but he managed to retain some of his father's early successes. Given his dire military situation at the end, the final settlement was not completely unfavorable to him; he had, in fact, gotten off quite lightly. The failure of many Habsburg objectives during the war, together with the (allegedly) improved position of the princes following the Westphalian settlement, used to be taken as evidence for the general decline in imperial power and as an explanation for the emperor's apparent growing concentration on purely dynastic interests. However, scholars are beginning to call this reasoning into question, although this debate has just started. The Holy Roman Empire was far from moribund after 1648. It not only survived but revived during the long reign of Leopold I (ruled 1658–1705).

Despite huge expenditures and much effort, France had achieved little. Mazarin failed to reduce the power of the emperor significantly, and he failed to increase French influence in Germany to any degree. Some historians gloss over this by suggesting that Mazarin laid the foundations for future success by obtaining territory with ill-defined jurisdictions over adjacent lands. Still others praise him for excluding Spain from the settlement, but this was not the case, because Spain had not wanted to be part of the treaty anyway. Mazarin himself was clearly disappointed with the peace; he wanted the war to continue. The real reason for the hurried nature of the settlement was the collapse of governmental authority and the outbreak of civil disorder in France itself, events for which Mazarin must, to some extent, take the blame. As far as Sweden was concerned, Queen Christina's desire for a quick settlement did undoubtedly lessen her country's chances of a satisfactory outcome, but compared with, say, Swedish aims in 1630 or the difficult times between 1634 and 1638, the outcome was highly satisfactory. Sweden was now more secure, although it could be argued that Christina had simply extended her responsibilities and given herself more problems The Peace of Westphalia created a loose framework for religious and political coexistence in Germany that stood the test of time remarkably well, though after 1648 Germany was further away than ever from economic and political unity (if that was a desirable, or even desired, outcome). Clearly, whether or not the Thirty Years' War retarded German development is itself a moot point. Political divisions were perpetuated and, religiously, Germany was divided roughly into a Protestant north and a Catholic south (although Münster and Cologne in the north and Württemberg in the south were major exceptions). In the process Protestantism had survived and the Counter-Reformation had been checked.

The Peace of Westphalia was actually innovative in many ways. It was the first pan-European peace congress, and there was a genuine attempt to resolve a multitude of disputes in the hope that there would be a general settlement and lasting peace. Most experts believe it was a success.

*See also* **Austria; Bohemia; Catholic League (France); Christina (Sweden); Counter-Reformation; Dutch Republic; Ferdinand III (Holy Roman Empire); France; Frederick William (Brandenburg); Fronde; Habsburg Dynasty; Holy Roman Empire; Leopold I (Holy Roman Empire); Mazarin, Jules; Palatinate; Richelieu, Armand-Jean Du Plessis, cardinal; Spain; Sweden; Thirty Years' War (1618–1648); Tilly, Johann Tserclaes of; Wallenstein, A. W. E. von.**

BIBLIOGRAPHY

Asch, Ronald G. *The Thirty Years' War: The Holy Roman Empire and Europe, 1618–1648.* New York and London, 1997. An up-to-date survey of the war of manageable length that keeps the focus on Germany. See Chapter 5 for the peace.

Croxton, Derek. *Peacemaking in Early Modern Europe: Cardinal Mazarin and the Congress of Westphalia, 1643–1648.* Selinsgrove, Pa., and London, 1999. This restores Mazarin to a central role.

Croxton, Derek, and Anuschka Tischer. *The Peace of Westphalia: A Historical Dictionary.* Westport, Conn., 2002. This has over 300 detailed entries.

Darby, Graham. *The Thirty Years' War.* London, 2001. A concise introduction to the conflict; a good place to start. See Chapter 6.

Parker, Geoffrey, ed. *The Thirty Years' War.* 2nd ed. London and New York, 1997. Currently the definitive work on the war, with a full set of notes and a comprehensive bibliography that lists all the essential works in German. For Westphalia, see especially the bibliographical essay, pp. 266–268.

Symcox, G., ed. *War, Diplomacy, and Imperialism, 1618–1763.* New York, 1973. The terms of the peace are summarized in English on pp. 39–62.

GRAHAM DARBY

# WIDOWS AND WIDOWHOOD.

*Vedova, viuda, veuve, Witwe, widow:* all are words derived from the Indo-European base meaning 'to separate', and early modern Europeans were very familiar with the grief of a separation by the death of one's spouse. But these words also represent something else about widowhood. They are female forms, for widowhood affected women far more than it did men. Male words for widowhood—for example the English *widower*—derived from the female form and were infrequently used in the early modern period. Widows always outnumbered widowers: in Castile by up to 12 to 1, in Tuscany by more than 5 to 1, in England by 2 to 1. Wives, generally younger than their husbands, usually outlived them, and the dangers of childbirth were more than balanced by violence and occupational hazards experienced by men. Widowers were also at least twice as likely to remarry, and remarry quickly, driven by the domestic problems consequent on the absence of a wife. Their marital status was rarely remarked in literature and legal records, their occupational, financial, and public roles little altered by bereavement.

On the other hand, great cultural and economic change usually marked a woman's transition to widowhood. Widows were a large, identifiable, and problematic social group. In fifteenth-century Florence, for example, a quarter of females over age twelve were widows. Even in England, where age differences between husbands and wives were usually relatively small, widows constituted almost a tenth of the female population.

## CULTURE AND IDEAS

For a few of these women, widowhood conveyed wealth and independence; for most, it meant increased poverty. But whether rich or poor, widows challenged the fundamental premise of patriarchal order. Not only did every widow remind each man of his own mortality, a widow heading her own household also represented a lapse of the universal idea that women should be controlled by men. There were alternatives to this dangerous independence. Where Roman law was influential, widows sometimes, at least in theory, continued under male guardianship of father or brother or brother-in-law. Traditional Christian admiration for celibacy extended to chaste widowhood, and some Catholic widows took the opportunity of bereavement to enter (and in the case of some wealthy widows, to found) religious houses to secure an honorable home. Remarriage was another solution, but it suggested disloyalty to the dead husband, threatened his property and his children, and was generally criticized except for young childless women. The remarrying widow was a standard subject for jokes, satire, and gossip. But widows who did not marry were equally subject to criticism: as sexually rapacious, as subversive advisors to potentially rebellious wives, as aggressive and irritating borrowers and beggars, or, at best, as pathetic objects of charity. In the eighteenth century this last idea developed into the sentimentalized image of the permanently grieving and helpless widow, replacing the disorderly crone. Works of advice for widows prescribed a private life of chaste loyalty to the dead husband as the only defense against these negative images.

## PROPERTY AND WORK

Of course, most widows did not and could not retire into helpless passivity. How did they live? Across Europe, most widows had some rights by law or custom, but variations were complex. One factor was the nature of conjugal estate in the area. Where tradition emphasized the separated unit of husband, wife, and children, the widow was more likely to succeed to headship of an independent household, with all the opportunities and problems that implied; where integration of the conjugal unit into a lineage was stronger, the widow would more likely make her home with her dead husband's successors, or return to her own male kin. Widows' rights to the

couple's property also varied. At one extreme, a wife's estate (that is, the wealth she brought to the marriage as dowry, the parallel gift from her husband's family to her, and what she earned) remained all or partly under her own control during and after the marriage. Wives who traded in their own right in London, women in the Netherlands who chose to manage their own wealth (like many Jewish and Muslim women), and noble wives in Russia who gained the right to acquire their own lands during the eighteenth century probably experienced very little economic change in the transition to widowhood. In other systems, for example in Valencia, the property that a bride brought to her marriage remained hers but under her husband's control, until his death allowed the wife/widow to reclaim her contribution. In Florence a widow could, if she chose, take her wealth back and return to her own kin. But her children, part of her husband's lineage, stayed with his family, and by retrieving her wealth, she was potentially depriving them of both herself and her wealth. Even where, as in England, the wife's contribution in cash or goods belonged, notoriously, to her husband, some latent tradition remained by *legitime* of a guaranteed customary widow's share of the husband's goods. A widow could also claim a share of his real property (one-third by common-law dower, sometimes more, according to local custom). It was hers for life, but she could not sell it or bequeath it by will. An English husband had a corresponding right to his dead wife's real property, provided a child had been born to the couple. Similar rules of life estate have been studied in Paris, in parts of the Netherlands, and in Poland and elsewhere. For many wives the crucial document was the husband's will. A large, but declining, proportion of husbands conveyed substantial control by making their wives executors; but a will could also be used to reduce customary rights. Indeed, during the early modern period, widows' traditional rights tended almost everywhere to become more attenuated, sometimes replaced by negotiated contractual protections. Historians have been surprised by the energy with which widows used the courts, often successfully, to defend their customary or individual rights.

Rural widows thus sometimes had access to land and continued to farm. In some localities, up to a quarter of the land might be under widows' control.

In towns and cities, wives of craftsmen and merchants also commonly carried on their husbands' businesses. Glikl bas Judah Leib of Hameln, whose memoirs have made her one of the best known of early modern widows, continued her Jewish family's trade in jewels during her first widowhood. Tax records and family letters reveal the lives of many other economically active widows. Even where there was no custom of wives' separate trading, most women had their own occupations that they continued in widowhood. Access to work encouraged widows to migrate and perhaps discouraged make-do remarriage; thus, the proportions of widows in lace-making communities, for example, tended to be higher than in other parts of rural France. But like rights of succession to land, widows' rights to practice their husbands' trades became more circumscribed through the period, and women's opportunities to be trained for a profitable separate occupation were also reduced.

## HOME AND CHILDREN

The presence or absence of children made a huge difference. The desire to protect children's inheritances sometimes discouraged widowers from remarrying, despite the problems of single parenthood. Although patriarchal ideals theoretically favored a dying husband's right to control the guardianship of his children, in practice, respect for mothers' capabilities and high male mortality meant that widows often found themselves responsible for at least some young children, for educating them and arranging good marriages. It might be presumed that adult children would ease a widow's problems, but widows competed with children for resources, residence in a child's home was not necessarily attractive, and in the mobile early modern world adult children were often far away.

Widow-headed households were common (almost 14 percent in fifteenth-century Florence, 12 percent in sixteenth-century Paris, 13 percent in England) and although very few widows acquired any public authority by their headship (royal widows such as Catherine de Médicis and Anne of Austria were uniquely famous exceptions), having her own home could give a widow a novel opportunity for informal power in her family and community. But most widows succeeded to little property. If they headed their own households, they would inevitably be poor, and widow-headed households are overrepresented among the poorest groups in most communities for which we have records.

## POVERTY

However much widows were vilified in popular literature, in practice, early modern societies generally also regarded poor widows as deserving objects of charity and relief. Asylums and almshouses were endowed to care for them; giving charity to one's widowed neighbor was a duty. Where state-funded poor relief was established, widows were among those deemed, almost by definition, eligible recipients, and they dominated the relief lists. While wills, deeds, tax lists, and the records of law courts record the lives of propertied widows, the lives of the poorest are documented in the records of the asylums that gave them shelter or in the tiny sums doled out week after week to support a few widowed men, and a vast group of widows. These records evoke the generosity of early modern communities and, at the same time, mark the consequences of patriarchal structures that subordinated women and made most widows poor and vulnerable.

*See also* **Family; Inheritance and Wills; Marriage; Patriarchy and Paternalism; Poverty; Women.**

BIBLIOGRAPHY

*Primary Source*
Glikl bas Judah Leib. *Memoirs of Glükel of Hameln.* Translated by Marvin Lowenthal. New York, 1977.

*Secondary Sources*
Bremmer, Jan, and Lourens van den Bosch, eds. *Between Poverty and the Pyre: Moments in the History of Widowhood.* London, 1995. Provides useful extra-European perspective.

Cavallo, Sandra, and Lyndan Warner, eds. *Widowhood in Medieval and Early Modern Europe.* London, 1998. This fine collection is the best place to start; it also includes an excellent bibliography.

Diefendorf, Barbara. "Widowhood and Remarriage in Sixteenth-Century Paris." *Journal of Family History* 7 (1982): 379–395.

Hardwick, Julia. "Widowhood and Patriarchy in Seventeenth-Century France" *Journal of Social History* 26 (1992): 133–148.

Hufton, Olwen. "Widowhood." Chap. 6 in her *The Prospect Before Her: History of Women in Western Europe.* Vol. I, *1500–1800.* London, 1995. Excellent overview.

Klapisch-Zuper, Christiane. "The Cruel Mother." In *Women, Family and Ritual in Renaissance Italy,* pp. 117–131. Chicago, 1985. A classic essay.

Maresse, Michelle. *A Woman's Kingdom: Noblewomen and the Control of Property in Russia, 1700–1861.* Ithaca, N.Y., 2002.

Vassberg, David E. "The Status of Widows in Sixteenth-Century Castile." In *Poor Women and Children in the European Past,* edited by John Henderson and Richard Wall, pp. 180–195. London, 1994.

Wall, Richard, ed. "Widows in European Society." Special edition of *History of the Family* 7, no. 1 (2002).

BARBARA J. TODD

---

# WIELAND, CHRISTOPH MARTIN

(1733–1813), German writer, publisher, and classicist and one of the most influential literary figures of the German Enlightenment. The son of a Lutheran minister, Christoph Martin Wieland was born in Oberholzheim, Upper Swabia, near the imperial city of Biberach on 5 September 1733. At the age of thirteen, after attending the local public school of Biberach, Wieland was sent to Klosterbergen in the vicinity of Magdeburg, one of the most prestigious boarding schools of the time. Already an avid reader, Wieland acquired the reputation of a freethinker and, not surprisingly, his literary interests proved stronger than his dedication to his law studies at Tübingen (1750–1751). From 1752 to 1759, he was a student of the literary polemicist Johann Jakob Bodmer (1698–1783) in Zurich. After working as a private tutor in Bern (1759–1760) and as a professor of philosophy at the University of Erfurt (1769–1772), Wieland became the tutor of Karl August, the future duke of Weimar, in 1772.

Many of Wieland's works reflect his love of the classics and his profound knowledge of European literature, both of which become evident through his numerous commentaries and his often-criticized Shakespeare translations. Influenced by Bodmer (the teacher of the German poet Friedrich Gottlieb Klopstock [1724–1803]), Wieland's early works such as *Die Natur der Dinge* (1751; The nature of things) are profoundly religious in character, whereas his later works become more frivolous and suggestive in tone. Autobiographical elements appear with striking frequency in most of Wieland's writings. From 1760 to 1769, for example, Wieland served as municipal administrator in Biberach. Some of his experiences as a public administrator reappear in comic form in his later work *Die Geschichte der Abderiten* (1781; translated as The republic of fools, 1861), which belongs to the category of fools' literature and pointedly ridicules bourgeois pettiness and the fruitlessness of religious quarrels. Probably the first socially critical novel, *Die Geschichte der Abderiten* systematically portrays life in the Republic of Abdera, the ancient Greek symbol of folly, where things happen in reversal of what one would consider normal. His earlier works *Der Sieg der Natur über die Schwärmerey, oder die Abenteuer des Don Sylvio von Rosalva* (1764; translated as Reason triumphant over fancy, exemplified in the singular adventures of Don Sylvio de Rosalva, 1773) and *Der goldene Spiegel* (1772; The golden mirror) reveal Wieland's potential as a future novelist. Scholars view his most famous work, *Die Geschichte des Agathon* (1766/1767; The history of Agathon), which appeared in several revised editions between 1773 and 1793, as the first and one of the finest examples of the genre of the Bildungsroman (novel concerned with the intellectual or spiritual development of the main character). Influenced by Euripides's play *Ion,* *Die Geschichte des Agathon* uses a classical setting and focuses on the discrepancy between youthful idealism and the harsh realities of life. Kidnapped by pirates from his sheltered home at Delphi, its hero Agathon, who arguably could be seen as a reflection of Wieland's own youthful self, endures a long odyssey of fruitless searching for wisdom and happiness. As a disillusioned old man, Agathon eventually realizes that human beings rarely act the way they should and that the purpose of life must be to find a compromise between head and heart, which means between rational thought and human passions.

Many of Wieland's works, such as his *Die Geschichte der Abderiten,* first appeared as sequels in his own literary journal *Der teutsche Merkur* (The German Mercury). Wieland had cultivated the idea of creating a literary journal for a considerable time and was able to realize this goal with the help of the Jacobi brothers in 1772, during his time in Weimar. Wieland's presence at Weimar contributed to the duchy's rise to prominence as Germany's cultural capital because it attracted figures such as Johann Wolfgang von Goethe (1749–1832) and Friedrich von Schiller (1759–1805) as well. Wieland's relationship to Goethe and Schiller became strained over the years and eventually culminated in a polemic campaign against the aging poet. Proponents of the Sturm und Drang (Storm and Stress) movement initiated the campaign against Wieland and were joined at a later stage by adherents of the rising Romantic movement. Nonetheless, during his final years, Wieland's residence at Weimar became a place of pilgrimage for Germany's most noted and promising writers.

Wieland's reputation as one of the most prominent writers of his age is probably best illustrated by the poet's decoration with the Cross of the Legion of Merit in 1808 by Napoleon Bonaparte. Celebrated as the "German Voltaire" during his lifetime, Wieland's literary contribution fell into near oblivion in the nineteenth century, and scholars have only recently come to view him as one of the most important literary figures of the German Enlightenment as well as a precursor of German classicism and Romanticism.

*See also* **Enlightenment; German Literature and Language.**

BIBLIOGRAPHY

*Primary Sources*

Wieland, Christoph Martin. *Gesammelte Schriften*. Edited by Deutsche Akademie der Wissenschaften. Hildesheim, 1986–1987.

———. *The History of Agathon*. Translated from the German. London, 1773.

———. *History of the Abderites*. Translated and with an introduction by Max Dufner. Bethlehem, Pa., 1993.

———. *Musarion and Other Rococo Tales*. Translated and with an introduction by Thomas C. Starnes. Columbia, S.C., 1991.

———. *Oberon: A Poem from the German by Wieland*. Translated by William Sotheby. New York, 1978. Originally published London, 1798.

———. *Sämtliche Werke*. Edited by Heinrich Düntzer. 40 vols. Berlin, 1879.

*Secondary Sources*

Baldwin, Claire. *The Emergence of the Modern German Novel: Christoph Martin Wieland, Sophie von La Roche, and Maria Anna Sagar*. Rochester, N.Y., 2002.

Budde, Bernhard. *Aufklärung als Dialog: Wieland's antithetische Prosa*. Tübingen, 2000.

Erhart, Walter. *Entzweiung und Selbstaufklärung. Christoph Martin Wieland's "Agathon" Projekt*. Tübingen, 1991.

Günther, Gottfried, and Heidi Zeilinger. *Wieland-Bibliographie*. Berlin, 1983.

Jørgensen, Sven-Aage et al. *Christoph Martin Wieland: Epoche-Werk-Wirkung*. Munich, 1994.

Kurth-Voigt, Lieselotte E. *Perspectives and Points of View: The Early Works of Wieland and their Background*. Baltimore, 1974.

Mayer, Gerhart. *Der deutsche Bildungsroman: Von der Aufklärung bis zur Gegenwart*. Stuttgart, 1992.

McCarthy, John A. *Christoph Martin Wieland*. Boston, 1979.

Schelle, Hansjörg, ed. *Christoph Martin Wieland: Nordamerikanische Forschungsbeiträge zur 250. Wiederkehr seines Geburtstages 1983*. Tübingen, 1984.

Shookman, Ellis. *Noble Lies, Slant Truths, Necessary Angels: Aspects of Fictionality in the Novels of Christoph Martin Wieland*. Chapel Hill, N.C., 1997.

ULRICH GROETSCH

**WILKINS, JOHN** (1614–1672), an important figure in the history of science, religion, literature, and linguistics. As his many publications suggest, Wilkins possessed a wide-ranging intellect. His contributions to natural philosophy include the popularization of science, development of English scientific organization, creation of a universal language, and demonstration of the compatibility of religion and science. *The Discovery of a World in the Moone* (1638) and *A Discourse concerning a New World and Another Planet* (1640) introduced lay readers to Copernicanism and the implications of Galileo's telescopic observations, but literary figures satirized his speculations about the possibility of lunar flight and lunar inhabitants. He also proposed solutions to possible conflicts with Scripture, which he suggested God had "accommodated" to the capacity of the common people. Natural knowledge was determined by "Sensible Experiments and Necessary Demonstration"; science was an independent body of knowledge verifiable by its own standards of investigation. *Mercury, or the Secret and Swift Messenger* (1641) explores the nature of codes and secret communications and proposes a "Universal Character" and language. *Mathematical Magick, or the wonders that may be performed by mechanical geometry* (1648) explains fundamental principles of mechanics and suggests both practical and fanciful devices utilizing these principles.

While warden of Wadham College, Oxford, Wilkins defended universities against the attacks of Thomas Hobbes and the radical sects, and insisted that the universities were hospitable to recent developments in natural philosophy. He recruited to Wadham a group of naturalists of differing religious and political persuasions to pursue a wide-ranging, cooperative, and experimental program that was the forerunner of the Royal Society, which he helped to found, serving as one of its secretaries and supervising the composition of Thomas Sprat's *The History of the Royal Society* (1667). His long-standing interest in language and linguistics culminated in *An Essay towards a Real Character, and a Philosophical Language* (1668), which describes a universal language he designed to facilitate scientific communication and trade and reduce religious misunderstanding.

Wilkins also made important contributions to religion and wrote frequently reprinted works on the organization and presentation of preaching and prayer. In *A Discourse concerning the Beauty of Providence and All the Rugged Passages of It* (1649) he advised acceptance of recent political changes. During the Restoration he became a key figure in the development of latitudinarian theology and natural religion and a staunch advocate of comprehension, a policy intended to broaden the established church. His adoption of an epistemology that emphasized the probabilistic nature of human knowledge led him to advocate tentativeness and moderation in both religion and natural philosophy, and he expounded these views from the pulpit of St. Laurence Jewry, London, as Dean of Ripon and as Bishop of Chester, and in his *Sermons Preached upon Several Occasions before the King at White-Hall* (1677) and *Of the Principles and Duties of Natural Religion* (1675), completed by his son-in-law, John Tillotson.

Wilkins's diverse interests made him a significant figure in the intellectual and cultural life of his time, and his contributions to Interregnum and Restoration natural philosophy and scientific organization remain important. Historians interested in the relationship between religion and science have investigated his religious views, variously identified as Puritan or latitudinarian, while literary scholars and linguists read his work in connection with the development of prose style and linguistics.

*See also* **Academies, Learned; Astronomy; Bible: Interpretation; Copernicus, Nicolaus; Galileo Galilei; Hobbes, Thomas; Philosophy; Preaching and Sermons; Scientific Method.**

BIBLIOGRAPHY

Cohen, I. Bernard. *Puritanism and the Rise of Modern Science: The Merton Thesis.* New Brunswick, N.J., 1990.

Moss, Joan Dietz. *Novelties in the Heavens: Rhetoric and Science in the Copernican Controversy.* Chicago, 1993.

Shapiro, Barbara J. *John Wilkins 1614–1672: An Intellectual Biography.* Berkeley and Los Angeles, 1968.

———. *Probability and Certainty in Seventeenth-Century England: A Study of the Relationships between Natural Science, Religion, History, Law, and Literature.* Princeton, 1983.

Slaughter, M. M. *Universal Languages and Scientific Taxonomy in the Seventeenth Century.* Cambridge, U.K., 1982.

Subbiondo, Joseph L., ed. *John Wilkins and 17th-Century British Linguistics.* Amsterdam and Philadelphia, 1992.

BARBARA SHAPIRO

**WILLIAM AND MARY** (William III, 1650–1702; ruled 1689–1702), king of England, Scotland, and Ireland; (Mary II, 1662–1694; ruled 1689–1694), queen of England, Scotland, and Ireland. William III of Orange, stadtholder of the United Provinces, was born 4 November 1650, the son of William II of Orange (1626–1650), who died shortly before the birth, and Mary Stuart (1631–1660), eldest daughter of Charles I of England. Fiercely anti-French, the future William III led the Dutch in the war against France of 1672–1678 following the revolution of 1672 that revived the stadtholderate. The future Mary II was born on 30 April 1662, the eldest daughter of James, duke of York (James II; ruled 1685–1688), and his first wife, Anne Hyde (1638–1671). William and Mary were married on 4 November 1677 as part of the scheme of Thomas Osborne (1632–1712), earl of Danby, to move England out of the French orbit and to secure the Protestant succession in the wake of York's conversion to Catholicism. At the time Mary was second in line to the throne after her father, and William was fourth.

Alarmed by political developments under James II after 1685 and determined to bring England into his anti-French alliance, William offered to invade England by April 1688 if he could be assured of the necessary support. The birth of a Prince of Wales to James II's second wife on 10 June 1688, however, provided the immediate cue for action. A group of seven Whig and Tory politicians sent William a signed invitation to come to England's rescue. William, using the rumor that the baby was not really the queen's but had been smuggled into the bedchamber in a warming pan as a pretext, alleged that James therefore was guilty of trying to defraud William and his wife of their inheritance rights. The Glorious Revolution of 1688–1689 that followed resulted in the overthrow of James II and the installment of William and Mary as joint sovereigns of England, Scotland, and Ireland, though with full regal power invested in William alone.

William's accession brought England into the Continental alliance to prevent the expansionist ambitions of Louis XIV (ruled 1643–1715) in Europe. William first secured Ireland, defeating James II's Franco-Irish army at the River Boyne on 1 July 1690 (though Jacobite resistance in Ireland did not finally collapse for another year). William then led the Continental campaign in the Low Countries, but the War of the League of Augsburg (1688–1697) ended inconclusively with the Treaty of Ryswick (Rijswijk) in 1697, leaving the crucial question of the fate of the Spanish inheritance undecided. In 1698–1700 William negotiated two treaties with France to partition the Spanish empire upon the death of the Spanish king Charles II (ruled 1665–1700). But when Charles died in October 1700, leaving his entire empire to Louis XIV's grandson Philip of Anjou (ruled 1700–1724, 1724–1746 as Philip V), Louis reneged on the agreement, prompting William to forge a new Grand Alliance (August 1701) to secure partition by force. The War of the Spanish Succession (1701–1714) broke out shortly after William's death.

The expense of war necessitated a financial revolution and the establishment of the Bank of England in 1694. Setting up the national debt, which needed to be serviced by regular grants of parliamentary taxation, did more than anything else to make the English monarchy dependent on Parliament. William's reign also saw the passage of the Triennial Act in 1694 (guaranteeing new Parliaments every three years) and the lapsing of the Licensing Act in 1695 (thereby establishing freedom of the press), while William's repeated absences in conducting war on the Continent led to the beginnings of the cabinet system of government. However, Mary was not a complete political nonentity. An act of May 1690 made her regent during her husband's absences, and she showed considerable adroitness in dealing with various crises that emerged until her premature death from smallpox in December 1694. Mary died childless, and her sister Anne's sole surviving child, the duke of Gloucester, died in 1700. Consequently in 1701 Parliament passed the Act of Settlement, which conferred the succession on the house of Hanover once the Protestant Stuart line died out, established that future monarchs had to be communicating members of the Church of England, and placed limits on the crown's ability to involve England in war fought in defense of the monarchy's possessions abroad.

In Scotland, William achieved notoriety for authorizing the massacre of the MacDonald clan at Glencoe in 1692, when the clan accidentally missed the deadline for swearing allegiance to the new regime by five days. In Ireland, William's regime presided over the passage of a series of penal laws designed to strike at the Catholic faith that were in clear breach of the Treaty of Limerick, which had ended the Jacobite War in 1691. With his health already deteriorating—he had long suffered badly from asthma—William fell and broke his collarbone when his horse stumbled on a molehill in Hampton Court Park on 20 February 1702. He died from pleurisy on 8 March. Jacobite legend attributes his demise to "the little gentleman in black velvet."

*See also* **Church of England; Glorious Revolution; Jacobitism; League of Augsburg, War of the (1688–1697); Louis XIV (France); Spanish Succession, War of the (1701–1714); Stuart Dynasty (England and Scotland).**

BIBLIOGRAPHY

Baxter, Stephen B. *William III*. London, 1966.

Claydon, Tony. *William III*. London and New York, 2002.

———. *William III and the Godly Revolution*. Cambridge, U.K., 1996.

Holmes, Geoffrey, ed. *Britain after the Glorious Revolution, 1689–1714*. London, 1969.

Hopkins, Paul. *Glencoe and the End of the Highland War*. Edinburgh, 1986.

Horwitz, Henry. *Parliament, Policy, and Politics in the Reign of William III.* Manchester, U.K., 1977.

———. "The 1690s Revisited: Recent Work on Politics and Political Ideas in the Reign of William III." *Parliamentary History* 15 (1996): 361–377.

Rose, Craig. *England in the 1690s: Revolution, Religion, and War.* Oxford, 1999.

Speck, W. A. *Reluctant Revolutionaries: Englishmen and the Revolution of 1688.* Oxford, 1988.

———. "William—and Mary?" In *The Revolution of 1688– 1689: Changing Perspectives,* edited by Lois G. Schwoerer, pp. 131–146. Cambridge, U.K., and New York, 1992.

TIM HARRIS

# WILLIAM OF ORANGE (1533–1584),

Dutch statesman, leader of the Dutch Revolt, and founding father of the Dutch Republic. Also known as William the Silent, William of Orange was the oldest son of the German count of Nassau, William the Rich, and Juliana of Stolbergen. His life was changed by the cannonball that killed his childless uncle René of Chalons during the Habsburg siege of the French town of Saint-Didier in 1544. As the last representative of the house of Nassau-Breda, Chalons had appointed his young nephew as his heir. The heritage included not only large possessions in the Netherlands, but also the principality of Orange in southern France. From now on, William was no longer the son of an insignificant German count, but a prince by blood. Emperor Charles V (ruled 1519–1556) summoned the young boy from his family's castle at Dillenburg to the Netherlands, where he became a page at the imperial court and was raised as a loyal and Catholic nobleman. The years that followed saw the remarkable transformation of the son of a Lutheran German count into a French-speaking Burgundian *grand seigneur,* ready to serve the Habsburgs. A brilliant career followed, with honorable military charges, an appointment in the Council of State, admittance to the Order of the Golden Fleece, and, in 1559, the office of governor or stadtholder of Holland, Zeeland, and Utrecht. William of Orange had become one of the wealthiest and mightiest noblemen in the Netherlands. His 1558 marriage to Anna van Buren of the Egmont family confirmed his new standing.

**William of Orange.** LIBRARY OF CONGRESS

In the 1560s, under the regime of Charles V's successor, Philip II of Spain (ruled 1556–1598), everything changed dramatically. From being a central pillar of royal authority, William of Orange became the leader of an armed opposition to Habsburg rule in the Low Countries. In hindsight, it is clear that the split between Orange and the regime started in 1561, with William's second marriage to Anna of Saxony, the niece of the elector of Saxony. It was a prestigious but hardly tactful marriage. Anna had many powerful relatives, but they were all Lutherans, and most of them were old enemies of the Habsburgs. In order to profit fully from his new German connections, Orange was, according to some historians, forced to become more critical of the persecutions and executions of Protestants in the Netherlands and, in the end, of Catholicism itself. Certainly, the marriage heightened the suspicions in government circles concerning the prince's religious loyalty. Lacking strong commitment to any confession, Orange himself became more and more convinced of the disastrous consequences of Philip II's stubborn religious policy. Instead, he championed a policy of religious compromise. In December 1564, in a famous speech to the members of the Council of State, Orange criticized frankly those rulers who sought to force the consciences of their subjects.

In politics William of Orange was above all an ambitious nobleman, seeking power and prestige. And as a natural advisor in military and political issues, he felt himself under the new regime more and more excluded from all-important decision making. In the figure of Philip II's new right-hand man in Brussels, Antoine Perrenot de Granvelle, Orange and his noble friends found their *bête noire*. For a traditional nobleman such as Orange, Granvelle was nothing more than an upstart civil servant from the Franche-Comté, an example of the rising new bureaucrats of non-noble background. And as the new archbishop of Malines, he was the personification of the new bishoprics, by many falsely associated with the Spanish Inquisition.

Orange and other nobles formed an anti-Granvelle league. By the end of 1563 Granvelle had lost the game in Madrid, and on 13 March 1564 he left the Netherlands. But William of Orange and his fellow noblemen never managed either to overcome the paralysis into which the government had fallen or to moderate Philip's policy. In the end, the king's reinforced religious persecutions sparked rebellion: in 1566 the Netherlands witnessed a profound political crisis, with rebellious Protestant members of the middling and lower nobility (the League of Compromise), a wave of iconoclasm (the *Beeldenstorm*), and military actions of the league of armed nobles known as the *Gueux* ('beggars').

As a *politique,* 'mediator between extremes', Orange tried to steer a middle course during the upheaval. He supported the political opposition but tried at the same time to prevent social unrest and chaos and to maintain good relations with the government. His attempt failed. Both sides mistrusted him. In April 1567, with the opposition in the Netherlands losing momentum and Don Fernando Alvarez de Toledo, third duke of Alba, at the head of ten thousand Spanish troops on the way, William of Orange fled to the Dillenburg to find rest and peace among his friends.

He was not to find it. His property was confiscated when he refused Alba's summons to appear before the Council of Blood, and his eldest son, Philips William, had been seized by the royalists at the university town of Louvain and taken to Spain. William of Orange had become a dishonorable exile. In an attempt to redeem his lost reputation, and that of the house of Nassau, Orange decided on armed opposition to Habsburg rule in the Netherlands, and in 1568 he launched a military campaign. It was accompanied by a stream of well-crafted propaganda, elaborating on "Spanish cruelty" and tyranny, and stressing the godliness and heroism of William of Orange. In military affairs, however, Orange was no match for Alba. The campaign was a failure, and in the years that followed Orange was unable to mount further large-scale invasions to save the "worthy inhabitants who enjoyed freedom in former times from unbearable slavery," as he had promised.

On 1 April 1572, however, six hundred Sea Beggars, pirates carrying letters of marque by William of Orange, seized the small port of Brill. In the months that followed, one town after another in Holland and Zeeland opened its gates for Orange and the Sea Beggars, with the notable exception of Amsterdam, which stayed in the royalist camp until 1578. Alienated by Alba's tax policy and unwilling to billet Spanish garrisons, the citizenry choose what they thought was the lesser of two evils. At least the troops of the Sea Beggars included some countrymen and exiled townsmen who had fled the Netherlands in 1567. The Estates of Holland took matters into their own hands. On 19 July the Orangist Holland towns assembled at Dordrecht and accepted William of Orange as their stadtholder, recognizing him "in the absence of His Royal Majesty" as "Protector" of the Netherlands as a whole. In exchange, Orange promised through his secretary Philips Marnix, Lord of St. Aldegonde, that he would not govern Holland without the consent of the States. In the autumn of 1572, Orange, whose own efforts to stir up the cities of Brabant and Flanders had failed, decided to withdraw to Holland, convinced that he would find his grave there.

Dark years of civil war followed, including religious cleansing, mutual atrocities, and massacres of nuns, monks, and priests. Orange was powerless to prevent the elimination of Catholicism in Holland and Zeeland as an officially tolerated church, in spite of his own tolerant attitudes in religion. In the autumn of 1573 he became a Calvinist.

As a political leader, however, William of Orange experienced his finest hour. He proved to be a charismatic leader, pragmatic, keen, unwilling to compromise, and provided with an unflagging faith in God. It was largely as a result of his leadership that the rebels overcame their differences and continued their military struggle. Seizing the opportunities caused by the large-scale mutinies of the unpaid and unsupplied Spanish troops, the rebellious provinces of Holland and Zeeland in 1576 signed a treaty with the States-General, the Pacification of Ghent. It seemed a victory for Orange, the first step toward a reunification of the Netherlands under a new constitution. In September 1577 Orange entered Brussels in triumph, as a new "messiah." But the new coalition was too fragile; Orange never managed to overcome the differences between Holland and the moderate noblemen in the south, or to moderate the demands of the radical Calvinists in Brabant and Flanders. In the end, north and south drifted apart, as was illustrated by the two "Unions" concluded in 1578: the Union of Arras, which aimed to reconcile the State of the Catholic-dominated provinces in the southern Netherlands with the king of Spain, and the Union of Utrecht, which was meant as a military alliance among the rebellious provinces "for all time."

In September 1583 William of Orange returned to Holland from Antwerp. Declared a traitor and outlawed by Philip II, who had in 1581 promised a reward for the assassination of the prince, and confronted by the steady military advance of the new governor-general, Alexander Farnese, duke of Parma, Orange faced an insecure future. He defended himself in a fierce *Apologia*, but his popularity had reached rock bottom, largely because of his disastrous pro-French policy. He had always been convinced that the revolt could only succeed with the help of the French and had in 1580 offered the governor-generalship of the Netherlands to Francis, the duke of Anjou and Alençon, who was the brother of the French king. The eventual result was political crisis and mutinous soldiers (the French Fury of January 1583). Orange's pro-French politics was symbolized in his private life by his marriage with Louise de Coligny in 1582. It was his fourth marriage, after Anna van Buren, the disastrous affair with Anna of Saxony, from whom he was divorced in 1575, and Charlotte de Bourbon. Louise de Col-

igny would give birth to Frederik Hendrik, Orange's youngest son, after Philips William from his first marriage and Maurice from his second. He had six daughters with Charlotte de Bourbon.

When on 10 July 1584 the French Catholic zealot Balthazar Gérard fired his fatal pistol shots in Delft, the realization of Orange's goals for the Netherlands seemed farther away than ever. No wonder therefore, that an English visitor, Fyne Moryson, described the original grave of the prince as "the poorest that ever I saw for such a person, being only of rough stones and mortar, with posts of wood, colored over with black, and very little erected from the ground" (quoted in Swart, forthcoming). It was only some twenty years later that the newly founded Dutch Republic erected the monument that William of Orange deserved as the founding father of a new state and the advocate of religious tolerance—Hendrick de Keyser's monumental tomb in the Nieuwe Kerk in Delft.

*See also* **Alba, Fernando Álvarez de Toledo, duke of; Charles V (Holy Roman Empire); Dutch Republic; Dutch Revolt; Huygens Family; Oldenbarneveldt, Johan van; Philip II (Spain); Sea Beggars.**

BIBLIOGRAPHY

Israel, Jonathan. *The Dutch Republic: Its Rise, Greatness, and Fall, 1477–1806.* Oxford, 1995.

Motley, J. L. *The Rise of the Dutch Republic: A History.* 3 vols. London, 1929.

Parker, Geoffrey. *The Dutch Revolt.* London, 1977.

Swart, K. W. *William of Orange and the Dutch Revolt, 1572–1584.* Forthcoming.

———. *William the Silent and the Revolt of the Netherlands.* London, 1978.

Wedgwood, C. V. *William the Silent, William of Nassau, Prince of Orange 1533–1584.* London, 1944.

PAUL KNEVEL

**WILLS.** *See* **Inheritance and Wills.**

# WINCKELMANN, JOHANN JOACHIM (1717–1768), German art historian, archaeologist, and philosopher of aesthetics, and one of the leading proponents of neoclassicism. Winck-

elmann is regarded as the first modern historian of art for his systematic treatment of ancient art as an expression of historical conditions, rather than as a tradition of artistic skills and ideas passed from one generation of artists to the next, which was the art-historical approach practiced by Giorgio Vasari (1511–1574), Karl van Mander (1548–1606), and Giovanni Pietro Bellori (1613–1696) in their *Lives* of artists.

Winckelmann was born on 9 December 1717 in Stendal, a town between Hannover and Berlin. The son of an impoverished cobbler, he sought, as a young man, to better his conditions through devotion to academic study, and fell in love with the literature of classical antiquity. In hopes of securing a measure of financial security, and on the advice of his father, Winckelmann pursued a course of study in theology, mathematics, and medicine, as well as Greek and Latin, at the Universities of Jena and Halle. At Halle, Winckelmann was a student of Alexander Baumgarten (1714–1762), the founder of

**Johann Joachim Winckelmann.** LIBRARY OF CONGRESS

modern aesthetics, and developed his own philosophy of beauty, involving the direct experience of beautiful objects, in reaction to Baumgarten's rather cold (in Winckelmann's own opinion) philosophical formalism.

Not finding theology or medicine his calling, Winckelmann left the university and continued to pursue the study of ancient literature and contemporary aesthetics privately, while serving in various positions as a tutor and schoolteacher. A student tutored by him, F. W. Peter Lamprecht, became one of the great loves of his life and followed him to Seehausen after Winckelmann accepted a position as a teacher of Classics there in 1743. In 1748 Winckelmann left Seehausen to work as a librarian and researcher for Count Heinrich von Bünau in Nöthnitz, near Dresden. Lamprecht did not follow, although Winckelmann would continue to lavish his affections upon his former student in private correspondence for years to come. In 1754 he moved to Dresden to work as librarian to Cardinal Passionei, a position that afforded him access to works of literature, art objects, and contemporary cultural debate previously unavailable to him in the provinces where he had been raised and schooled. It was during this period in Dresden that Winckelmann wrote what would, in retrospect, count as the manifesto for the rest of his scholarly life: the brief but powerful and influential essay *Gedanken über die Nachahmung der griechischen Werke in der Malerei und Bildhauerkunst* (1755; Reflections on the imitation of the painting and sculpture of ancient Greeks). The essay took up a long-running debate in eighteenth-century European intellectual circles, called "The Battle of the Books" in London and the "Querelle des Anciens et des Modernes" in Paris, about which culture was superior—ancient or modern—and why. Winckelmann argued that ancient art was clearly superior and that, for the moderns, the only art worth making is the imitation of the art of the ancients, but added (in a rhetorical flourish typical of Winckelmann's style of argument) that the art of the ancients is so superior to the moderns that it is inimitable. He therefore counseled his artistic contemporaries that, since they are doomed to the ineradicable falseness of painting and sculpture in modern times, they should imitate that which is inimitable. Winckelmann reinforces his valuation of the impossible imitability of the Greeks by being the first art historian to discriminate between Greek originals and their inferior Roman copies.

Winckelmann's *Reflections* were quickly translated into several languages and found a wide audience. In 1755, with his intellectual reputation established, Winckelmann, encouraged by a group of Jesuit dignitaries visiting Dresden, moved to Rome, where he would be able to pursue his studies and personal inclinations more freely. By 1763, with Cardinal Alessandro Albani (1692–1779), the Vatican's chief librarian and a leading patron of the arts, as his sponsor and confidant, Winckelmann became papal antiquary, a position that included escorting visiting dignitaries through Rome's art and antiquities collections. In Rome, Winckelmann set to work on his most important book, *Geschichte der Kunst des Altertums* (1764; The history of ancient art), an ambitious, multivolume account of the art of antiquity in Egypt, Greece, and Rome, written in a style that mixes the sentimental with the clinical and the platonic. Winckelmann narrated the course of each of these cultures as a kind of life cycle showing "the origin, progress, change and downfall of art, together with the different styles of nations, periods and artists," and drew for his studies upon the concentrations of collections of antique art and artifacts in Rome. Elaborating on the thesis first offered in his *Reflections,* he argued that the felicitous cultural situation of ancient Greece—including political freedoms and unfettered opportunities to view and appreciate the naked body—could not be repeated in modern times. Following a logic reminiscent of the Socratic doctrines of love and beauty, he lamented the passing of Greek art and the beautiful male bodies that inspired it, but found consolation in the historian's ambition to know about it.

Winckelmann met with an untimely death at the hands of an unemployed cook and thief, Francesco Arcangeli, in a hotel in Trieste on 8 June, 1768, while on a diplomatic mission. The motive for the murder was never determined, although speculation about this and other details of Winckelmann's very public private life has inspired numerous literary treatments and plays.

*See also* **Ancients and Moderns; Art: Art Theory, Criticism, and Historiography; Dresden; Early Modern Period: Art Historical Interpretations; Neoclassicism; Rome, Art in; Sculpture.**

BIBLIOGRAPHY

*Primary Sources*

Winckelmann, Johann Joachim. *History of Ancient Art.* Translated by G. Henry Lodge. Boston, 1849; reprinted New York, 1969. Translation of *Geschichte der Kunst des Altertums* (1764).

———. *Reflections on the Imitation of Greek Works in Painting and Sculpture.* Translated by Elfriede Heyer and Roger C. Norton. La Salle, Ill., 1987. Translation of *Gedanken über die Nachahmung der griechischen Werke in der Malerei und Bildhauerkunst* (1755).

*Secondary Sources*

Fried, Michael. "Antiquity Now: Reading Winckelmann on Imitation." *October* 37 (1986): 87–97.

Leppmann, Wolfgang. *Winckelmann.* New York, 1970.

Morrison, Jeffrey. *Winckelmann and the Notion of Aesthetic Education.* Oxford and New York, 1996.

Parker, Kevin. "Winckelmann, Historical Difference and the Problem of the Boy." *Eighteenth-Century Studies* 25, no. 4 (1992): 523–544.

Potts, Alex. *Flesh and the Ideal: Winckelmann and the Origins of Art History.* New Haven and London, 1994; reprinted, 2000.

KEVIN PARKER

# WITCHCRAFT.

**WITCHCRAFT.** Despite a generation of excellent research, the history of witchcraft remains bedeviled by a host of misperceptions. Ordinary readers often assume that the major witch-hunts occurred in the Middle Ages, that they were conducted by the Catholic Church, and that they reflected the prescientific notions and sexual fantasies of fanatics and neurotics. Elsewhere one can read that huge chain reaction witch trials constituted a "women's holocaust" accounting for millions of deaths, and that the witch-hunters especially targeted midwives and female healers. All of these conclusions are both wrong and misleading. The great age of witchcraft trials came after 1430, and primarily after 1570. The prosecuting magistrates were almost always secular officials, imbued with the best thinking of prominent theologians, philosophers, and even scientists. The numbers of those executed have often been exaggerated by a factor of one or two hundred. Men made up perhaps a quarter of those executed, and there is little evidence that midwives or healers were singled out for suspicion anywhere. But historical prejudices are hard to uproot.

## UNDERSTANDINGS OF WITCHCRAFT

Depending on one's definition, various histories of witchcraft are defensible. It was once common, for example, to understand the crime of witchcraft as consisting essentially of having a pact with the devil, an agreement in which one exchanged one's eternal soul for monstrous powers. Such a crime of diabolism had not existed in the ancient world and only slowly emerged from the medieval campaign against magic and heresy, especially against medieval heretics such as the Cathars and Waldensians, groups who challenged both Catholic doctrines and papal jurisdiction. By the late fourteenth century, however, canon lawyers, prominent inquisitors, learned academics, and several popes came to agree that by means of a contract with the devil, whether explicit or only implicit, a magician might work genuine harm in this world. These theorists also gradually worked out a composite view of all the different sorts of crimes and activities their heresy involved. It was increasingly believed that witch-heretics flew off to a "sabbath" where they renounced their Christian faith and baptism, worshipped the devil, danced together, and enjoyed a cannibalistic feast, devouring children whom they had killed while using their fat or other body parts to make loathsome potions. They were also thought to receive instruction in working harmful magic by which they might destroy their neighbors' crops, interfere with the fertility of their cattle, and with the sex lives of those around them. Most luridly, witches were thought to have sexual relations with the devil or with lesser demons. During the fifteenth century large numbers of heretical "witches" or sorcerers began to be discovered, and increasingly they were women.

Another definition of witchcraft emphasizes the continuity of magical practices that witches had used in the West ever since classical times and the similarities between such practices and those found all around the world. On such an understanding, witchcraft is the belief in and use of unusual, secret, or even supernatural forces in order to force or promote specific desired ends. The ancient Greeks had believed in such magic but had not seen it as much of a daily threat. They originally thought that "magic" (*mageia*) was the strange, foreign religious practice of Persian priests (the magi) and of beggars or other dishonorable Greeks. Magic

seemed both alien and disreputable. In Greek literature, the figure of the witch included characters such as Circe and Medea, women who used destructive magic to express their anger, lust, and frustration, but magic does not seem to have been a prominent fear among the Greeks. With the ancient Romans, however, harmful magic (*maleficium*) was forbidden in the earliest set of laws (the Twelve Tables, 451 B.C.E.) and was punished with increasing severity. The Roman historian Livy (*History* 39.41.5 and 40.43.2f) recounts episodes when apparently thousands of persons were executed by jittery judicial officials, and, in the late first century C.E., the Romans began to crack down on fraudulent *magicae vanitates* ('worthless magic'), practices that included healing, divination, and astrology. Thus, this understanding of witchcraft did not require a devil or a pact but insisted on the dangers lurking in the hidden practices of lustful and vengeful witches.

A third notion of witchcraft may be found in the injunctions of the Old Testament, in which the authors of Exodus, Leviticus, Deuteronomy, and Kings, for example, forbade necromancy and divination, practices that competed with the rituals of the Levites and sacrificial priests while also challenging God's sovereignty over the dead and the future. From this point of view, witchcraft represented not diabolism or a physical danger but an abomination, not a conspiracy in league with the devil but impiety, a denial of God's omnipotent control over blessings, punishments, and history (and hence the future as well); such witchcraft constituted an attempt to gain knowledge or advantages that were for God alone. Over time the Israelites intensified their prohibitions against magic, sorcery, divination, and consulting the dead (necromancy), which all hinted at popular polytheism during the exilic and post-exilic period.

All of these notions of witchcraft blended together in various proportions during the late Middle Ages and early modern periods. Some jurists and demonologists were more concerned about a supposed Satanic conspiracy, whose goal seemed to be the destruction of humankind and Christianity. Others remained convinced that witches were primarily a physical danger to their neighbors. Still others were inspired by the image of idolatrous or irreligious magicians who did not constitute a physical danger to anyone and were not members of some hideous conspiracy, but were committed to "heathenish practices" and to foretelling the future by means of astrology, numerology, or other illicit means. In the seventeenth century some writers began to think that the basic crime of witchcraft consisted in being antisocial, regardless of any actual harm done or religious error.

## THE GROWTH OF FEARS OF WITCHCRAFT

In the early Middle Ages, these components had not yet blended to any extent, and so one finds approaches to the crime of witchcraft concentrating on the old Roman or Germanic fear of harmful magic, while churchmen felt free to express deep skepticism about other elements of witchcraft. In perhaps the most important early medieval text, the *Canon Episcopi* (c. 910; "Bishops," a title taken from the first word of this admonition), Regino of Prüm condemned *maleficium* ('wrongdoing') and *sortilegium* (harmful magic and 'fortune-telling') harshly in his first paragraph, but also went on to express deep doubts about the stories told of women who supposedly went out at night to ride on the backs of beasts with the goddess Diana. Such persons were dreaming or hallucinating, he thought, and any Christian who believed these tales was guilty of conceding too much power to a pagan goddess. This canon found a prominent place in Gratian's *Decretum* (1140; Resolution), the most important medieval codification of canon law. From then on, all commentators had to concede that anyone who thought he or she flew might well be deluded.

Following the notion of witchcraft as diabolical heresy, one can trace the rise to prominence of an ecclesiastically flavored fear of a new and growing sect of witches. In the early fourteenth century, Pope John XXII (reigned 1316–1334), for example, repeatedly condemned his enemies for using charms, wax figures, and incantations in their efforts to kill him. In a couple of papal bulls aimed at combating these threats, Pope John widened the understanding of heresy to claim that sorcery involved heresy and a pact with the devil. It was once thought that his reign also witnessed the beginnings of large-scale witchcraft trials with hundreds of executions in southern France, but research in the mid-1970s established that the sources purportedly de-scribing these trials are in fact nineteenth-century forgeries. Consequently, historians over the past twenty-five years have relocated the beginnings of major witch-hunts to the fifteenth century, and especially to the 1430s.

## THE EARLIEST WITCHCRAFT TRIALS

The earliest trials seem to have sprung up around Lake Geneva, to the east in the Valais and Vaud, to the north in Fribourg, Neuchâtel, and Basel, and to the southeast in Leventina (Ticino) and Valle d'Aosta (Italy). During that decade, several authors elaborated the notion of the witches' sabbath and expressed a sharpened sense of the dangers of a witches' conspiracy. For example, the Dominican Johannes Nider (c. 1380–1438) wrote extensively in favor of church reform and against witchcraft. Although he maintained a skeptical attitude toward the flight of witches, he helped propagate the view that witches assembled for dancing, feasting, and sexual orgies and for murdering babies and eating their flesh. Gradually the notion took hold that witches gathered regularly at meetings called *sabbaths* or *synagogues,* terms that make the parallel with Jewish assemblies obvious. Frequently, however, these newly detected witches were seen as analogous to medieval heretics, especially to the Cathars and Waldensians. One treatise (c. 1450) described the "heresies" of the witches under the title *Errores Gazariorum* (The errors of the Cathars, referring to the dualist heretics), while many texts referred to fifteenth-century witches as Vaudois (Waldensians, another prominent medieval heresy). Although the concept of witchcraft drew on ideas of how medieval Jews and heretics were organized, there is no credible evidence that the European witchcraft trials were actually directed at Jews or surviving pockets of heresy or paganism.

## THE MALLEUS MALEFICARUM

By the late fifteenth century many ecclesiastical writers had concluded that witchcraft was a fairly new heresy with its origins in the 1380s. In 1484 Pope Innocent VIII (reigned 1484–1492) issued a papal bull, *Summis desiderantes affectibus,* reporting the wide extent of the threat and authorizing two Dominicans, Jacob Sprenger (c. 1436–1495) and Heinrich Kramer (for centuries called *Institoris* [Latin for 'merchant']; c. 1430–1505) as inquisitors to root out the heretics, especially in southern

Germany and in the alpine regions of Tyrol. Secular magistrates were to cease obstructing their efforts and offer their assistance. Despite the bull, Kramer continued to have trouble prosecuting witches, partly because of continued secular and ecclesiastical resistance to his haughty and brutal methods. In the diocese of Constance, Kramer seems to have overseen the conviction and execution of at least forty-eight women, but at Ravensburg he secured the conviction of only two, while many other suspects were released. In 1485, Bishop Georg II Golser of Bressanone quashed Kramer's investigations at Innsbruck and exiled Kramer, noting that he seemed credulous, unethical, and perhaps crazy in his use of torture and in his wild imaginings of what witches did.

While licking his wounds, Kramer composed what is perhaps the most famous treatise on witchcraft, the *Malleus Maleficarum* (late 1486 or early 1487; The hammer of witches), in an effort to justify his fear that witchcraft was gaining ground against Christendom and that lustful women were naturally attracted or seduced into a life of devil worship, demonic sex, and harmful magic. Historians have often thought that the more distinguished Cologne theologian and coinquisitor, Jacob Sprenger, was the coauthor of this book, but the evidence for this collaboration is thin. It is worth noting that Kramer's *Malleus* never embodied accepted Catholic doctrine and that Kramer himself, after being banned from Innsbruck, was rusticated to the mission fields of Bohemia, where he died in obscurity in 1505.

In the *Malleus* Kramer laid out both the new theological understanding of witchcraft and the harsh inquisitorial methods by which one could force suspects to confess and to implicate others in their heresy-crime. Kramer also pleaded successfully for the intervention of secular officials in the prosecution of witchcraft, and, indeed, after 1500 most of the trials north of the Mediterranean were run by secular magistrates and according to secular laws. The vast majority of witchcraft executions came at the hands of ordinary secular magistrates who enforced secular laws and did not follow the prescriptions or share the peculiar phobias of the *Malleus*.

## HERESY OR HARM?

Those who define *witchcraft* as a sort of heresy have often argued that by the end of the Middle Ages the construction of the crime was complete and that the great witch-hunts that followed in the sixteenth and seventeenth centuries were only the automatic result of this late medieval construction. On this view, common among certain medievalists, the "great witch craze" merely combined this fantastic crime with the supposedly relentless procedures of the Inquisition. Those who have emphasized the nature of witchcraft as harmful magic, however, have thought that the emphasis on heresy and inquisition seriously underestimates the fear of witchcraft among humble villagers, who were always more concerned about their crops, herds, and families than any supposed deviations in belief, and point to the slow adoption of witchcraft statutes by the civil authorities of northern Europe. Emperor Charles V's (ruled 1519–1556) imperial penal code (*Constitutio Criminalis Carolina*, 1532; The criminal code of the Emperor Charles), valid for the whole Holy Roman Empire, described the crime in these words: "When someone harms people or brings them trouble by witchcraft, one should punish them with death, and one should use the punishment of death by fire. When, however, someone uses witchcraft and yet does no one any harm with it, that person should be punished otherwise, according to the custom of the case" (Article 109). There was no mention of pacts with the devil, no sabbath, cannibalism, flight, or heresy. This secular code was obviously most concerned with *maleficium*, 'harmful magic'.

A similar emphasis is visible in the English statute of 1563, which threatened the death penalty for any witchcraft, enchantment, charming, or sorcery if it resulted in the death of a human being; but if these dark arts were less successful (if the victim was maimed or if animals were killed), the witch was to be punished with only a year's imprisonment. Reduced penalties were introduced for the lesser crimes of using magic to find lost or stolen goods, or to incite someone to illicit love. Other secular states also continued to consider witchcraft as first and foremost an attack on others by magical, supernatural means; it was only in the seventeenth century that some of these northern European states finally adopted a fully diabolized understanding of witchcraft, one that made it a capital crime to "consult, covenant with, entertain, employ, feed, or reward any evil and wicked spirit to or for any intent or purpose," as the English statute of 1604 put it. Just as most secular states in northern Europe continued to place *maleficium* at the heart of witchcraft accusations, so too most jurisdictions under an ecclesiastical law (for example, the Mediterranean regions of Italy, Spain, and Portugal) persisted in the sixteenth and seventeenth centuries in seeing witchcraft mainly as a spiritual offense. But that did not mean that the inquisitorial regimes were fiercer. Rather, it meant that throughout southern Europe the scrutiny of witchcraft rumors, accusations, and confessions was more intense, and executions for the crime of witchcraft correspondingly scarce.

## VARIATIONS IN TIME AND SPACE

The wave of recent research into witchcraft trials across Europe has underscored dramatic variations from time to time and from place to place. No region was ever subject to a hundred years of terror; the worst witch-hunts came in waves or spasms, starting in the 1560s and 1570s in southern Germany and in Lorraine, rising again in the 1590s, again in the 1610s and late 1620s, and coming to an end in the 1660s. Across the Holy Roman Empire, the largest persecutions occurred in smaller territories, especially those under the secular jurisdiction of a prelate, an imperial abbot, or some other ecclesiastical administrator. The bishoprics and archbishoprics of Trier, Mainz, Cologne, Augsburg, Würzburg, Bamberg, and Eichstätt were among the fiercest in all of Europe, while the Duchy of Lorraine was perhaps the worst secular territory. Together they accounted for about 10,000 executions.

It was not only Catholic territories that proved to be zealous prosecutors of witchcraft. The Swiss territory of Vaud (under the general control of Bern) conducted perhaps the most extensive witchcraft trials in any Protestant land (perhaps 2,000 executed in all), but the reformed courts of Scotland probably executed 1,000 witches as well. Lutheran Mecklenburg, a land of splintered jurisdictions and widespread noble autonomy, may well have executed 2,000 of the approximately 3,700 persons tried there for witchcraft. In these large persecutions, village accusations of witchcraft usually proliferated in the wake of some climatic disaster, a late

frost or a cold, rainy summer that ruined crops, as was common in Germany in 1626, "the year with no summer."

Magistrates responded to local pressures demanding punishment for the witches thought responsible for these disasters; by the seventeenth century some magistrates were ready to interpret such crop failures and the resulting famine as the consequence of a satanic conspiracy. Thus, village suspicions were reinforced by elite fears. In general, however, it appears that larger secular territories with better-developed appeals courts were able to contain the panic of witchcraft more effectively. The Electoral Palatinate, for example, never carried out witch-hunts of any magnitude, and Bavaria after the 1590s also displayed an increasing skepticism. The Parlement of Paris, the appeals court responsible for a huge jurisdiction that took in most of northern France, became increasingly skeptical from the 1580s onward and, after 1624, made the prosecution of witchcraft almost impossible. After a high point in much of Central Europe in the 1620s, another wave of witchcraft trials erupted in the 1660s from Germany north to Sweden, but then became rare except in Poland, where trials continued until about 1725. By then, witchcraft trials were long over elsewhere. It was long supposed that the last German execution for witchcraft occurred in 1775 in Kempten, but it is now known that the suspect there, though condemned, was not actually executed. In 1782 the Protestant canton of Uri executed a woman as a witch, and a few Polish trials resulted in executions even after that.

Witchcraft remained a crime mainly prosecuted in Catholic and Protestant Europe. The thoroughly developed notion of the pact with the devil was never introduced into the lands of Eastern Orthodoxy, so there were basically few trials (and no massive chain-reaction trials) in Russia. Even in Catholic Poland it appears that earlier accounts of huge witchcraft trials are seriously exaggerated. Suspicions of magic and a variety of other popular spiritual beliefs remained common among the Russian peasantry, however, right down to the twentieth century. Altogether, for all of Europe and over a period of about 300 years, scholars now estimate that perhaps 40,000 to 50,000 people were executed for the crime of witchcraft, a large number to be sure, but small compared to estimates that suggest nine million executions, a number for which there is no basis.

Variations in the severity of witch-hunts and punishments imposed on those accused of the crime-heresy of witchcraft seem to have depended on whether local convictions could be appealed to a distant (and usually more skeptical) court. Where local courts could act autonomously, local excesses were difficult to moderate. It may even be that the term *witch-hunt* is misleading because, in many of the worst cases, magistrates were not actively hunting anyone but were, instead, responding to accusations that bubbled up from neighborhood suspicions. In a surprising number of cases, the original accusations were launched by village women against one or more other women suspected, sometimes for decades, of causing local harm.

### WITCHCRAFT AS "SUPERSTITION"
The third definition of *witchcraft* as impiety surfaced in early modern Europe among magistrates who reacted in horror at the "superstition" of common villagers whose impious attitudes, magical practices, illicit charms, and devotion to local magical healers or shamanlike prophets seemed to prove their adherence to irreligion and witchcraft. Such "superstitious" peasants seemed to deny God's omnipotence, omniscience, and sovereignty over the future and over all blessings and troubles. From this point of view, witchcraft accusations seem connected to efforts of churchmen and magistrates to enforce severe reforms of parish and devotional life. This pattern has been found in Friuli, north of Venice, among villagers who confessed that some of their neighbors regularly went forth "in the spirit" at night to combat the witches who threatened their fields.

Another study has examined the similar case of an alpine horse wrangler who confessed that he traveled with the "phantoms of the night" to learn the secrets of life and death and to gain healing powers. Pastors and priests, however, complained that their parishioners were too quick to blame their pains on witchcraft instead of recognizing the ways that God tested and punished them for their deviation from the devotion expected of them. So the common notion that ordinary people were "superstitious" did not automatically lead to charges of witchcraft among them. Instead, it often happened

that elite judges sitting in provincial or national capitals disdained to take seriously accusations or convictions at the village level.

### SOCIOLOGY OF WITCHCRAFT TRIALS
Much recent research has concentrated on the sociology of the victims of witchcraft trials. The old notion that midwives and popular healers were singled out for repression has faded in the light of evidence that most of those convicted were more often women and men who failed in their neighborly obligations. The fantasies and tensions that led some women to accuse other women of witchcraft, for example, have been examined. In the German lands and in Britain about three-quarters of the executed were women, but elsewhere the proportion of men could be higher. In northern France men and women seem to have been executed in about equal numbers, while in Iceland and Finland men made up the majority of convictions. It was once held that women were the targets of misogynistic (and supposedly celibate) inquisitors, but it has become clear that most magistrates responded to pressures for witch trials from below and that the Mediterranean lands of the Inquisition (together with Ireland) were among the safest places to suffer local suspicions. There is also little evidence that those suspected of witchcraft were mentally ill or "hysterical." Many of those convicted may, however, have seemed like "bad neighbors," quarrelsome or dangerous, isolated and suspected of harboring vengeful feelings toward fellow villagers.

### THE RISE OF SKEPTICISM
There was never a time when "everyone believed in witchcraft." Even at the height of witchcraft trials, some people expressed doubts about the crime itself, about details (for example, whether witches could really fly to the sabbath), or about judicial procedures (whether torture could reliably force suspects to confess the truth). Johann Weyer (Wier; 1515–1588), personal physician to the Duke of Jülich-Cleves-Berg, reacted to the renewal of witchcraft trials by publishing *De Praestigiis Daemonum* (1563; On the deceits of demons), which questioned whether the crime of witchcraft was even possible. Although Weyer conceded large powers to the devil, in his view magic could never be effective (and therefore *maleficium* could never harm anyone); no one could really have a binding pact with

**Giovanni Battista Tiepolo.** Mercury, messenger of the gods, detail from ceiling fresco in the staircase of the Residenz, Würzburg. ©ERICH LESSING/ART RESOURCE, N.Y.

**RIGHT: Titian.** *Bacchus and Ariadne,* one of three "Bacchanals" created by Titian between 1518 and 1524, all of which portray the classical world as a place of sensual delight. ©ERICH LESSING/ART RESOURCE.

**BELOW: Jacopo Tintoretto.** *The Annunciation,* 1581–1582. This masterpiece of the artist's maturity beautifully illustrates his use of naturalism to create realistic scenes that powerfully suggest the presence of the divine. ©CAMERAPHOTO/ART RESOURCE, N.Y.

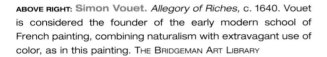

**ABOVE RIGHT:** Simon Vouet. *Allegory of Riches,* c. 1640. Vouet is considered the founder of the early modern school of French painting, combining naturalism with extravagant use of color, as in this painting. THE BRIDGEMAN ART LIBRARY

**BELOW RIGHT:** Jean-Antoine Watteau. *Gilles,* 1717. Although typical in style, this later depiction of a standard commedia dell'arte character reflects the artist's more mature vision in the contrast between the character's festive dress and melancholy expression. THE ART ARCHIVE/MUSÉE DU LOUVRE PARIS/DAGLI ORTI (A)

**OPPOSITE PAGE:** Jan Vermeer. *The Milkmaid* is typical of Vermeer's intimate interiors.

**LEFT:** Art in Venice. *Apotheosis of Venice,* 1585, by Veronese, painted on the ceiling of the Sala del Maggior Consiglio in the doge's palace, Venice. ©SCALA/ART RESOURCE, N.Y.

**BELOW LEFT:** Veronese. The coronation of Esther as Queen of Ahasuerus, ceiling decoration in the Church of San Sebastiano, Venice, painted c. 1556. ©CAMERAPHOTO/ART RESOURCE, N.Y.

**BELOW RIGHT:** Elisabeth Vigée-Lebrun. Portrait of Marie-Antoinette, 1788. Vigée-Lebrun was favored by the queen for her ability to lend an informal air to royal portraits; this is one of several portraits of the queen painted by Vigée-Lebrun between 1778 and 1793. ©GIRAUDON/ART RESOURCE

**LEFT:** Women and Art. Angelica Kauffmann, *Self-Portrait*, 1787. An enormously successful artist, Kauffmann was one of only two women among the founders of the British Royal Academy. ©ARTE & IMMAGINI SRL/CORBIS

**BELOW LEFT:** Women and Art. Clara Peeters, *Table with Pitcher and Dish of Dried Fruit*. THE ART ARCHIVE/MUSEO DEL PRADO MADRID

**BELOW RIGHT:** Women and Art. Adélaide Labille-Guïard, portrait of Marie Adélaide of France, 1787. A noted portraitist, Labille-Guïard ran a studio for women in Paris and at one point asked the French academy to raise the quota of four female academicians. THE ART ARCHIVE/MUSÉE DU CHÂTEAU DE VERSAILLES/DAGLI ORTI

the devil, and so confessions of guilt suggested that the suspected witch (usually an old woman) was actually melancholy (mad). In 1584 Reginald Scot (1538?–1599), a Kentish gentleman, published his *Discoverie of Witchcraft,* an even more radical rejection of witchcraft that questioned even the power of demons to produce wonders or harm of any sort. During the seventeenth century these sorts of skepticism were reinforced by a growing procedural skepticism of the sort expressed anonymously by Frederick Spee, S.J. (1591–1635), in his *Cautio Criminalis* (1631; A warning concerning criminal cases). Spee movingly criticized the brutal employment of torture, the reliance on perjured testimony, and twisted interpretations of the law, so that in his view no one once accused could expect to escape conviction. Doubts like these finally made an impression all across northern Europe, so that the secular courts there became as skeptical as the Roman and Spanish Inquisitions had been ever since the mid-sixteenth century. Only after witchcraft trials had almost died away did a more fundamental skepticism spread, a philosophical or theological doubt that spirits of any sort could have any physical effects in this world. Here we may point to the example of Balthasar Bekker (1634–1698), the Dutch reformed theologian, whose *Betoverde Weereld* (1691; The world bewitched) did not challenge the existence of demons but tried to show that they could not affect human affairs or the natural world. In his view the doctrine of demons had crept into Catholic Christianity from the pagans and needed to be thoroughly reformed. Christian Thomasius (1655–1728), a celebrated jurist of the University of Halle, took a similar position in *De Crimine Magiae* (1701; Regarding the crime of magic).

It is noteworthy that witchcraft remained controversial, at least among theologians, well after the crime of witchcraft was essentially no longer pursued. The Netherlands had ceased prosecuting this crime around 1600 and the Parlement of Paris had made witchcraft hard to prove by the early seventeenth century, but it was not until 1682 that King Louis XIV (ruled 1643–1715) prohibited witchcraft trials in France, while England did not abolish the crime until 1736, and Austria and Hungary waited until 1755 and 1768, respectively, for this step. Even after these legal reforms were imposed,

certain theologians and many villagers continued to believe in magic and to fear the powers of witchcraft.

*See also* **Astrology; Charles V (Holy Roman Empire); Crime and Punishment; Folk Tales and Fairy Tales; Inquisition; Magic; Midwives; Popular Culture; Religious Piety; Thomasius, Christian; Women.**

BIBLIOGRAPHY

Ankarloo, Bengt, and Gustav Henningsen, eds. *Early Modern European Witchcraft: Centres and Peripheries.* Oxford, 1990.

Bailey, Michael D. *Battling Demons: Witchcraft, Heresy, and Reform in the Late Middle Ages.* University Park, Pa., 2003.

Behringer, Wolfgang. *Shaman of Oberstdorf: Chonrad Stoeckhlin and the Phantoms of the Night.* Translated by H. C. Erik Midelfort. Charlottesville, Va., 1998.

Briggs, Robin. *Witches and Neighbors: The Social and Cultural Context of Early Modern Witchcraft.* New York, 1996.

Clark, Stuart. *Thinking with Demons: The Idea of Witchcraft in Early Modern Europe.* Oxford, 1997.

Clark, Stuart, ed. *Languages of Witchcraft: Narrative, Ideology, and Meaning in Early Modern Culture.* London, 2001.

Cohn, Norman. *Europe's Inner Demons: An Enquiry Inspired by the Great Witch-Hunt.* London, 1975.

Davies, Owen. *Witchcraft, Magic, and Culture, 1736–1951.* Manchester, U.K., 1999.

Ginzburg, Carlo. *The Night Battles: Witchcraft and Agrarian Cults in the Sixteenth and Seventeenth Centuries.* Translated by J. and A. Tedeschi. Baltimore, 1983.

Henningsen, Gustav. *The Witches' Advocate: Basque Witchcraft and the Spanish Inquisition (1609–1614).* Reno, Nev., 1980.

Kieckhefer, Richard. *European Witch Trials: Their Foundation in Popular and Learned Culture, 1300–1500.* Berkeley, 1976.

Levack, Brian. *The Witch-Hunt in Early Modern Europe.* 2nd ed. London, 1995.

Pócs, Éva. *Fairies and Witches at the Boundary of South-Eastern and Central Europe.* Helsinki, 1989.

Roper, Lyndal. *Oedipus and the Devil: Witchcraft, Sexuality, and Religion in Early Modern Europe.* London, 1994.

Sharpe, James A. *Instruments of Darkness: Witchcraft in Early Modern England.* Philadelphia, 1997.

Soman, Alfred. *Sorcellerie et justice criminelle: Le Parlement de Paris (16e–18e Siècles).* Aldershot, U.K., 1992.

Thomas, Keith. *Religion and the Decline of Magic: Studies in Popular Beliefs in Sixteenth- and Seventeenth-Century England.* 2nd ed. London, 1997.

Zika, Charles. *Exorcising Our Demons: Magic, Witchcraft, and Visual Culture in Early Modern Europe.* Leiden, Netherlands, 2003.

H. C. Erik Midelfort

---

# WITT, JOHAN AND CORNELIS DE

(Johan 1625–1672; Cornelis 1623–1672), Dutch statesmen and patriots. The de Witt brothers, leading statesmen of the Dutch Republic and opponents of the House of Orange from 1653 to 1672, were born in Dordrecht, a city in the south of the province of Holland, where their father, Jacob de Witt, had already served several times as alderman and burgomaster. Together Johan and Cornelis went to the Latin School and studied law at the University of Leiden. They completed their education with a grand tour through France and England. About this time it was evident that Johan possessed extraordinary mental powers, notably in the field of mathematics. In the course of his busy life he would find time to publish a pioneering work on geometry, *The Elements of Curved Lines* (1659), and his masterpiece, *The Worth of Life Annuities Compared to Redemption Bonds* (1671), which is regarded today by historians of insurance as the foundation of modern actuarial science.

The brothers started their careers in a turbulent time when international developments and national events created unprecedented opportunities. First there was the Peace of Westphalia (1648), which ended the wars the Dutch had fought for eighty years (1568–1648) against the Spanish oppressor. The treaty was an official recognition of the Dutch territory as the United Provinces. The treaty also brought peace, and it was precisely this peace that caused havoc. The princes of Orange had led the army against the Spanish, and the cities had provided the funds, but now the peace broke up their confluence of interests. The merchants wanted to reduce the army budget and use their money for investments in trade and for the reduction of their enormous debts, but the young prince of Orange, William II (1626–1650), could not accept the prospect of being stripped of this glamorous part of the family heritage.

The second development took place across the English Channel, where Oliver Cromwell had put an end to the kingship of Charles I, William II's father-in-law. When Charles was beheaded in 1649, William wanted to bring the Stuarts back to power, which meant starting a new war. This was anathema to the regents of Holland, the wealthy non-noble patricians of the cities. The conflict between the prince of Orange and the cities of Holland therefore escalated rapidly. In 1650 William incarcerated several leading regents, one of whom was Jacob de Witt, and tried in vain to conquer Amsterdam. William died of smallpox that same year, and a collective aversion to monarchical power surfaced among the regents. This mood was not tempered by the birth of William III eight days after the death of his father. Holland and the six other provinces decided that the Dutch Republic could do without a singular authority, that the state would be governed by the city aristocracies, and proudly called this "True Freedom" *(de Ware Vrijheid)*. Along with it came a tolerant attitude toward various religious groups and a keen eye for the connection between peace and prosperity. Of this set of values Johan de Witt became the eloquent spokesman.

Johan and Cornelis went separate ways, but both achieved powerful positions. Cornelis became a foremost member of the administration of his hometown of Dordrecht and married the daughter of an important aristocrat from Rotterdam. With the help of his brother, he became chief justice of a large area. Johan's star rose higher. On 30 July 1653, at the age of 28, he was appointed *raadpensionaris* or grand pensionary of Holland, chairman of the assembly of the States of Holland. Because this province was by far the wealthiest and most powerful of the Dutch Republic, it dominated the assembly of the States-General, so Johan became in fact the political leader of the nation. In 1655 he married Wendela Bicker, whose father was the most influential regent of Amsterdam and had been the leader of the resistance against William II.

Before Johan started his term as grand pensionary, the First Anglo-Dutch War (1652–1654) broke out. Johan managed to strengthen the navy and to conclude the war as quickly as possible, but he paid a high price for the peace: the Act of Seclusion (1654), a secret concession to Cromwell, which stated that no prince of Orange was to be stadtholder or captain-general. When the other six provinces learned about it, a storm of indignation came down on Johan's head. Much of the hatred that was later directed at him originated from this act. During the twenty years of his rule, Johan tried to curtail the power of William III. But the older the prince became, the more difficult it was to contain support for him. The gap between the proponents of the "true freedom" and the supporters of the prince, many of whom saw him as a kind of messiah, became unsurmountable.

The Restoration (1660) in England brought Charles II, William's brother-in-law, to power. Charles grew into a dedicated enemy of the Dutch Republic and of Johan personally, whose domestic position he tried to undermine by persuading the Orangist party that the grand pensionary had denied William his family rights. When the Second Anglo-Dutch War (1665–1667) broke out, Johan sailed several times with the fleet to encourage the commanders to take offensive action. In the summer of 1667 Cornelis de Witt executed a bold plan devised by Johan: with a flotilla he raided the Chatham Dockyards and not only destroyed the biggest ships, but also towed home the *Royal Charles*. After this humiliation, Charles was forced to sign the peace, the Treaty of Breda.

Meanwhile, Louis XIV of France was usurping large parts of the Spanish Netherlands in the War of Devolution; this was the territory that Johan wanted to keep as a buffer against mighty France. On 23 January 1668 he concluded the Triple Alliance with England and Sweden, and the war ended with the Treaty of Aachen (Aix-la-Chapelle) in May 1668. But two years later Louis and Charles entered into the secret Treaty of Dover, by which the latter promised the former to assist in a full-scale attack on the Dutch Republic.

For more than a year Johan did not recognize the bad omens. He was too much of a rationalist and counted completely on the balance of power, believing that both France and England would be at a disadvantage when the other got hold of the United Provinces. He was incapable of understanding that the French and English kings would work together in destroying the Dutch Republic, because he thought it would be fatal to their own interests. He also did not grasp the fact that kings could start

wars out of injured pride. When the assault came in June 1672, it was too late. Louis XIV invaded Holland and began the third of the Anglo-Dutch Wars. The Dutch defeated the English and French navies, but the immense French army crushed its opponent in a matter of weeks. Panic raged through the republic and a hunt for scapegoats ensued. Popular feeling suddenly turned in favor of William III, and he was made stadtholder by popular acclaim. Hatred against the De Witt brothers resulted in an attempt on Johan's life and the detention of Cornelis, who was accused of planning to assassinate William III. On 20 August Johan, who was visiting his brother in prison, and Cornelis were lynched by the people of The Hague; in the frenzy the bodies were mutilated, bowels were eaten, and fingers and tongues collected as souvenirs. Among scholars it is still a matter of dispute whether Prince William III was behind the bloodbath.

*See also* **Anglo-Dutch Naval Wars; Devolution, War of (1667–1668); Dutch Republic; Louis XIV (France); Netherlands, Southern; Westphalia, Peace of (1648); William and Mary.**

BIBLIOGRAPHY

Geddes, James. *History of the Administration of John de Witt, Grand Pensionary of Holland.* Vol. I (only vol. published). New York, 1880.

Geyl, Pieter. *Orange and Stuart 1641–1672.* Translated from the Dutch by A. Pomerans. London, 1969.

Levèvre-Pontalis, Germain Antonin. *John de Witt, Grand Pensionary of Holland, or Twenty Years of a Parliamentary Republic.* Translated from the French by S. E. and E. Stephenson. 2 vols. London, 1885.

Rowen, Herbert H. *John de Witt, Grand Pensionary of Holland 1625–1672.* Princeton, 1978.

LUC PANHUYSEN

# WITTELSBACH DYNASTY (BAVARIA).

The Wittelsbachs were one of the more important dynasties in European history. They ruled Bavaria (1180–1918), the Palatinate (1214–1918), and Electoral Cologne (1583–1761), as well as half a dozen prince-bishoprics (Freising, Liège, Münster, Osnabrück, Paderborn, and Regensburg), and they held up to three electoral votes in the Holy Roman Empire during the early modern period. Three Wittelsbachs were elected Holy Roman emperor (1314–1347, 1400–1410, 1742–1745), some ruled as counts of Holland and Friesland (1349–1425), one became king of Denmark, Sweden, and Norway (1440–1448), two became kings of Bohemia (1619–1620, 1741–1745), four succeeded to the throne of Sweden (1654–1720), and one was made king of Greece (1832–1862). An attempt to succeed the Habsburgs in Spain failed in 1699, as did other attempts to assume the status of a major dynasty. The Wittelsbachs rose to princely status as supporters of the Hohenstaufen dynasty in the twelfth century, deriving their name from the tiny castle of Oberwittelsbach in Bavaria (in the district of Aichach, near Augsburg).

## THE BAVARIAN WITTELSBACHS

The Wittelsbachs molded the history of Bavaria, which they ruled as dukes (1180–1623), prince-electors (1623–1806), and later kings (1806–1918). Otto I von Wittelsbach, appointed by Emperor Frederick I Barbarossa in 1180, and his son Louis I, who received the Palatinate in 1214 from Emperor Frederick II von Hohenstaufen, were the founding fathers of the dynasty. The Wittelsbach coat of arms, assembled during this period, includes the Hohenstaufen lion as well as the colors white and blue from the counts of Bogen, inherited through Ludmilla of Bogen (daughter of Frederick Přemysl, duke of Bohemia), and Elisabeth of Hungary, the wife of Louis I.

The first Wittelsbach emperor, Louis IV (ruled 1314–1347), attracted Franciscan celebrities and philosophers like William of Ockham and Marsilius of Padua to his court at Munich; Pope John XXII disdainfully branded him Ludovicus Bavarus (Louis the Bavarian). The emperor married Margaret of Holland, and his numerous children married into the dynasties of Lancaster, Cleves, Denmark, Mecklenburg, Poland, Brzeg, Bohemia, Hungary, Nuremberg (the Hohenzollerns), Hohenlohe, Lower Bavaria, the Tyrol, Verona (the della Scala, or Scaliger, family), and Sicily. The emperor's attempt to spread Wittelsbach rule over large parts of Europe—with his sons ruling over Holland, Zeeland, Friesland, Hainaut (Hennegouwen), Brandenburg, Bavaria, and the Tyrol—failed, but Louis's legacy influenced Bavarian politics in the early modern period, raising ambitions and inspiring historiography.

More concretely, the Treaty of Pavia (1329), in which Louis divided the Wittelsbachs into a Bavarian and a Palatine branch, actually maintained dynastic unity in order to secure mutual succession, concluding with the unification of the house of Wittelsbach in 1777 and 1799.

Throughout the early modern period the Bavarian Wittelsbachs based their politics on their core territory, securing it carefully with dynastic and religious alliances. They managed to bring about sustained development and to create not only a modern territorial state, but even a Bavarian nation. Albert IV the Wise of Bavaria-Munich (ruled 1465–1508), married to a Habsburg princess, obtained territorial unity in the Bavarian War of Succession (1504) and by issuing a law of primogeniture (1506). William IV (ruled 1508–1550) molded a policy of absolute Catholicity in the period of the Reformation. Bavarian princes married exclusively Catholic princesses, primarily of the houses of Habsburg, Lorraine, and Savoy. The dynastic alliance of Albert V (ruled 1550–1579) and Anna of Austria guaranteed an austere Counter-Reformation. Catholicism was indeed transformed into a state ideology. William V the Pious (ruled 1579–1597) compensated for his weak character with religious determination, guided by Jesuit advisers. He intervened in the Cologne War (1583), leading his territory close to bankruptcy, and had to resign. However, he secured the Bavarian secundogeniture in the Lower Rhine region and Bavarian rule over the ecclesiastical lands of Cologne, Münster, Hildesheim, Paderborn, Osnabrück, Liège, and the abbacies of Stavelot and Malmedy.

Maximilian I (ruled 1597–1651) was the most powerful of all the Wittelsbachs. Like his Lorraine cousins in France, he managed to assume leadership, and he forged a Catholic League in Germany (1610). He defeated his Wittelsbach cousin in Bohemia (1620), gained the Palatine dignity of prince-elector (1623), and annexed the Upper Palatinate (1628), leading his country through the horrors of the Thirty Years' War and eventually supporting the Peace of Westphalia. His son Ferdinand Maria (ruled 1651–1679) consolidated the country during the postwar depression and introduced the culture of the baroque, together with his wife Henriette Adelaide of Savoy. Maximilian II Emanuel (ruled 1679–1726), the "blue prince," fought successfully in the wars against the Turks and served as a governor in the Spanish Netherlands from 1691, but failed in his aspirations to the secure the Spanish succession for his son by Maria Antonia of Spain, prince Joseph Ferdinand (1692–1699), who died at the most unfavorable moment. Charles Albert, Maximilian II's son by a Polish princess, was elected king of Bohemia and became Emperor Charles VII (ruled 1742–1745), his rule marked by war and financial exhaustion. Maximilian III Joseph (ruled 1745–1777), an enlightened prince and astute reformer, became the last prince-elector of the Bavarian line. According to the Treaty of Pavia (1329), he was succeeded by a Palatine prince.

## THE PALATINE WITTELSBACHS

The history of the Palatine Wittelsbachs is much more complicated and confused, as their territory remained fragmented throughout the early modern period, and the dynasty suffered from endless divisions. This creative chaos had its positive sides, as it guaranteed a plurality of voices and eventually secured the survival of the Wittelsbach dynasty. The Wittelsbach electoral vote was given to the Palatines by the Golden Bull of 1356. Rupert III managed to become German king (Rupert I von der Pfalz, or 'of the Palatinate'; ruled 1400–1410). As in the case of the Bavarian emperor, after his death the land was divided into four lines—the electoral line (*Kurpfalz*, or Electoral Palatinate), Palatinate-Neumarkt, Palatinate-Simmern, and Palatinate-Mosbach—with a good number of subdivisions. Of growing importance were the line Palatinate-Simmern, which succeeded to the electoral line with Frederick III (ruled 1559–1576), and its sideline Palatinate-Zweibrücken (founded 1459), which branched out into Palatinate-Neuburg (1614), Palatinate-Zweibrücken-Birkenfeld (1569), and Palatinate-Sulzbach (1614).

Some of the Palatine Wittelsbachs adopted Protestantism, and the elector palatine assumed leadership of the Protestant party (Heidelberg Catechism, 1563) in the Holy Roman Empire. The Calvinist Frederick V (ruled 1610–1632), son-in-law of James I of England through his 1613 marriage to Elizabeth Stuart, was elected king of Bohemia (4 November 1619) but—despite Dutch, English, and Danish support—was deposed by his Bavarian cousin in 1620; he is thus remembered as the

"Winter King." His son Rupert (1619–1682) fought as a general in the English Civil War, became privy councillor to Charles II, and discovered Rupert's Land (the drainage basin of Hudson's Bay) in Canada. The Palatine Wittelsbachs won back their territory in 1648, along with an additional (eighth) electoral vote. Charles I Louis (ruled 1648–1680) introduced toleration, admitting Lutherans, Mennonites, Jews, and Catholics to the Palatinate. His son remained childless, however, and his daughter Elizabeth Charlotte's (1652–1722) marriage to Duke Philip I of Orléans was utilized by France as a pretext to invade and devastate the Palatinate in the War of the Palatine Succession (1688–1697).

In 1685 the Electoral Palatinate was inherited by the Catholic Palatinate-Neuburg line. Wolfgang William of Palatinate-Neuburg (ruled 1610–1653), who had been raised as a Lutheran, had maintained his claims in the Jülich-Cleves Succession War and converted to Catholicism after marrying a sister of Maximilian of Bavaria in 1613. The new Palatine ruler in Düsseldorf, the ruler of the duchies of Jülich and Berg, married a princess of Palatinate-Zweibrücken, confirming his line's claim of succession in the Electoral Palatinate. The Neuburgers eventually succeeded to the main electoral line in Heidelberg in 1685/1699 with Elector Philip William. Their policy of re-Catholicization drove many subjects to emigrate, some to North America. When the Neuburger line ended with Elector Charles III Philip in 1742, they were succeeded by the princes of Palatinate-Sulzbach, a sideline of the Neuburgers, famous for their Rosicrucian commitment under Prince Christian August (1622–1708). Although married to a Calvinist princess of Nassau, Christian August personally converted to Catholicism but admitted all confessions and invited the Jews into his territory.

The Sulzbacher elector palatine Charles Theodore (ruled 1743–1799) inherited Bavaria in 1777 and shifted the Palatine court to Munich, but he remained childless. In the end the count of the tiny Palatinate-Zweibrücken-Birkenfeld inherited not only all the Palatine lines (1795 Zweibrücken, 1799 Electorial Palatinate), but also the throne in Munich. For the first time since 1329 all the Wittelsbach territories were united under one single ruler, after 470 years. After the collapse of the Holy Roman Empire in 1806, Maximilian IV Joseph (ruled 1799–1825), supported by Napoleon I, gained territorial independence and became King Maximilian I Joseph of Bavaria. His descendents stayed in power in an enlarged kingdom of Bavaria (with added lands from Swabia and Franconia) until the revolution of 1918. The Wittelsbach family, despite the official abolition of nobility, is still honored by the Bavarian government to the present day.

An offshoot of the Palatine Wittelsbachs became kings of Sweden in the seventeenth century, when the younger son of the Calvinist prince John I of Palatinate-Zweibrücken, John Casimir of Palatinate-Kleeburg in Alsace, married Catherine, a daughter of King Charles IX of Sweden. After Queen Christina Vasa converted to Catholicism and abdicated in 1654, the son of John Casimir and Catherine, educated as a Lutheran, came to the Swedish throne as Charles X Gustav (ruled 1654–1660). Under the Wittelsbach ruler Charles XI (ruled 1660/1672–1697) Sweden became the hegemonic power in northern Europe, ruling over Finland, Estonia, Latvia, Livonia, and Pomerania. Charles XII (ruled 1697–1718) maintained this position in the Great Northern War, but remained without an heir and was briefly succeeded by his sister Ulrika Eleonora (ruled 1718–1720). Her husband Frederick of Hessen-Kassel (ruled as Frederick I, 1720–1751) was elected Swedish king in 1720. All Wittelsbach rulers, even the Swedish kings, shared the titles of duke of Bavaria and Count Palatine of the Rhine.

*See also* **Bavaria; Charles X Gustav (Sweden); Holy Roman Empire; Palatinate; Reformation, Catholic; Reformation, Protestant; Thirty Years' War (1618–1648).**

BIBLIOGRAPHY

Glaser, Hermann, ed. *Wittelsbach und Bayern.* Munich, 1980.

Rall, Hans, and Marga Rall. *Die Wittelsbacher in Lebensbildern.* Graz, Austria, and Regensburg, Germany, 1986.

Spindler, Max, ed. *Handbuch der bayerischen Geschichte.* 4 vols. Munich, 1967–1975.

Straub, Eberhard. *Die Wittelsbacher.* Berlin, 1994.

WOLFGANG BEHRINGER

# WŁADYSŁAW II JAGIEŁŁO (POLAND) (Lithuanian: Jogaila; c. 1351–1434), grand duke of Lithuania (1377–1401) and king of Poland (1386–1434); son of Grand Duke Algirdas of Lithuania (d. 1375) and Yuliana, princess of Tver; and founder of the Jagiellon dynasty in Poland. In 1382 Jogaila imprisoned his uncle Kêstutis, with whom he had ruled jointly, and assumed full power in Lithuania; he later had Kêstutis murdered. That same year, threatened by the Order of Teutonic Knights, he concluded an armistice with them on the Dubysa River, in which he gave up the western part of Samogitia and promised to adopt the Christian faith. The agreement was broken in 1383 and Jogaila, seeing that a union with Poland would give him support against the Teutonic Knights, negotiated a union between the Grand Duchy of Lithuania and Poland at Krewo (14 August 1385). In return for the hand of Queen Jadwiga of Poland, he promised to Christianize the Grand Duchy, associate (*applicare* in Latin) its territories with Poland, and recover the territories lost by Poland (Gdańsk, Pomerania, Kujavia, Silesia, Halicz Ruthenia).

In 1388 Jogaila, now King Władysław Jagiełło, restored Mazovia's feudal dependence on Poland. From 1388 to 1392 he waged war against the Teutonic Knights and their ally, his cousin Vytautas (Witold). The war was brought to an end in 1392 by an agreement making Vytautas viceroy of the Grand Duchy of Lithuania. The Teutonic Order's attempts to conquer Lithuania and sever its union with Poland achieved partial success when Vytautas gave up Samogitia in 1398 (confirmed by treaty at Raciąż in 1404). In 1409 the Teutonic Knights resumed the war but were routed by Polish-Lithuanian forces under Jagiełło's command at the battle of Grunwald (Tannenberg; 15 July 1410). Even though the Poles did not take advantage of their victory militarily or politically (the Treaty of Toruń, concluded in 1411, was unfavorable to Poland), the battle marked the beginning of the decline of the Teutonic state's power. The fighting against the Teutonic Knights in the years that followed proved successful for the Polish-Lithuanian side.

The childless death of Queen Jadwiga (1399) weakened Jagiełło's position as king of Poland and made it necessary to renew the union with the Grand Duchy of Lithuania and settle the question of succession to the throne. The Treaty of Vilnius (1401) confirmed the union of the two states and recognized Vytautas as grand duke of Lithuania; the union was further strengthened by a new treaty concluded at Horodo on 2 October 1413. Jagiełło's second marriage, with Anna, princess of Cilli (1402) and granddaughter of King Casimir III the Great, was meant to strengthen his legal position in Poland.

In 1421 the Hussites urged Jagiełło to accept the Bohemian throne, but he declined the offer and in 1424 issued an edict condemning Hussitism and threatening severe punishment for its believers and adherents. Having no male heir (Anna died in 1416, and his third wife, Elizabeth Granowska, died in 1420), Jagiełło contracted a fourth marriage (1422) with Sophia Holszańska, who bore him two sons, who became Władysław III Warneńczyk (ruled 1434–1444) and Casimir IV Jagiellończyk (ruled 1447–1492). In order to gain the nobility's support and secure the throne for his dynasty, the king confirmed the nobles' privileges in an act signed at Jedno (1430). In addition to his successes in foreign policy, Jagiełło also deserves credit for the restoration of the university in Cracow (1400). He was buried in the cathedral on Wawel Hill.

*See also* **Jadwiga (Poland); Jagiellon Dynasty; Lithuania, Grand Duchy of, to 1569; Lublin, Union of (1569); Poland to 1569.**

BIBLIOGRAPHY

Krzyżaniakowa, Jadwiga, and Jerzy Ochmański. *Władysław Jagiełło.* Wrocław, 1990.

MARCIN KAMLER

---

# WOLFF, CHRISTIAN (1679–1754), German philosopher. Born on 24 January 1679 in predominantly Catholic Breslau, Silesia (now Wrocław, Poland), the son of a Lutheran tanner who wanted him to become a minister, Wolff soon developed an interest in philosophy. After receiving a solid grounding in Scholasticism and Cartesianism under Jesuit supervision at the local *Gymnasium* (college preparatory school), Wolff began to study theology, mathematics, and philosophy at the University of Jena. He eventually earned his master's degree from the University of Leipzig in 1703, where his interest had shifted increasingly toward mathematics and philosophy, both of which he regarded as useful disciplines to solve religious disputes. His dissertation, *De philosophia practica universali methodo mathematica conscripta* (1702; Practical philosophy according to mathematical methods), drew the attention of Gottfried Wilhelm Leibniz (1646–1716), whose letter of recommendation helped Wolff secure a professorship in mathematics at the University of Halle in 1706.

Although officially a professor of mathematics, Wolff lectured on experimental and theoretical physics, metaphysics, moral philosophy, and logic. At Halle, he published his most important works in philosophy including *Vernünfftige Gedancken von den Kräfften des menschlichen Verstandes* (1713; Rational thoughts on the powers of human understanding), *Vernünfftige Gedancken von Gott, der Welt, und der Seele des Menschen, auch allen Dingen überhaupt* (1720; Rational thoughts on God, the world, and the human soul, and all things in general), and *Vernünfftige Gedancken von der Menschen Thun und Lassen, zu Beförderung ihrer Glückseeligkeit, den Liebhabern der Wahrheit mitgetheilet* (1720; Rational thoughts on human conduct for the purpose of their happiness, told to those who love the truth), all of which were written in German. Ever since, Wolff has been regarded as the founder of a German philosophical language. His fame, however, did not save him from attacks by leading Pietist members of the theological faculty at Halle, such as Joachim Lange (1670–1744), who viewed Wolff as an advocate of a deterministic universe and as a potential danger to Christian dogma. The conflict escalated on the occasion of Wolff's public lecture, "De Sinarum philosophia practica" (1721; On the practical philosophy of the Chinese), which emphasized that revelation was not essential for arriving at sound moral principles. His opponents successfully appealed to King Frederick William I of Prussia (ruled 1713–1740), who issued an official warrant on 8 November 1723, demanding his departure from Halle within forty-eight hours under the threat of death by hanging. Wolff subsequently accepted a position as professor of philosophy at the University of Marburg until 1740, when the new King Frederick II of Prussia (ruled 1740–1786) invited him to return to Halle. At the time of his death on 9 April 1754, Wolff held the position of chancellor of the University of Halle and was privy councillor of Prussia, vice president of the Academy of St. Petersburg, and baron of the Holy Roman Empire.

Wolff's philosophical system builds on mathematical principles. He regarded the "mathematical method" as a guarantor for clarity because it connected premises and deductions into a chain of closely intertwined demonstrations. Although his philosophy was labeled as "Leibniz-Wolffian" as early as 1724—probably by one of his students, Georg Bernhard Bilfinger (1693–1750)—Wolff himself rejected this adjective without denying Leibniz's profound influence on him. He surpassed his famous predecessor by developing a more comprehensive system of philosophy, thereby linking all the individual disciplines with each other. He viewed philosophy as the science of all possible things. By *possible* Wolff meant anything that does not contain a logical contradiction, which is a lack of sufficient reason. In contrast to theology, which concerns itself with the supernatural, philosophy represents world wisdom. This marked a shift away from his predecessor Leibniz, who had always tried to prevent philosophy and theology from going their separate ways. Because, according to Wolff, attributes of the visible world proved God's existence, one branch of theology, the *theologia naturalis* ('natural theology') can, in accordance with the laws of reason, engage in determining God's qualities. Although he asserted that Christianity is based on the only true revelation, he nonetheless claimed that, at least in theory, certain standards must apply as well in order to distinguish it from false revelation. By making this suggestion, Wolff laid the foundation for a critical (rational) examination of revealed religion.

Christian Wolff was certainly the most important German philosopher between Leibniz and Immanuel Kant (1724–1804). In his *Kritik der reinen Vernunft* (1781; Critique of pure reason), Kant praised him as the "founder of the spirit of thoroughness in Germany." Wolff was the first modern thinker to write extensively in German. The rigor and clarity of his methodology helped emancipate philosophy from theology as an independent discipline. Wolffian principles, such as his emphasis on sufficient reason, encouraged radical biblical critics such as Johann Lorenz Schmidt (1702–1749) and

Hermann Samuel Reimarus (1694–1768) to examine and reject Christian revelation by subjecting Scripture to its rational principles. Nonetheless, one should not forget that Wolff's incorporation of Scholastic elements in his system and his conservative metaphysics made his philosophy equally appealing to Protestants and Catholics alike, both of whom viewed it as a useful defense against atheism and deism.

Wolff's influence reached even beyond the German territories. The concept of philosophy, as it appears in Diderot's and d'Alembert's *Encyclopédie*, can almost be called a precise copy of his definition of philosophy from his *Discursus praeliminaris de philosophia in genere* (1728; Preliminary discourse on philosophy in general).

*See also* **Alembert, Jean Le Rond d'; Atheism; Cartesianism; Deism; Descartes, René; Diderot, Denis; *Encyclopédie*; Enlightenment; Frederick II (Prussia); Frederick William I (Prussia); Kant, Immanuel; Leibniz, Gottfried Wilhelm; Logic; Mathematics; Philosophy; Physics; Pietism; Theology.**

BIBLIOGRAPHY

*Primary Sources*

Wolff, Christian. *Gesammelte Werke*. Edited by Jean École, et al. Hildesheim and New York, 1962–.

———. *Preliminary Discourse on Philosophy in General*. Translated by R. J. Blackwell. Indianapolis, 1963.

———. "Reasonable Thoughts on the Actions of Men, for the Promotion of Their Happiness." In *Moral Philosophy from Montaigne to Kant*, vol. 1, edited by J. B. Schneewind, pp. 333–350. Cambridge, Mass., 1990.

*Secondary Sources*

Blackwell, Richard. "The Structure of Wolffian Philosophy." *Modern Schoolman* 38 (1961): 203–218.

Carboncini, Sonia. *Transzendentale Wahrheit und Traum: Christian Wolffs Antwort auf die Herausforderung durch den cartesianischen Zweifel*. Stuttgart-Bad Cannstatt, 1991.

École, Jean. "Wolff était-il un Aufklärer?" In *Aufklärung als praktische Philosophie*, edited by Frank Gunert, et al., pp. 31–44. Tübingen, 1998.

Frängsmyr, Tore. "Christian Wolff's Mathematical Method and Its Impact on the Eighteenth Century." *Journal of the History of Ideas* 36 (1975): 653–668.

Morrison, J. C. "Christian Wolff's Criticism of Spinoza." *Journal of the History of Philosophy* 31 (1993): 182–213.

Saine, Thomas P. *The Problem of Being Modern, or, the German Pursuit of Enlightenment from Leibniz to the French Revolution*. Detroit, Mich., 1997.

Schneiders, Werner, ed. *Christian Wolff, 1679–1754: Interpretationen zu seiner Philosophie und deren Wirkung.* Hamburg, 1983.

Wundt, Max. *Die Deutsche Schulphilosophie im Zeitalter der Aufklärung.* Tübingen, 1945. Reprint, Hildesheim, 1964.

ULRICH GROETSCH

**WOMEN.** As they have in all the world's cultures, women made up about half the population in early modern Europe, and their experiences were thus nearly as varied as those of men. Like those of men, women's experiences differed according to social class, geographic location, religious affiliation, ethnicity, and rural or urban setting. The life of Queen Elizabeth of England—probably the most powerful and famous woman from this period—was far more like that of her male relatives than like that of a peasant woman in Poland or the Ottoman Empire, or even a peasant woman on one of Elizabeth's own estates. She was highly educated, spoke many languages, held legitimate authority over many people, ate well, and lived quite comfortably, while peasant women—and men—had none of these advantages.

The great changes of the period had widely varying effects on women, creating greater opportunities for some women in some places while lessening opportunities for other women elsewhere. The expansion of rural cloth production, for example, created better-paying work for single women in parts of France, but lessened the demand for cloth made by married Irish women. Leaders of the Protestant Reformation supported teaching girls to read the Bible, but also advocated the closing of convents that provided a place where learned women could study and teach. Urban women in western Europe were increasingly able to obtain cheaper and more diverse consumer goods, but these were often produced in Europe's overseas colonies by men and women working in horrific conditions.

Despite this variety, however, all women in Europe lived in a society that regarded women as inferior to men. This idea undergirded and shaped legal systems, family relationships, inheritance patterns, religious doctrine and institutions, educational opportunities, and structures of work throughout all of Europe. Even Queen Elizabeth was not excluded from this, for her life—and the course of English history—would have been very different had she been a man. Many women, from Queen Elizabeth on down, were able to shape their lives to a great extent despite restrictive ideas and systems, but their actions did not upset the underlying hierarchy of gender. This essay will first examine trends in the way that women's history of the early modern period has been conceptualized and studied, and then explore three realms of life that were especially important in shaping early modern women's situation and experiences: legal systems, work, and religious life.

### EARLY MODERN WOMEN'S HISTORY

Intensive study of women in the early modern period, as in most periods, began in the 1970s by asking what women contributed to developments regarded as central to the period, such as the Renaissance, the Reformation, the development of capitalism, the creation of colonial empires, or the rise of the centralized state: Who were the great women artists/musicians/scientists/rulers? How did women's work serve capitalist expansion? What was women's role in political movements such as the English Civil War or other seventeenth-century revolts? Along with this, historians investigated what effects the developments of the early modern period had on women: What was the impact of the Reformation on women's lives? How did the scientific revolution or the Enlightenment shape ideas about women's place? What new products or opportunities were offered to women because of overseas empires?

Both these original lines of questioning continue, particularly for parts of Europe or groups of women that were slower to be studied, such as eastern Europe, Jewish women, or peasant women. They have been augmented more recently by quite different types of questions, as historians have realized the limitations of simply trying to fit women into historical developments largely derived from the male experience (an approach rather sarcastically described as "add women and stir"). Such questions often center on women's physical experiences—menstruation, pregnancy, motherhood—and the ways in which women gave meaning to these experiences, and on private or domestic matters, such as friendship networks, family devotional practices, or unpaid household labor. Because so little of this was documented in public sources during the early modern period, this research has required a great amount of archival digging and the use of literary and artistic sources.

To these older and newer lines of inquiry historians have also added questions about the symbolic role of gender, that is, how qualities judged masculine and feminine are differently valued and then used in discussions that do not explicitly relate to men and women, but that still reinforce women's secondary status. Investigations of the real and symbolic relations between gender and power have usually not been based on new types of sources, but have approached some of the most traditional types of historical sources—political treatises, public speeches by monarchs, state documents, religious tracts, and sermons—with new questions.

Taken together, these investigations have resulted in hundreds of books and thousands of articles on many aspects of the lives of early modern women. This is still far less, of course, than the number of books and articles on men, but it has created a much more complex—and interesting—picture than historians of women could have imagined thirty years ago and has changed the way we view many features of early modern life.

## LAW AND LEGAL SYSTEMS

Traditional medieval law codes in Europe accorded women a secondary legal status, based generally on their inability to perform feudal military service; the oldest legal codes required every woman who was not married to have a male legal guardian who could undergo such procedures as trial by combat or trial by ordeal for her. This gender-based guardianship gradually died out in the later Middle Ages as court proceedings replaced physical trials, and unmarried women and widows generally gained the right to hold land on their own and to appear in court on their own behalf. In most parts of Europe, unmarried women and widows could make wills, serve as executors for the wills of others, and serve as witnesses in civil and criminal cases, though they could not serve as witnesses to a will.

Limitations on women's legal rights because of feudal obligations thus lessened in the late Middle Ages, but marriage provided another reason for restricting women's legal role. Marriage was cited as the key reason for excluding women from public offices and duties, for their duty to obey their husbands prevented them from acting as independent persons; the fact that an unmarried woman or widow might possibly get married meant that they, too, were included in this exclusion. A married woman was legally subject to her husband in all things; she could not sue, make contracts, or go to court for any reason without his approval, and in many areas of Europe could not be sued or charged with any civil crime on her own. However, Russian law codes and Islamic law in the Ottoman Empire recognized women's right to sue and be sued as well as certain property and inheritance rights. In many parts of Europe, all goods or property that a wife brought into a marriage and all wages she earned during the marriage were considered the property of her husband, a situation that did not change legally until the nineteenth century.

The husband's control of his wife's property could be modified somewhat by a marriage contract that gave her legal ownership of the dowry she brought into the marriage, or, in some cities, by her declaring herself unmarried (*femme sole*) for legal purposes, such as borrowing and loaning money or making contracts. In the sixteenth century, wives were also gradually allowed to retain control over some family property if they could prove that their husbands were squandering everything through drink, gambling, or bad investments. In addition to these exceptions provided through law codes, it is clear from court records that women often actively managed their dowry property and carried out legal transactions without getting special approval. The proliferation of exceptions and the fact that women were often able to slip through the cracks of urban law codes began to bother jurists who were becoming educated in Roman law with its goals of comprehensiveness and uniformity. Roman law also gave them additional grounds for women's secondary legal status, for it based this not on feudal obligations or a wife's duty to obey her husband but on women's alleged physical and mental weaknesses, their "fragility, imbecility, irresponsibility, and ignorance," in the words of Justinian's sixth-century code. Along with peasants and the simple-minded, women were regarded as not legally responsible for all of their own actions and could not be compelled to appear before a court; in all cases their testimony was regarded as less credible than a man's. These ideas led jurists in many parts of Europe to recommend, and in some cases implement, the reintroduction of gender-based guardianship; unmarried adult women and widows were again given male guardians and were prohibited from making any financial decisions, even donations to religious institutions, without their approval. In many parts of Europe, women lost the right of guardianship over their own children if they remarried.

Increasing restrictions on unmarried and married women continued throughout the early modern period. In 1731, for example, the Paris Parlement passed the *Ordonnance des donations,* which reemphasized the power of the husband over the wife; its provisions limiting women's legal rights later became part of the *Code Napoléon* of the early nineteenth century. The fact that court records show that fewer and fewer women appeared on their own behalf indicates that male guardianship was enforced. Governments generally became less willing to make exceptions in the case of women, as they felt any laxness might disrupt public order.

The spread of Roman law thus had a largely negative effect on women's civil legal status in the early modern period because of both the views of women that jurists chose to adopt from it and the stricter enforcement of existing laws to which it gave rise. Its impact on criminal law was less gender-specific, as was criminal law itself. In general, women throughout Europe were responsible for their own criminal actions and could be tortured and executed just like men. Women were often executed in a manner different from men, buried alive or drowned instead of being beheaded, largely because city executioners thought women would faint at the sight of the sword or ax and make their job more difficult. In Germany, a wife was often included in her husband's banishment for criminal actions—including banishment for adultery!—while the opposite was not the case. In Russia under Ivan the Terrible (ruled 1547–1584), the execution of a husband or father usually meant death for the victim's wife and children as well.

Along with concepts of feudal obligation, wifely obedience, and Roman law, one additional idea was essential in shaping women's legal rights in early modern Europe—the notion of honor. Honor in this period was highly gender-specific, and for women, honor was largely a sexual matter. In most parts of Europe, women of all classes were allowed to bring defamation suits to court for insults to their honor, and it is clear from court records that they did this. Because of ideas of female sinfulness, irrationality, and weakness, however, women, particularly those in the middle and upper classes, were never regarded as able to defend their own honor completely without male assistance. Lower-class women might trade insults or physically fight one another, but middle- and upper-class women were expected to internalize notions of honor and shame and shape their behavior accordingly, depending on male relatives to carry out any public defense of their honor.

## WORK

Though the actual work that men and women performed in the early modern economy was often very similar or the same, their relationships to work and their work identities were very different. Male work rhythms and a man's position in the economy were to a large degree determined by age, class, and training, with boys and men often moving as a group from one level of employment to the next. Female work rhythms were also determined by age and class, but even more so by individual biological and social events such as marriage, motherhood, and widowhood, all of which were experienced by women individually and over which they might have little control. Women often changed occupations several times during their lives or performed many different types of jobs at once, so that their identification with any one occupation was not strong.

Women rarely received formal training in a trade, and during the early modern period many occupations were professionalized, setting up required amounts of formal training and a licensing procedure before one could claim an occupational title. Thus in the Middle Ages both male and female practitioners of medicine were often called "physicians," but by the sixteenth century, although women still healed people, only men who had attended university medical school could be called "physicians." This professionalism trickled down to occupations that did not require university training; women might brew herbal remedies, but only men could use the title "apothecary." Professionalization did not simply affect titles, but also the fees people could charge for their services; a university-trained physician, for example, could easily make ten times the annual salary of a female medical practitioner.

During the early modern period, gender also became an important factor in separating what was considered skilled from what was considered unskilled work. Women were judged to be unfit for certain tasks, such as glass cutting, because they were too clumsy and "unskilled," yet those same women made lace or silk thread, jobs that required an even higher level of dexterity than glass cutting. The gendered notion of work meant that women's work was always valued less and generally paid less than men's. All economies need both structure and flexibility, and during the early modern period these qualities became gender-identified: male labor provided the structure, so that it was regulated, tied to a training process, and lifelong; female labor provided the flexibility, so that it was discontinuous, alternately encouraged or suppressed, not linked to formal training, and generally badly paid. Women's work was thus both marginal and irreplaceable.

Despite enormous economic changes during the early modern period, the vast majority of people in almost all parts of Europe continued to live in the countryside, producing agricultural products for their own use and for the use of their landlords. Agricultural tasks were highly, though not completely, gender-specific, though exactly which tasks were regarded as female and which as male varied widely throughout Europe. These gender divisions were partly the result of physical differences, with men generally doing tasks that required a great deal of upper-body strength, such as cutting grain with a scythe; they were partly the result of women's greater responsibility for child care, so that women carried out tasks closer to the house that could be more easily interrupted for nursing or tending children; they were partly the result of cultural beliefs, so that women in parts of Norway, for example, sowed all grain because people felt this would ensure a bigger harvest. Whatever their source, gender divisions meant that the proper functioning of a rural household required at least one adult male and one adult female; remarriage after the death of a

spouse was much faster in the countryside than in the cities. Women's labor changed as new types of crops and agricultural products were introduced and as agriculture became more specialized. Women in parts of Italy, for example, tended and harvested olive trees and grape vines, and carried out most of the tasks associated with the production of silk: gathering leaves from mulberry trees, raising the silk cocoons, and processing cocoons into raw silk by reeling and spinning. Women also worked as day laborers in agriculture; from wage regulations, we can see that female agricultural laborers were to be paid about half of what men were, and were also to be given less and poorer quality food.

Women also found work in rural areas in non-agricultural tasks, particularly in mining in central Europe and by the sixteenth century in domestic industry. In mining, women carried ore, wood, and salt, sorted and washed ore, and prepared charcoal briquets for use in smelting. In domestic industry, they produced wool, linen, and later cotton thread or cloth (or cloth that was a mixture of these), and were hired by capitalist investors, especially in parts of France, southern Germany, and northern Italy, as part of a household or as an individual. In areas of Europe where whole households were hired, domestic industry often broke down gender divisions, for men, women, and children who were old enough all worked at the same tasks; labor became a more important economic commodity than property, which led to earlier marriage, weaker parental control over children, and more power to women in family decision making. In parts of Europe where women were hired as individuals, men's agricultural tasks were more highly paid, so men continued to make most of the decisions in the family, and there was little change in women's status.

In the cities, domestic service was probably the largest employer of women throughout the period. Girls might begin service as young as seven or eight, traveling from their home village to a nearby town. Cities also offered other types of service employment on a daily or short-term basis. Many of these jobs were viewed as extensions of a woman's functions and tasks in the home—cleaning, cooking, laundering, caring for children and old people, nursing the sick, preparing bodies for burial, mourning the dead. The hospitals, orphanages, and infirmaries run by the Catholic Church were largely staffed by women, as were similar secular institutions that many cities set up beginning in the fifteenth century. In most parts of Europe, women continued to dominate midwifery, the one female occupation whose practitioners developed a sense of work identity nearly as strong as that of men.

The city marketplace, the economic as well as geographic center of most cities, was filled with women; along with rural women with their agricultural and animal products there were city women with sausage, pretzels, meat pies, cookies, candles, soap, and wooden implements they had made. Women sold fresh and salted fish that their husbands had caught or that they had purchased from fishermen, game and fowl they had bought from hunters, and imported food items such as oranges, and, in the eighteenth century, tea and coffee bought from international merchants. Women also ran small retail establishments throughout the city. They made beer, mead, and hard cider, and ran taverns and inns to dispense their beverages and provide sleeping quarters for those too poor to stay in the more established inns. Among Muslim populations in Ottoman urban centers, a number of women vendors, many of them Christians and Jews, catered to upper-class harem women.

Domestic industry provided employment for increasing numbers of urban as well as rural women, particularly in spinning. Early modern techniques of cloth production necessitated up to twenty carders and spinners per weaver, so that cloth centers like Florence, Augsburg, or Antwerp could keep many people employed. The identification of women and spinning became very strong in the early modern period, and by the seventeenth century unmarried women in England came to be called "spinsters."

Women increasingly turned to spinning as other employment avenues were closed to them, particularly in craft guilds, which continued to dominate the production and distribution of most products throughout the early modern period. There were a few all-female guilds in cities with highly specialized economies such as Cologne, Paris, and Rouen, but in general the guilds were male organizations and followed the male life cycle. One became an apprentice at puberty, became a journeyman four to ten years later, traveled around learning from a number of masters, then settled down, married, opened one's own shop, and worked at the same craft full-time until one died or got too old to work any longer. Women fit into guilds much more informally, largely through their relationship to a master as his wife, daughter, or domestic servant. Masters' widows ran shops after the death of their husbands, and were expected to pay all guild fees, though they could not participate in running the guild. As the result of economic decline, the competition of rural and urban proto-industrial development, the increasingly political nature of the guilds, and notions of guild honor, even this informal participation began to be restricted in the fifteenth century on the Continent, however, and women largely lost this relatively high-status work opportunity.

## RELIGION

In Christianity, Judaism, and Islam, the early modern period was a time when the domestic nature of women's acceptable religious activities was reinforced. The proper sphere for the expression of women's religious ideas was a household, whether the secular household of a Jewish, Orthodox, Catholic, Protestant, or Muslim marriage, or the spiritual household of an enclosed Catholic or Orthodox convent. Times of emergency and instability, such as the expulsion of the Jews and Muslims from Spain, the first years of the Protestant Reformation, the English Civil War, or the Schism Crisis in Russia, offered women opportunities to play a public religious role, but these were clearly regarded as extraordinary by male religious thinkers and by many of the women who wrote or spoke publicly during these times. Women who were too assertive in expressing themselves during more stable times, or who were too individualistic in their ideas, risked being termed insane or being imprisoned by religious or secular courts.

Christianity, Judaism, and Islam all contain strong streaks of misogyny and were in the early modern period totally controlled by male hierarchies with the highest (or all) levels of the clergy reserved for men. In all three, God is thought of as male, the account of Creation appears to ascribe or ordain a secondary status for women, and women are instructed to be obedient and subservient; all three religious traditions were used by men as buttresses for male authority in all realms of life, not simply religion. Nevertheless, it was the language of religious texts, and the examples of pious women who preceded them, that were used most often by women to subvert or directly oppose male directives.

Before the Reformation in western Europe and throughout the early modern period in eastern Europe, the most powerful and in many ways independent women in Christianity were the abbesses of certain convents, who controlled large amounts of property and often had jurisdiction over many subjects. Convents had widely varying levels of religious devotion and intellectual life; many were little more than dumping grounds for unmarriagable daughters, while others were important centers of piety and learning. In the fifteenth century many underwent a process of reform designed to enforce strict rules of conduct and higher standards of spirituality. These reforms put convents more closely under the control of a local male bishop, taking away some of the abbess's independent power, but also built up a strong sense of group cohesion among the nuns and gave them a greater sense of the spiritual worth of their lives. In addition to living in convents, a number of women in the late Middle Ages lived in less structured religious communities, supporting themselves by weaving, sewing, or caring for the sick.

Like Christianity itself, the Protestant Reformation both expanded and diminished women's opportunities. The period in which women were most active was the decade or so immediately following an area's decision to break with the Catholic Church, or while this decision was being made. In Germany and many other parts of Europe, that decision was made by a political leader—a prince, duke, king, or city council—who then had to create an alternative religious structure. During this period, many groups and individuals tried to shape the new religious institutions. Sometimes this popular pressure took the form of religious riots, in which women and men destroyed paintings, statues, stained-glass windows, or other objects that symbolized the old religion, or protected such objects from destruction at the hands of government officials; in 1536 at Exeter in England, for example, a group of women armed with shovels and pikes attacked workers who had been hired by the government to dismantle a monastery. Sometimes this popular pressure took the form of writing, when women and men who did not have formal theological training took the notion of the "priesthood of all believers" literally and preached or published polemical religious literature explaining their own ideas.

Women's preaching or publishing religious material stood in direct opposition to the words ascribed to St. Paul (1 Timothy 2:11–15), which ordered women not to teach or preach, so that all women who published felt it necessary to justify their actions. Once Protestant churches were institutionalized, polemical writings by women (and untrained men) largely stopped. Women continued to write hymns and devotional literature, but these were often published posthumously or were designed for private use. Women's actions as well as their writings in the first years of the Reformation upset political and religious authorities. Many cities prohibited women from even getting together to discuss religious matters, and in 1543 an act of Parliament in England banned all women except those of the gentry and nobility from reading the Bible; upper-class women were also prohibited from reading the Bible aloud to others.

Once the Reformation was established, most women expressed their religious convictions in a domestic, rather than public, setting. They prayed and recited the catechism with children and servants, attended sermons, read the Bible or other devotional literature if they were literate, served meals that no longer followed Catholic fast prescriptions, and provided religious instruction for their children. Women's domestic religion frequently took them beyond the household, however, for they gave charitable donations to the needy and often assisted in caring for the ill and indigent. Such domestic and charitable activities were widely praised by Protestant reformers as long as husband and wife agreed in their religious opinions. If there was disagreement, however, most Protestants generally urged the wife to obey her husband rather than what she perceived as God's will.

The Protestant rejection of celibacy had a great impact on female religious, both cloistered nuns and women who lived in less formal religious communities. In most areas becoming Protestant, monasteries and convents were closed; nuns got very small pensions and were expected to return to their families. In parts of Germany where convents had long been powerful, nuns became the most vocal and resolute opponents of the Protestant Reformation; the nuns' firmness combined with other religious and political factors to allow many convents to survive for centuries as Catholic establishments within Protestant territories or even as Lutheran institutions, redefined as educational centers for young women.

The response of the Catholic Church to the Protestant Reformation is often described as two interrelated movements, a Counter-Reformation that attempted to win territory and people back to loyalty to Rome and prevent further spread of Protestant ideas, and a reform of abuses and problems within the Catholic Church that had been recognized as problems by many long before the Protestant Reformation. Women were actively involved in both movements, but their actions were generally judged more acceptable when they were part of a reform drive; even more than the medieval crusades, the fight against Protestants, which was generally couched in very military language and could involve secret missions into "enemy" territory, was to be a masculine affair. Women who felt God had called them to oppose Protestants directly through missionary work, or to carry out the type of active service to the world in schools and hospitals that the Franciscans, Dominicans, and the new orders like the Jesuits were making increasingly popular with men, were largely opposed by the church hierarchy. The Council of Trent, the church council that met between 1545 and 1563 to define what Catholic positions would be on matters of doctrine and discipline, reaffirmed the necessity of cloister for all women religious, though enforcement of this decree came slowly. The only active apostolate left open to religious women was the instruction of girls, and that only within the convent. No nuns were sent to the foreign missions for any public duties, though once colonies were established in the New World and Asia cloistered convents quickly followed.

Some analysts see the period of the later seventeenth and early eighteenth centuries as a time when western European religion was feminized, as large numbers of people turned to groups that emphasized personal conversion, direct communication with God, and moral regeneration. Many of these groups were inspired by or even founded by women, and had a disproportionate number of women among their followers. Women prophesied, published religious works, and even occasionally preached during the English Civil War, and also organized prayer meetings and conventicles in their houses. Quaker women preached throughout England and the English colonies in the New World, and were active as missionaries also in Ireland and Continental Europe well into the eighteenth century. Jansenism, a movement primarily within the French Catholic Church that emphasized personal holiness and spiritual renewal, attracted many women, and the convent of Port-Royal in Paris became the movement's spiritual center. In Germany, Pietism developed as a grass-roots movement of lay people who met in prayer circles and conventicles, among which were many women.

Judaism and Islam were minority religions in western Europe and Russia in the early modern period, and Jewish and Muslim women, along with men, were often the targets of persecution. Jewish women as well as men were questioned, tortured, physically punished, and in some cases executed by the Inquisition in Spain, leading Jews in other parts of Europe to make special efforts to help women of Jewish ancestry leave Spain and Portugal. Jewish women were excluded from public religious life, but they did have specific religious duties relating to the household and special prayers to say when they carried out these duties. Like Jewish women, Spanish Muslim women (termed "Moriscas") carried out religious rituals in their homes and taught them to their children. According to the records of the Inquisition, Moriscas observed the Muslim holy month of Ramadan, performed daily prayers, hid religious books and amulets written in Arabic in their clothing and furniture, taught Muslim ideas and practices to Christian women who married Muslim men, and organized funerals, weddings, and other ceremonies.

Women's lives involved much more than legal systems, work, and religious life, of course, but it is as impossible to cover all aspects of their lives in a relatively brief article as it would be those of men's lives. In fact, including a separate article on women—without a corresponding article on men—goes to some degree against recent research, which has emphasized the diversity more than the commonalities in women's experience across Europe. Even the experience of the relatively small group of women who held political power was diverse. Elizabeth I's situation was very different from that of queen mothers in France such as Marie de Médicis, female rulers of eastern Europe such as Maria Theresa, tsarinas such as Catherine the Great, or mothers of the sultans (known as the *valide-sultan*) in the Ottoman Empire. Thus perhaps the only generalization safe to make is that gender shaped the lives of all early modern Europeans in complex ways, and that every development of the period was shaped by, and in turn shaped, ideas about or structures of gender.

*See also* **Bassi, Laura; Behn, Aphra; Catherine II (Russia); Concubinage; Cornaro Piscopia, Elena Lucrezia; Divorce; Elizabeth I (England); Feminism; Gender; Gentileschi, Artemisia; Harem; Inheritance and Wills; Jansenism; Maria Theresa (Holy Roman Empire); Marie de Médicis; Marriage; Midwives; Motherhood and Childbearing; Pietism; Quakers; Quietism; Reformation, Catholic; Reformation, Protestant; Salons; Widows and Widowhood; Witchcraft; Women and Art.**

BIBLIOGRAPHY

Amussen, Susan D., and Adele Seeff, eds. *Attending to Early Modern Women.* Newark, Del., 1998.

Bennett, Judith. *Ale, Beer, and Brewsters in England: Women's Work in a Changing World, 1300–1600.* New York, 1996.

Cohn, Samuel K., Jr. *Women in the Streets: Essays On Sex and Power in Renaissance Italy.* Baltimore, 1996.

Davis, Natalie Zemon. *Women on the Margins: Three Seventeenth-Century Lives.* Cambridge, Mass., 1995.

Davis, Natalie Zemon, and Arlette Farge, eds. *Renaissance and Enlightenment Paradoxes.* Vol. 3 of *A History of Women in the West,* edited by Georges Duby and Michelle Perrot. Cambridge, Mass., 1993.

Gowing, Laura. *Domestic Dangers: Women, Words, and Sex in Early Modern London.* Oxford, 1996.

Hafter, Daryl M., ed. *European Women and Preindustrial Craft.* Bloomington, Ind., 1995.

Hufton, Olwen. *The Prospect Before Her: A History of Women in Western Europe.* London, 1995.

King, Margaret. *Women of the Renaissance.* Chicago, 1991.

Kuehn, Thomas. *Law, Family, and Women: Toward a Legal Anthropology of Renaissance Italy.* Chicago, 1992.

Levin, Eve. *Sex and Society in the World of the Orthodox Slavs, 900–1700.* Ithaca, N.Y., 1989.

MacCurtain, Margaret, and Mary O'Dowd, eds. *Women in Early Modern Ireland, 1500–1800.* Edinburgh, 1991.

Marshall, Sherrin, ed. *Women in Reformation and Counter-Reformation Europe: Public and Private Worlds.* Bloomington, Ind., 1989.

Mendelson, Sara, and Patricia Crawford. *Women in Early Modern England, 1550–1720.* Oxford and New York, 1998.

Pierce, Leslie. *The Imperial Harem: Women and Sovereignty in the Ottoman Empire.* New York, 1993.

Roper, Lyndal. *The Holy Household: Women and Morals in Reformation Augsburg.* Oxford, 1989.

Sánchez, Magdalena S., and Alain Saint-Saëns, eds. *Spanish Women in the Golden Age: Images and Realities.* Westport, Conn., 1996.

Sperling, Jutta. *Convents and the Body Politic in Renaissance Venice.* Chicago, 1999.

Stretton, Tim. *Women Waging Law in Elizabethan England.* Cambridge, U.K., 1998.

Vickery, Amanda. *The Gentleman's Daughter: Women's Lives in Georgian England.* New Haven, 1998.

Wiesner, Merry E. *Women and Gender in Early Modern Europe.* 2nd ed. Cambridge, U.K., 2000.

Wunder, Heide. *He Is the Sun, She Is the Moon: Women in Early Modern Germany.* Translated by Thomas Dunlap. Cambridge, Mass., 1998.

MERRY WIESNER-HANKS

---

**WOMEN AND ART.** Although women certainly produced art in previous centuries, it is in the sixteenth century that we first find strong biographical information on female artists. In the second edition of his *Lives of the Artists* (1568), Giorgio Vasari mentions a number of Flemish and Italian female artists, including the Bolognese sculptor Properzia De' Rossi (c. 1490–c. 1530), Sister Plautilla (1523–1588; prioress of the Florentine convent of Santa Caterina da Siena), a Madonna Lucrezia, wife of Count Clemente Pietra, and Sofonisba Anguissola (1527–1625). Nonetheless, the sixteenth and seventeenth centuries also witnessed a progressive exclusion of women from membership in guilds and the newly established art academies. The latter elevated painting, sculpture, and architecture above the status of craft by linking them to fields of knowledge—mathematics, geometry, human anatomy and study from living models, as well as a deep understanding of classical literary and visual sources—largely inaccessible to women.

## FATHERS AND DAUGHTERS

Until the modern period women rarely achieved success in sculpture or architecture, although De' Rossi, who won a reputation for miniature curiosities comprising elaborate scenes carved on peach stones and later received public commissions in stone for the Church of San Petronio in Bologna, is a notable exception. Vasari emphasizes her accomplishment in household management and her physical beauty along with her artistry as a carver. According to Vasari, her relief of *The Temptation of Joseph by Potiphar's Wife* (c. 1526–1530), was "esteemed by all to be most beautiful," emphasizing that "the wife of the Pharao's Chamberlain" is seen stripping Joseph's garment from him "with a womanly grace that defies description."

Occasionally, educated aristocratic women achieved great success as courtiers and artists. The career of Sofonisba Anguissola is, in this regard, paradigmatic. She was the daughter of a noble family of Cremona. Her father, Amilcare Anguissola, educated all his seven children in music, painting, and Latin. He also sent Sofonisba, together with her sister Elena, to spend three years (1546–1549) in the household of the painter Bernardino Campi, and she subsequently studied with another Cremonese painter, Bernadino Gatti. Sofonisba, in turn, trained three of her sisters—Lucia, Europa, and Anna Maria—to paint. Anguissola was celebrated for her informal portraits and self-portraits, singled out by Vasari as "breathing likenesses." An extraordinary painting depicting three of her sisters playing chess while a maid looks on (1555, *The Chess Game*) stands out for its striking attention to detail and for its natural rendition of physiognomy and gestural expression. While still in her twenties, Anguissola was invited to join the retinue of Philip II in Madrid, where she resided for over ten years (1559–1573), working as court painter and lady-in-waiting to Queen Isabel of Valois and subsequently Queen Anne of Austria.

Although some aristocratic women, like Anguissola, received an education that prepared them to pursue a career in the arts, more often than not the women who achieved success as artists benefited from a relative in the trade. Antwerp artist Catharina van Hemessen (1527/28–after 1566?), court painter to Mary of Hungary, came to be known for her small panels of religious subjects in the mode of

her father, the artist Jan van Hemessen. Levina Teerlinc (c. 1510–1576) followed the profession of her father, the miniaturist Simon Bining (or Bennick), and was called to the court of Henry VIII. Barbara Longhi (1552–1638), painter of small-scale devotional images, was trained by her father, Luca, in Ravenna; similarly, Venetian Marietta Robusti (1560–1590) was a vital member of the workshop of her father, Jacopo Robusti (called Tintoretto, c. 1518–1594). The Bolognese artists Lavinia Fontana (1552–1614) and Elisabetta Sirani (1638–1665) were also taught by their fathers, Prospero and Giovanni Andrea, respectively. Bologna, in fact, appears to have been an environment marked by progressive attitudes toward women in general (its university admitted female students already in the thirteenth century) and by its relative openness to female professional artists: no fewer than twenty-three female painters are recorded as active in Bologna during the sixteenth and seventeenth centuries. Sirani even opened a school for female artists in her native Bologna, allowing the possibility for women of non-artistic families to pursue a career in the arts.

## SELF AND OTHERS

These forms of alternative education became more widespread in the following centuries. Yet with the powerful presence of the art academy in the seventeenth and eighteenth centuries and the limitations placed on female admissions, it was still very difficult for women to study art and therefore to become professional artists. Women could hardly aspire to produce the highest genre within the academic hierarchy, history painting, since they were barred from the life classes where the nude (and especially the male body) could be studied. This form of study was perceived as a prerequisite for the complex figurative compositions that history painting demanded. One way to circumvent this limitation was by copying from casts, statues, and skeletons, with which most studios were equipped. In a striking self-portrait of 1579, Lavinia Fontana shows herself seated with an air of intellectual seriousness at her desk, surrounded by a small nude figure and casts of body parts. Fontana, who in her lifetime amassed an impressive collection of antiques, gained success as a portraitist but also became known for her many ambitious religious and mythological scenes. Her marriage and eleven children did not hinder her

**Women and Art.** Properzia De' Rossi, *The Temptation of Joseph by Potiphar's Wife,* marble relief, Bologna, Museo di San Petronio. ©ART RESOURCE, N.Y.

career; she became official painter at the court of Clement VII and was elected to the Roman Academy. Her history paintings include a large-scale altarpiece of the *Consecration of the Virgin* (1599) and the full-length nude depiction of *Minerva Dress-* *ing Herself* (1613) commissioned by the major Roman art collector Cardinal Scipione Borghese. This image of the goddess-warrior and patron of the arts is the first documented single-figure painting of a female nude by a female artist.

Another female artist who managed to produce a large body of work, including history paintings, was Artemisia Gentileschi (c. 1597–after 1651). Trained in the style of Caravaggio by her father, Orazio Gentileschi (c. 1562–c. 1647), and by Agostino Tassi, Gentileschi produced a great number of mythological and biblical scenes for patrons in Florence, Rome, Naples, and London. Products of one of the most powerful of female artists, Gentileschi's impressive heroines have been linked to her own biography, particularly with regard to the assault she suffered at the hands of her teacher Tassi. Her *Judith Decapitating Holofernes* (1615–1620; Pitti Palace, Florence) shows a dramatic nocturnal scene: the Old Testament heroine Judith has secretly entered the enemy camp and, with the help of her maid, cuts the throat of the Assyrian general. Although this iconography was painted by many of Gentileschi's contemporaries—including Caravaggio, Sirani, and her own father—no other artist achieved such a convincing rendition of sheer bodily force and psychological tension. We know from surviving letters that Gentileschi privately hired female models. The first extant studies of a male nude by a female artist are, however, a series of exquisite drawings by the Venetian painter Giulia Lama (1681–1747) and the roughly contemporary life studies by Susanna Maria von Sandrart (1658–1716), a graphic artist from Nuremberg.

Female artists often turned their attention to the mimetic genres of portraiture and still life painting, where academic training mattered less and which permitted women to work in the privacy of their own homes. In these fields, female artists were often highly innovative. Dutch artists such as Clara Peeters (1594–after 1657) and Rachel Ruysch (1664–1750) specialized in still life painting. Ruysch's marvelous, minutely rendered flower pictures were much sought after and fetched more than double the price of what Rembrandt could ask for his canvases. With her meticulous and painstakingly detailed renditions of insect specimens and plants in watercolor on vellum, the German-born Maria Sibylla Merian (1647–1717) contributed fundamentally to the fields of entomology and botany. Born in Frankfurt am Main and living much of her adult life in the Netherlands, Merian spent two years with her sister in the Dutch colony of Suriname in South America, where she catalogued indigenous insects, plants, and animals. Other female baroque still life painters include the Italian Giovanna Garzoni (1600–1670), who became a member of the Academy of Saint Luke in Rome, Josefa de Obidos (1630–1684) in Portugal, and the Parisian child prodigy Louise Moillon (1615/16–after 1674), known for her originative combining of genre and still life scenes.

As a painter of intimate domestic genre scenes, Judith Leyster (1609–1660) deserves special mention. She presumably studied painting in the workshop of Frans Pietersz de Grebber, a renowned portrait painter in Haarlem, before becoming a member of the Haarlem Guild of St. Luke in 1633. The membership in the painters' guild enabled Leyster to establish her own studio, to which she also admitted a number of male students. Her paintings have often been confused with those of her contemporary Frans Hals. Leyster's successful career ended when she married an artist colleague and became a mother.

### THE EIGHTEENTH CENTURY

The belief that women's ability to bear children paralleled their ability to reproduce nature mimetically bears upon the products of women artists throughout early modernity. From the sixteenth through the eighteenth centuries, female artists were particularly prized as portraitists. Mary Beale (1633–1699), England's first documented professional female artist, made a name for herself as a prolific painter of clerical portraits in the London of Charles II, competing with Peter Lely and Godfrey Kneller. A generation later, the Venetian Rosalba Carriera (1675–1757), who began her career illustrating snuff boxes, won international repute for her skillful portraits in pastels. Her light and effervescent manner not only helped raise pastel to a fine art, but—following her visit to Paris in 1720–1721 (on the invitation of the important patron Pierre Crozat)—her technique and style also had a decisive impact on the development of the rococo. Carriera captured her sitters in flattering portraits of brilliant luminous color and introduced a degree of informality that suited the taste of her international clientele and was quickly emulated by other artists throughout Europe. She became the first foreign woman to be elected to the French Academy of Fine Arts. Felicità Sartori, Carriera's best student, also won international acclaim; she worked for August III, elector of Saxony and king of Poland, at his court in Dresden. In France, many female artists achieved success in and around the Bourbon court and in the Paris salons, including Anne Vallayer-Coster (1744–1818), Adélaïde Labille-Guïard (1749–1803), Marie Gabrielle Capet (1761–1818), the sculptor Marie-Anne Collot (student of M. E. Falconet), and the German painter Anna Dorothea Lisiewska-Therbusch (1721–1782).

But the most successful female French artist of the late eighteenth century was undoubtedly Elisabeth Vigée-Lebrun (1755–1842). One of the foremost painters of her time and court painter to Queen Marie Antoinette, she is remembered for her animated portraits and her equally lively autobiographical *Souvenirs* (1835–1837), which describe her coming of age in the *ancien régime,* her European travels, and her life in Napoleonic Paris. In this book, Vigée-Lebrun records her awareness of female artists both past and present: she notes studying works by Carriera in Venice and expresses pride at seeing the *Self-Portrait* of Angelica Kauffmann (1741–1807) in the Uffizi gallery. Indeed, during the second half of the eighteenth century Vigée-Lebrun's fame was matched only by the Swiss-born Kauffmann, who lived most of her life in Italy, but who spent a productive decade and a half in London. In 1768 Kauffmann became one of only two female founding members of the British Royal Academy, along with Mary Moser (1744–1819), a flower and subject painter. Kauffmann was enormously successful as a history painter of ambitious ancient and modern themes, while many of her smaller allegorical and mythological subjects were picked up by the print trade and reproduced on furniture, wall panels, and fabrics, causing one critic to exclaim that "the whole world is Angelicamad." It was, however, through her portraits that Kauffmann, like Vigée-Lebrun and Carriera, secured an international clientele. Capitalizing on contemporary notions that promoted women's "sensibility," Kauffmann's portraits came to be seen as particularly profound comments on the sitters' interior states.

Given that female artists had to negotiate their identities in a profession that for the most part shunned them, it is perhaps not surprising that as a group they produced such a large number of self-portraits. One of the earliest known self-portraits by a female artist is that by a young Dutch woman, who emerges from a dark background holding a thin brush in her hand. The painting is inscribed "I, Catharina van Hemessen, painted myself in 1548 at the age of 20." Sofonisba Anguissola's father sent out some of his daughter's many self-portraits to patrons as advertisements of her beauty and her talent, and Clara Peeters sometimes captured multiple self-reflections, holding brush and palette, in the surface of shiny objects in her meticulous still lifes. With the advent of the public art market and the unavoidable visibility of artists in the competitive annual academy exhibitions, self-portraiture had, by the eighteenth century, become a vital genre for female artists. It allowed them to craft public personae in a time when invisibility and private virtues (associated with modesty and domesticity) constituted ideal femininity. In the year that Vigée-Lebrun exhibited her monumental portrait of *Marie Antoinette and Her Children* (1787), an effort to counter the slander identifying the queen as a "bad mother," the artist also showed her own *Self-Portrait with Daughter Julie.* Emulating a Madonna painting by Raphael, Vigée-Lebrun advertises her role as mother while simultaneously competing artistically with her celebrated male predecessor.

It also became a matter of pride—and self-advertisement—for professional women to show themselves with their female students, as in Carriera's *Self-Portrait* in which the artist works on a pastel portrait of her sister, whom Carriera had trained as her assistant. The accomplished painting by Marie-Victoire Lemoine (1754–1820), *Atelier of a Painter, Probably Mme Vigée Le Brun and Her Pupil* (1796), shows the artist as a student, learning to draw under the guidance of her celebrated teacher. After 1780, Vigée-Lebrun's chief female competitor and co-academician in Paris, Adélaïde Labille-Guïard, ran a private studio for women and in September 1790 approached the academy to raise the established quota of four female academicians. In her celebrated painting *Self-Portrait with Two Tulips,* Labille-Guïard depicts herself life-size in a dazzling dress at work on a monumental canvas, framed by attentive pupils Marie Gabrielle Capet (d. 1818) and Garreaux de Rosemond (d. 1788).

## THE SALON: PATRONAGE AND PERSONALITIES

Since the appearance of Baldassare Castiglione's *The Courtier* (1528), the idea of art as a component of ideal feminine comportment had become widespread, reaching its greatest extent in the eighteenth century when the status of the amateur artist became broadly accepted as a norm. It was common practice for female artists to instruct aristocratic pupils, thereby cultivating a network of female patrons. Indeed, many female artists found particular success with powerful female patrons. This was certainly true for Vigée-Lebrun, Kauffmann, and Labille-Guïard, all of whom prospered from female protectors. There was, in fact, a long tradition of female aristocratic patronage, from the voracious collector and patron Isabella d'Este in sixteenth-century Ferrara to Rubens's great patron, Marie de Médicis, in seventeenth-century Paris. It was, however, in the eighteenth century that female patrons emerged as a powerful force in determining the development of art. For example, the extensive patronage of Catherine II the Great of Russia (ruled 1762–1796) helped transform St. Petersburg into a European city. In France, the sociable patronage of Jeanne Antoinette Poisson, Dame Le Normant d'Étioles, Marquise de Pompadour (1721–1764) deserves mention. The mistress of Louis XV, Pompadour shaped the cultural life of France between 1744 and her death in 1764. She collected art, commissioned paintings, and influenced the king's architectural patronage. By promoting certain artists, notably François Boucher, Pompadour supported the novel rococo forms, which defined the art of her age. Pompadour was also at the vanguard of what was to become the public expression of the new theory of aesthetics: the private salon. In line with contemporary notions privileging the cultivation of taste, salons were social gatherings staged for the polite cultured exchange that was increasingly thought to represent the foundation of civilized society. Women, long associated with the private sphere, played a major role in this development. Important salons were held by Marie de Rabutin-Chantal Marquise de Sévigné, Marie-Madeleine Marquise de La Fayette, Anne (called Ninon) de Lenclos, Claudine Alexandrine Guérin de Tencin, and Jeanne Françoise Julie Adélaïde Récamier. Germany lacked the cultural and social climate of France but similar attempts to institute salons were made by Dorthea Caroline Albertine von Schelling (later Schlegel) and Henriette Julie Herz. These informal social gatherings also often provided the space for artistic expression by women; for example, Emma Hart (later Lady Hamilton) became famous throughout Europe for her performance of "attitudes," a series of poses emulating different ancient works of art.

When the female body entered representation in the early modern era, it often negotiated a long tradition of accepted figural, social, and moral models. Given prevailing Christian conceptions of female virtue and vice in representation women were often seen to embody the virginal/maternal qualities of Mary or the seductive worldliness of Eve. Early modern portraits of female sitters—almost always patrician or aristocratic—shift between these two poles, with images of courtesans enticing assumed male spectators on the one hand, or, on the other, enacting the roles of "happy mothers" who appear to embrace a domestic ideal. This ambivalence runs through all genres and media. It is made more complex by the enduring fascination with Greco-Roman mythology. The reclining female nude, a staple of Renaissance, baroque, rococo, and neoclassical art, produced an alternate moral axis. For while the woman represented might be a courtesan elevated to the status of Venus, the mythological guise could also be donned by aristocratic women—but referring only to their beauty, not to their moral state. In fact, given the ease with which the female body could pass into abstraction, many representations of women in early modernity tend to fluctuate between fixed reference to a particular individual and/or character, and an embodiment of an abstract principle. This is perhaps most evident in the baroque art associated with the courts of Rome and Paris in the seventeenth century, but it also can be seen in contemporary Dutch paintings of domestic scenes. The women represented within the apparently unpretentious Netherlandish interiors are taken by some scholars as images of actual women, while other scholars insist that these women are types, operating within various moralizing tales.

Although often hindered by misogynistic opinions and obstacles, women in early modern Europe were active as artists and patrons, contributing decisively to the development of major artistic movements. The work they produced is, in fact, intriguing in part on account of the manner in which these women responded to the complex restrictions they faced.

*See also* **Anguissola, Sofonisba; Art: The Conception and Status of the Artist; Art: Artistic Patronage; Art: The Art Market and Collecting; Baroque; Carriera, Rosalba; Early Modern Period: Art Historical Interpretations; Gender; Gentileschi, Artemisia; Kauffmann, Angelica; Merian, Maria Sibylla; Painting; Ruysch, Rachel; Salons; Vigée-Lebrun, Elisabeth; Women.**

BIBLIOGRAPHY

Baillio, Joseph. *Elisabeth Louise Vigée Le Brun, 1755–1842.* Exh. cat. Fort Worth, 1982.

Bermingham, Ann. *Learning to Draw: Studies in the Cultural History of a Polite and Useful Art.* New Haven and London, 2000.

Borzello, Frances. *A World of Our Own: Women as Artists since the Renaissance.* New York, 2000.

Chadwick, Whitney. *Women, Art, and Society.* 3rd ed. London and New York, 2002.

*Dictionary of Women Artists.* Edited by Delia Gaze. 2 vols. London and Chicago, 1997.

Fortunati, Vera. *Lavinia Fontana of Bologna, 1552–1614.* Exh. cat. Milan, 1998.

Garrard, Mary D. *Artemisia Gentileschi: The Image of the Female Hero in Italian Baroque Art.* Princeton, 1989.

Gere, Charlotte, and Marina Vaizey. *Great Women Collectors.* New York, 1999.

Gorsen, Peter, Gislind Nabakowski, and Helka Sander. *Frauen in der Kunst.* 2 vols. Frankfurt am Main, 1980.

Greer, Germaine. *The Obstacle Race: The Fortunes of Women Painters and Their Work.* London, 1979.

Heller, Nancy G. *Women Artists: An Illustrated History.* New York, 1987.

Jürgs, Britta, ed. *Sammeln nur um zu besitzen?: Berühmte Kunstsammlerinnen von Isabella d'Este bis Peggy Guggenheim.* Berlin, 2000.

Nochlin, Linda, and Ann Sutherland Harris. *Women Artists, 1550–1950.* Exh. cat. Los Angeles and New York, 1976.

Parker, Rozsika, and Griselda Pollock. *Old Mistresses: Women, Art, and Ideology.* London and New York, 1981.

Perlingieri, Ilya Sandra. *Sofonisba Anguissola: The First Great Woman Artist of the Renaissance.* New York, 1992.

Pointon, Marcia. *Strategies for Showing: Women, Possession, and Representation in English Visual Culture, 1665–1800.* Oxford and New York, 1997.

Rosenthal, Angela. *Angelika Kauffmann: Bildnismalerei im 18. Jahrhundert.* Berlin, 1996.

Roworth, Wendy Wassyng, ed. *Angelica Kauffmann: A Continental Artist in Georgian England.* London, 1992.

Sani, Bernardina. *Rosalba Carriera.* Turin, 1988.

Sheriff, Mary D. *The Exceptional Woman: Elisabeth Vigée-Lebrun and the Cultural Politics of Art.* Chicago and London, 1996.

Slatkin, Wendy. *Women Artists in History: From Antiquity to the Present.* 2nd ed. Upper Saddle River, N.J., 1997.

Tufts, Eleanor. *Our Hidden Heritage: Five Centuries of Women Artists.* New York and London, 1974.

Vasari, Giorgio. *Lives of the Painters, Sculptors and Architects.* Translated by Gaston du C. de Vere. 2 vols. New York, 1996.

ANGELA H. ROSENTHAL

---

**WOODLANDS.** *See* **Forests and Woodlands.**

---

**WORK.** *See* **Artisans; Laborers; Peasantry; Wages.**

---

**WREN, CHRISTOPHER** (1632–1723), English architect. Sir Christopher Wren was an English scientist and architect, important for confirming, in what later was jokingly referred to as the "Wrenaissance," a tradition of classical architecture in England in the seventeenth century that lasted for two centuries. His father was a distinguished cleric, and Wren was well educated, coming into contact while a student at Oxford with a group of scientists who were later, in 1661, to found the Royal Society. His interests at this time were science and astronomy; after receiving his degrees, he was elected a member of All Souls College and in 1661 he became the Savilian professor of astronomy at Oxford.

Gradually, however, Wren became interested in architecture, then considered a part of mathematics. When in 1663 his uncle, the bishop of Ely, asked him to design a chapel at Pembroke College, Cambridge, he was able to produce an adequate design, simple and classical in its forms. A year later he began the Sheldonian Theatre, Oxford, a complex structure, taken as to be expected from the design of

**Christopher Wren.** St. Paul's Cathedral, London, view from the northwest. ©DAVID REED/CORBIS

**Christopher Wren.** The Wren Library, Trinity College, Cambridge. THE ART ARCHIVE/JARROLD PUBLISHING

classical theaters, but roofed with a new truss system without columns, based on a floor plan devised by John Wallis, formerly professor of geometry at Oxford. It was in 1665 that Wren made his only visit abroad, to Paris, where he visited the new classical buildings and met, if briefly, the Italian architect Gian Lorenzo Bernini.

On his return to London, Wren began further restorations at St. Paul's Cathedral. But in 1666 came the Great Fire, and with it an opportunity for him not only to rebuild the fabric of the cathedral, but also to redesign the whole city of London on a regular and ordered plan. As one of the commissioners appointed to survey the areas destroyed, Wren was very much involved in the restoration of London; when in 1668 he was also appointed surveyor general of the king's works, he resigned from Oxford and turned all his attention to architecture. Of the project for London, which was taken from some of the new plans for Rome, little was realized, commerce and expediency requiring that everything

in the city be quickly rebuilt along the existing patterns of streets. Wren was also involved in rebuilding more than fifty local city churches. Their designs, varied and distinct as they were in their plans, established a new form for the Protestant church, with open galleries inside and bell towers outside, often set apart from the basic structure and effectively recalling, in all their classical details, the spires of the older medieval churches that had earlier been present at the same sites.

Wren's design for St. Paul's Cathedral was equally important. Its great dome, with the colonnade running around the drum, taken from a design by Donato Bramante for St. Peter's, was a model for many later buildings—such as the Capitol in Washington, D.C.—where a dome was to be used for purely secular buildings. Wren also worked on several projects for King Charles II. Although many of his designs for Winchester Palace, Whitehall, and Hampton Court were never realized, at the Royal Hospital, Chelsea (begun in 1682), and at the Royal

Hospital for Seamen, Greenwich (1696 onward), he defined an ideal of monumental architecture, deeply influential on architects of the next generation. In addition, Wren again worked for the universities, notably at the library of Trinity College, Cambridge (1676–1684) and at Tom Tower at Christ Church, Oxford (1681–1682), which, following what he called customary rather than natural beauty, was constructed in a Gothic style to complement its older architectural surroundings.

The last years of Wren's life were not happy. His supervision of the Office of Works became haphazard, and in 1718 he was dismissed, retaining only his surveyorship at St. Paul's and at Westminster Abbey. It was then that the Palladian group, led by Lord Burlington, took charge of this office, arguing for a new native style of architecture, based on the theories of Andrea Palladio and Inigo Jones, to replace the more pragmatic baroque style of Wren and his followers. But what Wren had done was of immense importance. And if his designs never reached the quality of those executed by Sir John Vanbrugh and Nicholas Hawksmoor, who had begun his career in Wren's office, his ideas about his work, carefully preserved by his son, served to demonstrate, in ways now compatible with the experimental approaches he learned as a scientist, how architecture and its history could be seriously thought about and seen as part of a design tradition that dated back to Italy and antiquity.

*See also* **Britain, Architecture in; Classicism; Jones, Inigo; London; Palladio, Andrea, and Palladianism.**

BIBLIOGRAPHY

*Primary Sources*

Soo, Lydia M. *Wren's "Tracts" on Architecture and Other Writings.* New York and Cambridge, U.K., 1998.

Wren, Stephen. *Parentalia, or Memoirs of the Family of the Wrens.* Reprint. Hampshire, U.K., 1965. Originally published London, 1750.

*Secondary Sources*

Bennett, J. A. *The Mathematical Science of Sir Christopher Wren.* Cambridge, U.K., 1982.

Jardine, Lisa. *On a Grander Scale: The Outstanding Career of Christopher Wren.* London, 2002.

Jeffery, Paul. *The City Churches of Sir Christopher Wren.* London and Rio Grande, Ohio, 1996.

Whinney, Margaret. *Christopher Wren.* New York, 1971.

DAVID CAST

**WÜRTTEMBERG, DUCHY OF.** Early modern Württemberg had a flourishing agricultural economy, a highly developed administrative structure, and superb cultural achievements, yet its prime location in the southwest corner of the Holy Roman Empire also made it a target for imperial ambitions and invasions. For administrative and taxation purposes, the territory of almost 3,500 square miles (9,000 square kilometers) was divided up into districts (*Ämter* or *Vogteien*) that varied greatly in size and whose number rose from thirty-eight in 1442 to fifty-eight by 1600. Württemberg's total population during the sixteenth century was between three and four hundred thousand, with 70 percent of the populace living in the countryside and 30 percent in the towns. The capital was Stuttgart, the largest town by far with a population of about nine thousand inhabitants. Württemberg's economy rested primarily on wine, rye, barley, hay, and oats, although its merchants also traded in wood, wool, cloth, linen, glass, and metal. Small property ownership by landlords who charged their tenants rent (*Grundherrschaft*) remained the rule, rather than the large landed estates (*Gutsherrschaften*) common in other German territories.

A series of wars during the seventeenth century and the early eighteenth century had a devastating impact on the region's social, economic, and cultural life. While the duchy was at first little touched by the Thirty Years' War (1618–1648), large-scale invasions by imperial troops following the Battle of Nördlingen in 1634 led to a decline in the duchy's population from 415,000 to 97,000 by 1639. The wars of Louis XIV (ruled 1643–1715) continued to suppress population levels, and it was not until the Treaty of Utrecht of 1713 that an era of relative peace and prosperity ensued.

**GOVERNMENT**

Territorial administration existed on several levels. Rulers came from the House of Württemberg, which had governed the territory since the eleventh century. Count Eberhard im Bart ("the Bearded," 1445–1496) became a duke following the elevation of Württemberg to a duchy by Emperor Maximilian I (ruled 1493–1519) at the Diet of Worms in 1495. For advice on policy, subsequent dukes surrounded themselves with burgher and noble councillors, many of whom were educated at Tübingen University, founded in 1477.

The majority of councillors came from the urban notables *(Ehrbarkeit)*, a relatively diverse administrative group holding positions at the local and district levels. Most local positions, such as village mayor *(Schultheiss)*, burgomaster, and town clerk, arose during the thirteenth century. At the district level the position of the commissioner *(Vogt)* split into two separate positions, junior commissioner and senior commissioner *(Untervogt* and *Obervogt)*, by the late fifteenth century. The junior commissioner, typically a burgher, worked with the district court to maintain law and order and supervise taxation, whereas the senior commissioner, almost always a noble, had a military role, although this position became essentially honorary by the early seventeenth century.

The notables also dominated the Estates, which first met in 1457 and comprised the territory's representative body. With 75 percent of the representatives coming from the towns, the Estates comprised lesser nobles, burghers, and prelates and served as a counterbalance to the higher nobility, the knights *(Reichsritter)*, who gradually exempted themselves from Württemberg's state control. While the ruler had to call the Estates to assembly, two committees, the Small and Large Committees, could convene on their own authority. The Estates claimed some early victories, such as the 1514 Treaty of Tübingen that affirmed citizens' privileges, but it rose to even greater heights during the seventeenth century, particularly following the Thirty Years' War, when the duke needed the Estates to raise more revenue. A combination of the diversity and power of the notables, the long-term presence of the Estates, and rigorous Lutheran reforms contributed to the relative unity of Württemberg's territories over time.

### RELIGION AND CULTURE

After fifteen years of Austrian occupation, Württembergers witnessed two seminal events: the triumphant return in 1534 of Duke Ulrich (1487–1550) with the aid of Landgrave Philip of Hesse (1504–1567) and the Schmalkaldic League, and the ushering in of the Lutheran Reformation. A confiscation of church property ensued, which initially brought in over 100,000 gulden annually, although the monasteries were not dissolved. The principal reformer, the humanist scholar and theologian Johannes Brenz (1499–1570), cofounded the visitation to instruct the faithful and enforce church discipline. The church council *(Kirchenrat)*, created in 1553 under Duke Christoph (1515–1568), subsumed these and other duties, such as collecting rents from church lands, distributing loans or grants to the poor and to university students, and paying the salaries of court musicians.

The Pietist movement, based on the theology of Johann Valentin Andreae (1586–1654) and Philipp Jacob Spener (1635–1705), arose during the 1680s and 1690s, when the Württemberg court moved toward a hedonistic lifestyle patterned after Versailles and reveled in opera, dance, and Carnival. Pietism offered a "passive, antiabsolutist" stance and provided a corollary to English Puritanism but was less political in its manifestations. Pietists' disapproval of the court increased strongly while Württemberg had Catholic dukes from 1733 to 1797, beginning with Carl Alexander (1684–1737), who had converted in 1712 and established close ties with the Habsburgs. His son and successor Carl Eugen (1728–1793), who ruled for almost fifty years, seemed to personify the "petty absolutist" and was in continual conflict with the Estates. Court life inspired the territory's greatest Enlightenment figure, Friedrich Schiller (1759–1805), who attended the duke's military academy and rebelled openly against the pomposity and vainglory of the age through drama and verse.

Notable achievements in the fine arts included the establishment of a music ensemble *(Hofkapelle* or court chapel) in 1496 under Duke Eberhard II (1447–1504). Consisting at its peak of fifty-nine instrumentalists and a boys' choir, the music ensemble became renowned throughout Europe during the sixteenth and seventeenth centuries, and performed at both sacred and secular occasions. It attracted many foreign musicians, including the English lutenist John Price (d. 1641) and the Hungarian composer Samuel Capricornus (1628–1665), who served as music director (kapellmeister) from 1657 to 1665. The territory's most famous artist, Hans Baldung-Grien (c. 1484–1545), was an apprentice to Albrecht Dürer (1471–1528) before he moved to Strasbourg to become one of the leading figures of the northern Renaissance. In his paintings, stained glass, drawings, woodcuts, and engravings, Baldung depicted a broad array of subjects, from traditional Christian iconography and secular portraiture to witchcraft and death.

*See also* **Maximilian I (Holy Roman Empire); Pietism; Reformation, Protestant; Representative Institutions; Schiller, Johann Christoph Friedrich von; Thirty Years' War (1618–1648).**

BIBLIOGRAPHY

Brecht, Martin, and Hermann Ehmer. *Südwestdeutsche Reformationsgeschichte: Zur Einführung der Reformation im Herzogtum Württemberg 1534.* Stuttgart, 1984.

Fulbrook, Mary. *Piety and Politics: Religion and the Rise of Absolutism in England, Württemberg, and Prussia.* Cambridge, U.K., 1983.

Grube, Walter. *Der Stuttgarter Landtag, 1457–1957.* Stuttgart, 1957.

Marcus, Kenneth H. "Music Patronage of the Württemberg *Hofkapelle,* c. 1500–1650." *German History* 13, no. 2 (1995): 151–162.

———. *The Politics of Power: Elites of an Early Modern State in Germany.* Mainz, 2000.

Scribner, Bob. "Police and the Territorial State in Sixteenth-Century Württemberg." In *Politics and Society in Reformation Europe: Essays for Sir Geoffrey Elton on His Sixty-fifth Birthday,* edited by E. I. Kouri and Tom Scott, pp. 103–120. Basingstoke, U.K., 1987.

Vann, James Allen. *The Making of a State: Württemberg, 1593–1793.* Ithaca, N.Y., 1984.

Wilson, Peter H. *War, State, and Society in Württemberg, 1677–1793.* Cambridge, U.K., 1995.

Zull, Gertraud. "Die höfischen Feste." In *Die Renaissance im Deutschen Südwesten zwischen Reformation und Dreissigjährigem Krieg.* Vol. 2, pp. 913–925. Karlsruhe, 1986.

KENNETH H. MARCUS

# XYZ

**YOUTH.** The transitional phase of life between childhood and adulthood in early modern Europe is not easily fixed chronologically. Traditionally childhood ended around age seven, but since full adulthood was usually marked by marriage, "youth" (Latin *iuventus*) could last as little as ten years and as long as twenty-five or more years. Consequently, terms for male youths, such as lad or knave, *garçon* (French), or *Knabe* (German), could refer to someone as young as seven years old or as old as thirty-five. The same is true of the female maid or maiden, *jeune fille* (French) or *Jungfrau* (German), as well as the forms of address of Miss, Mademoiselle, and Fräulein. Early modern legal codes similarly varied widely on the age of majority, ranging from twelve in canon law to twenty-five in Roman law and its later imitators.

The onset of youth, on the other hand, enjoyed broader consensus in European societies and was reinforced by the ecclesiastical tradition established by Lateran IV (1215) of establishing seven as the age of discretion (Latin *anni discretionis*), when a child was intellectually and morally competent to receive the Eucharist. Puberty certainly fell within this life stage but was rarely a formalized marker within itself, not only because of its individual character but also because the average age of menarche was at least sixteen or seventeen, and many males continued to grow physically into their twenties. Occasionally, certain rituals marked the transition from childhood to youth, such as the bestowing of a knife or sword on a boy, or distinctive jewelry,

headwear, or a new hairstyle among girls. In general, though, early modern "youth" is best measured in chronologically flexible terms of an individual's position in various groups, principally relating to his or her immediate family, employer, and peers.

## WORK AND SCHOOL

Most boys and girls left their homes at some point before marriage for apprenticeships or domestic service positions with relatives or strangers. Few departed before the age of seven and some not until their late teens. By the time youths had reached their early twenties, though, at least two-thirds and sometimes three-quarters of them had left their parents' homes. Ostensibly the main purpose of the arrangement, typically lasting three to seven years, was for a boy to learn certain marketable skills and for a girl to earn the money for her dowry. The sojourn away from home, however, also had the effect of reducing a household's expenditures while the child was away. Some returned at the end of their contractual period, awaiting an inheritance (in the case of a son), a dowry and/or marriage prospect (in the case of a daughter), or a new position. The same expectations held for the large number of youths who had never left home in the first place (particularly in the countryside) and who in the meantime worked to contribute to the family's income. Meanwhile, the remainder had married and usually set up their own households, a universally recognized sign of adulthood.

Education received a powerful boost from both the Renaissance and Catholic and Protestant Reformations, but schooling remained a minority experience among European youths until at least the eighteenth century. The majority of those boys and girls who did attend school usually received no more than a few years of instruction from parish or private schools in basic vernacular literacy and some fundamental arithmetic. Well-to-do and intellectually gifted boys were able to attend Latin grammar schools, with many continuing their studies at a university. Often, pupils, like apprentices, moved into the homes of their masters. Among the wealthy, either tutors took up lodging with their students' families, instructing their charges in a variety of subjects, or teenagers attended exclusive boarding schools. In Catholic countries, the new religious orders of the Catholic Reformation, notably the Jesuits, Barnabites, Piarists, and others, offered free education in Latin schools found in every major city and many towns. Those boys who were able to continue their studies at a university were forbidden to marry before completing their degrees and were controlled in other ways by their masters, who acted in loco parentis and continued to set strict rules and discipline with the rod.

One of the initial benefits of the Reformation for girls was the opening of many mixed and single-sex schools that they might attend in Protestant lands. Among Catholics, new teaching orders such as the Ursulines undertook a similar mission to educate girls and young women. In addition, in Catholic countries many girls received educations as long-term boarders in convents or as novices (future nuns). The majority received limited vernacular reading and writing skills plus sewing and singing lessons. A few convent boarders and future nuns received good Latin educations. Unfortunately, both movements coincided with a greater restriction against and eventually prohibition of non-accredited "cranny schools," the more affordable and thus more common site of education for early modern girls. The reforms and advances among Protestants must also be weighed against the closure of all convent and other girls' schools run by nuns. Consequently, only a minority of girls enjoyed the fruits of the education boom of the early modern era and even those who did, with the exception of the privileged few, gained little more than the most fundamental of literary and mathematical skills.

## GROUP ACTIVITIES

Rural fraternities or youth groups were known by a variety of names: *iunores* (Latin), *Bürschen* (German), *garçons de village* (France), *gioventù* (Italian). All were exclusively male, rarely accepted anyone younger than sixteen, and sometimes required experience as an apprentice or soldier. Their leaders might be known as "abbots" (in the case of France's *abbayes de la jeunesse,* or 'youth abbies'), "captains," "kings," and so forth. Initiation usually involved some sort of extended and humiliating hazing, after which new members swore their allegiance to the group and received their own secret nicknames. Some fraternities maintained their own written law as well as primitive courts for handing out fines and other punishments. As everywhere in early modern society, a strict hierarchy ruled, with older boys at the top charged with introducing younger males to the adult male culture. Drinking, gambling, and cursing constituted the main pastimes, but the principal focus of such groups was the regulation of sexual activities in the community. For the most part this meant finding eligible girls for one another and possibly organizing dances. However, such bands of rural youths also ritually harassed other members of the community who had transgressed local mores (such as widows who remarried too soon or shrewish wives), failed sexually (presumed impotence or sterility), or were beginning a sexual union (newlyweds). The youths' loud verbal abuse, lewd songs, and crudeness—known as *charivaris,* 'rough music', or *Katzenmusik* (German)—served an important communal function of expressing popular approval or disapproval of what modern people would consider private matters. Surviving modern customs, such as putting tin cans and signs on the groom's car, have largely lost such meaning in the contemporary world but continue to survive as obscure relics of communal approval of some sort.

In cities, male youths could join a number of groups. The best organized were probably the journeymen's associations (German *Gesellenverbände;* French *compagnonnages*), distinguished by craft. Like rural fraternities, these groups were characterized by prolonged hazing and other mischief as well as drinking and gambling. Because of their extensive European networks as well as growing association with assorted acts of violence, journeymen's associations were banned in France in the early sixteenth century and were prohibited in the Holy Roman Empire in 1730.

University fraternities were also a prominent part of urban life, with students originally divided into "nations" (based on common languages), but by the eighteenth century organized by a variety of purposes and identities, including religious groups such as the John Wesley's Holy Club at Oxford, derided by other students as "Methodists." In Britain the college constituted a central corporate identity for most students and continues in this role to a lesser degree today, albeit with an increasingly heterogeneous undergraduate population. Still another type of young male organization were the secular fool societies (French *sociétés joyeuses*), groups that played key roles in all secular pageantry (especially at Mardi Gras) and reveled in mocking their elders and playing pranks on them. The most famous of these was the Parisian *Enfants sans souci* ('carefree children'), closely rivaled by the Kingdom of Basoche, composed of the clerks of the Parlement of Paris.

Male groups tended to gather at local inns as well as at private homes or barns. In addition to their *charivari* activity, they were especially visible during public holidays, when they would engage in various ball sports, archery, wrestling, boxing, card-playing, cock fighting, and dog tossing. Often competitions became quite heated and led to serious injuries and occasionally deaths. In England Guy Fawkes Day (5 November) was renowned as the prompter of many violent town versus gown riots in Oxford and Cambridge. Ritualistic raids on brothels were also common, though more so at the beginning and end of the early modern period.

Single-sex gatherings of young women, by contrast, were both less formalized and less publicly visible than those of their male counterparts. This reflected the typical public-private expectations in gender relations. Among Catholics, convent schools and cloisters themselves were the most obvious centers of exclusively female societies, in both instances removed from the public sphere. Some Protestant girls formed prayer groups, particularly during the later seventeenth and eighteenth centuries. Otherwise, spinning at home with female relatives or communally with other women provided opportunities for young women to become acculturated to their society's expectations of them as adults. Such gatherings also provided important companionship and conversation with peers, without any of the prolonged rituals of initiation or formalized aggression of male groups. On the other hand, segregation of teenage boys and girls shared one important goal, the finding and securing of an acceptable mate, an objective that simultaneously reinforced and (if successful) undermined the coherency of single-sex groups.

## RELATIONS BETWEEN THE SEXES

The numerous festivals and wedding feasts provided a host of opportunities for young men and women to meet and court. In addition to local village or town holidays, youths were especially prominent in the festivities of St. Valentine's Day (England), Shrove Tuesday (Mardi Gras), May Day, Midsummer (June 24), and Christmas. According to the historian Michael Mitterauer, "These were social institutions which virtually forced adolescents into contact with the opposite sex." Males were almost always expected to initiate contact with the opposite sex, though in a few cases girls were customarily allowed to organize dances and collect boys, such as the St. Catherine's Day Ball in France (25 November) and the German *Jungferntanz* ('maidens' dance'). In rural Bulgaria, the feast of St. Lazarus, before Palm Sunday, marked the ritual transition of young girls (*lazarki*) into eligible young women, known as *lazarouvané*. Following a collective withdrawal of adolescent girls from the village, they would return to sing outside the house of every bachelor, donning new festive dresses that signified their right to take part in all of the village's public festivities. More typically, teenage boys and girls met under more informal circumstances: through relatives, in the marketplace, or (especially in the case of domestic maids and males of the house) in the home. In fact this last pairing—including masters, their sons, and male servants—accounted for more of the illegitimate children born than any other type of relationship. Sometimes the sex was consensual; often it was coerced, either through threats of dismissal or outright rape. It rarely resulted in marriage and usually meant dismissal and disgrace for the pregnant young woman. As in cases of incest between stepfathers and stepdaughters, we have no reliable statistics on the actual frequency of such situations since families usually shrouded themselves in conspiracies of silence.

After first contact, youths normally began a courting process, varying in formality by social status, whose ostensible final goal was marriage. Throughout Europe, we hear of the practice of youths visiting girlfriends in their bedrooms at night, a custom variously known as "night visiting" in the south of England and "sitting up" in the north, "nights of watching" in Wales, *Kiltgang* ('dusking') or *Fensterln* (climbing in through a window) in German lands, and *nattelöpere* ('night-runners') in Norway. Sometimes these visits involved kissing, petting, or even intercourse, but given the possibility of parental interruption, sex was not always involved. Parental attitudes toward this ubiquitous practice varied widely, with some mothers and fathers turning a blind eye if they thought the two youths well-matched for marriage, while others (particularly in Scotland) strongly condemning such meetings on moral and religious grounds. The same divergence characterized parental attitudes toward premarital sex in general, with most of Europe's parents apparently tolerant even of premarital cohabitation as long as they were assured that a suitable formal union and public ceremony were forthcoming. If parental disapproval was known or feared, young people might meet at the homes of friends, secluded places, or the boisterous gatherings known as "spinning rooms" (German *Spinnstuben* or *Gunkeln;* French *veilles;* Russian *posidelki*), smoky rooms at private residences or inns where women of all ages gathered in the evening to spin cloth and gossip, visited by young men who drank, sang, and occasionally danced with their female counterparts. Often such encounters led to engagement and eventually marriage; other times they could result in unwanted pregnancy and rushed marriage, abortion, abandonment, or infanticide.

### "MASTERLESS YOUNG PEOPLE"

Complaints about "youth these days" are as old as civilization itself. The early modern period was no exception, with unceasing laments from every region about a world "full of ill-advised and ill-nurtured youth" (Griffiths, p. 111). Some of these concerns may be tied to the attempted Protestant and Catholic reforms of morals through catechization and other educational means. It is thus difficult to assess whether there truly were more problems with young people or simply higher expectations. Clearly, economic instability during the entire early modern period also contributed to the perceived laziness of youths at any given time. Changes in the common practice of tramping (German *Wanderjahre;* French *tour de France*), for instance, illustrate some of this transformation at work. Since the Middle Ages, most young journeymen spent their late teens and twenties traveling the countryside, sometimes staying at established houses of call for their profession (referred to in France as "mother houses"), but more often renting a small room or bed and getting by on whatever work was available. Ideally, those already trained in crafts would be accordingly employed, but by the late sixteenth century such temporary positions were increasingly difficult to find, and becoming a master was a near impossibility for someone without family connections. Instead, many youths turned to day labor or, what was more lucrative still, begging. Countless ordinances throughout Europe complained of a pandemic of "able-bodied beggars," whose tactics were often quite physically aggressive and extortionate of passersby. References to what we might call "gangs" of youths had been common since at least the late Middle Ages, but during the early modern period scuffles increasingly went beyond turf battles. Violence could also be turned against property, yielding vandalism such as breaking or stealing street lanterns, damaging conduits, rolling timber onto the highways, and committing widespread graffiti. Some of these unemployed and "masterless" youths made the more serious turn to professional crime, principally burglary and robbery, but occasionally arson and murder.

In response, some parents succeeded in having their unruly children incarcerated in new "bridewells" and workhouses. During the seventeenth century, punishment of both juvenile delinquents and sturdy beggars grew in intensity, with magistrates increasingly relying on chain gangs, galley sentences, military impressments, and "transportation" to foreign colonies. Repeated petty thefts were also often treated as capital offenses. Despite such extreme measures, the number of "masterless" young people continued to grow in Europe, particularly in burgeoning cities. Philanthropic endeavors approached the problem from a different perspective and had some successes but were no match for the enormity of the economic and social crisis underway.

## CONCLUSION

While early modern youths throughout Europe shared many experiences, it would be misleading to speak of a uniform youth culture. Friends and other peers were merely one of several social groups to which a young person belonged, and their influence—admittedly strong during the teens and early twenties—was not the only shaper of individual identity and values. The transition from childhood to adulthood involved many biological, cultural, economic, and political changes that occurred at different ages for each youth. Some events, such as entering the world of work or school, proved more significant in the social development of some young people than others. Only marriage could be described as a universally recognized sign of adulthood, and even here an independent household might still be years away. Thus while clearly an important stage in every individual's life cycle, the phase known as youth often remained ambiguous as to both rights and responsibilities—a situation not completely unfamiliar in the modern West.

*See also* **Childhood and Childrearing; Crime and Punishment; Education; Family; Festivals; Guilds; Marriage; Sexuality and Sexual Behavior; Vagrants and Beggars.**

BIBLIOGRAPHY

Ben-Amos, Ilana Krausman. *Adolescence and Youth in Early Modern England*. New Haven, 1994.

Cox, Pamela, and Heather Shore, eds. *Becoming Delinquent: British and European Youth, 1650–1950*. Aldershot, U.K., and Burlington, Vt., 2002.

Davis, Natalie Zemon. "The Reasons of Misrule." In *Society and Culture in Early Modern France: Eight Essays*, pp. 97–123. Stanford, 1975.

Eisenbichler, Konrad, ed. *The Premodern Teenager: Youth in Society, 1150–1650*. Toronto, 2002.

Gillis, John R. *Youth and History: Tradition and Change in European Age Relations, 1770–Present*. Expanded Student Edition. New York, 1981.

Griffiths, Paul. *Youth and Authority: Formative Experiences in England, 1560–1640*. Oxford and New York, 1996.

Levi, Giovanni, and Jean-Claude Schmitt, eds. *A History of Young People in the West. Volume 2: Stormy Evolution to Modern Times*. Translated by Carol Volk. Cambridge, Mass., 1997.

Mitterauer, Michael. *A History of Youth*. Translated by Graeme Dunphy. Oxford and Cambridge, Mass., 1993.

Ozment, Steven, ed. *Three Behaim Boys: Growing Up in Early Modern Germany: A Chronicle of Their Lives*. New Haven, 1990.

JOEL F. HARRINGTON

---

**ZINZENDORF, NIKOLAUS LUDWIG VON** (1700–1760), poet, preacher, theologian, and religious leader. Count Zinzendorf was a controversial figure within German Pietism in the first half of the eighteenth century. He advocated a nonrational approach to Christianity that he called "religion of the heart." In addition to being a creative theologian and author, he was the founder of a dynamic religious community known as the Brüdergemeine (Community of Brethren, now commonly called the Moravian Church) that established communities on four continents.

Zinzendorf was the son of George Ludwig von Zinzendorf, a counsellor in the court of the king of Saxony, and Charlotte Justine von Gersdorf. Because of the early death of his father, Zinzendorf was raised primarily by his grandmother, Henrietta Catherine, Baroness von Gersdorf (1648–1726), who was closely connected to the leaders of the Pietist movement, Philipp Jacob Spener (1635–1705) and August Hermann Francke (1663–1727).

When he was ten, Zinzendorf was sent to Francke's school in Halle, where he developed a strong interest in the Pietist program. He was then sent to the University of Wittenberg for advanced education to broaden his perspective, but Zinzendorf devoted himself to theological and religious pursuits rather than to politics and law.

After his marriage to Erdmuth Dorothea von Reuss (1700–1756) in 1722, Zinzendorf became deeply involved with a group of Protestant refugees from neighboring Moravia who claimed to be a remnant of the Unitas Fratrum (Unity of Brethren), a pre-Reformation Protestant church with roots in the Hussite movement. In addition to offering the Moravians protection from persecution, Zinzendorf organized their village of Herrnhut as a unique religious community.

The Brotherly Agreement of 1727 subordinated secular activities to a religious mission. Women assumed leadership roles almost equal to those of men. Artisans held leadership posts alongside nobles. Several distinctive Moravian practices originated in Herrnhut, such as the Daily Texts drawn from the Bible, making or confirming decisions through the lot, the Easter dawn confession of faith, foot washing, and love feasts. Through schools, publications, and Herrnhut-style communities, the Moravians established a strong presence throughout Protestant Europe, especially in Germany, Switzerland, the Baltic, the Netherlands, and the British Isles.

In 1735 Zinzendorf was ordained as a Lutheran minister, although he never held an official position in the church. Also in 1735 he arranged for the ordination of one of his Moravian followers as a bishop of the nearly defunct Unitas Fratrum. In 1737 Zinzendorf was consecrated a Moravian bishop.

Inspired by Zinzendorf, the first Moravian missionaries left for Saint Thomas (Virgin Islands) in 1732. Soon mission work was established among the Inuit in Greenland and Labrador, the Khoi Khoi in South Africa, the Delaware in British North America, and many other tribal peoples in the Atlantic world. On his voyage to Georgia, John Wesley (1703–1791) met Moravian missionaries and became interested in Zinzendorf's theology. Zinzendorf's writings played an important role in the early development of the Methodist movement.

Controversy swirled around Zinzendorf throughout his career. In 1736 he was exiled from Saxony because he sheltered religious refugees from Habsburg lands. Subsequently Zinzendorf traveled extensively, including two trips to North America, where he preached to slaves and tribal people.

During the 1740s Zinzendorf developed some of his most creative and controversial ideas. Among them were the "choir system" that replaced traditional family structures in Moravian communities with groupings according to age and gender. He also promoted a positive attitude toward sexuality. For instance, he argued that the incarnation of Christ made both male and female genitalia holy since Christ was born of a woman and had male organs. He also taught married couples to view sexual intercourse as a sacramental act symbolizing the mystical union of the soul with Christ. In addition, Zinzendorf encouraged his followers to worship the Holy Spirit as "Mother," and he maintained that all churches are expressions of the true, invisible church. Most controversial was his promotion of a Lutheran "theology of the cross" through a highly evocative worship of the wounds of Christ.

In 1747, Zinzendorf's banishment from Saxony was lifted and the following year, the Moravians received official recognition in Saxony because they had proven to be good subjects. In 1749 Zinzendorf persuaded the British Parliament to recognize the Moravian Church as "an ancient and apostolic church," paving the way for further mission work in the British colonies.

Also in 1749 Zinzendorf experienced the greatest blow to his work when Count Ernst Casimir of Ysenburg-Büdingen (ruled 1708–1749), the secular overlord of the Moravian community of Herrnhaag in the Wetterau, died. His son and successor Gustav Friedrich Casimir (ruled 1749–1768) ordered the Moravians in his realm to swear their fealty to him and repudiate their allegiance to Zinzendorf. Reports of eroticism connected to the veneration of the wounds of Christ among the Single Brothers in the late 1740s (the so-called Sifting Time) may have contributed to this crisis. Over a thousand Moravians chose to relocate in 1750 rather than reject Zinzendorf. They were forced to abandon Herrnhaag's expensive buildings, and the resulting financial crisis nearly destroyed the church.

In 1755 Zinzendorf returned to Herrnhut, where he edited and republished his works. Following the death of Erdmuth in 1756, he married his lifelong co-worker Anna Nitschmann in 1757. Zinzendorf's death in 1760 was a severe blow to the church. Under the leadership of August Gottlieb Spangenberg (1704–1792), the church became increasingly conservative in orientation.

Zinzendorf left a multifaceted legacy. He was a forerunner of the modern subjective theology exemplified in Friedrich Schleiermacher (1768–1834), and he was an early Romantic poet. Moreover, his unusual understanding of race, gender, sexuality, and society attracts attention and even admiration. He established important Moravian communities in Bethlehem, Pa., and Salem, N.C., that continue to be centers of Moravian work in America. By the early twenty-first century the bulk of his followers were in eastern Africa, thanks to the Moravian mission effort.

*See also* **Methodism; Moravian Brethren; Pietism.**

BIBLIOGRAPHY

*Primary Sources*

Zinzendorf, Nikolaus Ludwig von. *A Collection of Sermons from Zinzendorf's Pennsylvania Journey 1741–42.* Edited by Craig D. Atwood, translated by Julie Tomberlin Weber. Bethlehem, Pa., 2002.

———. *Ergänzungsbände zu den Hauptschriften.* Edited by Erich Beyreuther and Gerhard Meyer. Hildesheim, 1965–1971.

———. *Hauptschriften in sechs Bänden.* Edited by Erich Beyreuther and Gerhard Meyer. Hildesheim, 1962–1965.

———. *Nine Public Lectures on Important Subjects in Religion, Preached in Fetter Lane Chapel in London in the Year 1746.* Edited and translated by George W. Forell. Iowa City, 1973; paperback, 1998.

*Secondary Sources*

Atwood, Craig D. *Community of the Cross: Moravian Piety in Colonial Bethlehem.* University Park, Pa., forthcoming. Includes a discussion of Zinzendorf's theology and its impact on his followers.

Freeman, Arthur J. *An Ecumenical Theology of the Heart: The Theology of Count Nicholas Ludwig von Zinzendorf.* Bethlehem, Pa., 1998.

Kinkel, Gary Steven. *Our Dear Mother the Spirit: An Investigation of Count Zinzendorf's Theology and Praxis.* Lanham, Md., 1990.

Meyer, Dietrich, ed. *Bibliographisches Handbuch zur Zinzendorf-Forschung.* Düsseldorf, 1987. An invaluable guide to research on Zinzendorf.

Meyer, Dietrich, and Paul Peucker, eds. *Graf ohne Grenzen: Leben und Werk von Nikolaus Ludwig Graf von Zinzendorf.* Herrnhut, 2000. A beautiful and informative text produced in connection with an exhibit for Zinzendorf's three-hundredth birthday.

Weinlick, John R. *Count Zinzendorf.* New York, 1956; reprint, Bethlehem, Pa., 1989. An English-language biography.

CRAIG D. ATWOOD

**ZOOLOGY.** For much of the sixteenth century, as in earlier periods, animals were valued for use or for their symbolic or allegorical meaning. Medieval bestiaries, based on the *Natural History* of Pliny and the encyclopedic works of such early church fathers as Isidore of Seville, mingled naturalistic description, uses, and symbolic significance in their accounts of animals, and did not clearly demarcate real from mythological beasts. Conrad Gessner's *Historia Animalium* (Description of animals) of 1551, the era's most comprehensive text on animals, continued this mode of description, still evident fifty years later in Edward Topsell's revised translation, *A History of Four-Footed Beastes* (1607). Animals were classified in hierarchical terms centered on the notion of the great chain of being. However, the voyages of discovery and the intellectual changes associated with the scientific revolution began to strip away the layers of symbol and allegory from animals and made them objects of study in themselves.

Animals had been used as surrogates for humans in the training of physicians and surgeons since the twelfth century. Even after human dissection began to be practiced in the fourteenth century, medical schools continued to use animals, especially pigs, dogs, and cats, to teach human anatomy by means of both dissection and vivisection. The beginnings of comparative anatomy are usually dated to the appearance in 1551 of Pierre Belon's (1517–1564) work on the anatomy of cetaceans, soon followed by his comparison of a human skeleton to that of a bird (1555). Volker Coiter (1534–1576) established comparative anatomy as an autonomous field of study in the 1570s, and while animals continued to function as human proxies, numerous works appeared on animal anatomy and physiology as well.

Exotic animals were a form of diplomatic exchange dating back to Roman times. Medieval monarchs established menageries such as that at the Tower of London, which during the sixteenth century included lions, leopards, a tiger, a lynx, an eagle, and a porcupine. Animals in menageries were often used for sport in the form of animal combats or baiting. Louis XIV of France established a menagerie at his palace at Versailles; when the animals died, they were dissected before the Paris Academy of Sciences, and many of them were described in Claude Perrault's (1613–1688) *Mémoires pour servir à l'histoire naturelle des animaux* (1671–

1676; Memoirs for a natural history of animals). After death, these animals graced natural history cabinets (among which Gessner's was famous), which also included plants, antiquities, minerals, and curiosities. These predecessors of the modern natural history museum attempted to make sense of a rapidly expanding world by means of analogies, etymologies, and seemingly odd juxtapositions and also served important social and cultural roles in an aristocratic society based on status and patronage.

The work of Perrault's team and others such as Edward Tyson (1651–1708) made great strides in comparative anatomy. However, the main use of animals in science from the end of the sixteenth century onward was to demonstrate aspects of human (and animal) anatomy and physiology, for instruction and especially for research. William Harvey (1578–1657) demonstrated the circulation of the blood, published in 1628, by means of hundreds of experiments on live animals ranging from fish to dogs. Experimenters in universities and academies all over Europe embraced Harvey's experimental techniques, which included injection and inflation as well as vivisection. Notable examples included the work of Marcello Malpighi (1628–1694) on the structure of the lungs and the capillary circulation, Robert Hooke (1635–1704) on the process of respiration, Regnier de Graaf (1641–1673) on the glands, and Nicolaus Steno (1638–1686) on the structure of the muscles. Hooke and Robert Boyle (1627–1691) placed small animals in a vacuum pump of their design and demonstrated the body's need for fresh air to sustain life. Antoni van Leeuwenhoek (1632–1723) revealed the possibilities of the microscope, also used successfully by Malpighi and Hooke.

Most seventeenth-century natural philosophers regarded animals as machines, although few went as far as René Descartes (1596–1650) in denying their mental capacity to experience pain. Vitalist philosophies revived in the eighteenth century, although the mechanical philosophy continued to influence views of animal function. The work of Stephen Hales (1671–1767) on blood pressure was mechanistic, but by mid-century, Albrecht von Haller (1708–1777) exemplified the new emphasis on vital function with his work on the sensibility and irritability of the nerves. At the beginning of his 1752 treatise on this topic, Haller also displayed a new sensibility toward animals when he apologized for causing them pain.

By the end of the seventeenth century, concepts of classification had reached a crisis. The seemingly chaotic organization of cabinets and collections reflected a lack of consensus on classification schemes. The great influx of animals from the New World and other areas disrupted the old notion of a chain of being that was both full and complete, but there was little agreement about what might be a proper criterion for classification. Although Aristotle had attempted to establish a natural system of classification based on essential features and natural affinities, he also believed in a natural hierarchy. Various theories of plant classification multiplied, but the classification of animals lagged behind. At the end of the seventeenth century, John Ray (1627–1705) attempted a natural classification of animals, but its complexity did not bode well for future endeavors. In 1735, Carl Linnaeus (1707–1778) described a classification of plants based on sexual parts in his *Systema Naturae* (System of nature), which also presented a scheme for classifying animals, organizing them in six broad classes. In the 1779 edition of *Systema Naturae*, he described nearly six thousand species of animals. His system was artificial, aimed at establishing order rather than reproducing nature's plan, and its use of the binomial nomenclature was widely adopted.

Linnaeus's system of classification was challenged by Georges-Louis Leclerc, comte de Buffon (1707–1788), whose *Histoire naturelle* (1749–1788; Natural history) was the most comprehensive (and best-known) work on natural history in the eighteenth century. Buffon argued that any system of classification was by definition arbitrary and artificial, and that reality resided in individuals, not in species. While he modified his views over the course of his life, adopting many Linnaean categories, Buffon is especially important for introducing the concept of time into the discussion of taxonomy, finding variability of species over time but constancy of form at higher taxonomic levels.

By the end of the eighteenth century, animals had lost much of their earlier symbolic meaning. But in both laboratories and natural history museums they were, more than ever, objects of scientific scrutiny.

*See also* Academies, Learned; Biology; Botany; Boyle, Robert; Buffon, Georges Louis Leclerc; Descartes, René; Harvey, William; Hooke, Robert; Leeuwenhoek, Antoni van; Linnaeus, Carl; Louis XIV (France); Malpighi, Marcello; Medicine; Natural History; Ray, John; Scientific Instruments; Scientific Method; Scientific Revolution.

BIBLIOGRAPHY

Cole, F. J. *A History of Comparative Anatomy from Aristotle to the Eighteenth Century.* New York, 1975.

Findlen, Paula. *Possessing Nature. Museums, Collecting, and Scientific Culture in Early Modern Italy.* Berkeley, 1994.

George, Wilma. "Sources and Background to Discoveries of New Animals in the Sixteenth and Seventeenth Centuries." *History of Science* 18 (1980): 79–104.

Guerrini, Anita. "The Ethics of Animal Experimentation in Seventeenth-Century England." *Journal of the History of Ideas* 50, no. 3 (1989): 391–407.

Larson, James L. *Reason and Experience. The Representation of Natural Order in the Work of Carl von Linné.* Berkeley, 1971.

ANITA GUERRINI

---

# ZURBARÁN, FRANCISCO DE (born

Francisco de Zurbarán Márquez [or Salazar]; 1598–1664), Spanish painter. Francisco de Zurbarán was born in Fuentedecantos (Extremadura), an agricultural village. At considerable expense, his father, a shopkeeper, sent him in 1614 to Seville, where he was an apprentice to Pedro Díaz Villanueva, an obscure artist. In 1617 he established a workshop in Llerena, a large Extremaduran market town; no paintings before 1627 have been located. By 1630 he was living in Seville.

In 1626 Zurbarán contracted with the Dominican monastery of San Pablo el Real, Seville, to produce twenty-one paintings for the relatively modest sum of 4,000 reales. Displayed in an oratory chapel of this monastery, *Christ on the Cross* (1627, Art Institute of Chicago), his earliest dated painting, made him famous. Against the dark background, strong illumination accentuates the sculptural qualities of the naturalistically rendered figure. The exceptional stillness of the body indicates death, but dramatic tension is introduced by its leftward sag, which causes Christ's head to fall against his shoulder. Zurbarán probably developed his distinctive style by studying the work of the Italian painter Caravaggio (born Michelangelo Merisi, 1573–1610) and the Spanish sculptor Juan Martínez Montañes (1568–1649).

From 1628 until approximately 1640, Zurbarán was regarded as the leading artist of Andalusia, and he received commissions from monasteries and convents throughout Spain. Apparently jealous of his success, officers of the painters' guild, led by Alonso Cano (1601–1667), ordered him on 23 May 1630 to take the examination for master painters in Seville. Zurbarán appealed to the city council, which denied the guild's authority on 8 June 1630.

Many of Zurbarán's major pictorial programs concern the lives of the most famous saints of the monastic orders that had commissioned them. Thus, for the Monastery of the Merced Calzada, Seville, he produced twenty-two paintings that illustrate the life of Saint Peter Nolasco, the founder of the order. *Saint Peter Nolasco's Vision of the Crucified Saint Peter the Apostle* (1628, Prado, Madrid) eloquently reveals his ability to make the supernatural seem believable. Zurbarán's eight paintings for the Sacristy of the Monastery of Saint Jerome, Guadalupe (1638–1639; still in situ), were unusual because they all depicted residents of that house, such as Bishop Gonzalo de Illescas. His commission for the Carthusian Monastery of Jerez de la Frontera included four large altarpieces depicting Christ's early life. In *Adoration of the Magi* (1639–1640, Musée du Peinture et de Sculpture, Grenoble), he created spectacular effects through the use of glowing colors and lavish still life details.

In 1634 Zurbarán went to Madrid in order to undertake a royal commission, which had been awarded to him through the intervention of Diego Rodriguez de Silva Velázquez (1599–1660). For the Hall of Realms in the Buen Retiro Palace, he painted ten pictures of the Labors of Hercules and a battle scene, *The Defense of Cádiz against the English* (all in the Prado, Madrid). In contrast to most seventeenth-century painters, Zurbarán did not base his images of Hercules on famous classical statues. Instead, he infused Hercules' Labors with an earthy vitality by depicting Hercules as a rugged, awkward man of exceptional strength.

**Francisco de Zurbarán.** *Christ on the Cross.* ©CHRISTIE'S IMAGES/CORBIS

In addition to large-scale programs, Zurbarán also produced many single paintings, including over forty images of Saint Francis of Assisi. As does *Saint Francis in Meditation* (c. 1635–1640, National Gallery, London, National Gallery), most prominently feature a skull, a symbol of penitence; upturned eyes and open mouth express the saint's mystical ecstasy. The "close-up" depiction of the isolated figure against a neutral background still makes a strong impact. In his few still life paintings, such as *Still Life with Lemons, Oranges, and a Rose* (1633, Norton Simon Foundation, Pasadena, Calif.), Zurbarán endowed humble objects with transcendent importance.

After 1640 Zurbarán's career underwent an irreversible decline. The collapse of the Spanish economy greatly limited the expenditures of Spanish monasteries and convents, his primary clients. Moreover, his austere style did not correspond with the increasing emphasis on tender piety in Spanish religious life. To compensate for the loss of clients in Spain, Zurbarán expanded his workshop's production of images for export to the Americas. Moreover, he responded to the changed spiritual mood by creating images such as *Christ Carrying the Cross* (1653, Cathedral at Orléans) that invokes the pity of its spectator. In 1658 Zurbarán moved to Madrid, where he imitated Velázquez's style in portraits such as *Doctor of Laws* (c. 1658–1660, Gardner Museum, Boston).

In 1838 the modern revival of interest in Zurbarán's work resulted from the display of eighty of his paintings in the Galerie Espagnole of the Louvre. His paintings were copied by Édouard Manet (1832–1883) and many other nineteenth-century artists.

*See also* **Spain, Art in.**

BIBLIOGRAPHY

Baticle, Jeannine, ed. *Zurbarán.* New York, 1987. Catalogue of a major exhibition held 1987–1988 at The Metropolitan Museum of Art, New York; Galeries Nationales du Grand Palais, Paris; and Museo del Prado, Madrid; with scholarly studies by leading experts.

Brown, Jonathan. *Francisco de Zurbarán.* New York, 1974. A well-illustrated overview of the artist's career, intended for the general reader.

Soria, Martin S. *Zurbarán.* London, 1953. This catalogue of the artist's entire oeuvre is still useful.

RICHARD G. MANN

---

**ZURICH.** Although there is evidence of settlement around Zurich from the Bronze Age, the Romans were the first to fortify the site and named it Turicum. The legend of the city's foundation dates from the martyrdom of Felix and Regula, Roman Christians and the patron saints of Zurich, who fled to the city from the massacre of their legion in Valais in the third century C.E. They were martyred by decapitation for refusing to pray to Roman gods, whereupon they picked up their heads and carried them up the hill to the spot where they wished to be buried. The Wasserkirche in Zurich marks the spot where they are thought to have been executed. During the eleventh and twelfth centuries, Zurich's traders exploited the favorable location of the city between the Alpine passes and the Rhine to build the city's wealth from textiles, such as wool and silk. In 1336 the Bürgermeister Rudolf Brun led a revolt that shifted power from the patrician families into the hands of the thirteen guilds. Shortly thereafter, in 1351, still under Brunn's direction, Zurich joined the Swiss Confederation, though it remained an imperial city under the direct authority of the emperor. During the fifteenth century Zurich repeatedly attempted to centralize the Confederation under its control, and the result was civil wars such as the Old Zurich War (1439–1450).

Although it lay in the vast diocese of Constance, Zurich was fairly independent of the bishop and had three major ecclesiastical bodies: the Grossmünster, the Fraumünster, and St. Peterskirche. Huldrych Zwingli (1484–1531) arrived in Zurich in 1519 and gradually built a reform movement that gained minority, although influential, support from leading families and the guilds. In April 1525 the Reformation was formally adopted and the Reformed church established. It was an institution that remained under the control of the magistrates throughout the early modern period. Zurich developed provision for higher education, but not a university. It remained an important center of trade and a key member of the international Reformed church, but during the seventeenth and eighteenth centuries

Zurich was a provincial city with little influence beyond the Swiss Confederation.

*See also* **Switzerland; Zwingli, Huldrych.**

BIBLIOGRAPHY

Flüeler, Niklaus, and Marianne Flüeler-Grauwiler, eds. *Geschichte des Kantons Zürich*. Vol. 2, *Frühe Neuzeit, 16. bis 18. Jahrhundert*. Zurich, 1996.

Gordon, Bruce. *The Swiss Reformation*. Manchester, U.K., 2002.

BRUCE GORDON

## ZWINGLI, HULDRYCH (1484–1531),

Swiss reformer and church leader. Born into a peasant family in Toggenburg, an Alpine valley in the eastern part of modern-day Switzerland, Zwingli studied at the universities of Vienna and Basel (1498–1506), where he was exposed to the major currents that would shape his theology: late medieval Scholasticism and humanism. Research beginning in the late twentieth century has pointed to the particular importance of Desiderius Erasmus (1466?–1536) and John Duns Scotus (c. 1266–1308) to his theological formation. Zwingli was ordained to the priesthood and served first in Glarus, one of the smallest cantons of the Swiss Confederation, before going to the great Benedictine monastery of Einsiedeln (1516), whose rich library resources afforded the young priest the opportunity to deepen his knowledge of patristic and medieval writers. He preached at the yearly official pilgrimages made by the citizens of Zurich to the Black Madonna of Einsiedeln, and his sermons made him well known in the city. In 1519 he was called to the Grossmünster in Zurich as a stipendiary priest.

Zwingli's preaching, in which he denounced corruption and called on the people to purify themselves before God, created the mood for reform, but it was a small circle of like-minded priests, printers, and magistrates who pushed the movement forward. Events took shape around two disputations in 1523 for which Zwingli wrote his *Sixty-seven Theses*, his first major work. Zwingli sought to reform church and society, but he recognized that to do this he required the support of Zurich's magistrates, who in turn needed to be reassured that reform did not imply social revolution. His vision of Christian government was drawn from the Old Testament, with the prophet (Zwingli) advising the ruler (the Zurich town council), who was responsible for enforcing the laws of the state.

Zwingli's position in Zurich was never wholly secure. The establishment of the new Reformed order in Zurich at Easter 1525 was largely due to the influence of a couple of key magistrates who backed Zwingli. At the center of Zwingli's vision was the reform of worship, and the Reformation commenced in Zurich with a celebration of the new liturgy of the Lord's Supper. His reforms, however, revealed a mixture of late medieval and Erasmian impulses; institutional changes, as well as moral legislation, were drawn from the reform councils of the fifteenth century, and, like Erasmus, Zwingli believed that education was the key to the creation of a Christian society.

Institutional reform under Zwingli was halting, largely because from 1525 until his death he was involved in a series of heated polemical exchanges. Zwingli faced opposition from Catholics, his former mentor Erasmus, the so-called Anabaptists, and most famously, from Martin Luther. Virtually all of Zwingli's theological writings were hastily compiled responses to particular crises or attacks. Thus his work cannot be treated as systematic theology. The three major events in Zwingli's career after 1525 were the Baden disputation (1526), which he refused to attend for fear of being arrested and executed, the Bern disputation (1528), which saw the Reformation adopted in major parts of the Swiss Confederation, and the Colloquy of Marburg (1529), where he and Luther came face to face. Zwingli's desire to bring the Reformation to the rest of the Swiss Confederation led to alliance building that made war with the Catholic states probable. This led to the disastrous First and Second Kappel Wars of 1529 and 1531. Zwingli was killed in a surprise attack on the night of 11 October 1531.

On account of their acrimonious falling out with respect to the celebration of the Lord's Supper, specifically the nature of Christ's presence in the Eucharist, the question of Luther's influence on Zwingli has remained, for confessional reasons, highly contentious. Certainly Zwingli keenly followed the "Luther affair" of 1517–1521, and read all the German reformer's works, which were being printed in Basel. On key theological points, such as "faith alone" and "scripture alone," they were in agreement, but Zwingli had an entirely different agenda, which led to a theology of a different character. Zwingli's theology was shaped by two crucial aspects: first, his experience of serving in military campaigns (1513–1515) and observing with horror the effects of the mercenary trade on the Swiss; and second, the form of Christian humanism prevalent in southwestern Germany and the Swiss lands. The type of humanism that shaped Zwingli's thought concentrated on the practical Christian life and reform of the church, emphasizing the role of the Old Testament. To this we can attribute most of the major themes in Zwingli's thought: the utter sovereignty of God, the covenantal nature of God's relationship with humanity, God's demand that his people be "pure," and the centrality of ethics and the life of the regenerated Christian.

Zwingli was not a national reformer; his cause was closely linked with the particular aspirations of Zurich. Nevertheless, the clarity of his thought carried his ideas across Europe, and there can be no doubt that he was the founder of the Reformed tradition.

*See also* **Bullinger, Heinrich; Erasmus, Desiderius; Luther, Martin; Lutheranism; Marburg, Colloquy of; Reformation, Protestant; Zurich.**

BIBLIOGRAPHY

Gordon, Bruce. *The Swiss Reformation*. Manchester, U.K., 2002.

Potter, G. R. *Zwingli*. Cambridge, U.K., and New York, 1976.

Stephens, W. P. *The Theology of Huldrych Zwingli*. Oxford and New York, 1986.

BRUCE GORDON

# SYSTEMATIC OUTLINE
# OF CONTENTS

This outline provides a general overview of the conceptual scheme of the *Encyclopedia,* listing the titles of each entry and subentry. Because the section headings are not mutually exclusive, certain entries in the *Encyclopedia* are listed in more than one section. Monarchs of the same name are listed first by their country, and then numerically. Thus, for example, Henry VII and Henry VIII of England precede Henry II of France.

Passarowitz, Peace of (1718)
Pyrenees, Peace of the (1659)
Utrecht, Peace of (1713)
Westphalia, Peace of (1648)

---

## 10 RELIGION

Anabaptism
Anticlericalism
Apocalypticism
Atheism
Augsburg, Religious Peace of
Bible
    Interpretation
    Translations and Editions
Cabala
Calvinism
Catholic Spirituality and Mysticism
Catholicism
Church and State Relations
Church of England
Clergy
    Protestant Clergy
    Roman Catholic Clergy
    Russian Orthodox Clergy
Confraternities
*Conversos*
Deism
Dissenters, English
Febronianism
Gallicanism
Hagiography
Haskalah (Jewish Enlightenment)
Huguenots
Hussites
Hymns
Inquisition
Inquisition, Roman
Inquisition, Spanish
Islam in the Ottoman Empire
Jansenism
Jesuits
Jews, Attitudes toward
Jews and Judaism
Josephinism
Lutheranism
Marburg, Colloquy of
Martyrs and Martyrology
Messianism, Jewish

Methodism
Miracles
Missions, Parish
Missions and Missionaries
    Asia
    Spanish America
Moravian Brethren
Moriscos
Nantes, Edict of
Old Believers
Orthodoxy, Greek
Orthodoxy, Russian
Papacy and Papal States
Pietism
Poissy, Colloquy of
Preaching and Sermons
Puritanism
Quakers
Quietism
Reformation, Catholic
Reformation, Protestant
Reformations in Eastern Europe: Protestant,
    Catholic, and Orthodox
Religious Orders
Religious Piety
Seminary
Swedenborgianism
Theology
Toleration
Trent, Council of
Uniates
Union of Brest (1596)
Witchcraft

---

## 11 ART AND CULTURE

Academies of Art
Architecture
Art
    Art Exhibitions
    The Art Market and Collecting
    Art Theory, Criticism, and
        Historiography
    Artistic Patronage
    The Conception and Status of the Artist
Baroque
Biography and Autobiography
Britain, Architecture in
Britain, Art in

Hungary
Ireland
Italy
Kalmar, Union of
Lithuania, Grand Duchy of, to 1569
Lorraine, Duchy of
Milan
Naples, Kingdom of
Netherlands, Southern
Ottoman Empire
Palatinate
Parma
Poland to 1569
Poland-Lithuania, Commonwealth of,
    1569–1795
Portugal
Prussia
Roma (Gypsies)
Romania
Russia
Savoy, duchy of
Saxony
Scotland
Serbia
Silesia
Spain
Sweden
Switzerland
Teutonic Knights
Ukraine
Venice
Württemberg, duchy of

## 18.2 CITIES
Amsterdam
Antwerp
Augsburg
Barcelona
Berlin
Bordeaux
Boston
Budapest
Buenos Aires
Cádiz
Charleston
Cologne
Constantinople
Cracow
Dresden
Dublin

Edinburgh
Florence
Frankfurt am Main
Free and Imperial Cities
Gdańsk
Geneva
Genoa
Goa
Granada
Hamburg
Hanover
Jülich-Cleves-Berg
Kiev
La Rochelle
Leipzig
Lima
Lisbon
London
Lübeck
Lviv
Lyon
Macau
Madrid
Manila
Mantua
Marseille
Mexico City
Moscow
Munich
Münster
New York
Nuremberg
Paris
Philadelphia
Potosí
Prague
Rome
St. Petersburg
Seville
Smyrna (İzmir)
Stockholm
Strasbourg
Toledo
Topkapi Palace
Versailles
Vienna
Vilnius
Warsaw
Zurich

# 19 BIOGRAPHIES

# DIRECTORY OF CONTRIBUTORS

**O. W. ABI-MERSHED**
*Georgetown University*
Africa: North Africa

**ANN JENSEN ADAMS**
*University of California, Santa Barbara*
Netherlands, Art in the: Art in Flanders, 1585–1700
Netherlands, Art in the: Art in the Netherlands, 1500–1585
Netherlands, Art in the: Art in the Northern Netherlands, 1585–1700
Rembrandt van Rijn

**CHRISTINE ADAMS**
*St. Mary's College*
Bordeaux
Bourgeoisie

**GÁBOR ÁGOSTON**
*Georgetown University*
Budapest
Hungarian Literature and Language
Hungary
Rákóczi Revolt
Vienna, Sieges of

**VIRGINIA H. AKSAN**
*McMaster University*
Sultan
Vizier

**KEN ALBALA**
*University of the Pacific*
Consumption

**AMIR ALEXANDER**
Author of *Geometrical Landscapes: The Voyages of Discovery and the Transformation of Mathematical Practice*
Euler, Leonhard
Lagrange, Joseph-Louis
Mathematics
Viète, François

**MICHAEL J. B. ALLEN**
*University of California, Los Angeles*
Neoplatonism

**GLENN J. AMES**
*University of Toledo*
Colbert, Jean-Baptiste
French Colonies: India
Gama, Vasco da
Mercantilism

**WILDA CHRISTINE ANDERSON**
*Johns Hopkins University*
Condorcet, Marie-Jean Caritat, marquis de
Lavoisier, Antoine

**WALTER G. ANDREWS**
*University of Washington*
Turkish Literature and Language

**WILBUR APPLEBAUM**
*Illinois Institute of Technology*
Copernicus, Nicolaus

**KARL APPUHN**
*University of Oregon*
Genoa

**IAN W. ARCHER**
*Keble College, Oxford University*
London

**ROGER ARIEW**
*Virginia Polytechnic Institute and University*
Aristotelianism

**RONALD G. ASCH**
*University of Osnabrück*
Aristocracy and Gentry
Court and Courtiers
Thirty Years' War (1618–1648)

**WILLIAM B. ASHWORTH, JR.**
*University of Missouri*
    Leeuwenhoek, Antoni van
    Steno, Nicolaus

**CHRISTOPHER D. M. ATKINS**
*Museum of Fine Arts, Boston*
    Hals, Frans
    Ruysch, Rachel
    Vermeer, Jan

**CRAIG D. ATWOOD**
Author of *Community of the Cross: Moravian Piety in Colonial Bethlehem*
    Zinzendorf, Nikolaus
        Ludwig von

**MICHAEL AUSTIN**
*Shepherd College*
    Pepys, Samuel

**DAMIAN BACICH**
*University of California, Los Angeles*
    Vives, Juan Luis

**MARTHA BALDWIN**
*Stonehill College*
    Chronometer
    Clocks and Watches
    Gilbert, William

**PETER BARKER**
*University of Oklahoma*
    Cosmology
    Kepler, Johannes
    Stoicism

**G. J. BARKER-BENFIELD**
*University at Albany, State University of New York*
    Sensibility

**ROBIN B. BARNES**
*Davidson College*
    Apocalypticism
    Prophecy

**PAUL BAROLSKY**
*University of Virginia*
    Vasari, Giorgio

**M. ELIZABETH C. BARTLET**
*Duke University*
    Gluck, Christoph
        Willibald von
    Rameau, Jean-Philippe

**GEORGE C. BAUER**
**ASSOCIATE EDITOR**
*University of California, Irvine*
    Academies of Art
    Bernini, Gian Lorenzo
    Caricature and Cartoon
    Prints and Popular Imagery:
        Later Prints and
        Printmaking

**LINDA F. BAUER**
**ASSOCIATE EDITOR**
*University of California, Irvine*
    Forgeries, Copies, and Casts
    Maulbertsch, Franz Anton

**FREDERIC J. BAUMGARTNER**
*Virginia Polytechnic Institute and State University*
    Anne of Brittany
    Authority, Concept of
    Charles VIII (France)
    Charles the Bold
        (Burgundy)
    Francis I (France)
    Henry II (France)
    Louis XII (France)

**CHARLES BEDDINGTON**
*Beddington and Blackman Ltd., London*
    Veduta (View Painting)

**WOLFGANG BEHRINGER**
*University of York, U.K.*
    Bavaria
    Postal Systems
    Wittelsbach Dynasty
        (Bavaria)

**WILLIAM BEIK**
*Emory University*
    Popular Protest and
        Rebellions

**KEITH R. BENSON**
*National Science Foundation*
    Buffon, Georges Louis
        Leclerc

**CRISTIAN BERCO**
*University of Toronto*
    Moriscos
    Moriscos, Expulsion of

**ROBERT W. BERGER**
Author of *A Royal Passion: Louis XIV as Patron of Architecture*
    Art: Art Exhibitions

**JOSEPH BERGIN**
*University of Manchester*
    Marillac, Michel de
    Richelieu, Armand-Jean Du
        Plessis, cardinal

**ZVI BIENER**
*University of Pittsburgh*
    Physics

**ROBERT BIRELEY**
*Loyola University*
    Ferdinand II (Holy
        Roman Empire)

**JEREMY BLACK**
*University of Exeter*
    Anne (England)
    Cateau-Cambrésis (1559)
    England
    George I (Great Britain)
    George II (Great Britain)
    George III (Great Britain)
    Gibbon, Edward
    Grand Tour
    Habsburg-Valois Wars
    Laud, William
    Pyrenees, Peace of the
        (1659)

**CONSTANCE BLACKWELL**
*Foundation for Intellectual History*
Logic

**ANN BLAIR**
*Harvard University*
Dictionaries and
Encyclopedias

**BRIAN BOECK**
*Harvard University*
Fur Trade: Russia
Imperial Expansion, Russia
Serfdom in Russia

**DONNA BOHANAN**
*Auburn University*
Marseille

**REBECCA BOONE**
*Lamar University*
Cambrai, League of (1508)
Gentleman
Savoy, duchy of

**PETER BORSAY**
*University of Wales, Lampeter*
Spas and Resorts

**GAIL BOSSENGA**
*University of Kansas*
Citizenship

**RUTH BOTTIGHEIMER**
*State University of New York
at Stony Brook*
Folk Tales and Fairy Tales

**D'A. J. D. BOULTON**
*University of Notre Dame*
Heraldry

**CYNTHIA BOUTON**
*Texas A & M University*
Food Riots

**BARBARA C. BOWEN**
*Vanderbilt University*
Humor

**JAMES M. BOYDEN**
*Tulane University*
Éboli, Ruy Gómez de Silva,
prince of
Philip II (Spain)

**JOHN K. BRACKETT**
*University of Cincinnati*
Crime and Punishment

**THOMAS A. BRADY, JR.**
*University of California, Berkeley*
Augsburg, Religious Peace
of (1555)
Germany, Idea of
Holy Roman Empire
Institutions

**KATHRYN BRAMMALL**
*Truman State University*
Museums

**CAROL M. BRESNAHAN**
*University of Toledo*
Daily Life
Florence
Medici Family
Pawning

**DANIEL BREWER**
*University of Minnesota*
*Encyclopédie*
Philosophes

**THOMAS H. BROMAN**
*University of Wisconsin, Madison*
Medicine

**DAVID BROMWICH**
*Yale University*
Burke, Edmund
Sublime, Idea of the

**KENDALL W. BROWN**
*Brigham Young University*
Cortés, Hernán
Pizarro Brothers
Potosí

**STUART BROWN**
*Open University, U.K.*
Empiricism

**DANIEL BROWNSTEIN**
*Independent Scholar, Bologna*
Cartography and Geography

**GAYLE K. BRUNELLE**
*California State University,
Fullerton*
Communication and
Transportation

**LAWRENCE M. BRYANT**
*California State University,
Chico*
Ritual, Civic and Royal

**ALMUT BUES**
*German Historical Institute,
Warsaw*
Baltic Nations

**DOROTHEA BURNS**
*Harvard College Libraries*
Pastel

**PAUL BUSKOVITCH**
*Yale University*
Alexis I (Russia)
Boris Godunov (Russia)
Duma
Ivan III (Muscovy)
Ivan IV, "the Terrible"
(Russia)
Michael Romanov (Russia)
Oprichnina
Romanov Dynasty (Russia)
Russia
Sofiia Alekseevna
Vasilii III (Muscovy)

**WILLIAM CAFERRO**
*Vanderbilt University*
Accounting and
Bookkeeping
Banking and Credit
Late Middle Ages
Mercenaries

**EUAN K. CAMERON**
*Union Theological Seminary*
Clergy: Protestant Clergy

**JODI CAMPBELL**
*Texas Christian University*
Calderón de la Barca, Pedro
Charles II (Spain)
Drama: Spanish and
Portuguese
Vega, Lope de

**JORGE CAÑIZAZES-ESGUERRA**
*University at Buffalo, State*
*University of New York*
Race, Theories of

**BERNARD CAPP**
*University of Warwick*
English Civil War Radicalism

**MICHAEL CARHART**
*University of Neveda, Reno*
Ethnography
Herder, Johann
Gottfried von
Noble Savage
Travel and Travel Literature

**MARYBETH CARLSON**
*University of Dayton*
Servants

**CHARLES CARLTON**
*North Carolina State University*
Charles I (England)

**ANN CARMICHAEL**
*Indiana University*
Plague

**DAVID W. CARRITHERS**
*University of Tennessee,*
*Chattanooga*
Montesquieu, Charles-Louis
de Secondat de

**LINDA L. CARROLL**
*Tulane University*
Carnival

Casanova, Giacomo
Girolamo
Drama: Italian
Goldoni, Carlo
Italian Literature
and Language

**STUART CARROLL**
*University of York, U.K.*
Catherine de Médicis
Catholic League (France)
Coligny Family
Guise Family
Henry III (France)
L'Hôpital, Michel de

**DAVID CAST**
*Bryn Mawr College*
Britain, Architecture in
Jones, Inigo
Wren, Christopher

**FRANCESCO C. CESAREO**
*John Carroll University*
Bellarmine, Robert
Borromeo, Carlo
Catholic Spirituality
and Mysticism
Reformation, Catholic
Theology

**SARA E. CHAPMAN**
*Oakland University*
Bossuet, Jacques-Bénigne
Fénelon, François
Mazarin, Jules

**LESLIE CHOQUETTE**
*Assumption College*
French Colonies:
North America

**ALVIN L. CLARK, JR.**
*Fogg Art Museum, Harvard*
Callot, Jacques
Claude Lorrain (Gellée)
Le Brun, Charles
Poussin, Nicolas
Vouet, Simon

**GEOFFREY CLARK**
*State University of New York*
*at Potsdam*
Insurance

**HENRY CLARK**
*Canisius College*
La Rochefoucauld,
François, duc de

**RICHARD CLEARY**
*University of Texas at Austin*
City Planning
Ledoux, Claude-Nicolas

**JAMES CLIFTON**
*Museum of Fine Arts, Houston*
Naples, Art in

**LOUISE GEORGE CLUBB**
*University of California, Berkeley*
Commedia dell'Arte

**NICHOLAS H. CLULEE**
*Frostburg State University*
Dee, John

**TIMOTHY J. COATES**
*College of Charleston*
Goa
Macau
Portuguese Colonies: The
Indian Ocean and Asia

**MICHAEL COLE**
*University of North Carolina*
Cellini, Benvenuto
Giambologna (Giovanni
da Bologna)

**JAMES B. COLLINS**
*Georgetown University*
Absolutism
Brittany
Class, Status, and Order

**MARSHA S. COLLINS**
*University of North Carolina*
Góngora y Argote, Luis de

**STEPHEN L. COLLINS**
*Babson College*
Reason

**WILLIAM CONNELL**
*Seton Hall University*
Grotius, Hugo

**NOBLE DAVID COOK**
*Florida International University*
Spanish Colonies: Peru

**J. P. D. COOPER**
*University of Sussex*
Edward VI (England)

**BERNARD DOV COOPERMAN**
*University of Maryland*
Messianism, Jewish
Nasi Family

**KEVIN L. COPE**
*Louisiana State University*
Pope, Alexander

**LESLEY CORMACK**
*University of Alberta*
Arctic and Antarctic
Surveying

**FANNY COSANDEY**
*University of Nantes*
Queens and Empresses

**ALLISON P. COUDERT**
*Princeton University*
Cabala
Magic

**EDWARD COUNTRYMAN**
*Southern Methodist University*
American Independence,
War of (1775–1783)

**HOWARD COUTTS**
*Josephine & John Bowes Museum*
Ceramics, Pottery, and
Porcelain

**SARAH COVINGTON**
*Elizabethtown College*
Clothing

Sports

**ALEXANDER COWAN**
*Northumbria University, U.K.*
Lübeck

**DAVID L. COWEN**
*Rutgers University (Emeritus)*
Apothecaries

**KATHERINE CRAWFORD**
*Vanderbilt University*
Sexuality and Sexual
Behavior

**DANIEL A. CREWS**
*Central Missouri State University*
Cobos, Francisco de los

**DAVID M. CROWE**
*Elon College*
Roma (Gypsies)

**JOHN CUNNALLY**
*Iowa State University*
Coins and Medals

**NICHOLAS P. CUSHNER**
*State University of New York,
Empire State College*
Spanish Colonies:
The Philippines

**DAVID DANIELL**
*University of London (Emeritus)*
Bible: Interpretation
Bible: Translations
and Editions

**GRAHAM DARBY**
*King Edward VI School,
Bournemouth, U.K.*
Wallenstein, A. W. E. von
Westphalia, Peace of (1648)

**BRIAN DAVIES**
*University of Texas*
Andrusovo, Truce of (1667)
Black Sea Steppe
False Dmitrii, First
Livonian War (1558–1583)

Razin, Stepan
Russo-Polish Wars
Time of Troubles (Russia)

**J. M. DE BUJANDA**
*University of Sherbrooke, Quebec*
Index of Prohibited Books

**MICHEL DE WAELE**
*University of Quebec, Chicoutimi*
Anne of Austria
Assassination
Fronde
Officeholding

**DAVID J. DENBY**
*Dublin City University*
Passions

**DENNIS DES CHENE**
*Washington University, St. Louis*
Determinism
Mechanism
Psychology

**DOMINIQUE DESLANDRES**
*University of Montreal*
Bérulle, Pierre de
François de Sales
Marie de l'Incarnation
Missions, Parish
Quietism
Seminary
Vincent de Paul

**JONATHAN DEWALD**
**EDITOR IN CHIEF**
*University at Buffalo, State
University of New York*
Bourbon Dynasty (France)
Diamond Necklace, Affair of
Espionage
France
Industrial Revolution
Rentiers
Valois Dynasty (France)

**DONALD R. DICKSON**
*Texas A & M University*
Utopia

**BARBARA B. DIEFENDORF**
*Boston University*
St. Bartholomew's
Day Massacre

**THOMAS DIPIERO**
*University of Rochester*
Sade, Donatien-Alphonse-
François de

**SIMON DITCHFIELD**
*University of York, U.K.*
Hagiography

**WILLIAM DONOVAN**
*Loyola College*
Lisbon

**BRENDAN DOOLEY**
*International University, Bremen*
Gianonne, Pietro
Muratori, Ludovico Antonio
Printing and Publishing

**SUSAN DORAN**
*Christ Church College,*
*Oxford University*
Church of England

**MICHAEL D. DRIEDGER**
*Brock University*
Anabaptism
Hamburg
Pietism

**ROBERT S. DUPLESSIS**
*Swarthmore College*
Crisis of the Seventeenth
Century

**FRANCIS A. DUTRA**
*University of California,*
*Santa Barbara*
Portugal
Portuguese Colonies: Brazil
Portuguese Colonies:
Madeira and the Azores

**WILLIAM EAMON**
*New Mexico State University*
Secrets, Books of

**THERESA EARENFIGHT**
*Seattle University*
Ferdinand of Aragón

**GLENN EHRSTINE**
*University of Iowa*
Brant, Sebastian
German Literature
and Language

**EMLYN EISENACH**
*Independent Scholar*
Concubinage
Divorce
Marriage

**MARTIN MALCOLM ELBL**
*Trent University, Otonabee*
*College*
Portuguese Colonies: Africa

**J. H. ELLIOTT**
*Oriel College, Oxford University*
Olivares, Gaspar de Guzmán
y Pimentel, Count of

**LEE MATTHEW ESCANDON**
*Princeton University*
Victoria, Tomás Luis de

**DOREEN EVENDEN**
*McMaster University*
Motherhood and
Childbearing

**JAMES R. FARR**
*Purdue University*
Artisans
Guilds
Proto-Industry
Strikes

**GAIL FEIGENBAUM**
*Getty Research Institute*
Carracci Family

**PALOMA FERNÁNDEZ-PÉREZ**
*University of Barcelona*
Cádiz
Charles III (Spain)

**ZIRKA ZAREMBA FILIPCZAK**
*Williams College*
Rubens, Peter Paul
Van Dyck, Anthony

**NENAD FILIPOVIC**
*Princeton University*
Balkans
Porte

**MAX FINCHER**
*Independent Scholar,*
*Aylesbury, U.K.*
Addison, Joseph
Fielding, Henry
Johnson, Samuel
Richardson, Samuel
Steele, Richard
Swift, Jonathan

**PAULA FINDLEN**
*Stanford University*
Academies, Learned
Aldrovandi, Ulisse
Bassi, Laura
Kircher, Athanasius
Pornography

**MARY FISCHER**
*Napier University*
Teutonic Knights

**MARY E. FISSELL**
*Johns Hopkins University*
Midwives
Obstetrics and Gynecology
Sexual Difference,
Theories of

**KATE FLEET**
*Newnham College, Cambridge*
*University*
Levant
Mehmed II
(Ottoman Empire)
Ottoman Dynasty

**BENEDETTO FONTANA**
*Baruch College*
Democracy

KRISTINE K. FORNEY
*California State University,*
*Long Beach*
    Gabrieli, Andrea and
        Giovanni
    Lasso, Orlando di

MARC FORSTER
*Connecticut College*
    Febronianism

JULIAN H. FRANKLIN
*Columbia University*
    Bodin, Jean

DAVID FRICK
*University of California, Berkeley*
    Cracow
    Gdańsk
    Kiev
    Kochanowski, Jan
    Kołłątaj, Hugo
    Lithuania, Grand Duchy of,
        to 1569
    Lithuanian Literature
        and Language
    Lviv
    Mohyla, Peter
    Polish Literature
        and Language
    Reformations in Eastern
        Europe: Protestant,
        Catholic, and Orthodox
    Sarmatism
    Smotrytskyi, Meletii
    Ukrainian Literature
        and Language
    Vilnius
    Warsaw

J. WILLIAM FROST
*Swarthmore College (Emeritus)*
    Quakers

ROBERT I. FROST
*King's College London*
    Northern Wars

THOMAS A. FUDGE
*University of Canterbury,*
*New Zealand*
    Hussites

RADEK FUKALA
*Silesian University at Opava*
    Silesia

JOHN G. GAGLIARDO
*Boston University*
    Enlightened Despotism

ALISON GAMES
*Georgetown University*
    Atlantic Ocean

ELENI GARA
*University of the Aegean,*
*Mytilene, Greece*
    Greece

JOHN GARRIGUS
*Jacksonville University*
    French Colonies:
        The Caribbean

HILARY GATTI
*University of Rome, La Sapienza*
    Bruno, Giordano

SUZANNE GEARHART
*University of California, Irvine*
    Prévost d'Exiles,
        Antoine-François

TOBY GELFAND
*University of Ottawa*
    Surgeons

IAN GENTLES
*Glendon College, York*
*University, Toronto*
    Cromwell, Oliver
    English Civil War and
        Interregnum

JANIS M. GIBBS
*Hope College*
    Cologne

GUIDO GIGLIONI
*Massachusetts Institute of*
*Technology*
    Anatomy and Physiology
    Harvey, William
    Malpighi, Marcello
    Vesalius, Andreas

EMMA GILBY
*Gonville and Caius College,*
*Cambridge University*
    Pascal, Blaise

JULIANNE GILLAND
*University of California, Berkeley*
    Ensenada, Cenón
        Somodevilla,
        marqués de la
    Floridablanca, José Moñino,
        count of

JOHN R. GILLIS
*Rutgers University*
    Islands

JAN GLETE
*Stockholm University*
    Navy

THOMAS F. GLICK
*Boston University*
    Colonialism
    Magellan, Ferdinand
    Scientific Instruments

DANIEL GOFFMAN
*Ball State University*
    Smyrna (İzmir)

ELIZABETH C. GOLDSMITH
*Boston University*
    La Fayette,
        Marie-Madeleine de
    Molière
    Scudéry, Madeleine de
    Sévigné, Marie de

JAMES L. GOLDSMITH
*University of Oklahoma*
    Economic Crises
    Feudalism

**JAMES GOODALE**
*Bucknell University*
Augustus II the Strong
(Saxony and Poland)
Saxony

**BRUCE GORDON**
*University of St. Andrews,
Scotland*
Bullinger, Heinrich
Zurich
Zwingli, Huldrych

**DAVID M. GORDON**
*University of Maryland*
Africa: Sub-Saharan

**MICHAH GOTTLIEB**
*Brown University*
Mendelssohn, Moses

**KENNETH GOUWENS**
*University of Connecticut*
Rome
Rome, Sack of

**PAOLO GOZZA**
*University of Bologna*
Acoustics

**LISA JANE GRAHAM**
*Haverford College*
Lettre de Cachet

**MARK GRANQUIST**
*Gustavus Adolphus College*
Swedenborgianism

**RICHARD L. GREAVES**
*Florida State University*
Bunyan, John

**MOLLY GREENE**
*Princeton University*
Mediterranean Basin
Piracy

**MARK GREENGRASS**
*University of Sheffield*
Comenius, Jan Amos
Condé Family

Hartlib, Samuel
Huguenots

**TOBIAS GREGORY**
*University of California,
Northridge*
Tasso, Torquato

**PAUL F. GRENDLER
ASSOCIATE EDITOR**
*University of Toronto (Emeritus)*
Advice and Etiquette Books
Benedict XIV (pope)
Censorship
City-State
Cornaro Piscopia,
Elena Lucrezia
Education
Machiavelli, Niccolò
Mantua
Parma
Progress
Renaissance
Universities

**JACQUES M. GRES-GAYER**
*Catholic University of America,
Washington*
Gallicanism
Jansenism
Urban VIII (pope)

**EVA GRIFFITH**
*King's College London*
Jonson, Ben
Marlowe, Christopher
Shakespeare, William

**ULRICH GROETSCH**
*Rutgers University*
Lessing, Gotthold Ephraim
Wieland, Christoph Martin
Wolff, Christian

**EDDY GROOTES**
*University of Amsterdam
(Emeritus)*
Dutch Literature
and Language

**EMILY R. GROSHOLZ**
*Pennsylvania State University*
Leibniz, Gottfried Wilhelm

**DAVID GRUMMITT**
*History of Parliament Trust,
London*
Cecil Family
Henry VII (England)
James I and VI
(England and Scotland)
Star Chamber
Stuart Dynasty
(England and Scotland)
Tudor Dynasty (England)

**ANITA GUERRINI**
*University of California,
Santa Barbara*
Zoology

**GAY GULLICKSON**
*University of Maryland*
Textile Industry

**CHARLES D. GUNNOE, JR.**
*Aquinas College*
Palatinate

**BRUCE GUSTAFSON**
*Franklin and Marshall College*
Lully, Jean-Baptiste

**DOROTHY METZGER HABEL**
*University of Tennessee*
Rome, Architecture in

**ERIK J. HADLEY**
*University at Buffalo, State
University of New York*
National Identity

**MICHAEL HAKKENBERG**
*Roanoke University*
Dort, Synod of

**MARY HOYT HALAVAIS**
*Sonoma State University*
Madrid

**MARCIA B. HALL**
*Temple University*
Mannerism

**FIONA DEANS HALLORAN**
*University of California,*
*Los Angeles*
Boston
Charleston
New York
Philadelphia

**MICHAEL HAMMER**
*University of California,*
*Los Angeles*
Spanish Literature
and Language

**RACHEL HAMMERSLEY**
*University of Sussex*
Harrington, James
Idealism

**GREGORY HANLON**
*Dalhousie University*
Italian Wars (1494–1559)
Italy
Milan

**JAMES D. HARDY, JR.**
*Louisiana State University*
Frederick II (Prussia)
Frederick William I (Prussia)
Joseph II (Holy
Roman Empire)

**DONALD J. HARRELD**
*Brigham Young University*
Dutch Revolt (1568–1648)

**JOEL F. HARRINGTON**
*Vanderbilt University*
Childhood and Childrearing
Family
Nuremberg
Youth

**ALICE K. HARRIS**
*Georgia State University*
Granada

**TIM HARRIS**
*Brown University*
Exclusion Crisis
Glorious Revolution
(Britain)
James II (England)
Political Parties in England
William and Mary

**PETER HARRISON**
*Bond University, Australia*
Design
Enthusiasm

**GARY HATFIELD**
*University of Pennsylvania*
Epistemology

**JOHN B. HATTENDORF**
*U.S. Naval War College*
Anglo-Dutch Naval Wars

**J. MICHAEL HAYDEN**
*University of Saskatchewan*
Estates-General,
French: 1614

**PATRICK MARSHALL**
**HAYDEN-ROY**
*Nebraska Wesleyan University*
Franck, Sebastian

**DAVID L. HAYS**
*University of Illinois*
Gardens and Parks
Picturesque

**RANDOLPH C. HEAD**
*University of California,*
*Riverside*
Reformation, Protestant
Switzerland

**LEX HEERMA VAN VOSS**
*International Institute of Social*
*History, Netherlands*
Baltic and North Seas

**WENDY HELLER**
*Princeton University*
Monteverdi, Claudio

Palestrina, Giovanni
Pierluigi da
Schütz, Heinrich
Vivaldi, Antonio

**MARY HENNINGER-VOSS**
*Princeton University*
Engineering: Civil
Engineering: Military
Technology

**JOHN HENRY**
*University of Edinburgh*
Glisson, Francis
Hooke, Robert
Matter, Theories of
Scientific Revolution

**WILLIAM L. HINE**
*York University, Toronto*
Mersenne, Marin

**KEITH HITCHINS**
*University of Illinois*
Romania

**LOTHAR HÖBELT**
*University of Vienna*
Ferdinand III (Holy
Roman Empire)

**TIMOTHY HOCHSTRASSER**
*London School of Economics*
Thomasius, Christian

**PHILIP T. HOFFMAN**
*California Institute of Technology*
Agriculture
Spanish Colonies: Other
American Colonies

**PAUL M. HOHENBERG**
*Rensselaer Polytechnic Institute*
Cities and Urban Life

**THOMAS HOLDEN**
*Syracuse University*
Philosophy

**MACK P. HOLT**
*George Mason University*
Burgundy
Wars of Religion, French

**R. P. HOME**
*University of Melbourne*
Coulomb, Charles-
Augustin de

**ROSAMOND HOOPER-
HAMERSLEY**
*New Jersey City University*
Geoffrin, Marie-Thérèse
Marie Antoinette
Pompadour, Jeanne-
Antoinette Poisson

**R. A. HOUSTON**
*University of St. Andrews*
Capitalism
Edinburgh
Literacy and Reading
Scotland

**JEREMY HOWARD**
*University of St. Andrews*
Central Europe, Art in

**WILLIAM V. HUDON**
*Bloomsburg University*
Catholicism
Church and State Relations

**MARK HULLIUNG**
*Brandeis University*
Helvétius, Claude-Adrien

**ALAN HUNT**
*Carleton University*
Sumptuary Laws

**JOHN J. HURT**
*University of Delaware*
Law's System
Parlements
Regency

**JANE CAMPBELL
HUTCHISON**
*University of Wisconsin*
Cranach Family

Dürer, Albrecht
Holbein, Hans, the Younger
Prints and Popular Imagery:
Early Popular Imagery

**RONALD HUTTON**
*Bristol University*
Charles II (England)

**SARAH HUTTON**
*Middlesex University*
Cambridge Platonists
More, Henry
Oldenburg, Henry
Vaughan, Thomas

**MELISSA HYDE**
*University of Florida*
Boucher, François
Rococo

**ROB ILIFFE**
*Imperial College, London*
Astronomy

**COLIN IMBER**
*University of Manchester*
Islam in the
Ottoman Empire
Ottoman Empire
Suleiman I

**CHARLES INGRAO**
*Purdue University*
Austria
Joseph I (Holy
Roman Empire)

**MALCOLM JACK**
Author of *Sintra: A Glorious
Eden*
Mandeville, Bernard

**K. DAVID JACKSON**
*Yale University*
Portuguese Literature
and Language

**FREDRIKA H. JACOBS**
*Virginia Commonwealth
University*
Anguissola, Sofonisba

**BRUCE B. JANZ**
*University of Central Florida*
Jacob Boehme

**MARK JENNER**
*University of York, U.K.*
Sanitation

**DE LAMAR JENSEN**
*Brigham Young University
(Emeritus)*
Diplomacy

**CHRISTOPHER M. S. JOHNS**
*University of Virginia*
Canova, Antonio
Mengs, Anton Raphael
Neoclassicism

**DOROTHY JOHNSON**
*University of Iowa*
David, Jacques-Louis
Greuze, Jean-Baptiste

**JAMES JOHNSON**
*Boston University*
Music
Opera

**ROBERT JÜTTE**
*Institute for the History of
Medicine, Stuttgart*
Banditry
Vagrants and Beggars

**ÇİĞDEM KAFESCIOĞLU**
*Bogazici University, Istanbul*
Sinan
Topkapi Palace

**FRANK KAFKER**
*University of Cincinnati
(Emeritus)*
Holbach, Paul Thiry,
baron d'

**MICHAEL KAISER**
*University of Cologne*
Tilly, Johann Tserclaes of

**THOMAS E. KAISER**
*University of Arkansas*
Property

**MARCIN KAMLER**
*Independent Scholar, Warsaw*
Jadwiga (Poland)
Jagiełłon Dynasty
(Poland-Lithuania)
Lublin, Union of (1569)
Poland to 1569
Poland-Lithuania,
Commonwealth of,
1569–1795
Poniatowski, Stanisław II
Augustus
Sigismund II Augustus
(Poland, Lithuania)
Stephen Báthory
3 May Constitution
Władysław II Jagiełło
(Poland)

**SUSAN C. KARANT-NUNN**
*University of Arizona*
Ritual, Religious

**JONATHAN KARP**
*State University of New York,
Binghamton*
Jews, Attitudes toward
Jews and Judaism

**DONALD KELLEY
ASSOCIATE EDITOR**
*Rutgers University*
Republic of Letters
Sleidanus, Johannes

**JAMES KELLY**
*Dublin City University*
Dublin

**EDMUND M. KERN**
*Lawrence University*
Habsburg Territories

**SHARON KETTERING**
*Montgomery College, Maryland
(Emerita)*
Patronage

**TANYA KEVORKIAN**
*Millersville University*
Bach Family
Leipzig

**MARIE SEONG-HAK KIM**
*St. Cloud State University*
Law: Lawyers
Poissy, Colloquy of

**MARGARET L. KING**
*Brooklyn College, City University
of New York*
Venice

**JAMES M. KITTELSON**
*Luther Seminary*
Luther, Martin
Lutheranism

**HANNES KLEINEKE**
*History of Parliament Trust,
London*
Hanoverian Dynasty
(Great Britain)

**WIM KLOOSTER**
*University of Southern Maine*
Dutch Colonies:
The Americas
Trading Companies
Triangular Trade Pattern

**LOUIS KNAFLA**
*University of Calgary*
Ramus, Petrus
Violence

**PAUL KNEVEL**
*University of Amsterdam*
Oldenbarneveldt, Johan van
Sea Beggars
William of Orange

**ZENON KOHUT**
*University of Alberta*
Hetmanate (Ukraine)
Mazepa, Ivan

**ROBERT KOLB**
*Concordia Seminary*
Melanchthon, Philipp

**JACK KOLLMANN**
*Stanford University*
Clergy: Russian Orthodox
Clergy
Moscow
Orthodoxy, Russian
Russia, Architecture in
Russia, Art in
St. Petersburg

**MILTON KOOISTRA**
*University of Toronto*
Ancient World
Latin

**CRAIG KOSLOFSKY**
*University of Illinois*
Holy Roman Empire

**JOSEPH W. KOTERSKI**
*Fordham University*
More, Thomas

**ELMAR KREMER**
*University of Toronto (Emeritus)*
Free Will

**MARK KROLL**
*Boston University*
Monteverdi, Claudio
Palestrina, Giovanni
Pierluigi da
Schütz, Heinrich
Vivaldi, Antonio

**ROGER KUIN**
*York University, Toronto*
Sidney, Philip

**MICHAEL KWASS**
*University of Georgia*
Equality and Inequality

Taxation

**CHRIS R. KYLE**
*Henry E. Huntington Library,*
*San Marino, Calif.*
Parliament

**JOHN CHRISTIAN LAURSEN**
*University of California,*
*Riverside*
Skepticism: Academic
and Pyrrhonian

**T. J. A. LE GOFF**
*York University, Toronto*
Intendants
Louis XV (France)
Louis XVI (France)

**NATHALIE LECOMTE**
*Independent Scholar,*
*Palaiseau, France*
Dance

**DAVID LEDERER**
*Institute for European Cultural*
*History, Augsburg*
Popular Culture

**ELIZABETH LEHFELDT**
*Cleveland State University*
Joanna I, "the Mad"
(Spain)

**CHRISTOPHER I. LEHRICH**
*Boston University*
Hermeticism
Occult Philosophy

**HOWARD LEITHEAD**
*Trinity College, Cambridge*
*University*
Cromwell, Thomas

**THOMAS M. LENNON**
*Talbot College, University of*
*Western Ontario*
Bayle, Pierre

**MICHAEL LEVIN**
*University of Akron*
Gattinara, Mercurino

**JOSEPH M. LEVINE**
*Syracuse University*
Ancients and Moderns

**MARY L. LEVKOFF**
*Los Angeles County*
*Museum of Art*
Clouet, François
Fontainebleau, School of
Pilon, Germain

**VICTOR MORALES LEZCANO**
*Institute for Historical Research–*
*UNED, Madrid*
Spanish Colonies: Africa and
the Canary Islands

**CHARLES LILLEY**
Asia

**MARY LINDEMANN**
*Carnegie Mellon University*
Public Health

**CHARLES LIPP**
*University at Buffalo, State*
*University of New York*
Lorraine, Duchy of

**PEGGY K. LISS**
Author of *Isabel the Queen:*
*Life and Times*
Cisneros, Cardinal
Francisco Jiménez de
Isabella of Castile

**DONALD W. LIVINGSTON**
*Emory University*
Hume, David

**MICHAEL LOBBAN**
*Queen Mary College,*
*University of London*
Law: Common Law

**PAUL DOUGLAS LOCKHART**
*Wright State University*
Denmark

**PAMELA O. LONG**
Author of *Openness, Secrecy,*
*Authorship: Technical Arts and*
*the Culture of Knowledge from*
*Antiquity to the Renaissance*
Communication, Scientific
Nature
Scientific Method

**CAROLYN C. LOUGEE**
*Stanford University*
Salons

**HOWARD LOUTHAN**
*University of Florida*
Bohemia

**THOMAS M. LUCKETT**
*Portland State University*
Interest

**MARVIN LUNENFELD**
*State University of New York,*
*Fredonia*
Las Casas, Bartolomé de
Sepúlveda, Juan Ginés de

**WALLACE MACCAFFREY**
*Cambridge University*
Elizabeth I (England)

**DIARMAID MACCULLOCH**
*St. Cross College,*
*Oxford University*
Knox, John
Mary I (England)

**PETER MACHAMER**
*University of Pittsburgh*
Physics

DIRECTORY OF CONTRIBUTORS

**RUTH MACKAY**
Author of *The Limits of Royal Authority: Resistance and Obedience in Seventeenth-Century Castile*
    Catalonia, Revolt of
        (1640–1652)
    Lerma, Francisco Gómez de
        Sandoval y Rojas,
        1st duke of
    Mariana, Juan de
    Philip III (Spain)
    Philip IV (Spain)
    Salamanca, School of

**RICHARD MACKENNEY**
*University of Edinburgh*
    Industry

**KERRY V. MAGRUDER**
*University of Oklahoma*
    Earth, Theories of the
    Geology

**MICHAEL W. MAHER**
*St. Louis University*
    Clergy: Roman Catholic
        Clergy
    Ignatius of Loyola
    Jesuits
    Religious Orders

**WALTRAUD MAIERHOFER**
*University of Iowa*
    Goethe, Johann
        Wolfgang von

**GEORGE P. MAJESKA**
*University of Maryland*
    Orthodoxy, Greek

**ANDREW MAJESKE**
*University of California, Davis*
    Hooker, Richard

**GREGORY MALDONADO**
*California State University, Long Beach*
    Buxtehude, Dietrich
    Scarlatti, Domenico
        and Alessandro

**WILLY MALEY**
*University of Glasgow*
    Spenser, Edmund

**WILLIAM S. MALTBY**
*University of Missouri, St. Louis (Emeritus)*
    Alba, Fernando Álvarez de
        Toledo, duke of
    Charles V (Holy
        Roman Empire)

**ELIZABETH MANCKE**
*University of Akron*
    Utrecht, Peace of (1713)

**JUDITH MANN**
*St. Louis Art Museum*
    Gentileschi, Artemisia

**RICHARD G. MANN**
*San Francisco State University*
    El Greco
    Murillo, Bartolomé Esteban
    Velázquez, Diego
    Zurbarán, Francisco de

**KENNETH H. MARCUS**
*University of La Verne*
    Württemberg, duchy of

**JOHN A. MARINO**
*University of California, San Diego*
    Naples, Kingdom of
    Naples, Revolt of (1647)

**GARY MARKER**
*State University of New York at Stony Brook*
    Anna (Russia)
    Catherine II (Russia)
    Dashkova, Princess
        Catherine
    Elizabeth (Russia)
    Novikov, Nikolai Ivanovich
    Paul I (Russia)
    Peter I (Russia)
    Prokopovich, Feofan
    Pugachev Revolt
        (1773–1775)

    Russian Literature
        and Language

**GUIDO MARNEF**
*University of Antwerp*
    Antwerp

**PETER MARSHALL**
*University of Warwick*
    Death and Dying

**CARLOS MARTÍNEZ-SHAW**
*Universidad Nacional de Educación a Distancia*
    Bourbon Dynasty (Spain)
    Farnese, Isabel (Spain)
    Ferdinand VI (Spain)
    Patiño y Morales, José
    Philip V (Spain)

**LINDA MARTZ**
*Independent Scholar, Bethesda, Maryland*
    *Comuneros* Revolt
        (1520–1521)
    *Conversos*
    Toledo

**ANNE E. C. MCCANTS**
*Massachusetts Institute of Technology*
    Orphans and Foundlings
    Poverty

**DIANE KELSEY MCCOLLEY**
*Rutgers University (Emerita)*
    Milton, John

**ANITA MCCONNELL**
*Oxford University Press, U.K.*
    Barometer

**WILLIAM MCCUAIG**
*Independent Scholar, Toronto*
    Beccaria, Cesare Bonesana,
        marquis of
    Guicciardini, Francesco
    Republicanism
    Sarpi, Paolo (Pietro)

**RORY MCENTEGART**
*American College, Dublin*
   Henry VIII (England)

**JOHN MCERLEAN**
*York University, Toronto*
   Corsica

**FREDERICK J. MCGINNESS**
*Mount Holyoke College*
   Anticlericalism
   Nepotism
   Paul III (pope)
   Paul V (pope)
   Pius IV (pope)
   Pius V (pope)
   Preaching and Sermons
   Sixtus V (pope)

**ANTONY MCKENNA**
*Jean-Monnet University*
   Arnauld Family

**ANNE MCLAREN**
*University of Liverpool*
   Divine Right Kingship

**SUSAN MCMAHON**
*Independent Scholar,*
*Cochrane, Alberta*
   Ray, John

**DAVID O. MCNEIL**
*San Jose State University*
   Budé, Guillaume

**MARK A. MEADOW**
*University of California,*
*Santa Barbara*
   Art: The Art Market
     and Collecting
   Bruegel Family

**JAMES VAN HORN MELTON**
*Emory University*
   Freemasonry
   Haydn, Franz Joseph
   Mozart, Wolfgang Amadeus

**SARA H. MENDELSON**
*McMaster University*
   Diaries

**MICHAEL P. MEZZATESTA**
*Duke University*
   Sculpture

**GEORG MICHELS**
*University of California,*
*Riverside*
   Avvakum Petrovich
   Morozova, Boiarynia
   Nikon, patriarch
   Old Believers

**RICHARD MIDDLETON**
*Queens University, Belfast*
   British Colonies:
     North America
   Navigation Acts

**H. C. ERIK MIDELFORT**
**ASSOCIATE EDITOR**
*University of Virginia*
   Habsburg Dynasty: Austria
   Jülich-Cleves-Berg
   Madness and Melancholy
   Prague, Defenestration of
   Suicide
   Witchcraft

**JENNIFER D. MILAM**
*University of Sydney*
   Fragonard, Jean-Honoré
   Games and Play
   Vigée-Lebrun, Elisabeth

**MARGARET M. MILES**
*University of California, Irvine*
   Archaeology
   Pompeii and Herculaneum

**GORDON L. MILLER**
*University of Seattle*
   Browne, Thomas

**NICHOLAS J. MILLER**
*Boise State University*
   Serbia

**PETER N. MILLER**
*Bard College*
   Peiresc, Nicolas-Claude
     Fabri de

**NELSON H. MINNICH**
*Catholic University of America*
   Leo X (pope)
   Papacy and Papal States
   Trent, Council of

**VERNON HYDE MINOR**
*University of Colorado, Boulder*
   Early Modern Period: Art
     Historical Interpretations

**BONNER MITCHELL**
*University of Missouri–Columbia*
   Festivals
   Tournament

**LYNN WOOD MOLLENAUER**
*University of North Carolina*
   Poisons, Affair of the
   Versailles

**W. GREGORY MONAHAN**
*Eastern Oregon State College*
   Camisard Revolt
   Lyon

**MICHAEL L. MONHEIT**
*University of South Alabama*
   Calvin, John

**PAUL MONOD**
*Middlebury College*
   Monarchy
   Political Secularization
   Representative Institutions

**GEORGE MONTEIRO**
*Brown University*
   Camões, Luís Vaz de

**WILLIAM MONTER**
*Northwestern University*
   Calvinism
   Geneva

**BRUCE T. MORAN**
*University of Nevada, Reno*
Alchemy
Helmont, Jean Baptiste van
Paracelsus

**JENNIFER MORI**
*University of Toronto*
Pitt, William the Elder and
William the Younger
Walpole, Horace

**JAVIER MORILLO-ALICEA**
*Macalaster College*
Spanish Colonies:
The Caribbean

**JEAN DIETZ MOSS**
*Catholic University of America*
Rhetoric

**JAMES MULDOON**
*The John Carter Brown Library*
Europe and the World
Law: Canon Law
Law: International Law

**STAFFAN MÜLLER-WILLE**
*Max-Planck-Institute for the
History of Science, Berlin*
Linnaeus, Carl

**D. E. MUNGELLO**
*Baylor University*
Missions and Missionaries:
Asia

**JOHN H. MUNRO**
*University of Toronto*
Inflation
Money and Coinage:
Western Europe

**LUCY MUNRO**
*King's College London*
Beaumont and Fletcher
Behn, Aphra
Donne, John
Drama: English
Dryden, John

English Literature
and Language

**STEVEN NADLER**
*University of Wisconsin*
Atheism
Cartesianism
Descartes, René
Spinoza, Baruch

**SARA TILGHMAN NALLE**
*William Paterson University*
Inquisition
Inquisition, Spanish

**CHARLES G. NAUERT**
*University of Missouri (Emeritus)*
Humanists and Humanism

**LARRY D. NEAL**
*University of Illinois,
Champaign-Urbana*
Stock Exchanges

**CARY J. NEDERMAN**
*Texas A&M University*
Deism
Liberty
Rights, Natural
Political Philosophy
Toleration
Virtue

**PAUL NEEDHAM**
*Princeton University Library*
Caxton, William
Gutenberg, Johannes

**PAUL NELLES**
*Carleton University*
Dissemination of Knowledge
Libraries

**JANICE L. NERI**
*University of California, Irvine*
Camera Obscura
Merian, Maria Sibylla
Scientific Illustration

**DANIEL NEXON**
*Georgetown University*
State and Bureaucracy

**TOM NICHOLS**
*King's College, Aberdeen*
Giorgione
Tintoretto
Titian
Venice, Art in
Veronese (Paolo Caliari)

**KATHRYN NORBERG**
*University of California,
Los Angeles*
Prostitution

**BYRON J. NORDSTROM**
*Gustavus Adolphus College*
Charles X Gustav (Sweden)
Charles XII (Sweden)
Christina (Sweden)
Gustavus II Adolphus
(Sweden)
Oxenstierna, Axel
Sweden
Vasa Dynasty (Sweden)

**PAUL NORLÉN**
*University of Washington*
Stockholm
Swedish Literature
and Language

**WM. ARCTANDER O'BRIEN**
*University of California,
San Diego*
Novalis

**JENS E. OLESEN**
*Ernst-Moritz-Arndt University*
Kalmar, Union of

**EDWARD J. OLSZEWSKI**
*Case Western Reserve University*
Art: Artistic Patronage

**MARGARET OSLER**
*University of Calgary*
Charleton, Walter
Gassendi, Pierre

**SUSANNAH OTTAWAY**
*Carleton College*
Old Age

**JAMES R. OTTESON**
*University of Alabama*
Smith, Adam

**CHRISTIAN OTTO**
*Cornell University*
Asam Family
Dientzenhofer Family
Fischer von Erlach, Johann
Bernhard
Neumann, Balthasar

**JAMES R. PALMITESSA**
*Western Michigan University*
Prague

**LUC PANHUYSEN**
Author of *De Beloofde Stad [The
Promised City]*
Leyden, Jan van
Witt, Johan and Cornelis de

**KATHERINE PARK**
*Harvard University*
Marvels and Wonders

**DAVID PARKER**
*University of Leeds*
La Rochelle

**KEVIN PARKER**
*University of North Carolina*
Winckelmann, Johann
Joachim

**DAVID PARROTT**
*New College, Oxford University*
Devolution, War of
(1667–1668)
Dutch War (1672–1678)
League of Augsburg, War of
the (1688–1697)
Mantuan Succession, War of
the (1627–1631)

Military:
Armies: Recruitment,
Organization, and Social
Composition
Military: Battle Tactics and
Campaign Strategy
Military: Early Modern
Military Theory
Military: Historiography
Spanish Succession, War of
the (1701–1714)

**KATHLEEN A. PARROW**
*Black Hills State University*
Law: Roman Law
Resistance, Theory of

**JOSEPH F. PATROUCH**
*Florida International University*
Ferdinand I (Holy
Roman Empire)
Matthias (Holy
Roman Empire)
Maximilian I (Holy
Roman Empire)
Maximilian II (Holy
Roman Empire)
Vienna

**ALINA PAYNE**
*University of Toronto*
Venice, Architecture in

**SUE PEABODY**
*Washington State University*
Slavery and the Slave Trade

**ELIZABETH A. PERGAM**
*Metropolitan Museum of Art*
Britain, Art in
Gainsborough, Thomas
Reynolds, Joshua

**JUAN JAVIER PESCADOR**
*Michigan State University*
Basque Country

**CARLA RAHN PHILLIPS
ASSOCIATE EDITOR**
*University of Minnesota*
Exploration

**ROD PHILLIPS**
*Carleton University*
Food and Drink

**WILLIAM D. PHILLIPS, JR.**
*University of Minnesota*
Columbus, Christopher

**PETER PIERSON**
*Santa Clara University
(Emeritus)*
Armada, Spanish
Estates and Country Houses
Habsburg Dynasty: Spain
Isabel Clara Eugenia and
Albert of Habsburg
Juan de Austria, Don
Medina Sidonia, Alonso
Pérez de Guzmán,
7th duke of
Netherlands, Southern
Parma, Alexander Farnese,
duke of
Santa Cruz, Álvaro de
Bazán, first marquis of
Spain

**HEIKKI PIHLAJAMÄKI**
*University of Helsinki*
Torture

**JULIE ANNE PLAX**
*University of Arizona*
France, Art in
Watteau, Antoine

**SERHII PLOKHY**
*University of Alberta*
Belarus
Ukraine

**MARJORIE E. PLUMMER**
*Western Kentucky University*
Augsburg

**MARTHA POLLAK**
*University of Illinois, Chicago*
Architecture

ROBERT POOLE
*St. Martin's College, U.K.*
Calendar

JEREMY POPKIN
*University of Kentucky*
Journalism, Newspapers,
and Newssheets

DAVID M. POSNER
*Loyola University, Chicago*
French Literature
and Language
Montaigne, Michel de
Rabelais, François
Racine, Jean

JEAN-PIERRE POUSSOU
*University of Paris, Sorbonne*
Mobility, Geographic
Mobility, Social

MAARTEN PRAK
*University of Utrecht*
Amsterdam
Dutch Republic
Tulips

OM PRAKASH
*Delhi School of Economics*
British Colonies: India

CYNTHIA PYLE
*New York University*
Gessner, Conrad

PAULA REA RADISICH
*Whittier College*
Chardin, Jean-Baptiste-
Siméon

DAVID RANDALL
*Rutgers University*
Providence

BENJAMIN RAVID
*Brandeis University*
Ghetto

KAREN REEDS
*Princeton Research Forum*
Botany

EILEEN REEVES
*Princeton University*
Galileo Galilei

GERDA REITH
*University of Glasgow*
Gambling
Lottery

PIERRE-CLAUDE REYNARD
*University of Western Ontario*
Environment
Weather and Climate

THOMAS E. RIDENHOUR, JR.
*University of Virginia*
Schmalkaldic War
(1546–1547)

PATRICK RILEY
*Harvard University*
Rousseau, Jean-Jacques

PATRICK RILEY, JR.
*Colgate University*
Alembert, Jean Le Rond d'
Diderot, Denis
Voltaire

GUENTER B. RISSE
*University of California,
San Francisco (Emeritus)*
Cullen, William
Hospitals

LISSA ROBERTS
*University of Twente,
Netherlands*
Boerhaave, Herman
Chemistry

JAMES ROBERTSON
*University of the West Indies,
Mona*
British Colonies:
The Caribbean

THOMAS ROBISHEAUX
*Duke University*
Peasants' War, German

SHIRLEY A. ROE
*University of Connecticut*
Haller, Albrecht von

SHELLEY E. ROFF
*University of Texas, San Antonio*
Barcelona
Catalonia

KARL A. ROIDER
*Louisiana State University*
Charles VI (Holy
Roman Empire)
Francis II (Holy
Roman Empire)
Frederick I (Prussia)
Frederick William
(Brandenburg)
Frederick William II
(Prussia)
Hohenzollern Dynasty
Maria Theresa (Holy
Roman Empire)
Rudolf II (Holy
Roman Empire)

LEONARD N. ROSENBAND
*Utah State University*
Balloons
Laborers

ANGELA H. ROSENTHAL
*Dartmouth College*
Hogarth, William
Women and Art

JEAN-LAURENT ROSENTHAL
*University of California,
Los Angeles*
Wages

DANIEL ROWLAND
*University of Kentucky*
Autocracy

**INGRID ROWLAND**
*American Academy in Rome*
    Leonardo da Vinci
    Raphael
    Rome, Art in

**GUY ROWLANDS**
*Newnham College, Cambridge University*
    Austrian Succession, War of
        the (1740–1748)
    Louis XIV (France)
    Louvois, François Le Tellier,
        marquis de
    Seven Years' War
        (1756–1763)

**A. R. ROWLEY**
*University of York, U.K.*
    Tobacco

**JULIUS R. RUFF**
*Marquette University*
    Police

**ERIKA RUMMEL**
*Wilfrid Laurier University, Toronto*
    Erasmus, Desiderius

**ANDREA RUSNOCK**
*University of Rhode Island*
    Graunt, John
    Petty, William
    Statistics

**KATHLEEN RUSSO**
*Florida Atlantic University*
    Carriera, Rosalba
    Kauffmann, Angelica

**DAVID RYDEN**
*University of Houston, Downtown*
    Sugar

**THOMAS MAX SAFLEY**
*University of Pennsylvania*
    Bankruptcy
    Charity and Poor Relief
    Commerce and Markets

    Frederick III (Holy
        Roman Empire)
    Fugger Family
    Monopoly
    Shops and Shopkeeping

**J. H. M. SALMON**
*Bryn Mawr College (Emeritus)*
    Constitutionalism
    Sovereignty, Theory of
    Tyranny, Theory of

**BRIAN SANDBERG**
*European University Institute*
    Firearms

**VICTORIA SANGER**
*Columbia University*
    France, Architecture in
    Mansart, François

**RICHARD E. SCHADE**
*University of Cincinnati*
    Drama: German
    German Literature
        and Language

**STEPHAN K. SCHINDLER**
*Washington University, St. Louis*
    Klopstock, Friedrich
        Gottlieb

**J. B. SCHNEEWIND**
*Johns Hopkins University*
    Kant, Immanuel
    Moral Philosophy and Ethics

**ROBERT A. SCHNEIDER**
*Catholic University of America*
    Duel
    Journals, Literary
    Louis XIII (France)
    Marie de Médicis
    Paris

**ZOE A. SCHNEIDER**
*Georgetown University*
    Landholding
    Law: Courts
    Villages

**GORDON SCHOCHET**
*Rutgers University*
    Hobbes, Thomas
    Locke, John
    Natural Law
    Patriarchy and Paternalism

**JOHN F. SCHWALLER**
*University of Minnesota, Morris*
    Mexico City
    Missions and Missionaries:
        Spanish America
    Spanish Colonies: Mexico

**A. TRUMAN SCHWARTZ**
*Macalester College*
    Priestley, Joseph

**STUART B. SCHWARTZ**
*Yale University*
    Restoration, Portuguese War
        of (1640–1668)

**KARL W. SCHWEIZER**
*New Jersey Institute of Technology*
    Churchill, John,
        duke of Marlborough
    Harley, Robert
    Hastings, Warren
    Jenkins' Ear, War of
        (1739–1748)

**JOHN BELDON SCOTT**
*University of Iowa*
    Borromini, Francesco

**TOM SCOTT**
*University of Liverpool*
    Peasantry

**PAUL S. SEAVER**
*Stanford University (Emeritus)*
    Puritanism

**JOHN SEWELL**
*Arizona State University*
    Magic

**JOLE SHACKELFORD**
*University of Minnesota*
    Brahe, Tycho

Rosicrucianism

**BARBARA SHAPIRO**
*University of California, Berkeley*
Sprat, Thomas
Wilkins, John

**LESLEY SHARPE**
*University of Bristol*
Schiller, Johann Christoph
Friedrich von

**CHRISTINE SHAW**
*University of Warwick*
Julius II (pope)

**ANITA SHELTON**
*Eastern Illinois University*
Czech Literature
and Language

**NIKKI SHEPARDSON**
*Rider College*
Bèze, Théodore de
Martyrs and Martyrology

**JOHN SHOVLIN**
*Hobart and William Smith Colleges*
Physiocrats and Physiocracy

**DAVID SIMPSON**
*University of California, Davis*
Romanticism

**NANCY SINKOFF**
*Rutgers University*
Haskalah
(Jewish Enlightenment)

**CAROLE SLADE**
*Columbia University*
Teresa of Ávila

**A. MARK SMITH**
*University of Missouri*
Optics

**JEFFREY SMITTEN**
*Utah State University*
Robertson, William

**JIM SMYTH**
*University of Notre Dame*
Ireland

**STEPHEN D. SNOBELEN**
*University of King's College, Halifax*
Newton, Isaac

**SUSAN M. SOCOLOW**
*Emory University*
Buenos Aires

**PHILIP M. SOERGEL**
*Arizona State University*
Miracles
Munich
Religious Piety

**PHILIP L. SOHM**
*University of Toronto*
Art: Art Theory, Criticism,
and Historiography
Baroque

**GERALD L. SOLIDAY**
*University of Texas, Dallas*
Frankfurt am Main
Hesse, Landgraviate of

**JACOB SOLL**
*Rutgers University*
Lipsius, Justus

**JULIE ROBIN SOLOMON**
*American University*
Bacon, Francis
Cavendish, Margaret

**ELISABETH SOMMER**
Author of *Serving Two Masters: The Moravian Brethren in Germany and North Carolina 1727–1801*
Moravian Brethren

**NICHOLAS SPADACCINI**
*University of Minnesota*
Cervantes, Miguel de

**JACK SPALDING**
*Fordham University*
Florence, Art in

**E. C. SPARY**
*Independent Scholar, Cambridge, U.K.*
Natural History

**JOHN P. SPIELMAN**
*Haverford College*
Leopold I (Holy
Roman Empire)

**JOHN SPURR**
*University of Wales, Swansea*
Baxter, Richard
Dissenters, English

**GOVIND P. SREENIVASAN**
*Brandeis University*
Census
Inheritance and Wills
Serfdom

**GRETCHEN D. STARR-LEBEAU**
*University of Kentucky*
Jews, Expulsion of
(Spain; Portugal)
Persecution

**MALINA STEFANOVSKA**
*University of California, Los Angeles*
Biography and
Autobiography
Saint-Simon, Louis de
Rouvroy

**MATTHEW STEGGLE**
*Sheffield Hallam University*
Sheridan, Richard Brinsley

**ALISON STENTON**
*King's College, London*
Boswell, James
Burney, Frances
Defoe, Daniel
Smollett, Tobias
Sterne, Laurence

**BARBARA STEPHENSON**
*Mount Holyoke College*
　Marguerite de Navarre

**JAMIE STEPHENSON**
*University of Minnesota*
　Lima

**DAVID M. STONE**
*University of Delaware*
　Caravaggio and Caravaggism

**SIEP STUURMAN**
*Erasmus University, Rotterdam*
　Feminism

**DONALD SUTHERLAND**
*University of Maryland*
　Ancien Régime
　Estates-General,
　　French: 1789
　Revolutions, Age of

**JULIAN SWANN**
*Birkbeck College, University of
London*
　Provincial Government

**FRANK E. SYSYN**
*University of Alberta*
　Cossacks
　Khmelnytsky, Bohdan
　Khmelnytsky Uprising
　Uniates
　Union of Brest (1596)

**FRANZ SZABO**
*University of Alberta*
　Josephinism

**DANIEL SZECHI**
*Auburn University*
　Jacobitism

**LYNNE TATLOCK**
*Washington University, St. Louis*
　Grimmelshausen,
　　H. J. C. von

**KENNETH L. TAYLOR**
*University of Oklahoma*
　Earth, Theories of the
　Geology

**SCOTT TAYLOR**
*Siena College*
　Honor

**WAYNE TE BRAKE**
*Purchase College, State
University of New York*
　Patriot Revolution

**JOHN TEDESCHI**
*University of Wisconsin*
　Inquisition, Roman

**NICHOLAS TEMPERLEY**
*University of Illinois*
　Handel, George Frideric
　Hymns
　Purcell, Henry

**NICHOLAS TERPSTRA**
*University of Toronto*
　Confraternities

**JOHN THEIBAULT**
*Author of German Villages in
Crisis: Rural Life in Hesse-Kassel
and the Thirty Years' War,
1580–1720*
　Housing
　Hunting
　Salzburg Explusion

**FREDERICK J. THORPE**
*Curator Emeritus, Canadian
Museum of Civilization*
　Fur Trade: North America

**BARBARA J. TODD**
*University of Toronto*
　Widows and Widowhood

**JANIS TOMLINSON**
*National Academy of Sciences*
　Goya y Lucientes,
　　Francisco de
　Spain, Art in

**ERNEST TUCKER**
*U.S. Naval Academy*
　Austro-Ottoman Wars
　Galleys
　Holy Leagues
　Janissary
　Lepanto, Battle of
　Passarowitz, Peace of (1718)
　Russo-Ottoman Wars

**JAMES B. TUELLER**
*Brigham Young University*
　Manila
　Pacific Ocean

**A. J. TURNER**
*Independent Scholar, Le Mesnil
le Roi, France*
　Time, Measurement of

**RICHARD W. UNGER**
*University of British Columbia*
　Hansa
　Shipbuilding and Navigation
　Shipping

**MARY VACCARO**
*University of Texas, Arlington*
　Correggio

**PETER VAN DEN DUNGEN**
*University of Bradford*
　Pacifism

**THEO VAN DER MEER**
*Independent Scholar, Amsterdam*
　Homosexuality

**STEVEN VANDEN BROECKE**
*Johns Hopkins University*
　Astrology

**JOHN VARRIANO**
*Mount Holyoke College*
　Palladio, Andrea,
　　and Palladianism

**DONALD PHILLIP VERENE**
*Emory University*
　Vico, Giovanni Battista

**RICK VERNIER**
*Purdue University, Calumet*
Liberalism, Economic

**MARKUS P. M. VINK**
*State University of New York, Fredonia*
Dutch Colonies:
The East Indies

**DIANE WAGGONER**
*Huntington Library, Art Collections, and Botanical Gardens*
Portrait Miniatures

**STEFANIE WALKER**
*Bard College*
Decorative Arts
Jewelry

**WILLIAM A. WALLACE**
*University of Maryland*
Scholasticism

**WILLIAM E. WALLACE**
*Washington University, St. Louis*
Michelangelo Buonarroti

**PETER WALMSLEY**
*McMaster University*
Berkeley, George

**PAUL WARDE**
*Pembroke College, Cambridge University*
Enclosure
Forests and Woodlands

**HELEN WATANABE-O'KELLY**
*Exeter College, Oxford University*
Dresden

**ELISSA B. WEAVER**
*University of Chicago*
Castiglione, Baldassare

**WILLIAM WEBER**
**ASSOCIATE EDITOR**
*California State University, Long Beach*
Music Criticism

Songs, Popular

**GEORGE G. WEICKHARDT**
*Ropers, Majeski, Kohn & Bentley*
Law: Russian Law

**KATHLEEN WELLMAN**
*Southern Methodist University*
La Mettrie, Julien Offroy de

**CATHERINE WHISTLER**
*Ashmolean Museum, Oxford*
Tiepolo, Giovanni Battista

**MERRY WIESNER-HANKS**
*University of Wisconsin, Milwaukee*
Gender
Women

**ELIZABETH A. WILLIAMS**
*Oklahoma State University*
Biology
Mesmer, Franz Anton

**GLORIA WILLIAMS**
*Norton Simon Museum, Pasadena*
Painting

**PETER H. WILSON**
*University of Sunderland, U.K.*
Berlin
Brandenburg
Free and Imperial Cities
Hanover
Münster
Prussia
Strasbourg

**JOHN WILTON-ELY**
*University of Hull (Emeritus)*
Piranesi, Giovanni Battista

**JAN W. WOJCIK**
*Auburn University*
Boyle, Robert

**MICHAEL WOLFE**
*Pennsylvania State University, Altoona*
Henry IV (France)
Nantes, Edict of

**ALLEN G. WOOD**
*Purdue University*
Boileau-Despréaux, Nicolas
Corneille, Pierre
Grimm, Friedrich
Melchior von
La Bruyère, Jean de
La Fontaine, Jean de
Laclos, Pierre Ambroise
Choderlos de
Perrault, Charles

**JOANNA WOODS-MARSDEN**
*University of California, Los Angeles*
Art: The Conception and
Status of the Artist

**D. R. WOOLF**
*University of Alberta*
Historiography

**JOHNSON KENT WRIGHT**
*Arizona State University*
Enlightenment
Public Opinion

**W. J. WRIGHT**
*University of Tennessee*
Marburg, Colloquy of

**AMANDA WUNDER**
*University of Wisconsin*
Seville

**ANDRZEJ WYCZAŃSKI**
*Polish Academy of Sciences (Emeritus)*
Serfdom in East
Central Europe

**WANDA WYPORSKA**
*Hertford College, Oxford University*
Poland, Partitions of

Polish Succession, War of the (1733–1738)

**JOELLA G. YODER**
Author of *Unrolling Time: Christiaan Huygens and the Mathematization of Nature*
Huygens Family

**CHARLES YRIGOYEN, JR.**
*General Commission on Archives and History, United Methodist Church*
Methodism

Wesley Family

**AVIHU ZAKAI**
*Hebrew University of Jerusalem*
Refugees, Exiles, and Émigrés

**FARIBA ZARINEBAF**
*Northwestern University*
Constantinople
Harem
Odalisque

**MADELINE C. ZILFI**
**ASSOCIATE EDITOR**
*University of Maryland*
Shabbetai Tzevi
Tulip Era
(Ottoman Empire)

**RONALD EDWARD ZUPKO**
*Marquette University (Emeritus)*
Weights and Measures

# INDEX

Page references are preceded by the volume number in boldface. Page numbers in boldface refer to the main entry on the subject. Page numbers in italics refer to illustrations, tables, and maps; tables are further indicated by *t*. A volume designation followed by *pl*. indicates the color plate section of that volume.

## A

Aachen. *See* Aix-la-Chapelle
Aachen, Hans von, **1**:444
*Aan het Volk van Nederland,* **4**:418
abacus school, **3**:482
Abarca, Pedro, count of Aranda, **2**:408
Abbasids
  harems of, **3**:132
  and viziers, **6**:180
Abbot, George, **5**:114
*Abdelazer; or the Moor's Revenge* (Behn), **1**:243
*Abduction from the Seraglio* (Mozart), **5**:545
Abdülhamid I (Ottoman Empire), **4**:352
*Abecedario pittorico* (Orlandi), **1**:115
Abel, Carl Friedrich, **4**:229
Abelove, Henry, **5**:395
*Abenteuerliche Simplicissimus, Der* (Grimmelshausen), **3**:51, 93; **4**:117–118
*Abenteuerlichen Simplicissimi Ewig-währender Calender, Des* (Grimmelshausen), **3**:94
*Abhandlung über den Ursprung der Sprache* (Herder), **3**:163
Abner of Burgos, **2**:53
abolitionism, **5**:435–437
abortion
  marriage and, **4**:42

midwives and, **4**:113
Abravanel, Isaac, **3**:356
  Jewish messianism and, **4**:104
*Abrégé de la philosophie de Gassendi* (Bernier), **3**:22
*Abrégé de l'histoire de Port-Royal* (Racine), **5**:131–132
*Abridgement of Mr. Baxter's History of His Life and Times, An* (Calamy), **1**:237
*Absalom and Achitophel* (Dryden), **2**:177, 294
absolutism, **1**:1–7; **2**:362; **4**:168–169
  armies and, **4**:136–137
  baroque art and, **1**:227–230
  biology study and, **1**:265–266
  Bodin on, **1**:271; **5**:447–448
  bourgeoisie and, **1**:299–300, 301
  in Brandenburg-Prussia, **2**:462
  canon law and, **3**:443–444
  civil engineering and, **2**:260–261
  common law and, **3**:445
  in Denmark, **2**:127–128
  divine right kingship and, **2**:158–159
  English Civil War and, **2**:276–277, 285
  enlightened despotism and, **2**:296–298
  Enlightenment and, **2**:299 300
  and inability to tax at will, **6**:3
  and increase in migration, **5**:162
  interior decoration and, **2**:114

John V (Portugal), **3**:515
Locke on, **3**:527
mercantilism and, **4**:96–99
Milton on, **4**:138
Montesquieu on, **4**:189–191
papacy and, **3**:436–437
personal projects of monarchs, **1**:4–5
of popes, **1**:420
power *versus* authority, **1**:2
prince's prerogatives, **1**:1
in Prussia, **2**:463; **5**:96–97
rise of, **1**:3–4
Roman law and, **3**:466
in Savoy, **5**:316–317
and social, political and religious unification, **5**:162
in Spain, **5**:456
Sweden, **5**:553
abstinence, sexual, **5**:396–397
*Absurda Comica oder Herr Peter Squentz* (Gryphius), **2**:168; **3**:50
Abulafia, Abraham, **1**:350
  magic and, **4**:14
*Academia* (Talon), **5**:427
Academia das Ciências, **5**:43
Academia dos Singulares, **5**:43
Academia Parisiensis, **4**:102
*Academica* (Cicero), **5**:426, 427
*Academica* (Valencia), **5**:427
Académie de Saint-Luc (Paris)
  Chardin member of, **1**:451
  Vigée-Lebrun member of, **6**:160

# C

Cock, Hieronymus, **1**:330

Cockayne, Aston, **1**:240

Cocks, Mayken, **1**:330

Codazzi, Viviano
in Naples, **4**:235
and view painting, **6**:122

*Code* (Justinian), **3**:464

*Codex* (Behem), **1**:441

codex and ciphers in diplomacy, **2**:150

Coelho, Gonçalo, **5**:30

*Coeli et Terri* (papal bull), **5**:8

Coello, Alonso Sánchez, **1**:67

Coen, Jan Pieterszoon, **1**:138, 139, 140

coffee, **2**:15–16, 51, 419
in daily life, **2**:103
elites and, **1**:521
plantations on French Caribbean colonies, **2**:474, 475
slave trade and, **5**:433

*Coffee Cantata* (Bach), **2**:419

coffeehouses, **2**:303
Bach in, **1**:188
in daily life, **2**:103

*Coffer, The* (Ariosta), **3**:301

Cogswell, Thomas, **4**:402

Cohen, Gerson, **4**:105

Cohen, Sherrill, **1**:456

Coimbra, University of, **5**:25

Coimbra commentaries, **3**:530, 531

Coimbrans (Conimbricenses), **1**:103

coins and medals, **1**:551–554

Coiter, Volker, **6**:259

Coke, Edward, **4**:416
on common law, **3**:444, 445, 446
and constitutionalism, **2**:47–48
on law codes, **3**:455

*Col Tempo* (Giorgione), **3**:68

Colbert, Charles, **2**:147–148

Colbert, Jean-Baptiste, **1**:554–555; **2**:437–438
and Académie Royale de Peinture et de Sculpture, **1**:10
art patronage of, **1**:124
and Asian trade, **2**:477
and Canal du Midi, **2**:25
Dutch War and, **2**:215–217
economic liberalism and, **3**:497
economic regulation, **3**:99
on increased litigation, **3**:463
and intendants, **3**:277–278
library of, **3**:510
Louis XIV and, **3**:544, 546
Mansart and, **4**:21
Marseille under, **4**:43
Mazarin and, **4**:67
mercantilism and, **4**:97–98
on North African captives, **4**:88

and patronage, **4**:421
portrait by Lefebvre, **1**:*555*
and procurement of the money for Versailles, **6**:146
protector of Charles Perrault, **4**:439
reform of manufactures, **3**:256
and roads, **2**:28
slavery as punishment and, **5**:432
statistics and, **5**:520
and urban improvement in Paris, **4**:395–396

Colbert, Seignelay, **3**:544

Cole, Elisha, **2**:291

Coleridge, Samuel Taylor, **6**:69
Swedenborgianism and, **5**:557

Colet, John, **5**:152
adoption of Erasmus curriculum, **5**:219
Bible lectures, **1**:257
condemnation of war, **4**:362
Erasmus and, **2**:322
More and, **4**:201
St. Paul's school and, **2**:233

Coligny, Gaspard de, **1**:411, 555, *556*; **2**:435
assassination, **3**:103, 156; **6**:193, 194
Catherine de Médicis and, **1**:416
Louis I de Bourbon, prince de Condé and, **2**:33
St. Bartholomew's Day Massacre, **5**:299

Coligny, Gaspard II de, **1**:555
and Protestants, **3**:214

Coligny, Gaspard III de, **1**:557

Coligny, Odet de, **1**:555

Coligny family, **1**:555–557

Colijer, Jacob, **4**:409

"Colin Clout" (Skelton), **2**:294

*Colin Clout's Come Home Again* (Spenser), **2**:295; **5**:504

Collé, Charles, **5**:447

*Collection of Rules of Slavonic Grammar* (Smotrytskyi), **6**:93

*Collection of Sundrie Statutes* (Pulton), **5**:510

*Collection of Voyages and Travels* (John and Awnsham Churchill), **6**:68

collections, **2**:52. *See also* art markets and collecting
books of secrets and, **5**:365–366
and natural history, **4**:246, 247
public, **4**:248
scientific illustration and, **5**:333
scientific instrument, **5**:338
scientific revolution and, **5**:350

collective action, classic definition of, **5**:16

Collège de Clermont, **2**:238

Collège de Pharmacie, **1**:82

Collège Louis le Grand, **2**:238

Collegio Romano, **4**:391; **5**:252
Kircher at, **3**:406

Collegio Urbano (Rome), **4**:390

Collegium Musicum (Augsburg), **1**:168

Colley, Linda, **4**:245

Colli, Bonifacio de', **5**:166

Collier, Jeremy, **4**:230–231

Collier, Mary, **2**:295

*Colliget* (Averroes), **1**:54

Collins, William, **2**:295

Collodi, Carlo, **1**:230

*Colloquies* (Erasmus), **2**:323
anticlericalism of, **1**:74
and humor, **3**:224

*Colloquium Heptaplomeres de Rerum Sublimium Arcanis Abditis* (Bodin), **1**:271; **6**:53

*Colloquium to the Missionaries* (Vincent de Paul), **6**:170

Colloredo, Hieronymus, **4**:215, 228

Collot, Marie-Anne, **5**:289; **6**:244

Colocci, Angelo, **5**:137

Cologne, **1**:505; **2**:1–2
archbishop as imperial elector, **3**:192
as city-state, **1**:515
fairs, **2**:11
as imperial city, **2**:467
Münster and, **4**:218
printing in, **5**:63
witchcraft persecution, **6**:223

Cologne, University of, **2**:2

Cologne War, Bavaria and, **1**:234

Colombia as Spanish colony, **5**:480–491

Colombo, Realdo, **1**:54; **3**:139

Colombo, Treaty of (1766), **2**:193

*Colonel Jack* (Defoe), **2**:119

colonial missions. *See* missions and missionaries

colonialism, **2**:2–5
biology study and, **1**:265–266
bullion shortages and, **3**:434
colonization process in French North American colonies, **2**:478–479
diseases and, **2**:342, 349
the environment and, **2**:312
geographic mobility in, **4**:154
international law and, **3**:456–458
Las Casas and, **3**:430–431
mercantilism and, **4**:96–97
missions and, **4**:148–151
Roman law and, **3**:466
shipping and, **5**:414–415
social mobility and, **4**:157–158

copies. *See* forgeries
Coppe, Abiezer, **2:**287
copper coinage, **1:**552; **4:**175
 introduced in Spain, **4:**454
copper production, **2:**423
 Fugger family and, **2:**498
Coptic Catholic Church, **4:**389
copyright laws, **5:**107
Coques, Gonzales, **4:**276
Coquille, Guy, **2:**46
Coram, Thomas, **4:***333*
Cordemoy, Géraud de, **2:**468
 Cartesianism of, **1:**398
Cordier, Mathurin, **1:**359
Córdoba, Gonzalo Fernández de, the
 Great Captain, **4:**238
 Pavia and, **4:**125
Cordovero, Moses, **3:**366
Corelli, Arcangelo, **1:**125
 Scarlatti and, **5:**320
Corenzio, Belisario, **4:**235
 and Certosa di San Martino, **4:**237
Corfu under Venetian rule, **3:**88
*Corn Harvest, The* (Pieter Bruegel the
 Elder), **4:***430*
*Cornard Wood* or *Gainsborough's
 Forest* (Gainsborough), **3:***3, pl.*
Cornaro, Alvise, **2:**263
Cornaro Piscopia, Elena Lucrezia,
 **2:**57–58, 367
Corneille, Jean-Baptiste, **3:**471
Corneille, Michel I, **6:**185
Corneille, Michel II, **3:**471
Corneille, Pierre, **2:**58–59, *59*, 489
 Dutch influence of, **2:**199
 Lully and, **3:**559
Corneille, Thomas, **2:**58
Cornelisz van Haarlem, Cornelis,
 **4:**277
 mannerism of, **4:**365
Corner, Giovanni, **6:**37
*Cornucopiae* (Perotti), **2:**142
Cornwallis, Charles, **1:**42, 43
Cornysh, William, **4:**225
*Coronation of the Emperor Napoleon I,
 The* (David), **2:**110
coronations, **3:**24; **4:**166; **5:**231–232
 of Frederick I of Prussia by himself,
 **2:**458
 in Moscow, **4:**210
 as oath binding king and his people,
 **5:**201–202
 order of procession in Britain, **5:***232*
Corot, Jean-Baptiste Camille, **1:**530
corporatism, guilds and, **3:**98–99
Corps de Ponts et Chaussées, **2:**264
*Corpus Christi Procession, Cuzco,*
 **5:***489*
Corpus Christi processions, **5:**236

*Corpus iuris civilis* (Justinian), **3:**464,
 465; **6:**57
 Budé's historical study, **1:**335–336
 on slavery, **5:**433–434
corpuscular philosophy, **4:**56, 57–58
 mechanism and, **4:**68–69
 scientific revolution and, **5:**348
corrective lenses, **4:**329
Correggio (Antonio Allegri),
 **2:**59–61, 405
 *Assumption of the Virgin,* **2:***pl.*
 Camera di San Paolo, **2:***60*
 and Gioanna da Piacenza, **1:**123
Correia, Gaspar, **5:**41
*Correspondance littéraire, philosophique
 et critique* (Grimm), **3:**92–93
correspondence
 business, **2:**18
 of Catherine the Great, **1:**412
 and climatic information, **6:**200
 dissemination of knowledge
 through, **2:**154
 English, **2:**293
 of Erasmus, **2:**154, *323*
 of Hartlib, **3:**137–138
 of Horace Walpole, **6:**191
 of Peiresc, **4:**436–437, *437*
 and Republic of Letters, **3:**171;
 **5:**193, 194
 rhetoric in letters meant to be read
 aloud, **2:**22–23
 and scientific communication,
 **2:**20–21
 of Sévigné, **5:**390–391
 as urban pursuits, **1:**507
 of Vives, **6:**179
Corsi, Jacopo, **4:**324
Corsica, **2:**61–63, 431
 France and, **3:**153
 purchased by French from Genoa,
 **3:**319
 sold by Genoa to France, **3:**33
Corsini, Lorenzo, **2:**406
Corsini family, **1:**518
Corso, Sampiero, **2:**62
Cort, Cornelis, **5:**71
Cort, Henry, **6:**15
Corte, Juan de la, **5:***229*
*Corte Giana, La* (Aretino), **2:**171
*Corte na Aldeia* (Lobo), **5:**43
*Cortegiano, Il* (Castiglione). *See Book
 of the Courtier* (Castiglione)
Corte-Real, Gaspar, **2:**349
Corte-Real, Miguel, **2:**349
Cortes, **5:**456–457
Cortés, Hernán, **1:**160; **2:**63–65,
 349
 entering Tenochtitlán, **2:***65*
 Mexico City and, **4:**108

 Mexico under, **5:**473
 missions and, **4:**149
Cortese, Gregorio, **5:**147
Cortese, Isabella, **5:**366
Cortona, Pietro da. *See* Pietro da
 Cortona
Coruds, Valerius, **3:**60
*corvée*
 in east central Europe, **5:**378–380
 landholding and, **3:**429
 in Mexico, **5:**476
 serfdom and, **5:**375–377
Cosattini, Giovanni Giuseppe, **1:***504*
*Così fan tutte* (Mozart), **4:**215
cosmogonies, chemical, **3:**40
*Cosmographia* (Münster), **1:**400;
 **2:**143, *466*; **3:***30*
*Cosmographiae Introductio*
 (Waldseemüller), **5:**64
*Cosmographie universelle* (Thévet),
 **2:**143
cosmology, **2:**66–70
 Brahe on, **1:**303–304
 Bruno on, **1:**332–333
 Descartes, **2:**130
 madness and, **4:**6
 matter theories and, **4:**54
 Stoicism and, **5:**530
 theories of the Earth, **2:**222–226
Cossacks, **2:**70–71
 histories of, **6:**94
 Mazepa and, **4:**67–68
 Michael Romanov and, **4:**109–110
 nobility integrated in Russian
 imperial nobility, **5:**282
 and restoration of Orthodox
 hierarchy in Ukraine, **6:**90–91
 Russia and, **3:**246
 serfdom and, **5:**382
 transformation into new society,
 **6:**90–91
 uprisings
 against the Lithuanian-Polish
 Commonwealth, **6:**91
 Pugachev revolt, **1:**412;
 **5:**109–110
Costa, Angelo Maria, **4:**237
Coster, Salomon, **1:**542
Costerman Tax Riots (1690), **4:**17
Costin, Miron, **3:**169; **5:**246
Cosway, Richard
 and portrait miniatures, **5:**23
 *Sir Frederick Augustus d'Este,* **5:***24*
Coton, Peter, **1:**254
cottage industries. *See* proto-
 industrialization
Cotton, Robert, **3:**510
cotton industry, **6:**19–20, 21–22, 23
 British colonies and, **1:**317

cotton industry *(continued)*
  cloth, **3:**261
  from colonies, **2:**51
  East India Company and, **1:**141
  in French Caribbean colonies,
    **2:**473, 474, 475
  slave trade and, **5:**433
Coudray, Angélique Marguerite le
    Boursier du, **4:**211, 306, 307
Coulomb, Charles-Augustin de,
    **2:**71–72
Coulomb's laws, **2:**71
Council of Conscience (France),
    **6:**170
Council of the Indies
  in Peru, **5:**483–484, 484
  Sepúlveda and, **5:**372–373
*Counterblaste to Tobacco, A* (James I
    and VI), **6:**48
Counter-Reformation. *See*
    Reformation, Catholic
Counter-Remonstrants, **1:**367
*Countess's Morning Levee, The*
    (Hogarth), **3:***pl.*
Count's War (1534–1536), **2:**126
Cour de Monnaies, **3:**448
Cour des Aides, **3:**448
Cour des Miracles (Paris), **4:**396
Courcillon, Philippe de, **5:**304
*coureurs de bois,* **2:**480–481, 500
Courland, Duchy of, **1:**210–211
*Cours de chymie* (Lémery), **1:**85
*Course of Experimental Philosophy*
    (Desagulier), **4:**472
*Course of the Exchange, The*
    (periodical), **3:**282
court and courtiers, **2:**72–77;
    **4:**169–171
  and capital cities, **1:**506
  court Jews, **3:**359–360
  courtier as gentleman, **3:**36
  decorative arts and, **2:**114–115
  and distribution of patronage, **4:**420
  entertainments, **2:**382–383
  etiquette, **1:**521
  inequality in court culture,
    **2:**317–318
  interior decoration and, **2:**114–115
  Mantua, **4:**23
  political culture of, **2:**73–74
  Prussian, **5:**98
  in Russia
    under Peter I, **4:**444, 445; **5:**278
    Prokopovich and, **5:**77
    theater, **5:**280
  Saint-Simon on, **5:**303–305
  scientific revolution and, **5:**349
  in Spain
    art and, **5:**462

Ferdinand and Isabella, **5:**494
  sports and, **5:**506–507
  state building and, **5:**516
  in Sweden, **5:**556–557
  at Versailles, **6:**147–149
  as vital center for artistic production,
    **4:**271
  in Württemberg, **6:**250
*Court Journals* (Burney), **1:**346
court memoirs, **4:**171
Court of Chancery, **3:**445–446
Court of Common Pleas, **3:**445,
    449–450, 456
Court of High Commission, **3:**450;
    **5:**510
*Courtesan, The* (Aretino), **3:**302
courtesans, **5:**83
  and writing, **3:**303
*Courtier, The* (Castiglione). *See Book
    of the Courtier, The* (Castiglione)
courting and courtship, **6:**256
  nocturnal visits, **5:**5
courts of law, **3:**447–456. *See also*
    ecclesiastical courts
  in Balkans, **1:**197
  common law in, **3:**445–446
  England, **3:**445–446
  feudal, **2:**387
  France, **2:**437
    *chambre ardente,* **3:**153
*Judge and Three Advocates, A,* **3:**449
  judicial reform
    Beccaria on, **1:**241–242
    Joseph II, **3:**379
  juries
    England, **3:**452–453
    grand *versus* petty, **3:**452–453
  jurisdiction of nobles at local level,
    **1:**100
  in Mexico, **5:**473
  monarchy and, **4:**171–172
  Parliament as highest court, **4:**401
  in Peru, **5:**483, 484
  secular courts and witchcraft trials,
    **6:**222
  Spanish, **5:**456
  Star Chamber, **5:**510
  Stephen Báthory and, **5:**525
  in villages, **6:**165
  women and, **6:**234
Couto, Diogo do, **5:**41, 42
*Coutumes du pays et duché de
    Nivernais* (Coquille), **2:**46
Covent Garden (London), **3:**374
*Covent-Garden Journal, The*
    (periodical), **2:**389
Coverdale, Miles, **1:**262
Cowley, Abraham, **5:**509
Cowper, Sarah, **2:**139

Cowper, William, **2:**295; **6:**69
Cox, Richard, **2:**243
*Coxcomb, The* (Beaumont and
    Fletcher), **1:**240
Coya, Beatriz, **5:**489
Coypel, Antoine, **1:**396
  Le Brun and, **3:**471
Coypel, Noël Nicolas, **1:**451
Coysevox, Antoine
  bronze bust of the Grand Condé,
    **2:**34
  *Neptune,* **2:***447*
Cózsa, György, **5:**380
Crabbe, George, **2:**295
  and Romanticism, **5:**248
Cracow, **2:**77–78
  university as center of science and
    culture, **4:**500
  Wawel Castle, **1:**441; **2:**77
  Berreci and Sigismund Chapel,
    **1:**441
Cracow Academy
  and Protestant Reformation, **5:**158
  reform of, **3:**411
crafts
  in cities, **1:**503
  craft economy, **1:**128–130
*Crafty Cromwell* (play), **2:**166
Cranach, Augustin, **2:**78
Cranach, Lucas the Elder, **2:**78
  *Christi and Antichirsti,* **5:**69
  loss of church patronage, **1:**123
  Luther portrait, **3:***561*
  *The Pope/Antichrist Selling
    Indulgences,* **5:***153*
Cranach, Lucas the Younger, **2:**78
Cranach, Lucas III, **2:**78
Cranach family, **2:**78–79
Cranmer, Thomas, **3:**151, 152
  Edward VI and, **2:**243–244
  and English Book of Common
    Prayer, **1:**496
  Knox and, **3:**410
  Thomas Cromwell and, **2:**96
Crashaw, Richard, **5:**420
*Creation of the Rococo, The* (Kimball),
    **5:**242
credit. *See* banking and credit
Crema conquered by Venice, **6:**130
*Cremonensium Orationes III Adversus
    Papienses in Controversia
    Principatus* (Vida), **1:**66
Crépy, Peace of (1544), **1:**411; **3:**121
Crespin, Jean, **3:**31, 168, 216
  Bèze and, **1:**255, 256
  martyrology, **3:**122; **4:**46
Cresques, Jefuda, **2:**13
Crete, **3:**88. *See also* Levant
Crétin, Guillaume, **2:**484

Diderot, Denis *(continued)*
  on Fragonard, **2**:428
  on Greuze, **3**:91
  Grimm and, **3**:92
  La Mettrie and, **3**:418
  laughter and eroticism, **3**:225
  as overt Baconian, **6**:12
  on reason, **5**:144
  Rousseau and, **5**:267
  at salon of Mme Geoffrin, **3**:38
  on sensibility of organic molecules, **5**:103
  social mobility of, **4**:159
  on surgeons, **5**:550
*Dido and Aeneas* (Purcell), **4**:227, 325; **5**:111
*Dido, Queen of Carthage* (Marlowe and Nashe), **4**:37–38
Diemen, Anthony van, **1**:138
Dientzenhofer, Kilian Ignaz, **1**:287
Dientzenhofer family, **2**:146–147
diet, **2**:102–103
  meat in, **2**:102
  medicine and, **4**:73
  melancholy/madness and, **4**:6
  of newborns, **4**:213–214
  in Sweden, **5**:556
*Dietwalts und Amelinden anmuthige Lieb- und Leids-Beschreibung* (Grimmelshausen), **3**:93–94
*Difesa del savio in corte* (Peregrini), **2**:74
*Differences in Judgment about Water Baptism* (Bunyan), **1**:341–342
Digby, Kenelm, **4**:57
*Digests* (Justinian), **3**:454–455, 464
Diggers, **1**:78; **2**:287
  egalitarianism and, **2**:320
  and history, **3**:171
Digges, Leonard, **5**:552
*Digression sur les anciens et les modernes* (Fontenelle), **5**:74
Dijon, artisans in, **1**:128
Dilettanti Society, **5**:402
Dilthey, Wilhelm, **3**:513
Din, Aruh al-, **1**:20
Din, Kahayr al-, **1**:20
Dinglinger, Georg Christoph, **2**:175
Dinglinger, Georg Friedrich, **2**:175
Dinglinger, Johann Melchior, **2**:175
Diodati, Charles, **4**:139
Diogenes Laertius, **5**:531
Dionysius of Phocaea, **5**:536
Dionysius the Areopagite, **4**:269
*Dioptrice* (Kepler), **3**:6; **4**:330
*Dioptrique* (Descartes), **4**:330
Dioscorides, **1**:84
  on botany, **1**:291
  Mattioli on, **1**:292

diplomacy, **2**:147–152
  ambassadors, **2**:147–151
  development during Renaissance, **5**:182
  espionage in, **2**:324–327
  exotic animals as form of diplomatic exchange, **6**:259
  Ferdinand of Aragón and, **2**:379
  Jesuits and, **4**:146–147
  Mazepa and, **4**:67–68
  Montaigne in, **4**:187
  More and, **4**:201
  of Ottoman Empire, **6**:78
  Sidney in, **5**:420, 421
  Vatican diplomatic service, **5**:251
diplomatic immunity, **2**:149, 151
Diplomatic Revolution (1756), **2**:460
  Louis XV and, **3**:549
  Maria Theresa and, **4**:29
  Pompadour and, **4**:521–522
*Directions to Servants* (Swift), **5**:562
*Directorium Inquisitorum* (Eimeric), **3**:267, 272
*Directory for Publique Worship in the Three Kingdoms, A*, **5**:238
*Disasters of War* (Goya), **3**:83
*Disciplina clericalis* (Petrus Alphonsus), **2**:409
*Discorsi sopra la prima deca di Tito Livio* (Machiavelli), **1**:508; **3**:98; **4**:3–4, 515, 518; **5**:182
*Discorso di Logrogno* (Guicciardini), **3**:97
*Discorso intorno alle imagini sacre e profane* (Paleotti), **1**:68
*Discours admirables* (Palissy), **2**:224
*Discours contre Machiavel* (Gentillet), **4**:4
*Discours de la méthode* (Descartes), **1**:526; **2**:130, 131, 488; **4**:460
  on mathematics, **4**:51
  use of the first person, **3**:529
*Discours de la servitude volontaire* (La Boétie), **6**:85
*Discours de l'état et des grandeurs de Jésus* (Bérulle), **1**:254
*Discours de métaphysique* (Leibniz), **3**:478
*Discours des misères de ce temps* (Ronsard), **2**:487
*Discours of Trade* (Barbon), **3**:499
*Discours politiques et militaires* (La Noue), **4**:130
*Discours préliminaire* (Alembert), **2**:253
*Discours sur le bonheur, Le* (La Mettrie), **3**:418
*Discours sur l'économie politique* (Rousseau), **6**:176

*Discours sur les sciences et les arts* (Rousseau), **2**:492; **4**:462; **5**:267
  ethnography in, **2**:338
*Discours sur l'origine et les fondements de l'inégalité parmi les hommes* (Rousseau), **2**:492; **4**:462; **5**:267
  ethnography in, **2**:338
  on virtue, **6**:176
*Discourse concerning a New World and Another Planet, A* (Wilkins), **6**:212
*Discourse concerning the Beauty of Providence and All the Rugged Passages of It, A* (Wilkins), **6**:213
"Discourse concerning the Original and Progress of Satire, A" (Dryden), **2**:294
*Discourse concerning the Origins and Properties of Wind* (Bohun), **1**:226
*Discourse of Things above Reason, A* (Boyle), **1**:302
*Discourse of Trade* (Barbon), **3**:499
*Discourse on Dramatic Poetry* (Diderot), **2**:145
*Discourse on the Anatomy of the Brain* (Steno), **5**:523
*Discourse on the Cause of Heaviness* (Huygens), **4**:470
*Discourse on Universal History* (Bossuet), **1**:288
*Discourses concerning Government* (Sidney), **2**:48; **6**:86
*Discourses concerning Two New Sciences* (Galileo), **2**:261
  on gunnery, **2**:267
  revival of Archimedean mechanical physics, **4**:469
  translation by Mersenne, **4**:102
*Discourses on Art* (Reynolds), **1**:315; **5**:216
"Discourses on Dramatic Poetry" (Corneille), **2**:58
*Discourses on the First Ten Books of Livy* (Machiavelli). *See Discorso sopra la prima deca di Tito Livio* (Machiavelli)
*Discourses upon Trade* (North), **3**:499–500
*Discoverie of Witchcraft* (Scot), **6**:225
*Discovery of a World in the Moone, The* (Wilkins), **6**:212
*Discovery of the True Causes Why Ireland Was Never Entirely Subdued* (Davies), **3**:286
*Discurso de los grandes defectos que hay en la forma del govierno de los Jesuitas* (Mariana), **4**:31–32

Dönmes, **1:**196; **5:**403

*Donna Giustiniani Barbaro with Old Nurse* (Veronese) (Villa Barbaro), **6:***145*

Donne, Henry, **2:**161–162

Donne, John, **2:161–163**
Constantijn Huygens and, **3:**238
erotica by, **2:**295
metaphysical poetry, **2:**294
Sidney and, **5:**420
on suicide, **5:**539

Doria, Andrea, **3:**31

Doria, Paolo Mattia, **4:**240

Dorigny, Michel, **6:**185

*Dormition of the Virgin* (El Greco), **2:**244

Doroshenko, Peter, **6:**91
Mazepa and, **4:**67

*Dorotea, La* (Lope de Vega), **6:**124

Dort, Synod of, **1:**367; **2:**163

Dositheus, Patriarch of Jerusalem, **4:**337

Dostoevsky, Fyodor
on Holbein's *The Body of the Dead Christ in the Tomb,* **3:**180–181
on St. Petersburg, **5:**300, 302–303

Dou, Gerrit (Gerard), **1:**113, 451; **4:**278, 368

Douai as center of Catholic learning, **3:**289

Douay Old Testament, **1:**262

Douglas, Gavin, **2:**290

Douglas, John, **6:**70

Dover, Treaty of (1670), **1:**65

Dovizi, Bernardo (Il Bibbiena), **1:**406; **2:**171; **3:**301

Down Survey and mapping of Irish lands, **4:**447

Downs, Battle of the (1639), **4:**282; **6:**32

dowries, **2:**102
divorce and, **2:**159–160
legal disputes over, **3:**460
marriage and, **4:**38
negotiations, **4:**40
widows and, **6:**209

"Draft of an Imperial Reformation" (Weifgandt), **4:**435

Drake, Francis, **1:**93, 96
country house of, **2:**329
Elizabeth I and, **2:**249
exploration by, **2:**350
Medina Sidonia and, **4:**81
raids by, **2:**274; **4:**360
report included in *Principal Navigations, Traffiques and Discoveries* (Hakluyt), **6:**68
San Juan and, **5:**472
Santa Cruz and, **5:**312

and Spanish Armada, **1:**104, 105

Drake, Judith, **2:**367

drama, **2:164–175.** *See also* comedy; tragedy; individual dramatists
Behn, **1:**242–244
Carnival and, **1:**392
"closet" tragedy, **2:**165
and clothing, **1:**548
comic theater, **3:**224
dance in, **2:**107
domestic tragedy, **2:**165
dramatic unities
Boileau-Despréaux on, **1:**281
"quarrel of *Le Cid,*" **2:**58
Racine and, **5:**132
Dutch, **2:**196, 197–198
English, **2:164–167**
*Diary of Samuel Pepys* as important primary text, **4:**438
Dryden, **2:**177
Restoration comedy, **2:**165
Shakespeare, **5:**405–407
theatrical dance in, **2:**107
French, **2:**483, 489, 492
Diderot reforms in, **4:**461
drame bougeois, **4:**461
farces, **2:**484
Voltaire as playwright, **6:**183
German, **2:167–171; 3:**50, 53–54
baroque vernacular, **3:**51
comic drama, **3:**52
Jesuit, **3:**50
Middle Ages, **3:**48
Schiller, **5:**323–324
*Schuldrama,* **2:**167, 169
heroic drama, **2:**165
influence of commedia dell'arte on, **2:**9
Italian, **2:171–173; 3:**301–302
comedy, **3:**301–302
melodrama, **2:**171
reform of the commedia dell'arte tradition, **3:**79
Lessing, **3:**489–491
Marlowe, **4:**37–38
Poniatowski's promotion of, **4:**524
popular songs in, **5:**446
Portuguese, **2:173–175; 5:**42, 43
puppet theater, **5:**43
Russian, **1:**41; **5:**280
Sheridan, **5:**407–408
Spanish, **2:173–175; 5:**458, 497–498; **6:**124
*auto sacramental,* **2:**174
*comedia* established by Lope de Vega, **6:**124
Philip IV's patronage of, **4:**457
Steele, **5:**522–523
Swedish, **5:**558, 560

and tournaments, **6:**63
tragicomedy, **2:**165
*Le Cid,* **2:**58

Drapentier, Jan, **4:***259*

*Drapier Letters, The* (Swift), **5:**561

Draskovich, Georg, **6:**73

drawing
Claude Lorrain and, **1:**529
importance of, **4:**365
in private art academies, **1:**10
of Tiepolo, **6:**37
of Vouet, **6:**184

Drayton, Michael, **2:**294
pastorals by, **2:**295

"Dreams of a Spirit-Seer" (Kant), **5:**557

Drebbel, Cornelis, **6:**13
Constantiun Huygens and, **3:**238

Drescher, Seymour, **5:**433

Dresden, **2:175–177**
arts in, **1:**443
china factories, **3:**261
Old Market Square by Canaletto, **2:***176*
Saxony and, **5:**317
Schütz and, **5:**330–331
Thirty Year's War and, **5:**331

Dresden, Treaty of (1745), **2:**460

Drina Bridge (Visegrad), **5:**425

Drottningholm, **5:**556

*Drummer, The* (Addison), **1:**15

Drummond, William
on Jonson, **3:**375
reporting Jonson on Spenser, **2:**291

*Drunken Bacchus* (Caravaggio), **1:**384

Drury, Robert, **2:**162

Drużbacka, Elżbieta, **4:**510

Dryden, John, **2:177–178; 4:**325
on Beaumont and Fletcher, **2:**291
English language and, **2:**291
and heroic drama, **2:**165
and noble savage, **4:**295
satires, **2:**294; **3:**225
Virgil translated by, **2:**290

Du Barry, Jeanne, **3:**474, 475

Du Bellay, Joachim, **2:**486; **3:**154
Lasso settings of, **3:**432
Spenser translations of, **5:**503

Du Bos, Jean-Baptiste, **1:**118

Du Broeucq, Jacques, **3:**63

*Du contrat social* (Rousseau), **1:**510–511; **2:**492; **5:**267
on civil religion, **5:**108
critical of Grotius, **3:**96
on monarchy, **4:**169
on slavery, **5:**435
on sovereignty, **5:**449–450

*Du droit des magistrats* (Bèze), **6:**85
and theory of resistance, **5:**202

*Eikonoklastes* (Milton), **4**:138

Eimeric, Nicolau, **3**:267, 272

Eisenberg, Ruth, **3**:397

Eisenstein, Elizabeth, **2**:20

*ekphrasis*, **1**:118–119

El Greco (Doménikos Theotokópoulos), **2**:244–247; **5**:458, 463–464

   *Assumption of the Virgin*, **2**:*pl.*

   *The Burial of the Count of Orgaz*, **2**:*245*

   in mannerism, **4**:19

   and Tintoretto, **6**:44

   *View of Toledo, 1604*, **6**:*51*

El Pardo, Treaty of (1777–1778), **5**:28

*Elberta* (Burney), **1**:346

Elbing (Elblag), **5**:94

Elcano, Sebastián, **2**:349

Eleanor of Aquitaine, **1**:281–282

Eleanor of Portugal, **2**:450, 457

Eleazar of Worms, **1**:349

elected heads of state

   emperor, **3**:184

   king of Bohemia, **5**:56; **6**:29

   tsar of Russia, **5**:247

electrical machines, **5**:337

*Elegances of the Latin Language* (Valla), **1**:525; **3**:219, 438

"Elegie aux nymphes de Vaux" (La Fontaine), **3**:415

*Elegies* (Donne), **2**:162

"Elegy Written in a Country Church-yard" (Gray), **2**:295

*Elementa Physiologiae Corporis Humani* (Haller), **1**:58; **3**:124

*Elements* (Euclid)

   Dee translation of, **2**:117

   modern editions of, **4**:468

*Éléments de musique théorique et pratique suivant les principes de M. Rameau* (d'Alembert), **1**:37; **5**:135

*Elements of Curved Lines, The* (Johan de Witt), **6**:226

*Elements of Euclid* (Dee), **4**:49

*Elements of Myology* (Steno), **5**:524

*Elements of Newtonian Philosophy* (Voltaire), **4**:472

*Elements of the Law* (Hobbes), **3**:174

*Eleonora of Gonzaga* (Titian), **6**:46

*Eleonora of Toledo and Her Son Giovanni de' Medici* (Bronzino), **1**:*97;* **2**:404

*Elephant Obelisk* (Bernini), **5**:363

*Élévation à Jésus-Christ sur ses principaux états et mystères, L'* (Bérulle), **1**:254

Elias, Norbert, **2**:81

   on the civilizing process, **6**:171

      Romanticism and resistance to, **5**:249

   and passions, **4**:412

   and popular culture, **5**:3

   on rituals of Louis XIV's court, **6**:149

   on sensibility, **5**:370

Eliezer, Abraham ben, **4**:104

Elijah ben Solomon (Elijah Gaon), **6**:168

Elizabeth I (England), **2**:247–250, 248; **5**:120

   and censorship, **1**:435

   charity and poor relief under, **2**:229

   clothing of, **1**:546

   court of, **2**:75

      and portrait miniatures, **5**:22

   as Deborah, prophetess and savior of her people, **5**:81

   Dee and, **2**:117

   drama under, **2**:165

   Dutch Revolt and, **2**:213

   East India Company and, **1**:320

   education of, **5**:122

   *Elizabeth I Addresses the House of Lords*, **4**:*164*

   English Reformation, **1**:496, 497

   espionage under, **2**:325

   excommunication of, **4**:386, 488

   Gilbert and, **3**:66

   government changes by, **2**:273–274

   grand entries, **2**:381, 382

   and hunting, **3**:234

   lotteries and, **3**:539

   love poetry and, **2**:294

   Mary I and, **4**:48, 49

   Maximilian II and, **4**:65

   and membership of the House of Lords, **4**:401

   mercantilism and, **4**:97

   monetary debasements and, **4**:175

   monopolies and, **4**:186

   and Parliament, **4**:403

   patronage of, **4**:421

   piracy and, **4**:85–86, 87–88

   portraits, **2**:*248*

      "Ditchley" portrait, **1**:312

      "Pelican" portrait (Hilliard), **1**:312, *312*

   and prophesyings, **5**:113

   Sea Beggars and, **5**:365

   Sidney and, **5**:420

   Spain and, **5**:459

   Spenser and, **5**:503

   state building and, **5**:514

   and Stuart dynasty, **5**:535

   and Tudor dynasty, **6**:77

*Elizabeth I Addresses the House of Lords*, **4**:*164*

Elizabeth Petrovna (Russia), **2**:250–251, 460; **5**:121, 247–248, 287

   law courts under, **3**:450

   portrait by Grooth, **2**:*251*

   St. Petersburg and, **5**:302

   Seven Years' War and, **5**:387, 389–390, *390*

Elizabethan Settlement

   legitimization by Hooker, **3**:203

   and Puritanism, **5**:112

Elliott, J. H., **2**:90; **4**:457; **5**:462

elocution and rethoric, **5**:220

*El-Rei Seleuco* (Camões), **1**:375

Elstrack, Renold, **1**:*432*

Elton, Geoffrey R., **2**:158; **4**:402

   on Mary I, **4**:49

Elyot, Thomas, **5**:508

   dictionary of, **2**:140

Elzevier, Louis, **5**:64

Emanuel Philibert (Piedmont), **3**:317

*Embajador, El* (Vera), **2**:151

*Embarkation for Cythera, The* (Watteau), **6**:*199*

emblem books, **2**:197

*Emblemata* (Alciati), **4**:246

Emden, synod of (1571), **1**:366

*Émile, ou Traité de l'éducation* (Rousseau), **1**:483; **2**:121, 241, 368, 492; **3**:16, 163; **4**:462; **5**:267

   on Index of Prohibited Books, **4**:388

   on salons, **5**:308

   on virtue, **6**:176

*Emilia Galotti* (Lessing), **2**:169; **3**:53–54, 489–490

Emiliani, Jerome, **5**:167

*Emperor of the Moon, The* (Behn), **1**:243

empiricism, **2**:252–255

   Bacon, **1**:189–190

   Boyle on, **1**:302

   as distinguished from rationalism, **4**:464–465

   Enlightenment and, **2**:299–300

   influence on the philosophes, **4**:461

   Locke on, **3**:526–527

   mathematics and, **4**:51–52

   and passions, **4**:411

   scientific method and, **5**:342

   seasonal, **3**:423

Empson, Robert, **3**:149, 150

enameling, **2**:114

   and portrait miniatures, **5**:22, 23

*Enchiridion Metaphysicum* (More), **1**:371; **4**:200

France *(continued)*
native *versus* foreigners, **1**:508, 509
navy, **4**:261, *261 t2,* 263, *263 t3,*
*263 t4*
Battle of Port Mahon, Minorca,
1756, **4**:*262*
galley navy, **4**:260, *260 t1*
rebuilt by Colbert, **1**:554
sailing navy, **4**:260–261
newspapers in, **3**:381
nobility, **1**:518
*noblesse de robe,* **1**:100
and Ottomans, **1**:200–201; **4**:85
and Papal States in Avignon and
Comtat Venaisin, **4**:382
and Peace of Utrecht, **6**:108
and Peace of Westphalia, **6**:205,
206, 207
peasantry, **4**:428
efforts of landlords to shorten
leases, **4**:429
revolts, **5**:12
penal colonies, **2**:88
and piracy, **4**:481
police, **2**:86
*gendarmerie nationale,* **4**:507
*Maréchaussée,* **4**:506–507
postal system, **5**:46
prostitution, criminalization of, **5**:83
Protestant Reformation, **5**:156
proto-industrialization in, **5**:85
provincial government, **5**:90, 91
provincial estates, **5**:92
public opinion in, **5**:108–109
quarrel of ancients and moderns,
**1**:62
Quietism in, **5**:124
regencies
Anne of Austria, **5**:164
Catherine de Médicis, **5**:163–164
Louise of Savoy, **5**:163
Marie de Médicis, **5**:164
Philippe, duke of Orléans, **5**:164
relation with papacy, **1**:491
religious confrontations over rituals
and symbols, **5**:16
rentiers in, **5**:185–186
roads, **2**:28
rococo in, **5**:240
Roma in, **5**:244
Roman law in, **3**:465–466
Romanticism in, **5**:249
royal power
1453–1589, **2**:433–435
1589–1789, **2**:435–437
royal rituals, **5**:230
as models of kingships, **5**:230–231
and rites of personality, **5**:233
royal funeral ceremonies, **5**:231

*Te Deum* services, **4**:171
salons in, **5**:306–309
Savoy and, **5**:315
scientific instruments in, **5**:337
seigneurial courts in, **3**:453, 454
seminaries in, **5**:368
serfdom in, **5**:377
skilled *versus* unskilled labor in,
**3**:422
slave trade, **1**:23, *24 t2*
slavery, **5**:434, 435
as punishment, **5**:432
and smoking, **6**:49
social mobility and, **4**:159
sovereign courts in, **3**:448–450
Spanish literature and, **5**:493, 498
spas and resorts in, **5**:502
strikes in, **5**:535
Switzerland and, **5**:564, 565–566
taxation, **6**:4
capitation, **6**:8
direct taxes, **6**:7–8
fiscal system criticized by
Physiocrats, **4**:474
indirect taxes, **6**:7
peasants and, **4**:432
*taille,* **6**:5, 8
tax rebellions, **5**:14–15; **6**:6
tax surveys, **1**:438
in Thirty Years' War, **6**:31
financing of army, **6**:32
three estates, **1**:519–520
and trade in Ottoman Empire,
**4**:347
training of clerics in, **1**:537
transportation, **2**:28
universities in, **6**:98
Urban VII (Maffeo Barberini) as
nuncio to, **6**:103
vagrancy in, **6**:112
punishment, **6**:113
violence in, **6**:173, 174
and War of American Independence,
**1**:42, 43
and War of the Austrian Succession,
**1**:174, 175, 176
and War of the League of Augsburg
(1688–1697), **3**:471–472
and War of the Polish Succession,
**4**:512
and War of the Spanish Succession,
**5**:499–501
Westphalia on, **2**:150
woodlands in, **2**:423
youth violence, **6**:172
France, architecture in, **2**:439–443.
*See also* Versailles
Amboise, château of, **1**:464
Anet, château of, **2**:441; **3**:154

Arc de Triomphe du Carrousel
(Paris), **4**:268
Balleroy château (Mansart), **4**:21
Blois, château of, **1**:88; **2**:411, 440
gardens, **3**:19
Louis XII and, **3**:540
Mansart and, **4**:21, 22–23
Chambord, château of, **2**:329, 411,
440, 450
country houses, **2**:329, 330–331
domestic, **2**:441
Fontainebleau, château of, **2**:450
Galerie François I, **2**:*411,* 412
gardens, **3**:19
Henry II and, **3**:154
Gaillon, château of, **3**:19
Hôtel des Invalides (Paris), **4**:121
Louis XIV and, **3**:547
Louvre (Paris), **1**:92; **2**:441; **4**:222,
395
Colbert and, **1**:555
Fragonard and, **2**:429
great gallery, **3**:158–159
Mansart and, **4**:21
reconstruction under Henry II,
**3**:154
Luxembourg Palace, **4**:36, 395
Maison Lafitte, **4**:21, *22*
Maisons, château, **1**:88; **2**:441
Malmaison, château of, **1**:377
religious, **2**:441–442
Saint-Germain-en-Laye, château of,
**3**:19–20
Tuileries (Paris), **3**:20, 159
urban renewal of Paris under Henry
IV, **3**:158
Vaux-le-Vicomte, château of (Le
Vau and Hardouin-Mansart),
**2**:329, *331,* 441, *442;* **3**:20
Le Brun and, **3**:469
France, art in, **2**:444–449;
**4**:370–371
academic French style, **4**:367–368
art books, **1**:116
art patronage, **1**:124
astronomy, **1**:152
exhibitions, **1**:109–110
Francesco di Giorgio
and cabala, **1**:351
and engineering and hydraulics,
**6**:11
military architecture by, **2**:265–266
Franche-Comté, **2**:431
*Franciade, La* (Ronsard), **2**:486
Francis, Phillip, **3**:144
Francis I (France), **2**:433, **449–451**
and architecture, **2**:440
Budé and, **1**:335, 336
Burgundy under, **1**:342–343

# H

*History of the Peloponnesian Wars* (Thucydides), **3:**174
*History of the Rebellion and Civil Wars* (Hyde), **3:**173
*History of the Reformation of Religion within the Realm of Scotland* (Knox), **3:**410
*History of the Reign of the Emperor Charles V, The* (Robertson), **5:**240
*History of the Royal Society, The* (Sprat), **5:**508–510; **6:**213
*History of the Worthies of England* (Fuller), **2:**293
*History of Travayle, The* (Willes), **6:**68
Hoare, Henry, **4:***476*
Hoare, William, **3:**3
Hobbes, Thomas, **3:**171, **174–176**
  and Aristotelianism, **1:**104
  atheism of, **1:**154–155
  and Bodin's definition of sovereignty, **1:**2
  on citizenship, **1:**509
  Civil War and, **2:**292
  clockwork metaphor, **1:**543
  democracy and, **2:**124
  on freedom of belief, **6:**53
  Gassendi and, **3:**22
  human freedom, **2:**469
  identification of religion as source of political conflict, **4:**516
  influence on Cavendish, **1:**428
  on laughter, **3:**224
  on liberty, **3:**506
  Locke on, **3:**527
  on London, **2:**279
  matter theories and, **4:**57
  and modernity, **1:**61
  on monarchy, **4:**163, 169
  on moral philosophy, **4:**195
  More on, **4:**200
  and natural law, **4:**251
  and noble savage, **4:**295
  on passions, **4:**411
  on paterfamilias, **2:**362
  Petty and, **3:**500
  portrait by Dobson, **3:**175
  and restriction of the influence of religion, **4:**519
  Rousseau's critique of, **5:**267
  scientific revolution and, **5:**348
  Selden's influence on, **5:**226
  and social contract, **4:**465
  on sovereignty, **5:**449
  state building and, **5:**517
  and state of nature, **4:**251–252, 294
  study of power, **4:**516
Hobsbawm, Eric J.
  on banditry, **1:**212, 213

on crisis of the seventeenth century, **2:**89, 90
  definition of nationalism, **4:**243
*Hobson-Jobson*, **5:**40
Hoby, Margaret, **2:**293
Hoby, Thomas, **2:**291
Hocart, A. M., **2:**157
Höchstetter bankruptcy, **1:**219–220
hockey, **5:**508
Hoefnagel, Joris, **5:**333
Høegh-Guldberg, Ove, **2:**129
Hofbibliothek, **3:**509
Hofburg (Vienna), **2:**75
Hoffmann, E. T. A., **2:**409
Hofmann (Hoffmann), Melchior, **1:**51
  and apocalypticism, **1:**78
  Leyden and, **3:**494
Hofmannswaldau, Christian Hofmann, **3:**50
"Hofwijck" (Huygens), **2:**198
Hogarth, William, **1:**116, 125, 314–315; **3:**176–178; **4:**370, 371
  and caricatures, **1:**389
  *The Countess's Morning Levee*, **3:***pl.*
  and engraving, **5:**71
  *Harlot's Progress, A*, **3:***176*
  and satire, **3:**225
Hogenberg's engravings, **3:***127, 215*
  assassination of Duke Henry of Guise, **6:***195*
  Dijon, Burgundy, surrenders to King Henry IV, May 1595, **6:***196*
  massacre of Huguenots by Catholics in Sens, **6:***193*
Hohenzollern, Frederick of, **3:**178
Hohenzollern, George William, **5:**95, 96
Hohenzollern dynasty, **3:**178
  Berlin and, **1:**249–250
  Brandenburg in, **1:**305–306
  Sigismund II Augustus and, **5:**422
  Silesia and, **5:**423–424
  territories 1640–1795, **3:***115*
Hohenzollern Prussia, **5:**95–96
Holanda, Francisco de, **5:**41
Holbach, Paul Thiry, baron d', **3:**178–180, *179;* **4:**461
  atheism of, **1:**155, 156
  *Encyclopédie* article, **2:**260
  and Helvétius, **3:**148
  La Mettrie and, **3:**418
  on morality and ethics, **4:**196
  on passions, **4:**411
Holbein, Ambrosius, **3:**180
Holbein, Hans, the Elder, **1:**166; **3:**180

Holbein, Hans, the Younger, **3:180–182**
  in Britain, **1:**311–312; **4:**371
  Edward VI portrait, **2:***243*, 244
  Erasmus portrait by, **2:***322*
  frontispiece of Luther Bible, **5:***155*
  loss of church patronage, **1:**123
  and portrait miniatures, **5:**22
  portrait of Henry VIII, **3:***151*
  portrait of Thomas Cromwell, **2:***96*
  soldier imagery, **5:**70
Holbein, Sigismund, **3:**180
Holberg, Ludwig, **2:**128
Hölderlin, Friedrich, **3:**409
holding companies, **1:**216
holidays
  holy days celebrations in villages, **6:**165
  music and, **4:**224
  in Ottoman Empire during Tulip Era, **6:**78
  of Reformed Protestantism, **1:**369
  religious holidays, **5:**172
Holinshed, Raphael, **3:**168
Holl, Elias, **1:**168
Holland
  Boehme's influence in, **1:**273
  bourgeoisie in, **1:**297
  canal building, **2:**26–27
  Jews readmitted, **3:**358
  newspapers in, **3:**381
Holland, Henry, **1:**311
Holland, Nathaniel Dance, **4:***169*
Holland school of painting, **2:**206–207
*Hollandsche Spectator, De* (journal), **2:**199; **3:**386
Hollar, Wenceslaus, **2:***82*
Holles, Denzil, **2:**278
  Civil War and, **2:**281
Hollis, Thomas, **3:**137
Hollonius, Ludwig, **2:**168
Holmes, Robert, **1:**64, 65
Holstein, feudalism in, **2:**387
Holstein-Segeberg as Denmark, **2:**126
Holstenius, Lucs, **4:**437
Holy, Prokop, **3:**236
*Holy City, The* (Bunyan), **1:**341
Holy Club, Methodism and, **4:**106–107
*Holy Family* (Anguissola), **1:**66
*Holy Family with Saint Anne and the Young John the Baptist* (Anguissola), **1:**68
Holy League, **1:**173, 370–371
  Battle of Lepanto and, **3:**485–487
  Budapest under, **1:**334
  Ferdinand of Aragón and, **2:**379

Huygens, Christiaan *(continued)*
as mechanical philosopher, **4:**69, 469–470
member of the Académie Royale des Sciences, **3:**238
member of the Royal Society of London, **3:**238
on pastel, **4:**413–414
pendulum clock, **6:**14
pendulum theory, **1:**542; **6:**40
scientific method and, **5:**341
statistics and, **5:**521
theory of light, **4:**331
Huygens, Christiaan the Elder, **3:**237
Huygens, Constantijn, **2:**198; **3:**238
on pastel, **4:**413–414
and Rembrandt, **5:**175
Huygens, Constantijn Jr., **3:**238
Huygens, Maurits, **3:**238
Huygens family, **3:237–239**
Huyghen van Linschoten, Jan, **1:**138
Huysman, Roelof (Rodolphus Agricola)
and curriculum, **5:**219
work furthered by Ramus, **5:**136
Hyde, Edward, **3:**173
on the navy, **2:**278
hydraulic engineering. *See* engineering: hydraulic
hydraulic organ, **3:**407
*Hydriotaphia, or Urn Burial* (Browne), **1:**329
hygrometer, **5:**337
hylomorphism, **4:**54–55, 57–58
*Hymenaei: or the Solemnities of Masque and Barriers at a Marriage,* **6:**63
*Hymnen an die Nacht* (Novalis), **4:**299, 301
hymns, **3:239–240**
Buxtehude and, **1:**348
Catholic, **3:**50
Protestant singing of, **4:**226
Swedish, **5:**559
written by women, **6:**238
*Hypnerotomachia Poliphili* (Colonna), **3:**17; **5:**64
hypnosis, Mesmer and, **4:**103
hysteria, **4:**8

# I

*I Ching,* Leibniz on, **4:**147
*I Will Pray with the Spirit* (Bunyan), **1:**341
Iam Zapol'skii, Treaty of (1582), **4:**297, 501

iatrochemistry, **1:**55–56, 293
Helmont and, **3:**491
iatrophysics, **1:**56, 57
and microscopic observation, **1:**56
Iavorskii, Sefan, **5:**278
Iberia. *See also* Portugal; Spain
expulsion of the Jews, **3:**350–351
merchants in France, **2:**439
Iberville, Pierre le Moyne d', **2:**352
Ibn Ezra, Abraham, **3:**350
Ibn Khaldun, **5:**544
Ibrahim I (Ottoman Empire), **3:**297; **4:**345, 350
Ibrahim of Aleppo, **3:**294
*Ibrahim ou l'illustre Bassa* (Scudéry), **5:**357
Ibrahim Pasha, **4:**346
Iceland as Denmark, **2:**126
*Icones* (Gessner), **3:**60
iconoclasm of Reformation, **1:**123
Dutch Republic, **4:**441
Netherlands, **5:**15–16; **6:**216
women and, **6:**238
*Iconography,* **5:**71; **6:**117
*Iconologia or Moral Emblems* (Ripa), **3:**397
iconostasis, **5:**285–286
icons, **5:**285–286
of the Crucifixion, **4:***340*
icon of the holy doors, **5:***287*
importance in Greek Orthodoxy, **4:**338
ideal eternal history, conception of, **6:**151–152
"Ideal und das Leben, Das" (Schiller), **5:**324
idealism, **3:241–242**
*Idea's Mirror* (Drayton), **2:**294
*Ideen zur Philosophie der Geschichte der Menschheit* (Herder), **3:**163, 164
Idel, Moshe, **1:**351
*Idéologie* (Destutt de Tracy), **5:**102
ideology
influence on the writing of history, **3:**171
neoclassicism and, **4:**265
Idle Institutions, Edict on (1780), **3:**379
*Idler, The* (Johnson), **3:**372
Ignatieff, Michael, **1:**456
*Ignatius His Conclave* (Donne), **2:**162
Ignatius of Loyola, **1:**103, 418, 423; **3:242–244**, 343; **5:**147–148
as Basque, **1:**232
beatification of, **4:**426
and Constitutions of the Jesuits, **1:**535; **3:**344

critical of the clergy, **1:**73
education, **1:**536; **2:**237
missions, **4:**149
Paul III and, **1:**421
portrait by Rubens, **3:***243*
Ihones, Richard, **5:***47*
Illinois, French in, **2:**479, 481
*illiterati,* **3:**520
*Ill-Matched Lovers* (Massys), **4:**271
Illuminati in Bavaria, **1:**236
*Illusion comique, L'* (Corneille), **2:**58
illustrations. *See also* prints and popular imagery; scientific illustration
in print, **5:**64
Illustrious Theater, Molière and, **4:**161–162
*Illustrium Maioris Britanniae Scriptorum* (Bale), **3:**509
Illyrian peninsula. *See* Balkans
*Image of Ireland* (Derricke), **4:***119*
*Imitation of Christ, The* (Thomas à Kempis), **2:**454; **5:**67
and revival of religious orders, **5:**165
translations
by Corneille, **2:**59
by Marillac, **4:**36
*Immaculate Conception* (Murillo), **4:**221; **5:***pl.*
*Immaculate Conception with SS. Dominic and Francis of Paola* (Caracciolo), **4:**235
immaterialism of Berkeley, **1:**248–249
*Immortality of the Human Soul, Demonstrated by the Light of Nature, The* (Charleton), **1:**476
Imperato, Ferranto, natural history collection of, **4:**247
Imperial Academy of Sciences (Russia), **1:**69
Imperial Aulic Council, **3:**189, 191
Imperial Cameral Court, **3:**186, 189
Imperial Chamber Court, **3:**191
Schmalkaldic League and, **5:**325
Imperial Council of Regency, **5:**317
imperial electors, **3:**186, 191
imperial expansion, Russia, **3:244–246**, *245*
Imperial Governance Council, **3:**186, 191
imperial princes, college of, **3:**186, 191–192
Imperial Trades Edict (1731), **3:**189
*Impiété des déistes, L'* (Mersenne), **4:**102
impotence, **5:**397–398
Imprimerie Royale, **5:**224
*Impromptu de Versailles, L'* (Molière), **4:**162

## K

## M

mining *(continued)*
women in, **6:**236
Ministers of the Sick (Fathers of a
Good Death), **1:**417
*Minna von Barnhelm oder das
Soldatenglück* (Lessing), **2:**169;
**3:**53
Minshull, Elizabeth, **4:**138
Miquelon, **2:**483
Mir Ali Şir Nevaî, **6:**83
Mirabeau, Honoré-Gabriel Riqueti,
count of, **1:**5
on lettre de cachet, **3:**491–492
Mirabeau, Victor Riqueti, marquis de
critical of intendants, **3:**279
and physiocracy, **4:**473
Mirabelli, Domenico Nani, **2:**142
*Miracle of Saint Ignatius Loyola, The*
(Rubens), **5:**270, *271*
oil sketch, **5:***269*
*Miracle of the Slave* (Tintoretto), **6:**43
miracles, **4:**141–143; **5:**170
Mersenne on, **4:**102
museums and, **4:**222–223
Miranda, Bartolomé de. *See* Carranza,
Bartolomé de
Miranda, Francisco de Sá de, **5:**39
*Mirandolina* (Goldoni), **3:**79
*Miroir de l'âme pécheresse, Le*
(Marguerite de Navarre), **2:**486;
**4:**27
*Mirror for Magistrates* (Ferrers and
Baldwin), **2:**293–294
mirrors
in paintings, **2:**51
techniques for quicksilvering, **6:**10
Mirrors for Princes, **4:**168
Miruelo, Diego de, **5:**477
*Misanthrope, Le* (Molière), **4:**162
caricature of Robert Arnauld
d'Andilly, **1:**107
*Misantrope, Le* (journal), **2:**199;
**3:**386
*Miscellaneous Discourses concerning the
Dissolution of the World* (Ray),
**5:**140
*Miscellanies* (Fielding), **2:**389
Misericórdia (confraternity), **2:**38–39
*Miseries of War* (Callot), **1:***359;*
**2:**393, *393*
*Misfortunes of Virtue, The* (Sade),
**5:**298
Mishnah, **3:**365
misrule and subversion rites
at Carnival, **1:**391
at festivals, **2:**383–384
*Miss Sara Sampson* (Lessing), **2:**169;
**3:**53, 489
*Missa Pro Victoria* (Victoria), **6:**153

Missal, **3:**122
revision of by papacy, **4:**391, 488;
**5:**149; **6:**75
Misselden, Edward, **3:**498
*Mission Principles* (Valignano), **3:**346
missions, parish, **4:**143–144
Lazarists and, **6:**169
missions and missionaries, **4:**144–151
Asia, **4:**144–148
of Catholics, **1:**425
of the Jesuits, **3:**345–346
Marie de l'Incarnation, **4:**33–34
of Moravians, **6:**258
non-Christian support of the papacy,
**4:**389–390
Paul II and, **4:**425
Paul V and, **4:**426
Spanish America, **4:**148–151
training, **4:**390
Mississippi Company of John Law,
**2:**477
Law and, **3:**468–469
Mississippi Bubble (1720) and stock
exchanges, **5:**528
Missy, Rousset de, **2:**151
*Mithridate* (Racine), **5:**131
Mitrofanovic, Djordje, **1:**441
Mnischówna, Marina, **2:**356
Mniszech, Jerzy, **2:**355
mobility, geographic, **4:**151–156. *See
also* migrations
Baltic and North Seas, **1:**207–208
Basque, **1:**232
under Mehmed II, **4:**90
missions and, **4:**150
Moriscos and, **4:**203
in Serbia, **5:**374–375
serfdom and, **5:**377–378, 379
strikes and, **5:**534
of villagers, **6:**166, 173
mobility, social, **4:**156–160
of architects, **3:**473–474
bourgeoisie and, **1:**297–298
concubinage as strategy of
advancement, **2:**33
of conversos, **2:**53–54
law courts in, **3:**447, 449
lawyers in, **3:**461–462
and literary art in Ottoman Empire,
**6:**83
marriage and, **4:**39
during Renaissance, **5:**184
of villagers, **6:**164–165
Modena, Leone, **3:**367–368
Modena, papacy and, **4:**381
moderns. *See also* ancients and
moderns
Enlightenment and modernization,
**2:**299, 305–306

*Modest Defence of Publick Stews, A*
(Mandeville), **4:**18
*Modest Proposal, A* (Swift), **2:**293;
**5:**562
Modrzewski, Andrzej Frycz (Fricius
Modrevius), **4:**509
Mohács, Battle of (1526), **1:**177, *178;*
**4:**349
and apocalyptic fear of "the Turks,"
**4:**356
and division of Hungary, **3:**227,
228–229
Janissaries in, **3:**337
Mohyla, Peter, **3:**405; **4:**160–161,
337
correction of liturgical books in
Church Slavonic, **6:**93
and reform of Orthodox
Christianity, **6:**90
Moillon, Louise, **6:**243
Mokyr, Joel, **3:**251, 253
Molcho, Solomon, **3:**368; **4:**105
Moldavia. *See also* Romania
higher schools for Greeks in, **4:**336
historiography, **3:**169
Roma in, **5:**244
Molière (Jean-Baptiste Poquelin),
**2:**489; **4:**161–163
Boileau-Despréaux and, **1:**280
on the bourgeoisie, **1:**300
Houdon bust of, **5:***363*
humor of, **3:**224
Italian companies' influence on, **2:**9
Lully and, **3:**558
on manners, **2:**104
Mignard buste, **4:***162*
and *Plaisirs de l'île enchantée*, **2:**383
portrait as a character, **4:***163*
Racine and, **5:**131
on salons, **5:**308
sexuality in, **5:**402
Molina, Luis de, **3:**345
and constitutionalism, **2:**46
on determinism, **2:**134
dispute between Jesuits and
Dominicans over teachings of,
**4:**387
drama of, **5:**498
on free will, **2:**470
Salamanca school and, **5:**305
Molina, Tirso de, **4:**240; **5:**458
on Seville, **5:**392
Molinet, Jean, **2:**484
Molinism, **3:**341
Molinos, Miguel de, **3:**247; **4:**387;
**5:**124
Molitor, Franz Josef, **1:**352
Moll, Herman, **5:**485
*Moll Flanders* (Defoe), **2:**119, 292

Netherlands *(continued)*
  Synod of Dort on, **2:**163
  taxation in, **6:**4
  and Thirty Years' War, **6:**29
  urbanization in, **1:**207
  violence in, **6:**173
  War of the Austrian Succession and, **1:**176
  War of the Spanish Succession and, **5:**499–501
  and water-lifting machines, **6:**15
  Westphalia on, **2:**150
Netherlands, art in the, **4:**271–279
  art in Flanders, 1585–1700, **4:**274–276, 368
  art in the Netherlands, 1500–1585, **4:**271–274
  art in the northern Netherlands, 1585–1700, **4:**276–279
Netherlands, southern, **4:**279–284, 281–283
  Alba in, **1:**32; **4:**451
  duke of Parma in, **4:**406
  Juan de Austria governor of, **3:**387–388
  police in, **4:**507
networks
  confraternal, **2:**38–39
  elite confraternities and merging of church and state, **2:**38
  established by Sufi orders, **3:**296
  merchants, **1:**200
Neuber, Friederike Caroline, **3:**53
Neuburg, Eleanora Magdalena of, **3:**484
Neuburg, Johann of, **5:**438
Neuburg, Mariana of, **1:**468
  marriage to Philip IV (Spain), **3:**110
*Neueröffnete Orchestre, Das* (Mattheson), **4:**231
*Neues Blumenbuch* (Merian), **4:**101
Neuf-Brisach as military garrison town, **1:**513
Neufville, Nicolas de, **3:**543
Neuhof, Theodor von, **2:**62
Neumann, (Johann) Balthasar, **3:**189; **4:**284–287
  Borromini and, **1:**287
Neumann, Caspar, **1:**85
neutrality
  Hamburg in Thirty Years' War, **3:**126
  Nuremberg and politique of, **4:**303
  Prussia and, **2:**462
*Neveu de Rameau, Le* (Diderot), **2:**145, 491
Neveux, Hughes, **5:**16
Neville, Henry, **6:**86
  on Machiavelli, **4:**4

Nevşehirli Ibrahim, **2:**44; **6:**78
New Amsterdam. *See* New York
*New and Universal History, Description and Survey of the Cities of London and Westminster* (Harrison), **3:**535
*New Arcadia* (Sidney), **5:**421
*New Art of Writing Plays in Our Time, The* (Lope de Vega), **2:**174; **6:**125
*New Astronomy, Based on Causes, or Celestial Physics, A* (Kepler), **3:**398, 399
*New Atlantis* (Bacon), **1:**8, 190; **6:**105
  and ideal technological and moral society, **6:**13
New Christians. *See* conversos
New Construction, **4:**64–65
*New Cyneas, The* (Crucé), **4:**363
*New Experiments Physico-Mechanicall, Touching the Spring of the Air and Its Effects* (Boyle), **1:**302; **4:**470
New Jerusalem Church, **5:**557
*New Law of Righteousness, The* (Winstanley), **2:**292
New Model Army (England), **2:**92, 280–281, 286
  egalitarianism and, **2:**320
  Levellers and, **2:**286–287
*New Play Called Canterbury His Change of Diet, A*, **2:**166
New River Company, **5:**311
New Room (Bristol), **4:**106
*New Science, The* (Vico), **3:**173, 304; **4:**240
*New Sett of Maps Both of Ancient and Present Geography, A* (Wells), **4:**351
  map of Spain, **5:**457
New Spain. *See* Mexico
*New Theory of the Earth* (Whiston), **2:**223
*New Voyage round the World, A* (Dampier), **6:**68
*New Way to Pay Old Debts, A* (Massinger), **2:**165
*New World Chronicles* (Peter Martyr d'Anghiera), **2:**337
New York, **4:**287
  Stock Exchange, **5:**528
Newcomen, Thomas, **3:**251
newspapers. *See* journalism, newspapers, and newssheets
Newton, Isaac, **1:**8, 14, 56; **3:**22; **4:**287–292
  on air resistance, **2:**267
  and alchemy, **1:**34–35; **6:**12

  and astronomy, **1:**152
  belief in ancient wisdom, **1:**61
  Berkeley and, **1:**249
  and biblical prophecy, **1:**80
  Buffon and, **1:**337, 338, 339
  on calculus, **4:**52–53, 288
  on causation, **5:**89
  Charleton's influence on, **1:**475
  and chemistry, **1:**477
  on the cosmos, **2:**68
  d'Alembert and, **1:**39
  on design, **2:**132
  empiricism and, **2:**253
  epistemology of, **2:**315
  Gilbert's influence on, **3:**67
  Hooke and, **3:**201
  and Huygens, **3:**239
  influence on the philosophes, **4:**461
  influence on Voltaire, **6:**182
  and Kepler, **2:**67; **3:**400
  language in, **3:**438
  Latin used by, **2:**234
  Leibniz and, **3:**478
  on lenses, **4:**331–332
  matter theories and, **4:**56, 57
  mechanism and, **4:**68, 70
  More and, **4:**200
  nerve theory of, **5:**369
  and the new physics, **4:**471–472
  notes and illustrations by, **4:***290*
  popularization of, **4:**472; **6:**182
  portrait by Kneller, **4:***289*
  and prophecy, **5:**82
  on religion, **5:**351
  Scholasticism and, **5:**329
  scientific method and, **5:**341
  scientific revolution and, **5:**345, 346–348, 348
  Stoicism and, **5:**531
  telescope and, **5:***335*
  theory of light, **4:**331
  three laws of motion, **4:**257, 471
  Universal Gravitational Constant, **2:**68
*Newtonianism for Ladies* (Algarotti), **1:**232
*Nibelungenlied*, **3:**48
Niccoli, Niccolò de', **3:**508
Nice, **2:**431
Nice, Peace of (1538), **1:**551
Nicholas II (Russia), **4:**210
Nicholas V (pope), **3:**508
Nicholas of Cusa, **1:**60
Nicholas of Dresden, **3:**236
*Nicholas Ruts* (Rembrandt), **5:**175
Nicodemism, **1:**51; **4:**46
Nicola da Urbino, **1:**446
Nicolai, Philipp, **3:**240

Pasek, Jan Crhyzostom, **4**:510

pasha. *See* Vizier

Pashazade, Kemal, **3**:296

Pasqually, Martines de, **1**:352

Pasquier, Étienne

and constitutionalism, **2**:46

and national myth, **3**:170

*Pasquin* (Fielding), **2**:389

Passarowitz, Peace of (1718), **1**:179, 196, 467; **3**:8; **4**:409–410

and Ottoman Empire, **4**:352, 356

Passau, Treaty of (1552), **5**:327

Passerini, Silvio, **4**:420

*Passional Christi und Antichristi* (Luther), **5**:*153*

passions, **4**:410–413

examination by Vives, **6**:179

violence and, **6**:172

*Past and Present* (journal), **2**:89

pastel, **4**:413–414, *pl.*

Pastor, Ludwig von, **5**:146

"Pastoral Instruction in the Form of Dialog on the System of Hansenius" (Fénelon), **2**:371–372

*Pastoral Landscape* (Claude Lorrain), **1**:529

*Pastorale Officium* (Paul III), **4**:389

pastorals

country houses and, **2**:328

English, **2**:295

Italian, **2**:171, 172; **3**:303

*Pastorals* (Pope), **4**:525, 526

Patel, Pierre, **6**:185

aerial view of Versailles, **1**:*90*

patents, **4**:186

Pater, Baptiste-Joseph, **6**:198

paterfamilias, **1**:181; **2**:362

royal authority and, **3**:27

Patin, Carla, **1**:118

Patinir, Joachim

*The Battle of Pavia, Feb. 24 1525*, **3**:*308*

Bruegel (Pieter the Elder) compared with, **1**:330

and landscape painting, **4**:272

Patiño y Morales, José, **4**:414–415

Ensenada and, **2**:307

and Philip V, **4**:458

Patkul, Johann Reinhold von, **1**:211

*Patriarcha* (Filmer), **2**:362; **4**:416

Patriarchal Academy (Constantinople), **4**:335

patriarchalism

Locke on, **3**:506, 527

scientific revolution and, **5**:345

sexual difference theories and, **5**:394

patriarchy and paternalism, **4**:415–417

honor and, **3**:200

paternal imagery and monarchy, **3**:27

servants and, **5**:385

widows and, **6**:209

Patrick, John, **1**:225

Patriot Revolution (Dutch Republic, 1786–1787), **2**:208; **4**:417–418

Mennonites in, **1**:53

Patriotic Society (Hamburg), **1**:9

patriotism and Estates, **5**:190

patristic scholarship, **3**:221; **6**:26

patristic theology, **6**:25–26

Patrizi, Francesco, **3**:171

encyclopedia of natural philosophy, **4**:254, 255

and Neoplatonism, **4**:269

theory of the Earth, **2**:223

Patrona Halil Rebellion (1730), **2**:44; **4**:352

and end of the Tulip Era, **6**:78–79

patronage, **2**:188–189; **4**:418–423.

*See also* artistic patronage

courts and, **2**:74

of early scientists, **2**:69

ecclesiastical of Guise family, **3**:102

of Louis XIV, **3**:546–547; **6**:149

Medici family, **4**:72

monarchy and, **4**:170–171

of Pompadour, **4**:521–522

of Rudolf II, **5**:272–273

scientific revolution and, **5**:349

Spain, **5**:462

state building and, **5**:515, 516

terminology of, **4**:419

Patte, Pierre, **1**:513

Paul, Lewis, **6**:23

Paul, Thomas, **1**:341

Paul I (Russia), **4**:423–424; **5**:248, 282

centralization of Russian government, **5**:274–275

Dashkova and, **2**:108

portrait by Batoni, **4**:*423*

Paul II (pope)

and fortification of Rome, **5**:252

and problems of the clergy, **1**:536

Paul III (pope; Alessandro Farnese), **1**:420, 491; **4**:382, 424–426

appointment of reform-minded cardinals, **4**:384

approval of Jesuits, **3**:243

and Catholic Reformation, **5**:148

and Cellini, **1**:123

condemnation of enslavement of native, **4**:389

and Council of Trent, **1**:420, 421; **6**:71

and direct rule in Papal States, **4**:381

and Jesuits, **3**:344

portrait by Titian, **4**:*425*

and Roman Inquisition, **3**:267, 270

special congregations, **4**:384

Paul IV (pope; Giovanni Pietro Carafa), **1**:420

and Council of Trent, **1**:421

first Roman Index, **3**:246

in Habsburg-Valois Wars, **3**:122

and Italian Wars, **3**:309

on Jewish ghettos, **3**:61

and Jews, **3**:352

Mary I and, **4**:49

Philip II and, **4**:450

and Roman ghetto, **1**:424

Roman Seminary, **1**:537

Sixtus V and, **5**:425

and Theatines, **5**:166

Paul V (pope; Camillo Borghese), **4**:426–427

centralizing politics, **1**:491

condemnation of Gallicanism, **4**:383

and expansion of St. Peter's, **5**:255

on Jesuit-Dominican dispute over Molina, **4**:387

and Vatican Library, **4**:391

Paul de Gondi, Jean François, **5**:391

Paulet, Amias, **1**:189

Paulze, Marie, **3**:440

Paumgartner, Balthasar, **2**:23, 28

Pauw, Adriaen, **6**:80

Pavel of Kolomna, **4**:318

Pavia, Battle of (1525), **3**:120, 308

*The Battle of Pavia, Feb. 24 1525* (Patnir), **3**:*308*

battle tactics in, **4**:125

Marguerite de Navarre and, **4**:28

Pavia, Treaty of (1329), **4**:373

Pawel of Krosno (Paulus Crosnensis), **4**:509

pawning, **4**:427–428

banking and, **1**:218–219

pawnshops, **1**:453

"Pax Gulielmi Auspiciis Europae Reddita" (Addison), **1**:15

Pax Hispanica, **4**:454

Pázmány, Péter, **3**:226

"Peace of the Church," **3**:339

*Peaceable Principles* (Bunyan), **1**:341–342

*Pearl Fishers* (Allori), **2**:404

*Peasant Dance* (Pieter Bruegel the Elder), **1**:*330*

*Peasant Family in an Interior* (Le Nain), **2**:444

# S

Smith, Adam, **3**:261; **5:439–441**
  and belletrism, **5**:220
  critical of Locke's natural rights,
    **5**:228
  on design, **2**:132
  on interest, **3**:280, 283
  La Rochefoucauld and, **3**:418
  on leisure preference, **3**:423
  on liberty, **3**:507
  Mandeville and, **4**:18
  member of the Literary Club, **3**:372
  on mercantilism, **2**:230; **4**:98
  on monopolies, **4**:184
  self-interest
    contribution to general welfare,
      **5**:75
    as a social motive, **4**:411
  on sensibility, **5**:369, 371–372
  shipping and, **5**:413
  system of liberty in, **2**:302
Smith, John, **1**:371
Smith, Joseph, **1**:395
  patron of Canaletto, **6**:123
Smith, Thomas
  and constitutionalism, **2**:47
  serfdom and, **5**:377
smoking, **6**:48
  effort to curb recreational use of
    tobacco, **6**:49
Smolensk capture by Muscovy, **6**:121
Smolensk War (1632–1634),
  **4**:109–110
Smollett, Tobias George, **2**:292;
  **5:441–443**
Smotrytskyi, Meletii, **4**:160–161;
  **5:443–444**; **6**:90, 93, 94
  Ruthenian translation of Old
    Slavonic Homiliary Gospel, **6**:93
smuggling
  British colonies in, **1**:316
  Buenos Aires and, **1**:337
  Mexico and, **5**:475
Smyrna (İzmir), **3**:89; **5:444–445**
  urbanization of, **4**:87
Smyth, Craig Hugh, **4**:19
Smythson, Robert, **1**:309
  Hardwick House, **2**:329, *330*
Snyders, Frans, **4**:276
  and eagle in Rubens's *Prometheus,*
    **5**:271
Soane, John, **1**:311
  Piranesi and, **4**:482
Soarez, Cipriano, **5**:218
Soarez, João, **6**:73
sobriquets, **1**:520
soccer, **5**:507
sociability, gentlemen and, **3**:37
social banditry, **1**:212–214

social classes. *See also* class, status and
    order
  and consumerism, **2**:49
  and consumption of meat,
    **2**:414–415
  death and, **2**:112–113
  height and, **2**:103
  Jansenism and, **3**:341–342
  and jewelry, **3**:348
  joining in French tax revolts, **6**:6
  in Moravian Church, **6**:258
  officeholding and, **4**:314
  Protestant clergy and, **1**:532
  social differentiation, **1**:520–523
  and variation in diets, **2**:419
social contract theory, **1**:510–511;
    **2**:301–302; **4**:465, 516
  in Beccaria, **1**:242
  Burke on, **1**:344
  democracy and, **2**:125
social control
  in Russia, **5**:276–277
  sumptuary laws and, **1**:545
social drama, **2**:166
social ills, Hogarth's perspective on,
    **3**:177
social mobility. *See* mobility, social
social sciences
  Enlightenment, **2**:302
  environment and, **2**:313
  Montesquieu on, **4**:189–190
social welfare
  state building and, **5**:517
  statistics and, **5**:520–522
  Vincent de Paul and, **6**:170
Société des Missions Étrangères,
  **4**:390
Société Dieppoise, **2**:477
societies, learned. *See* academies,
    learned; literary societies;
    scientific societies
Society for Effecting the Abolition of
    the Slave Trade, **5**:436
Society for the Reformation of
    Manners, **5**:400
Society for the Translation of Foreign
    Books (Russia), **5**:280
Society of Apothecaries, **1**:82
Society of Artists in London, **3**:3
  Reynolds and, **5**:216
Society of Berbice, **2**:189
Society of Friends. *See* Quakers
Society of Jesus. *See* Jesuits
Society of Suriname, **2**:189
Society of Universal Harmony, **4**:103
Socrates, **5**:426, 427
Sodalitas Litteraria Vistulana, **4**:509
sodomy, **5**:400–401. *See also*
    homosexuality

Sofiia Alekseevna, **5:445–446**
  and development of Russian high
    literature, **5**:288
  regent for Peter I, **5**:247
Sofiia Paleologue
  marriage to Ivan III, **3**:321
  mother of Vasilii III, **6**:121
Sohm, Philip, **4**:20
Sokollu Mehmed Pasha, **4**:349
Sokolovic, Makarije, **1**:198
Sokoly, Mustafa, **1**:439
Solander, Daniel, **6**:70
  exploration of South Pacific, **6**:70
Solari, Pietro Antonio, **3**:322
Soldani-Benzi, Massimiliano, **1**:553
soldier imagery, **5**:70
*Soledades* (Góngora), **3**:80–81; **5**:497
Solemn League and Covenant (1643),
  **2**:279
Soler, Antonio, **5**:458
  Scarlatti and, **5**:322
Solimena, Francesco, **4**:235, 236, 240
  and portraiture, **4**:237
Solis, Juan de, **4**:11
solitaires. *See* Port-Royal des Champs,
    convent of
"Solitude of Alexander Selkirk, The"
    (Cowper), **6**:69
*Solomon* (Handel), **3**:129
Solothurn as city-state, **1**:515
Soly, Hugo, **1**:456
  on poverty, **5**:53
Somachi, **5**:167
*Some Considerations of the
    Consequences of the Lowering of
    Interest and Raising the Value of
    Money* (Locke), **3**:499
*Some Reasons for an European State*
    (Bellers), **4**:363
*Some Thoughts concerning Education*
    (Locke), **1**:483; **2**:239; **3**:16
Somer, Paul van, **1**:312
  portrait of Bacon, **1**:*190*
  portrait of James I and VI, **3**:*333*
Somko, Iakiv, **6**:91
*Sommersby* (film), **5**:4
*Somnium* (Kepler), **3**:400
*Somnium Vitae Humanae*
    (Hollonius), **2**:168
Somodevilla, Zenón de, **5**:461
*Sonate pian e forte* (G. Gabrieli), **3**:2
Sonenscher, Michael, **3**:423; **5**:86
"Song of Ostrov, The," **2**:98
Songhay kingdom, **1**:22
*Songs* (Kochanowski), **3**:411
songs, popular, **5:446–447**
  songs of protest as source for studies
    of popular culture, **5**:5
  Spanish, **5**:494

# U

*Underwoods* (Jonson), 3:376
unemployment
  and poverty, 2:85
  and vagrancy, 6:113
*Unfortunate Traveller, The; or, the
  Life of Jack Wilton* (Nashe),
  2:292
Ungler, Florian, 2:77
Uniate Armenian Mechtarist, 6:96
Uniates, 4:335, 505; **6:95–96**, 168
  Mohyla and, 4:160–161
  Smotrytskyi and, 5:443–444
uniformity, Joseph II and, 3:378
unigeniture in Russia, 4:446
*Unigenitus Dei Filius* (Clement XI),
  3:10, 340, 341; 4:387
  condemnation of Jansenism, 4:387
  Louis XIV and, 3:548
Union of Brest (1596), 4:504–505;
  5:160; 6:89, 95, **96–98**
  attempt to unite Eastern and
    Western Christianity, 4:339
  Cossack resistance to, 2:70
  and revival of Orthodox religious
    traditions and culture, 6:89
  Smotrytskyi and, 5:443
Union of England and Scotland
  (1707), 2:276
Union of Hadiach (1658), 6:95
Unitas Fratrum (Unity of Brethren),
  **6:257.** *See also* Moravian
  Brethren
United Belgian States, 4:284
United East India Company
  (English), 1:141
United East India Company
  (Vereenigde Oost-Indische
  Compagnie or VOC). *See* Dutch
  East India Company
United Provinces of the Netherlands.
  *See* Dutch Republic
United State of Belgium, 5:207
United States
  Methodism in, 4:106
  Scholasticism and, 5:329
  as slave society, 5:430
  Spanish colonies in, 5:477–480,
    478–480
  stock exchanges in, 5:528
Unity of Brethren (Moravians),
  3:236; 4:478
*Universal Chronicle, or Weekly
  Gazette,* 3:372
universal gravitation, theory of, 4:289
universal human nature, search for,
  4:294
*Universallexikon* (Zedler), 2:143; 5:5
universities, **6:98–103**
  in Bavaria, 1:234

  in Bohemia, 1:276
  curriculum
    humanist influence, 2:20; 4:254;
      6:100
    Ramus and, 5:135
  defended by Wilkins against
    Hobbes, 6:213
  dissemination of knowledge, 2:153
  education in, 2:237
  fraternities, 6:255
  geographic mobility of students,
    4:156
  Leipzig, 3:479
  map, 6:99
  northern
    introduction of humanistic studies,
      6:100–101
    *versus* Italian, 6:98–99
  in Papal States, 4:391
  reformed in Lutheran states, 1:532
  during Renaissance, 5:180
  in Saxony, 5:319
  Scholasticism and, 5:328
  scientific method and, 5:339
  scientific revolution and, 5:349–350
  in Scotland, 5:353–354
  size of, 6:99
  Swedish, 5:557
  and Thomism, 6:25
  women and, 2:368
    Cornaro Piscopia, 2:57–58
*Unknown New World* (Montanus),
  5:480
unnatural, category of, 4:255
Unterberger, Michael Angelo, 1:444
Uppsala University, 3:512–513
*Urania* (Wroth), 2:291
Uraniborg, 1:304
Urban VI (pope), 3:436
Urban VIII (pope; Maffeo Barberini),
  4:382; **6:103–105**
  Bernini portrait, 6:104
  Bernini work for, 1:251
  Mazarin and, 4:65–66
  and missions, 4:389–390
  on smoking, 6:49
  Smotrytskyi and, 5:443
urban planning. *See* city planning
urban revolts, 5:12, 14–15
urbanization. *See also* cities and urban
  life
  abolitionism and, 5:435–437
  Bach family and, 1:187–189
  Balkans, 1:191–192
  Baltic and North Seas, 1:207–208
  Basque, 1:231, 232
  bourgeoisie and, 1:296–301
  civil engineering in, 2:260–265
  daily life and, 2:101–105

  Dublin, 2:178
  Dutch Republic, 2:204
  Edinburgh, 2:232
  education and, 2:234
  England, 2:270–271
  environment and, 2:310–311,
    312–313
  geographic mobility and, 4:152
  inequality and, 2:317–318
  London, 3:532–537
  Ottoman, 4:86–87
  pattern in 1700, 1:505
  plague and, 3:434
  sanitation and, 5:310–311
  in Scotland, 5:355
  servants and, 5:383–384
  in Seville, 5:393
  shipping and, 5:415
  in Spain, 5:453
  state building and, 5:513–516
  suicide and, 5:541
  sumptuary laws and, 5:546–547
  in Sweden, 5:556
Urbarial Patent (1767), 3:231
Urbino, duchy of
  annexed by Urban VIII, 6:103
  papacy and, 4:382
  ruling dynasty, 3:311 t1
Urdaneta, Andrès de, 4:359
Urdinola, Francisco de, 1:232
Urfé, Honoré d', 2:487
Urquhart, Thomas, 2:291
Ursulines, 1:417, 423; 5:168
  begun as a confraternity, 2:38
  and education, 1:482; 5:148
Urusova, Evdokiia, 4:206
Ushakov, Simon, 5:287
Ussher, James
  Baxter and, 1:237
  biblical chronology and, 4:147
usury, 1:216. *See also* interest
  as crime, 2:84
  laws, 3:280
Utenhoven, Jan, 1:206
Utens, Giusto, 3:19
utilitarianism, 4:196, 197
  Beccaria, 1:242
  Swift, 5:562
utopia, **6:105–106**
  Bacon, 1:190
  Enlightenment, 2:305–306
  and islands, 3:300
  neoclassicism and, 4:268
*Utopia* (More), 2:85, 290; 4:201;
  6:105
  on suicide, 5:539
Utraquism, 3:236
  Bohemia, 1:276–277
  Prague, 5:54

30°W  20°W  10°W  0°  10°E  70

60°N

50°N

40°N

ICELAND
(Denmark)

Faroe
Islands

Shetland
Islands

Orkney
Islands

NORWAY
(Denmark)
Christiania

Lake Va/nern

Lake
Va/ttern

Scotland

Firth of Forth
Edinburgh

North
Sea

DENMARK
Copenhagen

Isle of
Man

Dublin

Ireland

GREAT
BRITAIN

Wales

England

Bristol
London

Shannon

Trent

Severn

Thames

Amsterdam

NETHERLANDS

Brussels
Austrian
Netherlands

Cologne

Rhine

Frankfurt

Hanover

Elbe

Weser

Berlin

Saxony

Saale

P

Bohem

Prague

Main

HOLY ROMAN
EMPIRE

Neckar

Danube

Bavaria
Munich

HA

Aus

ATLANTIC
OCEAN

Aisne

Seine
Paris

Meuse

FRANCE

Loire

Lyon

Rhône

Garonne

SWISS
CONFED.

Milan

MILAN

Turin

SARDINIA

Genoa

PARMA

MODENA

GENOA

LUCCA

Arno

TUSCANY

Po

VENICE
Venice

Appennines

Adriatic

Pyrenees

ANDORRA

Ebro

Marseille

PAPAL
STATES

Rome

Tiber

NA

PORTUGAL

Douro

Madrid

SPAIN

Tagus

Barcelona

Balearic Islands

Iviza
(Spain)

Majorca
(Spain)

Minorca
(Great Britain)

Corsica
(France)

SARDINIA

Naples

Lisbon

Seville

Mediterranean Sea

Sicily

AFRICA

Malta